Benjamin Franklin in Portraiture
by Charles Coleman Sellers

More than either a biography or a catalogue, this study of Franklin's portraits shows how his interest in portraiture was influential throughout his life, presents a wealth of new information about early American portraitists and their art, and brings together for the first time all known likenesses of Franklin.

Part One is a review of Franklin's life as revealed in painting, sculpture, caricature, and other media, with full histories of the important pieces. Part Two is a descriptive catalogue, including over 200 works, of which 27 are life portraits and 17 are the originals of the portrait types from which the present-day conception of Franklin's appearance has been formed. The portraits are arranged by types and fully illustrated in a final section.

Of primary value to all who are interested in Franklin, this volume is an essential companion piece to *The Papers of Benjamin Franklin* now being published by Yale University Press.

Charles Coleman Sellers is the librarian of Dickinson College and an authority on Frankliniana.

BENJAMIN FRANKLIN IN PORTRAITURE

Benjamin Franklin, ca. 1782   miniature in enamel by Jean
Baptiste Weyler (WEYLER, no. 1)   Courtesy of Charles Clore,
London; photo courtesy of Edward Speelman, Ltd.

Charles Coleman Sellers

BENJAMIN FRANKLIN
IN PORTRAITURE

New Haven & London: Yale University Press: 1962

Published in cooperation with
the American Philosophical Society

PREFACE

MY PURPOSE in this study has been to define the appearance and character of Benjamin Franklin as revealed in portraiture. A secondary aim has been to show something of the historical role of the portraits themselves in spreading his fame and sustaining the philosophy, the policies, and the nation he represented. My interest has been both in the man and in the symbol.

The method used is more historical than critical. Much evidence (and some speculation) is presented, and many points of interest left without a definitive conclusion. It is offered as a contribution to knowledge put together in the full awareness that others may be expected to add or amend as light is given to them to do so. It is really no more than the story of a search. Often enough I have found the writers before me employing the circumlocutions of hesitancy, "undoubtedly," "in all likelihood," or "très vraisemblablement," and often enough have pegged a statement of my own in the same way. Days or weeks of systematic search have frequently yielded no absolutely sure result, and an appalling amount of honest labor has led only to negative proof and complete dismissal. Some firm results, to be sure, are here, and even that irregular type of research which Whitfield Bell so aptly calls "haystacking" has sometimes brought a needle to light.

A search inevitably ranging so far to serve its narrow central theme has inevitably had its ups and downs of triumph and despair. My marriage, at the outset of the work, to a lady long familiar with both the tribulations and the allure of art history, gave to it, how-

v

ever, a certain equilibrium, doubling its pleasures and halving its pains. The whole of this fortunate alliance has thus been passed with Franklin's face above it, and the two travelers for ten full years walked in that benign and auspicious light.

The study was first suggested, late in 1951, by Dr. William E. Lingelbach, Librarian of the American Philosophical Society. In June 1952 it had the support of a grant of $1,500 made by the Society from the Penrose Fund, and the Society, in the purchase of books and materials, has given it continuing aid throughout. The first year's work brought the subject in hand, but revealed also the number of unsolved problems and obscure details, and how far from easy access so many of the answers to them were. It was continued, as time allowed, through the following year. With the launching of the project for the complete publication of the Franklin Papers under the auspices of the Society and of Yale University, formally announced on January 6, 1954, our pursuit of the portraits project was relaxed, in order to gain full advantage of the work of the larger undertaking. That advantage was amply realized. The editors of the Papers, Leonard W. Labaree and Whitfield J. Bell, Jr., not only made all their accumulation of materials available, but watched over this incidental matter and supported it at every opportunity. The study of the portraits was enormously aided by this association, and would never have been carried so far without it.

In the autumn of 1957 a visit to England and Scotland was made possible through the interest and generosity of Mrs. Waldron Phoenix Belknap and of the Henry Francis du Pont Winterthur Museum, an assistance related also to my position as Librarian of the Belknap Library at Winterthur. Through 1959, 1960, and 1961 the final research and the preparation of the manuscript were carried forward as rapidly as was possible in the time which could be spared from my work as the Librarian of Dickinson College.

The book is divided into three parts. The first is a general survey in nine chapters telling the story of the life portraits from young manhood to old age. The second is a descriptive catalogue of them, with the addition of other works selected from the great mass of Franklin portraiture because they document the originals or have some other incidental interest. The third is the illustrative material which is composed of a smaller selection of originals and related pieces. More material has of course been assembled than can be printed, and the residue will be available in the Library of the American Philosophical Society for the use of those with a continuing interest in the subject.

To my colleagues on the staff of the Dickinson College Library I owe much, particularly to Arthur C. Flandreau (now Librarian of Concord College) and to Miss Nancy J. Loughridge. It was of course upon the larger library institutions that the search most depended. Constant support came from the libraries of the American Philosophical Society and Yale University, and from the Franklin Papers project. Dr. Whitfield J. Bell, Jr., was here the principal one of the many friendly points of liaison, giving most generously of his time and trouble, unearthing and transmitting material of all sorts. It was he who discovered in London the identity of the artist of Nini's "fur cap" medallion, the most famous and perhaps the most influential of all the Franklin portraits, and this was but one item in the steady flow caught by his eye and hand.

The project owes a deep obligation also to the Frick Art Reference Library, always the best starting point as well as the constant support of such an enterprise, and to the Philadelphia Museum of Art, whose Print Department and Library were a source of guidance and information throughout. The Manuscripts Department of the Princeton University Library brought to my attention at the outset the George Simpson Eddy Papers. In the 1920s George Simpson Eddy had worked with William Smith Mason on the formation of the great collection of Frankliniana which now forms the heart and main resource of the "Franklin factory" at Yale. His correspondence, notes, and photographs contain the first truly scholarly appraisal of the Franklin portraits as a whole. My association with the Henry Francis du Pont Winterthur Museum, 1956–59, brought with it both the opportunity to make full use of its collections and library, and the encouragement and stimulation of the Winterthur climate.

In Britain particularly valuable assistance was rendered by the British Museum's Library and Department of Prints and Drawings, the National Portrait Gallery, the Victoria and Albert Museum, the Witt Library of the Courtauld Institute, and the Scottish National Portrait Gallery. The British research is memorable on the one hand for its concentrated activity, and on the other for the kindness of more people and institutions than can be named here, all of whom were so ready to aid and indulge the mad preoccupation of the visitor. The French research at the Bibliothèque Nationale and elsewhere was accomplished both by direct correspondence and through the expert services of Abel Doysié who had been George Simpson Eddy's investigator in this same area, and who, in the intervening years, has advanced the work of so many American scholars.

Other institutions which have in various ways rendered particular assistance are: Addison Gallery of American Art; American Numismatic Society; American Scenic and Historic Preservation Society; Andersonian Library, Royal College of Science and Technology, Glasgow; Boston Athenaeum; Boston Public Library; Buten Museum of Wedgwood; Chicago Historical Society; Corcoran Gallery of Art; Fogg Art Museum; Free Library of Philadelphia; Grand Lodge, Free and Accepted Masons of Pennsylvania; Friends Historical Library, Swarthmore; Haverford College, Quaker Collection; Henry E. Huntington Library and Art Gallery; Historical Society of Pennsylvania; Independence Hall National Historical Park; Institut Tessin, Paris; Lewis–Walpole Library, Farmington; Library Company of Philadelphia; Library of Congress; Manufacture Nationale de Sèvres; Massachusetts Historical Society; Missouri Historical Society; Mount Vernon Ladies' Association of the Union; Musée Cantonal des Beaux-Arts, Lausanne; Musée Calvet, Avignon; Musée d'Art et d'Histoire, Geneva; Musée de la Coopération Franco-Américaine de Blérancourt; Musée des Beaux-Arts, Ville d'Angers; Musée Municipale, Carpentras; Musée Nationale d'Histoire de France, Chateau de Versailles; Museum of Fine Arts, Boston; National Archives and Records Service, Washington; Nationalmuseum, Stockholm; New-York Historical Society; New York Public Library; New York State Library; Pennsylvania Academy of the Fine Arts; Robbins Library, Arlington, Mass.; Royal Society of Arts; Thomas Jefferson Memorial Foundation; United States Naval Academy; University of Pennsylvania; Wedgwood Museum, Josiah Wedgwood and Sons; The White House, Washington; Zentralbibliothek, Zurich.

Much of this work has of necessity been carried on by correspondence, and in this and other ways has been dependent upon the interest and good nature of other people, drawing, sometimes quite liberally, upon their knowledge and their time. A grateful acknowledgment is due to those who have in one way or another made a special effort to further it: Kingsley Adams; Winslow Ames; the Earl of Albemarle; John V. Alcott; John Alden; Alfred Owen Aldridge; Alexander J. Alexander; D. G. C. Allan; M. O. Anderson; Mrs. Harry Armstrong; H. H. Arnason; Miss Caroline D. Bache; Franklin Greene Balch; Miss Dorothy C. Barck; Mme. Hélène Barland; Malcolm Barnes; James A. Bear, Jr.; Miss Helen R. Belknap; Mrs. Waldron Phoenix Belknap; Michel Benisovich; William Billington; Charles W. Black; Theodore Bolton; Frances M. Bradford; James S. Bradford; J. C. Brash; Ralph Brown; Mrs. David F. Brubaker; Mlle. Marcelle Brunet; Alan Burroughs; Alfred L. Bush; Harry M. Buten; Mrs. Genevieve B. Butterfield; Lyman H. Butterfield; George E. Byford; Dr. Williams B. Cadwalader; Jean Cailleux; Mrs. James M. Castle, Jr.; Barney Chesnick; Mrs. Edmund R. Childs; Gilbert Chinard; Miss Elizabeth Clare; Alexander P. Clark; P. F. Clausey; William S. Coleman; John Coolidge; Miss Joyce C. Cooper; Edward Croft-Murray; Mrs. Anne E. Crosby; W. F. Davidson; J. Morgan Denison; Mrs. Clara Louise Dentler; Ulysse Desportes; Mlle. Anne Dumur; Mrs. Ruth A. Duncan; Henry Francis du Pont; Milton W. Eddy; Donald Drew Egbert; L. P. Eisnehart; Alvin Eisenman; Allan Ellénius; Mrs. William H. Emory; John Eppstein; Stuart Paul Field; Mrs. Helene H. Fineman; Joseph P. Flaherty; John Fleming; James Thomas Flexner; Henry Wilder Foote; Miss Edith A. Ford; Joseph T. Fraser, Jr.; Miss Kathryn E. Gamble; Mlle. Suzanne Gervaix; Milo Sargent Gibbs; Mrs. F. Warrington Gillet; Donald E. Gordon; Mrs. Arthur M. Greenwood; Miss Florence M. Greim; Paul L. Grigaut; Henry Grunthal; M. Gukovsky; Charles Hamilton; T. E. Hanley; Ernest E. Harding; Miss Lucy T. Hare; Mrs. G. Roger Harvey; John Davis Hatch, Jr.; Francis W. Hawcroft; Bartlett H. Hayes, Jr.; E. H. Heckett; Mrs. Gertrude D. Hess; Norman Hirschl; T. W. Hodgkinson; D. Holland; Herbert Hoover; King V. Hostick; George L. Howe; Mrs. Henry W. Howell, Jr.; R. P. Howgrave-Graham; Sidney C. Hutchinson; R. E. Hutchison; Mrs. Horace H. F. Jayne; I. Kaye; Miss Winifred

Kennedy; A. J. B. Kiddell; W. Wright Kirk; Mrs. Benjamin R. Kittredge; Herbert S. Klickstein; Mrs. Irving Lavin; James Lawrence; Charles Le Gras; John Frederick Lewis; Wilmarth Sheldon Lewis; Miss Frances Lichten; Lady M. Longmore; Mrs. Robert Sabatino Lopez; Georges de Loÿe; Gunnar W. Lundberg; Tom Lyth; William H. McCarthy, Jr.; Mrs. Norman A. MacColl; Charles H. Mace; John P. McGowan; David McKibbin; Samuel Herbert McVitty; Henri Marceau; Ferdinando Dante Maurino; A. Hyatt Mayor; Thomas N. Maytham; Mrs. Louis Wardlaw Miles; Jesse C. Mills; Charles F. Montgomery; Henry de Morant; T. R. Mordaunt-Hare; Junius S. Morgan; James M. Mulcahy; Milo M. Naeve; Miss Yvonne Noble; Gardner Osborn; Antonio Pace; Mrs. Haven Parker; William J. Paterson; Edward H. Payne; Mrs. John N. Pearce; T. Morris Perot, III; Mrs. R. E. Phillips; David Piper; Mrs. A. Wright Post; John W. Pratt; Mr. Edmund A. Prentis; Mrs. Granville T. Prior; Mr. and Mrs. Russell J. Quandt; Kenneth J. Rayburn; Graham Reynolds; Howard C. Rice, Jr.; Edgar P. Richardson; Mlle. Micheline Marie Ricois; John Beverly Riggs; Edward M. Riley; Stephen T. Riley; Lloyd M. Rives; Mrs. Barbara S. Roberts; Miss Lydia S. M. Robinson; Mrs. Theodore Douglas Robinson; T. Glen Rogers; Marvin C. Ross; Claude Rossel; Miss Elizabeth E. Roth; Miss Anna Wells Rutledge; Robert E. Schofield; Miss Margaret Scriven; Russell A. Scully; Murray Seasongood; Miss Josephine Setze; Mrs. B. Shell; J. G. Shelley; Richard H. Shryock; Mr. and Mrs. Wharton Sinkler; Theodore Sizer; Max Slater; Murphy D. Smith; Miss Eugenie Söderberg; Edward Speelman; Mrs. Frances H. Stadler; the Earl Stanhope; Miss Mildred Steinbach; Damie Stillman; H. C. Strippel; Mrs. Robert M. Tappan; Max Terrier; Frederick B. Tolles; Mlle. Estelle Trépanier; Harry S. Truman; Franklyn C. Upham; Preston Upham; R. W. G. Vail; George Vaux; J. L. Vellekoop; Helmut von Errfa; Robert C. Vose, Jr.; S. Morton Vose; Richard Wadleigh; Charles C. Wall; A. Dayle Wallace; David H. Wallace; Robert R. Wark; Mrs. Annie Reese Wedgwood; Herbert Weissberger; A. H. Westwood; Georges Wildenstein; Richard Norris Williams, II; Alice Winchester; Edwin Wolf, II; Miss Juliet Wolohan; C. G. Wood; the Earl of Yarborough; Carl Zigrosser.

CONTENTS

ABBREVIATIONS

A.P.S.   American Philosophical Society

H.S.P.   Historical Society of Pennsylvania

L.C.   Library of Congress

M.H.S.   Massachusetts Historical Society

N.Y.H.S.   New-York Historical Society

P.M.H.B.   *Pennsylvania Magazine of History and Biography*

1 BENJAMIN FRANKLIN AND THE PORTRAITIST'S ART

•

IN THESE tumultuous latter-days the art of portraiture has lost the deep involvement with our lives that it held in former times. The portrait image has been an element of human history, whether in ancient, magical shapes and mysteries or as reflected truth. It has moved populations to reverence. It has been an implement of substantiation and a weapon of attack. This is a study of the portraits of one man who lived at a time when the image still held some of that age-old fascination and power.

I shall try to show him as he actually was, as he appeared in the sensitive eyes of the artist, and in the representation of him as the symbol which gave visual form to his varied and far-reaching thought. He was depicted as a friend, as an enemy, as the "genius" of an embattled nation, and, at the last, benign and old, as the living emblem of a new world's birth and of the liberation of the mind. Only very rarely were his portraits wholly true to him, yet even where his appearance is obscured we learn something of his brightly-mirrored universality. To the artists of his climactic years he posed a baffling problem: a figure impressive in his lack of impressiveness. They had their traditional and fixed devices for the representation of portentous human values, and portentous people acted out the poses in life: the body's carriage, the noble gesture, the head held high above the splendor of costume. In the lift and turn of a hand was seen the strong direction of a persuasive and commanding mind, and the "piercing eye" revealed its intellectual power. Dress and physical bearing were elements of domination and success. Never before, however, had they encountered a figure of such monumental importance with so little monumentality and so total a disregard for "presence." Some did their best to create it for him. Some tried to conjure it up by symbolic stage properties and allegorical attendant figures. Their subject gave them no cooperation and no criticism but his smile.

To the casual visitor it was the same. It is profoundly significant that in an age intensely interested in the characters of its great men not one contemporary has left us a complete and adequate description of Franklin's appearance. For all the interest, excitement, and controversy surrounding him, his face, figure, and habitual manner received only cursory or superficial remark. Apparently there was something in the big mouth and friendly eyes, lighted always by humor and understanding, which drew you immediately into the world of his learning, his wisdom, and his feeling. If you came, as many did, to gaze with awe upon the great man, this objective attitude would be quickly dispelled by his warm acceptance of you and his readiness to share all his interests with you. You met the man himself. You came away with the friendliest admiration but with only a secondary impression of personal appearance.

We know that in young manhood he stood an inch or two short of a full six feet, was heavy-set and muscular. His eyes were hazel, but seemed gray in some lights. His peculiarly wide mouth had in it much strength and a denial of any daintiness. It was not the mouth of a frequent and forceful speaker, but it was shaped to give emphasis either to serious thought or to a pleasantry. His was a large head on a large body. Deborah Logan tells us this, though when she noticed it the stoop of age had reduced his height. She was an acute observer with a sense of history, and her description is worth quoting even though it is the recollection, half a century later, of what a child of thirteen had seen. "He was fat, square built, and wore his own hair, thin and gray: but he looked healthy and vigorous. His head was remarkably large in proportion to his figure, and his countenance mild, firm, and expressive. He was friendly and agreeable in conversation, which he suited to his company, appearing to wish to benefit all his hearers."[1]

In youth his hair was dark brown. As a successful young tradesman he wore an inexpensive wig of the same color. During the English years, from 1757 to 1775, he covered his head with a heavily fashionable gray wig. This he discarded altogether in 1775, finding that to do so relieved a scalp irritation which had troubled him for two years. After that, his long iron-gray locks, gradually whitening, gave him distinction. A middle-aged stoutness had come on in his forties after he had retired from business and relaxed his youthful austerities. At the age of fifty-one he described himself as a "fat old fellow."[2] He used spectacles in those years, and after 1776 wore them continually, a thing then unusual even among the elderly. Stoutness and the rounding shoulders of old age reduced his height, but there always remained in his bearing some of his former vigor and monumentality.

A few second-generation descriptions have value, though based on recollections of his later years. E. D. Ingraham was told by his mother and aunt that the Doctor "was about 5 feet 9 inches high, stout made and well formed, and inclining to fat, and that he grew fatter as he grew older, but he was not a fat, short man, on the contrary, when old his appearance was very impressive and venerable." Along with this description, found in Jared Sparks' papers at Harvard University, is Dr. Franklin Bache's statement of January 30, 1840, "that Dr. Franklin was five feet, ten or eleven inches high, strongly made but not so as to have a heavy appearance. He had particularly a very handsome leg. Bishop White, I think, told me this. When he became old, he became fat." A quite independent source of the same period, Madame Tussaud's ghostwriter, gives us "a stout man, about five feet ten inches in height; his eyes were gray, his complexion light."[3]

The writers tell us little. The painters and sculptors, from whom explicit statement is surely to be expected, are remarkably diver-

---

1. *Historical Magazine,* 2d ser. *4* (1868), 280.
2. Paul Leicester Ford, *The Many-Sided Franklin* (New York, 1899), p. 57.
3. Francis Hervé, ed., *Madame Tussaud's Memoirs and Reminiscences of France* (London, 1838), p. 13.

gent. In copies of copies, as they recede from the original, the likeness becomes hopelessly blurred. In late copies the mouth becomes formalized, the moles on the left cheek and lower lip disappear, and the strong lines of the face are softened away. An astonishingly large number of painted or sculptured portraits of other individuals have been identified and accepted with absolute faith over periods of years as portraits of this great man, and are so firmly established that they must needs have a special place of their own in this volume. It is clear that the painters and sculptors, like the diarists and letter writers, have been beguiled by Franklin's charm and universality and that their admiration for his greatness has often led them away from the simplicity which is so much a part of it. Here was a large, hale, and hearty man, but one quite without the kind of physical majesty which artists and writers have conveyed in their descriptions of Washington, for example. A few have depicted Franklin superlatively well. Of the others who worked from life or from intimate knowledge of him, not one can be disregarded as unimportant. A portrait may be deficient as an exact statement, but it can nonetheless tell us how the world regarded its subject—with candor, reverence, or mockery; how the sensitive artist reacted to him as a person; how he himself wished to be seen in the world's eyes; and how he stood in the ancient conventions of the art.

Those conventions, and Franklin's awareness of them, are a fundamental part of this history. Portraiture had survived the Reformation to become the dominant art of England and America. Protestantism and democracy, advancing together, found it the most congenial and least suspect of the arts. It sustained that new feeling for the worth of the individual and it went well with social climbing. The portrait, always an attribute of nobility and a mark of family status, had been taken over by the well-to-do bourgeois families and was touching the lives of the tradesman class. Puritan inhibitions and the fear of involvement in the sin of vanity had been calmed, and the portrait was invested with a morality of its own. Samuel Johnson, who with such solid emphasis could define the feeling of the Englishman of his day, denied that "national selfishness" was the reason for British artists being almost wholly employed in painting portraits, and went on to explain the matter:

4

Whoever is delighted with his own picture must derive his pleasure from the pleasure of another. Every man is always present to himself, and has, therefore, little need of his own resemblance, nor can desire it, but for the sake of those whom he loves, and by whom he hopes to be remembered. The use of this art is a natural and reasonable consequence of affection; and though, like other human actions, it is often complicated with pride, yet even such pride is more laudable than that by which palaces are covered with pictures, that, however excellent, neither imply the owner's virtue, nor excite it.

Genius is chiefly exerted in historical pictures; and the art of the painter of portraits is often lost in the obscurity of his subject. But it is in painting as in life; what is greatest is not always best. I should grieve to see Reynolds transfer to heroes and to goddesses, to empty splendour and to airy fiction, that art which is now employed in diffusing friendship, in reviving tenderness, in quickening the affections of the absent, and continuing the presence of the dead.[4]

Benjamin Franklin, in just this spirit, was to take pleasure in having his own portrait made and in giving it away to others, a thing which he did far more liberally than any other American of his time. He regarded it as a social amenity, a way of visiting distant friends "in person." He knew also how the personal image gave strength to feelings and ideas, knew its value to the writer and statesman. He was equally alert to the fact that family portraits reinforced social status, an area in which, without any taint of pretentiousness whatever, he was determined to maintain his position as a gentleman of family. He did so successfully and without disturbing the Poor Richard concept in which much of his wide influence was rooted. It was with him a sense of social worth, something whose attributes in America any successful man might readily assume. In England greater emphasis lay in the length of a distinguished pedi-

4. *Idler*, No. 45, Feb. 24, 1759.

gree, and it is significant that in 1758, the first summer of his long residence in England, Franklin toured northward to search out the family genealogy, poring over the Ecton parish records and copying the gravestone inscription. Always proud of belonging to an armigerous line, he had long been sealing his letters with the Franklin coat of arms, which was engraved also on his brother John's bookplate and stamped on the product of John Franklin's soap manufactory. And almost at once on his arrival in London he had embarked on a plan either to "get all our little family drawn in one conversation piece" or to have painted a group of individual family portraits.[5]

It would be unfair to suppose that Franklin's feeling for portraiture was, in Dr. Johnson's phrase, "complicated with pride." It was, however, complicated by a trait of innocence. The vast range of his understanding did not penetrate far into the arts. He regarded the artist as a tradesman like himself whose craft, like the printer's, was compounded of industry, technical skill, and some feeling for design. He had no appreciation of the artist's virtuosity, nor any ability to distinguish the subtleties of a sensitive and powerful work. He knew the persuasive force of pictures and used it, but never sought to acquire sophistication in art. He hardly seemed aware that such sophistication existed. Poor Richard shared Dr. Johnson's preference for portraiture and was even less responsive to empty splendor and airy fiction. His few statements on works of art relate to their obvious content and never probe farther or echo that liturgical jargon in which writers on art perennially involve themselves and which Sir Joshua Reynolds called "the cant of criticism." We see artists reacting in agony or anger to his blind disregard for those things which were to them so essential, so sacred. Throughout his life, he had little concern with the poetry of art but much with its content.

His feeling for family portraits came with middle life, retirement in comfortable circumstances, and a circle of English friends. But that naïve, rather touching acceptance of the portrait image as a thing of heart-to-heart responses goes back much further and was more deeply felt. Benjamin Franklin, as natural and reasonable a creature as ever breathed, discovered that "the use of the art is a nat-

5. Albert Henry Smyth, *The Writings of Benjamin Franklin, 3* (New York, 1905), 423, 439.

ural and reasonable consequence of affection" more than twenty years before Johnson's *Idler* was printed. At the time of his first experience with art and artist, he was a young tradesman, aged thirty. His little, four-year-old son had suddenly been taken from him by a terrible disease, and he had had a portrait painted of the child, a large gaudy and fanciful thing but, for all that, a heart's monument and one to be cherished in private through all his long years. As it brought him warmth and solace, he tolerated its conventional artificialities for which he naturally felt a plain man's dislike. We find him ruling them out of his own portraits wherever he had the chance, but he was ready at other times to put up with them as a painters' mystery which had, at least in that first experience of 1736, brought comfort. Although in later years he watched with interest as England and France, rivals in the arts as in war, strove to outdo each other in this highest manifestation of national culture, nothing from the academies of London or Paris could have touched him more poignantly than the painted image of Franky Franklin, the little boy with upraised, beckoning arm, who gazes out upon us from a fairyland of mountains, brightly colored birds, and flowing water.

2 LITTLE FRANKY IN ELYSIUM

FRANCIS Folger Franklin, named Francis for what friend or by what whim we do not know, and Folger for the Nantucket family of his grandmother, Josiah Franklin's wife, was born on October 20, 1732. His father was then twenty-six, a master printer newly cleared of debt, and prospering. *The Pennsylvania Gazette,* which Benjamin Franklin had been writing, editing, and printing for three years, was an established success. He held investments in other newspapers in colonies to the north and south. He was printer to the province of Pennsylvania and would soon have the official printing of Delaware, New Jersey, and Maryland as well. And in December of that year he had issued his first *Poor Richard's Almanac.*

Gazette and *Almanac* alike can do much to dispel whatever misconceptions Franklin's autobiography and some of his biographers may have given us as to the calculating asceticism on which he supposedly founded his career. The young man had clearly put some bridle on his abundant natural appetites, and yet he was abundantly enjoying himself. In both the world is seen with his cool, objective eye and his warm participation, so full of zest and fellow feeling, assurance, understanding, fun. His *Gazette* may at any time snicker by including some casual news or commercial item, or break into laughter by giving up the best part of an issue to some such foolery as the "Drinker's Dictionary."[1] The *Almanac* laughed at all the fol-

1. Jan. 6, 1737.

lies of mankind, almanacs among them. At that time Franklin's was a life of long swims in the Delaware, long hours of talk with friends, of thought with books, long hours at the press, with eyes alight and feet on the ground, denying himself nothing but a retreat from reality. There was no Puritanism here, no stern discipline imposed at home. He took an uninhibited, naïve delight in his two sons, those extensions of his own being, and petted and indulged them. When death took the younger from him, it was as if a strand of his own life had been cut away.

It happened in November 1736. On November 11 the *Gazette* had advertised the *Poor Richard* for 1737 as then on sale. In that almanac the verses heading the January calendar are a jocose reflection of Franklin's strong advocacy of inoculation against the smallpox:

> God offer'd to the Jews Salvation
> And 'twas refus'd by half the Nation:
> Thus, (tho' 'tis Life's great Preservation)
> Many oppose *Inoculation*.
>   We're told by one of the black Robe
> The Devil inoculated Job:
> Suppose 'tis true, what does he tell:
> Pray, Neighbours, *Did not Job do Well?*

Within a few days the disease was running its course in his own home. There were then five people in the family, all living upstairs over "the New Printing Office, near the Market," in Philadelphia —Deborah and Benjamin, Deborah's mother, the "Widow Read," and the two children, five-year-old William and his younger brother Franky, petted, delicate, and deliciously gay. Downstairs in the shop the *Gazette* came out on schedule and the shop accounts show no break in the daily business: books and "stationary-ware" were on sale as usual, with ink horns, pen knives, and quills, ciphering slates and pencils, lampblack and linseed oil and specialties such as the "super fine Crown Soap" manufactured by brothers John and Peter Franklin, and the arcane salves and ointments compounded in their own kitchen by Mrs. Read.

On November 21 Franky died, and on the next day he was laid in the earth of Christ Church burying ground. Any buyer of the newly issued almanac, looking ahead to the verses for February, would have found there lines strangely attuned to mourning and the broken circle:

> The *Thracian* Infant, entring into Life,
> Both Parents mourn for, both receive with Grief:
> The *Thracian* Infant snatched by Death Away,
> Both Parents to the Grave with Joy convey.
> This, *Greece* and *Rome,* you with derision view;
> This is meer *Thracian* ignorance to you:
> But if you weigh the Custom you despise,
> This *Thracian* Ignorance may teach the wise.[2]

The father, now a public figure and one who had spoken out more strongly in simple prose than in rhyme for "Life's great Preservation," soon learned that rumors of his personal tragedy were injuring his cause. The *Gazette* of December 13, 1736, carried his rebuttal:

> UNDERSTANDING 'tis a current Report, that my Son *Francis,* who died lately of the Small Pox, had it by Inoculation; and it being desired to satisfy the Publick in that Particular; inasmuch as some People are, by that Report (join'd with others of the like kind, and perhaps equally groundless) deter'd from having that Operation perform'd on their Children, I do hereby sincerely declare, that he was not inoculated, but receiv'd the Distemper in the common Way of Infection: And I suppose the Re-port could only arise from its being my known Opinion, that Inoculation was a safe and beneficial Practice; and from my having said among my Acquaintance, that I intended to have my Child inoculated, as soon as he should have recovered sufficient strength from a Flux with which he had been long afflicted.
>
> B. FRANKLIN.

2. Robert Newcomb in *The Sources of Benjamin Franklin's Sayings of Poor Richard* (University of Maryland Ph.D. dissertation, 1957), p. 184, has shown that the verses on "The Thracian Infant" were taken verbatim from *A Collection of Epigrams* (London, 1735–37), No. CCXL, and that the last four lines of the rhyme on inoculation come from the same source.

This for the public. For himself he had a picture painted of the child. It is a reasonable supposition that a majority of the children whose static little faces peer back at us from early American portraits were actually painted after death, cheeks blooming, eyes opened, toys or flowers about them in the posthumous reconstruction. Almost every family experienced this tragedy. It was a part of the limner's craft to deal with it. He was the expert at reviving tenderness, quickening the affections of the absent, and continuing the presence of the dead. The painter who came to the New Printing Office on this business found a father eager to have the best and ready to pay for it. Fullface, the most difficult and expensive pose of the head, was in order, along with the complete figure, both hands, and a "distance" of scenic background. This little child of four was to have the artistic treatment usually accorded to high station and great wealth. The painter's first problem was to catch a facial likeness to the satisfaction of his client. After that he would, in the usual procedure, work everything else out in the privacy of his painting room.

The likeness in a case such as this would necessarily be painted from someone with a family resemblance, amended by family recollections. It could not have been hard to "hit," since, as has been acknowledged, father and son had looked so much alike. Since it is virtually certain that Franklin himself posed for it, I can cite this canvas, though guardedly, as the first portrait of Benjamin Franklin. I must admit that the wide-eyed little face also compares interestingly to the portrait of the child's mother, and that the wear of more than two hundred years has deprived the paint surface of the sharpness of detail on which a final judgment should depend. But one can still see something there of the lines of Benjamin Franklin's mouth, the feature which, more than all the others, determines his likeness.

The painting stands at the beginning of this history for another reason: as Franklin's first experience with the arts, it may have fixed the pattern of his feeling for them. For Benjamin and Deborah this picture filled a profound emotional need, and thus may have made Benjamin Franklin somewhat more tolerant of its baroque artificiality and somewhat less aware of the truly poetic subtleties in the painting of his time. It must certainly have been marked by the practical approach in which his warm sentimentality was always framed. Throughout his life he ordered a painter's work as he would a printer's. He was particular that features should be correctly stated, but asked no more. A copy saved time and trouble for all concerned and was therefore preferable, in his mind, to a life portrait. The rest of the picture he could, with complacent resignation, leave to the limner's fancy.

In the portrait of Franky his son's face looked back upon him, but the little boy was more glamorously robed and cloaked than ever in life, and stood half in woodland shadow, a tropical bird perched near his upraised hand. Across the sunny meadow beside him rose the pinnacles of a marble palace, and beyond, blue mountains framed the scene. He probably never knew how in this instance the painter's fancy had been inspired. Our knowledge of it is due to a discovery made by Waldron Phoenix Belknap, Jr., some years ago, of the manner in which British mezzotint portraits of court figures and other popular characters became part of the stock in trade of almost every early American portrait painter.[3] From these they borrowed details, attributes, poses, and sometimes even copied everything, only substituting the colonial for the British face. The great Sir Godfrey Kneller was shown to have had, through this medium, a vast and hitherto unsuspected influence in the foundations of American art. Thus guided, my search for the source of Franky's picture was quickly rewarded. It was a mezzotint of "The Lord Euston"— a bar sinister grandson of the Merry Monarch, engraved by John Smith in 1689 after Kneller's painting of 1685.[4] The print appears to have been enormously popular. A mezzotint copy of it was published at Amsterdam as a sentimental idealization of childhood and without subject identification.[5]

Franky's face must have been completed before the artist selected his print, since the print calls for a three-quarter view of the face,

3. Waldron Phoenix Belknap, Jr., *American Colonial Painting: Materials for a History* (Cambridge, Mass., 1959), pp. 273–77.

4. Charles Fitzroy, Duke of Grafton, Earl of Euston and Arlington, Viscount Ipswich, Baron of Sudbury, &c., was born on Oct. 25, 1683, and died in 1757. He figures in history also as Lord Lieutenant of Ireland. He was a grandson of Charles II and Barbara Villiers.

5. Engraved in mezzotint by Petrus Schenck. Composition reversed.

> Contre un si grand Vainqueur, quel Coeur peut se défendre
> On voit à son Pouvoir les plus grand Dieux se rendre.

looking upward toward the bird. But as Americans had a distinct preference for portraits which returned the spectator's gaze, it is not at all unusual to find the sentiment or action of an original design altered in this way.

The print is 12¼ inches high and 10 inches wide. The canvas is 33 by 25 inches, but may have been cut down from the standard "kit-kat" size, 36 by 27, or even from the 50 by 40 in which a large proportion of the formal portraiture of the time appears. The painter seems to have made some slight concessions to Philadelphia simplicity. He entirely omitted the richly chased collar and clasp of a little princeling, so that the blue cloak worn over the ethereal Franky's red dress is held at the shoulder by nothing at all and would have fallen off had he but stirred. The morning-glory vine and waterfall were perhaps omitted as demanding too much of the artist's hand and palette. The bank on which the little elbow rests is simplified to a reddish brown rock. Behind it, at the left, a stretch of olive-green lawn leads the eye away toward distant blue hills and sky, with the marble palace rising midway between. The macaw is brought closer to the child as if demanding the attention which, in the mezzotint original, is the theme of the picture. Of the bird, as the picture stands today, only a trace of its beak and a flash of brilliant red feathering can be seen. The face, too, is blurred. The curling sandy hair looks as if it might have originally had a tint of red. But Benjamin Franklin's mouth is there, and above it are Deborah's dark brown eyes.

As for the identity of the artist, little stylistic evidence can now be found in the painting itself. His use of the print suggests a professional limner, but one of the native-born, "painter in general" class. In New York there were several whose wholesale dependence on mezzotints has been made clear by Waldron Belknap, and one of them might have been in Philadelphia. The picture could conceivably be a very early work of Robert Feke, though this must be judged unlikely on various counts. If we look for a painter whom Franklin knew and to whom he might have turned in this personal need, there are three possibilities: Gustavus Hesselius, Hesselius' partner, John Winter, and Samuel Johnson.

Hesselius is a likely choice from the viewpoint of personal association, and an unlikely one from that of his background and mature

13

style. He had come to America in 1712, aged thirty, a professional portrait painter trained in Stockholm. For the first few years he had lived in Philadelphia, so that he had known the city well long before Franklin's arrival there. One may suppose that he met Franklin first in the winter of 1732–33, after his return from a sojourn of some years in Maryland. He was then fifty-one and Franklin twenty-seven. In a letter written in the spring of that year James Logan calls him "no bad hand" as a painter, but goes on to describe his portraits as so truthful and unflattering that "the fair sex" would not sit for him.[6] Franklin, whose feeling would have been opposite to that of the fair sex, gave him credit at his shop. The entries begin on January 15, 1733, with a book binding job and the purchase of some gold leaf.

One can imagine the two together. Hesselius' face was like Franklin's in its strong chin and the sensitive yet firm mouth. The curled gray wig he wears in his self-portrait was light in weight, just wig enough to mark him as a gentleman, and I can imagine it slightly askew in moments of earnest discussion. He was musical and well-read as was the young tradesman. He was the brother of a clergyman and nephew of a bishop, and yet in all probability a different sort of churchman from the others Franklin knew. The books he bought at the shop were mostly religious, though we find among them the two fat octavo volumes of the "Polygraphic Dictionary."[7] When he bought Whitefield's sermons and the journal of Whitefield's companion, William Seward, we may be reasonably sure that he did so on Franklin's cordial recommendation.

The slowly lengthening columns in Ledgers A, B, and D show him in Franklin's debt for pasteboard, paper and lampblack, pounce boxes, gold and silver leaf, for Bibles and other books, for "Binding a parcel of Swede books" and "binding a book of Pictures," this last entry confirming the reasonable assumption that Hesselius owned a collection of prints.[8] Most of the items are small, though on October

6. Frederick B. Tolles, "A Contemporary Comment on Gustavus Hesselius," *Art Quarterly, 17* (1954), 271–72. The letter is dated May 31, 1733, and addressed to Logan's brother in England.

7. *Dictionarium Polygraphicum: or, The Whole Body of Arts Regularly Digested*, 2 vols., London, 1735. The text in both volumes is headed "Polygraphick Dictionary."

8. The ledgers are in the library of the A.P.S., Philadelphia.

24, 1748, he bought one of Franklin's fireplaces for five pounds. He had at about the same time earned four pounds painting the gun carriages of the militia battery organized at Franklin's call.[9] In 1749 the account was carried into Ledger E, which has been lost. In those sixteen years there was no credit entered for a portrait and only one small item of two shillings crossed out as paid. A painter would have charged five to seven pounds for such a picture as Franky's, and as early as 1737 Hesselius owed considerably more than that. The portrait may, of course, have been paid for in cash or have been a gift of the artist, and yet it remains difficult to believe that so servile and awkward an imitation could have come from this hand.

Gustavus Hesselius was not at all a first-rate painter. Some portraits based upon mezzotint prototypes have been attributed to him, but the work for which he is known is of a far more respectable character. His justly famous portraits of the Indian chiefs Lapowinsa and Tishcohan, owned by the Historical Society of Pennsylvania, bear out James Logan's characterization of the painter, as the portrait of Franky does not. They were painted in 1735, a full year before Franky's picture. Circumstances may have called for an unrealistic treatment of the child, but this may be said also of the Indians. The negotiation of the infamous "Walking Purchase" from the Lenni Lenape was under way and John Penn, I assume, commissioned these portraits not as ethnological documents but in accordance with the long-established European custom of so complimenting the heads of state with whom a treaty was in the making. Hesselius must have understood these formalities well, and could have satisfied them better by showing his subjects in regal poses drawn from his print collection as other artists in like circumstances had done.

If Hesselius is more or less disqualified in this inquiry by his sincerity and competence as a painter, his younger business associate appears to possess all the necessary ineptitude. If John Winter be the man, however, the picture must have been painted at least four years after Franky's death, which is in itself largely improbable. On March 12, 1740, the following advertisement appeared in the *Penn-*

9. The bill, with John Hesselius' receipt, dated Jan. 11, 1749/50, is in the Edgar Fahs Smith Library of the History of Chemistry, University of Pennsylvania.

15

sylvania Gazette and was repeated in the issues of March 20, March 27, and April 3:

> DONE by *John Winter,* Painter, from *London,* at the Sign of the easy Chair in *Chestnut-Street,* Landskip and Coach-Painting, Coats of Arms, Signs, Shewboards, Gilding, Writing in Gold or common Colours and Ornaments of all Kinds very reasonable.
>
> N.B. He has a very good Sign of the King's Arms to dispose of very cheap.

And on September 25, 1740, the *Gazette* published the following, repeating it in the issues of October 9, 16, 23, and December 11:

> PAINTING done in the best manner, by GUSTAVUS HESSELIUS, from Stockholm, and JOHN WINTER, from London, viz. Coats of Arms drawn on Coaches, Chaises, &c. or any other kind of Ornaments, Landskips, Signs, Shew-boards, Ship and House Painting, Gilding of all sorts, Writing in Gold or Colour, old Pictures clean'd and mended, &c.

George Whitefield had preached in Philadelphia that spring. The *Gazette* reflects in almost exuberant fashion the response of the public—and of its printer—to the preacher's warm Christian humanitarianism. This spirit, and Franklin himself, may have had some influence in bringing the two painters from competition into partnership. The advertisements, incidentally, are that one item in Hesselius' long account for which he paid cash.

It is possible that John Winter had been in Philadelphia in 1736, though the evidence shows him as an immigrant from London in 1740. There is no painting known to have come from his hand, and we have only grounds for conjecture that he painted portraits at all. That portraits are not mentioned in either advertisement means little, since portraiture was a very special branch of the trade, adapted to the wishes and feelings of the wealthy, and patronage was rarely sought by such means in the early eighteenth century. Hesselius had described himself as a portrait painter upon his arrival in Delaware long years before and, writing the opening sentence of his will in

1750, with dignity declared himself "I, Gustavus Hesselius of the City of Philadelphia, Face-Painter . . ."[10] At that later date John Winter publicly professed himself a "Landskip painter." The following was in the *Gazettes* of June 7 and 21, 1750:

> DRawing in perspective, as building, figures, landskips, &c. ornaments of all kinds, proper for those who intend to be painters, carvers, engravers, or for pleasure, &c. taught by
>
> JOHN WINTER
>
> Landskip painter, and in general; next door to Mr. George Heap's, in Third-street.
>
> N.B. School hours from 5 a clock to 7 or longer, if required. Some have already begun learning to draw.

This was printed just after Thomas Penn's commission for a view of Philadelphia, to be published in London, had been given to another painter, James Claypoole. Claypoole labored haplessly with the difficult task; then Winter fretted over it and abandoned it to his neighbor, George Heap. Heap died as he was leaving for England with his drawing, and it was Winter at the last who gained some fame and profit by making an improved copy from which the now well-known engraving was cut in 1754.[11]

Winter died at the close of the year 1782, and the inventory of his estate, taken January 6, 1783, gives us at last a feeling that that phrase in the advertisement of 1750, "and in general," included, as surely it must somewhere in the course of his life, the painting of faces.[12] Along with the paint stone and muller, the thirty small boxes of powdered paint, the palettes and brushes, the "16 Boards painted," there were also "Picture frames and back boards" and "Pieces of Oyl cloth on stretching frames," and these are the materials of the portrait rather than the sign painter. At the head of the column of artist's equipment is an item of "18 Doz. and 5 Prints."

10. Christian Brinton, "Gustavus Hesselius," in *Gustavus Hesselius, 1682–1755. An Exhibition held at the Philadelphia Museum of Art* (Philadelphia, 1938), p. 13. Original in the office of the Register of Wills, City Hall, Philadelphia.

11. Nicholas B. Wainwright, "Scull & Heap's East Prospect of Philadelphia," *P.M.H.B., 73* (1949), 20–21.

12. Register of Wills, Philadelphia.

These must have been mezzotints, the tone process of engraving which was so popular in England and which were so easily translatable into paint. The majority of the mezzotints were portrait or figure pieces, and, futile though the speculation be, one of these may have been the Lord Euston reaching for his bird, the source of Franky Franklin's portrait.

Early in November 1743, while the partnership of his friends Hesselius and Winter was presumably still flourishing, another painter stepped into Franklin's shop and purchased a pound of lampblack, for which he was given credit. The entries in Ledger D were written in red ink, now faded to a pale salmon color:

Saml. Johnston (Boston)   Dr.
1743.   Novr. 7.   1 lb. Lampblack   —   5.

Both this entry and its duplicate in the index to the ledger were altered by later insertions in black ink to read, "Saml. Johnston (*formerly of* Boston, *Painter*)." According to Whitfield J. Bell, Jr., whose eye and authority none may question, the original entry does not appear to be in Franklin's hand, nor in Deborah's, while the insertions which amend it are "indisputably" Franklin's. We must suppose, therefore, that a journeyman in the shop made the sale and that the buyer, in asking for credit, presented himself as a Boston compatriot of the master printer.

Actually, this Bostonian had been a resident of Philadelphia longer than Franklin, longer than Hesselius, and had been living within half a block of where the printer's shop now stood for more than thirty years. Franklin knew him well. It cannot be proven that he painted the fanciful portrait of Benjamin Franklin's son, but he is a more likely candidate than either Hesselius or Winter for he meets the three necessary conditions: a painter-in-general of little skill, a friend, and one who was at hand to do this service in 1736. Because his story is a curious one, never before set down in the annals of our native art, it is perhaps worth telling here in some detail.

He was one of a family of Johnsons whose migration from Kentish farms and towns to the Massachusetts Bay country had begun in 1630, continuing for a number of years thereafter. They were a knotty race, and have left their mark upon our history. Samuel was a younger son of Timothy Johnson, a farmer of Andover, Massachusetts. He was born on July 25, 1684.[13] His father died in 1688, when he was but four and his eldest brother eleven. In the great witchcraft delusion of 1692 his mother had been one of those accused of secret dealings with the devil, but happily the popular frenzy subsided in time to spare her life. On February 22, 1698, raiding Indians stormed the farmhouse, and gunfire and satanic yells sounded near and far upon the frosty air, while bullets hammered at the shuttered windows. Penelope Johnson, a girl of nineteen, was killed. After a time the two older brothers, John and Timothy, married and bound their lives to the earth and walls of Andover. Samuel, the third and youngest, turned to city life as a boy emerging from so turbulent a childhood might well have yearned to do, and found himself in more comfortable circumstances.

We may guess that he learned his trade of painter in the usual way, by apprenticeship. That surmise places him in Boston between the ages of fourteen, the year of the Indian raid, and 1705, when he turned twenty-one. He next appears, however, in Philadelphia where, in about 1710, he married Sarah Hodgson, a widow, and a sister of James Sherman, a Boston clergyman. She had married Daniel Hodgson, "practitioner of physick,"[14] in 1696, and he had brought her from Boston to Penn's new and prospering town. Here the doctor had prospered also, for at his death in 1709 he was the owner of several landed properties in and about the city. Sarah did not long survive her remarriage, and by 1712 Samuel Johnson had another wife, Mary Burch.[15] He and Mary lived in one of the Hodgson houses in Black Horse Alley, collecting rentals from their other holdings in the neighborhood. It was but a step around the corner to High Street, the markets, and the "New Printing Office."

13. William W. Johnson, *Johnson Genealogy, Records of the Descendants of John Johnson of Ipswich and Andover, Mass., 1635–1892* (North Greenfield, Wisconsin, 1892), p. 124.

Samuel Johnson's mother was Rebecca Aslett, born in Andover on May 6, 1652. Further records of the family may be found in: Abiel Abbott, *History of Andover*, Andover, 1829; Sarah Loring Bailey, *Historical Sketches of Andover*, Boston, 1880; Topsfield Historical Society, *Vital Records of Andover, Mass.*, Topsfield, 1912.

14. "Daniel Hodson & Sarah Sherman were married by Mr. James Allen." Boston, Mass. Record Commissioners. *9th Report . . . Containing Boston Births, Baptisms, Marriages and Deaths, 1630–99* (Boston, 1883), p. 229.

15. The transactions noted here and below are recorded in the offices of the Recorder of Deeds and Register of Wills, City Hall, Philadelphia.

In all recorded transactions he is "Samuel Johnson, Painter," in evidence that he had plied his trade steadily through the years. In the spring of 1717 there had been a mass enrollment of citizens, enticed into the payment of appropriate fees by what had been termed "the Priviledges & advantages of the ffreemen of this City." Samuel Johnson joined the roster on May 27 with a payment of 15*s*. 6*d*.[16] Three other painters followed suit, Aaron Huliot and Peter Luolie at the same fee, and Peter Cooper at 5*s*. 6*d*.[17]

Records remain of three painting jobs performed by Samuel Johnson, and of these two may have gone to him on the recommendation of Benjamin Franklin. In 1723 he earned £7. 2*s*. painting the city's new market house.[18] In September 1741 the Union Fire Company, of which Franklin had been one of the founders in 1736, had ordered new fire hooks and poles, and 10*s*. had been paid to "Samuel Johnson for painting the poles."[19] In 1748 and 1749, £12. 7*s*. 9*d*. had been paid to "Samuel Johnston, Painter," for work on the new batteries at Wicaco and on Atwood's Wharf, the defenses being erected by the militia association organized by Franklin.[20] Gustavus Hesselius' bill for painting "four Field cariages" bears Franklin's endorsement urging its prompt payment.[21] But as evidence that Samuel Johnson's skill in his craft embraced upon occasion the painting of a portrait, that it may have been he who brought the printer's son to life in those green fields, we have only a few clues in his will and in the will of his wife: showing him as a friend of Franklin, as associated with that class of Philadelphians among whom a portrait painter would find employment, and as the owner of family pictures of his own and a portrait of himself.

Samuel Johnson made his bequests on May 25, 1755, and the will was probated eight days later. He named as executors Benjamin Franklin, Thomas Bourne, and his wife. To Mary he bequeathed the house in which they lived and the house next door to it. Other

16. *Minutes of the Common Council of the City of Philadelphia, 1704 to 1776* (Philadelphia, 1847), p. 129.

17. Ibid., pp. 131, 135, 134.

18. Ibid., p. 239.

19. Harold E. Gillingham, "Philadelphia's First Fire Defences," *P.M.H.B., 56* (1932), 365.

20. *Philadelphia Lottery Accounts* (Philadelphia, 1752), pp. 9, 14.

21. Edgar Fahs Smith Library of the History of Chemistry, University of Pennsylvania.

property went to his niece, Phebe, "the wife of James Trumble," and to his nephews, John and Samuel Johnson. The nephew Samuel was at hand to witness the document, along with the Rev. William Sturgeon, then a lodger in the painter's home and the assistant minister at Christ Church, of which Mr. Bourne was an active member, associations which link the painter to the Anglican group, more liberal in matters of art than the dissenters. The inventory accompanying his will brings us again, as old inventories do, intimately into the home in that hushed pause between one generation and another. Pictures of any sort were rare in eighteenth-century American life but here, in the two rooms occupied by the elderly couple, there were thirty-four of them and of these at least two, and perhaps all, were paintings. Three were stored away. Fifteen adorned the "lower room." In the large "chamber" above stood the bed in which the painter died, with tester and enclosing curtains. There was another bed nearby, a couch, a card table, a tea table with glass and china, two other tables with "sundry old books," and a tall chest of drawers. Three curtained windows let in the soft light of summer. Two mirrors gleamed among the sixteen "old pictures" spread around the walls.[22]

Mary Johnson lived there for five years more, and in her will, dated October 15, 1760 and proved on May 15, 1761, the first bequest is "unto James Trumbal of Charles-town in New England the Picture of my dear late Husband Samuel Johnson." Now the inventory lists "20 small Picturs," "1 Stand and 4 Picturs," and "2 Famley Picturs." One of the family pictures must have been her husband's portrait and the other, almost certainly, a companion piece of herself. Christopher Ludwick, that adventurous spirit, at this time a baker of gingerbread men around the corner in Letitia Court and later Baker-General to the Continental army, had witnessed her will, helped to make the inventory, and finally purchased the Black

22. The documents in Mary's estate are where they should be, in Philadelphia City Hall. Samuel's, with hundreds of other papers, were recently stolen and sold to separate institutions, leaving behind only a defective transcript of the will. It is to be hoped that this may be the last great raid on public archives. Its detection, largely accomplished by the prompt action of Richard Norris Williams of the H.S.P. and Edwin Wolf of the Library Co. of Philadelphia, has been followed by measures which have restored a part of the loot and may lead to protective and procedural reforms and to further restitutions.

Horse Alley property from Mary's principal heir, her brother, Thomas Burch, a planter from Caroline County, Virginia. If, therefore, we should ever find an authentic painting from Samuel Johnson's hand, it may be in Philadelphia, in Massachusetts, or by the rivers flowing south toward Yorktown.

One link of possible significance does not appear in wills or elsewhere. Though Samuel Johnson had remained in touch with his old home and continued to announce himself as a Bostonian, I have found no evidence allying him to the well-known Boston family of painters, Thomas Johnston and his sons, who may well have been related to him and with whom he may also have had a relationship of training in the craft.[23]

I therefore suggest three painters, Hesselius, Winter, and Johnson, one of whom may have made the portrait of Franky Franklin. For those who insist upon a tidy conclusion, I offer Samuel Johnson as the one most favored by the evidence at hand. But even if it be none of them, these three were still Benjamin Franklin's introduction to the world of art and artists. They were his friends, and in them we may see the basis for the cordial, forthright acceptance with which he faced all such folk thereafter. It all began with these three and with the picture of a little boy romping in Elysium, a lost happiness ever recalled to mind from the painting's misty unreality. In 1758, at the beginning of Franklin's long residence in England, Franky's portrait or a small copy of it was sent to him there. The original was in the Philadelphia house in 1770, for we have a pretty glimpse of it there in a letter of Deborah's written on June 13 to her "Dear Child," as she called her husband, in London. Her "King Bird"—Benjamin Franklin Bache, their grandson whom Benjamin Franklin had not yet seen—was ten months old then, and the Baches were living with her, as was William Franklin. "Billey," she wrote,

> is very fond of the Child and thinkes he is like Frankey
> Folger. I thoute so too and had the pickter broute
> down to look and every bodey thinkes as much as thow
> it had been drawn for him. When we show it to the
> Child and tell him he is his little unkill he will pat it

23. Frederick W. Coburn, "The Johnstons of Boston," *Art in America, 21* (1932–33), 27–36, 132–38.

and kiss it and clope his hand to it and every morning
he crowes and clopes to his Grandadey but I wonte
say aney more now.[24]

Others wrote in praise of his grandson to Franklin in London,
bringing pleasure but also the pang of loneliness, bringing "often
afresh to my mind the idea of my son Franky, though now dead
thirty-six years, whom I have seldom since seen equalled in every
thing, and whom to this day I cannot think of without a sigh."[25] It
was a recollection which, as the years passed and as his other son
emerged as a powerful enemy, must have become more sharply dear.

When Franky's grave was new in Christ Church burying ground,
his father had placed there a little stone of the native marble, close
beside the spot where he and Deborah would lie. This epitaph was
carved upon it:

> FRANCIS F.
> Son of Benjamin & Deborah
> FRANKLIN
> Deceased Nov. 21, 1736
> aged 4 Years, 1 Mon. & 1 Day.
> The DELIGHT of all that knew him.

The stone, small and white, crumbled into nothing long ago.[26] All
one sees now is the broad slab with those two names of the parents
united into one. Only the painting remains as a monument to this
love and sorrow, the lighted eyes and laughter of the child.

24. Letter and painting are both owned by Franklin's direct descendant, Mrs.
James Manderson Castle, Jr., Wilmington, Del.

25. Carl Van Doren, ed., *The Letters of Benjamin Franklin & Jane Mecom*
(Princeton, 1950), p. 134. The letter is dated Jan. 13, 1772.

26. The stone is illustrated in Ford, *The Many-sided Franklin*, pp. 39, 509.

3 THE AMERICAN GENTLEMAN

THERE IS an auction scene in *The School for Scandal* in which a young spendthrift puts his ancestral portraits up for sale, with his rich uncle (in disguise) as the only bidder. "Ay, ay," he says to get the thing started,

> these are done in the true spirit of portrait painting;—
> no *volontier grace* and expression. Not like the work
> of your modern Raphaels, who give you the strongest
> resemblance, yet contrive to make your portrait inde-
> pendent of you, so that you may sink the original
> and not hurt the picture. No, no; the merit of these is
> the inveterate likeness—all stiff and awkward as the
> originals, and like nothing in human nature besides.

It is one of the most adroit scenes in English comedy, and uses as its denouement the portrait's part in strengthening the ties of family and friendship, that which in Dr. Johnson's estimation compensated for its "complication with pride." People were still aware of the deep recollections a portrait or a statue could evoke, and were still sensitive to them. The American colonial knew that he was perpetuating a pagan and a Romish practice but had no fear (save among Quakers and the like) of the taint of idolatry. Formalism, "all stiff and awkward," made the image more remote and more compelling. Little Franky's picture was successful in part because the remembered face looked out from that iconlike unreality. The earliest portrait we have of Franky's father, painted about ten years later, is in the fashion of mannered stiffness with all its stately emphasis. Curiously, however, this first portrait of Benjamin Franklin came at a turning point in art history, at a time in the mid-eighteenth century when a resurgence of humanism was transforming the English portrait into a more factual, rational image. Men of this spirit, and Franklin was superlatively one of them, responded more readily to the clean and clear-cut statement and were repelled by reverence-demanding poses. But when John Franklin of Boston had an artist paint a picture of his beloved younger brother, Benjamin, American art had not yet begun to catch reflections of Sir Joshua Reynolds' graceful naturalism, and Benjamin is introduced to us within the old pattern of static dignity.

The painting is in the large, standard, three-quarter size, fifty inches high and forty wide. In it is the usual standing figure, in a composition based upon straight, vertical lines, upright, suave, and firm in tradition. He wears a suit of dark green, almost black, and a dark green waistcoat. His body is to the right; his head is turned a little more toward the spectator; and his dark eyes are full upon him. His right arm extends straight downward, the hand in a pointing gesture. His hat is under the other arm, his hand in the waistcoat. The tightly curled wig is brown and reflected light is painted upon every curl. He stands against a brown wall, and at the right the picture opens into a strangely barren landscape of hills, piling up into gray-white clouds and a gray-blue sky.

It may be said of the study of portraiture that few other areas of research bring the student so intimately into the historical past. The personal tastes and habits of both painter and subject become matters of fascination to him. He enters a man's home, peers into his wardrobe, studies the character of his friends, watches the recession of his hair line. He gives minute consideration to George Washington's false teeth and finds himself studying the First Citizen's double chin as if upon it hung the fate of civilization. Now it is Benjamin Franklin's wig, a brown wig, what was called a "natural," though of course none of the wigs pretended to imitate natural hair. It was their deliberate artificiality, artistically related to the wearer's walk of life, which perpetuated the fashion through so many years. This wig is simply a cloth cap, covering the ears and dropping to the neckline, covered all over with rows of tightly curled brown hair. I think that Franklin did wear such a wig, and that this is not in any essential respect an addition of the painter's. White and gray wigs were more expensive than brown and indicated an advanced station in society. The painter has done this much: he has covered it with a profusion of highlights, thus giving his subject a more distinguished air. More expensive wigs had also more shape and more depth to the hair. This wig is very similar to that worn by Figg, the prize-fighter, in the second scene of Hogarth's *Rake's Progress,* painted in 1735, a scene which affords a good contrast in character and rank as expressed in wig styles.

Franklin's wig is a somewhat debased version of William Penn's in his later years. It has a shapeless simplicity and lack of flair which may have accorded well with Quaker feeling, and certainly we find the type well represented in early Philadelphia portraits. The portraits of James Logan and Charles Norris show it,[1] as does Gustavus Hesselius' self-portrait of about 1740 and the Hesselius portrait of Robert Morris, Sr., of about 1748.[2] West has shown Dr. Samuel Boudé, about 1755, with a late, up-country survival of it.[3] As for the date of Franklin's wig, I would place it before his retirement from business in 1747. He may have worn it longer than that, but his degree of affluence and his growing involvement in public affairs and association with men of learning would probably have been reflected in his dress and head cover. Franklin's famous simplicity in dress belongs to a later period. In a society where status and costume went together he took the straightforward, sensible view—dressed according to his rank, never below it, and never so far above it as to appear pretentious. Then, too, the style in wigs was changing at that time. In the new modes with which the long history of wig-wearing was to close, the hair was parted at the center and flowed down into a wider mass below or else into a few tight horizontal curls over the ears. These were the "full-bottomed" and the "bob" wigs. After 1750 the older fashion was worn mostly by men of advanced age, clinging to old ways.

1. For illust. see Albert Cook Myers, ed., *Hannah Logan's Courtship* (Philadelphia, 1904), pp. 16, 50.
2. For illust. see *Gustavus Hesselius, 1682–1755,* pl. 7.
3. For illust. see *P.M.H.B., 62* (1938), no. 11.

Given the masculine position in such matters, fashions in dress are much less helpful in dating a man's portrait than a woman's. Nevertheless, what this wig tells us and what the rest of the costume bears out is of profound significance, and it is strange indeed that this picture, studied so much because of its famous subject, has received no particular attention here. What we see in the portrait is that the subject chose to dress in the style of a successful tradesman, neither wearing his own hair as many contemporaries did, nor assuming the wig style of professional men and gentlemen of leisure. The other wigs I have cited are white or gray. The painter has lightened the tone of this one as much as he could with his highlights and would have been delighted, had he been permitted to do so, to have represented his subject in a finer style. A waistcoat of a rich, contrasting color, white satin, perhaps, a more shapely wig, a binding of gold lace on the hat, all would have made it a far more striking and attractive picture. Instead, we have here—and in this painting alone —the ordinary citizen, the small businessman, of the 1740s. As such, it is a unique social document. As such, it offsets the legend then current in France, of a Franklin scorning the artificialities of dress which obscure the natural man. He was too alert and intelligent a leader of men for that. His portraits show him costumed neatly within his social rank. As wealth and public office raised him to higher station, he assumed an appearance appropriate to it, wig included. When at last he put off his wig it was for personal comfort and at a time the public was quite ready to accept and even extol the act.

Earlier, Franklin might have worn a somewhat deeper cuff and, very likely, the long-popular straight white "Steenkirk" cravat which we see in James Logan's portrait and which by 1740 had largely given way again to the frilled shirt ruffle. More decisive as to date is the pose of the figure. If the costume is bourgeois, this at least is aristocratic. It is the ancient tradition of formal portraiture in its politely Anglicized application, yet expressed according to a personal formula wholly characteristic of one certain painter, all of whose known work lies in the decade of the 1740s. The erect carriage, the lift of the head, the gesture of one hand, and the easy concealment of the other are all in the manner of Robert Feke, that seafaring man turned artist, that ever mysterious figure of the little towns, the wild coast, and the islands. So too is the background, with the unusual depth of window opening to show a greater reach of hill and sky. Feke, self-trained so far as we know, had a style of his own, a "force of genius" as one contemporary put it, a comprehension of both his sitter and his paints. Long, slender fingers guided his brush; his dark eyes were intent; his hair hung in dark curls to the shoulder[4] for men who fared out upon the windy seas did not wear wigs, and there was bred in them the habit of perceptive watchfulness.

We have no evidence that Franklin and the painter ever met. They had, however, mutual acquaintances and three possible meeting places, Philadelphia, Boston, and the Rhode Island town of Newport. Henry Wilder Foote, in his biography of Feke, points out also that Feke's having copied in oils a frontispiece engraving from one of Shaftesbury's works suggests a common viewpoint with the free-thinking Philadelphian.[5] Waldron Belknap, defending the general accuracy of Dr. Foote's work, brought to light new material on the painter's early life, including a rebellious hegira similar to Franklin's early escapade.[6] From this account we know that Robert Feke was born in Oyster Bay, Long Island, between 1706 and 1710, the son of a yeoman and blacksmith of the same name. On December 12, 1730, he filed in the Oyster Bay records a survey of lands owned by his uncle, Silvanus Wright, a transaction which Waldron Belknap gently avers to have had "the characteristics of a youthful prank," but which disrupted the little community and was condemned by a specially called town meeting as "Contrayry to ye Coustoum." The young man then disappears entirely from the Oyster Bay records. He may have gone at once to Newport, a town in which he had relatives and doubtless friends as well, but of the next few years of his life we have only family legends of distant voyages, of a capture at sea and imprisonment in Spain.[7] Sometime between 1738 and 1741, in Philadelphia, he painted the portraits of Tench Francis and his wife, whose likenesses he again portrayed in 1746. The first written record of his professional career is his own inscrip-

4. Self-portraits illustrated in Henry Wilder Foote, *Robert Feke, Colonial Portrait Painter* (Cambridge, 1930), frontispiece and opp. p. 96.
5. Ibid., p. 49.
6. Waldron Phoenix Belknap, Jr., "The Identity of Robert Feke," *Art Bulletin*, 29 (1947), 203.
7. Ibid., pp. 203–04.

tion on the back of his group portrait of the Royall family of Boston, dated September 15, 1741.

There follows a period of settled life in Newport. There, on September 23, 1742, he was married to Eleanor Cozzens whose brother, Charles, was later to marry one of his sisters in Oyster Bay.[8] He was painting portraits in Philadelphia in 1746, and his daughter, Philadelphia Feke, was perhaps born there at that time. He was in Boston in 1748 and in Philadelphia again in 1750. No doubt there were other trips afield of which we are unaware, but after 1750 there is only the legend of a voyage to one of the southern islands from which he never returned. He left behind unfinished portraits of his wife and himself in costumes of about 1750. He chose to show himself here with palette and brushes in hand, to be remembered as a painter, though at his daughter's marriage in 1767 they wrote him down in the certificate as "mariner, deceased," and it is doubtless true that the family had enjoyed a higher social standing on this count than on the other.[9]

Newport was a seafaring island town of considerable wealth, with opportunities for both mariner and limner. The aristocratic face-painter's art had arrived there in 1729, when Dean Berkeley had been wafted into port with John Smibert in his entourage, bestowing on it, as it were, the blessing of both church and state. Smibert's work had influenced Feke, but it is not the principal source of his style. Smibert had more influence, first in Newport, then in Boston, as the painter who gave portraiture a new attractiveness and a sophistication within the grasp of the prospering New Englander. John Franklin of Newport and Boston was the first of his family to adopt the amenities of higher station: a library, portraits on his walls, his letters sealed with the Franklin coat of arms, and the coat of arms elaborately engraved upon his bookplate. Benjamin, fifteen years his junior but prospering more rapidly, followed close behind. Yet I doubt if John Franklin was ready for the expensive and sentimental luxury of paintings as early as 1733, when Benjamin visited Boston and, stopping in Newport on his way home, was reconciled with his brother James, the printer from whose service he had

8. Ibid., p. 205.
9. Ibid., p. 207. Foote, *Robert Feke,* p. 100.

run away ten years before. It is scarcely possible, moreover, to believe that Feke had matured his style so early.

We know that Newport was Feke's home through the 1740s. The Franklin connection with Newport had been longer. John Franklin with his young bride, Mary Gooch, had gone there from Boston and had been admitted a freeman of the colony on May 3, 1715.[10] John and Peter were the two sons whom Josiah Franklin had bred to his own trade of tallow chandler. They made the crown soap which Benjamin sold in his Philadelphia shop, and they sold his almanacs in theirs. As the father aged, John gave more time to the Boston business but continued to have Newport interests. In 1736 both John and Josiah, along with James Trumble and many others, were listed as subscribers to Prince's *Chronology,* and John seems to have been then considered a resident of Boston.[11] Peter, meanwhile, had settled in Newport, keeping a stock of imported merchandise in addition to his regular trade.[12] Peter, a seagoing businessman who fancied himself a poet, was surely a kindred spirit of the painter's. James Franklin had died in Newport in 1735, but his widow continued the printing business there until her son, the younger James Franklin, could be trained in the craft at his uncle's Philadelphia office.

Benjamin Franklin was in Boston again in May 1743, and back at home in July. In late July or early August, John had come up from Newport to Boston, and the brothers must have been together at one place or both. In 1746, as we know from his signed and dated paintings, Feke was busy in Philadelphia. In mid-October of that year, Franklin set out again for New England and did not return until late in December. He had young James Franklin with him in Boston, so that he may have returned by way of Newport to leave the boy there with his mother. Of places and dates at which the painter and the subject of this portrait may have been together we have therefore the following from which to choose: Philadelphia, between 1738 and 1740; Boston or Newport in the summer of 1743; Philadelphia, Boston, or Newport in 1746.

10. John R. Bartlett, ed., *Records of the Colony of Rhode Island, 4* (Providence, 1859), 183.

11. *New England Historical and Genealogical Register, 6* (1852), 193.

12. Account book and ledger, Library of the A.P.S.

Dr. Foote included the portrait of Franklin in his catalogue of the work of Robert Feke, thus corroborating in 1930 an attribution first made by Lawrence Park in 1923.[13] Both agreed upon 1746 as the probable date. Dr. Foote's conjecture that John Franklin may have commissioned the painter to do the work while in Philadelphia is obviously a reasonable one. So is his feeling that Franklin may at that time have introduced Feke to his close friend, Thomas Hopkinson, president of the recently organized American Philosophical Society, although Feke's portrait of Hopkinson, now in the National Gallery, was more probably painted in 1750 than in 1746.[14]

The rather fumbling brushwork in the painting has been a topic of much discussion, and may be used as an argument for an early date. It might be suggested that Feke painted this picture on his first visit to Philadelphia, and painted little Franky's at the same time. One is a possible, the other a doubtful, conjecture. The picture of Franky is an awkward, charmingly earnest effort to reproduce the outmoded elegance in which the little Lord Euston had been enshrined fifty years before. His early portrait of Tench Francis is modish, sincere, and marked by Feke's characteristic independence. He did at times borrow a composition from a print, but was not an abject follower. Franky's portraitist had obviously put in the head before he selected his mezzotint, but from there on he had groped his way devoutly after Kneller, and any departures are due simply to his own ineptitude.

Another factor argues also for an early date. Elizabeth Partridge, who will be described below in the roster of the portrait's owners, believed it to have been painted in London in 1726. She herself, born in 1728, was probably in her late teens or early twenties when her mother became John Franklin's second wife and the portrait was brought into her home. Her statement, to be sure, was probably made in the 1790s, and was not put into writing until 1839.[15] One must make due allowances for such a stretch between the spoken and the written word. What remains at least fairly certain is that in the years of Benjamin Franklin's rising fame, as early as 1755 to 1760,

13. Lawrence Park, "A Portrait of Franklin by Robert Feke," *Art in America, 12* (1923), 29–32.
14. Foote, *Robert Feke,* p. 159.
15. Sparks Papers (Harvard), *18,* no. 148.

this picture was regarded in Boston as an old one, coming from a former period in his career.

Having determined the probable painter of this picture and fixed its date within an eight-year span, nothing remains but to discuss a possible attribution to either of two other painters rather than to Robert Feke, and to again raise the doubt—here advancing a new and more plausible theory on the subject—as to whether it is a portrait of Benjamin Franklin to start with. To do this it is necessary to look more closely at the household in which we first find the picture and at those others in which it afterward had a place.

The dates of the death of John Franklin's first wife, Mary Gooch, and of his marriage to Mrs. Elizabeth Gooch Hubbart are unknown. These dates would be helpful clues, since the establishment of a new home was so often an occasion for the painting of portraits. Captain John Hubbart had died in 1734 and Elizabeth was still "Widow Hubbart" on December 16, 1740.[16] John and Elizabeth Franklin, as man and wife, were executors of a kinsman's will on December 20, 1752.[17] The marriage took place sometime in those twelve years, perhaps in 1746, a year when Benjamin Franklin visited Newport and Boston. The Hubbarts were Boston people. John Franklin, childless now, moved into his wife's house on Cornhill, with a pleasant and mature group of stepchildren around him. There, on the wall, he hung the portraits of Elizabeth, of himself, and of his brother Benjamin. Benjamin was with them there in person in 1753 and 1754, organizing the postal service for the northern colonies. He made John postmaster for Boston. There, on January 30, 1756, John Franklin died. He left his widow with a fair provision, to which Benjamin added by putting her in charge of the post office. John had written his will on January 22, and on January 24 added a codicil of smaller bequests: a silver porringer, the two volumes of Chambers' *Dictionary,* the three volumes of Bacon's *Works,* and the portraits:

> I give to my well Beloved Wife my large Picture
> likewise my Brother Benjamins Picture during her

16. Frank Austin Gooch, *The History of a Surname* (New Haven, 1926), p. 102.
17. Ibid.

Natural life, and after her Decease I give my Picture
to William Franklin of Philadelphia the son of my
Brother Benjamin Franklin Esqr. and I give my
Brother Benjamin Franklins Picture to James Franklin of Newport the Son of my Brother James Franklin Deceased.[18]

The inventory of John Franklin's estate lists "three family Pictures," valued together at four pounds.[19] The third, not mentioned
in his will, can only have been the portrait of Elizabeth.

As in detective stories, where a conveniently isolated coterie of
suspects is presented for our attention, we have only to consider four
pictures with interrelated histories: John's three, and one, long lost
to sight, of Benjamin. The puzzle is to determine, on a basis of probability at least, the artist and the date of the Harvard portrait and,
most important of all, whether it is a portrait of Benjamin Franklin
or (and this is really the only permissible alternative) a portrait of
his brother John. The four portraits are:

1 *Benjamin Franklin.* Owned by John Franklin (Pl. I).

2 *John Franklin.* Owned by Benjamin Franklin. These two may
well represent an exchange, as tokens of fraternal affection. Deborah
Franklin wrote to her husband in 1765 describing the furnishings of
the new Philadelphia house: "In the north room where we sit, we
have a small Scotch carpet, the small bookcase, brother John's picture and one of the King and Queen."[20] There is no other record of
the painting.

3 *John Franklin.* Owned by himself, and possibly a replica of the
above. John obviously bequeathed this portrait to Benjamin's son,
William, because in 1756 Benjamin already had one. That phrase
in the will, "my large Picture," may possibly mark his own portrait
as larger than that of his brother. Or it may distinguish this portrait
of himself from a smaller one, perhaps a locket miniature kept and
worn by his wife. This "large Picture" has been unrecorded since
1853.

18. Suffolk County probate records, Boston, Mass., transcripts, Vol. 51.
19. Mrs. Russel Hastings, "Some Franklin Memorabilia Emerge in Los Angeles,"
Antiques, 36 (1939), 225.
20. John F. Watson, *Annals of Philadelphia, 1* (Philadelphia, 1891), 206.

4   *Mrs. John Franklin* (Pl. I). Elizabeth's portrait, lost to sight for a century, was rediscovered in 1939. Mrs. Russel Hastings, corresponding secretary of the Santa Barbara Historical Society, in the course of investigating a group of Franklin heirlooms which had turned up in California, found it among the portraits of members of the Gooch family which the Brooklyn Museum had purchased from a descendant in 1927.[21] Her research procedure was similar to that of Waldron Belknap, discoverer of the influence of the mezzotints in American painting, and one of whose warm friends she later became. Both, in studying family portraits, reconstructed the pattern of owners and possible subjects and into this fitted their critical judgment of each canvas. This portrait had long been identified as that of another, earlier Elizabeth Gooch. Its identification as the second Mrs. John Franklin is now accepted without question.

Compare this portrait of Elizabeth Franklin to the Harvard portrait. The gentleman faces to the right, the lady to the left. His canvas is 50 by 40 inches in size, hers only 36 by 28⅜, but you will notice that her head and hand are uncomfortably close to the margins. Granting that hers has been cut down in size—about six inches trimmed off all around—they would stand perfectly as a pair, with the figure in hers of the right proportions to match the figure in his. Her portrait was relined before coming to the museum, so that we no longer have a margin showing its original size. The composition is also similar and carries out the feeling that one may have been painted as pendant to the other.

As for the man's likeness, could it not be John Franklin as well as Benjamin? They were full brothers, though one the first and the other the last of Josiah Franklin's sons by his second wife. Benjamin's eyes were hazel, and although painters have read them differently, from yellowish to gray, the eyes of his life portraits are light in tone. The eyes in this portrait are dark. The fact is significant, but by no means conclusive, since in early American portraiture a strongly defined eye was thought to add vastly to the force and character of the piece. People were impressed by an image which could hold them in its fixed, mysterious regard. One of Feke's portraits had the eyeballs scratched out by a woman who was frightened by

21. Hastings, "Franklin Memorabilia," p. 226.

its watchfulness, and it is worth noting that there appear to be more dark eyes in those early portraits than anyone could expect to find in a random selection of acquaintances.

Mrs. Hastings, quoting William Sawitzky's positive opinion, attributed the portrait of Elizabeth Franklin to a young Bostonian of good family and convivial habits, John Greenwood.[22] Some have felt it to be more characteristic of Joseph Badger.[23] They were rival hacks in Boston, and their styles have points of similarity. The case for Greenwood is bolstered by the attribution to him of other portraits of ladies identical with this one in almost every detail but the face. The Harvard portrait has also been attributed to Greenwood and never, with absolute certainty, to Feke.[24] The poverty of its coloring and a tyro's fumbling hesitation in the brushwork point to Greenwood and, obliquely, to Badger. The pose and composition, on the other hand, are Feke's. Greenwood, if he imitated them here, never did so again. Badger, an older man, adhered the more fixedly to his own clumsy formulas.

Greenwood had learned his craft in the shop of that Thomas Johnston, the painter-decorator who may have been a kinsman of Franklin's friend, Samuel Johnson of Philadelphia.[25] The earliest of his portraits known today is signed and dated 1745.[26] He left Boston late in 1752 for Surinam, turned up in Holland five years later, and finally, in 1762, settled in London as an art dealer and auctioneer. He called on Benjamin Franklin in Paris in 1777 bringing news of importance which Franklin sent to America as from "Mr. Greenwood, a Painter formerly of Boston."[27] The incident implies a previous acquaintance, though whether they met first at Boston, London, or Paris we cannot know.

If Greenwood painted Benjamin Franklin it could only have

22. Ibid., p. 223.

23. Alan Burroughs, *John Greenwood in America, 1745–1752* (Andover, 1943), pp. 37–40, 73. The Frick Art Reference Library records attributions to Badger by Lawrence Park and, in an altered opinion, William Sawitzky.

24. Alan Burroughs, ed., *Harvard Portraits* (Cambridge, Mass., 1936), p. 59. Burroughs, *John Greenwood*, pp. 35–36.

25. Burroughs, *John Greenwood*, p. 12. Frederick W. Coburn, "The Johnstons of Boston," *Art in America, 21* (1932), p. 32.

26. Burroughs, *John Greenwood*, pp. 16–17.

27. Benjamin Franklin to Thomas Cushing, May 1, 1777 (Franklin Papers, L.C., 358). Greenwood to Franklin, 1777 (Franklin Papers, A.P.S., *40*, no. 31).

been in Boston in 1746. The case for him is the stronger if the portrait is actually that of John and therefore presumably painted at the same time as its companion piece. Happily, in facing the mystery as to which brother looks down upon us from the Harvard wall, we have unusually clear and authentic data on former ownerships over the whole of its history. The roster of ownership follows, and is accompanied by a chart of the family showing more simply the descent of John Franklin's three paintings from generation to generation through these two centuries. In these we can see at what points a change might have occurred, what family continuity there was to work against it, and how old portraits, now greatly treasured, were once passed on as lightly as those of the Surface family in *The School for Scandal:*

1   *John Franklin* (1690–1756). John Franklin either received the gift of a portrait from his brother or commissioned a painter to make one. Probably at the same time he gave a portrait of himself to Benjamin, retaining a replica of it in his own home.

2   *Mrs. John Franklin* (1698–1768). Period of ownership, 12 years, 1756–68.

3   *Tuthill Hubbart* (1720–1808). Period of ownership, 40 years, 1768–1808. Tuthill was the third of Mrs. John Franklin's sons by her first husband. He lived with her and shared the duties of the post office. After her death Benjamin Franklin appointed him postmaster in her place. The house on Cornhill became his, and with it the three portraits. A few years later Jane Mecom, filling a letter to her brother Benjamin with gossip of the Boston family, expressed her belief that "Tuthill Has no Thoughts of Matreymony."[28] Tuthill maintained this viewpoint throughout his life, giving strict attention to his business as an insurance underwriter and acquiring a fairly substantial fortune. He was a successful, trusted businessman, though regarded as somewhat eccentric, a judgment which, in that day, his bachelorhood alone would have brought upon him. He had been the administrator of his mother's estate but had not carried out his stepfather's wishes as to two of the pictures. That of Benjamin Franklin he could not send to James Franklin of Newport, for he

28. Van Doren, *Benjamin Franklin & Jane Mecom,* p. 120.

had died, childless, in 1762. William Franklin had returned to America as Governor of New Jersey and was living there in 1768. The portrait of John was not sent to him for reasons we do not know. It may not have been thought worth the cost of shipment to Perth Amboy. Perhaps Benjamin Franklin sent his portrait of John there instead.

During Tuthill's long period of ownership, Benjamin Franklin reached his climactic fame as architect of the French alliance and became, with his death in 1790, one of the immortal heroes of the nation, one of the most revered fathers of his native city. As far as I can observe, these changes appear hardly to have entered into the thinking of Tuthill Hubbart at all, and the portraits of the Franklin brothers continued to represent to him simply one of the foundations of his own prosperity. He was not a social type, and the paintings cannot have been seen by many. It is a curious fact that in these years of intense and increasing veneration for the hero and sage, with a commensurate demand for his likeness, the publishers in Boston never made use of this portrait and had recourse instead to such foreign prints as came their way. The old picture, which might have had so much to recommend it, was passed by. Indeed, Boston was not aware of having any original portrait of Benjamin Franklin at all until 1828 when the Athenaeum acquired what was believed to be one—the portrait, actually an inferior copy from Duplessis, which Thomas Jefferson had brought back with him from France. The fanfare accompanying this transaction appears to have awakened the first real interest shown by the Hubbart family in their own picture.

Tuthill Hubbart died, intestate, on February 8, 1808. One entry in his inventory lists "11 Pictures" at $3.00, and another, "1 glass & 3 Pictures" at $4.00.[29] From the latter one may infer that the three portraits had hung together in a room with a mirror. The estate was divided among the heirs at law. Only one of his own generation remained, his sister, Elizabeth, and the three portraits passed to her, leaving for the first time the house in which they had hung so long.

4 *Mrs. Samuel Partridge* (1728–1814). Period of ownership, 6 years, 1808–14. Elizabeth Hubbart had been married to Captain

29. Suffolk County probate records, transcripts, Vol. 106.

Samuel Partridge on December 13, 1768, the year in which her mother, Mrs. John Franklin, had died. In the gossipy letter of a year or two later that has already been quoted, Jane Mecom repeats what the neighbors had been saying: that before the birth of her first child, Betsy Partridge had lain abed awaiting the event with her hair done up in formal style and adorned with a plume.[30] From other sources as well, one catches the sparkle of a lady with a mind of her own. The fact that her stepuncle, Benjamin Franklin, was in touch with her up to his last years, writing her some of his wittiest and most delightful letters, bears out the impression, as does her portrait, in which she appears well-dressed, intelligent, a book in hand.[31]

It was Betsy Partridge, then an elderly widow living in Brookline, who gave Thomas Waldron Sumner her opinion of the early origin of Benjamin Franklin's portrait. "I had it from Mrs. Partridge," he wrote in 1839, "that the portrait . . . was painted in London the first time he went there."[32] It is thus, so often, that a spoken recollection or surmise is transformed into the written presumption of historical fact.

It was natural that the three portraits should have gone to Mrs. Partridge in 1808, since she was the last who had known and loved the two brothers, and was her mother's namesake as well. With her death in 1814 the pictures came for the first time into the possession of a generation too young to have any recollection of the people represented. It was here also that the portrait of Mrs. John Franklin was separated from the other two.

Mrs. Partridge's effects were dispersed at a public sale. Among the older people who attended it was William Gooch, a son of Mrs. John Franklin's half brother. He himself had married into the Hubbart family, and his daughter had married a grandson of Mrs. Partridge. Out of respect for this multiple relationship, he bought "two family pictures" for $6.00 each and "one family picture" for $5.50.[33] Mrs. Hastings' inference that the first item represents the pendant portraits of Mr. and Mrs. Samuel Partridge now at the

30. Van Doren, *Benjamin Franklin & Jane Mecom*, p. 120.
31. Brooklyn Museum. Illust. in Hastings, "Franklin Memorabilia," p. 218.
32. Sparks Papers, *18*, no. 148.
33. Hastings, "Franklin Memorabilia," p. 226.

Brooklyn Museum, and the second that of Mrs. John Franklin, fits so perfectly into the pattern of family relationships, the artistic styles, and the history of the seven paintings acquired by Brooklyn in 1927, that there can be no doubt of its accuracy.

Stephen Bean, whose wife had been Susan Hubbart, a younger sister of Mrs. William Gooch, bought the portrait of Benjamin Franklin. A Mr. Hubbart purchased that of John. The price for each was $3.50.[34] Both, apparently, were given to Susan, since she was in possession of them at the time of her death. There seems to have been a feeling in the family that the pictures of the two brothers should be kept, as always, together.

5 *Mrs. Stephen Bean* (1761–1828). Period of ownership, 14 years, 1814–28. Susan Hubbart had married Stephen Bean on May 4, 1808, three months after the death of her rich uncle Tuthill, one of whose heirs she was. Prosperity, however, was not to be theirs. Her husband died insolvent in 1825, and she followed him after a penurious widowhood. The inventory of her estate does, at least, show an increase in the value of the pictures, and for the first time, Benjamin's is rated as worth more than that of John, the one at $12.00 and the other at $5.00.[35] This was in 1828, the year in which with some fanfare the Boston Athenaeum had purchased its French portrait of Franklin from one of Thomas Jefferson's heirs, and we may suppose that Thomas Waldron Sumner, the executor of Mrs. Bean's estate, was alert to the growing value of the pictures. He was the husband of Elizabeth Hubbart, Susan Bean's younger sister, and became the next owner of the two paintings.

6 *Thomas Waldron Sumner* (1768–1849). Period of ownership, 21 years, 1828–49. They had been married at her home in Weston on October 22, 1793.[36] The Boston directories list him as a "housewright" from 1807 to 1823, and from 1825 to 1832, as occupant of a counting room in Merchants Row. He represented Boston in the Massachusetts legislature for eight years between 1805 and 1817. He was a member and officer of the Massachusetts Charitable Me-

34. Ibid., p. 225.
35. Ibid.
36. Weston, Mass., *Births, Deaths and Marriages, 1707–1850* (Boston, 1901), p. 171. See also William S. Appleton, *Record of the Descendants of William Sumner,* Boston, 1879.

chanic Association, in which master mechanics and manufacturers united for benevolent purposes and which had its own special reverence for the name of Franklin.[37] Late in life the couple retired to Brookline, where she died on July 13, 1839, and he on May 29, ten years later.

They had first met in 1792, and in that year he had first seen the portraits of John and Benjamin hanging in the home of his fiancée's uncle, Tuthill Hubbart.[38] Her aunt, Betsy Partridge, for whom they named their first child, told them that the portrait of Benjamin Franklin had been "painted in London the first time he went there."[39] Years later, when it was hanging in their Brookline home, Jared Sparks, President of Harvard, discovered it while compiling his ten-volume *Works of Benjamin Franklin*. He may have heard of it from their son, who had graduated from the college in 1826.[40] At all events, he had it engraved by G. F. Storm in November 1837, and it appeared as the frontispiece in the first volume of the *Works* in 1840. At Mr. Sumner's death, because of this publication, the picture had become the outstanding thing in his estate. Edward Everett, a month after the funeral on July 2, 1849, was consulting with the Massachusetts Historical Society on the chances of purchasing it.[41] William I. Bowditch, the executor, held out for a high price. On January 19, 1850, Mr. Bowditch offered it to Dr. Sparks, whose reply shows such a complete mastery of the cautious approach that it is worth quoting in full:

> Dear Sir,
>
> I have received your note concerning the portrait of Franklin. I will lay it before the Corporation of the College, but I do not think they will be disposed to purchase it. The portrait is interesting as being the

37. *Annals of the Massachusetts Charitable Mechanic Association, 1795–1892* (Boston, 1892), pp. 589, 593. In 1827 the association had participated in placing an obelisk over the grave of Franklin's parents. See *Proceedings on the Occasion of Laying the Cornerstone of a Building for the Use of the Mass. Charitable Mechanic Association,* (Boston, 1857), p. 7. The first proposal for a statue of Franklin in Boston was made by Robert C. Winthrop, *Archimedes and Franklin,* Boston, 1853.

38. Sparks Papers, *38,* no. 148.

39. Ibid.

40. Capt. Thomas Hubbart Sumner (1807–76), author of *A New and Accurate Method of Finding a Ship's Position at Sea* (Boston, 1843).

41. Everett Papers (M.H.S.).

earliest one known of Franklin, but as a work of art it has little to commend it.

I suppose it would be difficult to prove with certainty that it is a portrait of Benj. Franklin. I was satisfied, however, that the evidence rendered this assumption in a high degree probable, amounting as nearly to a certainty as the nature of the testimony would admit.

Although I cannot give any encouragement to the expectation, that the Corporation will buy this portrait, yet I should be much pleased to know what price is set upon it; and also upon the portrait of John Franklin, which formerly hung by its side in Mr. Sumner's house.

> I am, &c.
> Jared Sparks.[42]

In March, Mr. Bowditch advertised an auction to be held on June 6, featuring "that very valuable ORIGINAL PORTRAIT OF DR. BENJAMIN FRANKLIN from which was taken the engraving prefixed to the first volume of Pres. Spark's edition of the Life and Works of Dr. Franklin; a portrait of Dr. Franklin's brother, John Franklin, and twenty-five pieces of beautiful china, cups, Plates, &c. which formerly belonged to Dr. Franklin."[43] The sale seems not to have attracted bidders, for on September 7 Mr. Bowditch wrote to Dr. John C. Warren, refusing an offer of $400 for the painting.[44] He insisted upon $500, and may have received it, for Dr. Warren became the next owner of the portrait, which here, for the first time, was separated from that of the older brother.

7   *Dr. John Collins Warren* (1778–1856). Period of ownership, 6 years, 1850–56. Dr. Warren, a Harvard graduate in the class of 1797, was a wealthy physician whose various properties in Boston included a museum and a "Mastodon Building" on Chestnut Street, housing the most complete skeleton of the American mastodon discovered up to that time. The Franklin portrait he kept in his home

42. Sparks Papers, *147 i,* nos. 128–29.
43. Hastings, "Franklin Memorabilia," p. 225.
44. J. C. Warren Papers (M.H.S.).

at 2 Park Street. At his death it was presented, by his wish, to Harvard.

8 *Harvard University.* Owned from 1856 to the present. The transfer was made by a brief note from Dr. Warren's son to the President and Fellows:

> Gentlemen:
>
> My father, Dr. Warren, directed an original portrait of Dr. Franklin executed in London in 1720, to be given to Harvard College. The picture is large and the frame fragile. Will you be kind enough to take charge of the same or give me your directions concerning it, and oblige your very obt. servant,
>
> J. S. Warren, 2 Park Street, Boston.[45]

With the portrait safely on a college wall, Dr. Sparks expressed his absolute certainty of its genuineness.[46] This sense of confidence, however, faded with time as a later generation looked with less assurance on Sparks' monumental *oeuvre*. Sparks had not accepted the early date given the picture but, with a courteous consideration for its owners, had deferred to them by leaving this matter undiscussed. In 1896, however, Charles Henry Hart, then the leading authority on American art, made much of this point and used it to condemn the whole work as spurious, vehemently pointing out the manifest absurdity that in 1726 a poor apprentice in London would have had his own portrait painted in such style.[47] To Hart's thorough and accurate studies we owe much but, like others of his time, he was also a professional expert and dealer, functions which, when operating, open the mind persuasively to wishful thinking. In this particular instance, while decrying the Harvard portrait as "mythical," he was on the next page advancing Matthew Pratt's likeness of Franklin (owned by himself and later sold to Alexander Smith Cochran) as

45. Quoted from the records of the corporation by Park, "Portrait of Franklin," pp. 30–31.
46. Sparks to D. Tilton, March 3, 1864 (Harvard MSS).
47. Charles Henry Hart, "Life Portraits of Great Americans. Benjamin Franklin," *McClure's Magazine, 8* (1897), 264.

painted "about 1756" and "the earliest authentic portrait of Franklin."[48]

The Fogg Museum, present custodian of the portrait, has reached, as of today, by its own objective inquiry and technical examination, an almost equally devastating conclusion about the picture: "that it has been considerably overcleaned and repainted and that it is no longer possible to determine anything . . . except that it is contemporaneous with Benjamin Franklin."[49] A museum's rigid standard of excellence may require the rejection of any conjectural stand, yet it is impossible for me to believe the matter so heavily overclouded as this last statement suggests. Dr. Henry Wilder Foote and Mr. Alan Burroughs, whose knowledge of the artists of this period is far more comprehensive than mine, have with great kindness re-examined the subject for me.

In 1930 Dr. Foote included the portrait in his work on Robert Feke with a cautionary note that it is "not particularly characteristic" of the painter.[50] He was nonetheless positive in his attribution, and has continued so. In 1959 he examined the canvas again, "to look at it with a freshly critical eye."[51] He could still see "some room for doubt as to the painter. The head does not seem very characteristic of Feke's work, yet, if he was not the painter, I find it even more difficult to say to what other artist of the period it could possibly be attributed with any reasonable probability."

In 1936 Mr. Burroughs had also expressed doubts as to Feke's authorship, feeling that the brushwork and color pointed to Greenwood—"the black and white coloring . . . especially foreign to Feke's delicate adjustments of tone."[52] In 1958, however, his opinion "now veers towards Feke. The surface *is* bleak and may have been tampered with, but the x-ray shadowgraph shows the original modelling, which is surely less suave than Feke's usual work, yet after all not so rough as Greenwood's.[53] Giving due prominence to the *de-*

48. Raymond H. Torrey, "Philipse Manor Hall and the Cochran Art Collection," *Scenic and Historic America, 4* (1935), 3.

49. John Coolidge, director, to the author, Dec. 17, 1958.

50. Foote, *Robert Feke,* p. 152 n.

51. Henry Wilder Foote to the author, Feb. 25, 1959.

52. Burroughs, *Harvard Portraits,* p. 59.

53. Illust. in Burroughs, *John Greenwood,* p. 84.

sign, as opposed to the handling, I now believe it was more likely to have been Feke who struggled with the modelling."[54]

As for the identity of the subject, Hart's condemnation of the picture as wholly spurious because of an unreasonable claim as to date is unjustified. Its pedigree of owners leaves no doubt that it must be either Benjamin or John Franklin. A switch in identities, especially after the removal of the portrait of Mrs. John, would represent a common enough sort of occurrence. The larger, more commanding figure might have been accepted as that of the more famous brother. However, the weight of evidence against this is enormously increased when you consider that Thomas Waldron Sumner had seen the picture in 1792, two years after Franklin's death, that Franklin's climactic fame must have impressed the likeness on his mind, and that his recollection bridges all the later vicissitudes. It was he who, when Dr. Sparks became interested in the picture, had for the first time an identifying label placed upon the frame. The identification is primarily his, and what little we know of his life indicates a man of probity and exactitude.

Another factor is the subject's apparent youthfulness. Old portraits are often deceptive in this regard, yet it argues strongly for Benjamin rather than John. There were sixteen years between the brothers' ages, and it is more credible that this is a man in his thirties, or a little beyond them, than one of fifty to sixty.

Only the reappearance of that other painting can confirm or shake the obvious inferences. The portrait of John Franklin which Benjamin had owned must be presumed destroyed. If given to William Franklin as I have surmised, it would have been burned with other of William's belongings in a British army warehouse. But John's own portrait of himself may yet be rediscovered; for it may be extant as an unknown or, as Mrs. Hastings has suggested, "masquerading as someone else."[55] We have but one tantalizing glimpse of it after it was offered for sale in March 1850. In 1853 the catalogue of the Boston Athenaeum's annual exhibition lists a "Portrait of James Franklin, brother of Benjamin Franklin," as loaned by "J. B. Up-

---

54. Alan Burroughs to the author, Dec. 8, 1958.
55. Hastings, "Franklin Memorabilia," p. 225.

ham."[56] There can be no doubt whatever that "James" is an error in the listing for "John." It would seem that after Dr. Warren had bought the one picture for his collection another, much younger Boston physician had taken the second. Dr. Jabez Baxter Upham (1820–1902) prospered in Boston for a number of years and then, apparently after some reverses, moved to New York, where he died. No portrait of this period has descended to his heirs or is recollected by them.

It is the duty of the student of these matters both to present all evidence indicating doubt or certainty and also to venture some sort of conclusion—that is, having placed the scimitar in his readers' hands, to extend his neck. To my mind, the assumption that this is a portrait of Benjamin Franklin, painted by Robert Feke between the years 1738 and 1746, will stand up to all questioning. Doubts will remain to add interest to the topic, as doubts always do. There are other possible conjectural positions, but little reason for me to speculate upon them here. One, however, I might mention briefly—the possibility (and heavens knows it has happened often enough) that when John Franklin had Elizabeth's portrait made for their new home he asked the man to "freshen up" the other old one of his brother, an act which would have altered the picture in some respects without destroying the composition and that pose of erect dignity so characteristic of the Newport painter.

So there he stands before us, "all stiff and awkward as the original." It is an image which, like Franky's, was created as a service of affection, an appeal to the heart. Perhaps it is appropriate to mention here that in Jared Sparks' private notes Franky's is described as "a beautiful picture,"[57] its archaic exuberance so impressing a New England sophisticate of a century later, and the truth is that formalism, unreality, and tricks of artifice are everywhere inherent in the image-maker's art and that the painted portrait, however archaic, can draw from them a power of its own.

56. *Catalogue of the Twenty-sixth Exhibition of Paintings and Statuary at the Athenaeum Gallery* (Boston, 1853), p. 5, no. 42.
57. Sparks Papers, *18,* no. 147.

4 FROM A PRIVATE
TO A PUBLIC IMAGE

T HE MOST natural, manly, useful, noble, and, however apparently easy, the most difficult of arts is portrait painting. Love first discovered this heavenly art. Without love what could it perform?" This highly rhetorical question is asked by Lavater in his *Essay on Physiognomy,* a work which stands as one of the monuments of the eighteenth century's preoccupation with human character.[1] To Benjamin Franklin, without the need of a book to tell him so, portrait painting was indisputably one of the arts of friendship and personal association. He gave prints, paintings, and sculptures of himself to friends more freely than almost anyone else of the time, and always with the feeling that it was done in the nature of a personal visit, a form of vicarious intimacy, just as the portraits of others around him brought their lives and friendship closer to him. Those whom he approached in this way responded with an answering warmth, elders regarding the image with reverence and affection, young women kissing it as ardently as they might the original.

The publication of the *Observations on Electricity* in London in 1751 and the much-publicized experiments in Paris confirming the Philadelphian's identification of lightning as electricity and his discovery of a safeguard against this danger brought him international eminence. His likeness, therefore, must needs represent not only the man, as before, but his accomplishment. To British artists, who still

1. Johann Kaspar Lavater, *Essays on Physiognomy,* trans. Henry Hunter, 2 (London, 1789), 73.

saw him as a private gentleman eminent in science rather than in his diplomatic role as a colonial agent, this marked no very great change. Later, for the French artists, it would pose a greater problem. To them he had become not only the living symbol of the new enlightenment, but was the official representative of a young and vigorous power, with armies, cities, and vast territories in his control. There were conventions of pose, dress, and gesture by which such power was expressed in art, but Franklin's simple clothes, plain manner, and even his uncomplicated, forthright diplomacy belied them. In France as in England the public portrait extolled and did homage to greatness. Yet here was a great political figure whose private and public lives were almost identical, and the artists had therefore to solve their quandaries each according to his own taste and his own feeling for the man's character and significance.

When Franklin left Philadelphia in the spring of 1757 to represent the province of Pennsylvania as its agent in London, he knew that his absence might be a long one. He could not know how prolonged it was actually to be, nor how congenial he would find English life. Deborah was of no mind to make the voyage, nor could this simple creature have stood well beside him there. So he left Sarah, his "Sally," with her, and took with him William, then a young man of twenty-six. The rift in "our little family" troubled him, and his first letters from London show him seeking to heal the wound with pictures. Indeed, he had brought Sally's with him from Philadelphia. The household accounts there show entries which may be dated 1756 or 1757, one a payment of £2 10s. to "B. West for drawing Sally's Picture," and another of the same sum—clearly the usual first and final half-payments for a portrait.[2] Sally's picture, it appears, did not please either parent at all, a fact which may explain something of the later relationship between Franklin and this artist. They seem to have associated on cordial terms after the painter came to London from Italy in 1764, but there is no life portrait of Franklin by Benjamin West.

Thus, with his son beside him and this dim reflection of his other child to place upon the wall, he arrived in London on July 26, 1757, and found a new home at 7 Craven Street, Mrs. Margaret Stevenson's boarding house. He seems to have written home to Deborah al-

2. Franklin Papers (A.P.S.), 66, no. 24.

most in journal-letter form, a correspondence of which many fragments, some undated, have survived. The following autumn an illness, an "intermittent fever" which continued in spite of Dr. Fothergill's and Mrs. Stevenson's watchful care, brought some interruption. It was painful and debilitating with periods of recovery followed by lapses into weakness and occasional delirium, and it must have heightened his sense of loneliness and estrangement. It was during this siege that he had a miniature painter make his likeness. The only record of the transaction is an entry in his accounts for October 31, 1757, "Paid Mr. Dixon for B. F's picture £6.6.0."[3] It gives us not only a date but the surname of an artist hitherto known only by the two letters with which he signed his ivories. Basil S. Long has described several examples of the work of "C. D.," all of which "had a certain naiveté but expressed a good deal of character without any attempt at flattery. They were not painted with great freedom; the style varied a good deal; the body was in some cases weakly drawn."[4] Long dates these works between 1750 and 1767, and suggests that the artist may have had patronage in Scotland, perhaps in Bath. Certainly he had not established himself in London, and must have been a provincial or itinerant. The records of the Society of Artists reveal only a miniature exhibited by "Dixon" in 1771 and a portrait by "Miss Dixon" at the same time.[5] Indeed, there seems almost to have been a provincial family of the name, dedicated to the craft of painting.

One of the best English miniaturists of the seventeenth century had been Nicholas Dixon, who signed his ivories, "N. D." It is possible that he may have been a brother of the portrait painter Matthew Dixon (active ca. 1670–1712), and possible that these were related to the pastelist, John Dixon. John, a pupil of the court painter, Sir Peter Lely, became himself "keeper of the King's picture closet." George Vertue's notes in the British Museum record these facts, the "great excellence" of his likenesses, and his retirement after 1698 "to a small estate at Thwait near Bungay in Suffolk where

3. A.P.S. See also, George Simpson Eddy, ed., "Account Book of Benjamin Franklin kept by him during his First Mission to England as Provincial Agent, 1757–1762," *P.M.H.B., 55* (1931), 104.

4. *British Miniaturists* (London, Geoffrey Bles, 1929), p. 113.

5. Algernon Graves, *A Dictionary of Artists who have Exhibited Works in the Principal London Exhibitions from 1760 to 1893* (London, 1901), p. 81.

his widow and children are still [ca. 1730] living. . . . He died about 10 years ago. His father and grandfather painted in oyl from the life."[6]

Enticed by this puzzle and anxious to add a name to the other initial, I visited Thwaite in the autumn of 1957 and through the kindness of the Rev. Edward H. Payne, was able to search the records of the parish. These revealed an interesting family of Dixons, including Matthew who in 1691 married a lady touchingly described as "the last of the Gostlings," but an exhaustive pursuit of the family through these and the probate records in London failed of its purpose. It is still "C. Dixon," and no more. In London, however, Mr. G. Reynolds of the Victoria and Albert Museum's Department of Paintings had information which more than offset this disappointment. A short while before, a lady, unnamed, had brought to Sotheby's for sale a small group of miniatures of her ancestors, including two self-portraits of "C. D.," a forebear of whose full name she, too, was ignorant. Sotheby's had presented these to the museum. One is on ivory and one a poorly-fired enamel on copper. This discovery brings us what easily compensates for any lacunae as to name and history—a glimpse of the painter's face. We see an earnest young man with a pleasant mouth and a rather Boswellian nose, wearing a powdered bob wig, a blue coat with gilded buttons, and a waistcoat of a paler blue, trimmed with gold lace. Set the pictures of artist and subject side by side and you have half the history of a portrait—the two faces which once so thoughtfully regarded one another, one in active concentration, one in acceptance of the other's studious attention, both absorbed in the task of duplication.

Miniature painting has been traditionally a private art and one in which informal costume appears more frequently than elsewhere. Franklin here wears a reddish purple banyan or dressing gown beneath which one sees his yellow waistcoat and white shirt, and on his head is the turbanlike white cap which a gentleman wore in the privacy of his home, as a comfortable substitute for the wig. The costume is not necessarily that of the sick room, and the pallor of the

6. Charles Henry Collins Baker, *Lely and the Stuart Portrait Painters. A Study of English Portraiture before and after Van Dyck, 2* (Boston, Small Maynard, 1913), 193–94. See also Horace Walpole, *Anecdotes of Painting in England, 3* (London, 1782), 120.

face may be laid to faded colors, yet for all that it is reasonable to suppose that the picture shows Franklin as Dixon must have found him that autumn, ailing and confined, a picture which Franklin may have intended then as a possible last memento for Deborah, so far away.

It was not sent to Deborah until after his recovery and then, curiously, with the request that she pass it on to his sister, Jane Mecom. "When you write to Boston," he added in a postscript to his letter of January 21, 1758, "give my love to sister Jenny, as I have not often time to write to her. If you please, you may send her the inclosed little picture."[7] He mentioned the gift again in what was probably his next letter, written late that month or early in February, "I wrote you by a Man of War lately sailing for New York, & sent you my Picture in Miniature."[8] That the miniature should have been for Jane rather than for Deborah raises the question of whether Deborah may not have had a portrait of him already in the house. More probably, he was expecting at this time to send her a large portrait of himself and was giving the miniature to Jane as a thing which could easily be forwarded to her.

At all events, it arrived in Philadelphia presumably in March or April. James Turner, the engraver who had made John Franklin's bookplate and had cut the armorial seals for Benjamin and John, was in Philadelphia at the time and was shown the piece. He wrote to Deborah on May 1, 1758, begging her not to let it out of her hands until he might have an opportunity to reproduce it in mezzotint.[9] His letter stands as the first recognition, by an artist, of Franklin as a public figure, the charm of its ingenuous enthusiasm heightened by that sense of both personal and public gratitude which Franklin so often inspired:

> Ever since I have been resident in Philadelphia, I have entertained thoughts of performing a piece of mezzotinto, which I have several times practiced in

7. Smyth, *Writings, 3,* 430. Original unlocated.
8. Franklin Papers (A.P.S.), *46,* no. 103.
9. William Temple Franklin, ed., *The Works of Dr. Benjamin Franklin, 6* (Philadelphia, 1817), 30–33.

Boston, and which, so far as I know, has never yet been done in this city...

And when I considered which way I should direct my choice for such a subject, my grateful sense of the many instances of Mr. Franklin's goodness to myself, his benevolent endeavors in private life, to promote the interest of any person, though no way connected with his own, and to advance by his candid remarks and wise advice every useful art in America; the great obligations which the whole learned world confess themselves to be under to him for his important philosophical discoveries; his honest steady and undaunted zeal in the cause of Liberty; his knowledge of the true interests, and his wise counsels and unwearied labours for the real service of this province—of America in general—of his nation and his king—manifesting the invaluable friend, the eminent philosopher, the true patriot, the loyal subject, the honest, the truly great and good man—the boast of Boston, his native place —the blessing of Pennsylvania—the admiration of the world! all these considerations bursting upon my mind at once with irresistible conviction, left me no room to hesitate before I fixed my choice; not that I imagine that any poor endeavors of mine can add to or help to perpetuate the fame of my proposed subject; that is already sufficiently extended, and will never be forgotten so long as the lightning's *flash* and the thunder's *roar* continue to remind mankind who it was that explained to them the nature, and taught them how to guard against the effects of that terrifying meteor....

... The truth is, that when I began to write, I intended only a few lines, but being once engaged, the gratitude and veneration that dilates my heart, whenever I think or speak of Mr. Franklin, and the pride also, I will confess, springing from the reflection that I could call such a man my countryman, would force to themselves utterance, almost whether I would or

not, and I could not without a great deal of pain have
withheld my real sentiments.

He planned a mezzotint "on a copperplate of the usual size, viz.
about fourteen inches long and ten inches broad." He would have
carried out the plan long before, he confessed, had he been able, "for
though I profess myself capable of imitating a good draught, yet I
have no pretensions to drawing after the life."

The miniature, as far as I know unique and original, was sent on
by Deborah to Jane Mecom as Franklin had requested. Among
Jane's Rhode Island and Massachusetts heirs it remained in an obscurity even deeper than that which for so long surrounded the Harvard portrait; indeed, its importance remained unrecognized until, quite recently, its documentation in the Franklin Papers at the
American Philosophical Society was revealed.[10]

On November 22, 1757, after the Dixon miniature had been
painted but before it had been sent to Philadelphia, Franklin had
written as follows to Deborah on his plan for portraits of all the
family:

> I hear there has a miniature painter gone over to Phil-
> adelphia, a relation to John Reynolds. If Sally's pic-
> ture is not done to your mind by the young man, and
> the other gentleman is a good hand and follows the
> business, suppose you get Sally's done by him, and
> send it to me with your small picture, that I may here
> get all our little family drawn in one conversation
> piece.[11]

Months later, June 10, 1758, Deborah's "small picture" had arrived, but he had still only the unsatisfactory one, by West, of Sally:

> I fancy I see more likeness in her Picture than I did at
> first, and I look at it with Pleasure, as at least it re-
> minds me of her. Yours is at the Painter's, who is to

10. Charles Coleman Sellers, "Jane Mecom's Little Picture," *Proceedings of the
A.P.S., 99* (1955), 433–35. The author's surmise of the existence of a replica of the
miniature is based on an erroneous dating of the Franklin letter cited, and may be
dismissed.

11. Smyth, *Writings, 3,* 423. John Reynolds, with an important business on Front
St., had been a frequent advertiser in Franklin's *Pennsylvania Gazette.*

> copy it, and do one of me of the same Size; but as to
> Family Pieces, it is said they never look well, and are
> quite out of Fashion; and I find the limner very un-
> willing to undertake anything of the kind. However,
> when Franky's comes, and that of Sally by young Hes-
> selius, I shall see what can be done.[12]

Conversation pieces, of course, had not gone out of fashion. We must realize that a London painter with a reputation to guard was being asked to produce one of these graceful family groups with only a father and son to pose for him, the rest to be compounded from the portrait of Sally by John Hesselius, the "small picture" of Deborah probably by the same, and the piece of Franky in Elysium which he had not seen but could doubtless imagine. The man's lack of enthusiasm is understandable, as well as his prediction that it would not "look well."

Of these sources, the portrait of Franky has survived and the two of Sally have vanished.[13] Of Deborah, one remains, the portrait which, as Franklin said afterward, had been left "a sort of widow" when his in 1778 had been stolen from the room by a British officer. That his is signed "B. Wilson 1759" and almost exactly the size of hers indicates that both are the work of Benjamin Wilson (1721–88), the painter to whom Franklin would inevitably have gone, first of all, after his arrival in England. Wilson had published in 1746 a little treatise on electricity which Franklin, in 1752, had read and praised.[14] He was now living in Great Queen Street in the house which Sir Godfrey Kneller had formerly occupied, and earning a reputed £1500 a year as a painter. He had followed Franklin's electrical discoveries with equal interest, and was still deeply engrossed in the matter. They would have sought one another out at once.

Soon after writing to Deborah about the portraits, Franklin set

---

12. Ibid., p. 439.

13. The destruction of a portrait of Sarah, probably that by John Hesselius, is recorded by Mrs. E. D. Gillespie in her *Book of Remembrance* (Philadelphia, 1901), p. 28. A third portrait, painted for her brother in 1766, was presumably destroyed by fire with the rest of William Franklin's American possessions.

14. Benjamin Wilson, *An Essay towards an Explication of the Phenomena of Electricity, Deduced from the Aether of Sir Isaac Newton,* London, 1746. Franklin to Colden, Sept. 14, 1752, and Colden to Franklin, Oct. 24, 1752, originals at N.Y.H.S.

out on his genealogical tour to the north, to establish his English family background. He probably did not pose for Wilson until fall, when he was back in town and catching up on neglected affairs—among other things, writing to his sister in Boston: "I wonder you have had no letter from me since my being in England. I have wrote you at least two, and I think a third before this, and what was next to waiting on you in person, sent you my picture."[15] His new portrait was probably finished in the spring. There is a letter from Wilson to Franklin of April 8, 1759, which shows them together at that time. "I have been considering Mr. Colden's expt. which we tried on saturday last, and the appearances it affords seem not now so surprising, or indeed, curious as I at first imagined. . . . I will endeavor to satisfy you that this is probably the fact by an expt. or two which are easily made when I see you next."[16] The letter reveals a man who, impressed by Franklin's demonstration of Cadwallader Colden's experiment on Saturday, had by Monday worked out a way to reduce it to the commonplace. He probably did not know that Colden's opinion of his own work was not a particularly flattering one. He subscribed his letter to Franklin "most affectionately," and yet it carries a hint of an attitude of competitive superiority, foreign to Franklin, which was in time to mar their relationship. Wilson was later to emerge as the proponent of a theory on lightning rods rivaling Franklin's, the theory that the rod should end in a knob rather than a point. It is related that during the war George III tried to establish this as the official view, until the Royal Society persuaded him that the laws of nature could not be revised upon political considerations. In art, too, Wilson was to emerge as a rival of sorts to Benjamin West, with a "Belshazzar's Feast," a "Jairus' Daughter," and other "historical" pieces.[17] When he painted Franklin his work in portraiture was thought to rival Reynolds. It was dark, exciting, Rembrandtesque, bringing to contemporaries but not at all to later

15. Sept. 16, 1758. Smyth, *Writings, 3,* 458.

16. Franklin Papers (A.P.S.).

17. Algernon Graves, *The Royal Academy of Arts, a Complete Dictionary of Contributors and Their Work from Its Foundation in 1769 to 1904, 8* (London, 1905), 305. Sir Robert Thomas Wilson, *Life of General Sir Robert Wilson* (London, 1862), pp. 26–27. Wilson's biography includes passages from Benjamin Wilson's autobiography, the MS of which was, according to the Whitley Papers in the British Museum, in the hands of Messrs. John Lane for publication in April 1916. The firm has now no record of it.

generations a sense of power and imagination. He had amused the town, too, by making an etching in Rembrandt's manner good enough to fool the connoisseurs, whom he entertained lavishly at dinner with the money they had paid him for the supposed discovery.[18]

Although of a size, Wilson's portraits of Benjamin and Deborah are not a pair. At the time, there could have been no thought of hanging them together. Hers was for his rooms in Craven Street. His was to go at once to Philadelphia, to show the family there how he appeared in his new London wig and to represent the master of the house upon its wall. Work did not move rapidly out of a fashionable artist's studio, and his portrait was probably not shipped until 1760. It would have gone at the same time as a replica which Franklin ordered for his friend, Dr. Thomas Bond. Franklin saw Dr. Bond's when he returned to Philadelphia in 1762. There is no record of that in his own house until Deborah's letter of June 13, 1770, when she told how little Benjamin Franklin Bache would "clope to his grandadey" in the morning. Furthermore, along with these two, Wilson was working on a third, the same likeness but in three-quarter length, with added still life appropriate to an electrician. Franklin had, therefore, done well as his colleague's patron, ordering two portraits of himself, one of Deborah, one of William, and possibly one of Sally. In addition to this, Wilson expected to publish a print from his own large piece which, with the sale of both painting and print, should profit him most of all. The print was a joint venture with James McArdell, then at the top of the profession as an engraver in mezzotint. It was ready for sale in 1761.

The print must have been successful, for its subject's fame was rising and the circle of his friends continually enlarging. His degree of Doctor of Laws had been awarded him in February 1759. In the summer and fall of that year he had traveled across England and then north to Edinburgh and Glasgow, a journey which enormously widened the pattern of his influence. He met Matthew Boulton of Birmingham, founder of the great Soho manufactory there, James Watt's partner in the development of the steam engine and, later, owner of the private mint which, with the collaboration of Benja-

18. Wilson, *Wilson*, p. 13.

min West, Augustin Dupré, and others, raised the medallic art in Britain to a new standard of excellence. It may have been at this time also that he made the acquaintance of Boulton's counterpart in the field of ceramic production and design, Josiah Wedgwood, who was in later years to honor Franklin repeatedly in his series of portrait medallions of "illustrious moderns."

Wilson's larger portrait in contrast to his half-length of Franklin illustrates the often fine and sometimes imperceptible difference between public and private portraiture. The half-length is not quite the usual seated figure, relaxed and appropriate to the home atmosphere. It almost appears so, but no chair back is shown and the background is entirely one of night sky with a long stream of lightning flashing down from a stormhead above to a huddled town below. In the three-quarter length the figure clearly stands erect in the commanding pose considered suitable for a public edifice. Franklin holds a book in his right hand (in the print it is identified as "Electricl. Expts."), while his left hovers over it in a here-is-everything-between-two-covers gesture. The background is the same, but as the lightning flash is longer, it falls upon the cowering hamlet with more dramatic force. The foreground table with pen and paper on it and the green curtain rising above it on the right side of the canvas are not, of course, properties one would expect the leading actor to have about him abroad on a stormy night, but they were undoubtedly acceptable to contemporaries accustomed to viewing these things as the products of a poetic imagination.

We can only speculate upon whether Franklin himself disliked being posed in this manner. When another artist, in the year after the publication of the Wilson-McArdell print, painted another three-quarter length from which another print was made, showing Franklin seated comfortably indoors, making calculated observations upon the thunderstorm raging outside, Franklin ordered a replica of the painting and purchased a very considerable number of the prints. These he gave away, far and wide, to friends, while there is no record of his ever having purchased or given away the Wilson print. My own feeling is that Franklin neither liked the rather stilted pose Wilson had given him, nor found it particularly objectionable. It is more likely that he had some objection to the artist, and most likely that the new picture appealed to him because of the friend who had sponsored it and the fact that his son seems to have agreed to underwrite the publication of the new mezzotint.

At the time of the Wilson-McArdell venture Franklin knew that he should soon return to America. Reluctant to go and with all his friends urging him to remain, he delayed his departure until August 1762. In the meantime Oxford awarded him the degree of Doctor of Civil Law, and William was appointed Governor of New Jersey. The elevation of the young man to this importance was reflected in an immediate keen interest in all the appurtenances of high office, including paintings of the King, the Queen, his father, and himself, which were to adorn the walls of the prospective governor's mansion. Franklin commissioned one of the new portraits for William. A letter of two years later to Jonathan Williams, Sr., in Boston showed how he viewed the matter:

> Just before I left London, a Gentleman requested I would sit for a Picture to be drawn of me for him by a Painter of his choosing. I did so and the Portrait was reckon'd a very fine one. Since I came away, the Painter has had a Print done from it, of which he has sent a Parcel here for sale. I have taken a Dozen of them to send to Boston & it being the only way in which I am now likely to visit my Friends there, I hope a long Visit in this shape will not be disagreeable to them.

He added a list of the friends to whom he thought they might go, the Rev. Dr. Mayhew, the Rev. Mr. Byles, Mr. Winthrop of Cambridge, Miss Betsy Hubbart (afterward Mrs. Partridge), his sister, and others.[19]

The friend who had invited him to pose had been Colonel Philip Ludwell, III, of Virginia, a gentleman who in middle life had come to London two years before and settled there permanently. The painter of his own choosing was Mason Chamberlin, a solid sort of limner with a reputation for accurate likenesses and none of Wilson's flair or ambition. Admiration and friendship are reasons enough for Colonel Ludwell's action. It is possible also, however,

19. Philadelphia, Feb. 24, 1764 (A.P.S.).

that the artist was giving him special terms in consideration of the print and William Franklin's willingness to purchase a large quantity for sale in America. One can never be quite sure which one of the parties involved may have initiated an affair of this sort. A popular mezzotint portrait could have been worth appreciably more than the price of the painting it was taken from, and the painting, by its exhibition, the critics' praise, and the satisfaction of its owner, would itself have promoted sales of the print.

William Franklin's marriage took place that September, after his father's departure and in the midst of his own preparations for removal to America. In November 1762 he wrote from Hampshire to William Strahan who had agreed to look after their affairs in London about the miniatures ordered from Jeremiah Meyer and to be set as bracelets for his wife, about the painting of the king due to him as a royal governor "which I would have done by Mr. Ramsay one of the King's Painters" and in the hope that a portrait of the Queen would also be allowed him:

> The Print from Mr. Chamberlyne's Picture of my Father was not done when I came away, but I told him that if the Execution was approv'd of by Mr. Ludwell & Mr. Myers, that I would take 100 of them; in which case I must desire that you would receive them of Mr. Chambe. & forward them to me by the first Opportunity, in two different Vessels; and I will as soon as they come to hand remit you the Money in order to pay him.[20]

He runs on about the chapel plate and furniture granted him by the government, concluding with a hope expressed that the people of New Jersey would be willing to add a chapel to his official residence —early evidence of the divergence of father and son. A year later, Franklin gave William a replica of the Chamberlin portrait, he himself continuing over the next eight or nine years to place orders for the prints, giving them away happily and affectionately far and near.

Whether or not the Wilson portraits pleased Franklin, there is every reason to believe that this new piece was made exactly to his

20. Yale University Library.

taste. Mason Chamberlin, "Portrait Painter. Stuart-street, Spital-fields," to quote the London directory of 1763, was the sort of crafts-man with whom he could see eye to eye. He made sound observations and had a head for business. Chamberlin's will, proved on February 14, 1787, reveals him as the owner of two houses and the savings of a prosperous professional career, adding to that two clergymen as brothers-in-law and a brother of his own, William Chamberlin, settled in the English colony at Saint Petersburg, Russia.[21] His early life as a merchant's clerk had trained him in prudence and good management. He was exhibiting regularly with the Society of Artists and in 1764 won their second prize for historical painting, but his reputation really depended upon his solid likenesses of sub-stantial people, Dr. William Hunter, the surgeon, Dr. Richard Chandler, the archaeologist, and the like.[22]

In Dr. Johnson's *Idler,* Number 76, September 29, 1759, Sir Joshua Reynolds asks the reader not to take literally the "continu-ally inculcated" insistence that the artist should imitate nature, and warned that if he actually did so, imagination, freedom, and poetry would be banished from the art of painting. He restated a position which artists and critics had taken before. Nature must be the art-ist's guide, not his master. Benjamin Wilson would readily have agreed. Chamberlin represents a more strictly factual approach, one more in line with the feeling of men of Franklin's character. He shows Franklin seated, pen in one hand, papers in the other. His eyes are not upon the spectator. He is turning in his chair to watch an arrangement of wires and bells which has been affected by the electrical storm raging outside. All this is coolly realistic. In the storm itself, seen through a window at the right, the artist has ven-tured to heighten the drama by showing a steeple rent asunder and a house in the same instant torn apart by the stroke of lightning which, in the philosopher's study, merely rings a bell.

Mezzotints often sharpened the realism of a painting, and Mc-Ardell's print from Wilson's picture had done exactly that. To be sure, it was scarcely realistic to have added a static electricity ma-

21. Somerset House, London. Prerogative Court of Canterbury. Will book Major, 1787, fol. 59.

22. William Sandby, *History of the Royal Academy of Arts, 1* (London, 1862), 97.

chine to the still life on the table, with the subject out-of-doors at night and a thunderstorm raging. More precise definition weakened the artist's poetic concept. With Chamberlin's more matter-of-fact work this did not occur. His engraver was Edward Fisher, a competent craftsman, Irish-born like McArdell, whose dated prints run between 1758 and 1781.[23] He lived in Leicester Square in the house in which a fleetingly notorious Swiss painter, Theodore Gardelle, had in 1761 murdered his landlady in a shocking manner. He must have known Franklin by sight, at least, though all the orders for prints went to Chamberlin. Chamberlin's original painting, after Colonel Ludwell's death in 1767, was inherited by one of his three daughters, Lucy, the wife of John Paradise. John Paradise was one link between Franklin and the group of Samuel Johnson's club, and Franklin must have enjoyed Lucy Paradise, too, an unusually small, trim, and sharply witty woman, whose verbal battle with Mrs. Mary Lloyd, the flower painter, at Mrs. Nollekins' tea table brought from Dr. Johnson a heavy "Fie, fie, my dears" and an "Off with your mufflers and fight it fairly out!"[24]

Along with this bit of information, Nollekins' biographer brings us what is probably the best characterization of Franklin's Craven Street neighbor, Caleb Whitefoord, wine merchant, wit and dabbler in the arts. Whitefoord enclosed a caricature of Franklin, which may have been drawn from life, in a letter to Philadelphia written very shortly after his friend's departure from London. The drawing has disappeared, doubtless from being passed about and enjoyed by too many people, and all we know of it is contained in Franklin's reply to Whitefoord, written on December 7, 1762:

> I thank you for the humourous and sensible Print you
> sent me, which afforded me and several of my Friends
> great Pleasure. The Piece from your own Pencil is ac-
> knowledged to bear a strong and striking Likeness,
> but it is otherwise such a picture of your Friend, as
> Dr. Smith would have drawn, *black, and all black*. I
> think you'll hardly understand this remark, but your

23. John Chaloner Smith, *British Mezzotinto Portraits, 2* (London, 1883), 485.
24. John Thomas Smith, *Nollekins and His Times: Comprehending a Life of that Celebrated Sculptor; and Memoirs of Several Contemporary Artists, 1* (London, 1828), 347–48.

Neighbour [good] Mrs. Stevenson can explain it.
Painting has yet scarce made her Appearance among
us; but her Sister Art, Poetry, has some Votaries. I
send you a few Blossoms of American Verse, the Lisp-
ings of our young Muses.[25]

The allusion to Dr. Smith carried a small note of triumph. William Smith of Philadelphia had been in England spreading malicious rumors which Franklin had denied without silencing them,
and which on his return home had proved wholly untrue. The con-
text of the letter makes it clear that Whitefoord's more friendly
comment was in pictorial form rather than, as one might otherwise
suspect, a literary piece. Externally, Whitefoord was an opposite to
Franklin, a slight, thin-faced, sharp-eyed figure, "rather foppishly
dressed," with the "true Garrick cut wig" (five rows of curls on
each side) and a habit of shrugging his shoulders in conversation.
Oliver Goldsmith and Dr. Johnson saw in his wit a literary talent
wasted. He was an amateur artist as well, and a collector of old
paintings which he was said, by unkind gossip, to touch up occasionally with his own brush by way of improving them.[26] This was
Franklin's friend next door, at Craven Street, the master of persiflage whose life had but one peak of enduring fame—when he came
to Passy, twenty years later, as one of the commissioners to negotiate
a treaty of peace with Franklin.

Whitefoord's wit was often directed toward exposing the humorous aspects of the political turmoil around him. It was a viewpoint
which Franklin could share, though he was soon to find himself in
circumstances which left little room for humor or objectivity of any
sort. This American interlude lasted exactly two years, from his arrival at Philadelphia on November 1, 1762, until his departure
again on November 7, 1764. It began pleasantly. He saw his son
happily established as Governor of New Jersey. He toured the New
England post offices, renewing old acquaintances, with Sally as
company. He planned and began the building of a new house. And
then his peace was broken by those climactic events, the Paxton mur-

25. Smyth, *Writings, 4,* 184.
26. As acidulously described by John Thomas Smith in *A Book for a Rainy Day, or
Recollections of the Events of the Years 1766–1833,* (London, 1905), pp. 113–14, and
in *Nollekins and His Times, 1,* 333–40.

ders and the turbulent election of 1764, bringing a flood of mass emotion which spilled over in the form of political appeal and diatribe, mock-epic verse, mock-tragic drama, and copperplate caricatures of men and events in which Franklin was featured at least four times. This literature and art is so full of bantering that it is hard to realize that its source had been a bloody Indian war and the savage murder by white men, in December 1763, of the peaceful Conestoga Indians. They were a remnant of those who had met with William Penn by the Treaty Elm, and their death marked the end of Pennsylvania's policy of peace. The "Paxton Boys," about five hundred strong, marched on Philadelphia to murder also the Christian Indians who had taken refuge there. Franklin denounced them in the boldest terms of all, organized military resistance in the city, and when they came, was one of those who met and persuaded them to go back to their homes.

The fright of the town, the training of a cannon one night on supposed invaders who turned out to be only a company of German butchers and porters joining the defense, the spectacle of soldiers taking refuge (from the rain) in the Quaker meeting house, the surprisingly large number of Quakers who appeared under arms, all made for humorous and sardonic treatment. Most of the humor came from the Presbyterians of the frontier and their partisans. Under it lay the sense of communal guilt and the eagerness to laugh it off or cover it over by fixing equal guilt on others. The emotions of that year sparked a little blaze of prose, poetry, drama, and art in the province. The first piece had been Franklin's *Narrative of the Late Massacres in Lancaster County,* written in January. He had returned from London a popular hero because of his triumph over the Penns in securing for the Assembly the right to tax their lands. The *Narrative,* with its sharp, lucid, moving defense of reason and humanity, now suddenly brought upon him the fierce hostility of the Scotch-Irish, involving him in a double mesh of controversy. "Plain Dealer," one of the pamphleteers, accused him of trying "to set this province on fire, that he may have an opportunity of gathering the spoil."[27] The cartoonists depicted him with the same cynicism as the master of a bear-baiting:

27. John R. Dunbar, ed., *The Paxton Papers* (The Hague, Nijhoff, 1957), p. 380.

Fight Dog! fight Bear! you're all my Friends.
By you I shall attain my Ends:
For I can never be content
Till I have got the Government.
But if in this Attempt I fall,
Then let the Devil take you all.

Of the few caricatures which have survived from this famous year in Pennsylvania history, Franklin appears in four, three relating to the conflicts between Presbyterians, Quakers, Germans, and Indians, and the fourth to the hard-fought election of October 1, 1764, in which he was defeated as a candidate for a seat in the Assembly.

In the election piece Franklin is shown with the winged devil hovering at his back and addressing him familiarly as "Ben." His name does not appear in any of the others, the public being expected to recognize him instantly by the likeness. To facilitate this, the large mole on his left cheek was carefully emphasized. Obviously, it was well-known. It appears also in a profile of the right side of his face, but one must bear in mind that the artist might simply have forgotten that printing would reverse his plate, or perhaps just did not care as long as he had the disfigurement somewhere securely in his picture. In two of the plates Franklin wears spectacles, something which was henceforth to be an even more distinguishing feature. In one they appear as dark glasses, either to depict him as blind or just to make him more conspicuous. As portraiture, the greatest value of these pieces is in the figure. Chamberlin had shown not long before how fleshy Franklin had become, but only one of these prints even suggests a similar *embonpoint*. In the others the body is erect and trim. Perhaps he had become slimmer after a year and a half in America or perhaps, as a strong, athletic man, he carried himself on the street in a manner which concealed it. Certainly he was not, in 1764, betraying an obesity which a hostile caricaturist could use either for ridicule or special recognition.

Franklin lost in the election, but his party won a majority of the seats and promptly elected him agent to represent the province again in London and to continue there to combat the power of the proprietors. He had looked forward to this, but had not expected it so soon. The return to London was more like a homecoming than a depar-

63

ture. Deborah would not accompany him nor would she permit Sally to go, and he left them behind in the still unfinished house, its novel arrangement of stoves still unexplained to them. She had his portrait on the wall, and hers presumably returned with him to Craven Street.

This portrait of Deborah is interesting if only from the sentimental point of view, for where affection and loyalty are so deeply involved, the face of one partner in time reflects the other's. The picture now owned by the American Philosophical Society is the only one recorded as belonging to any member of the Franklin family. I believe it to be by Benjamin Wilson, copied in 1759 from the small original which had been sent from Philadelphia. It was, however, attributed to the Philadelphia painter, Matthew Pratt, first in 1898 by Sidney George Fisher in his *True Benjamin Franklin*.[28] William Sawitzky included it in his study of Pratt, in confirmation of a generally accepted attribution.[29] Young Pratt began painting in Philadelphia in June 1758. This is just too late for it to have been a picture of his sent to London in that year. Furthermore, the painting we have is a sophisticated work which could only be attributed to Pratt after he had had the advantage of English training. Sawitzky dates it between 1768 and 1770, after Pratt's return to Philadelphia from England and before his visit to England and Ireland in 1770.

It seems hardly in character for Mrs. Franklin to have ordered a portrait of herself for her own home. William had Sarah's portrait made, but that was for his own house, and his relationship with Deborah was not wholly cordial. Stylistically, the painting has that shadowy quality of Wilson's and a deep-brown background akin to that in the picture of Benjamin. The size of the canvas is 29¾ by 27⅞ inches, a fractional difference from the other which may have occurred in relining. Serious paint losses in the lower third of the picture were filled in as early as 1835 or 1836, though apparently without affecting the likeness or general coloring.[30] This preceded its appearance, engraved by Joseph Andrews of Boston, as frontispiece to Volume VII of Jared Sparks' edition of Franklin's works

28. Philadelphia (1899), p. 14.
29. William Sawitzky, *Matthew Pratt, 1734–1805. A Study of His Work* (New York, 1942), pp. 56–57.
30. A label of Earle's Gallery, Philadelphia, attached to the back, suggests that the work may have been done there.

in 1838. Professor Charles Hodge, then its owner, wrote as follows to Sparks, October 19, 1835:

> I am glad to be able to inform you, in reply to your letter of the 13th, that the portrait of Dr. Franklin's wife, about which you inquire, is in Mrs. Hodge's possession; & that she will be happy to place it at your command for the purpose of being engraved. It has unfortunately in its transmission through the different members of the family experienced a large measure of the fate common to such pictures. Old Mrs. Bache (Dr. Franklin's daughter) used to say "It was great nonesense for a woman to have her portrait taken; she was sure to find herself, by the next generation, in a garret window grinning at a north wester." Though the picture in question has been a good deal defaced it may still answer your purpose.[31]

Franklin had her picture, but was never to see Deborah again. She died ten years later while he was still in London. In those ten years his standing in the world's eyes had changed. Other colonies had joined with Pennsylvania in appointing him their agent, and he had come to represent not a distant provincial party but a continent, for whose vast future potential he thought and spoke. He fostered its particular interests but with them brought into English thinking a plan of imperial consolidation and growth. It was only when all hope had passed of this plan's becoming public policy that he turned, with equal boldness, to independence. In these ten years, new portraits of him had been made in answer to widening public interest and respect. After he had gone and the war begun, his face, as reflected in some of these, became vainly and fleetingly the symbol of a hope for reform, for reconciliation under his leadership, and for a newly enlightened empire.

31. Harvard. Hodge wrote, on Dec. 18, 1836, that the painting had been sent to Philadelphia "to be put in some kind of order." Mrs. Bache's opinion on portraiture is similarly quoted by Gillespie, *A Book of Remembrance,* p. 28.

5 FROM SAVANT
TO CHILD OF NATURE

DURING those two years in America Franklin had been continuously in touch with his English friends, a fact rather
mysteriously borne out in one of the Paxton cartoons in which he is
shown holding a scroll addressed "To Doctr. Pringle." William
Hogarth, whose death came suddenly on October 25, 1764, had on
that day received a letter from Franklin and had been drafting a reply to it when stricken. Franklin's letter, mailed probably in September, may have contained one of the Paxton caricatures. Franklin
was missed by his friends in England, and he himself was hopeful of
returning to them. David Hume had written to him on May 10,
1762, regretting his impending departure and declaring that of all
the good things sent out from America, "you are the first Philosopher and indeed the first Great Man of Letters for whom we are beholden to her."[1] Franklin's close friend, William Strahan, was
Hume's publisher, and instrumental in bringing them together.
Hume was not in London when Franklin arrived there early in December, 1764, and they did not meet until something over a year
later. Hume's life, however, in those thirteen or fourteen months, is
related in so many peculiar ways to the Franklin iconography as to
deserve a place in this chronicle.

1. Franklin Papers (A.P.S.), *1,* no. 68.

The Peace of Paris had ended the Seven Years' War in February 1763, and in that October the new ambassador went to Paris with David Hume as his personal secretary. Hume later became Embassy Secretary and Chargé d'Affaires. He had gone to France in part as a refuge from the hostility which his freedom of thought had stirred up against him in England and Scotland. To everyone's surprise the tall and portly Scotsman now became, for Paris, the hero of the year. The aristocracy, even the Dauphin, professed their ardent admiration. He was looked up to everywhere as a liberated philosopher and extolled for his naïveté, simplicity of manners, candor, and mildness.[2] Charles Nicolas Cochin drew his profile, published as a popular engraving by Simon Charles Miger in 1764; Louis Carrogis, called Carmontelle, made another.[3] Turgot paid tribute, as did Helvétius and his charming wife and Mme. Geoffrin and the Comtesse de Boufflers, patroness of Jean Jacques Rousseau, and indeed, as Mme. d'Epinay wrote, "All the pretty women have taken possession of him; he goes to all the smart suppers and no feast is complete without him."[4]

It surprised and irritated the Englishmen, but it lasted as long as Hume remained in Paris. Lord Charlemont observed that "The ladies in France gave the *ton,* and the *ton* was Deism."[5] In despotic France the women, enjoying the immunities and freedoms of their sex, could be the guardians and nourishers of a liberal movement. Encyclopedists and philosophers might live in fear of suppression, but the ladies of the *salons,* as Franklin was to learn ten years later, presided over little unassailable islands of the revolutionary spirit. Horace Walpole watched the Paris of 1765 with distaste, considering both Hume and Rousseau ridiculous. Rousseau, he wrote, "attempted to give himself the airs of an old philosopher, he showed himself at the Opera, in the coffee-houses, and in public promenades, first in an old greatcoat, and then in the habit of an Armenian, but neither his dirty wig nor the stick of Diogenes, nor his fur cap

2. Ernest Campbell Mossner, *The Life of David Hume* (Austin, Texas, 1954), p. 444.

3. Ibid., p. 482.

4. Ibid., p. 444.

5. Janet Aldis, *Madame Geoffrin. Her Salon and Her Times. 1750–1777* (London, 1906), p. 213.

arrested the passers-by."[6] Hume was too thoughtful to share all of Boswell's admiration for "the wild illustrious philosopher," but Rousseau with his famous paradox on the superiority of the savage state, his shattering affirmation of the natural goodness of man—the romantic, introspective sentimentalist who felt rather than thought and who uttered truth instinctively—had taken Europe by storm. There could be no doubt that he had changed and was changing history. He had been banished from Switzerland. Official France was becoming impatient of his presence. David Hume, quitting his diplomatic post, offered a haven in England. He consulted the Comtesse de Boufflers about the little man's rumored variability of temper and, reassured by her, set out upon the adventure which he was soon to regret profoundly.

They arrived in London on January 13, 1766. England welcomed the exile with warmth of feeling but with more curiosity than adulation. They made a strange pair, the big, open-faced, splendidly clad Scot, and the stooping little figure in his long "Armenian" robe of purple trimmed with dark fur, a fur cap on his head shading the searching, troubled eyes. Jean Jacques had adopted the costume at Motiers-Travers in 1762 or 1763 for reasons, it was said, of health— that is, because of an incontinence which made a robe more practicable than trousers. Sympathetic crowds of English people gathered to see him. Young King George was approached as to a pension and, proving himself for the moment at least a true son of the Enlightenment, expressed favor. With Allan Ramsay, the King's painter and Hume's close friend, at work on portraits of both Rousseau and Hume, it was the King himself who suggested that Rousseau's be given to the public as an engraving.[7]

Rousseau was in Scottish hands and to be seen through Scottish eyes, for both Ramsay and his principal assistant, David Martin, were natives of the northern kingdom. Martin, a painter and engraver, was to make the mezzotint from Ramsay's portrait. While they were at work James Boswell arrived in town with Thérèse Le Vasseur, bovine mistress of the great man, whom he had, with characteristic fervor, seduced en route from France. Ramsay, the poet's

6. Ibid., p. 238.
7. Mossner, *Hume,* p. 517.

son, was a political thinker and writer as well as painter. His *Essay on the Constitution of England* was published in that year of 1766. His pamphlets influenced the writing of the Pennsylvania constitution of 1776, framed by a convention of which Franklin was president.[8] He had been appointed portrait painter to George III in 1761, and by 1766 was doing very little more than turning out royal likenesses—a pair of which William Franklin had been so eager to obtain for his governor's mansion—the Harley Street studio full of them and a group of assistants at work. Martin started with Ramsay in 1752, at the age of fifteen, and continued with him until 1775. Starting so young, his painting style was inevitably an echo of Ramsay's, though at times in his independent work he did achieve a strength and individuality of his own.

For Hume and Rousseau Allan Ramsay made great portraits— Hume's broad, frank countenance set off by scarlet cloth and gold lace; Rousseau, in his strange costume of deep, exotic purple, a shadowy figure, intense and ominous—one personifying so well the rational enlightenment, the other its romantic tides.[9] The break which should have been expected soon appeared. Jean Jacques grew suspicious of David as, indeed, he did of every patron and friend. Suspicion was followed by repentance, the little man sitting on Hume's knee, his face flooded with tears, and then the dark, irrational resentments smoldered and flared again. As spring approached, a haven was found for him in the country, a retreat from abrasive city life to contemplation and solitude. Four days before he was to leave London, Hume arranged for another portrait. He introduced Isaac Gosset, a wax modeler of Huguenot descent, to Rousseau with the following note:

> Mars 1766. Le porteur de ce billet, M. Gosset, artiste, désire beaucoup faire votre portrait, à vive requête de plusieurs personnages qui veulent en orner leur cabinet: il m'assure qu'il ne vous demandera pas plus d'une demi-heure pour poser. Je ne pouver pas me

8. Chilton Williamson, "The Artist in Politics: Allan Ramsay and the Revolution in Pennsylvania," *P.M.H.B.,* 77 (1953), 452–56.

9. Hume's portrait is illustrated in color in Mossner, opp. p. 408. Rousseau's, at the National Gallery of Scotland, is represented here by Martin's mezzotint, Pl. 9 E.

refuser à une solicitation si raisonnable, et j'espère que
vous excuserez la liberté que je prise.[10]

Gosset, famous as a modeler of small profiles in wax, was also a
frame maker serving Ramsay, who had possibly recommended him
to Hume. His little portraits were quite as attractive as the ivory
carvings of an earlier generation which they imitated, though less
durable. He worked rapidly, so that the subject endured none of the
tedium of posing, and the facility of the technique enabled him to
really catch that definition of character which the profile so often
holds. His originals, too, could be duplicated easily. Rousseau himself was charmed by the piece. Hume gave him one and it was sent
at his request to a friend who, in his response, observed that he had
but one criticism of it: he thought the nose a shade too aquiline, a
small matter, and yet enough to injure the resemblance.[11] As far as I
can tell, no example of Gosset's wax "Rousseau" is extant today, but
this trifling distinction in the nose serves to identify its derivatives,
which in turn, are important here in two respects.

First, they established the fur cap as a symbol in the iconography
of the Enlightenment so well that a sculptor of eleven years later,
Jean Baptiste Nini, saw fit to crown the head of Franklin with it in
a similar bas-relief profile. Franklin had just arrived in France.
Nini, who probably never saw him in person, had a drawing by a
young Englishman to work from. The fame of Franklin's Canadian
fur cap had reached him, but if he knew anything of its warm and
shapeless contours he ignored them, and invested Franklin's head
with the fur cap of Jean Jacques Rousseau. The use of this symbol
and the enormous popularity of the Nini work strongly reinforced
the popular conception of Franklin, along with Rousseau, as a child
of truth and nature, a father of the liberation of the mind. Similarly,
and to an even greater extent, the fur collar of the Ramsay and Gosset portraits of Rousseau takes a symbolic place in the later por-

10. Quoted in Hippolyte Buffenoir, *Les Portraits de Jean-Jacques Rousseau*
(Paris, E. Leroux, 1913), pp. 138–39. For Gosset family and English connections, see
Mary H. Gosset, "A Family of Modellers in Wax," *Proceedings of the Huguenot
Society of London, 3* (1892), 540–68; William Thomas Whitley, *Artists and Their
Friends in England, 1700–1799, 2* (London and Boston, 1928), 22.
11. Buffenoir, pp. 139–41.

traiture of Franklin, Jefferson, and other imperial figures of liberal advance.

Secondly, two of the derivatives from Gosset's wax "Rousseau" of 1766, a Wedgwood medallion and a bronze uniface medal, may be matched to a Wedgwood medallion and a bronze uniface medal of Franklin, suggesting strongly that these works have the same approximate date of origin and are derived also from an original by Gosset. In 1766 public interest was concentrated upon Rousseau, but in both formal and popular portraiture Franklin appears as an object of peripheral attention. Ramsay's "Rousseau" was a major attraction at the exhibition of the Society of Artists which opened on April 21, 1766. Hume sent six impressions of the mezzotint from it to the Comtesse de Boufflers on May 6.[12] David Martin, who had made the mezzotint, was then, or soon would be, painting his "Franklin," also for a Scottish patron. All in all, a great deal of publicity that spring was given to philosophy and to the Jean Jacques of the Armenian costume, and although the strange dress was at this time permanently cast aside and its wearer soon returned to the Continent breathing vituperation against both Hume and the Ramsay-Martin *oeuvre*, something had been added to the Rousseau legend which Rousseau, try as he might, could never disclaim or obliterate.

Reflections appeared at once on the other side of the Channel. Gosset's wax "Rousseau" was the source of a print etched by Claude Henri Watelet (1718–86) after a drawing by Taraval. Watelet is remembered as a distinguished amateur of the arts. A pleasant afternoon at his "Moulin Joli" on an island in the Seine, in 1778, is commemorated in the first of the bagatelles written by Franklin for Mme. Brillon. The Taraval-Watelet engraving is the only derivative from Gosset bearing the correct date, 1766.[13] The bronze uniface medal, a little piece—6 centimeters, 2 millimeters in diameter —is inscribed, "JEAN JAQUES ROUSSEAU. L'Ami de la Nature. Frans Gabriel Leclerc, MDCCLXI." Buffenoir, in his study of Rous-

12. Ibid., p. 133.
13. Buffenoir, p. 109, describes a line engraving which according to its inscription was "Dessiné à Neuchâtel en 1765 & Gravé par J. B. Michel." He appears also to have been in error in accepting this date, however, as the print is advertised in the *Mercure de France,* April 1766, and may have been predated for competitive reasons.

seau's portraits, accepts the date 1761, though this antedates the adoption of the Armenian costume.[14] More probably, that carelessness by which the "C" was omitted in "JACQUES" also caused the omission of the "V" which would have corrected the date to MDCCLXVI.

Though Gosset's wax "Rousseau" is unrecorded, examples of the wax "Franklin," here attributed to him, have survived. This is the small wax profile which has for many years been attributed to Patience Wright, ca. 1775. I have never found contemporary evidence of any sort that Patience Wright, who nevertheless plays a major role in this history, ever made any waxwork but those life-sized, wholly realistic portraits for which she became so justly famous. A small wax profile of Washington has on somewhat better grounds been attributed to her, but the date would be many years later, and there is still no primary evidence to confirm it.

Isaac Gosset exhibited at the Society of Artists and Royal Academy from 1760 to 1776. He had made portraits of Lord Camden, General Wolfe, and other well-known persons. Franklin may have owned a number of his pieces, judging by the Rev. Mr. Cutler's description of the wax profiles over his mantel in the Philadelphia house late in his life.[15] Horace Walpole owned a number and Hume, who in his correspondence with Rousseau professed himself eager to own portraits of all his friends, doubtless did as well. Gosset had won a certain celebrity by persuading the reluctant Montesquieu to pose for him. When the great man had objected that to pose was evidence of vanity, the artist had replied, "Sir, is there not as much vanity in refusing?"[16] Gosset is known to have contributed to Wedgwood's series of "Illustrious Moderns," and the Wedgwood likeness of this "Franklin" with the heavy English wig is an important factor in attributing it to him. Josiah Wedgwood was at this time working experimentally on the small portrait medallions which after 1768 became a regular and increasingly popular part of his factory's output, at first all in one color, white or black, and after 1774 in the

14. P. 118. Also Buffenoir, "Les Médailles de Jean Jacques Rousseau," *Revue de l'art ancienne et moderne, 39* (1921), 196–97.

15. William Parker Cutler and Julia Perkins Cutler, *Life, Journals and Correspondence of Rev. Manasseh Cutler, LL.D., 2* (Cincinnati, 1888), 269.

16. Whitley Papers (British Museum), quoting *European Magazine,* 1795.

two-color "cameos."[17] I believe that Gosset made his "Franklin" at about the same time as his "Rousseau" and that both were reproduced soon after by Wedgwood, nor may it have been wholly a coincidence that this work of the Ramsay studio's wax-modeling frame maker was followed a few months after by a portrait of Franklin by its chief assistant, David Martin.[18] It appears that examples of the Wedgwood medallion, in varying sizes, were sent to Franklin in the autumn of 1766, and by him sent on to Philadelphia. Deborah wrote to him on December 13, 1766:

> The Profile is cume safe and is the thing as everey one ses that has seen it. I am verey much obliged to you for it everey bodey knows it that has seen it as to the candil sticks and corke screw they will doe when you return in the spring be so good as to give my love to Mrs. Stephenson and her Dahter tell me is Polley a going to be marreyed I think you sed sum such thing sum time a go when shee dos I hope it will be to one that will deserve her. It semes a dought with me wather Salley writes by this ship as shee is setting for her Pickter for her Brother shee is to be playing on the armonekey.[19]

And from Deborah again on May 16 or 17, 1767:

> My Dearest Dear Child
> on thusday last I reseved yours with one in closed to Salley with the Ring yours is dated March 17 you cante thing what pleshuer thees dear littel letters give to me as I know you think of me ofen . . .[20]

And from another of May 24:

> to mrs. West and I shold ased mr West I am in hopes

17. Samuel B. Oster, "Portraits by a Potter," *Antiques, 63* (1953), 52. Wedgwood to Bentley, Jan. 1, 1775, in Lady Katherine Eufemia Farrer, ed., *Letters of Josiah Wedgwood, 1771–1780* (London, 1903), p. 214.

18. Wedgwood "Rousseau" illustrated in John Meredith Graham II and Hensleigh Cecil Wedgwood, *Wedgwood* (Brooklyn, 1948), p. 33, pl. 24.

19. A.P.S.

20. Ibid.

Salley will be in time aneuf to write. I wold say sum-
thing a bought the Ring and letter hough [how] like
your self it is and what pleshuer it has given to many
of our friends. Mr. Ross wanted Salley to let him
have it but as he spoke to me I sed they mought send
to you to get them one. I rely wish that you would get
two of your shaid dun one for Mr. Roborts and one
for Billey.[21]

To which Franklin replied from London, June 22, 1767: "I send
you the little Shade that was copied from the great one. If it will be
acceptable to my good friend Mr. [Hugh] Roberts, pray give it to
him."[22]

This passage from his letter has been quoted frequently as referring either to a silhouette or to the wax profile supposedly by Patience Wright (who did not go to England until 1772), and may be
responsible through some obscure re-echoings for the inclusion of
Mrs. Wright among the silhouette cutters or painters of her time, a
totally unsupported assumption. Franklin used the words "shade"
or "shadow" for any sort of pictorial reflection. Clearly, he had sent
Sally a portrait of himself set in a ring, and in a form which could
easily be reproduced. The "great one" from which the "little Shade"
was copied might have been either one of the wax portraits or a
Wedgwood medallion. The latter conjecture is more probable since
the ceramic original would have been reduced to the size of a ring
setting by successive firing and remolding. It must have been one of
these Wedgwood pieces which Franklin sent to his sister Jane on
February 26, 1775, as "a Head they make here and sell at the China
Shops."[23] Wedgwood in later years repeated all the famous Franklin profiles, but this one seems to have been continued throughout,
popular even when outdated because of its good characterization
and its British background and dignity.

The Gosset wax gives us in profile, at approximately the same
time, the face which we see in a three-quarter view with lowered
eyes in what many would esteem as the greatest of all the Franklin
portraits, that painted by David Martin probably in 1766 and first

21. Ibid.
22. Franklin Papers (A.P.S.). Smyth, *Writings, 5,* 33.
23. Van Doren, *Benjamin Franklin & Jane Mecom,* p. 152n.

exhibited in April 1767. This also was a Scottish affair, stemming directly from Edinburgh. In his visit to that city in the autumn of 1759 Franklin had met Robert and William Alexander, sons of the Lord Provost, merchants like their father, with a steady eye also upon the arts and good living. Their graves in Roslin Chapel show them to have been members of the Anglican community. Alexander Carlyle remembered that one of the lesser lights of Edinburgh's famous Select Society, "Robert Alexander, wine merchant, a very worthy man, but a bad speaker, entertained us all with warm suppers and excellent claret, as a recompense for the patient bearing of his ineffectual attempts, when I thought he would beat his brains out on account of their constipation."[24] This glimpse of the gentleman in an intellectual group is perhaps not wholly fair. He and Franklin were guests together in 1759 at Prestonfield, home of the hospitable Sir Alexander Dick, and Franklin's poetic tribute to the "joys of Prestonfield" was afterward capped by Robert Alexander in sprightly lines in praise of Franklin and of their host and hostess.[25] Young Henry Marchant remembered meeting both Franklin and Hume in Edinburgh in 1771. "One Mr. Allexander one of the first Merchants in Edinburgh was also in Company—and displayed great Knowledge in ye Trade of Europe & America."[26] A year later another diarist, Sylas Neville, visited the home of the "Messrs. Alexander" and found "a pretty tolerable collection of pictures."[27] In short, Robert Alexander appears to have been a somewhat less effervescent northern version of that other wine-merchant-art-connoisseur, Caleb Whitefoord.

On May 14, 1765, David Martin published a mezzotint of the sculptor Louis François Roubiliac at work on his statue of Shakespeare. It was after a painting by Adrien Carpentiers, and bears the dedication, "To Robert Alexander Esqr This Plate from an Original Picture in his Possession at Edinburgh, is Inscribed by his

24. Quoted in Mossner, *Hume*, p. 282.

25. Mrs. Atholl Forbes, *Curiosities of a Scots Charta Chest, 1600–1800. With the Travels and Memoranda of Sir Alexander Dick, Baronet, of Prestonfield, Midlothian, Written by Himself* (Edinburgh, 1897), pp. 180–81.

26. Diary of Henry Marchant, quoted by J. Bennett Nolan, *Benjamin Franklin in Scotland and Ireland, 1759 and 1771* (Philadelphia, University of Pennsylvania, 1938), pp. 176–77.

27. Basil Cozens-Hardy, ed., *The Diary of Sylas Neville, 1767–1788* (London, Oxford University Press, 1950), p. 192.

Obliged & Obedient Humble Servant David Martin." Ramsay had made Hume a gift of the portrait of Rousseau, a fact brought out when the embittered Jean Jacques cited it as senseless extravagance. Especially when a print was contemplated, the painter of a famous man could well afford that much, and there may have been some similar understanding between Martin and Alexander. A friend sent word to Franklin from Edinburgh on September 2, 1765, that Robert Alexander would be a candidate for Parliament in the place of Sir Harry Erskine who had just died, standing for the borough of Anstruther.[28] Anstruther was David Martin's native place. He was not elected, but came to London anyway. Franklin's portrait was painted, and first seen by London at the opening of the Society of Artists exhibition on April 22, 1767, in the Great Room, Spring Gardens, Charing Cross. It is number 99 in the catalogue. Horace Walpole noted in his copy, "A great likeness. Now in the possession of Sir James Cockburn, Bart."[29]

My search for an explanation of Walpole's second note, conducted devoutly in the face of its being almost certainly no more than a piece of misinformation, found its reward in the Scottish Record Office in Edinburgh with a clue as to what words must have passed there in the hubbub of the Great Room with the crowd discoursing on the pictures that covered the walls from floor to ceiling. Papers on the estate of William Alexander, "Merchant and late Lord Provost," who had died in July, 1761,[30] record the transfer to his sons, Robert and William, on December 19, 1765, of a handsome legacy in capital stock of the Royal Bank of Scotland. "James Cockburn merchant in Edinburgh" was named as "cautioner"—that is, surety. Whether or not this James Cockburn accompanied Robert Alexander to London I cannot tell, but I can readily imagine the conversation before the picture in which his name may have been mentioned in a joking reference to the point of ownership, and Walpole have gone away with an impression that it belonged to the best known of the many holders of the name, Sir James Cockburn, third

28. John Balfour to Benjamin Franklin, Franklin Papers (A.P.S.), *1*, no. 157.
29. Original at National Portrait Gallery, London. Algernon Graves, *The Society of Artists of Great Britain, 1760–1791. The Free Society of Artists, 1761–1783* (London, 1907), p. 158.
30. Date 1763 is given by Charles Rogers in *Memorials of the Earl of Stirling and of the House of Alexander, 2* (Edinburgh, 1877), 33.

Baronet, a Scottish soldier who had served with Wolfe in America.

As to Martin himself who must have been there, his self-portrait shows us an attractive young man with red-gold hair and blue eyes, wearing a dark coat over a red waistcoat ornamented with gold braid.[31] He collected bows, arrows, pistols, and other weapons, and had a good library as well.[32] He was still Ramsay's assistant, but had had his own studio since 1765.[33] He also had painted a portrait of Rousseau.[34] Among his half dozen mezzotints are Ramsay's "Rousseau" and "Hume," 1766 and 1767, and one of Thomas Penn, after Davis, 1766. In 1775 he moved to Edinburgh as Chief Painter to the Prince of Wales for Scotland, but continued to exhibit at the Royal Academy. In his effort to face the public with a recognizable personal style he occasionally introduced into his portraits some large piece of sculpture vis-à-vis the subject. His "William Beckford" of 1766 is posed with a statue of Minerva, his "Dr. William Cullen" and "Earl of Mansfield" of 1776 and 1777, with huge bearded classic busts deemed appropriate to these gentlemen, his "Robert Cunninghame Graham," painted late in his career, with Nollekins' bust of Charles James Fox in heroic size. His choice for the "Franklin" was Roubiliac's bronze bust of Newton. Perhaps Robert Alexander, with his special interest in the sculptor, had suggested this. It is an intrusive but not too discordant object, and in every other respect the painting is most happily conceived. The pose of elbow on table and thumb under chin to hold the focus of his spectacles was characteristic of Franklin. Elkanah Watson, arriving early for a dinner engagement at Passy in 1781, found him in his study in exactly this attitude.[35]

Martin did not make a mezzotint of his "Franklin" probably because the McArdell and Fisher prints were still on the market and Franklin not interested in supporting the publication of a third. Franklin, however, did like the new portrait well enough to order

31. Presented by the Misses Bryce, of the artist's family, to the National Gallery of Scotland in 1910.

32. Catalogue of the sale of his estate, Jan. 14, 1799, and 20 days following. Copy at Scottish National Portrait Gallery.

33. The best account of his life is given by Alastair Smart, *The Life and Art of Allan Ramsay* (London, 1952).

34. Catalogue of sale, 1799.

35. Elkanah Watson, *Men and Times of the Revolution* (New York, 1857), p. 154.

a replica for himself. The two occasions upon which he did this give us a new opportunity to judge his taste. First with the Martin and then with the Duplessis of 1778, he asked for a somewhat less grandiose presentation than that which the artist had originally conceived. In Martin's original, Franklin is seated in a chair the back of which is ornately carved and gilded. The chair of the replica has a plain, round, upholstered back and has ceased to be a conspicuous feature of the painting. I believe that this was done upon Franklin's direction and that it simply expresses his preference for plain fact— that is, for a piece of furniture of the same quality as those he had in his rooms at Craven Street. Certainly, however, the change strengthens the painter's representation of a mood of thoughtfulness. One other point may or may not have been considered. In formal portraiture an ornate chair was used to symbolize high office, and Franklin held no high office at this time. Years later, when the original with the gilded chair had come to America, some other painter surmounted it with the carved figure of an eagle, thus more effectively representing, to his mind, the Minister Plenipotentiary to France, the President of the Supreme Executive Council of Pennsylvania.

The artist Joseph Moser mentions this picture in a reminiscence of Allan Ramsay:

> I have seen his *shewroom* crowded with portraits of his *Majesty* in every state of their operation.... Ramsay was an excellent scholar and an excellent painter. He was, perhaps, *too rich* to *devour letters* and the arts, and has been known to appear at the *East India House,* for instance, when an enthusiast would have thought that he ought to have been in his *painting room* or *library:* but were it necessary to show that he did not neglect the latter, I could, perhaps, refer to some excellent tracts, &c. of his writing; and with respect to the former, need only mention the half-length portrait of the *American* DR. FRANKLIN. In this picture, Ramsay, as he once justly observed, painted the *philosopher,* in which light he only viewed the subject

> of it; but leaving its graphic merit to the connoisseur,
> its highest praise was, that *"It seemed to think."*[36]

Ramsay had praised Martin's work rather than his own, and Moser's misrecollection has brought a portrait of Franklin inadvertently into the record of Ramsay's work.[37] The anecdote, however, is of positive interest in showing that Martin's portrait was probably painted in Ramsay's studio.

I believe that it was in its quality of thoughtfulness, calmness, and reserve that the picture appealed to Franklin himself. I should like to think that he ordered the replica and held it through the years for the very purpose to which at the last he assigned it in his will: to represent him in the government of Pennsylvania, the province and commonwealth whose interest he had served so long and so hopefully, and to remind his successors there of one who, thoughtful, untroubled, eyes and mind upon the business in hand, had so dealt with the crises of an earlier day. More than any other, this was the way he would see himself and wish to be seen. He would also have had, as time went on, a feeling for this portrait's association with the English years of self-realization, of harmony and advance, of friendships never overshadowed by the climactic events and triumphs that followed.

The Alexanders continued in Franklin's circle of friends. Robert never married, so that the portrait eventually passed to his brother, William, who had a young family about him. One catches another glimpse of the humor of these gentlemen and their liberation from the traditional proprieties in the christening of William's daughter, born in 1758. He named the child for the Jewish princess, Mariamne, daughter of Alexander and wife of Herod the Great, and the heroine of a tragedy by Voltaire. During the war Mariamne and her father lived in France where he was again involved in business connected with America. She, on her part, became the fiancée of Franklin's grandnephew, Jonathan Williams, whom she married in 1777. The portrait of Franklin, naturally, went to this couple and was brought by them to America.

36. *European Magazine and London Review, 64* (1813), 516.
37. Smart, *Ramsay,* pp. 124, 188.

David Martin made only one other replica of the portrait, identical with that owned by Franklin, and he later made a small oil sketch of the original. It was copied by others many times, both for its subject and as an example of great portraiture. It became popular in America as a tavern sign, perhaps better suggesting warmth and comfort than some of the other Franklin likenesses. I shall venture a guess that it inspired the composition of the portrait of another printer-philosopher, Pierre Samuel du Pont de Nemours, who is shown seated, writing, while on the table near him a large bust of Turgot (which he presented to the American Philosophical Society after his emigration to America in 1799) vies for attention much as does that of Newton in Franklin's picture. The eyes, however, look sharply into the distance in an active rather than a contemplative mood. The picture may be the work of an amateur, Anastasie Françoise Julienne de Reverony, a grandchild of Mme. du Pont by her first husband, Paul Poivre, and if influenced by the "Franklin" it must have been through the mezzotint which Edward Savage made in 1793 from Benjamin West's copy after Martin.

It is also conjectural whether or not, at the very time when Franklin's portrait in the character of philosopher was first being exhibited and admired, young Charles Willson Peale, then an art student in London, made a pencil sketch of him in the character of a philanderer. The sketch is in Peale's notebook of accounts and memoranda along with one of another couple in a similar pose and other jottings.[38] It shows a gentleman with a girl on his lap in amorous reciprocation. His costume is that of the Martin portrait. The face, in profile, is not convincing, though it might be Franklin's, and one could scarcely expect more on a page 3¾ by 6 inches and in a drawing which must have been made from immediate recollection rather than on the spot. The wig is the main point of doubt. It has the appearance of the subject's own hair, tied in a queue. Yet if one compares it with the wig in the Gosset or Tassie profiles, it is clear that the alteration only of a line or two could make it unmistakably Franklin's. If it indeed be Franklin, its value as portraiture is chiefly in the representation of the figure. Here it would confirm, as the few other sources do, that the weight to which he himself confessed was not excessive, and that he was still a stout man rather than

38. Peale-Sellers Papers (A.P.S.).

a fat one. There is no identification of the subject in his diary of that year, which is more a sketch and memorandum book than anything else. But in his diary of fifty years later, pointing up a moral that "only with men of little minds" is it necessary to stand upon formality, Peale recorded the meeting which had occurred at the time of the sketch:

> When I was in London studying painting with Mr. West . . . I wanted to be introduced to Doctr. Franklin, and not knowing who I could ask the favor of an introduction to the Doctr. I determined one day to call on him—and enquiring where he lodged I went alone to the House, being shewn into the Room where he was sitting with a young Lady on his knee, and in the dress of the Picture now in the Room of the Philosophical society in Philada. I asked the Doctr. if he remembered the name of Charles Peale who formerly lived in Maryland, the Doctr. replied that he remembered him well then I told him that I was the son of that Charles Peale—and having been in London some few months and not finding any Person offering to introduce me to him and having seen by the letters left by my father which had passed between you & him I have taken the liberty of waiting [upon] you. I then acquainted him that [with] the desire to improve myself in Painting I visited great Britain and was received very kindly by Mr. West. The Doctr. was very friendly to me, shewed me his experiments which he was then making, and desired me to call on him at any of my leisure moments and he would be always glad to see me.[39]

Nothing is more clearly established than the fact that another young Philadelphian, whom Peale addressed in friendly fashion as a "Brother Brush," painted a portrait of Franklin early in 1770, in time to get into the second exhibition of the Royal Academy in that spring, but beyond this clear record of origin the painting has totally disappeared, leaving a void into which claimant canvases from time

39. Ibid.

to time are thrust. Henry Benbridge, a portly, good-natured young man of twenty-five, had followed Benjamin West to Italy where he is said to have studied under Pompeo Girolamo Batoni and Anton Raphael Mengs.[40] He had acquired great technical competence and had developed a technique which, he boasted, enabled him to complete a portrait with unusual speed.[41] His name was already known in London, for his portrait of the Corsican patriot, Pasquale Paoli, commissioned by Boswell, had attracted crowds the year before. He arrived in November or December, 1769, and, presenting a letter of introduction from his father to Franklin, was introduced to young Thomas Coombe, another Philadelphian, who was lodging in the Craven Street house. Coombe, aged twenty-two, was a clergyman of promise, eloquent, interesting, with a feeling for poetry which led him later to compose an American echo to Goldsmith's *Deserted Village.*[42] Benbridge determined at once to paint them both for the coming exhibition as his introduction to the profession in London, promising to present the works afterward to Mrs. Franklin and to Mr. Coombe. They are numbers 14 and 15 in the catalogue. Number 14, "Portrait of a gentleman; half length," was identified by Horace Walpole in his catalogue as that of Dr. Franklin.[43]

In July Benbridge suddenly decided to return to America rather than follow the career in London open to him. There is no further mention anywhere of the two pictures. He carried a letter from Franklin to Deborah on July 19, 1770, but it says nothing of a portrait for her or for any other friend. He may have given it to someone in England. He had the Wilson and Martin portraits of himself, and William had the Chamberlin.

While not specified, the Martin was I am sure one of the paintings sent by Franklin from London to Philadelphia in 1771, where it was borrowed and copied by Charles Willson and James Peale. On

40. Charles Henry Hart, "The Gordon Family: Painted by Henry Benbridge," *Art in America,6* (1917–18), 192.

41. Ibid., p. 195.

42. Thomas Coombe, *Edwin: or the Emigrant. To which are added Three Other Poetical Sketches,* Philadelphia, 1775. Also Coombe, *The Peasant of Auburn, or the Emigrant, A Poem,* Philadelphia, 1784?

43. Algernon Graves, *The Royal Academy of Arts. A Complete Dictionary of Contributors and their Work from its Foundation in 1769 to 1904, 1* (London, 1905), 178.

April 20 he had written to William, "By this Ship I send the Picture that you left with Meyer. He has never yet finished the Miniatures. The other pictures I send with it are for my own house, but this you may take to yours."[44] The picture left with Meyer was the portrait of William which had been one of those painted by Benjamin Wilson in 1758 and 1759. To Meyer, Franklin wrote one of his rare angry letters:

> Dr. Franklin presents his Compliments to Mr. Meyer and prays him not to detain any longer the Picture from which he was to make a Miniature, but return it by the Bearer. Hopes Mr. Meyer will not think him impatient, as he has waited full Five Years, and has seen many of his Acquaintance, tho' applying later, serv'd before him. Wishes Mr. Meyer not to give himself the Trouble of making any more Apologies or to feel the least Pain on Acct. of his disappointing Dr. Franklin who assures him, he never was disappointed by him but once, not having for several years past since he has known the Character of his Veracity, had the smallest dependance upon it.[45]

The irritation caused by an expectation so disregarded is understandable. It is clear also, however, that Franklin's lack of any comprehension of the artist's viewpoint may itself have been an irritant, and William had the same failing. Jeremiah Meyer, a native of Wurtemberg, had been in England since the age of fourteen, had learned his craft thoroughly, and had been appointed enamel painter to George III and miniature painter to the Queen. His work on ivory stood with that of Reynolds on canvas. Redgrave praises him for truth and expression combined with a quiet refinement of color.[46] No artist is pleased to be asked to copy a contemporary's work. The Franklins sent him Wilson's portrait of a young man who might easily have come in to pose for an original. To be sure, the miniature must have been ordered early in 1762, when William's

44. Franklin Papers (A.P.S.), *45*, no. 37.
45. Ibid., *6*, no. 80. *P.M.H.B., 30* (1906), 107. Smyth, *Writings, 5,* 313.
46. Richard and Samuel Redgrave, *A Century of Painters of the English School, 1* (London, 1866), 419.

marriage and departure were impending. A year later he sent Strahan further directions which could well have increased the painter's rancor. "Please to tell Myers (if it is possible that he has not yet finished the Miniatures) that Mrs. Franklin would be glad to have them made a little fatter, as I have increased considerably in flesh since I left London. But care must be taken not to alter the likeness."[47] Such blindness to an artist's professional feeling, shared by both father and son, was not calculated to inspire a painter to his best efforts or, for that matter, to any effort at all.

Benbridge's lost portrait of Franklin is one of those which will live in chronicle only, to be known by their effect upon contemporaries rather than by our own estimate of them. This is also true of those of the American portraitist Patience Wright, whose art was almost as transient as that of the theater. Her life-sized sculptures of Franklin in wax almost certainly reproduced his appearance more faithfully than any others. Her role in his life and affairs, if not one of determining influence, was, at least, unique and surprising. She affords us, in watching the confrontation of artist and subject, a spectacle seen nowhere else. Her visionary political scheming might have involved him in serious embarrassment. Her plain friendship he returned and to her other attitudes opposed his sense of humor, an impenetrable armor.

Patience Wright, born Patience Lovell, came of an old family of Oyster Bay, Long Island, and numbered among her cousins Robert Feke, the painter of Franklin's first portrait. There are intermarriages in the record showing a tightly-knit group reaching from Oyster Bay down into New Jersey, as it did also to Newport where young Robert Feke had settled. Of the family of John Lovell and Patience Townsend it would be pleasant to know more. Their daughter's account may have been improved in the telling, but I think it fairly safe to accept the main points—that John Lovell was a Quaker, that he held his family to a strict vegetarian diet and backed it up by insisting that they all of them dress entirely in white, and that the children departed from strict Quaker custom by fashioning images, shaped or painted. Only two were fated to attract any notice by their gifts, Patience and Rachel, who became modelers in wax. Of the others (there may have been ten children in all) we

47. Hart in *P.M.H.B.*, *30*, 380.

have only the names of Rezine, who married first Ephraim Anderson of Trenton and then Ephraim Harris of Cumberland County, and who died in 1803; Anne, who married Nathaniel Farnsworth in 1749; Deborah, who became Deborah Ayres; and a sixth named in Patience's will of 1772 simply as "Sister Harker." Their one brother bore their father's name. Their will shows that even into the next generation they held shares in a Lovell estate at Oyster Bay.

Upon this background there is the story of a young Patience running away to Philadelphia in the belief that she would find there a great metropolitan center in which her artistic skill would find full scope and recognition. It is related, and quite possibly true, that Francis Hopkinson encouraged her.[48] He may have suggested wax as a better medium than bread dough or putty. Although matrimony steadied her course, she remained a lady with a mind of her own. It may be observed here that she was not related in any way to John Wesley. Wesley's sister, Hetty, had married William Wright in 1725 after she had been brought into disgrace by an overnight escapade with a young lawyer. William Temple Franklin calls her "Mrs. Mehitabel Wright" and a "niece of the celebrated John Wesley," an error which Dunlap and others followed.[49]

Patience Wright's skill as a wax modeler had certainly matured before her husband's death in 1769. Her youngest child was born soon after, and it was probably in this time of crisis that she and her sister Rachel began their public exhibitions. Waxwork shows had long been a popular amusement in America as in England. They were crudely fashioned and specialized in mythological or religious wonders with a sprinkling of royal splendor, horror subjects, and humor. In America Patience Wright originated the type of spectacle now associated with London and Mme. Tussaud: life-sized figures of well-known or typical contemporaries, made with such marvelous fidelity to nature and such marvelous detail that close inspection would reveal the wrinkled skin, the blood vessels under it, the hair on the back of a man's hand—all, of course, made with real hair, glass eyes, and costumes identical with those worn by the living individual, even to undergarments. The heads were built up on some sort of form, hollow and therefore light enough to rest

48. J. C. Long, *Mr. Pitt and America's Birthright* (New York, 1940), p. 504.
49. W. T. Franklin, *Works of Franklin, 6,* 87n.

safely on a lightly built figure. Summer, when the wax, which must normally be hard, was more malleable, was the time to work with this material. For added warmth and to the amazement of those who sat to her, Mrs. Wright would work with the wax in her lap, under her apron, both hands busy while her sharp eyes roved about her subject's features and her loud voice in a flow of emphatic and perspicacious statement kept the other's attention fixed upon her. William Dunlap saw her at work in London in this way in 1784, and though "too young and careless to observe her minutely," remembered the expression in her eye and the "energetic wildness in her manner."[50]

The two ladies seem to have visited all the seaboard cities. In Philadelphia Mrs. Wright knew the Franklin family well. She knew Jane Mecom in Boston and doubtless found kindred spirits in both her and Deborah, for all three spoke plainly. New York became home base for these operations. There, on the evening of June 3, 1771, when both ladies were away from home, one of the children set fire to the waxwork and nearly burned down the house. Only the "George Whitefield," the "John Dickinson," and a few others were saved. Most of the old and all of the new ones just brought from Charleston by Mrs. Wells were lost.[51] By August 5 the *New York Gazette*, or the *Weekly Post Boy* announced that they had made good the damage with new pieces of "superior Skill and Judge-

50. William Dunlap, *A History of the Rise and Progress of the Arts of Design in the United States, 1* (New York, 1834), 134. Charles Willson Peale in his autobiography (Peale-Sellers Collection, A.P.S.) gives a similar account as he received it from Benjamin West. Another account of Mrs. Wright's procedure is found in *The Observer* (London, 1785), p. 222. In the copy in the library of Wilmarth S. Lewis, Farmington, Conn., the author is identified in a contemporary notation as Richard Cumberland. The work described London society, with the identity of individuals disguised. Of Mrs. Wright: "There sat an ordinary woman in a black cloak by the fire side with her feet upon the fender and her knees up, who seemed employed upon a cushion or pillow, which she kept concealed under her apron, without once looking upon the work, she was upon. You have read of the Witch of Endor, says she to me (observing I had fixed my eyes upon her) I am a descendant of that old lady's, and can raise the dead as well as she could; immediately she put aside her apron, and produced a head moulded in wax so strikingly like my deceased friend, the father of Calliope, that the shock it gave me was too apparent to escape her: . . . You know this brave fellow, I perceive; says she, England never owned a better officer; he was my hero, and every line in his face is engraved in my heart."

51. *New York Gazette, or The Weekly Post-Boy,* June 10, 1771, quoted in William Kelby, *Notes on American Artists* (New York, 1922), p. 9.

ment," and added that "To both these extraordinary Geniuses, may without Impropriety be applied what Addison says of Kneller, a little varied.

> 'By Heav'n and Nature, not a Master taught,
> They give to Statues, Passion, Life and Thought.' "[52]

Perhaps inspired by this acclaim, Patience took a ship for England, leaving her family behind her. She wrote her will on board the ship *Nancy,* Captain Dillon, in New York harbor, on February 1, 1772 with Hercules Mulligan and another sailor as witnesses. The document is in part a testament and in somewhat larger measure a list of formal directions to "Aunt Wells" and the children.[53] From it we learn that the New York waxwork was her property, with Mrs. Wells receiving one quarter of the profits. Elizabeth, the eldest daughter, was manager. Phoebe was with her there. Joseph was in school in Philadelphia. Little Sally was with her Aunt Anderson. Three gentlemen were named advisors to the family, "Mr. James Bowne, Mr. Wm. Goforth my landlord, and Mr. Lindley Murray." Patience seemed always able to interest reputable and intelligent persons in her behalf. James Bowne, who must have been one of the Long Island cousins, was a substantial citizen of New York. So was Judge William Goforth, who appears in a military command and in touch with Franklin during the Canadian campaign of 1776.[54] Lindley Murray, the grammarian, had just returned from England and may have been the one who persuaded Mrs. Wright to seek her fortune there.

She had letters of recommendation and a good press to speed her away.[55] The crossing at this intemperate season was obviously so timed that she could be settled in London at the beginning of the warm weather necessary to her work. On March 30, 1772, Benjamin Franklin replied to the letter she had brought from his sister Jane. She may have arrived that day. She brought with her a bust of his friend Cadwallader Colden, and it remained for a while at

---

52. Ibid., pp. 9–10.

53. Will filed in Surrogate's Court of the County of New York, *Liber* 39, p. 133. Probated June 7, 1786.

54. Franklin Papers (A.P.S.), *4,* no. 80.

55. A. J. Wall, "Wax Portraiture," *N.Y.H.S. Quarterly Bulletin, 9* (1925), 5.

Craven Street, exciting admiration.[56] She had her bust of White-field, whom Franklin had so admired in his lifetime. Franklin had promised Jane to recommend the lady to his friends, and one can see the pattern of his introductions in her subsequent models: Mrs. Catherine Macaulay, whose English history from a new and liberal viewpoint was arousing great interest; David Garrick; the Earl of Chatham; Lord Temple; John Wilkes. And of course he sat to her himself. William Strahan printed a friendly notice in his *London Chronicle* of July 4–7:

> SIR,
>
> I doubt not but many of your Readers will receive pleasure by being informed, that the ingenious Mrs. Wright of New York, who is remarkable for expressing the exact likeness of the human face and passions of the soul, in wax work, is arrived in London. She has modelled the late Rev. Mr. George Whitefield in a sitting posture, as large as life, which is thought by all who have seen it, to be a striking resemblance. She has likewise modelled the present Lieutenant Governor of New York the learned Cadwallader Colden, Esq; and another of that excellent and public spirited Philosopher Dr. Benjamin Franklin, of Philadelphia. She is now forming a likeness of Mr. Garrick.

Patience, at 30 Great Suffolk Street, the Strand, had achieved success. Her children were sent over to her from New York. "And apropos of puppets," Horace Walpole wrote on February 11, 1773, to the Countess of Upper Ossory, "there is a Mrs. Wright arrived from America, to make figures in wax of Lord Chatham, Lord Lyttelton, and Mrs. Macaulay. Lady Aylesbury literally spoke to a waxen figure of a housemaid in the room, for the artistess has brought over a group, and Mrs. Fitzroy's aunt is one of them."[57] At about the same time, on April 6, 1773, Franklin wrote to Deborah

56. Henry Marchant saw it there on April 6 (diary, transcript at A.P.S.).
57. Mrs. Paget Toynbee, ed., *The Letters of Horace Walpole*, 8 (Oxford, 1904), 237. Mrs. Fitzroy's aunt was Anne de Lancey (1723–75), wife of John Watts, a prominent merchant of New York. (Information from Mrs. Genevieve B. Butterfield, Lewis-Walpole Library.)

that he had done all in his power to serve Mrs. Wright, but that he had somehow displeased her and she no longer came near him. That something untoward had occurred is apparent also from the fact that in all later references to Mrs. Wright's amazingly successful exhibition, in which at least a few of her subjects are named, there is no mention of a bust or figure of Franklin. The reason is not far to seek. Franklin was held in bitter political and personal enmity by the Penns. This great family had become patrons of the lady modeler, and it may well have been they who introduced her to the patronage of the King and Queen. They seem to have sensed the propaganda value of this more-than-photographic art in substituting for a name to which many Pennsylvanians were hostile a realization of the individual's actual form and presence. A bust was sent to Philadelphia, and its arrival recorded in the votes of the Assembly, September 24, 1773:

> The Speaker laid before the House an Extract of a Letter to the Reverend *Richard Peters* from Mrs. *Patient* [*sic*] *Wright,* in *London,* dated the 24th of *June* 1773, which was read and is as follows, *viz.* I Send you by Captain *Sutton* the Busto of the Proprietor *Thomas Penn,* Esq;—It is a Present from Lady *Juliana* his Wife to the People of *Pennsylvania,* to be lodged in the public Library.—Lady Juliana ordered me to send it to you, and to inform you she thought it a most excellent Performance, and that it was admired by the King and Queen and most of the Nobility in *England.* If any accident should happen in the Passage, or it may want any thing done to the Drapery, be pleased to apply to my Sister *Rachel Wells,* who has orders from me and Lady Juliana to inspect it and keep the Key of the Case, until she hears further from us, as a few alterations are intended to make it keep for Posterity, in memory of the *Penn* Family and of Mrs. Wright's Ingenuity.[58]

58. Quoted in "Notes and Queries," *P.M.H.B., 15* (1891), 122. A later announcement of the gift in the *New York Journal, or General Advertiser,* Oct. 14, 1773, is quoted in *P.M.H.B., 8* (1884), 433.

Whatever occurred it did not dim the appreciation and humor with which Franklin continued to regard Mrs. Wright. He did, much later, twit her lightly upon having included Lord North in the show. That lifelikeness which so impressed others he could only regard with amusement. It delighted him when, urging matrimony upon an English friend, Mr. Fitzmaurice replied that it would be more convenient to get "Mrs. Wright to make him a wax-work wife to sit at the head of his table."[59] Some Londoners were troubled by the deathlike stillness of the figures, "exceedingly well executed," as Mrs. Powys conceded in November 1773, "yet being as large as life, if of one's particular friends, 'tis rather a likeness strikingly unpleasing."[60] Their favorable impact upon the public at large, however, is beyond question. The trend in art was toward a new realism, with Reynolds leading it in portraiture and with West applying it in his "Death of Wolfe" and seeking in his classic themes a more authentic classicism.

I have compared Patience Wright's work to the drama in its transience. It was also close to the theater in another way. It had a kinship with that fidelity to real life which Garrick had brought to the Drury Lane and which itself was to influence painting in its direction as a popular, theatrical art. There was a final dramatic element in Patience herself, loud, crude, and bold. Her quickness of perception and total lack of inhibitions were twin wonders as great as her imitations of life. They called her "Sibyl" for her uncanny awareness of the people and motives under the courtly manner, a wilderness prophetess, another living exemplar of Rousseau's paradox.

Benjamin West had risen to fame upon that same faith in a purer genius emerging from primitive America. He was one of the lions of London now, the white-plumed champion of a new "History" painting which Englishmen saw as rivaling the effete, long dominant art of France. Patience must be seen in this mood of acceptance and against the background of the stilted sculpture of that day to realize how great an excitement she seemed to have brought the town. Her own account of her young life, as well as West's, was re-

59. Smyth, *Writings, 9*, 583.
60. Emily J. Climenson, ed., *Passages from the Diaries of Mrs. Philip Lybbe Powys of Hardwick House, Oxon., A.D. 1756–1808* (London, 1899), p. 153.

told enthusiastically by those eagerly dedicated to the simple child of nature theory. Such a one was, of all people, the vitriolic Philip Thicknesse, "discoverer" of Gainsborough and admirer of Robert Edge Pine, who found her, on tour, at Bath:

Mrs. WRIGHT, CHURCH YARD.

Among the Artists we must not omit to mention MRS. WRIGHT, Lady (*though born in the wilds of America*) who has a just Claim to the Notice of every Encourager of Arts, for her Talent in modelling Likenesses in Wax. Nor are her *Waxen* Figures the only Object worthy of Notice in her Apartments, *when she is present.* The Simplicity of her Manners, her strong, natural Sense, her Vivacity, and the open and honest Manner in which she indiscriminately discloses her political Sentiments, to Persons of whatever Rank, Condition, or Party, they are of, shews her to be a Native of the NEW WORLD, where she was taught, by virtuous Parents, to acknowledge no Distinction between Men, but that which is produced by superior Virtues, or distinguished Merit. This extraordinary Woman's Father was (for that part of *America* where he lived) esteemed among his Neighbors to be A VERY RICH, AND A VERY HONEST MAN; *i.e.* He had large Tracts of Land, Houses, Horses, Oxen, Sheep, Poultry, and, in short, every Kind of living Thing, and earthly Grain (*beside Ten Children*) which MAN can really want, for the Support and Comfort of Life; but being one of that Sect called *Quakers* (*I would to* GOD *we were all so*). He became so singularly conscientious, that he could not bring himself to believe, that GOD permitted Men to spill the Blood of animals for their daily Food. He therefore neither eat Flesh himself nor permitted it to be eaten by any one within his Gates. His ten Children were twice ten Years old, before they tasted Flesh. Instead of the modern Boarding-school education of *Britain,* the Daughters of this good man were instructed in the Arts of the Dairy, of Agriculture, and every Branch of such useful and Pastoral Knowledge as tended to make them good Wives to Men in the same humble and natural Way of Life their Father set before their Eyes.

The good Man of this *Arcadian* Family, nor any of his Household, ever appeared in any other Dress, from Head to Foot, than in white Apparel; and they became not only the Objects of Admiration, and Love, of their surrounding Neighbors, but the Fame of his singular Manner of Life, his virtuous Actions, and the general Ingenuity of his whole Family, was spread over ALL AMERICA. The Genius of his ten Children (*though they never eat Meat*) broke out in a Variety of Shapes; for though they were denied earthly Masters, they had the GREAT MASTER OF ALL NATURE FULL IN VIEW, and their imitative Powers burst forth like Fruits in their Season, and by the same hidden powers. They expressed Juice from the Herbs and Flowers of their Garden, and extracted Gums from the Trees of the Forest; with these they made Colours, and vied with each other, which should excel most in the Line of Genius they pursued. In short, the Sister-Arts in *America* were THEN *Ten in Number.* The fifth Daughter, our present BATH Artist, became a modeller in Clay, and at length, almost *made Man.* Her Desire of going to *Philadelphia* (where *she then conceived* all the Arts of the known World were to be seen) was so violent, that, for the first Time, she became a little disobedient, and got herself privately removed to that *Now City* of Sorrow and Sadness, but which, then, was the QUEEN of all the CITIES in AMERICA: But being straitened in Point of Circumstances, she soon after gave her hand to a substantial *Quaker,* who had nothing but *Age* and *Money* to *recommend* himself to her Favour. This Connection, however, enabled her to buy such Materials as she wanted, and to pursue the Bent of her Genius; and

while the old Gentleman produced her four living
Children, she modelled him an hundred in Clay, but
not one to his *Goût*. At length, Misfortunes befel him,
and he died, leaving his ingenious Wife, at the age of
35, little else to maintain her Family, but the Ingenuity of her Head, and the Cunning of her Finger.[61]

When this was written the war was on, Philadelphia had fallen
into enemy hands, and Patience was deeply involved in her country's plight. Franklin had again become a hero to her and she was
serving him in her famous, and I fear overrated, role of "spy." It
would seem to have been early in 1774 that she had first realized
how important a source of confidential information the crowds
coming and going from her exhibition rooms could be if carefully
mined. The Chatham Papers in the Public Record Office in London show her in touch with Lord Chatham and show that he on his
part received her missives, which certainly reveal more impetuosity
than regularity of mind, with respect. For all her rather confused
and increasingly apocalyptic style of communication she had certainly been industrious in gathering testimony from men about her
and from friends in New York. Lord Chatham, at the time of his
crucial conferences with Franklin, had already in hand a sizeable
dossier from Patience Wright. It is worth noting, in the light of
later events, that she was also taking as large a part as one in her
situation could in the parliamentary election of that autumn,
in close contact, I should judge, with Catherine Macaulay and her
brother, John Sawbridge, London alderman then running for Parliament. A new wind was blowing in British politics, one which had
fanned the fires in America as well—a new awareness of the power
of open, public meetings and a readiness to turn it against corrup-
tion in politics and to create a truly representative Parliament. Patience was not alone in hoping that a solution to the American crisis,
happy for all, might follow such reform. And in the meantime the
rage for her exhibition, now ensconced in rooms in Chudleigh Court,
Pall Mall, went on. *The London Magazine, or Gentleman's
Monthly Intelligencer* of November 1775 gave her a leading article

61. Philip Thicknesse, *New Prose Bath Guide for the Year 1778* (London and
Bath, 1778), pp. 51–53.

and an engraved portrait as "the Promethean Modeller," with "a new style of picturing, superior to statuary," her "art perfect as nature," and herself a model of "Integrity, virtue and a pure heart."[62]

West and Wright shared this integrity and virtue in the public esteem. I doubt if London, least of all in these last years of his residence there, regarded Franklin as embodying the same simplicity and purity of heart. But these qualities he assuredly shared with them, in fact and in imaginative popular concept, for he, too, was the product of an uncorrupted, natural environment. He and Rousseau had been thought of at once as kindred spirits, unlike as they were. And within a very short time Franklin was to be accepted in France with a tremendous and abiding fervor. All the world had to admire Franklin's simple, open integrity. But this new idea of the natural goodness of man invited participation as well, and was akin to those religious doctrines of a free and saving grace which were gathering strength at this time. Franklin came to France as a living example of what every man might be—outliving adversity, dangers, and the hand of time.

Patience was to make her own incongruous appearance in the French milieu. The portrait she made of him there and the one she had made in London each have a unique history. The London bust of 1772, as I have inferred, appears to have been taken out of the exhibition, but it was of little matter, for one had already been sent to America. This other probably followed it.[63] Their importance in the exhibitions of "Aunt Wells," to which Patience continued regularly to send her own "performances," was far greater than a bust or figure of Franklin at Chudleigh Court could have been. In America a perfectly realistic reproduction of himself, seen with others of the King, the Queen, William Pitt, George Whitefield, John Wesley, lords and ladies, and famous captains by land and sea, was visited and enjoyed and remembered by thousands of his country-

62. *London Magazine, 44* (1775), 555–56. Other contemporary accounts are in the *Gentleman's Magazine, 46* (1776), 214–15; *Morning Chronicle and London Advertiser,* No. 2172, May 7, 1776, p. 3; *The Diary of John Baker, Barrister* (London, 1931), p. 313, recording a visit to the exhibition on May 16, 1775.

63. News item from London, Dec. 1, 1772, in *New York Gazette and Weekly Mercury,* Feb. 15, 1773, quoted in Rita S. Gottesman, *The Arts and Crafts in New York* (New York, 1938), p. 393.

men through those long years of his absence when his broad and pleasant face might have faded so easily from recollection. No other portrait was seen by so many or could have carried with it so direct a feeling of the living presence of Poor Richard.

6 THE FACE OF
INSURGENT HUMANITY

THOUGH it has never to my knowledge been done, Franklin's life would lend itself peculiarly well to dramatization, by the cinema, preferably, if it could but compass the ease with which he used to hold vast issues within one line, one laugh. But the entrances and exits alone would make the play—his comings and goings from Boston and Philadelphia, every return and departure of the big, smiling man carrying with it its own wave of growing excitement and the historic impact of rising force. Of them all none was more electrically thrilling than his coming to France early in December 1776, the little armed sloop *Reprisal* fluttering into Quiberon Bay with two prizes captured off the English coast and aboard her the famous, indomitable old man. His two grandsons were at either hand, a boy of seven and a youth of seventeen. His grandnephew, Jonathan Williams, Jr., accompanied them to Paris. The city, alerted by flying rumors of his coming, watched for his entrance from day to day.

Old friends gathered round him and many new ones were at hand. They saw a stout figure, plainly and immaculately dressed, who wore, instead of a powdered wig, the warm, soft, shapeless cap of marten fur he had found on his journey to Canada the spring before. It covered his brow almost to the silver rims of his spectacles and from it on either side his thin, whitening hair fell to the shoulders. He wore no gold lace. He wore no sword, but carried a white walking stick. On an earlier visit to Paris he had bought a French wig, so that his heavy English one might not seem out of place. Formerly, he had always dressed so as to be inconspicuous and yet to command respect. When he had discarded wigs altogether on returning from England to America in 1775, he was on his way to a country where they were not at all a necessity of fashion. The change benefited a scalp irritation from which he had suffered for some time. But in London, while he might sit wigless by his window to relieve it, he would never have gone out into the street uncovered. Now, coming to Paris again, not as a visitor this time but upon a formal and official mission of the utmost importance, a wig was again in order, and it is significant that the first item in his accounts, after the expenses of landing had been paid, was a figure of 101 livres, 5 francs "for Wiggs."[1] This indicates a willingness to yield to fashion. But even then the coiffure of the fur cap with his own natural hair wisping out from under it was such a rousing success and so popular a symbol that the combination of national advantage and personal convenience must have been irresistible. It may have been an opportunistic, spur-of-the-moment decision, but nonetheless an inspired one. Here he had to dramatize himself before a people sensitive to drama. Barriers of language impeded a direct appeal, but his renown as a philosopher had preceded him. His role had to be that of age and wisdom, pitting forthright practical truth against the subtle maneuvers of Europe's most sophisticated capital, and his own personal simplicity against the "eau bénite du cour." The court had in it both hostile elements and a warm mood of acceptance, a balance which popular pressures might weigh in his favor.

Here was a foreign envoy whose costume, an unheard-of thing, discarded all outward pretension to eminence and power, and in so doing assumed the eminence common, as liberated minds believed, to all mankind. Here was an opponent of France's ancient enemy across the Channel who could only be seen, in his works and in his dress, as the champion of universal liberation. He had made himself as unique and significant a figure as Rousseau with his fur

1. Franklin MSS (H.S.P.), 7, 8. At the date of the entry, Jan. 26, 1777, Franklin was established in Paris and the fur cap in popularity. A large "Taylor's Bill" is recorded on Aug. 8, more than half of the expenditure being for clothes for William Temple Franklin. Franklin's fur cap is identified as "his Canadian Cap" in a letter from Edward Bancroft to Silas Deane, Feb. 21, 1777, in *Deane Papers,* Vol. 1, N.Y.H.S. Collections, *19* (N.Y., 1887), 496.

cap had been in London a decade before. He was well aware of the sensation he was creating and saw its value, though it would be absurd to believe that he was consciously taking his cue from Rousseau. There was another allusion supporting the symbolism of the fur cap which must have occurred at once to the Parisians, though Franklin may not have been aware of it at all. France was at this time deeply involved in Swedish foreign policy and politics, and Franklin's appearance must have sharply and directly called to mind the symbolism of Sweden's two long and bitterly embroiled political parties, the aristocratic "Hats," opposed to the popular, liberty-loving "Caps."

Now, too, for the first time we have verbal descriptions of Franklin's appearance, though not free from bias and all focused upon his new singularity. There is still a paucity of description in spite of the eighteenth century's admirable feeling for the objective recording of contemporary history. In one of the most detached, as well as one of the most frequently quoted and misquoted, accounts, dated January 15, 1777, the Abbé de Flamarens gives us a glimpse of the bland old man in the setting of popularity and excitement aroused by his first arrival at Paris:

> Ce quaker est dans tout le costume de sa secte. Il a une belle physionomie, des lunettes toujours sur les yeux, peu de cheveux, un bonnet de peau qu'il porte constamment sur sa tête, point de poudre, mais un air net, du linge extrêmement blanc, un habit brun, font toute sa parure. Il porte pour seule défense un baton à la main.[2]

2. *L'Espion Anglois, ou Correspondance secrète entre Milord All'eye et Milord All'ear, 5* (London, 1785), 5–6. (This Quaker is in the complete costume of his sect. He has handsome features, spectacles always over his eyes, little hair, a fur cap which he wears constantly, no powder but a very clean air, extremely white linen, a brown suit completes his apparel. His only defense is a cane in the hand.) The description of Franklin and an accompanying estimate of his popularity are here attributed to a bulletin on interesting occurrences in Paris sent privately to friends in the provinces and abroad by the Abbé de Flamarens. The Abbé was the twin brother of the Marquis de Flamarens, who became acquainted with Franklin, and may have owned a portrait of him by Duplessis. The description was echoed by Louis Petit de Bachaumont, *Mémoires, 10* (London, 1777–89), Feb. 4, 1777, 33, and is quoted by Edward Everett Hale and others as a police or spy's report on Franklin's arrival.

The Abbé goes on to say that Franklin's portrait had been engraved and was the popular New Year's gift of that season, but it was not, as he describes it, wholly appropriate to "the simple and singular costume of this grave personage." These must have been new impressions from Martinet's plate of 1773, made for the French edition of Franklin's *Works*.

We learn that Franklin at first wore the famous fur cap indoors as well as out while visiting in the city. Mme. du Deffand reported him so to Horace Walpole, at her house on December 31, 1776, Jean Baptiste Le Roy having introduced him there, together with Silas Deane.[3] The Duc de Croÿ, after calling on Franklin on January 23, tells us that he did not wear the cap at home, but put it on when going out. He describes a figure strong for his age, white-haired, his face very much like Martinet's print.[4] Two days later, young Jonathan Williams wrote from Nantes that the ladies there were dressing their hair "à la Franklin," that is, in imitation of the cap of marten fur.[5] The ladies rallied to Franklin as they had to Hume.

Franklin himself watched the response of those about him with relish, and on January 12 described to Mary Hewson the "odd figure" he was making.[6] He scolded Emma Thompson, also in England, for being a saucy hussy "in calling me *Rebel*," and went on to give her the same picture of his appearance and its effect, real and imagined:

> I know you wish you could see me; but as you can't,
> I will describe myself to you. Figure me in your mind
> as jolly as formerly, and as strong and hearty, only a
> few years older; being very plainly dress'd, wearing
> my thin gray strait hair, that peeps out from under my
> only *coiffure*, a fine Fur Cap, which comes down to
> my Forehead almost to my spectacles. Think how this
> must appear among the Powder'd Heads of Paris! I
> wish every gentleman and Lady in France would only

3. W. S. Lewis and W. H. Smith, ed., *Horace Walpole's Correspondence with Madame du Deffand and Wiart, 4* (New Haven, 1939), 385–86.
4. Vte. de Grouchy and Paul Cottin, ed., *Journal inédit du Duc de Croÿ, 1718–1784, 3* (Paris, 1906–07), 295.
5. Franklin Papers (A.P.S.), *37,* no. 45.
6. Smyth, *Writings, 7,* 10.

be so obliging as to follow my Fashion, comb their own Heads as I do mine, dismiss their *Friseurs,* and pay me half the Money they paid to them. You see, the gentry might well afford this, and I could then enlist those Friseurs, who are at least 100,000, and with the Money I would maintain them, make a Visit with them to England, and dress the Heads of your Ministers and Privy Councillors; which I conceive to be at present *un peu derangées.* Adieu, Madcap . . . [7]

The Duc de Croÿ, struck by Franklin's appearance, was even more strongly impressed by the conversation of this "beau veillard," always clear, precise, and energetic.[8] His unconventional costume emphasized the man, conveying no sense of concealment or pose. Another, Michel René Hilliard d'Auberteuil, also saw him so:

Everything in him announced the simplicity and innocence of primitive morals. . . . Franklin had laid aside the wig which formerly in England hid the nudity of his forehead and the useless adornment which would have left him at the level of the other English. He showed to the astonished multitude a head worthy of the brush of Guido [famous as a painter of old men] on an erect and vigorous body clad in the simplest of garments. His eyes were shadowed by large glasses and in his hand he carried a white cane. He spoke little. He knew how to be impolite without being rude, and his pride seemed to be that of nature. Such a person was made to excite the curiosity of Paris. The people clustered around as he passed and asked, "Who is this old peasant who has such a noble air?"[9]

Then the fur cap was discarded. Franklin seems to have worn it only during the winter of his arrival. Later, a hat and the long hair

7. Ibid., p. 26.
8. De Croÿ, *Journal, 3,* 301.
9. In Alfred Owen Aldridge, *Franklin and his French Contemporaries* (New York, New York University Press, 1957), p. 43.

falling to his shoulders were protection enough. Of Franklin's features at this time, his hair attracted the most remark. De Croÿ described it in 1777 as white, "la plus belle figure, aux grands cheveux blancs."[10] Félix Nogaret, a few years later, emphasizes his baldness, what hair remained hanging in carelessly untended locks to the shoulders.[11] The painters show it sometimes as white, but for the most part an iron gray, as Franklin himself had described it. Some portraits show a tint of brown. His baldness increased in these years, the forehead bare and a diminishing cover on the top of the head. Painters tended to strengthen this, and the sculptors, in the nature of their medium, had to do so or ignore it altogether.

Next in prominence were the spectacles, a reinforcement of nature which most of the artists chose to omit. Nini made a trial of showing them. Only Vanloo of the French artists accepted them as a feature of Franklin's face and adapted them to his characterization as successfully as Martin had done before and Peale was to do afterward. Caricaturists had seized upon them to suggest his inability to see. The French caricature, "Le Magnétisme Dévoilé," does not imply that, but it does convey the Frenchmen's feeling that it was ludicrous to appear so. The description of Franklin in *La Cassette Verte,* hostile and yet very much of the period, suggests that his bifocals excited the laughter of the French ladies, who believed that he was wearing cracked glasses as an emblem of economy and a white hat as an emblem of innocence.[12] Another English satire of 1779 has as its principal character a "French Louse," who

10. De Croÿ, *3,* 295.

11. Félix Nogaret, *L'Isle des sages, ou le Sceptre donné par les graces; esquisse anecdotique, mise en lumière* (Paris, 1785), pp. 112–13. Franklin is here described in a somewhat apocalyptic terminology and setting as "Richard-Saunders, Benjamin-Lincfran-Alopex," demi-god of a new world. The Greek "Alopex," or "fox," probably compliments his sagacity, but may, in this maze of allusions, take in "alopecie," the fox-evil, or baldness. The history of Nogaret's portrait of Franklin is discussed in Chap. 8.

12. *The Green Box of Monsieur de Sartine Found at Mademoiselle du Thé* (N.Y., 1916), pp. 24–25. The satirical attack on Franklin, originally published in 1779 as *La Cassette verte de Monsieur de Sartine,* is attributed to Richard Tickell (1751–93). Like the *Histoire d'un pou françois, ou l'Espion d'une nouvelle espèce* (Paris, 1779), it pretends to be a French work, and came as a counterthrust to John Almon's pro-American publications. The reference to Almon is on p. 30. Louis François Métra, in *Correspondance secrète, 8* (Paris, 1787–90), 267, describes under the date Aug. 23, 1779, the capture in England of a spy whom M. de Sartine, Minister of the Navy, had sent there to obtain information on troop movements.

sojourns for a while upon the head of Mlle. d'Eon, the famous transvestite, and from this vantage point is able to observe Franklin at dinner. The Louse notes that the glasses covered a third of His Excellency's face, comments on those moles on left cheek and left underlip, and in unkindly spirit compares his teeth to a rank of cloves driven into the jaw.[13] However hostile, the piece was certainly written by someone who had known Franklin by sight, and is evidence, at least, that he still had his own teeth at seventy-three. In the Wright portrait of four years later there is a suggestion of the losses usual in old age, while Rush's bust of 1787 shows a definite change in the structure of the mouth.

As to Franklin's dress in France, he adhered throughout to that standard of simplicity which represented his nation so well. His suits were brown, dull red, perhaps also gray. His linen had sometimes a simple pleated frill at the throat, sometimes a jabot similar to the old-fashioned steenkirk, and he sometimes knotted a white scarf about the open collar. It is worthy of note that there were others in Paris—philosophers, artists, writers, and the like—who followed the same simplicity of dress. The unique situation was not the costume but a statesman's wearing it. In this era, when dress and status were so united, the significant point is that Franklin was placing himself with the thinkers rather than with the representatives of political power.

In the freedom of his dress, too, one sees the license of old age. He was in his seventies now, and that "Né à Boston, Janvier, 1706" on so many of the French prints attests the wonder that he should have come so far in space and time. They saw a purity of character, the refinement of the years, proving his goodness and the worth of his philosophy as, had he appeared in worldly dress, it might not have done. Etienne Léon de Lamothe-Houdancourt writes in recollection of the prudence and the magic of his "verte veillesse":

Cet ambassadeur d'un nouveau genre eut un mérite

13. The *Histoire d'un Pou françois* was published simultaneously in English and by the same printer, as *History of a French Louse; or the Spy of a New Species,* London, 1779. The description of Franklin is on p. 26 of the French edition, pp. 19–20 of the English. On p. 40 of the one and p. 36 of the other "mon Aumônier" or "my almoner" is introduced into an absurd scene as a counterthrust at John Almon's publications friendly to Franklin.

très apprecié en France, celui de son étrangeté. Il par-
lait une langue toute nouvelle, celui de patriotisme:
il était enthousiaste dans sa reserve, hardi dans son
respect: il fascina nos raisonneurs, nos étourdis, les
hommes, les femmes; enfin il nous fut une religion
de la nécessité de l'indépendence de l'Amérique.[14]

In France the detestation of the English, the sting of earlier defeat, had reached a peak and with it, curiously, an admiration of
ideals essentially English. Franklin represented at once both sides
of this discordant image. It was a time, far more than ours, when
people thought of a cause in terms of a personality, and if he was
to be the personal image of America no one realized better than the
printer, Franklin, the necessity for giving it mass circulation. He
himself, of course, did nothing about it. His friends and his fame
acted for him. By March 1 he was settled at Passy, the pretty suburb
by the Seine, and Jacques Donatien Le Ray de Chaumont, who
had given him the use of the little house there in the garden of the
Hôtel Valentinois, was also producer of one of the first and most
popular of all the French reflections of him, the famous Nini medallion of "B. FRANKLIN, AMERICAIN."

Le Ray, of a bourgeois family of Nantes, had acquired the historic château of Chaumont with his marriage in 1750 and had
joined its name to his own. He had held various official posts, had
been "Intendant Honoraire des Invalides" when his own medallion
portrait had been made by Nini in 1771, but he was, primarily, a
businessman, warmhearted, optimistic, and successful. He had read
Rousseau with sympathy, had a feeling for the dignity of the common man, and it was characteristic that he should turn Chaumont,
disregarding the splendors and glories of its past, into a seat of local
industry, a manufactory of pottery and glass, of articles of utility
and beauty. Jean Baptiste Nini, a short, jovial Italian sculptor
whom he had found in Paris, had been in charge of the works since
1772. Nini, a man of sixty when the Franklin portrait was made,

14. "This new kind of ambassador had a merit fully appreciated in France, that
of his singularity. He spoke a new language, that of patriotism: he was an enthusiast
in his reserve, bold in his deference. He fascinated our intellectuals and nonintellec-
tuals, men and women. At the last he made us converts to the necessity for an independent America." (*Mémoires de Louis XVIII*, Paris, 1832, p. 165.)

had been an engraver in his time and was the son of an engraver. He was thoroughly competent, but not an original artist in the fullest sense. His Franklin medallions appear in five types, and I believe all of them, contrary to previous belief, are not actually his own designs but made from drawings sent to him from Paris, a hundred and twenty-two miles away. He was, after all, working in sculpture much as he had with the burin as an engraver.

The history of the origin of the Nini medallions takes us into the midst of the pro-American society in Paris, among people many of whom were financially involved in the insurgent cause. Chaumont not only had the chief American commissioner living under his wing at Passy, but was contracting for supplies, shipping gunpowder and other stores to America even before payment was assured, and all with a zeal both idealistic and speculative. There was a tightly-knit group of others, including young Jonathan Williams, concerned in the sale of prizes, and Franklin's Scottish friend, William Alexander, on the fringe of a complex of business dealings which extended from Paris to the major seaports and which was constantly stimulated by the hope of enormous profits and by the financial support, secretly given, of the French government. There was also Thomas Walpole, the English banker who had been concerned in Franklin's Vandalia speculation and who was now living in Paris with his son. They were cousins of Horace Walpole. Mme. du Deffand found them both charming, though the father's almost continuous laughter irritated her, and she liked to watch the young man, aged twenty-two in 1777, play lotto, winning regularly.[15] Franklin's letter of December 11, 1777, to the elder Walpole, establishes the fact that a drawing by the younger had gone to the Chaumont factory for the making of the famous terra cotta— "From a sketch Dr. B[ancroft] had which was drawn by your ingenious & valuable Son, they have made Medallions in *terre-cuit*" —and, having received a dozen for himself, he sent one to the artist.[16]

To Chaumont and to all of these others, Franklin was more than a warm personal friend: he was, looking at the matter from a materialistic point of view, a key figure in the success of their invest-

15. Lewis and Smith, *Walpole's Correspondence, 5,* 185, 189.
16. Mr. D. Holland, London.

ments, risked for high profits against heavy odds. It was necessary for them to establish him as a symbol, to "sell" him to the public. This was one object of the first Nini medallion and its success is indubitable. Its popularity has never waned, though the evidence points to its having been brought into being hurriedly and without much that could be called inspiration. Chaumont sent a profile drawing which Dr. Bancroft had given him to Nini. Nini, hearing of the rage for the fur cap, or perhaps simply being told by his employer to add one, added Rousseau's, copied from an engraving, as Allan Ramsay had painted it in London in 1766. This he sent to Paris for approval along with some other suggestions, a liberty cap, a face with spectacles, and a face without spectacles. These last were rejected and are now rarities. The accepted *bonnet de peau* had for the French a far deeper symbolism than the classic cap of liberty, and although not precisely true to what Franklin had been wearing, it hardly mattered, for the marten fur was laid aside by the time the piece appeared.

The intention of the first Nini is obviously to present a popular figure in homely, popular terms. The others that followed in the next two years were attuned to the recognition of the republic by the French court and the official dignity of a minister plenipoten-tiary. I have no doubt, however, that they were made in much the same way as the first, Nini receiving another drawing, more direc-tions, and, keeping his first design in view, making other pieces for his employer to accept or reject. The evidence as to other sources is not so secure as that which points to young Walpole, but there is good reason to believe that one of them may have come from an-other young habitué of the American circle, a friend of the mys-terious Pierre Augustin Caron de Beaumarchais, whose "Rodrique Hortalez and Company" had been supplying the rebel armies from Paris even before Franklin's arrival. This was Anne Vallayer-Coster (1744–1818), a Parisian artist, painter of genre, of flowers and still life, of portraits (often in profile), and of romantic heads with titles such as "Mélancolie" or "Une Vestale."[17]

17. Courtauld Institute, Witt Library, London. A pair of circular profile portraits in "pierre noire," marked "Dessiné par Mlle. Vallayer, 1778," are recorded as in the sale of May 23, 1928, Hôtel Drouot, Paris. "Un Amateur des Beaux-Arts" sings her praise in a "Vers à Mlle. Vallayer, Peintre du Roi," in the *Journal de Paris,* Feb. 25, 1779.

For our knowledge of her part we may thank the spirit of that assiduous gleaner and garnerer of historical fact, Benson J. Lossing.[18] In about 1850, when his *Pictorial Field Book of the Revolution* was published, he was snowbound on a stormy winter night in an old house in the lower Hudson Valley, the home of a family of Huguenot descent. Among the paintings on the walls he noticed a charming vineyard scene and a profile portrait of a young woman. He was given a portfolio of old letters in answer to his question about the artist. One of the family, a young bride then, had met her in 1774 at a ball celebrating the coronation of Louis XVI. Her husband is only identified as a friend of M. Cossoul of Nantes who was to become the business partner of young Elkanah Watson. Lossing copied the bride's letter on her meeting with Mlle. Vallayer:

> She is a charming little creature. Her modesty is almost diffidence, and her manners are as natural as those of a child. Her face is radiant with genius, that shines benignantly but almost silently upon us. She is a brunette, with sparkling dark eyes—short, plump and active. Her voice is like that of a singing-bird; and the pressure of her hand and of her lips on the cheek at meeting and parting testify that she has a warm heart and sympathetic nature. I am sure I shall love her. To-morrow my husband and I will dine with her at her father's—the only guests—when we shall see her pictures.[19]

They also had, it appeared, a common enthusiasm for America. Anne Vallayer was reported to have sensed in advance the duplicity of Arthur Lee and warned Beaumarchais of it, pled for the American cause with the Marquise de Lafayette, and, on the very next evening, in the winter of 1777, gone with Beaumarchais to Passy for her introduction to Franklin. Lossing, alas, tells this part without direct quotation from the letters:

> There she had her first interview with the venerable sage and diplomat, and charmed him with her en-

18. "Anna Vallayer Coster," *Harper's Magazine, 42* (1871), 719–24.
19. Ibid., p. 720.

thusiasm and personal magnetism. When, not long
afterward, she was passing an afternoon with the
philosopher, and receiving draughts of wisdom from
the deep well of his knowledge, she sketched that profile of him, with a fur cap on his head, which is seen
on the rare medals of the red clay of Passy which
Franklin's host caused to be struck in his honor. At
about the same time she also painted a profile likeness of the fine head of Beaumarchais, a copy of
which, with a long autograph letter of his to Alexander Hamilton, as his counsel, is before me as I
write. It was in profile portraiture that she most excelled.[20]

Small errors such as the "red clay of Passy" may be laid to Lossing's rounding-out of the story. He gives a description of Anne's
marriage to her childhood sweetheart, Lucien Coster, a week before Christmas 1779. Illness prevented Franklin's coming to the
wedding party, but he was represented by Elkanah Watson, John
Laurens, and "a young Livingston from the Manor."[21] John Laurens had arrived in Paris in March 1781, and was back for the
siege of Yorktown in October. Other details in the letters, such as
their author's dining with Jefferson and Trumbull the day before
Trumbull left Paris in 1786, tie in well with primary records.[22] I
can accept as fact that Vallayer-Coster made the design for a medallion, probably one of Nini's later versions, since the attribution
of the first to Walpole seems secure. Franklin's well-known letter
of June 3, 1779, to his daughter in Philadelphia, indicates that
Nini, Sèvres, perhaps Wedgwood, and other types were then enjoying a high vogue in Paris:

> The clay medallion of me you say you gave to Mr.
> Hopkinson was the first of the kind made in France.
> A variety of others have been made since of different
> sizes; some to be set in the lids of snuffboxes, and

20. Ibid., p. 721.
21. Ibid., pp. 722–23.
22. Sept. 13, "Trumbull left us three days ago." Julian P. Boyd, ed., *The Papers of Thomas Jefferson, 10* (Princeton, 1954), 363.

some so small as to be worn in rings; and the numbers sold are incredible. These, with the pictures, busts and prints, (of which copies upon copies are spread everywhere,) have made your father's face as well known as that of the moon, so that he durst not do anything that would oblige him to run away, as his phiz would discover him wherever he should venture to show it. It is said by learned etymologists, that the name *doll,* for the images children play with, is derived from the word IDOL. From the number of dolls now made of him, he may be truly said, *in that sense,* to be *i-doll-ized* in this country.[23]

The same simile occurred in another way to Jane Mecom as she compared one portrait to another. "If the Artists that have taken yr Face have varied a much from each other as that affixed to yr Philosophacal Papers done in France some years ago from the coppy, it will appear as changeable as the moon. However," she adds, comfortably, "if it is calld Dr Franklin it will be revered."[24]

That the Nini medallion came first there can be no doubt, and it is very doubtful that the Manufacture Royale would have published one until diplomatic recognition was at least assured. Mme. Campan's anecdote suggests that it came as something of a sensation when Franklin medallions appeared on sale in the regular Sèvres porcelain exhibit at Versailles, under the very eyes of the king. The Comtesse Diane de Polignac made this an occasion to attract attention to herself by lavish expressions of admiration for the sage, observing which His Majesty secretly ordered Sèvres to make for her a *vase de nuit,* its bottom to be ornamented both with the medallion and the epigram, *Eripuit coelo fulmen, septrumque tyrannis.* It came to her as a New Year's gift.[25]

Verses by Turgot, of similar tenor but in French, were to have

23. Smyth, *Writings, 7,* 347. Original at Dept. of State, Washington, D.C.
24. Van Doren, *Benjamin Franklin & Jane Mecom,* p. 200.
25. Jeanne Louise Henriette Genet Campan, *Memoirs of the Private Life of Marie Antoinette, 1* (London, 1823), 230. Similarly, Wedgwood, ca. 1763, had manufactured cuspidors with the portrait of William Pitt and the declaration:

We will spit
On Mr. Pitt.

In Samuel Smiles, *Josiah Wedgwood* (New York, 1895), p. 62.

been placed on Augustin de Saint Aubin's engraving of Franklin. They were suppressed by the censor. The memoirist, Grimm, noted the fact and printed them under the date, October 1777.[26] Turgot, statesman and writer, was also an *associé libre* of the Académie Royale. From every aspect, the first engraving of Franklin's diplomatic mission was on the highest level of professional performance, quite unlike the haphazard history of the medallions. The "fur cap" print was the work of one of France's most eminent engravers, after a drawing by Charles Nicolas Cochin the Younger, whom Carl Zigrosser describes as "one of the most charming and attractive personalities in the whole history of the graphic arts."[27] Cochin stands quite apart from such enthusiasts as Walpole or Vallayer-Coster, for he was sixty-two, an artist of long experience, high sensitivity, and sophistication, a conservative, and among the few who had dared to caricature Voltaire.[28] Saint Aubin, a younger man, was bookish, gentle, and sweet in character. He made over fifty portrait engravings after Cochin, many of them *en medaillons* in profile. The "Franklin" is a three-quarter view, with the fur cap just as Franklin himself and the others have described it. It is a work of perfect understanding and objectivity, with no idealization, its presentation of face and man strong and good. Its only fault may be said to be that it caused its innumerable copiers to somehow experience a singular lack of success, as if the artist had caught a glance, a moment, defying repetition.[29] The drawing must have been made soon after Franklin's arrival. Publication of the print was announced in the *Mercure de France* of July, 1777.

The Nini medallion and Cochin print had had, meanwhile, simultaneous counterparts across the English Channel in an engraving and a bronze medal which reflect a British view of Franklin

26. Friedrich Melchior Grimm, *Correspondance littéraire, philosophique et critique par Grimm, Diderot, Raynal, Meister, etc.*, ed. Maurice Tourneux, *12* (Paris, 1877–82), 1. Lewis and Smith, *Walpole's Correspondence, 5,* 413–14.

27. Carl Zigrosser, "Premier Dessinateur," *Philadelphia Museum Bulletin, 54* (1959), 41.

28. Edmond and Jules de Goncourt, *L'Art du dix-huitième siècle*, 2d ser. (Paris, 1909), p. 339.

29. Among the exceptions which may be taken to this statement is the small commemorative medal of ca. 1790 by J. M. Lageman of Amsterdam, an adaptation to profile, with the fur cap altered along sensible Dutch lines. It is reproduced in *Verslagen omtrent's rijks versamelingen van geschiedenis en kunst, 75* (1953), 108.

and a British conception of the part he might take in England's history. Sympathy for the American protest was then still strong and wide. War would diminish it. A war supported by a Franco-American alliance would virtually end it altogether. A year before, on January 1, 1776, the *London Evening Post* had denounced the story of the march of "one Arnold" to Quebec as a ministerial hoax intended to stimulate war measures against the colonies. By January 1777, English liberals could still envision a happy release from civil conflict and one which would bring with it both parliamentary reform and a strengthened empire. They could recall Franklin's earlier concept of the colonies "as so many nations" united to Britain.[30] His remarkable activity in America in 1775 and 1776 implied, in England as it did in France, leadership of the whole resistance movement. His arrival in France raised a hectic flurry of new reform activity in England, heightening the crisis and yet hopeful still of a peaceful settlement, with Franklin speaking for America. William Carmichael reported on January 24, 1777, a widespread belief in England that Franklin intended to negotiate a peace through the mediation of France.[31] At the end of May Lord Shelburne was supporting Chatham's motion in Parliament for an address to the Crown that might end hostilities in America, and William Strahan, the "Straney" of whom Franklin had been so fond, wrote to Franklin to directly express the hope that he had come to Paris with a plan for peace.[32]

The engraving of Franklin which appeared in the midst of all this was, in the good English fashion, attached to a book. The book was Volume V of *The Remembrancer,* a compilation of American documents issued in support of the American cause which had been begun in 1775 and was continued throughout the war. Its title recalls *The Remembrancer* of twenty-five years before which Franklin's friend, James Ralph, had edited as a weekly assault upon official policy. It was compiled and published by John Almon, whose trial for printing Junius' "Letter to the King" in the *London Musaeum* was fresher in memory and had been declared by the attorney general an act "to excite sedition and destruction in the

30. Franklin to William Shirley, Dec. 22, 1754 (in Smyth, *Writings, 3,* 240).
31. *Deane Papers, 1,* 472.
32. Franklin Papers (A.P.S.), *6,* no. 34.

kingdom, to divide one part of his Majesty's subjects against the other."[33] This volume of the *Remembrancer,* a veritable broadside for rebellious America, was the only one with a portrait engraving. Its frontispiece, dated April 21, 1777, is the work of John Lodge, an obscure engraver remembered for a few other American subjects. There was a public sufficient to support this as a publishing venture. Benjamin Vaughan was delaying his edition of Franklin's works only until he could add material. There was the same public to take up the bronze medal which, quite independently, appeared at about the same time.

The medal is dated "1777 +," a rather enigmatic designation seemingly intended to indicate that it honors what Franklin was expected to do in future rather than his past accomplishments. Like the print it records his L.L.D. [*sic*] and F.R.S. The likeness in both is based on Chamberlin's print, the most easily available source in London.[34] This gives the medal a more ambitious character, since a profile would have been simpler and more usual. On the medal there has been added to the head a loose cap and an open collar strongly suggestive of the Dixon miniature. I am convinced, rather, that this is no more than a British effort to recreate the famous fur cap at a time when it was talked of, but no Cochin or Nini had yet reached London. As a result there is an approximation of a gentleman's cap worn in lieu of a wig indoors at home and a costume appropriately décolleté. A possible hint of the medal's date is found in a letter from Edward Bancroft to Silas Deane, dated February 21, 1777: "You will see by the enclosed card (drawn by a son of 177 [Dr. Joseph Priestley]) what ideas are here formed of the appearance of 64 [Franklin] in his Canadian Cap. Make my most respectful compliments to him."[35] The Priestley son must have been Joseph, Jr., aged nine, and one must infer that the child was copying some other likeness "here formed of the appearance of 64 in his Canadian Cap."

It is tempting to conjecture that Dr. Bancroft, physician and naturalist, Fellow of the Royal Society, secretary to the American commissioners in Paris, and Franklin's trusted friend throughout

33. *Gentleman's Magazine, 41* (1771), 80.
34. See Catalogue, CHAMBERLIN, Nos. 4, 5.
35. *Deane Papers, 1,* 496.

the war, who was at the same time in the pay of the British secret service and constantly betraying the country he professed to serve, may have himself been the projector of the medal. He had owned the drawing by young Walpole which had gone to Chaumont for the making of the Nini medallion. He must have discerned Franklin's naïve pleasure in seeing the likeness of himself mechanically multiplied. Then, too, he retained a curious sense of friendship and respect for those he was conspiring to injure. At all events, it seems probable that Priestley had one of these medals in hand for the child to copy, and it may have been the same "brazen head" over which Josiah Wedgwood hesitated in July, unwilling to translate into pottery a work which might be construed as honoring an enemy of his country.

The medal's reverse shows a tree threatened by lightning and over it the motto "Non irrita fulmina curat" or "He stands impervious to the futile thunderbolt." These people, like the French, were groping for a few words of classic stability which would stand for Franklin just as "Vitam impendere vero" then did for Rousseau, the three words appended to almost every engraving of Jean Jacques, and at times rendering the addition of his name unnecessary.[36] In Paris at this time an eminent lawyer had another in mind, "Alterius orbis Vindex, utriusque Lumen," and proposed to place it under a portrait of Franklin painted for his own collection.[37] On March 8, 1777, at about the time when Sophie, the Chaumont daughter who spoke English, was getting the Franklin household in order at Passy, Jean Baptiste Jacques Elie de Beaumont asked the great American to pose again. Elie de Beaumont was famous for the literary quality of his briefs, for the simplicity and fresh, piquant gaiety of his conversation, and by those "fêtes de bonnes gens" by which he had recently begun to draw friends to his country estate in Normandy. From his letter and from the indefatigable reporting of Bachaumont he appears to have intended that Franklin should pose for Dufourny de Villiers, a very minor sculptor, and that this work was to serve as the model for a painted portrait—"me proposant ensuite de m'assurer d'après ce buste votre portrait pour

36. "To give one's life for the truth" (Juvenal, Satire 4, line 91).
37. "Liberator of the one world, light of both" (Quoted by Bachaumont, *Mémoires, 10,* July 25, 1777, 183).

le placer dans ma bibliothèque au rang des amis de leur patrie et de l'humanité."[38] As of June 30 and July 25 Bachaumont announced that the portrait was being made by no less a person than the great Jean Baptiste Greuze. Probably this arrangement was made after that with Dufourny. It seems incredible that so eminent a painter should be asked to follow the work of an inferior sculptor and would consent to do so, even though Franklin had been ill with the gout at this time and was at best an unwilling poser.

The portrait itself is suave, subtle, and profoundly interesting. One can feel in it the immediacy which distinguishes a life portrait, and yet it lacks the solid physical realism one might expect when such a subject faced the artist. Greuze, however, was not a literalist but a seeker of ideal and implication as well as fact. His statements came from a sense of superior intelligence and an enormous vanity. He was a man of genius, knew it, and defended it with stormy bursts of anger. For years he had refused to exhibit at the Salon because the Royal Academy had accepted him as a painter of genre, rather than of history. People had to come, as indeed they did, to his *logement* at the Louvre to see his work. With the "Franklin" at this time they saw the "Malédiction Paternelle" and that most lastingly popular of all his work, "La Cruche Cassée" or "The Broken Pitcher." He had felt a call to excel in portraiture and to transmit to posterity the great men of his time, yet only a few of his portraits appeared as prints and, disappointing public expectation, his "Franklin" was not given to an engraver.[39]

Greuze may or may not have had the Dufourny bust at his studio, but there can be no doubt whatever that his portrait is from life. The original study, retained by him, is a pastel, a medium perhaps chosen because in it he could work quickly from life. There is good evidence of a sitting, as well as of personal association soon after in Masonic affairs and elsewhere. In Franklin's papers there is an undated letter from Mme. Greuze introducing a friend and, also undated, a copy of some verses she had inscribed upon the porcelain

38. "Thus to assure my having your portrait after this bust to hang in my library among those of the friends of homeland and humanity" (Franklin Papers, A.P.S., *5,* no. 99). See Catalogue, Greuze, No. 2.

39. Bachaumont, *Mémoires, 11,* Jan. 19, 1778, 65; *10* (July 25, 1777), 183.

urn in which she preserved the bouquet of roses he had given her.[40] In this tender little incident lies a clue to the origin of the picture, for the verses, it would appear, had been written for her by a friend and were afterward printed in an obscure little book, with their date. On page fifty-nine of the *Nouveaux Opuscules de M. Feutry, de la Societé Philosophique de Philadelphie* will be found the author's "Inscription que Madame Greuze a mise sur une urne de porcelaine, où elle garde les restes d'un bouquet de roses, que M. Franklin lui a donné, en Juin, 1777." Bachaumont established the fact that the "sketch" of the Franklin portrait—undoubtedly the pastel—was finished and on view on June 30, 1777.[41] Thus there emerges, as clearly as one could wish, the story of a visit to Passy by the artist and his wife on a summer day when, in the gardens between the American pavilion and the Hôtel Valentinois, the roses were in bloom.

The poet Aimé Ambroise Joseph Feutry (1720–89) was a lawyer turned littérateur who wrote with charm and talent and who in those days tuned his lyre both to Greuze's art and Franklin's politics. He had asked and been promised membership in the American Philosophical Society, though not actually elected until 1786, after Franklin's return to Philadelphia. Lines on the same page of his little work hailing Franklin as an "Honneur du nouveau Monde & de l'Humanité" were politely called to the attention of their subject in a note of February 22, 1779.[42] Franklin responded by appointing Feutry poet of the July 4 celebration of that year and having his verses printed for the occasion.[43]

From the pastel, one replica in oil was for the library of Elie de Beaumont. Another went to a far more nicely discriminating collector and a profound admirer of the artist, the Abbé Joseph Alphonse de Véri (1724–99). The date of this painting is uncertain, but the known fact that each of these gentlemen owned a portrait of Franklin by Greuze has resulted in the names of artist and collectors being tagged for purposes of sale to innumerable old portraits, the earliest I can cite being that indifferent copy after Duplessis which

40. Franklin Papers (A.P.S.), *43*, no. 189; *51*, no. 81.
41. Ibid., *10*, no. 164.
42. Ibid., *13*, no. 136.
43. Ibid., "Family Expenses," *21*, 4.

was sold to Franklin's successor, Thomas Jefferson, as a Greuze from the collection of the Abbé de Véri. Since then it would seem as if every American diplomatic official in Paris has bought a portrait of Franklin, many of them by "Greuze" and most of them under circumstances similar to Jefferson's experience. By Véri's own account, written in 1780, Franklin had posed for this portrait expressly in order that he might become the owner of a characterization of him by this great master, and he counted the picture among his dearest possessions:

> Si je vieillis autant que ce bienfaiteur de l'humanité, je me vanterai, auprès de mes petits-neveux, d'avoir connu ce grand homme, de l'avoir souvent reçu chez moi et d'avoir obtenu de lui qu'il se laissât peindre par Greuze pour que j'eusse son portrait de la main de ce grand maître. Ce portrait me suivra partout jusqu'au tombeau. Je le chéris d'autant plus, qu'étant ressemblant, Greuze y a peint toute la noblesse d'une âme libre, toute la sagesse d'une tête bien organisée et toute la sagacité d'un homme d'état.[44]

The Abbé was himself an *homme d'état*. He had been a friend of Turgot and of Morellet ever since they had been fellow students at the Sorbonne. A man of influence and taste, eager to excel in diplomacy, he received his doctorate in theology and had influential connections everywhere. He was a sceptic, welcoming the new liberalism but at the same time loyal to Church and social order, a type both curiously close to Franklin and curiously apart. His own portrait had been painted twice by Duplessis whom he also greatly admired, and two portraits of him are attributed to Greuze.[45] His elder brother, the Marquis de Véri, was also a collector and a patron of Greuze. Their line ended with the Marquis' death, childless, in 1785. The catalogue of the sale of his paintings, dispersed shortly before Jefferson made his purchase, shows no "Franklin," though he had probably been the owner of at least the Simon Petit pastel

44. Jehan de Witte, ed., *Journal de l'Abbé de Véri, 1* (Paris, Jules Tallandieu, 1928–30), 21.

45. Jules Belleudy, *J. S. Duplessis, peintre du Roi, 1725–1802* (Chartres, 1913), pp. 47–48.

after Greuze. It is thus readily acceptable that the Abbé de Véri was one of those who brought Franklin and Greuze together, and may have taken the lead in doing so. He left Paris for Avignon in 1789, escaped the massacre of 1791, but was imprisoned in 1793 and 1794. He died there five years later, his paintings lost to sight, as were so many, in the swirling currents of the Revolution.

The Abbé de Véri's memoirs are still unpublished. A truly reciprocal attachment to Franklin seems unlikely, and yet it would be helpful to know more of those to whom Franklin may have turned for guidance in matters concerning the arts. Painters and sculptors were as busy around him as bees in summer, and while he obviously still thought it the part of friendliness and good policy to pose for all and any, his need for discrimination was to increase. Dufourny and Dejoux were making busts, as was a far better sculptor, Jean Jacques Caffiéri. Who in this instance brought artist and subject together is not recorded, nor how Caffiéri's superior standing was made clear to Franklin. I suspect that Caffiéri's bust may have been an early incident in Franklin's pleasant relationship with his dear friend and neighbor, Mme. Helvétius. In 1773 Caffiéri had made the marble bust of her husband, the philosopher Claude Adrien Helvétius, now at the Louvre. It had been a posthumous work, made two years after its subject's death, and yet it has a living, romantic verve and splendor about it. Its success as a memorial may have induced Franklin to give Caffiéri a commission authorized by Congress and important to his diplomatic mission, the monument to Richard Montgomery.

On learning of the death of the young general at Quebec, Congress had at once named Franklin and two others to consider a suitable memorial. On January 25, 1776, this committee had reported in favor of "a monument [to] be procured from Paris, or any other part of France, with an inscription sacred to his memory and expressive of his amiable character and heroic achievements."[46] That France rather than Italy was specified suggests Franklin's awareness that for a French artist to create and to exhibit at the Salon a tribute to the general who had given his life in an effort to drive the English from Canada would have persuasive force in a

46. Charles Henry Hart and Edward Biddle, *Memoirs of the Life and Works of Jean Antoine Houdon* (Philadelphia, 1911), pp. 63–64.

France still eager to avenge the humiliating peace of 1763. An obvious factor in the choice was that Caffiéri had long been a member in full standing of the Académie Royale de Peinture et de Sculpture, and such of his work as he chose to show was assured of a place in the Salon. On April 7, 1777, Franklin confirmed the commission for the Montgomery monument by a first payment to him.[47]

His own bust had probably just been completed at that time. In a brief note, dated Paris, March 26, 1777, Caffiéri had asked Franklin to name the day convenient to him for the final sitting.[48] The completed bust, in terra cotta, was duly included in the Salon of that autumn, together with Caffiéri's design for the monument to Montgomery and his busts of Pierre Corneille and the Maréchal de Muy. Furthermore, the censor, as censors will, had stimulated public interest in Montgomery by forbidding official publication of the fallen warrior's name and fame, facts which were, of course, soon spread by common bruit. Two years later, possibly at Franklin's behest, the design was engraved by Augustin de Saint Aubin and so brought to renewed attention.[49] The actual monument was sent to America in 1778 and erected in Saint Paul's Church, New York, in 1789. As for Caffiéri's "Franklin" of that Salon, it is the most solidly realistic of all the Franklin portraits, as if its maker had been on his mettle to meet Franklin's own taste for exactitude. There can be no doubt that it is the best reflection of Franklin's appearance, carefully and surely made by a competent artist, from life, the artist's compass verifying the judgments of his eye, a statement such as only true talent and long experience could bring into being. Here physical truth reveals the inward character in all its placid strength. Frenchmen looked upon its steady features and read into them the patriot's ennobling anger: "On voit son âme se soulever d'indignation sur sa physionomie, dont ce sentiment altère la douceur."[50]

47. Franklin Papers (A.P.S.), *19*, "Waste Book."

48. "M. Caffieri a l honneur de soiter le bon jour a Monsieur franklin et le pris de lui faire dire quel jour il voudra bien lui donné, pour la dernier seance. de Paris ce 26 mars 1777." (M. Caffiéri has the honor to wish Monsieur Franklin good morning and begs him to name the day he could best give for the final sitting.) Franklin Papers (A.P.S.), *72*, no. 30.

49. Reproduced in Hart and Biddle, *Houdon,* opp. p. 62.

50. Bachaumont, *Mémoires, 11, 52.*

An agreement existed between Franklin and Caffiéri the exact terms of which are unknown. Caffiéri believed that he had been given a closed monopoly upon all official sculptural work for the United States. Franklin appears to have given him such a promise as far as Congress and his own position were concerned, in order to make the Montgomery commission, for which only £300 had been appropriated, more attractive. He may also have agreed not to patronize other sculptors for his own portrait, and if this be the case, kept the agreement. William Temple Franklin states that his grandfather sat to Caffiéri at the earnest solicitation both of his own friends and of the artist. Caffiéri presented a cast from his bust to Franklin on December 9, 1777, asking in strong terms that no other artist be permitted to copy it. I would consider it quite possible that when Caffiéri had urged Franklin to pose, Franklin had suggested that he save himself trouble by copying Dufourny or Dejoux—which, if true, would explain his concern about the exposure of his own work to copyists.

The Caffiéri "Franklin" was purchased for the royal collections, though not assigned to any particular building, nor delivered by the artist, until two years after.[51] This was doubtless because it had preceded the French recognition of the United States, and the same reason may explain the fact that no exact model had been submitted for reproduction by the royal manufactory at Sèvres, as was commonly required at such times.

The bust will always be seen in contrast to that other by Jean Antoine Houdon, first exhibited two years later. To Caffiéri, Houdon's came as an effort to invade his supposed monopoly, and indeed his precautions may well have been taken with Houdon in mind. Caffiéri was then a man of fifty-two, the other, thirty-three. He had been a member of the Royal Academy since 1759. Houdon was not admitted until July 26, 1777, one obvious reason why he had not been recommended to Franklin at the outset. Caffiéri at an earlier day had shown kindness to Houdon, and they had been affectionate friends, a situation which had gradually changed to active rivalry and then, certainly on Caffiéri's part, to implacable jealous hatred.[52]

51. Jules Guiffrey, *Les Caffiéri* (Paris, 1877), p. 242.
52. Ibid.

Houdon was not formally introduced to Franklin until 1783.[53] He had had, however, frequent opportunities for observing him and had simply used them to make his bust of 1778, creating what is more a characterization than an accurate likeness, and yet a characterization holding all the charm of Franklin's humanity, wisdom, and humor. It had, and was intended to have, popular appeal. He then set about promoting its popularity in a manner which the older sculptor could only regard as insidious. He gave four casts of it to Franklin, to whom Caffiéri had given but one. He gave one to the Masonic lodge and others wherever there appeared to be a public ready to appreciate them. Sèvres published an exact reproduction in china, while Caffiéri's likeness had appeared there only in an altered copy. His other American commissions followed, culminating in the statue of Washington for the state of Virginia in 1785, the work for which he is best remembered. The Americans liked Houdon for the quality of vivid realism in his portraits, and for his personal forthright good nature. Caffiéri, maddened by the other's methods and success, wrote letters of angry accusation which first met a cruel rebuff from William Temple Franklin, and then a more gentle rebuttal from Franklin himself.[54] The two sculptors were rival portraitists also of Voltaire, Rousseau, and Molière. Houdon had all of these and his "Franklin" at the Salon of 1779. Most of the bitterness would seem to have centered about the rival "Franklins." As to their subject himself, despite a clearly expressed dissatisfaction with Caffiéri's claims and complaints, as well as his prices for casts and shipments, he showed no sign of ever doubting the superiority of Caffiéri's portrait. In response to requests from friends he purchased casts of it and never that of Houdon. He appears to have at once given away all of the four casts received from Houdon, retaining only the Caffiéri. Caffiéri's was at first the more generally copied, and for many years the Houdon type was the rarer of the two. It is now the more familiar, and has

53. Letter from Houdon, Nov. 8, 1783 (Franklin Papers A.P.S., *30*, no. 77).

54. Florence Ingersoll-Smouse, "Quelques Documents et Lettres Relatifs au Voyage (1785) et aux Oeuvres de Jean Antoine Houdon aux Etats Unis," *Bulletin de l'histoire de l'art français* (1914), pp. 11–31. The original letters are in the Franklin Papers (A.P.S.), with the exception of that from Franklin to Caffiéri, June 20, 1785 (L.C.).

been the basis of all of the more successful modern idealizations, such as James Earle Fraser's statue at the Franklin Institute in Philadelphia and Otto Grundmann's painting owned by the Boston Museum of Fine Arts.

The Caffiéri and the Houdon can be contrasted as "before and after." The first preceded and the other followed that memorable March 20, 1778, when Franklin, dressed in brown velvet, white stockings, white hat under his arm and spectacles on his nose, was received by the King. The censor had frowned upon the use of Turgot's famous epigram with the early Cochin print. A portrait alone was permissible but, after all, *Eripuit coelo fulmen, septrum-que tyrannis* was dangerous stuff until one could make a particular identification of the tyrants as British king and ministry. A simple portrait passed, but without honors or sentiments. The first Nini has only the identification "AMERICAIN," and it remained for that of 1779 to snatch the thunderbolt and scepter. In a similarly nice distinction, Josiah Wedgwood in 1777 refused to reproduce a medal at his pottery, thus specifically honoring a political enemy of his country, but was willing enough to turn out the noncommittal medallions, simple statements with no laureate aspect. In France allegorical prints were also strictly controlled. This was the picture with a message, the cartoon on a fine arts level. Here the artist of talent, with clenched fist or pointed finger, was a force to be feared. One such project, that of Antoine Borel, waited six months before it had a *nihil obstat* in May 1778.[55] This was two months beyond the date of official recognition, a hesitation which may reflect a reluctance to countenance rebellion anywhere. Gustavus III of Sweden, that liberal and enlightened monarch so close to the French in feeling, outspokenly condemned the Bourbon American adventure on this ground alone.

The allegory of the obscure Borel, "L'Amérique indépendante," stands inevitably, if not altogether happily, in contrast to that by Jean Honoré Fragonard. The two seem to have appeared almost simultaneously during that summer of 1778, though Borel's had been conceived earlier and months more were to pass by before his drawing was translated into the line engraving by Le Vasseur. Fragonard's, rendering Turgot's classic line in pictorial form, is

55. Bachaumont, *Mémoires, 11* (May 30, 1778), 281.

forceful and spontaneous, as alive with a sincere emotion as the other is labored and dull.

Borel, we must grant, was an able designer and an enthusiast for American liberty, but his wider reputation was made as the creator of *sujets galants,* pretty much in a class with the precious obscenities of another Franklin admirer, François Lainé, and wholly foreign to that delicacy and charm with which Fragonard could invest the themes of love. Borel's project was announced publicly on May 30, those who might wish to subscribe to the print being invited to view the drawing. On June 1 the artist wrote to Franklin, asking for a sitting in which to make the portrait for the piece. It is established that this likeness of Franklin, by a sound craftsman, son of a portrait painter and one who considered himself a portrait painter, was from life. It must be received with due respect for all its pomposity of pose and expression and in spite of the to-do of symbolic figures stationed around it. A sodden artificiality pervades it. As an effort favorable to his cause, the American minister had to offer encouragement, but between the lines of the correspondence one can read his distaste and his willingness to disassociate himself from it personally.

Fragonard's allegory also first appeared as a drawing (still extant) in which the face of Franklin was not yet a portrait likeness. In both his and Borel's compositions a figure of Minerva soars forward, her shield raised protectively over Franklin's head and her weapon wielded in his behalf. In both, a warrior charges forward upon two falling figures symbolic of British tyranny. Both have figures of America, though in Borel's piece she is so posed that the scene could best be interpreted as an anatomical lecture by Franklin, interrupted by an outbreak of rowdyism in the audience. Fragonard's group, on the other hand, is coherent and forceful, with all the unity and monumental splendor of the Latin words upon which it was built.

The likeness in Fragonard's print might be from life. There is no correspondence on the subject, as with Borel, but the two artists were in different situations, Fragonard being known and welcome in circles where he could readily find the opportunity he needed. It is probable, however, that he used the Caffiéri bust, which is accurate as to features and from which he might somewhat more easily have derived the expression of sublime anger that he needed. It is hard to imagine his doing so directly from the face of the pleasant old man. In another drawing, doubtless made soon after, he followed Houdon's bust, a likeness also not readily adaptable to the theme of the *Génie de Franklin*. A third allegory which appeared at about the same time is the Abbé de Saint Non's "Le Docteur Franklin Couronné par la Liberté." The signature on the original drawing from which his print was made, "fragonard," has been accepted as genuine, though the Abbé's letter on the undue prominence of the liberty cap in his aquatint implies that both drawing and print were his. Here the likeness of Franklin appears in the form of a bust, and it is Caffiéri's. It was made in the course of a morning to give Franklin a demonstration of the new aquatint process, the design having been prepared in advance and the finished print delivered to him later. The composition is certainly in Fragonard's style and in a mood of warm, poetic gentleness more characteristic of him than the Jovean concept of the *génie de Franklin*.

That spring and summer of 1778 are a pinnacle in Franklin's life, a time of absolute commitment, of triumph and acceptance. All eyes were upon him. He was lighted, as it were, from all sides, and the prints, the paintings, the sculpture, the pottery, the knickknacks, all are reflections caught in the watching eyes around him. Some are true, some are blurred, but all of them mirror the man who had become for so many both man and symbol, both common clay and far horizon. Among them is the canvas by the mysterious "J. F. De L'hospital," unrecorded anywhere other than in the artist's signature and date on a painting obviously made from life, and yet a curiously soft and feminine interpretation. This is a smiling, joking Franklin and, taking the picture as mirror of the artist as well, one can imagine someone humble, attentive, full of laughter on his own part. It is not essentially a public portrait, and never appeared as a print. Either De L'Hospital painted it for a fastidious private patron who did not care to publicize it, or the engravers thought it too weak an interpretation to be successful.

Franklin also, at this time, posed for an attractive young woman whose portrait has considerably more masculine vigor and was painted expressly for publication as a print. The artist was his neighbor, Mme. Filleul, who had come to live in Passy at about the same time as he.[56] After her marriage to Louis Filleul in 1777, the Queen had conferred upon her the office of concierge at the nearby château of La Muette. As Anne Rosalie Bocquet she had won favor at court as a miniaturist and a painter of portraits in oil and pastel.[57] This popularity, which she shared with her friend Vigée-Lebrun, was to lead to her death on the scaffold in the Terror. She painted less when a young housekeeper and mother, and the portrait of Franklin is one of her last works.[58] It must have been made at the behest of her father, Blaise Bocquet, a fan painter and proprietor of a Paris bric-a-brac shop where the print was placed on sale. Letters and notes in the Franklin Papers show the American minister enjoying a pleasant intimacy with the Filleuls until his departure from France in 1785. Louis Jacques Cathelin's engraving of the picture was exhibited at the Salon of 1779, he having been recently accepted into the Académie Royale. It is a line engraving, that stronger, sharper technique which had reached perfection in France. The moles on Franklin's face, for which I look as a gauge of an artist's frankness, are slurred over in the painting, but exactly inserted in the print, suggesting that Cathelin was himself familiar with his subject's face.

That Salon echoed the continuing roll of Franklin's popularity, with three portraits of him in three different media, Filleul, Houdon, and Duplessis. The Houdon bust is said to have had the Turgot epigram inscribed beneath it.[59] For all the finality of that sonorous line, the search for words expressive of the man's classic stature went on, not only in Paris but in London where, in 1779, Benjamin Vaughan's edition of Franklin's *Political, Philosophical and Miscellaneous Pieces* at last appeared, with one Latin line under an engraving after the Sèvres medallion and another across from it on the title page, Vaughan contributing one, the Bishop of Saint

56. Félix Bouvier, "Une Concierge de Passy en l'an II," *Bulletin de la Société historique d'Auteuil et de Passy, 5* (1905–06), 110–28.

57. Jules Guiffrey, "Histoire de l'Académie de Saint-Luc," *Archives de l'art français, 9* (1915), 192.

58. *Memoirs of Madame Vigée-Lebrun,* trans. Lionel Strachey (New York, 1903), p. 13.

59. Georges Giacometti, *Le Statuaire Jean Antoine Houdon et son époque, 3* (Paris, 1918–19), 239, 336.

Asaph the other. But at the Salon of that year Le Ray de Chaumont capped all others for pith and point with the painting which still remains in the big, elaborately carved, and gilded frame. Here the picture, painted for him by Joseph Siffred Duplessis, is surrounded by the insurgent symbols of rattlesnake, liberty cap, club of Hercules, a lion's skin trophy, wreaths of oak and laurel, and, on the plaque below (made by the carver for a much more fulsome inscription), the one word, "VIR."

7 VIR

EVERYONE who saw it in its central place at the Salon of 1779 seems to have joined in praising the Franklin portrait, its solid human splendor, and its dramatic summation in a single word. Triumph and nobility were in it, one man and the people of two hemispheres united in one world, France advancing to avenge an old humiliation and to open a new enlightenment, her ships and armies moving westward in response to this man's appeal, this old man, indomitable, defying by his life all the resolute immobility of the centuries, creating new hopes, a new resolution, and new powers. Duplessis took all the applause, leaving the other Franklin portraits in the exhibition—Houdon's delightfully pleasant bust and the engraving after Mme. Filleul—but little remarked. Bachaumont echoed the admiration, chiding Duplessis only for having painted Fontanel, of the *Mercure,* in his waistcoat and with an undignified air.[1] Young Elkanah Watson, who on September 14, 1779, and again on the following day, crowded into the galleries of the Louvre in the midst of "a prodigious current of human animals," was thrilled to find there that "master piece of painting representing our Illustrious Patron Doctr. Franklin, who is deposited (as a mark of particular respect) upon the left of his present Majesty. He is also represented in sculpture in various sizes."[2] He describes it elsewhere as upon the left of the portraits

1. Bachaumont, *Mémoires, 13,* 223.
2. New York State Library, MS journal of Elkanah Watson, *3,* 43, 55. See also Watson, *Men and Times of the Revolution,* 2d edition (New York, 1857), p. 106.

125

of the King and Queen, its neighbors actually being, probably, the portraits of Monsieur, the King's brother, and of the Duchess of Chartres. In the *livret* of the exhibition Duplessis' portraits are listed in the order of social precedence, with Franklin, as an untitled diplomat, ahead only of Fontanel. Elkanah seems by his notes to have received some misinformation on the pictures (he then understood no French), seeing Amédée Vanloo's elaborate allegory of Virtue, Vice, and Nature as a conflict between Love and Chastity, and recording other subjects not in the catalogue. He did not mention Mlle. Vallayer's "Vestale Couronnée de Roses," which belonged to the Queen and which had charmed that artist's American friends.[3] Grimm thought the portrait of Franklin Duplessis' masterpiece, holding a reservation upon one point only—that there was no clear indication as to whether the model was seated or standing.[4] This, to his eye, gave the figure an appearance of falling. The criticism may have had some effect upon later, altered, versions of the likeness, in which a chair back is indicated.

Pierre Samuel du Pont has left the best-known, most glowing comment upon the picture in one of his letters on the Salons to the Margrave Caroline Louise of Baden. Of Houdon's bust he only remarked that he preferred it to Caffiéri's.[5] But of the painting:

> Ce n'est pas assez de dire que *Franklin* est beau: il faut dire qu'il a été un des plus beaux hommes du monde et qu'on n'en connaît pas de son âge qui lui soit égal. Toutes ses proportions annoncent la vigueur d'Hercule et à soixante et quinze ans il a encore de la souplesse et de la légèreté. Son large front peint les fortes pensées et son col robuste la fermeté de son caractère. Il a dans les yeux l'égalité de l'âme et sur les lèvres le rire d'une inaltérable sérénité. Il ne parait pas que le travail ait jamais fatigué ses nerfs. Il a des rides gaies; il en a de tendres et de fières; il n'en a pas une de laborieuse. On voit qu'il a plus conçu qu'étu-

3. *Livret,* no. 102. There is a reference to David's praise of the picture and its influence on John Trumbull in *Harper's Magazine, 42* (1871), 72.

4. Grimm, *Correspondance littéraire, 12,* 327.

5. "Lettres sur les Salons de 1772, 1777 et 1779," *Archives de l'art français,* n.s. 2 (1908), 118–19.

dié, qu'il a joué avec les sciences, les hommes et les affaires. Et c'est encore presqu'en jouant qu'au déclin de ses ans il travaille à fonder la plus imposante république. On a mis au bas de son portrait cette laconique inscription, *Vir*. Il n'y a pas un trait de sa figure ni de sa vie qui la démente.[6]

In that day a few lines of verse were added beneath a portrait again and again, so that the sister arts of poetry and painting might in unison proclaim the theme. The *"Vir"* outshone them all, echoing Franklin's own terse directness, what the Duc de Croÿ called "son laconisme sublime."[7] The United States should ever recall with gratitude that it was Le Ray de Chaumont who had placed her minister and advocate so aptly in the public eye, first with the famous medallion and its sturdy *"B. Franklin, Américain,"* and then, in his hour of rising success, with this painting and the one breathtaking word. Le Ray had created a Franklin image to fire the imagination of the world, and those who came to Franklin with their business learned its truth. This was the Franklin who, when the Duc de Croÿ had called, March 1, 1779, to suggest that the insurgent ships of war give free passage to those of Captain Cook had replied, so simply, "Cela sera fait."[8]

I assume that Duplessis did not seek this commission, but was given it by Le Ray de Chaumont because he was the leading portrait painter of the court at that time. Certainly, patron and artist were united in their purpose to climax all earlier portraits with one which should hold the full vitality of a triumphant life. Duplessis

6. "It is not enough to say that Franklin is handsome. One must say that he has been one of the world's handsomest men and that one knows no man of his age who could equal him. All his proportions reveal the strength of Hercules and at seventy years he is still supple and light-footed. His large forehead suggests strength of mind and his robust neck the firmness of his character. Evenness of temper is in his eyes and on his lips the smile of an unshakeable serenity. Work seems never to fray his nerves. His wrinkles are gay; they are tender and proud, not one of them careworn. One can see that he has imagined more than he has studied, that he has played with the sciences, with men and affairs. And it is still almost as a game that in his declining years he labors to bring into being the greatest republic. They have put under his portrait that laconic inscription: *Vir*. There is not one trait in him nor in his life to belie it." (Ibid., 106–07.)

7. De Croÿ, *Journal, 4,* 167.

8. Ibid., p. 168.

the artist-scientist was probably as unknown to Franklin as to much of the busy world around him. A slow, intent worker, celibate, a drone, Duplessis had bad eyesight, difficult hearing, and few friends.[9] His work occupied eight or more rooms of the Galleries of the Louvre: reception room, studio, and rooms for his students and copyists.[10] He made only about ten portraits a year, charging one to three thousand livres, and brought in, with his royal pension, about 12,000 livres a year.[11] He lived somewhat beyond this income, wore lace and jewels, sent money to the blind mother living at his old home in Carpentras, and was known also to have lent money to a dissolute nobleman and to have lost money to robbers entering his studio.[12] By day he painted and by night worked with his tools and chemicals. He developed a secret formula for cleaning marble.[13] From 1779 to 1800 he studied the qualities and practical uses of rubber.[14] We have no evidence that Franklin knew of, or had any part in, launching this long and hopefully-pursued research.

Duplessis was at the height of his artistic career from 1771 to 1783. From 1788 on, he gave himself to museum work and to teaching, painting little beyond occasional replicas of the "Franklin" and a few other successes of the past, living in poverty, an artist of the old regime out of touch with the new, and honored in it only as the painter of Franklin. Of the many early repetitions of his great portrait, it is impossible for me to say how many are his and how many are copies. Belleudy's excellent biography does not list all of the type, and reflects the confusion of attributions with which a pioneering work must deal. It is certain that the painting was copied by other artists almost at once, partly in response to the demand for Franklin portraits, partly because Franklin himself encouraged it, and partly because it was regarded from the first as a model of strong portraiture. Due to the cataclysm of the French Revolution, only a very few have those clearly traced histories of

9. Belleudy, *J. S. Duplessis,* p. 97.

10. Ibid., p. 98.

11. Ibid., p. 252.

12. Ibid., pp. 154–55.

13. Michel N. Benisovich, "Duplessis in the United States," *Gazette des Beaux-Arts,* ser. 6, *29* (1946), 289.

14. Ibid., pp. 291–92.

ownership so helpful in tracing a work of art to the artist. There is not even any sure evidence that Duplessis kept in his own studio an original study from which replicas might be made.

As early as the time of the Salon, however, the portrait existed in two forms, and happily the originals of both have survived. One is the painting of the Salon, the "Fur Collar" type, signed and dated 1778, and now at the Metropolitan Museum. The other is the "Gray Coat" pastel, showing Franklin in much plainer dress but with an identical pose of the head. This, now at the New York Public Library, is dated only by the fact that a copy in miniature was made from it in August 1779. That was just before the Salon. The oil painting of the Salon, signed and dated 1778, may have been with Le Ray de Chaumont or, more probably, was at the studio of the engraver, Juste Chevillet. The pastel was almost certainly at Passy at that time. I list here my theories as to the origin of the pastel, and its relation to the oil, in the order of my preference for them.

1 The pastel, Duplessis' original study: By and large the most reasonable point of view, and that which fits most comfortably into the slender evidence at hand, is that the pastel is the original study for the portrait of the Salon, made in this medium because of its ease and quickness. A busy painter must catch the likeness of a busy subject, an elderly man to whom the act of holding a pose was, as he freely declared, both irksome and painful. This, it would appear, is just what Greuze had done the year before. Accepting this, one may or may not accept the pale Quaker gray as the color of Franklin's dress, though its cut is identical with that of the suit which Franklin gave to Elkanah Watson and which is now preserved at the Massachusetts Historical Society, even to the same self-covered buttons. He seems to have preferred darker colors, particularly the dark brown-red of the suit at the Historical Society and of other portraits, and the artist may simply have used in the pastel a color to please his taste. By the same token, we need not assume that the costume of the oil, while in Franklin's color, is in Franklin's cut. Franklin may well have had such a garment for chilly days, indoors or out, but one must remember that the painter of this era was creating a monument in the details of which emphasis and symbolism were far more important than reality. A skillful portrait

129

painter builds his picture about some one predominant feature, and here Duplessis saw his man in terms of the big head and intelligent brow set upon a strong, stout body. The body must be clothed in a way to suggest authority and power but not to obscure the element of broad humanity. But with dress so important an indication of status, a simple business suit would not do.

2   The pastel, a replica by Duplessis for Franklin: It is possible that Franklin, pleased with the portrait of the Salon, ordered a replica for himself, as he had done with Martin's work, but as with Martin, asked for some simplification, in this case of the costume.

3   The pastel, a copy for Franklin, possibly by Joseph Ducreux: Granting that Franklin ordered a simpler, cheaper version for himself, Duplessis might very reasonably have assigned the commission to one of his assistants or to a friend. That Joseph Ducreux (1737–1802), a pastellist of note, may have been the artist is supported only by the high quality of the work and by the fact that Ducreux exhibited a "Franklin" in pastel, of which there is no other record, at the Salon de la Correspondance in 1782. Both Benjamin Franklin and his grandson always referred to the pastel (and William Temple Franklin to the duplicate of it in oil which he himself owned) as by Duplessis. One cannot be sure, however, that they would not have so designated any work coming from Duplessis' studio or copied by another from his original, just as one names the author of a book regardless of whose hand may have multiplied the copies of it. That the portrait by Ducreux was never engraved supports the surmise that it was based on the work of another artist. Finally, its presence in the Salon de la Correspondance brings it more intimately into Franklin's circle. It appeared in this exhibition on June 7, 1782, and was shown for two weeks. The printed report of its presence lists it as: "Le Portrait de M. Franklin, peint au pastel, par M. Ducreux. *Du Cabinet d'un Particulier.* Ce Portrait, d'un homme toujours vu avec enthousiasme, est peint ici d'une manière savante et hardie."[15] To be told that the execution of the work was "masterly and bold" is unfortunately not very informa-

15. *Nouvelles de la Republique des Sciences et des Arts* (June 19, 1782), p. 180. The notice, lacking the second sentence, was also published in the issue of June 12, p. 171. The only known file of this journal is at the Bibliothèque Nationale, Paris.

tive, nor to learn that it came from a private collection. However, it is highly probable that if Franklin himself had been the lender, he would have chosen to do so anonymously.

Something should be interjected at this point regarding the Salon de la Correspondance, to which there will be further references. It is a story of the Enlightenment, and of the yearning of one human heart to bring all the brightening rays of science and art into a single focus. It was the dream of Mamès Claude Pahin de La Blancherie, a young man who had visited the French colonies in America, but had returned with a feeling of revulsion against the treatment of the Negroes there. He was twenty-five, and his plan had been some years in incubation when it burst into public notice as of May 20, 1778. A prospectus published on that day announces the approval of his project by a committee of the Académie Royale des Sciences, headed by Franklin. At the same time a notable roster of the nobility lent their names as patrons. The project was to establish at Paris a central headquarters for all art and learning. It was entitled the "Agence Générale de Correspondance pour les Sciences et les Arts," and La Blancherie, as "Agent Générale de Correspondance pour les Sciences et les Arts," opened his house to the learned and talented of all nations. In the middle of every week there was held there the "Assemblée Ordinaire des Sciences et des Arts," and this followed a few days later by a printed report, *Nouvelles de la République des Sciences et des Arts*. Each *Nouvelles* contained communications from learned men and institutions, with detailed descriptions of the models, painting, and sculpture shown at the Assemblées. The meetings and exhibits were held first at the Maison Neuve, rue de Tournon, later at the more spacious Hôtel Villayer, rue Saint André des Arts, where scientific and fine arts exhibits could be shown in separate galleries.

La Blancherie had an intelligent comprehension of the scientific, but his inclination was more firmly with the arts and he later became the author of a history of French painting.[16] From the first there was hostility to his enterprise, and in the arts it appears to have had the strongest official foundation. The Salon de la Correspondance,

16. *Essai d'un Tableau Historique des Peintre de l'Ecole Française, depuis Jean Cousin, en 1500, jusqu'au 1783.*

in spite of La Blancherie's deference to the Academicians, and the humbler quality of the work shown there, was nonetheless regarded as a threat to the Salon du Louvre and the monopolistic position of the Académie Royale de Peinture et de Sculpture. Two years before, the exhibitions of the ancient Académie de Saint Luc had been suppressed, and the rise of a new contemporary show was not welcomed. La Blancherie did his best to mollify his enemies, but they persisted and certainly contributed to the gradual loss of interest in his undertaking.[17] The *Nouvelles* reflect its decline, until publication ceased toward the end of 1787. With the outbreak of the Revolution, he emigrated to England, and died in London in 1811.[18] His Salon de la Correspondance had, in its heyday, offered a startling innovation by showing the work of young and untried artists side by side with those of established reputation, and though Franklin participated little in its activities his spirit and benign approval were there.

To return to Franklin and to Passy, we know at all events that there were two portraits there in the last years of his residence at Le Ray's estate: the pastel hanging in the "pavilion" where he lived and, across the garden in the hôtel, the oil in its sumptuously carved and gilded frame, the one distinguished by its simple "Quaker" gray, and the other in a costume deep and rich in color and design, wine-red and lined with fur. Fur trimming appears also in the Greuze and again in that beguilingly personal portrait which Amédée Vanloo made for Madame Helvétius, as well as in imitations of the Duplessis, and not forgetting, of course, the fur cap of Cochin and Rousseau. There seems to have been a new art convention in the making here, a necessary inherent symbolism for the prominent liberal, both to mark him out as the subjects of portraiture were expected to be marked, and to give him some of that special dignity which it was a duty of portraiture to bestow, a badge of status for the rejectors of status. Plain fur, rather fortui-

17. Bachaumont, in *Mémoires, 15* (May 8, 1780), 166, gloats over the fact that "une maladie de bourse" had obliged La Blancherie to discontinue publication and meetings. Julian P. Boyd, ed., *The Papers of Thomas Jefferson, 12* (Princeton, 1954), 98–99, 317–18, 333–34, 611, records other evidence of decline. See also Emile Bellier de Chavignerie, "Pahin de La Blancherie et le Salon de la Correspondance," *Revue universelle des arts, 19* (1864), 211–12.

18. Arnault, &c., *Biographie nouvelle des contemporains.*

tously, was coming into acceptance for this need. Ermine for kings. Bearskin for the bruins of the left.

Richard S. Greenough told Edward Everett Hale that Franklin's "fondness for fur in his pictures, was due to his supposing that fur was used as a professional badge by the early printers."[19] This conjecture has been much quoted. I have found no evidence that Franklin thought so or that he expressed any preference for the fur. It was customary to leave costume to the taste or imagination of the painter, and certainly Franklin was not much disposed to intervene. Years later, Rembrandt Peale painted Thomas Jefferson wearing a fur-collared coat, which may have been the artist's invention or may have been, as tradition has it, that which Kosciusko had brought from Europe and had presented to Jefferson on his departure from America in 1798.[20]

By and large, the French portraits agree in giving Franklin the simplicity of costume for which he had become famous and which he, in fact, preferred. As for his linen, the style of which sometimes distinguishes one portrait type from another (notably the Caffiéri and Houdon), we can assume that it was plain but varied. No long fine lace at the throat or wrists. The white scarf might be loosely knotted and was doubtless so worn informally, indoors. The shirt ruff of the Greuze, L'Hospital, and Duplessis portraits may have been in his wardrobe or may have been a touch of painter's elegance. None of the English portraits show it, nor does the Peale of 1785, though in making a formal enlargement of that picture Peale introduced it.

Duplessis' great French portrait was, as the great English portraits had been, supported by an engraving. In it Juste Chevillet strove to bring profit and honor to himself and his patrons and to meet the competition of the many other prints which Franklin's time of triumph had brought into being. It had, insofar as was possible, the character of an official likeness, reinforced by Duplessis' high standing, by the close association of Le Ray and Franklin, and by a laudatory poem which Feutry, now virtually poet laureate of the American embassy, had composed and sent to Franklin two years before:

19. Edward Everett Hale, *Franklin in France, 1* (Boston, 1887), xvi.
20. Information from Dr. Alfred L. Bush, Jefferson Papers, Princeton, 1959.

Vers
à mettre sous le Portrait
de
Monsieur de Franklin &c

honneur du nouveau monde et de l'humanité,
ce sage aimable et vrai les guide et les éclaire;
comme un autre mentor, il cache à l'oeil vulgaire,
sous les traits d'un mortel, une Divinité.

Passy, ce 27 avril, 1777
Par son très sincere
et très humble admirateur
Feutry.[21]

Le Ray's "Vir" would have been less striking on the small engraving than on the painting, and Feutry's four lines stood there with force and dignity. Le Ray probably selected them himself for the purpose. Certainly, Franklin had had nothing to do with it. A year later he sent one of the prints to Mrs. John Jay at her request, adding a cautionary note:

> The Verses at the Bottom are truly extravagant. But you must know that the Desire of pleasing by a perpetual use of Compliments in this polite Nation, has so us'd up all the common Expressions of Approbation, that they are become flat and insipid, and to use them almost implies Censure. Hence Musick, that formerly might be sufficiently prais'd when it was call'd *bonne,* to go a little farther they call'd it *excellente,* then *superbe, magnifique, exquise, celeste,* all of which being in their turns worn out, there remains only *divine;* and when that is grown as insignificant as its Predecessors, I think they must return to common Speech, and Common Sense: as from vying

21. "Honor of the New World and of humanity, this sage, beloved and true, guides and enlightens them both. He, like a new Mentor, in mortal form hides from the vulgar eye a divinity." (Franklin Papers, A.P.S., *51* (2), no. 24.) Feutry's is a literary form of the period, linking the arts of painting and poetry, and Franklin, though often honored in this way was by no means the only figure so extolled.

with one another in fine and costly Paintings on their Coaches, since I first knew the Country, not being able to go further in that way, they have return'd lately to plain Carriages, painted without Arms or figures, in one uniform Colour.[22]

In 1779 Franklin gave miniatures of himself to Georgiana Shipley and to Mariamne Williams. Duplessis was not a miniaturist and his work not at its best in small size.[23] Both, however, were copied by different artists from the "Gray Coat" pastel. In her glowing letter of appreciation Georgiana expressed herself as having been, before the arrival of the miniature, "perfectly happy and content with the small head you had the goodness to send me by Mr. Digges."[24] That had been one of the little Sèvres medallions which he kept by him in quantity and gave out as souvenirs to friends. It had been as cheap a gift as the other was expensive. Though Georgiana's miniature, mounted on a snuff box, one of those "boîtes aux portraits" so fashionable at the court, had cost less than in a gold setting, it was nevertheless a handsome present. Receiving from Betsy Partridge in Boston at about the same time a specific request for a miniature, he was then encouraged to take the thrifty course and send to her on October 11, 1779, "a little Head in China, more like, perhaps, than the Painting would be."[25] Betsy on her part was not pleased, having set her heart upon a painting "to Ware on the Neck," reporting back also that "the Paleness of the Countenance gives me Melancholy Ideas."[26]

A little-known miniaturist, Antoine Noël Benoît Graincourt, painted a "Franklin" in 1779 which may have been copied from the "Fur Collar" version of Duplessis. In the spring of 1780 Simon Pierre Fournier, from whom Franklin had been buying type for his Passy press, asked and was given permission to have a miniature

22. Franklin to John Jay, June 13, 1780 (L.C.).

23. A miniature of Franklin, owned by him and his descendants has a traditional attribution to Duplessis but is certainly a copy. Belleudy in his life of Duplessis ignores it. Joshua James Foster, *Dictionary of Painters of Miniatures* (London, 1926), lists Duplessis with this work alone cited.

24. A.P.S.

25. Princeton University.

26. Elizabeth Partridge to Benjamin Franklin, Dec. 6, 1781 (A.P.S). Her original request is dated Oct. 24, 1778 (ibid.).

made. In granting this, Franklin stated his willingness to pose, his strong aversion to doing so if it could be avoided, and suggested that a copy from Duplessis would be just the thing. But Fournier le Jeune (he was a son of the more famous typefounder) begged with warmth and enthusiasm for two or three sittings at least, and sent his miniaturist, another obscure figure, to Passy with the letter. How many times Alexis Judlin knocked in vain we do not know, but he was obliged at the last to ask for a painting to copy, saying that he would do his best, from that, to satisfy his patron's desire for an original work. While all this was going on, Thomas Digges, who had delivered Franklin's gift to Miss Shipley, wrote from England soliciting a portrait for himself. He received in reply the well-known letter in which Franklin sets down more explicitly than anywhere else his feeling about the making of portraits:

> I have at the request of Friends sat so much and so often to painters and Statuaries, that I am perfectly sick of it. I know of nothing so tedious as sitting hours in one fix'd posture. I would nevertheless do it once more to oblige you if it was necessary, but there are already so many good Likenesses of the Face, that if the best of them is copied it will probably be better than a new one, and the body is only that of a lusty man which need not be drawn from the Life; any artist can add such a Body to the face. Or it may be taken from Chamberlain's print. I hope therefore you will excuse me. The Face Miss Georgiana has is thought here to be the most perfect. Ornaments and emblems are best left to the Fancy of the Painter.[27]

He made his feeling quite clear to his friends in general, and one of them, a few years later, touched upon it in print:

> Tous les Peintres, tous les Sculpteurs voulurent faire
> le portrait de Lincfran, sans lunettes & avec lunettes.

27. Smyth, *Writings, 8,* 110. (Original in L.C.) It is not known that Mr. Digges followed this suggestion, and had the Shipley miniature either copied or enlarged on canvas with the addition of a body from the print after Chamberlin.

On en voyait des copies à tous les coins de rue. L'importunité alla au point qu'il demanda grace, disant qu'en huit jours de tems on lui avait donné vingt fois le torticolis. On prit en conséquence le parti de le saisir une bonne fois. On le frappa en argent, on le moula en biscuit; on le voit enfin, à cette heure, bien & fidellement rendu, en médaillons, en bracelets, sur des bonbonniéres, dans les médaillers & sur toutes les cheminée [*sic*] ni plus ni moins révéré qu'un Dieu Pénate.[28]

All in all, there was a finality about Duplessis' great painting which was as obvious to Franklin as to everyone else. Lesser men had tried their hands at it, but they could not outdo the King's painter. It gave Franklin a comfortable sense of justification in refusing to pose again. By his printer's estimate of the situation there was now a satisfactory type face which the artists in every technique need only copy, thus saving both themselves and their subject a great deal of trouble. Formerly, for the good of the cause, he had endured the tedium and discomfort of posing. From this time on he would yield but rarely. At the same time, he greatly enjoyed the multiplication of his image everywhere. It was a point of vanity, and yet redeemed by its naturalness and by his amused detachment. Those who sought to court him by the flattery of a portrait learned that they could indeed give him pleasure, but could gain nothing for themselves. On a woman's appeal, he might even agree to pose. Mme. Filleul succeeded. The Nogarets succeeded, too, though the appeal on behalf of Mme. Fournier fell short. That dubious character, Courtney Melmoth (more properly, Samuel Jackson Pratt), succeeded in gaining his confidence and a considerable sum of money by artfully using a pretty woman, his

---

28. "All the painters and sculptors wish to make the portrait of Lincfran, without and with spectacles. One sees copies at every street corner. The importunity has reached the point where he has pled for mercy, saying that in eight days' time they have given him twenty cases of crick in the neck. So they resign themselves to taking him once and for all. They strike him in silver, they mould him in china; one sees him now, at the last, well and faithfully rendered in medallions, in bracelets on bonbon boxes, in medals and on every mantlepiece worshipped no less than a household god." Nogaret, *L'Isle des sages*, pp. 118–19.

wife, and a gilded portrait. But the part of the plan by which Franklin was to have paid the artist of the gilded image appears to have failed.

By 1779, also, Franklin could well reflect that his portrait had accomplished its full share as promotion for the American cause. Franklin portraiture had played a substantial part in the build-up of the Franco-American alliance. Its political importance remained, but in a new way, and one less immediate to his diplomatic purposes. Both his presence in France and the spread of his portrait were serving in some measure to sustain those undercurrents of liberal thought which were carrying France toward revolution. For all that the Phrygian cap symbolized, this man's face was even more specifically a symbol. In it lay rejection of the traditions of the past and confident, sagacious discernment of the future—things no conventional symbols could represent as well as that broad mouth and those amused, attentive eyes. It was the first time in history that a half smile had meant so much or that the form of a corpulent old man signified the overthrow of empires.

Where a face and figure become symbolic it is generally in one popularly accepted likeness. The number and variety of the Franklin portraits prevented this, though the Duplessis and the many versions of it certainly gained an ascendancy. The Duplessis "Fur Collar" painting, with its dignity and intelligence, stands as the supreme public portrait of Franklin. It should be remembered in contrast to the greatest private portrait, intimate and perceptive, painted by Vanloo to capture not an era but a moment. This work is undated. Inference points to 1777 or 1778. Vanloo's genre piece, "Une Jeune Fille Electrisée," in the Salon of 1777, is suggestive, while his allegory in the Salon of 1779 reflects the climactic admiration for Franklin at that time, "Le Tems découvre les vertus, la sagesse détruit les vices, le soleil anime la nature."[29] The painting must surely mark the ripening of the friendly relationship of Franklin and Mme. Helvétius, for whom it was made, and I would date

29. *Livret,* no. 17. The inference must be drawn not from the idea that Franklin had inspired the artist's interest in electricity, but that a mutual attachment to science had helped to draw them together. Vanloo's "Un Oiseau dans la machine pneumatique" of 1771 evinces a subject interest akin to that of Wright of Derby in England.

it close after Franklin's famous summons to the lady, "Vengeons nous!" Perhaps a later date is argued by the fact that it holds so well that bantering, appealing smile which she had come to love. But as a private portrait, free of all symbolic purpose, as a personal mood and no more, the Vanloo is supreme.

In contrast, Carmontelle's print of 1780 has the qualities both of formal and of private portraiture. Franklin is seated, full-length and in profile, a reserved figure and yet showing, in the original drawing as one looks at it, that ever-present amusement of his. Though intended for no particular friend, and in spite of its background of ships and "Les Loix de Pensilvanie" on the table, it has the pleasant, unpretentious intimacy of all of this charming amateur's work. I am sure we have Franklin's balding head here as the artist saw it and with nothing added to grace forehead or pate. It shows Franklin's figure, too, something for which, in the French portraiture, we must depend upon this print, the caricature "Le Magnétisme Dévoilé," and the Lemire and Suzanne statuettes.

In France as in England the portrait of Franklin which almost certainly reproduced his features more faithfully than any other was the now-lost waxwork by Patience Wright. In reasonable conjecture also it stands as that which was seen by more people year after year, and had a larger part than any other in keeping his fame alive in Europe. It was made in 1781, and its history blends into that of the oil paintings by her son, painted in 1782. The origins of both are rooted in as strange a medley of odd characters and mad doings as ever graced the pages of history. On March 29, 1778, Patience had informed "Doctr Frankling" of a dream in which she had beheld his entrance into London as "the glorious deliverer, &c."[30] I suspect it to have been a subliminal echo of the hopes for a negotiation to which some of Franklin's English friends had briefly clung a year or more earlier. At any rate, the idea was now rooted in Patience's mind and continued there to the end of the war. On March 14, 1779, she wrote again to "my gardein Spirit the great Philosopher and american agent," confiding her thought of returning to America by way of France, and adding hopefully, "would to god you would sind for me—my services are worthy

30. Franklin Papers (A.P.S.), 5 (2), no. 128.

of the Pleneypotenterey of America." Franklin replied at once to disparage the scheme:

Passy, May 4, 1779.

Dear Madam,

I received your Favour of the 14th of March past, and, if you should continue in your Resolution of returning to America, thro' France, I shall certainly render you any of the little Services in my Power; but there are so many Difficulties at present in getting Passages from hence, particularly safe ones for Women, that methinks I should advise your Stay till more settled Times, and till a more frequent Intercourse is established.

As to the Exercise of your Art here, I am in doubt whether it would answer your Expectations. Here are two or three who profess it, and make a Show of their Works on the Boulevards; but it is not the Taste of Persons of Fashion to sit to these Artists for their Portraits; and both House Rent and Living at Paris are very expensive.

I thought that friendship required I should acquaint you with these Circumstances; after which you will use your Discretion. I am, Dear Madam

Your most obedient and most humble Servant

B. F.

P. S. My Grandson, whom you may remember when a little saucy boy at School, being my Amanuensis in writing the within letter, has been diverting me with his Remarks. He conceives, that your Figures cannot be pack'd up without Damage from anything you could fill the boxes with to keep them steady. He supposes, therefore, that you must put them into Postchaises, two and two, which will make a long train upon the road, and be a very expensive Conveyance; but, as they will eat nothing at the Inns, you may the better afford it. When they come to Dover, he is sure they are so like Life and Nature, that the Master of the Pacquet will not receive them on board without Passes; which you will do well to take out from the Secretary's Office, before you leave London; where they will cost you *only* the modest Price of Two Guineas and Sixpence each, which you will pay without Grumbling, because you are sure the Money will never be employ'd against your Country. It will require, he says, five or six of the long wicker French Stage Coaches to carry them as Passengers from Calais to Paris, and at least two large ships with good Accomodations to convey them to America; where all the World will wonder at your Clemency to Lord N——; that, having it in your Power to hang, or send him to the Lighters, you had generously repriev'd him for Transportation.[31]

Mrs. Wright did not come at once nor did she, on coming, bring her exhibition with her. She left that for her children's support and, as it turned out, did not leave them with it for long. She may have planned to launch a new waxwork in Paris, taking advantage of the popularity of Americans there. Or she may have had a subtler motive. At a later period Mrs. Wright's friend had much to say of her services as a spy for the American cause. The claim that she kept Franklin well informed on English military and diplomatic moves is not sustained by her surviving letters to him. William Temple Franklin gives her credit for so doing, but does not appear to write from the personal information he should have had.[32] The claim is that she picked up hints from important men visiting her show, and was then able to get details from their wives. John Williams, "Anthony Pasquin," affirms that "During the American War I wrote many letters to Mr. Hancock, Mr. Adams, &c. at the express desire and suggestions of this Lady, who maintained a correspondence, through me, with the Chiefs of the Congress."[33] Certainly information on troop movements should have gone in that direction rather than to Paris. Rachel Wells stated that she

31. Smyth, *Writings, 7,* 302–04.
32. W. T. Franklin, *Works of Benjamin Franklin, 6,* 87n.
33. Anthony Pasquin (John Williams), *Memoirs of the Royal Academicians* (London, 1796), p. 92.

herself had a part in its transmission, receiving the letters in the wax heads sent from London and passing them on. Her Philadelphia waxwork show was a popular attraction, though John Adams' description of it, as of May 10, 1777, mentions no piece which would have been made after the outbreak of hostilities—only the "Franklin" and other early portraits.[34] Patience may deserve due honor here, but the fact is that the vague, apocalyptic chaffering of her letters implies a call to command rather than accurate and intelligent service.

She was being borne along upon a popular current which had come into English and American life at about 1769, advocating public meetings for the expression of public opinion, the idea of popular representation carrying out the popular will, and the notion that a perfection of ancient Anglo-Saxon democratic procedure was vital to good government. These concepts had brought with them the hope of reforms from which a new, united empire might emerge. With conservative entrenchment, the prosecution of the war, and American successes, they acquired a lunatic fringe in which the waxwork artist flutters like a tassel. Parliament's repeal of the Roman Catholic disabilities brought popular agitation and riots in Scotland in 1779. The movement spread to London where, in December, Lord George Gordon accepted the presidency of the Protestant Association. The erratic nobleman's followers met in the auction salesroom of John Greenwood, the American painter, shaking the walls with their enthusiastic clamor.[35] I have no evidence of Mrs. Wright's direct participation at this time, but her letters are strongly anti-Romanist at times, and it is known that a few years later she was much in conference with Lord George.[36] An early supporter was William Bailston, an American veteran of the Boston Tea Party. He and Greenwood also knew Franklin well, and sought to involve him in their movement.[37] In the light

34. Charles Francis Adams, ed., *Familiar Letters of John Adams and His Wife, Abigail Adams, during the Revolution* (New York, 1876), p. 271.
35. Christopher Hibbert, *King Mob. The Story of Lord George Gordon and the London Riots of 1780* (Cleveland and New York, 1958), pp. 186–88.
36. Abigail Adams to Thomas Jefferson, June 6, 1785 (Boyd, *Papers of Thomas Jefferson, 8,* 180).
37. Hibbert, *King Mob,* p. 180.

of this, Patience's later letters to Franklin, urging him toward some undefined intervention in British affairs, are in a measure explained. Things were popping everywhere. The Royal Academy exhibition opened in April 1780 with a portrait of Patience by her twenty-four-year-old son, Joseph, number 202 in the catalogue, "Mrs. Wright Modelling a Head in Wax," and Horace Walpole crying out against the "lethargy of loyalty" by which it had been admitted to the show.[38] "A Lover of Decency" published his protest in the *Public Advertiser* of June 7. A favorable notice had appeared in the *London Courant and Westminster Review* of May 3. The rub was that Mrs. Wright had been shown modeling a head of King Charles I, watched as she did so by George III and his queen, her significant air implying that she was giving them a lesson not only in waxwork but in public policy:

> Wright on her lap sustains a trunkless head,
> And looks a wish—the King's was in its stead![39]

It was the Wrights' contribution to a movement in which the application of popular pressures replaced the appeal to established leadership, pressures which could easily take violent form and did so at just this moment in the devastating Gordon Riots of June 2–9, 1780. Thomas Digges wrote Franklin of the wreckage wrought in London by the blue cockade.[40] Franklin on his part expressed satisfaction at least in hearing that the houses of the ministers had been burned, making them, he thought, "sensible of the wanton malice with which they have encouraged the burning of Poor People's Houses in America!"[41] For those unknown persons who had sponsored the medal and engraving of 1777, and who may still have expected Franklin to exert some sort of leadership in the British liberal movement, his intervention was more impossible than ever. Already regarded as a possible accomplice in John the Painter's fantastic plot, he was now suspected of using French gold to burn London.

38. Horace Walpole to Rev. William Mason (Toynbee, *Letters of Horace Walpole, 11, 169*).
39. *Gazette,* May 16, 1780, quoted in Whitley Papers.
40. June 10, 1780 (H.S.P.).
41. Benjamin Franklin to Benjamin Vaughan, June 15, 1780 (L.C.).

Irish dissidents were hovering in the shadows. Mrs. Wright's laconic "Irland love you," cast in among other matters in a letter to Franklin, dated March 29, 1778, seems not a very constructive contribution to the conspiratorial effort, but we know that the Irish were in touch with Franklin in 1781, and that in 1785 Mrs. Wright was their channel of communication.[42]

The spring of 1780 had also seen the founding of the Society for Constitutional Information, with Major John Cartwright as its leading spirit and many old friends of Franklin prominent in its membership: Richard Price, Granville Sharp, Benjamin Vaughan, Thomas Bentley, and others.[43] This intelligent and influential group also had the madcap following which so often shakes its bells in the march of a liberal movement, and there we find the Wrights and with them another retired military officer, Major Peter Labilliere. This Major, descendant of a distinguished Huguenot family, is said to have recoiled from a disappointment in love into an erratic preoccupation with politics and religion.[44] While one group addressed itself to the intelligentsia, Patience and the Major, who I would judge had the larger following, conducted public meetings and sounded the trumpet, as she was pleased to put it, to the "tents o Isrell." One evidence of the Major's popular following is that Joseph Wright painted his portrait that year and a mezzotint from it by Henry Kingsbury was published on December 1. The "Christian Patriot & Citizen of the World" stares at us with eyes as bright as the buttons on his coat, surrounded by all the sources of his philosophy: Cartwright, Locke, Sidney, the Holy Bible, the Bishop of St. Asaph's sermon, the Magna Charta, and others. The British Museum's *Catalogue of Engraved British Portraits* lists it among the works of Joseph Wright of Derby, a quite different and much better painter. He

42. Patience Wright to Benjamin Franklin (Franklin Papers, A.P.S., Pt. II, *5*, no. 128). "Freedom" to William Temple Franklin, June 17, 1781 (ibid., *103*, no. 63). W. W. Seward to Thomas Jefferson, Oct. 25, 1785 (Boyd, *Papers of Thomas Jefferson, 8, 673*).

43. Frances Dorothy Cartwright, *The Life and Correspondence of Major Cartwright, 1* (London, 1826), 134–35.

44. John Timbs, *English Eccentrics and Eccentricities* (London, 1875), pp. 164–65. See also Francis P. de Labilliere, "History of a Cevenol Family," *Proceedings of the Huguenot Society of London, 2* (1889), 386.

was just coming into prominence in London, and while he is said to have added the "of Derby" to distinguish himself from Richard Wright of Liverpool,[45] I would think it much more likely that he eschewed any possible association with the young American.

In the midst of all the uproar in London, on July 8, 1780, Mrs. Wright's pretty daughter, Phoebe, was married at fashionable Saint George's Church, Hanover Square, to John Hoppner, the portrait painter. Major Labilliere was one of the witnesses to the register. Another was Juliet Ann Cozens, daughter of the artist, Alexander Cozens. It might as well be added, as part of all this zany background to a Franklin portrait, that Hoppner chose to encourage an unfounded rumor of his being a natural son of George III, that Alexander Cozens was similarly regarded as a son of Peter the Great, and that Juliet Ann later became the wife of Charles Roberts, pretender to an illegitimate connection with the Earls of Radnor.[46] Labilliere went back to his politico-preaching, which included, according to Mrs. Wright, setting "truth before the Solders —not to fight against ther conscience the Cause of america was the Cause of god."[47] Hoppner took his wife home to Mrs. Wright's new place in Cockspur Street, and Mrs. Wright bustled off to see Benjamin Franklin in France.[48] Midsummer was the waxwork artist's best creative season. As far as I know, however, Patience made only Franklin's portrait in Paris. It must have been he who persuaded the powerful Duchesse de Chartres to take the artist under her protection, though soon after, following a difference about money, we find this noble lady rated in Mrs. Wright's estimation as one of "those mean little minds."[49] Elkanah Watson came

45. William Bemrose, *The Life and Works of Joseph Wright, A.R.A., Commonly Called "Wright of Derby"* (London, 1885), p. 5.

46. Whitley Papers. A. P. Oppé, *Alexander & John Robert Cozens* (Cambridge, Mass., 1954), pp. 2–4.

47. Patience Wright to —— Adams, June 5, 1785 (Adams Papers, M.H.S.).

48. Dunlap, *Arts of Design, 1,* 135, 312. In his autobiography Charles Willson Peale quotes Benjamin West to the effect that Mrs. Wright had told Lord Bute to his face that a British victory in America was impossible. West warned her to be more cautious, or "*petticoats would not protect her,* and soon after she found it necessary to leave London and she went to france."

49. Benjamin West to Jean Baptiste Marie Pierre, Dec. 7, 1781 (*P.M.H.B., 32,* 1908, p. 17). Mrs. Wright quoted in Dunlap, *Arts of Design, 1,* 313.

upon her in Paris that summer, carrying on in her usual outgoing way:

I again mingled in the elegant festivities of the city, for two months, in the summer and autumn of '81.

I came oddly in contact with the eccentric Mrs. Wright, on my arrival at Paris, from Nantes. Giving orders, from the balcony of the Hotel d'York, to my English servant, I was assailed by a powerful female voice crying out from an upper story, "Who are you? An American, I hope!" "Yes, Madam," I replied, "and who are you?" In two minutes, she came blustering down stairs, with the familiarity of an old acquaintance. We were soon on the most excellent terms. I discovered that she was in the habit of daily intercourse with Franklin, and was visited by all the respectable Americans in Paris. She was a native of New Jersey, and by profession a moulder of wax figures. The wild flights of her powerful mind, stamped originality on all her acts and language. She was a tall and athletic figure; and walked with a firm, bold step, as erect as an Indian. Her complexion was somewhat sallow; her cheekbones, high; her face, furrowed; and her olive eyes keen, piercing, and expressive. Her sharp glance was appalling; it had almost the wildness of a maniac's. The vigor and originality of her conversation, corresponded with her manners and appearance. She would utter language, in her incessant volubility, as if unconscious to whom directed, that would put her hearers to the blush. She apparently possessed the utmost simplicity of heart and character.

With a head of wax upon her lap, she would mould the most accurate likenesses, by the mere force of a retentive recollection of the traits and lines of the countenance; she would form her likenesses by manipulating the wax with her thumb and finger. Whilst thus engaged, her strong mind poured forth an uninterrupted torrent of wild thought, and anecdotes and reminiscences of men and events. . . . The peculiarity of her character, and the excellence of her wax figures, made her rooms, in Pall Mall, a fashionable lounging-place for the nobility and distinguished men of England. Here her deep penetration and sagacity, cloaked by her apparent simplicity of purpose, enabled her to gather many facts and secrets important to "dear America,"—her uniform expression, in reference to her native land, which she dearly loved.

She was a genuine Republican, and ardent Whig. The King and Queen often visited her rooms; they would induce her to work upon her heads, regardless of their presence. She would often, as if forgetting herself, address them as George and Charlotte. This fact she often mentioned to me, herself. Whilst in England, she communicated much important information to Franklin, and remained in London until '75 or '76, engaged in that kind of intercourse with him and the American government, by which she was placed in positions of extreme hazard.

. . . Some time after my acquaintance with Mrs. Wright commenced, she informed me, that an eminent female chemist of Paris had written her a note, saying that she would make her a visit at twelve o'clock the next day, and announced also, that she could not speak English. Mrs. Wright desired me to act as interpreter. At the appointed hour, the thundering of a carriage in the court-yard announced the arrival of the French lady. She entered with much grace, in which Mrs. W. was no match for her. She was old, with a sharp nose, and with broad patches of vermillion spread over the deep furrows in her cheeks. I was placed in a chair, between the two originals. Their tongues flew with velocity, the one in English and the other in French, and neither understanding a word the other uttered. I saw no possibility of interpreting two such volleys of words, and at length abruptly commanded *silence for a moment.* I asked each—"Do you understand?" "Not a word," said Mrs. Wright. "N'importe," replied the chemist, bounding from her chair, in the midst of the floor; and, dropping a low courtesy, she was off. "What an old painted fool," said Mrs. W., in anger. It was evident, that this visit was not intended for an interchange of sentiment, but a mere act of civility, —a call.

I employed Mrs. W. to make the head of Franklin, which was often the source of much amusement to me. After it was completed, we were both invited to dine with Franklin, and I conveyed her to Passy in my carriage, she bearing the head upon her lap. No sooner in the presence of the Doctor, than she had placed one head by the side of the other. "There!" she exclaimed, "are twin brothers." The likeness was truly admirable; and, at the suggestion of Mrs. Wright, to give it more effect, Franklin sent me a suit of silk clothes which he wore in 1778. Many years afterward, the head was broken in Albany, and the clothes I presented to the "Historical Society of Massachusetts."

An adventure occurred to Mrs. Wright in connection with this head, ludicrous in the highest degree; but, although almost incredible, it is literally true. After the head had been modelled, she walked out to Passy, carrying it in a napkin, in order to compare it with the original. In returning in the evening, she was stopped at the barrier, to be searched for contraband goods; but, as her mind was as free as her native American air, she knew no restraint, nor the reason why she was detained. She resisted the attempt to examine her bundle, and broke out in the rage of a fury. The officers were amazed, as no explanation, in the absence of an interpreter, could take place. She was compelled, however, to yield to power. The bundle was opened; and, to the astonishment of the officials, exhibited the head of a dead man, as appeared to them in the obscurity of the night. They closed the bundle, without further examination, believing, as they afterward assured me, that she was an escaped maniac, who had committed murder, and was about concealing the head of her victim.

They were determined to convey her to the police station, when she made them comprehend her entreaties to be taken to the Hotel d'York. I was in my room; and, hearing in the passage a great uproar, and Mrs. W.'s voice pitched upon a higher key than usual, I rushed out, and found her in a terrible rage, her fine eye flashing. I thrust myself between her and the officers, exclaiming, "Ah, mon Dieu, qu'est ce qu'il y-a?" An explanation ensued. All except Mrs. W. were highly amused, at the singularity and absurdity of the affair.

The head and clothes I transmitted to Nantes; and they were the instruments of many frolics, not inappropriate to my youth, but perhaps it is hardly safe to advert to them in my age. A few I will venture to relate. On my arrival at Nantes, I caused the head to be properly adjusted to the dress, which was arranged in natural shape and dimensions. I had the figure placed in the corner of a large room, near a closet, and behind a table. Before it I laid an open atlas, the arm resting upon the table, and mathematical instruments strewn upon it. A handkerchief was thrown over the arm-stumps; and wires were extended to the closet, by which means the body could be elevated or depressed, and placed in various positions. Thus arranged, some ladies and gentlemen were invited to pay their respects to Dr. Franklin, by candle-light. For a moment, they were completely deceived, and all profoundly bowed and courtesied, which was reciprocated by the figure. Not a word being uttered, the trick was soon revealed.

A report soon circulated, that Doctor Franklin was at Monsieur Watson's. At eleven o'clock the next morning, the Mayor of Nantes came, in full dress, to call on the renowned philosopher. Cossoul, my worthy partner, being acquainted with the Mayor, favored the joke, for a moment, after their mutual salutations. Others came in; and all were disposed to gull their friends, in the same manner.[50]

I have searched in vain for some tangible link between Patience and Philippe Mathias Wilhelm Curtius, proprietor of the well-known waxwork on the Boulevard du Temple. They must certainly have known of one another. Mrs. Wright had made one substantial contribution to the art of waxwork: her figures were for the most part of people with whom her public was familiar, and visitors frequently mistook the imitation for one of themselves. In this Curtius appears to have imitated her, though contemporary descriptions are derisive of his workmanship. His figures seem never to have passed for reality. His public came of a lower class in society, paying their two sous to gape at a room set up "tout comme à Versailles," as well as at royalty, famous criminals, and the like. Later, the Curtius show flourished on the severed heads of victims of the Terror, then, in the hands of his niece, Mme. Tussaud, toured England and settled in London. There has always been a "Franklin" at Madame Tussaud's, destroyed but recreated after successive calamities. It has always been attributed to Tussaud herself, though the legend on which this delightful institution has prospered is, for the historian, easier to savor than to swallow. The story of young Marie Grosholtz (the future Tussaud), an intimate of royalty and philosophers alike, charming Franklin with her smile as she modeled this immortal work, is, as Parson Weems said in introducing the cherry tree story, "too valuable to be lost, and too true to be doubted." In any case, during the Revolution when his business was at its height,

50. Watson, *Men and Times,* pp. 137–42. The full figure which Mrs. Wright suggested was not actually made until after her return to England. Watson asked William Temple Franklin for the suit of clothes, writing from Nantes on Dec. 25, 1782 (Franklin Papers, A.P.S., *104,* no. 143). Had he planned the joke while with Mrs. Wright in Paris, the figure would have been provided with hands. Joseph Wright also stayed at the Hôtel d'York while in Paris (Dunlap, *Arts of Design, 1,* 312), as did William Alexander and many other English and American visitors.

Curtius had a "Franklin."[51] The late Tussaud version suggests a cast from Caffiéri. The source of its original, whether Curtius or Wright, cannot be identified.

In Paris, Patience received a disturbing letter from Phoebe. Mrs. Hoppner complained that her brother was spending his time in idleness, and spending the proceeds of the waxwork upon personal pleasures.[52] Later, George Washington was to describe the youth as "a little lazy."[53] Joe was dispatched to Paris, leaving apparently in December, after his mother had returned to London. He carried letters of introduction from Benjamin West to the distinguished French painter, Jean Baptiste Marie Pierre, and from Peter Labilliere to Benjamin Franklin.[54] The Major affirmed his belief in annual parliaments and universal suffrage as "the only constitutional Majesty," referred Franklin to the young artist for the details of his movement, and described himself "A Christian watchman for truth Do. Soldr. Do. Actor Do. Patriot, Citizen of the World."

Joseph remained in Paris until October 1782. For the first few months it may be assumed that he did nothing. Then, in April, the peace commissioners sent by Lord Shelburne began to meet with Franklin—first Richard Oswald, and then Franklin's old friend and neighbor, Caleb Whitefoord,

> Rare compound of oddity, frolic and fun,
> Who relish'd a joke, & rejoic'd in a pun.[55]

Richard Oswald, at once, apparently, asked for a portrait of Franklin. It was a gesture of marked respect and courtesy, an appeal for continuing friendship, and so regarded in the custom of the day. It was a flattering act with which to begin negotiations, but the character of the man and all the circumstances attest to the genuineness

51. *Dictionnaire de la conversation et de la lecture, 7* (Paris, 1853–58), 47. Jules Renouvier, *Histoire de l'art pendant la Révolution, considéré principalement dans les estampes* (Paris, 1863), p. 19.

52. Dunlap, *Arts of Design, 1,* 312.

53. Mount Vernon Ladies Association of the Union, "A Wright Profile," *Annual Report* (1959), p. 14.

54. West to Pierre, Dec. 7, 1781 (*P.M.H.B., 32,* 17). Peter Labilliere to Franklin, Dec. 8, 1781 (National Archives).

55. Oliver Goldsmith quoted in W. A. S. Hewins, ed., *The Whitefoord Papers* (Oxford, 1898), p. xxvii.

of the feeling it expressed. His first interview with Franklin was on April 15. On April 23 William Temple Franklin wrote to Félix Nogaret, a friendly connoisseur of the arts, asking the address of a painter, apparently one whom Nogaret had already recommended. They did not, however, employ that artist. They decided instead on Joseph Wright. He was an American. He was in need of money and in need of something to do. He could make his fortune by this. Being both young and beholden to Franklin, he could easily be overruled if there were any nonsense about sittings from life. The indolent Joe was therefore set to work. Nogaret's man, or another chosen by him, made a portrait independently which is discussed in the following chapter.

Both artists must have been aware that they were painting the greatest American in the culminating hour of personal and national triumph. The long American war was drawing to its close, and Franklin held the final issue in his hands. The world must be able to remember him as of this time. Joseph's plan, and it was his obvious course, was to hasten home with the original of his portrait, paint another of General Washington, and live in style for the rest of his days on the sale of replicas of both.

He encountered but one major difficulty. As usual, Franklin insisted in a friendly way that he wanted him to make a copy of the picture on the wall. Joseph had to make out as others had done, but he had at least a better opportunity to study his subject's face. He added some lines and shading to it which were either absent when the pastel was made four years before or ignored by the artist. In particular a shadow above the mouth, almost like a moustache, shows where the loss of teeth had taken support from the upper lip—an unsparing detail typically American in its factual intent, and one which Franklin would have approved. He also made the painting a little more his own by changing the color of coat and waistcoat to the deep red Franklin was wearing, and he added a clearly defined chair back behind the figure. His mother, in touch with all that was going on, wrote to Franklin on June 30, 1782, summoning him again to that role of leadership in the coming redemption of Britain and voicing her confident expectation that versions of Joseph's new portrait would soon be ordered for all the public buildings of the island:

I have the pleasure to tell you my hope is more fixt on you than ever. My Inthuzam encreases Evry day and from good authority can say my politicall Creed is well founded: you will be Very shortly calld upon by the People— ... I am very hapy to here by Mr Whitford and others that my son is Painting your Portraite. We expect a order from the Comon Councill very soon and so by these orders of the City or Part of them for your Picture to be Painted by Jos Wright and presented to those or to *whome* or *where* it may do most Honour ...

and so on.[56] But Joseph was better advised, and he had been offered free passage to America on one of the ships of Watson and Cossoul. In August he was ready to go, and wrote to William Temple Franklin in confused fashion of his plans:

I found at my return to Paris yesterday, that I am obliged to be detained a week longer, as every place was taken both in the Dilligence and Cabriolé and there being no other Conveyance before then—and as I receiv'd your Packet this Morning perhaps your letter to Mr. Williams may require an immediate conveyance. I return my sincere thanks for this continued instance of your grandfather's kindness. I could wish my situation here had put it in my Power to shew you that I had a sence of the friendship I have received from him and yourself, but I find I have only, more favours to ask. I could wish he would give me leave to make another Copy of his Picture either in small or Large—As I wish to make a Present of it to Mrs. Beech or whatever Person he should think fit. The last I did, Mr. Whitford has been pleased to take from me, I am fearful to ask, as I consider I may be in some measure troublesome, and he must be tired of seeing me so constantly.

I remain sr sincerely yours
Joseph Wright.

56. Patience Wright to Franklin (Franklin Papers, A.P.S., *25,* no. 143).

P. S. I had a great notion of making it the size of my
mothers, or the other little one you saw, as it will
be Portable, and yet sufficiently marked to keep the
Likeness.[57]

The "last" probably means the last remaining in his possession.
Without making one matrix portrait from which to produce others,
the young fellow had apparently each time copied the pastel, working in some element of life portraiture by having its original always near at hand. Whatever portrait he brought with him on the
voyage was lost in the shipwreck from which he barely escaped
with his life. All his originals went to Britain where, though not
copied as avidly as his mother had predicted, they were repeated
in both England and Scotland—the artist's name forgotten and the
work tagged as French, or, as with so many, labeled a "Greuze."

Patience meanwhile pursued in London her lively and incoherent
course, still hoping that her friend "the wisest man," would join
her there.[58] Franklin wisely remained at Passy, though strong rumors of his expected coming were current among his English
friends.[59] They flared into sudden, intense excitement when Elkanah Watson came to the city with his figure which he set up con-
spicuously at an open window.[60] Curiously, the wax head does not
seem to have been the basis for any other portraits. Benjamin West
was working on his painting of the peace commissioners, using
the Shipley miniature, the Whitefoord Wright, and the Sèvres medallion as his sources, and then, his thoughts recurring to earlier
and happier days, he painted his friend as he had known him before, an altered copy of the Martin portrait, with the large bagwig
and the eyes wholly preoccupied in philosophic speculation. That
was not the spirit of Patience Wright who was planning on her own
part to commemorate the work of the peace commissioners in an
ambitious group in wax: "To shame the English king, I would
go to any trouble."[61]

57. Franklin Papers (A.P.S.), *107,* no. 81.
58. Patience Wright to Franklin, March 29, 1779 (Franklin Papers, A.P.S., *5*
(*2*), no. 128).
59. John Sargent to Franklin, June 1, 1783 (A.P.S.).
60. Watson, *Men and Times,* pp. 142–43.
61. Patience Wright to Thomas Jefferson, Aug. 14, 1785 (Boyd, *Papers of
Thomas Jefferson, 8,* 380).

IN ONE portrait of Franklin, painted when peace was in the making and his long struggle nearly over, the artist has caught in pose and features the emotions of victory, the pride and triumph of the hour. Franklin may have assumed this pose and expression for a moment, although it is inconceivable that he would have held them, even briefly, for an artist. The body is to the front, the head and eyes looking sharply to the right. The hair seems tossed by a sudden motion of the head. A loose white kerchief is knotted at the neck, and the costume no more than a dark supporting mass. It is a quick and vigorous impression of the man. Others had shown him as the patient philosopher. Here patience is cast aside and he is the victor turning to his enemies to give them his terms. I cannot imagine his facing the friendly British commissioners in this manner, yet the valor and the anger of the staunch old man is in the picture.

Here the artist is without any doubt commemorating history, although the picture ostensibly came into being (if my reading of the slender evidence is correct) for a homely, Poor-Richard sort of reason: as a gift from her husband, with Franklin's blessing, to Mme. Elisabeth Nogaret of Versailles. In April 1782, as has been related, when the British commissioners were beginning their conferences at Passy, William Temple Franklin had written to Félix Nogaret asking for the address of an artist. I have inferred that one of the commissioners, Richard Oswald, had requested a portrait, and that young Joseph Wright, drifting into the embassy at the right moment, was given the commission. It was an unusual opportunity for any painter. The denouement of Franklin's years was evident: all his effort to strengthen and unite the empire, having been diverted to the fiery trial of war, was now emerging victorious. I cannot be sure to what extent young Wright, a careless lad, appreciated this, but even had it been in his mind I do not think that he would have painted otherwise than he did. His plain American impulse would have moved him only to paint with the greater care, to be the more reverently and meticulously truthful in his delineation of the features of his honored countryman.

A French artist would have seen the opportunity in quite a different light, and Félix Nogaret would have seen it above all as an occasion to be met by a French painter, one who could see and feel, one who would be inspired to bring into his work the emotions of a nation sternly taking vengeance on her ancient enemy, redeeming the defeat of twenty years before, of a world advancing on a stormy tide, of gods and tyrants overthrown together. A few weeks later, in June or July, 1782, a miniature suitable for a lady to wear was painted at Passy by the artist whom Félix Nogaret had sent there for the purpose. In the extant portrait which I believe to have come from that sitting, Gallic energy, pride, and power are all caught within the circle of gold and bursting from it like light from a jewel.

But of the two, I can have no doubt whatever that Franklin's own preference was for Joseph Wright's. The history of Wright's was for many years unknown and is still in parts obscure. The story of this other has remained even longer and more deeply enshrouded in mystery. It has remained for me to gather together what scattered bits of documentation I could find and fit them into a theory. Readers are free to form other conjectures or conclusions as they will or as new evidence comes to light. I know that Félix Nogaret commissioned a miniature and that it was painted. I have a likeness type in miniature of about the same date, but my assumption that the likeness is that sponsored by Nogaret is presumptive. If the presumption that it is his be correct, it may be assumed also that he had a nearly equal share with the artist in its making, and did everything in his power to give it such wide currency as it had. Nogaret, poet and wit, was like that, the possessor of a creative flame which burned both in the warmth of the court and the winds of the Enlightenment. The artists whom he knew and befriended were not those of established reputation, but rather those of a lesser sort who would willingly defer to the taste and putative genius of a rising littérateur. Some of the history of the origin of this portrait may well depend on the talent and tangled affairs of Nogaret.

François Félix Nogaret was born at Versailles on November 4, 1740, the third son of an official of the court.[1] His eldest brother, Armand Frédéric Ernest, was a godson of the Comte de Maurepas and under these favorable auspices rose to the post of treasurer-general of the Comte d'Artois, that pleasure-loving youngest brother of the King who in the next generation was to rule France as Charles X. Félix, small and sickly of body, not handsome but with intelligence and humor in his long, lean face, held only minor appointments to the court and owed these to his brother or to members of the noble family under whom his brother had risen to consequence. His facetious wit, some of his interest in science, and his friendship for the American cause may have been a reflection of Maurepas' or of Maurepas' relative, the Duc de La Vrillière, in whose household he was employed for a while. On August 2, 1769, he married Elisabeth Guillochin de la Chevallerie des Gaux, daughter of a successful haberdasher of Versailles. They made their home at 12 rue de Chenil, where Félix brought together a cabinet of natural history, entered into correspondence with Buffon, Voltaire, Malesherbes, and others, and turned his own quill to the production of original literary works. In 1771 he published his *Apologie de mon goût. Epitre en vers sur l'histoire naturelle,* with a dedication to Buffon. His *La Prodigue recompensée,* and *Les Voeux des cretois, histoire renouvelée des grecs,* followed and enjoyed popular success. He was elected to the academies of Angers and Marseilles. The King made him a New Year's gift of land. He was appointed librarian to the Comtesse d'Artois, thus returning in much improved station to that vast and powerful branch of the royal household of which his brother was a major functionary.

With their prosperity thus apparently assured, disaster overtook

1. The most complete biography of Nogaret is the study by Paul Fromageot, "Félix Nogaret (1740–1831)," *Revue de l'histoire de Versailles et de Seine-et-Oise* (1904), pp. 1–21, 137–51.

the elder brother and threatened the fortunes of the younger. One night in December 1778, Antoine Le Bel, secretary to the Chancellor of the Comte d'Artois, had been seized and taken to the Bastille.[2] There he remained through the months and years, implicating three others in the charges of maladministration and embezzlement which had been lodged against him. Prominent among the four defendants was the treasurer-general, Armand Nogaret, who, it was said, had not rendered an accounting in seven years and was believed to have stolen over 1,200,000 livres.[3] Bachaumont printed little biographies of the principals, telling of poor beginnings and sudden acquisitions of wealth, treating the affair both with indignation and the amusement befitting a default for which, after all, the fickleness of royalty was responsible.[4] To add to his woes, the Paris lodgings of the Sieur Armand Nogaret were swept by fire in the spring of 1781 and his collection of art treasures, including pictures of great value, was destroyed.[5] The court proceedings, in which Franklin's admirer, the famous advocate Elie de Beaumont, had a part, led at last to Armand's acquittal by a verdict issued on July 26, 1783, but his reputation had been ruined, his fortune swept away, and he never recovered from the disaster.[6]

The ruin of his brother in the "affaire Le Bel" lies in the background of Félix Nogaret's cultivation of Franklin's friendship and may explain in part some of his other activities. His venture into salacious literature brought him profit. It was published anonymously, probably to protect his position with the neglected little princess whom he served, but he was well known as the author. Along with this, a new interest in the publication of engravings may have been directed more toward securing the interest of influential persons than to yielding a profit. It was upon the matter of a new print that he opened his correspondence with Franklin.

His first letter, one of the few upon which he took the trouble to write a complete date, was sent from Versailles on March 2, 1781.

---

2. Bachaumont, *Mémoires, 14* (Aug. 3, 1779), 139. Fromageot, "Félix Nogaret," pp. 6–7.
3. Bachaumont, *15* (July 10, 1780), 216.
4. Ibid., *18* (Sept. 30, 1781), 76.
5. Ibid., *17* (May 13, 1781), 186–87.
6. Ibid., *23* (July 26, 1783), 76. Fromageot, "Félix Nogaret," p. 7.

It is one of the longest, and must surely have seemed to Franklin's eye one of the oddest, of all the missives received at the house in Passy. The letter shows us that Nogaret knew Franklin well by sight, and had probably spoken with him. It was apparently intended to inaugurate a friendly correspondence between two literary men. Such a rapport seemed doomed to failure by the very enthusiasm with which Nogaret launched into it. The eleven pages of his letter, addressed at their opening to "Sage et docte Excellence," are, for all the pomposity of their approach, deftly and gracefully composed. Franklin is told that the artists will, for better or for worse, catch his likeness as he passes, the writers celebrate his fame, and the public delight in the contemplation of his image. With Alexander the Great it was not so. The apotheosis of the tyrant is the creation of his hirelings. The sage wishes to live in obscurity, and he fails not for lack of power but because he has too much. The whole universe, admiring his modesty, casts itself at his feet. His likeness is repeated upon canvas in as great a variety of forms as it takes in the hearts of all people. By the grateful French, His Excellency will be painted and praised in a thousand variations. He continues:

> Un artiste s'est presenté chez moi ces Jours derniers. Cet homme a gravé le portrait de votre Excellence, et il se flatte, avec raison, d'en faire un grand débit. La tête a beaucoup de verité. Cependant comme cette estampe represente votre Excellence dans l'inaction, et que le tableau manque d'accessoires qui vous caractérisent, j'ai propose au graveur d'ajouter une table, sur laquelle on verrait une machine électrique, des volumes etc. Cette idée a été adopté. Maintenant il n'est plus question que de mettre un vers au bas du portrait; on veut que ce vers soit français, et l'on m'en charge.[7]

7. "An artist has called at my house these last few days. This man has engraved a portrait of your Excellency, and he flatters himself, with good reason, that it will have a large sale. The head is portrayed with truth. However, as this print represents your Excellency in inaction, and as the picture lacks accessories to characterize you, I have proposed to the engraver that he add a table on which one will see an electrical machine, books, etc. This idea has been adopted. Now it is only a question of placing a verse beneath the portrait; they want this verse to be in French, and have laid the matter in my hands." (Franklin Papers, A.P.S., *21,* no. 87.)

From this lofty peroration and small item of consequential news, he embarks upon an analysis of the problem of translating the famous *Eripuit coelo fulmen, septrumque tyrannis* into a single line, equally compact and eloquent, in his own tongue. In doing so he takes Franklin through the whole creative process within his own mind, by which he had fingered his way through to the solution, "On l'a vu désarmer les tyrans et les dieux." This is the line which appears under the engraving of Franklin the publication of which was announced on April 7, 1781.[8] We know, therefore, that the engraver was François Denis Née, and that Nogaret, preoccupied with his ideas about the inscription, failed to realize that the design was by Carmontelle and the engraver not actually at liberty to add the suggested electrical machine and books—a suggestion which reflects no credit upon the poet's taste or originality and which would have spoiled the delicately imaginative quality of the picture's pose and background. Nogaret's concern with the immediate and complex intricacies of poetic expression must excuse him, and these take up the remainder of his letter, leading from the problem of the one-line translation into a thirty-seven-line original composition, concluding with a briefer, climactic, "Vers pour mettre sous le Portrait de M. Franklin."

Franklin's reply, returned a week later, protested with some evident distaste the "Flood of Compliments." To Nogaret's plea for approval or criticism of the translation he replied, "If I were, which I really am not, sufficiently skilled in your excellent language, to be a proper Judge of its Poesy, the Supposition of my being the Subject, must restrain me from giving any Opinion on that line, except that it ascribes too much to me, especially in what relates to the Tyrant."[9] Nogaret's response was a gift of books, and a letter in which he was moved to declare himself corrected and, in the light of Franklin's modesty, more deeply his admirer than ever. He added, as a small note of personal triumph, that the print with the one-line inscription in French had appeared and was indeed, as he had predicted, making the fortune of the engraver.[10]

Those gifts of books must have included some of Nogaret's re-

8. *Mercure de France.* See Catalogue, CARMONTELLE.
9. March 8, 1781 (Smyth, *Writings, 8,* 214–15).
10. April 18, 1781 (Franklin Papers, A.P.S., *21,* no. 146).

cent anonymous works, his *Le Fruit de ma quête, ou L'Ouverture du sac* of 1779, and more surely his *Le Fond du sac, ou Restant des babioles de M. X...*, printed in Venice in 1780 in two volumes with illustrations by Pierre Louis Durand, and his more famous *L'Aristénète français* of the same year.[11] From this last work, recalling the style and substance of the letters of a Greek rhetorician of the early Christian era, he became known as the "French Aristenetos," a cognomen which no doubt suited his fancy for casual, amusing, polished whimsy, with the spice of eroticism and veiled authorship. It was esoteric in an advanced, sophisticated, yet also warmly personal way. Nogaret's dedication to the Masonic fraternity was wholly in character. It gave him a place in a ritual to which, for special occasions, he contributed solemn verse and prose, gave him an intellectual and social outlet, and, with these, an involvement in charitable good works which appealed strongly also to his humanity and good nature. He appears to have been one of the most active members of the Lodge of Patriotism of Versailles, and he was affiliated also with the Lodge of the Nine Sisters at Paris, in which Franklin held so prominent a place.

On October 9, 1781, he sent Franklin a small engraving, "Mon Allégorie en l'honneur de feue Marie Thérèse." The gift was delivered in a manner well calculated to appeal to the old man, brought to him by the little Nogaret daughter, accompanied by her nurse, and the letter with it explained how the child had been forever prattling happily of Franklin.[12] The print honors the memory of the Queen of Hungary and Bohemia, the mother of Marie Antoinette, who had died on November 28, 1780, and is expressive of the shadow of grief cast upon the nations by her pass-

11. Durand prepared illustrations for the second work, but they were not published with it until over a century later, in Nogaret's *L'Aristénète français, illustré de cinquante compositions de Durand, gravées à l'eau-forte par E. Champolion,* 2 vols. Paris, 1897. It is of particular significance here that Durand was an older artist who had been at the height of his career in the preceding reign, and who was also a miniaturist and an enamelist. Diderot in commenting on the Salon of 1761 had praised his work, stating that any gentleman who could procure from him an enamel after Greuze would have in effect an original work. "Une bonne copie en émail est presque regardée comme un original, et cette sorte de peinture est particulièrement destinée à copier." (Alphonse Maze-Sencier, *Le Livre des collectioneurs,* Paris, 1885, p. 511.) There is no evidence to connect Durand with the miniature painted for Nogaret, but he must certainly have influenced Nogaret's connoisseurship.

12. Franklin Papers (A.P.S.), *23,* no. 10.

ing.[13] Nogaret sent the original drawing as his gift to the Queen of France. This was aiming high for favor and, as it happened, just at the time when the Queen was about to gain her due distinction as mother of the royal heir. With the birth of a dauphin on October 22, 1781, Nogaret's patroness the Comtesse d'Artois, already the mother of two sons and a daughter, was deprived of her brief and only claim to historical importance.

This brings the story back to the spring of 1782 when, on April 23, Nogaret advised William Temple Franklin as to the address of a painter, and Joseph Wright was selected to paint the portrait for Mr. Oswald.[14] A month later, on May 24, Félix Nogaret made his own appeal for a new life portrait. It had to be from life so as to be worthy of the significance of the moment, reflect its sponsor's taste, and have true proprietary value. Getting the old man actually to pose was the rub. There is no telling whether or not he knew that Joseph's work was largely a copy, but he was as well aware as anyone of the difficulties. It had been apropos of one or another of the portraits, Duplessis' probably, that Franklin had told Nogaret how, in eight days' time, he had suffered twenty times with a cramp in the neck.[15] Nogaret made his appeal upon the grounds most likely to succeed: it was to be a miniature, a treasured gift for his wife who had been pleading for it long and earnestly, who wished to wear it upon her bosom in love and allegiance to the philosopher enshrined within her heart. He had in readiness a painter who could catch an accurate likeness in two hours only— and who would do the work for nothing. The letter of May 24, 1782, follows:

13. "Filiae, Uxori, Matrique Caesarum. / Delineavit P. L. Durand. Sculpsit M. Fessard, cum privilegio. / Praesentibus et Posteria / Offerebat Felix–Nogaret, Massilienis. et Andegavenis. Acad. socius, invor. / Anno MDCC, LXXXI. / Se trouve à Paris, chez Fessard, Graveur rue et Isle St. Louis, chez le Charon." Other Latin inscriptions occur within the design, which may be described as rococo effusion at its worst, and emphatically a conception of the pedantic poet. The plate size is 13 9/16 x 9 in. It is in marked contrast to the unity and dignity of the smaller print upon the same theme engraved by Jean Michel Moreau le Jeune after the design by Louis Jean Jacques Durameau. The latter is described and illustrated by Henri de Chennevières, "Les Archives de la Chalcographice du Louvre," *L'Art, 45* (1888), 50, 53.

14. The address of the unnamed painter given by Nogaret was the Comtesse d'Artois Inn, across from the Marc d'Or. (Franklin Papers, A.P.S., *107,* no. 86.)

15. Nogaret, *L'Isle des sages,* pp. 118–19.

Sage Docteur! homme pour qui c'est peu d'être en général utile au monde: Je vous dois des remercimens, et je vais vous demander une nouvelle faveur. Laissez nous ma femme et moi vous marquer notre reconnaissance par une preuve de notre vénération pour vous. Ma femme, depuis Longtems, me persecute pour que j'obtienne de vous la permission de vous laisser peindre en miniature: Elle desire vous avoir en médaillon pendu à son Col. Comme elle n'est pas jeune et que ses respectueux sentimens vous sont connus, quel inconvénient verriés vous à accorder cette grace à celle qui vous voit avec la tendresse d'une fille pour son Père, et l'admiration? Je me tais de peur de vous déplaire en disant quelque chose de plus. J'ai un peintre qui a le mérite de saisir parfaitement la ressemblance: Je viens de lui faire, il y a quinze jours le portrait de notre nouvel Archevêque M. de Juigné; Je lui ai fait peindre Mad. La Comtesse d'artois et Les Princes: je suis sûr de son talent, et je voudrais profiter du moment ou je puis disposer de lui. On ne vous volera pas plus de deux heures de votre tems; c'est beaucoup; Mais qu'est-ce que cela pour répondre au voeu de deux personnes dont le coeur est penetré de sensibilité? Qu'est-ce que pour répondre au désire pressant d'une femme jalouse de faire voir, par cette enseigne, qu'elle vous a gravé dans son esprit et dans son coeur? N'allez pas lui faire un refus dans l'intention de ménager sa bourse. Le peintre me doit son état, il me presse depuis longtems de lui fournir quelque occasion de nous marquer sa reconnaissance: il se trouvera heureux de saisir cette circonstance d'obliger ma femme; et il n'aura jamais aussi bien travaillé, ni d'aussi bon coeur.

Je suis à cette heure à Compiègne près de mon fils qui studie au college Royal de cette ville. Je serai à Versailles Le 20 Juin: J'aurai l'honneur de vous aller présenter mes hommages en passant. Vous me dirés quel jour enfin vous voulez bien prendre pour

163

sceller chez moi notre connaissance le verre en main.
Vous me dirés si vous permettés que le peintre se
rende chez vous quelque jour, et l'heure de votre com-
modité.

Accorde à ma femme ce qu'elle désire, et je m'engage à porter la reconnaissance jusqu'à ne vous rien
demander Jamais que la continuation d'un attache-
ment, qui nous honnore beaucoup sans doute, Mais
qui, j'ose dire, est pourtant du à l'affection et au respect avec lesquels j'ai l'honneur d'être, in nomine
amborum, totus tuus fidelis, et beneficiorum memor
felix nogaret[16]

Franklin acquiesced to this warm appeal soon after the miniature was made. Aglow with Masonic brotherhood, pride of pos-

16. "Wise doctor! Man to whom it is but little to be generally useful to the whole
world: I owe you my thanks and I seek a new favor from you. Permit us, my wife and
me, to confirm our gratitude by a demonstration of our veneration for you. My wife
has long pestered me to obtain your consent to be painted in miniature. She wishes to
have you hung en medaillon at her throat. As she is not young and as her feeling of
respect is known to you, what inconvenience can you see in granting this favor to one
who regards you with the tenderness of a daughter for her father, and a like admiration? Fearful of displeasing you, I hesitate to mention something more. I have a painter
who has the merit of making a perfect likeness. I just had him paint, fifteen days ago,
the portrait of our new Archbishop, M. de Juigné; I had him paint the portrait of Mad.
the Comtesse d'Artois and the Princes: I am sure of his talent, and am eager to profit
by the moment when he is at my command. It would not take more than two hours of
your time; that is a great deal; But what is it against the wish of two persons whose
hearts are infused with sensibility? What is it to answer the compelling desire of a
woman eager to declare, by this sign, that you are engraved in her soul and in her
heart? Do not refuse in order to spare expense. The painter owes his situation to me,
he has been urging me for a long time to give him an opportunity to show his gratitude:
he will be happy to take this occasion to oblige my wife; and he will never have worked
so well, or with a better heart.

"I am now at Compiegne with my son who is a student at the royal college in this
town. I will be at Versailles on June 20: I will have the honor of paying my respects in
passing. You will tell me at what date you can at last seal our acquaintance at my
house, glass in hand. You will tell me if you can permit the painter to call upon you
some day, and the hour that suits you.

"Grant my wife that which she desires, and I pledge to carry the acknowledgment
so far as never to ask anything more beyond the continuance of an attachment, which
honors us much without doubt, but which, I daresay, flows above all from the affection
and respect with which I have the honor to be, in the name of both, wholly faithful to
thee, and of favors mindful" (Franklin Papers, University of Pennsylvania, 6, no.
28). Postscripts add that the letter was accompanied by an epitaph on a frog, no doubt
in verse, and a printed letter in which Franklin is mentioned on p. 12.

session, and personal gratitude, Nogaret acknowledged its receipt from the painter in a letter dated July 1782:

Excellent Docteur et très cher f. ·.

Recevez nos sincères remercimens du cadeau sans prix que vous avez eu la bonté de nous faire. Le Peintre ne nous la remis qu'aujourd'hui jeudi. Puissiez vous vivre autant que durera votre portrait. Ce bijou devient un immeuble dont personne de nous ne peut jamais être tenté de se déffaire : il passera dans la famille de père en fils, et sera respecté des générations futures qui l'auront, quand la famille de son possesseur sera éteinte. Ma femme devrait vous aller assûrer, chez vous, de toute sa sensibilité; mais vous avez tant d'affaires, et nous sommes si peu sûrs de vous voir sans vous gêner, que nous croirons commetre une indiscretion, si nous entreprenions ce petit voyage, sans avoir obtenu de vous la faveur d'être avertis du jour où notre présence ne vous sera pas importune.

Permettez, Sage Docteur, Le plus vénérable de tous les V. ·. que je vous embrasse trois fois sur les deux joues, cinq, si vous voulez; et que je n'engage à avoir la gorge coupée plutôt que oublier jamais combien m'est précieuse votre amitié paternelle et fraternelle.

Tels sont les sentimens de votre respecteux et fidèle serviteur

f. ·. felix-Nogaret[17]

17. "Excellent Doctor and very dear F.·.

"Accept our sincere thanks for the priceless gift you have had the goodness to make us. The painter only just delivered it today, Thursday. May you live as long as your portrait will endure. This jewel becomes a personal possession from which not one of us can ever be tempted to part: it will pass in the family from father to son, and will be venerated in future generations when the family of its possessor will be extinct. My wife should call at your house to assure you of her heartfelt appreciation; but your affairs are so great, and we are so unsure of seeing you without inconveniencing you, that we fear we might commit an indiscretion if we undertook this little trip, without having obtained from you the favor of a word as to the day when our presence would not be inopportune.

Grant, Wise Doctor, the most venerable of all the V.·. that I kiss you three times on both cheeks, five, if you wish; and may my throat be cut rather than ever forget how precious your paternal and fraternal affection is to me." (Ibid., 7, no. 14.)

Unhappily, while this miniature may well endure through the years and even beyond the extinction of his family, just as Nogaret predicted that it would, I have as yet found no extant painting which can be identified with it beyond doubt. The problem is therefore to draw from these and from other letters what clues we can as to the artist and the character of the picture. His request for the sitting is a persuasive rather than informative document, and shows an awareness of even Franklin's sense of thrift. Yet there are here and in the letter of thanks some clues as to the character of the work and the identity of the artist. For example:

Letter of May 24, 1782
1   The painting was a miniature, to be worn by a lady "à son Col" —that is, either hung about her neck or as a brooch.
2   The painter, able to catch a perfect resemblance in the span of two hours, had made for Nogaret only fifteen days before a portrait of the new Archbishop of Paris, and had also painted for him the Comtesse d'Artois with her sons.
3   The painter owed his present standing to Nogaret and was eager to repay his patron with other works of art, suggesting, though with no certainty whatsoever, a young artist or a provincial.

The letter of July, 1782
1   While such an interpretation is not at all secure from doubt, Nogaret's emphasis upon his expectation that the miniature would endure forever suggests a miniature in the permanent medium, enamel.
2   His hesitation to express his gratitude in person appears to confirm his awareness that important conferences were in progress at the embassy.

The Archbishop's portrait is the clue to the painter. The King's appointment of Antoine Éléonore Léon Leclerc de Juigné to the archbishopric in December 1781 had been received with much acclaim. He was a churchman dedicated to piety and good works on the one hand, and holding a liberal view of the intellectual enlightenment, on the other. Upon both counts he would have commanded the admiration of Félix Nogaret. I have not been able to locate the miniature, but have found the engraving made from it. The publication of this ambitious print was announced by Bachaumont on November 21, 1782, and an impression of it had come to Franklin as a New Year's gift the following January.[18] I interpret it both as an act of genuine deference and as a courtier's gesture invoking favorable notice in a high quarter. It might also represent a publishing venture for profit, since the design was conceived by Nogaret himself and acknowledged to him on the plate. Here the Archbishop's portrait, oval, 6½ by 5⅜ inches in size, is surrounded by an arrangement of allegorical scenes, figures and symbols filling a plate of 16⅜ by 11¾ inches.[19] The name of the artist is engraved directly under the portrait in fine script, "Pinxit Castrique."

Of Castrique I have been able to find only the barest record. A humble figure he must have been if it is true that he stood indebted and in allegiance to so minor a courtier as the librarian of the Comtesse d'Artois. In the vast literature of the art he is described only as a miniature painter of the late eighteenth century who used a fine stroke technique and ran to gray tones—an estimate I would suspect to be based upon one or two works only and which is reinforced by no citation of actual paintings.[20] Even his given name is unknown. His *oeuvre* apparently reposes in anonymity or has been attributed to other artists. I have so far searched in vain for his miniature of the countess and the princes.[21]

In the letter of thanks there is only a warm note of satisfaction to answer the important question as to whether the artist had been successful in obtaining the requested sitting of two hours, or

18. Bachaumont, *Mémoires, 21,* 9–10 (198–200 in variant printing).

19. "Invenit F. Nogaret. Sculpsit M. Fessard cum Privilegio. / Virtutum remuneratori LUDOVICO XVI, / ob Archi-Episcopum sibi datum ANT. ELEON. LEON. LE CLERC DE JUIGNÉ. / grates agit Lutetia: / Interprete FEL. NOGARET Massiliensis et Andegavensis acad. Socio. / ANNO M.DCC.LXXXII. / AParis chez Fessard, rue et Isle St. Louis Maison de Charron vis-à-vis le Corps de Garde."

20. Leo Schidlof, *Bildnisminiaturen in Frankreich im XVII, XVIII und XIX Jahrhundert* (Wien und Leipzig, 1911), p. 274.

21. An engraving, "DEDIÉ ET PRESENTÉ À MADAME / LA COMTESSE D'ARTOIS / Par sa très humble et très Respecteuse Servante fem. Ingouf. / Gravé par P. C. Ingouf, d'après la Boîte donnée par cette Princesse à M. Busson son 1ʳ. Medecin. / A Paris chez Perrier au Collège Royal de Cambray, Place Cambray" reproduces a circular miniature of the princess and her three children. The three children appear also in a rectangular miniature attributed to Ignace Pie Victorien Campana and given the date 1780, illust. in Louis Gillet, ed., *Miniatures and Enamels from the D. David-Weill Collection* (Paris, 1957), p. 57.

whether he had been persuaded, as Joseph Wright and others perforce had been, to content himself with a copy, breathing as much new life into it as he could. If a copy, the miniature may be one of the exact or slightly variant versions of the Duplessis pastel now extant.[22] Our only recourse here is to look for an engraving. If it were a copy, there would be none. But if it were an original, there is every reason to suppose that Nogaret would have sought in one way or another to bring it to the attention of the public at large.

I move upward now into a purer air of conjecture. An engraving of a new likeness of Franklin, from a miniature, *was* published in the following year. It appeared in the second of the sumptuous and copiously illustrated volumes of Johann Kaspar Lavater's *Essai sur la physiognomie.* Lavater, a Swiss churchman and poet, came of an old family of Zurich, many of them physicians. He held a Protestant pastorate there, preaching a theology colored by the romantic mysticism of an *illuminé.* He had become known abroad by his poems and philosophical writings, was known in the arts also, and was a friend of Henry Fuseli. Félix Nogaret must have been familiar with the French version of his *Chants helvétiques,* if nothing else. In the massive work upon which his fame now rests—his study of character as revealed in the human countenance—he pursued an interest which had long been nourished in France by artists and connoisseurs. I would guess it to have been the emergence of a sublimated medical ambition. He undertook with acclaim if not with lasting success to establish this study as an exact science. His *Von der Physiognomik* of 1772 was expanded from two volumes to four in 1775–78, and from this the French translation was prepared in response to popular excitement, under his direct supervision and with three translators working from a new manuscript. The large quartos with their profusion of portrait engravings were printed at the Hague, the first appearing in 1781, the second, with the "Franklin," in 1783, its preface dated May 31, 1783.[23] From this

22. A miniature after Duplessis of this general description, grayish in tone and in a stroke technique, is owned by the A.P.S. Nogaret's statement in *L'Isle des sages* (see Chap. 7, n. 28) that the painters have resigned themselves to Franklin's unwillingness to pose, perhaps suggests that his may have done so.

23. Lavater, *Essai sur la physiognomie, destiné à faire connoître l'homme & à le faire aimer,* The Hague, 1781–1803. The Franklin portraits appear in Pt. II, pp. 280, 286.

set, completed in 1787, innumerable other editions and translations followed, the author having become famous throughout Europe as one who could, by a mere glance, discern the innermost weakness or the highest potential of any person.

There were two Franklin portraits in the volume of 1783, one a silhouette and the other that likeness type which I have described at the beginning of this chapter as intended to hold and express the emotions of victory. The portraits are printed some with names, some with identifications only in the index, and some with the identities withheld. The profile of Franklin on page 286 is not identified. The other portrait, on page 280, is unidentified in the text but listed as "Francklin" in the "Table Alphabétique" at the back of the volume. Curiously, in the English edition (London, 1792) the editors reversed this, the profile on page 318 (Vol. II, Pt. II) being listed in the table of contents as Franklin, and the other, probably because they were unable to accept the new likeness as Franklin's, as simply "portrait." However this may be, the arrangement of the book is obviously intended not as a scientific exposition of the subject so much as to show the great physiognomist in action. The pictures appear to be crowding to receive his judgments, just as people, known and unknown, came to his door, expecting their inner lives always to be revealed with the same perspicacious finality. In the book there is an added factor, itself to be marveled at: he not only characterizes the subject, but estimates the value of the artist's depiction of it.

I have no evidence that it was Nogaret who sent a copy of this new miniature to Lavater. I can merely conjecture that the whole procedure would have appealed to him. The thinly-veiled identities of many of the portraits, easily guessed by the cognoscenti, would pique curiosity and excite conversation here as the same procedure did with his own works. There is a Masonic flavor about it all, and indeed a Masonic connection may have existed. Dietholm Lavater (1741–1826), a physician and perhaps an elder brother of Johann, was Grand Master at Zurich. One cannot, of course, rely too heavily on this. As Marie Antoinette said of the Masons in 1781, "Tout le monde en est." But it fits into the pattern. Whoever did submit it had one specific and obvious purpose in doing so. This was a new likeness of a great man taken at an historic moment, but also at a time when other images of him had been well established in the minds of the public. Its action and vigor set it quite apart from those which had gone before, and every artist of the time knew the hazards of trying to gain acceptance for a variant pose and characterization of a widely-known figure. People would simply refuse to accept it as a correct resemblance. Some special effort was needed to fix it in popular favor, and nothing could have done so to better effect than its publication in Lavater's gigantic work-in-progress. It could have done so, that is, if Lavater had extolled the piece. Lavater, alas, did nothing of the sort, and the obscurity which has so long hung over this particular likeness may be ascribed to his emphatic condemnation of it.

He observes that the plate entitled "Addition G" presents a particularly difficult problem to the physiognomist, who must judge the subject from a portrait in which there is not one single element of exact truth. He concedes a certain unity of forehead, hair, and chin, but finds the wrinkles about the eyes insufficiently and incorrectly emphasized. Above all, the mouth should be less tightly compressed and its form less undulating. Having thus defined the faults of the picture, he then declares that he can perceive, in his own corrected vision of it, the character of a man who is not to be trifled with, and whose mere presence would expose and overawe men of venial spirit. One is almost compelled to believe that Lavater knew full well the identity of the subject, and had before him for comparison some of the earlier engravings of Franklin.

The Lavater engraving gives us our earliest dating of this portrait type. Allowing due intervals for communication between Paris, Zurich, and the Dutch printers, and for the making of the plate, the date moves back to 1782 and is approximately coincident with that of Nogaret's project. The Lavater engraving also gives us a clue to later repetitions of the likeness. I believe that the stronger and freer versions of it are not closer to the original, as one might normally conclude, but are the efforts of other artists to correct it along the lines of Lavater's criticism.

Of late years the type has been generally attributed to Jacques Thouron, a Swiss miniaturist, because of the existence at the Louvre of two similar versions, one on ivory and one on enamel, attributed to him. It has also been given to Jean Baptiste Weyler, an Alsatian following the same profession in Paris. The Thouron miniatures have been at the Louvre since 1832. The earliest recorded attribution of the type to Weyler is in the catalogue of the Lenoir sale, Paris, 1874. From the description there of its setting, this appears to be that which came later into the David-Weill collection in Paris. It is a tiny enamel in an elaborate Louis Seize setting of gold and pearls, fluent and dainty. The possibility of its having been the Nogaret heirloom is quite eligible. The attribution to Weyler is supported also by a curious yet substantial thread of contemporary evidence.

I have found in the Franklin Papers a formal communication with the engraved letterhead of the Masonic Lodge of Saint John at Carcassonne in which, under the date of June 24, 1783, Franklin is notified of his installation, *in absentia,* as a member.[24] In it M. Vidal de Saint Martial acknowledges Franklin's letter of March 1 accepting membership in the brotherhood at Carcassonne. That letter must have been one of genuine fraternal warmth, for we learn that the reading of it had been received "avec tous les transports de la joye la plus vive. Il étoit impossible de contenir nos fréres. Les applaudissements et les Vivats les plus rédoublés retentissoint de L'orient à L'occident." He explains that Franklin had been represented at the affair by his portrait, and extols the picture: "Un peintre excellent Italien et Maçon a copié votre portrait d'après Veilles peintre en mignature sur l'Émail à Paris. Ceux qui ont le bonheur de vous voir ne peuvent se méprendre à ses traits. C'est cette image qui a été apportée en Triomphe le jour de votre affiliation. Une deliberation de la Loge ordonne quelle ressera perpétuelement dans notre Temple."

I confess to having been mystified at the first by the attribution to "Veilles" of the work which the excellent Italian and Mason had

---

24. Franklin Papers (A.P.S.), *187,* no. 1. The reading of the letter from Franklin had been received "with the liveliest transports of joy. It was impossible to restrain our brothers. The most vociferous applause and cheering reechoed from east to west." Of the picture, "An excellent painter, an Italian and a Mason, has copied your portrait after Veilles, painter in miniature on enamel at Paris. Those who have had the good fortune to see you cannot fail to recognize its features. This is the image which has been carried in triumph on the day of your affiliation. A resolution of the Lodge ordains that it will remain forever in our Temple."

copied, and to have groped rather blindly in search of a painter, or indeed of anyone, with such a name. Considered phonetically, the answer at once appears. Weyler is the "painter in miniature on enamel at Paris," and this spelling is but one of various French efforts to deal with his Germanic name. The temple in which the copy was to repose forever vanished soon afterward in the whirlwind of events, and the painting, unless it be one recorded briefly at the time of the Franklin bicentennial, has long been lost to sight.

A self-portrait on canvas, now in the gallery at Versailles, shows us Weyler as a handsome, blue-eyed man of about thirty-five, hair curled and powdered but without undue care, shirt open at the throat, a plain rough greatcoat over his shoulders, and a large green portfolio held in hand and arm. He had studied his difficult art in his native Strasbourg, had come in 1763 to the studio of Joseph Marie Vien at Paris, and was admitted as an associate of the Académie Royale in 1775. Bachaumont, on September 23 of that year, praises the "productions de M. Weiler, nouveau concurrent, dont le pinceau brillant est surtout précieux par la vivacité du coloris & la vérité des étoffes," and later cites "Weyser" and Pierre Adolph Hall, the great Swedish miniaturist, as well-matched rivals in their work on ivory and in enamel.[25] I would attach some significance to the fact that he had painted an unusual number of prominent persons—of American interest, Lafayette as well as Franklin—and that in recognition of this he was, in 1785, authorized by the government to form a "Parthenon" of the great historic figures. After his death on July 25, 1791, this work was continued by his widow and former pupil, Louise Bourdic (later Mme. Kugler). During his lifetime Weyler exhibited regularly at the Salon, but the catalogues unfortunately list most of his work simply as miniatures grouped together under single numbers, and I have found no reference to his portrait of Franklin either in catalogue or critical comment. The *Livret* of 1789, however, does refer to his ambition to preserve in permanent form the likenesses of the great of his own and former times:

25. The "productions of M. Weiler, new associate, whose brilliant brush is above all superlative in animation of coloring and accurate rendering of materials." (Bachaumont, *Mémoires, 13,* 178; *24,* p. 35.) Weyler was admitted to full membership in 1779.

M. Weyler, voulant retracer à la France des grands
hommes qui ont illustré la nation, & ceux qui s'illus-
strent de nos jours, ne pouvant se procurer des origi-
naux qu'avec beaucoup de peine & de démarches,
invite instamment le Public, possesseur de ces trésors,
de vouloir bien les lui prêter. Les esquisses en pastel
qu'il a l'honneur d'offrir à ses regards, & qui doivent
être exécuter en émail, afin de porter leurs noms à la
postérité la plus reculée, sont toutes copiées d'après des
tableaux qui ont le grand mérite de la ressemblance,
mais peu sont peints par mains de maître. L'Auteur se
flatte qu'en faveur d'une enterprise dont il s'honore, le
Français s'empressera à lui épargner des recherches
qui nécessairement lui sont perdre un temps precieux.
Il espére témoigner sa reconnaissance au public ne le
faisant juge à toutes les expositions du Sallon du
Louvre de son application à remplir une tâche aussi
intéressante.[26]

In brief, it is possible that Weyler's dedication to the idea of preserving in enamel authentic portraits of the great, endorsed by the
government in 1785, had been privately pursued in 1782–83, and it
is possible that whoever contributed this new "victory" likeness of
Franklin to Lavater gave it also to Weyler, and from the same motive of gaining for it an immediate recognition.

Jacques Thouron, whose name has been most frequently attached
to the portrait, was almost of an age with Weyler. He had been
born at Geneva on March 6, 1749, and had learned his art there.
He was the son of a goldsmith, and his career was more wholly

26. "M. Weyler, wishing to recall to France the great men who have shed luster
on the nation and on our own times, able to procure originals only at great labor and
expense, now calls upon the owners of these treasures willingly to lend them to him.
The sketches in pastel which he has the honor of bringing to their attention, and which
should be executed in enamel, finally to carry their names to farthest posterity, are all
copied after pictures which have the great merit of resemblance, but are rarely from
the hands of masters. The artist trusts that to further an enterprise by which he honors
himself, the French people will be eager to lighten that burden of research which necessarily takes his precious time. He hopes to receive the recognition of the public without
facing, at all the exhibitions of the Salon of the Louvre, its judgment upon his application to the completion of so interesting a task." (*Livret,* Salon of 1789, no. 338, p. 58.)

given to the related craft of enamelist than was the other's. Weyler,
coming to the metropolis, had entered the studio of a front-ranking
painter. Thouron instead had formed a partnership with an enamelist already established there, and, concentrating on this, had
progressed from copied to original work. He achieved a high degree of success, becoming painter to Monsieur, the younger brother
of the King and elder brother of the Comte d'Artois. A brilliant
craftsman and artist, but moody and hypersensitive, he died on
March 13, 1789, reportedly as the result of an injustice or humiliation inflicted upon him by the Comte d'Artois.[27] Thouron was never
received into the Académie Royale. His exhibition record is confined to two appearances in La Blancherie's Salon de la Correspondance. In 1781 he showed there three enamels, all from subjects
after other artists, and in 1782 a "Portrait de M. Bourit, chantré
de l'église de Genève; émail d'après nature."[28] It would seem strange
that if he had made a miniature of Franklin in the summer of 1782
or thereabouts it was not shown at this Salon of which Franklin was
a prominent supporter and in which his portrait so frequently appeared.

Miniatures in a rough and vigorous style of painting, with
romantic dash and energy in the pose, lacking that delicate and
finished execution, that air of pleasant and settled well-being in
the subject typical of the time, are attributed to both Thouron
and Weyler. Thouron's portrait of an unknown old man, owned by
the Musée d'Art et d'Histoire in Geneva, has the same forceful,
wind-blown individuality as the "Franklin." Indeed, it resembled
Franklin more than some portraits which have been mistakenly
identified as his. Forcefully conceived in the same way is a miniature of Weyler's, recorded in the Mannheim sale of 1913 as a likeness of Franklin, actually a double miniature in enamel, "portraits
presumés de Franklin et de sa femme" (see Pl. 43).

The best documentation of a picture is of course the artist's signature, especially when he has had the good sense to add to it
the date. But in the Franklin portraits of this type, it is notably
lacking. There are no examples signed by Weyler or Thouron. Two

27. Henri Bouchot, *La Miniature française. 1750–1825, 1* (Paris, 1907), 82–83.
28. Emile Bellier de la Chavignerie, "Les Artistes français du XVIIIᵉ siècle oubliés
ou dédaignés," *Revue universelle des arts, 21* (1866), 108.

174

enamels are signed "D.C.," one dated 1785, and the other, "Avril, 1785," the year Franklin's departure from France brought a new demand for his portrait. "D.C." has never been identified beyond Clouzot's statement that he had been an apprentice in the studio of Thouron.[29] Louis François Aubry (1767–1851) left an example signed "Aubry pinxt.," but this cannot be dated earlier than the last years of the eighteenth century.[30] A signed piece by Abraham Constantin (1785–1855) is, of course, later still.[31]

An artist's signature is a matter of individual taste and pride not rigidly governed by custom. It is fairly safe to expect, however, that he would sign his first original but not (as with the Duplessis "Franklin") his replicas. It is only among the enamelists that one occasionally finds a signature placed by the maker upon his copy from another artist. The enamelists' complex technique places them in a different class from the other miniature painters. The artist had generally before him a completed work, his own or another's, from which, in the successive firings, he produced the new, jewel-like work in the permanent medium. The enamel was essentially a form of reproduction, as was the making of a copperplate for an engraving, and the problem of authorship is obscured by the frequency with which each craftsman made use of the work of others. In 1785 "D.C." made not only the likeness in question, but an enamel version of the Greuze "Franklin."[32] Individual style, sometimes as good as a signature, is here acceptable evidence only after careful study of the history of each piece.

It is impossible for me to offer a mature judgment on the basis of composition, pose and technique. The rough, bold style of the miniatures at the Louvre and of some other works attributed to Thouron is found also in Weyler's. Of the two Louvre miniatures, the ivory is the stronger and more free, while the enamel is defined with somewhat greater detail and its lines closer to the Lavater engrav-

29. Henri Clouzot, *Dictionnaire des miniaturistes sur émail* (Paris, 1924), p. 42.

30. Reproduced in *Sale of Rare Books, Manuscripts and Autograph Letters,* (Anderson Galleries, New York, Dec. 18, 1928), p. 31, no. 169. Another, perhaps the same, is recorded in Godefroy Mayer's catalogue, *No. 30. Old Paintings, Drawings, Miniatures* (Paris, 1910), p. 1.

31. Recorded in *Golden Jubilee Fiftieth Annual Exhibition of Miniatures* (Philadelphia, Pennsylvania Academy of the Fine Arts, 1951), p. 41, no. 190.

32. Sotheby and Co. sale catalogue (London, May 16, 1957), no. 37.

ing—suggesting that the ivory may not be the study from which the enamel was made, but rather an effort to strengthen it. The two "D.C." enamels are both close to the Lavater engraving.

One feature of this portrait type is the pure white of the hair. Franklin's hair was tinged with iron gray. Such a variation suggests at first that gradual deviation from truth which occurs in copies of copies; yet here I am willing to believe the color of the hair to be the artist's deliberate choice, so obviously and effectually does it support the flashing energy of the tiny picture.

Remote though the possibility of a connection may be, one other name should be mentioned as perhaps related to the history of this portrait. Joseph Ducreux, painter in oil and pastel, an artist whose portraits are sometimes marked by vigorous and unusual pose, exhibited a pastel of Franklin at the Salon de la Correspondance in 1782. I have been unable to learn anything of its origin, character, or later history. An elusive oil portrait attributed to Ducreux has turned out to be only another of the many erroneously identified as "Franklin." That Weyler's miniature was made from the Ducreux pastel, or the pastel from it, are unsupported thus far by any evidence.

From the evidence, fragmentary and fragile as it is, it is clear only that in 1782 a new likeness in miniature was made—dramatic, idealized, and yet with an authentic force. It was engraved for the enormously popular *Essai sur la physiognomie,* and was reproduced in enamel by Weyler. With this, there exists the strong, still unproven, possibility that it originated as the gift for Mme. Nogaret.

Félix Nogaret, at the time of the portrait, was looking about for a better sinecure than that which he held with the Savoyard princess. In a letter of April 1, 1783, he acknowledges Franklin's kindness in recommending him, as Buffon had already done, for the post of librarian to the Marquis de Serreul.[33] Poet and flatterer, plain citizen and courtier, cynic and sentimentalist, he continued to play a dual role through life, emerging anon as the Jacobin whose *Cantate à l'Eternelle* was chanted by its devotees before the Temple of Reason, and whose occupation was described in an official report

33. Franklin Papers (A.P.S.), *28,* no. 2. Nogaret is still described as "Bibliothécaire de Madame Comtesse d'Artois" on the title page of his *Fictions, discours, poèmes, lyriques,* published "A Memphis, 1787."

as "Poète pour chanter la Revolution."[34] Napoleon, finding in him a devout imperialist, made him dramatic censor, a duty which he executed with servile exactitude.[35] His last years were spent in Paris, supported by the small pension of a civil servant, a very old man who professed to find "encore dans la commerce des muses quelques consolations."[36] He died there on June 2, 1831.[37]

Presumably, the Franklin miniature had remained with him until the close of this long life, secure through all the perils and confusions of the Revolution. It cannot, however, be traced further. There is no evidence to link it to the two miniatures received by the Louvre in 1832, nor to the enamel so obviously made for a lady to wear, which came into the collection of Mme. Lenoir and was sold with it in 1874.

In summary, at least a date can be given to this portrait, and with it the names of three artists, Castrique, Weyler, and Thouron. Of the three, Castrique has perhaps the best claim to its original authorship.[38] We have Nogaret's letters to show that he painted a miniature of Franklin in June or July, 1782, and we have reason to believe that this miniature of the same date is his. Weyler and Thouron, in the light of the works attributed to them, might be credited with strengthening and improving the likeness. Lavater's criticism of the mouth is well taken, and in particular the miniature on ivory at the Louvre is truer both to Franklin and to the historic moment depicted.[39] A more distant echo is found in the little high-relief portraits in wax attributed to Curtius, an effort also to amend the Lavater engraving along the lines of Lavater's criticism.[40]

It is worth noting, however, that "D.C." in 1785 was making miniatures still close to the original as it is reflected in the Lavater engraving. That long-mysterious British miniaturist "C.D." was identified by the happy circumstance of his name's appearing in

34. Fromageot, "Félix Nogaret," p. 17.

35. Ibid., p. 139.

36. A. V. Arnault, &c., *Biographie nouvelle des contemporains 15* (Paris, 1824), 106–07.

37. Fromageot, "Félix Nogaret," p. 150.

38. The portrait is catalogued, below, under WEYLER, as its earliest actual documentation is in his name.

39. See Catalogue, WEYLER, No. 4, 5. Pl. 34 A, B.

40. See Catalogue, WEYLER, No. 9. Pl. 34 D.

Franklin's accounts, but no such stroke of luck has as yet revealed the identity of "D.C." Could this have been Castrique himself, turned enamelist and repeating his own likeness? It would be pleasant to think so, if only for the pleasure of imagining a young artist adhering strictly to his own personal vision of the great man, whatever writers might write or other painters paint to the contrary.

9 THE LAST SHADOW

THE PORTRAITURE of gods and famous men demands a standardization of the image. For deification to be successful, the worshipers must be of one mind upon the visual focal point. In the cult of liberty and of Franklin, Duplessis' painting assumed a certain ascendancy at once. Caffiéri's bust was borne toward this goal on the impetus of countless engravings and Sèvres profiles, passing the Nini in popularity. Then Houdon's, promoted by its author, accepted by the Masonic fraternity, sustained by Franklin's friendship for Houdon and, above all, by its success as a characterization, took first place. Houdon's gained acceptance as the best medallic profile, a use begun in Franklin's lifetime by Dupré and Bernier, and continued by many others. Though Houdon's is as near as we are likely to get, there is still no one, standard Franklin face, and I should like to think that not only the multiplicity of interpretations but the enduring, sensible, ever-various humanity of the man himself created this situation. It is as impossible to sum him up in a single portrait as in an epigram. He cannot be approached with reverence: as some images of the saints of old are said to have responded to their worshipers' adoration with physical movement, so would Franklin's big body have begun to shake with amusement at what was going on. Franklin is not to be worshiped but to be understood, and the portraits are true to him in the measure of their honesty and candor. Their historic significance lies in the strength of their symbolic appeal for the Enlightenment and for the Ameri-

179

can cause, and it lies in the fact that they gave concrete, human form, not to the power he held, but to the ideas and the fundamental honesty by which that power had been created.

Franklin returned to his beloved Philadelphia in the summer of 1785, after an absence of almost ten years. He had left behind with his friend Le Veillard the Duplessis pastel from which copies continued to be made for other friends in France. Later, Mme. Lavoisier painted one for herself and another as a gift for him. He had brought with him the miniature long attributed to Duplessis but which must actually be a copy, perhaps by Graincourt. Apparently he did not bring with him a cast of the Houdon bust, though he may have brought one of those by Caffiéri. He consented, soon after his arrival, to sit to Charles Willson Peale—a new portrait for Peale's new gallery of heroes of the Revolution. Here again was the straightforward reporting so appropriate to the picture's subject. It was seen by the public in "Peale's Museum" for the next seventy years, was published by Peale in a mezzotint of 1787, and repeated in an enlarged replica of 1789, becoming by far the best known of the American portraits. In Franklin's estimation it appears to have served in the same way as the Duplessis, relieving him of any further sense of obligation to pose formally for a painter.

Robert Edge Pine had certainly to content himself with a copy from Peale in spite of his mission as an historical painter. Franklin must, however, have posed for the miniature which I have here attributed to John Ramage. The miniature is wholly undocumented, beyond a history of ownership in the Franklin family. It is a full-face portrait, simple and direct, with the spectacles in heavy prominence. It was probably painted by Ramage in Philadelphia in 1787. Though there is no record of his having done so, Ramage may have come to the city from New York in order to pick up business among the Constitutional Convention dignitaries, the same public for whom Peale made his mezzotint. And at the same time we have a view of Franklin of a wholly different sort in the caricature of that year, "Zion Besieg'd & Attack'd 1787."[1]

The drafting of the federal constitution had stirred into action

1. Print and accompanying broadside description are owned by the Library Company of Philadelphia. See Pl. 38 B, 39 A.

the enemies of the radically democratic Pennsylvania state constitution of 1776. Merchants, bankers, and a long roll of first citizens had become increasingly hostile to it and were now beginning to unite in the effort that would lead to its final dissolution. In "Zion besieg'd & attack'd" the old state constitution is represented by a fortress on a rock. The large plate, 14 by 18 inches, is crowded with activity. Franklin, described as *the* Genius *of the State*," can be recognized upon the ramparts commanding the garrison, one of whom holds aloft the banner of "FRANKLIN & Liberty." We glimpse a shorter, stouter figure than in the past. It is a glimpse only, for the purpose of the cartoon is to ridicule the assailants, not to extol the defenders of this doomed Gibraltar. Gouverneur Morris, the farthest advanced in the scaling of the walls, has given the most explicit statement of the attackers' purpose: "This constitution is too democratic. The people are not virtuous enough to enjoy so much liberty. We are in the Gentleman's party and will keep down those plaebeans."

Early in this year, too, the last portrait in sculpture had been made. It had nothing to do with political events. A printer-bookseller in New Haven had asked Noah Webster, who intended to call upon Franklin in Philadelphia, to obtain it for his use as a shop sign. Young Noah gave the business to the shipcarver, William Rush. It was ordered on February 9, 1787, and dispatched north on April 14. It is certainly a life portrait, though I would doubt that Franklin agreed to any prolonged sittings for it. It is groping, primitive, but true. Rush had not yet mastered that warm assurance of his later busts. This is hard, literal statement, with the new shape of the mouth, once so broad and firm, now weakened by the deterioration of old age. But should the viewer read into it the kindly interpretation it deserves, he has here again the worldly-wise, cordial, obstinate old man with whom Noah Webster could not always agree but in whom he found a mutually enjoyable companion.

The Franklin of the Rush bust is seen again in the little painted silhouette, 2½ inches high, by young Joseph Sansom. It is inscribed "Ae. 84," which dates it about 1789 or 1790. This is the last shadow, the Franklin whom the new generation of his countrymen remembered, the Franklin whom Manasseh Cutler found sitting among his friends under the mulberry tree in the garden at Franklin Court:

> I felt as if I was going to be introduced to the presence of an European Monarch. But how were my ideas changed, when I saw a short, fat, trunched old man, in a plain Quaker dress, bald pate, and short white locks, sitting without his hat under the tree, and, as Mr. Gerry introduced me, rose from his chair, took me by the hand, expressed his joy to see me, welcomed me to the city, and begged me to seat myself close to him. His voice was low, but his countenance open, frank, and pleasing. He instantly reminded me of old Captain Cummings, for he is nearly of his pitch, and no more of the air of superiority about him. I delivered him my letters. After he had read them, he took me again by the hand, and, with the usual compliments, introduced me to the other gentlemen of the company.[2]

Joseph Sansom was born on February 13, 1767, and therefore about twenty-two when he drew Franklin's profile. He died on October 4, 1826, at the end of a quiet, unobtrusive life as connoisseur and gentleman which is well summed up by an old inscription on the back of his portrait, "a man of culture in his day and an early antiquarian."[3] The "Franklin" is number 82 in a series of silhouette portraits obviously made for publication as a book. Among the other subjects are Dr. Moses Barton, aged 23, Thomas Say, aged 82, Guillaume Comte de Cockburn, aged 84, William Savery, Owen Jones, Robert Proud, Daniel Carroll, Ashbel Green, James Madison, and Tsekuyeaathaw, or the man who keeps you awake, Chief Speaker of the Five Nations, aged 30. Its title and preface are our primary documentation of the work:

2. Manasseh Cutler, *Life, Journals and Correspondence of Rev. Manasseh Cutler,* *1* (Cincinnati, 1888), 267–68.
3. Charles Coleman Sellers, *Portraits and Miniatures by Charles Willson Peale* (Philadelphia, 1952), p. 190.

AN OCCASIONAL COLLECTION of
PHYSIOGNOMICAL SKETCHES,
chiefly North Americans, and drawn from
the life; designed to preserve the characteristic
features, personally, mentally, or officially [of]
REMARKABLE PERSONS, and the endeared Memory
of PRIVATE FRIENDS or PUBLIC BENEFACTORS, with
professional Notices &c. PHILADELPHIA, 1790,
91 & 92.

Preface by the Author

The following collection is not considered as a
regular or compleat Series, under any of the heads
into which it is divided in the title page, it being for
the most part occasional, as the persons presented;
and still wanting many Fellow Citizens of each character who would have been a valuable addition to it.
It is also defective in regard to relative proportion,
being drawn from memory, without the use of a scale,
the first stroke that conveyed a resemblance necessarily determined the size of the figure, as it was
dangerous to retouch. This however is in some degree obviated by the table of contents, where the
height of each is noted in general terms, with other
personal data.

It is principally intended as a memorial of particular friends, and remarkable Contemporaries; for
though a few of the sketches record nothing more than
personal peculiarity, or professional eminence, many
of them will long be dear to their Connections; and
some perhaps interesting to posterity.—If my pencil
may be thought to have owed this small tribute to their
various merits, it has been one of the amusements of
my youth partly to discharge the obligation.

Joseph Sansom

Philada. 1792.[4]

4. Title, preface and the greater part of the collection, including the "Franklin,"
are owned by T. Morris Perot, III, Philadelphia.

One may wonder whether to accept the "from the life" of the title or the "from memory" of the preface, but I am inclined to think of the preface chiefly as evidence of the artist's apologetic and retiring character, and to regard the collection as a whole as bearing out well his ability to catch with fidelity the profile's one sure line. Of Joseph Sansom we know only enough to be sure of his devout respect for the record and his aversion to any distortion of it. Within this we find him something of a romantic, as, indeed, many antiquarians are. In Rome, wandering into the Coliseum by moonlight, he was arrested and hailed away by the watch, a mishap which would not have occurred, he confessed, "if I had not been an incorrigible Amateur of the sublime, in the composition of which, unfortunately, terror we are told by one that understood it well, is an indispensable ingredient."[5]

On this European tour he purchased a bust of Franklin, described as a cast which John Flaxman had made from the Houdon, and which he presented in 1803 to the American Philosophical Society. From 1805 to 1807 he was designing and sponsoring "A History of the Revolution" in a series of medals, on two of which Franklin was honored.[6] He was a dilettante, a gentleman traveler who made drawings to illustrate his travels.[7] He was one of the few Americans of his day with an art collection. Professor Thomas Cooper of Dickinson College mentions his "Tribute Money" by Rubens.[8] He had become sophisticated far beyond that simple, priceless silhouette of 1789, and yet Sansom was one of the new romantics and even his excursion into the medallic art had something in it of the spirit of 1787–90, the greatest splurge into allegorical fantasy our country ever had, culminating in those celebrations of the ratification of the federal constitution. Franklin had played a great part in them, and was represented with an enthusiasm and an effulgence worthy of the French. The printers of New York marched under a banner on which his medallion was encircled by

5. Joseph Sansom, *Letters from Europe during a Tour through Switzerland and Italy, 1* (Philadelphia, 1805), 510.

6. See Catalogue, SANSOM, Nos. 5, 6.

7. His drawing "The Town of Sherburne in the Island of Nantucket" was engraved by Benjamin Tanner in 1811. His *Travels in Lower Canada* (London, 1820) bears a frontispiece plate of Quebec inscribed only "From memory."

8. *Port Folio,* 2d ser. 7 (1812), 539.

the motto, "Where Liberty dwells, there is my country," with the attendant figures of Fame blowing her trumpet and Liberty holding her cap above the sage's head with "the electric fluid darting from below."[9] *Bickerstaff's Boston Almanack, Or, The Federal Calendar, For the Year of Our Redemption, 1788* indulged in a woodcut of Franklin and Washington, seated together in a chariot drawn by thirteen freemen—"the sagacious and philosophical FRANKLIN sits attentive with Spectacles on, having scan'd over the GLORIOUS WORK." French and English manufacturers saw the market, and met it with similarly decorated goods.

It is difficult for us today, dwelling in the midst of so great a pictorial abundance, to appreciate fully the meaning and influence of pictures in an earlier age. We are by the same token easily deluded into believing that artists then always aimed at photographic realism and that engravings always faithfully reproduce their sources. The artist was even more jealous of individual expression then than now, since his influence when he asserted it was greater. Portrait galleries such as that at Peale's Museum had an attraction and an impact hardly conceivable now. A good portrait had still the magic of rarity. A good portrait of any time is an image caught in a magic mirror, revealing something more than one might see face to face with its subject. It may be an interpretation or it may be something of the artist's own character projected into his work. The artists' problem with Franklin, as many of them were well aware, was to reveal somehow the understanding and persuasive thought behind those homely features. They tried it by showing him in contemplation, in action, or in laureled splendor. Some realized that it does no harm at all to show one's subject simply in the act and fact of sitting for his portrait. Whatever the pose, it is for us to seek in each what the artist sought, the reflection of that profound intelligence which is part of our lives today and will remain so. Always those eyes will give their answer, and that wide, curiously shaped mouth hold its smile.

9. *Pennsylvania Journal* (Aug. 16, 1788), p. 2, col. 2.

CATALOGUE

CATALOGUE

THIS CATALOGUE describes, by artist, the matrix portraits of Benjamin Franklin from which all others are derived, and includes also certain authoritative contemporary works not from life and some later versions which serve to substantiate the histories of their originals. It does not list all portraits of Franklin, but only those related in one way or another to this study, the concern of which is Franklin's actual appearance. Its purpose is to explore not the whole but the foundations of that iconography which did so much to sustain Franklin's historic position and to prolong his popular fame.

"Replica" is here used to denote an artist's repetition of his own work, and "Copy" to denote repetition by a different hand.

Only the owners of unique works are identified.

ALIX, PIERRE MICHEL (1762–1817)
    Ca. 1790. Color aquatint. Pl. 23. See VANLOO, No. 2.

BACHE, BENJAMIN FRANKLIN (1769–98)
    1   Ca. 1790–98. Pen-and-ink sketch. Ht. 2½ in. On margin of a page of notes, 7¼ x 4½ in. *Owner:* A.P.S., Bache Collection, Philadelphia.

    2   Same. *Owner* (1933) : Franklin Bache.

Both sketches are posthumous and casual, the doodlings of a newspaper man during idle moments. They are also recollections of

189

Franklin's appearance by one who had every reason to remember him well. In both, the strong chin and humor of the mouth are emphasized. Both show the spectacles similarly placed. The larger, and perhaps earlier (No. 1), is crudely drawn. The other (No. 2), a more careful rendering, is illustrated in Bernard Faÿ's *The Two Franklins* (Boston, 1933), p. 158.

BARICOLO, FRANÇOIS
    1783. Painting. See DUPLESSIS, "Grey Coat," No. 9; see J. WRIGHT, No. 7.

BENBRIDGE, HENRY (1744–1812)
    1770. Painting. Oil on canvas. Dimensions unknown. Unlocated.

No portrait of Franklin has so brief a recorded history as that by Benbridge. In November or December, 1769, the portly young artist arrived in London. He was already known there, his full-length of Pasquale Paoli, commissioned by James Boswell, having attracted considerable attention in the preceding year. He carried a letter of introduction from his stepfather in Philadelphia to Franklin, asking that Franklin help him to establish himself in London. Benjamin West's wife was his cousin, and West was also well disposed to aid him. He wrote home soon after reaching the city and meeting his friends, "I believe I shall stay in London and intend to paint Mr. Coombs and Mr. Franklin to put in the exhibition next spring, which pictures I shall make a present of to them and you will see them upon those two gentlemen's return to Philadelphia."[1] Thomas Coombe, the young clergyman who was lodging with Franklin in Mrs. Stevenson's Craven Street house, was at about the same time writing to his father, also in Philadelphia, of what was going on. "Mr. Benbridge is arrived in Town from Italy, & is going to paint Dr. Franklin's Portrait & mine for the Exhibition next April. After that, the former will be presented to Mrs. Franklin, & the latter to yourself."[2] On Jan. 23, 1770, Benbridge reported home at greater length upon his plan:

    1. Hart, "The Gordon Family," p. 192.
    2. Jan. 3, 1770 (Coombe Papers, H.S.P.).

I waited upon Dr. Franklin with your letter of recommendation and he said any service he could do to
me, he would do with the greatest pleasure. I am now
preparing for the exhibition; Mr. Coombs (who is
very much esteemed in this Capitol and known almost
by all) I have made choice of for the subject of one
of my Pictures and I believe I shall do Mr. Franklin
for the other, for these two gentlemen are so exceedingly well known the making of strong likenesses will
be a great means of recommending me to business
and will do more than the recommendation of any
private gentleman whatever; and another thing is
that after an Exhibition, my friends have it more in
their power to say anything in favor of my Performances, when they have seen what I am able to do in
the Portrait way ... Mr. West intends to decline Portrait Painting and to follow that of History, which
will enable him to recommend me much stronger,
than if he was in the same way with myself. My own
picture he approves of and thinks it very like, as likewise that of Mr. Coombs; you'll see them both, God
Willing, in America and then you will be able to
judge of the advancement I have made in Art. If I
stay here I shall get money fast, or if I should come
to America I am not afraid but I shall do well there
too.[3]

The two portraits are in the catalogue of the Royal Academy
exhibition of that year, nos. 14 and 15, each entered as "Portrait of
a gentleman." Horace Walpole identified the first by a note
in his copy as that of Dr. Franklin.[4] There is no other record of
either. Benbridge, suddenly abandoning the idea of a career in
London, left for Philadelphia, bearing a letter, dated July 19, 1770,
from Benjamin to Deborah Franklin:

This will be delivered to you by our ingenious Coun-

3. Hart, "Gordon Family," p. 195.
4. Graves, The Royal Academy of Arts, 1, 178.

tryman Mr. Benbridge, who has so greatly improv'd himself in Italy as a Portrait Painter, that the Connoisseurs in that Art here think few or none excel him. I hope he will meet with due Encouragement in his own Country, and that we shall not lose him as we have lost Mr. West. For if Mr. Benbridge did not from Affection chuse to return and settle in Pensilvania, he certainly might live extreamly well in England by his Profession.[5]

Benbridge was elected to membership in the A.P.S. on Jan. 18, 1771. By 1773, after his marriage to Letitia Sage, a Philadelphia miniature painter, he had settled in Charleston, S.C., though he still returned from time to time to Philadelphia, and was living there at his death. Thomas Coombe returned to the city in 1772, serving as Assistant Minister of Christ Church and Saint Peter's until 1778, when he went again to England as a loyalist refugee. He may have taken his portrait with him. As for that of Franklin, in 1770 he had already sent his picture by Wilson to Philadelphia and was soon to send that by Martin. He could hardly have expected that Deborah would have room for a third. If he accepted Benbridge's kindness, it was probably to pass the picture on to some American or English friend.

BERNARD, (JEAN) JOSEPH (1740–1809)
> Ca. 1780. Pen-and-ink calligraphic drawing. Paper, 16¾ x 12½ inches. Profile, to left. Inscribed, "Franklin. Eripuit fulmen coelo sceptrum que tyrannis." Unlocated.

This portrait by the calligraphic artist commonly known as "Bernard de Paris," is recorded only in the catalogue of Americana issued about 1910 by Godefroy Mayer, dealer in old prints, Paris.[6] It is there described as a full bust, in profile, to left, within an ornamental frame, and as having been made between 1778 and 1780, when the artist was "Professeur et dessinateur des pages du Roi et de Mesdames Royales."

5. Franklin Papers (A.P.S.), *69*, no. 46.
6. *No. 30. Old Paintings, Drawings, Miniatures, Statuettes,* p. 3, no. 18.

An indirect association with Franklin may be seen in the exhibition of his portraits of the King and Queen and a "Tête de Femme" at La Blancherie's Salon de la Correspondance on Aug. 4, 1779. These are described in the *Nouvelles de la république des sciences et des arts* as in freehand, without counterdrawing or filling-in, "en traits de plume à main levée, sans calque ni remplissage."[1] The artist is here distinguished as "Maître d'Ecriture des Pages du feu Roi Stanislaus," and the drawings described as 20 inches in height and 16 in width. Bachaumont, under the date Nov. 24, 1781, gives considerable space to the public opening of the "bureau académique d'écriture," at which "M. Bernard, écrivain du cabinet du feu roi Stanislaus, créateur d'un genre de dessin en traits jété, parfaitement conformés à leurs vues," gave a demonstration of the skill and accuracy of his portraiture. It was explained that he did not work with the pen over a design previously established in crayon, but, having established the profile, drew in the remainder with an entirely free hand, working with marvelous virtuosity and accuracy in a technique in which correction was impossible.[2]

BERNIER, JEAN FRANÇOIS (ca. 1715–91)

> 1783. Medal. Silver or bronze, diam. 1 3/16 in. Obverse: profile of Franklin, to left; around edge: "BENJ. FRANKLIN MINIS^T PLEN^T DES ETATS UNIS DE L'AMERIQ. SEPT. MDCCLXXXIII"; under shoulder: "BERNIER"; reverse: the nine muses by a circular temple; around edge: "DE LEURS TRAVAUX NAITRA LEUR GLOIRE"; in exergue: "DES NEUF SOEURS." Pl. 22.

On Nov. 30, 1782, the Marquis de la Salle wrote to Franklin, whom he had succeeded as *Venerable* of the Masonic Lodge of the Nine Sisters, that the fraternity wished to congratulate him, through an official deputation, upon the conclusion of the war for independence.[3] A letter of the following summer, dated June 6, 1783, from the medalist Bernier to Franklin, reveals that he, with the approval of the Marquis de la Salle, was ready to reveal what he was pleased to call their "operations Effigiaires."[4] They were about to present,

1. August 10, 1779, p. 205.
2. Bachaumont, *Mémoires, 18*, 175–76.
3. Franklin Papers (A.P.S.), *26*, no. 79. Hale, *Franklin in France, 2*, 228.
4. Franklin Papers (A.P.S.), *28*, no. 146.

it would seem, the first examples of the small medal authorized by the lodge in his honor.

Bernier was admitted to the Academy of Saint Luc in 1768. He had designed some of the coinage of the realm and several Masonic medals. He was a member of the *Neuf Soeurs,* and its treasurer in 1778.[5] Though he must have known Franklin well, and though his signature attests an original likeness, the dress and arrangement of the hair suggests that the little profile had been influenced by the Houdon bust. The silver medal was distributed at various lodge functions in succeeding years.[6] Franklin brought some with him to Philadelphia, and sent one to his sister on Sept. 4, 1786.[7] It is repeated in numerous other medals, the first probably being that by Joseph Arnold Pingret (1798–1862), made for the *Neuf Soeurs* in 1828.[8]

BERRUER, PIERRE FRANÇOIS (1733–97)

> 1779. Bust. Stone, approx. life size. Signed and dated 1779. First described by Louis Réau in "Le Buste en marbre de Franklin par J. J. Caffiéri," *Gazette des Beaux Arts, 18* (1928), 167; illust. p. 169. *Owner* (1928) : J. de Saint Pierre, Paris.

Costume, drapery and likeness all appear to be based, with significant variations, upon the bust by DEJOUX. The artist was a sculptor of high professional standing in Paris, who in the year of the bust had exhibited a statue of Chancelor d'Aguesseau.[1] That the bust of Franklin was not exhibited and received no contemporary notice emphasized the probability that it was not an original portrait. The patron for whom it was made is unknown. Berruer had applied on July 19, 1777, for the position of keeper of the "Salle des Antiques." In 1785 he was appointed a professor of the Académie Royale.[2]

5. Louis Amiable, *Un Loge maçonnique d'avant 1789* (Paris, 1897), pp. 334, 390.

6. Nogaret, *L'Isle des sages,* pp. 207–09, and *Fictions, discours, poèmes, lyriques,* pp. 59–60.

7. Van Doren, *Benjamin Franklin & Jane Mecom,* p. 281.

8. Described and illustrated, "Medallic Memorials to Franklin," *Numismatist, 69* (1956), 1413–14.

1. *Archives de l'art français,* n. per. *1* (1907), 80–81.

2. Ibid.

BOREL, ANTOINE (1743–18–   )

1778. Line engraving by Jean Charles Le Vasseur (1734–1805), after a drawing by Borel. Engraved surface, 17 x 13¾ in. "A Borel invenit et delineavit 1778. J. C. le Vasseur Sculptor Regis et Majest^m. Imper^m. et Reg^m. Sculp. / L'AMÉRIQUE INDÉPENDANTE / Dediée au Congrès des Etats unis de l'Amérique / Par leur très humble et très obéissant / Serviteur Borel / A Paris ches l'Auteur rue Boucherat au coin de la rue Xaintonge." Original unlocated. Pl. 32.

Ten figures crowd the scene. Franklin, in Roman costume, his brow wreathed with oak leaves, stands beside the kneeling Indian maiden who represents America, one hand on her shoulder and his staff directed to her side. America is embracing the pedestal on which the statue of Liberty stands, while Minerva, above them all, rushes to guard Franklin with sword and shield. Prudence stands close to Franklin's shoulder, while Courage, wielding a savage club, has upset both Britain and Neptune into the water. At the left, Commerce and Agriculture watch the proceedings with satisfaction.

Bachaumont described the projected print on May 30, 1778, remarking that the government now found harmless an honor offered to the American insurgents which for the last six months it had refused to countenance.[3] The *Journal de Paris* on the next day printed a full description of the design and announced that subscriptions would be taken for the finished work until Aug. 20:

GRAVURE

L'AMÉRIQUE *indépendante, Dessin allegorique,*
executé par le sieur Borel.

Ce Dessin représente M. *Franklin,* qui affranchit l'Amérique : elle embrasse la Statue de la Liberté, & Minerve couvre le sage Legislateur de son égide. La Prudence & le Courage renversent leur ennemi, qui, dans sa chûte, entraine un Neptune, dont le trident est rompu. A la droite de la Liberté, l'Agriculture, le Commerce & les Arts applaudissent à cette heureuse révolution. Ce Dessin, gravé par M. *le Vasseur,*

3. *11,*281.

Graveur du Roi & de leurs Majestés Imperiales & Royales, formera une Estampe de seize pouces un quart de haut, sur treize pouces de large, sans le titre, & paroîtra à la fin de la présente année 1778.

Elle sera pour ceux qui souscriront, à commencer du 20 Mai jusqu'au 20 Août inclusivement, de *neuf livres; six livres* en souscrivant, & *trois livres* en la livrant. On suivra pour la livraison l'ordre des numéros de MM. les Souscriteurs. On souscrira à Paris chez M. Trutat, Notaire, rue de Condé. Ceux qui ne souscriront pas, la payeront *douze livres*. Le 20 Juin on pourra voir le Dessin chez M. *le Vasseur,* rue des Mathurins.[4]

Comparing this description with the plate, it appears that the engraver reversed the design, so that Commerce and Agriculture appear at the left, not the right. The action would have been somewhat more dramatic as originally conceived. Borel may have removed a figure of "les Arts," or it may be that the three faces briefly glimpsed behind Commerce, are those of Painting, Sculpture, and Architecture. Borel had come thus far without a likeness of Franklin, the principal actor. He wrote on June 1, 1778, asking for a few moments in which to make the portrait.[5] Franklin appears to have granted the "*quelques* moments," but, having doubtless read with some awe the description of the work, bridled at the prospect of having it dedicated to him. On June 24 he declined the invitation, suggesting that for his own name there be substituted the words,

4. No. 151, p. 602. "ENGRAVING. Independent America, allegorical drawing executed by the Sieur Borel. This drawing represents M. *Franklin,* who liberated America: She embraces the Statue of Liberty, & Minerva protects the wise legislator with her shield. Prudence & Courage overthrow their enemy who, in his fall, carries down Neptune, whose trident is broken. At the right of Liberty, Agriculture, Commerce and the Arts applaud this happy revolution. This drawing, engraved by M. le Vasseur, Engraver to the King and to their Imperial and Royal Majesties, will form a print 16¼ pouces high, and 13 pouces wide, not including title, and will appear at the end of the present year 1778. It will be, for subscribers, from May 20 to Aug. 20 inclusive, 9 livres; 6 livres on subscribing & 3 livres on receipt. Delivery will be in the order of subscription. Subscriptions at Paris will be taken by M. Trutat, notary, rue de Condé. Non-subscribers will pay 12 livres. On June 20 the drawing will be on view at M. le Vasseur's, rue des Mathurins."

5. Franklin Papers (University of Pennsylvania).

"le congrès representé par un senateur habillé à la romaine &c."[6] This must have been something of a blow to the artist, since the dedication of a print carried with it a certain financial obligation. Dedication to a congress was something quite new, in addition to holding less promise in the area of patronage. The drawing had not gone to the engraver until June 19.[7] On Aug. 3 Borel wrote Franklin that he had returned from the country to find the plate, "que j'ai l'honneur de vous presenter," well advanced, and asked for an appointment in which to make further revisions on the portrait.[8] The work dragged on. Through September and November he was pressing Franklin for the seal of the United States, without which he declared his design could not be complete. He was determined that it should have an official cast. Franklin supplied for the purpose two pieces of paper money, and Borel chose for his purpose the eight-dollar Continental with a harp surrounded by the motto, "Majora minoribus consonat" (the great are in harmony with the smaller). On Feb. 3, 1779, Borel wrote that he had been looking for Franklin at the Salon de la Correspondance, where several of his own works were on exhibition, to return the money. The loan may have been the only monetary support he received from his somewhat unwilling patron.

C..., D...
    1785. Miniature. See CASTRIQUE; see GREUZE, No. 10; see WEYLER, Nos. 7, 8.

CAFFIÉRI, JEAN JACQUES (1725–92)
    1   1777. Bust. Terra cotta, ht. 52 cm. (20.42 in.). Inscription written on the back in the clay before firing, "BENJAMIN FRANKLIN / né à Boston en Amerique / le xvii Janvier 1706 / fait par J. J. Caffiéri en 1777."[9] Owner: Bibliothèque Mazarine, Paris. Pl. 16.
Caffiéri's strong and authoritative portrait, from life, was com-

6. Franklin Papers (L.C.; A.P.S., *45*, no. 127; *42*, no. 182).
7. *Journal de Paris,* No. 170, June 19, 1778, p. 678.
8. Franklin Papers (A.P.S.), *11*, no. 14.
9. Réau, "Le Buste en Marbre," p. 170.

pleted toward the end of March, 1777 (see above, p. 117). It was first seen by the public in the autumn of that year at the Salon of the Académie Royale, where it was exhibited together with the same artist's marble busts of Pierre Corneille and the Maréchal de Muy, and his design for a memorial monument to General Richard Montgomery.[1] Earlier, Caffiéri had made a striking and romantically conceived bust of Claude Adrien Helvétius, and it is possible that his widow, now Franklin's friend and neighbor, may have been one of the friends who had urged him to sit for this portrait. The American pieces commanded much attention at the Salon. Bachaumont saw in the "Franklin's" calm aspect "un sage philanthrope" seeking a remedy for the evils which harassed his country, and discerned in its features the patriot's indignation.[2] The monument to Montgomery drew attention to the soldier who had given his life in an attempt to take from England the fortress which England had wrested from France.[3] The project had been authorized by Congress a year earlier, upon recommendation of a committee of which Franklin had been a member. Caffiéri's letters to Franklin of June 13 and 30, terse inquiries on the life and death of the General, suggest that the commission had been given him at the last sitting for the bust. In conversation during those sittings Caffiéri seems to have received from Franklin some sort of encouragement or promise which he misconstrued as an appointment as state sculptor to the new American republic. In 1780 he reminded Franklin of this promise as referring to "all the tombs," and in 1782 wrote again regarding monuments to heroes. Three years later, when he learned of Houdon's commission from the state of Virginia for a statue of Washington, he wrote again in bitter resentment. His angry persistence brought William Temple Franklin's cutting reply of April 3, 1785, assuring him of the emptiness of his pretensions, a letter which incidentally establishes the fact that

1. Nos. 216–19 in the *Livret* of the Salon, pp. 41–42. Hart and Biddle, *Life and Works of Houdon*, pp. 88–89. Most of Caffiéri's correspondence relating to the portrait is at the A.P.S., and most of it has been published by Florence Ingersoll-Smouse, "Lettres inédites de J. J. Caffiéri," *Bulletin de la société de l'histoire de l'art français* (1913), pp. 202–22.
2. Bachaumont, *Mémoires, 11,* 44.
3. Hart and Biddle, in *Houdon,* pp. 62–72, give a full account of the monument, illust.

Franklin had originally granted sittings to Caffiéri upon the urging both of his friends and of the artist.

The bust of Franklin, "fait d'après nature," is in a list of portraits of illustrious men drawn up by Caffiéri in 1778, probably for presentation to the *Directeur Générale des Bâtiments,* the official in charge of governmental purchases of works of art.[4] A note from Jean Baptiste Marie Pierre of August 1780 states that the bust had been acquired for the *Direction des Bâtiments,* that Caffiéri had delivered it almost two years before but had not yet received the 500 livres due, this being his charge for an original terra cotta.[5] In 1792 the revolutionary authorities sent the bust to the Hôtel de Nesle and then, in 1796, to the Bibliothèque Mazarine, where it has remained ever since.

The correspondence between Caffiéri and the Franklins contains eight references to plaster casts of the bust, the first a gift from the sculptor, the others purchased from him. In a letter of Oct. 29, 1783, Caffiéri reminds his patron that he is prepared to make as many casts as he had the year before: "Je vous prie de resouvenir que j'ay le copie du portrait de Monsieur franklin et que je puis en faire autant que l'an dernier."[6] Franklin placed an order following this appeal. By the correspondence, however, his last previous order had been in 1779, and we have no record of those of 1782–83.

Either because of its greater accuracy, or because of a promise to the sculptor, Franklin himself purchased for his friends and family only casts of the Caffiéri. It was the ascendant sculptured likeness for many years as, on the point of accuracy, it deserves to be. The phrenologists of the early and mid-19th century based their researches upon it under the leadership of George Combe, finding the subject highly developed in "Causality, Wit, and Order."[7] Gradually, it was replaced in popularity by the Houdon bust, a warmer and far more acceptable characterization. The bust has

4. Guiffrey, *Les Caffiéri,* p. 453.
5. Ibid., pp. 241–42.
6. Ingersoll-Smouse, "Lettres inédites," p. 212.
7. The mask, with the collections of the Edinburgh Phrenological Museum, is now in the Department of Anatomy, University of Edinburgh. Reference is made to the "Franklin" in George Combe's *System of Phrenology* (Edinburgh, 1836), pp. 516, 570, 585, 901. Information from Prof. J. C. Brash, University of Edinburgh, March 5, 1954.

been copied in marble many times, though there is no incontrovertible evidence that Caffiéri himself made such a replica. A bust sold at Sotheby's on March 27, 1945, as the property of R. T. Sands, is inscribed "FRANCLEN" and "fait par J. J. Caffieri 1777."[8] Of a marble made in that year there would surely have been contemporary confirmation. Another marble of the 18th century is at the Lomonosov Museum in Leningrad.[9] Others are described below.

The bust and its copies were copied many times by other sculptors, by the makers of pottery portraits, and by the engravers. It is not certain whether another sculptor or the maker of a cast first gave it that forward thrust of the head of many later versions, which makes it more suitable for a high pedestal but which, in any location, adds weight and thoughtfulness to the likeness. The Caffiéri is recognizable in all its variations, first, by the scarf about the neck, second, by the hair falling over the ears, and third, by the strong, surely modeled detail of the face.

2   1777. Cast. Unlocated.

Soon after the close of the Salon, on Dec. 9, 1777, the sculptor wrote to Benjamin Franklin, congratulating him upon the recent victories of the American army, and sending a bust as a gift to his grandson.[1] The young man endorsed the letter, "Caffieri with a Burst as a present." In a letter of July 18, 1817, William Temple Franklin stated that he was then the owner of a bust "large as life and executed by Caffieri an eminent artist at Paris from the life."[2] He sent with the letter a profile taken from it, probably an engraving. William died in Paris on May 25, 1823, where his widow, who had inherited most of his property, continued to live.

3, 4, 5   1779. Casts. Unlocated.

On March 17, 1779, Caffiéri wrote to William Temple Franklin that a bust had been hardened with wax and packed ready for shipment. A letter of June 16 mentions this and two additional casts

8. *Catalogue of Valuable Printed Books ... also a Marble Bust of Benjamin Franklin by J. J. Caffiéri* (Sotheby and Co.), no. 378.

9. *News; A Fortnightly Searchlight on World Events,* No. 8 (Moscow, Oct. 31, 1951), p. 21.

1. Franklin Papers (A.P.S.), 7, no. 140. Ingersoll-Smouse, "Lettres inédites," pp. 205–06.

2. To Samuel Starbuck (Franklin Papers, L.C.).

prepared and packed for shipment through customs.[3] Franklin's payment for the three on June 11 is entered in his Cash Book.[4] One certainly, and probably all three, were on their way to America.

Francis Hopkinson wrote from Philadelphia on Sept. 5, 1779, "Mrs. Bache tells me you have sent a Bust of yourself by Mr. Luzerne," and expressed his eagerness to see it.[5] Sally herself wrote in the same vein on the 16th to William.[6] But the bust had remained at L'Orient, Luzerne's frigate sailing without it, and Sally received nothing but the directions for careful unpacking.[7] On Sept. 14, 1781, William had at last to tell her that the bust had gone out with the *Marquis de Lafayette* and with her had been captured by the enemy. "At the Peace I will send you another."[8]

6, 7 1783. Casts. Unlocated.

On October 17, 1783, Sir Edward Newenham, of Dublin, asked Franklin for his bust.[9] The bust was lost on its way to Bordeaux, whence it was to have been shipped to Ireland. More than a year passed before the loss was discovered, a new cast being ordered on March 12, 1785. Sir Edward acknowledged its receipt with delight on June 4, adding that he was about to cross the Irish channel by balloon, masked and in fancy dress, and might be tempted to proceed as far as Paris. On Jan. 12, 1786, he reported his friends' admiration of the piece, together with a malicious rumor "that I bought an old bust of Lord Chancellor Newport and pretended it was yours, for that it was well known that you were so poor that you never sat for your Bust."[10] By an unconfirmed report, the bust was destroyed in the Irish insurrection of 1798.[11]

8 1785. Cast. *Owner:* Académie des Sciences, Paris.

Shortly before his return to America, Franklin ordered two more

3. Ingersoll-Smouse, "Lettres inédites," pp. 206–07.
4. Franklin Papers (A.P.S.).
5. Ibid., *15,* no. 170.
6. Ibid., *101,* no. 128.
7. William Temple Franklin to Sarah, Oct. 28, 1779 (Princeton University). Sarah to William, March 29, 1780 (Franklin Papers, A.P.S., *102,* no. 40), and June 22, 1781 (ibid., no. 66).
8. Franklin Papers (L.C.).
9. Hart and Biddle, *Houdon,* pp. 88–89. Correspondence at A.P.S.
10. Ibid., p. 90.
11. Ibid.

casts, a commission acknowledged in Caffiéri's letters of June 10 and 15, 1785. On June 20 Franklin asked that one be sent to Jean Baptiste Le Roy of the Académie des Sciences, and the other (see below) to William Carmichael, chargé d'affaires at Madrid.[1] That sent to M. Le Roy is now in the Institut de France, of which the Académie des Sciences is an affiliate.

9   1785. Cast. Unlocated.

The cast was ordered by Franklin in June 1785, as described above, in response to an appeal from William Carmichael, then on a diplomatic mission in Madrid: "If at your departure from Paris you should happen to have a bust of the many that have been made of you, I shall regard it as a particular mark of your esteem, if you would leave it at my disposition."[2] The cast was not to be delivered, but to be held by Caffiéri until Carmichael should call for it. Carmichael presumably carried it with him on his return to Madrid.

10   Ca. 1777–90. Cast. Plaster, ht. 30 in. (24 in. bust on 6 in. socle). Inscribed on the back (as part of the cast), "BENJAMIN FRANKLIN né à Boston en Amerique l[e xvii] / Janvier 1706 fait à Paris par J. H. Caffiéri en 1777." In center, below, "3." Damage at the tip of the nose has been repaired. The bust had been painted to resemble terra cotta, and this coloring has been removed. *Owner:* Royal Society of Arts, London. Pl. 16.

The bust was a gift to the Royal Society of Arts from Pahin de La Blancherie, organizer of the Salon de la Correspondance in which portraits of Franklin had often figured. Its receipt is recorded in the minutes of the society under the date Nov. 9, 1791: "The Secretary reported that Mons. de la Blancherie had delivered him a Bill of Lading for three Cases containing the Bust of Dr. Franklyn in terra cotta—a Bust of Mons. Peronner in Plaster and a Pedestal in Scagliola and of which Mr. de la Blancherie begs the Society's acceptance."

It may be supposed that La Blancherie, who lived out the remainder of his life as an emigré in London, had brought with him the artistic milieu in which he had moved as "Agent Générale de Correspondance pour les Sciences et les Arts." Among his efforts

1. Franklin Papers (L.C.). Ingersoll-Smouse, "Lettres Inédites," pp. 220–21.
2. April 4, 1784 (Franklin Papers, A.P.S., *33,* no. 69).

to revive the flagging fortunes of the Salon de la Correspondance was the establishment of a portrait gallery of famous men at the "chef-lieu."[3] Busts of Voltaire, Diderot, Rousseau, and others were soon acquired. On Feb. 20, 1783, these had been joined by two others contributed by William Temple Franklin: "21 & 22. Le Buste de M. Franklin, Ministre Plénipotentiare des Etats-Unis de l'Amérique, par M. Caffiéri, Sculpteur du Roi; un autre, par M. Houdon, Sculpteur du Roi; envoyé au Chef-lieu de la Correspondance, pour servir à la collection des hommes célebres, par M. Franklin, son petit-fils."[4]

What prompted Billy to this generous response is unknown. One can only infer that La Blancherie had brought both busts with him to England, and was disposing of one of the Franklins in this ingratiating manner.

11   Ca. 1777–85. Cast. Unlocated.

The minutes of the Philadelphia Library Co., Jan. 7, 1790, record that "The Committee appointed for the purpose report that a Bust of Doctor Franklin has been procured from the Managers of the Pennsylvania Hospital, which has been forwarded with a drawing of the Figure proposed and the necessary orders to Italy."[5] This cast was very probably the source not only of the Library Co. full-length statue by Lazzarini (see below) but of other early Italian copies in marble, of which that owned by the A.P.S. is an example.

12   1790–91. Statue, by Francesco Lazzarini. Full-length, in Carrara marble, ht. 98 in., on base 34 x 23 in. Standing figure with drapery over contemporary costume. In the right hand, "an inverted sceptre, an emblem of anti-monarchical principles; and in his left, a scroll of paper."[6] The right elbow rests on a pile of books. The statue is badly weathered

3. *Nouvelles de la république des sciences et des arts* (1782), pp. 270, 277.
4. Ibid., Feb. 26, 1783, p. 70; March 5, 1783, p. 78.
5. Minutes, *3*, 188. Charles E. Peterson, "Library Hall: Home of the Library Company of Philadelphia, 1790–1880," *Proceedings of the A.P.S., 43* (1953), 136.
6. William Temple Franklin, ed., *Memoirs of the Life and Writings of Benjamin Franklin, 1* (Philadelphia, 1818), 505. The account of the statue quoted here must have been sent from Philadelphia to the editor, in London. It may have come from John Vaughan. It gives the erroneous attribution of the likeness afterward repeated by William Vaughan (see CAFFIERI, No. 14), "the head is a copy from the excellent bust produced by the chisel of Houdon."

and has lost both hands. It originally stood in a niche in the façade of Library Hall. With the restoration of the building on the same site in 1959, to house the library of the A.P.S., an exact duplicate by Lewis Iselin, Jr., was placed in the same situation. *Owner:* Library Co. of Philadelphia.

The statue was the gift of Senator William Bingham to the Library Co., to adorn the front of its new building and to pay a signal honor to its founder, who, as all the city was aware, was then nearing the close of his long life. On Jan. 7, 1790, a committee of the library's directors reported that the order, with a bust for the likeness and a drawing for the figure, had been sent to Italy. A pen-and-ink drawing prepared for the sculptor's guidance, now at the Chicago Historical Society, shows us that they wished a tall and impressive figure, holding a scroll, draped in some sort of classic or semi-classic costume. Franklin had been consulted, and it must have been he who recommended the Caffiéri bust at the hospital. He was reported as preferring "A gown for his dress and a Roman head."[7] The physique was to be that of their founder, youthful and strong, rather than the heavy, stooping old man who had come back to them from France.

The commission was presumably forwarded by some commercial correspondent of Bingham's in Italy. Little is known of Francesco Lazzarini, who carried it out, other than that he came of a long line of Carraran sculptors.[8] He did as well as could be expected with the materials and directions offered him, adding books to the supporting pediment, and placing in Franklin's hand what might represent either a scroll or the scepter "snatched from the tyrants." Sculpture of this size had been rare in America, and such a commission was an event of great artistic importance and the greatest popular interest. It is curious that more careful thought had not been given to the matter. Houdon, who seems to have had a Franklin statue in mind, might have been consulted. If the order had not been sent so promptly, Giuseppe Ceracchi might have had it, for he was in America soon after and on friendly terms with William

7. Peterson, p. 136.

8. Antonio Pace, *Benjamin Franklin and Italy* (Philadelphia, 1948), p. 290. A bust of Louis XVI, "qui porte le nom de Francesco Lazari à Carrare," appears as no. 29 in the *Catalogue de tableaux, dessins, estampes et objets de haute curiosité . . . après cessation de commerce de M. Rolland,* Paris, March 22, 1830.

Bingham. The procedure, however, was what Franklin himself would have suggested: a head to copy, a sketch or something of the body, as the cheapest and most expeditious procedure.

The statue arrived in the spring of 1792. Senator Bingham addressed a graceful letter to the Library Co. on April 4, transmitting to it the work which was to perpetuate in Franklin's "fellow citizens the recollection of his public & private Virtues."[9] On the 7th the statue was raised into its niche on the front of Library Hall, to the accompaniment of much fanfare and much emphasis on the price (500 guineas) of the work. Badly damaged by the weather, it was taken down again on Aug. 25, 1879.[10]

> 13 Ca. 1790–1800. Bust, by unknown Italian sculptor. Marble, ht. 27¼ in. *Owner:* A.P.S., Philadelphia. Pl. 17.

The bust was presented to the A.P.S. by Joseph R. Smith on July 20, 1804:

> I have this day deposited in the Hall of the Society a marble bust of our venerable first President Dr. Franklin which I will thank you to beg the favour of the Society to accept from me.
>
> It is of Italian workmanship, executed at Florence, & from my imperfect recollection of the Doctor's features, would seem to be a good likeness.[1]

It is the earliest recorded copy in marble of any Franklin bust. It has the upright head of Caffiéri's original, indicating that it is probably a copy of the bust sent to Italy by the Library Co. (see above, No. 11).

> 14 Ca. 1785. Cast. *Owner:* Bowdoin College, Brunswick, Me.

In 1835 William Vaughan (1752–1850), London merchant and author, presented a bust of Franklin to Bowdoin College. His elder brother, Benjamin Vaughan (1751–1835), had settled at Hallowell, Me., after the war. It was Benjamin who had dared to pub-

9. H.S.P. The name of the artist and other details are recorded in the *Columbian Magazine, 1* (April, 1792), 284.
10. Diary of W. G. Armstrong (H.S.P.).
1. Smith to John Vaughan (archives, A.P.S.).

lish a volume of Franklin's writings in London in 1779 (see SÈVRES, No. 3). Benjamin mentions the gift in a letter to Parker Cleveland, dated Sept. 26, 1835.[2] He refers to it again in a letter to Jared Sparks, written on Dec. 6, 1835, the day before his death:

> I go now to Houdon. My brother Wm. V. said to me, in his letter accompanying this bust, that the bust had been in the family house in London *40 or 50 years*. De Ville, who you say had been 30 years in his trade, called to see the bust at my brother's desire, before it was packed up; but mentioned nothing peculiar (related to me) giving him any claim to the manufacture of the plaster of Paris bust. My brother expressly speaks of Houdon as the sculptor, & the tradition at the Phil. Society at Philadelphia as to the marble bust there is, that it was executed by Houdon.
>
> . . .
>
> I can remember to have been at the studio of Houdon at Paris, where he was in very good esteem.[3]

The Bowdoin bust, however, is of the Caffiéri type. The explicit attribution to Houdon appears to be in error, recalling the similar statement sent to William Temple Franklin from Philadelphia, perhaps by John Vaughan, that the head of the Lazzarini statue had been copied from a Houdon bust.

> 15   Undated. Bust by unknown artist. Marble, ht. 22¼ in. (bust, 16⅜; socle, 6⅛). *Owner:* Home Insurance Co., Philadelphia.

The marble appears to be of early date. The erect pose of the head relates it to Caffiéri's original rather than to a later derivation. The detail of the face is well defined, but the sculptor has altered details of hair and costume. Its pose and reduced size might relate it to the bust of Franklin shown in the 1801 engraving of Jefferson, full-

2. A.P.S.

3. Sparks Papers. J. S. Deville exhibited portrait busts at the Royal Academy, 1823–26. Elizabeth Bryant Johnston, *Original Portraits of Washington* (Boston, 1882), pp. 164, 168, describes him as a French artist who had a studio in London and who owned a Houdon "Washington" from which he made casts. The marble "Franklin" at the A.P.S. was not by Houdon (see CAFFIERI, No. 13).

length, after Rembrandt Peale.[4] While one can never expect any engraving to have photographic authority, the electrical machine also shown in the print appears to be one still preserved by the A.P.S.

The work was for many years the property of the Franklin Insurance Co. of Philadelphia (now absorbed into the Home Insurance Co.), perhaps since its founding in 1829. It was shown in the Franklin exhibition at the Masonic Temple, Philadelphia, in 1906.

> 16 Ca. 1790–1800. Bust, attributed to Giuseppe Ceracchi (1751–1804). Marble, ht. 23¼ in. The bust has the forward thrust of the head, the first significant variation from Caffiéri's original. The pupils of the eyes, shown in the original terra cotta, are not indicated in this copy. *Owner:* Pennsylvania Academy of the Fine Arts, Philadelphia. Pl. 17.

The earliest documentation on the bust is the record of its purchase in the minutes of the Pennsylvania Academy of the Fine Arts:

> *June 12, 1811.*
> Mr. Rush and Mr. Peale were appointed a committee to purchase of Mr. Chaudron for the Academy the marble Bust of Dr. Franklin now in the Academy.
> *July 8, 1811.*
> Mr. Rush from the committee appointed at the last meeting, reported, that they had purchased of Mr. Chaudron the marble Bust of Dr. Franklin for $120 and paid for it by a draft on the Treasurer.

In the academy's "Donations" book the transaction is recorded as of July 8, 1811, with the first identification of the sculptor, "Bust of Benjamin Franklin by Cerraci, purchased of — Chaudron." It was, for the young academy, a major acquisition. The exhibition of 1813 featured the work, together with a bust of Washington also attributed to Ceracchi:

> 2 Original Bust of Franklin. Marble. *Ceracchi.*
> In every future age
> Whilst History holds a pen,

4. "Thomas Jefferson / President of the United States. / Published by A. Day No. 38 Chestnut Street Philada." Information from Dr. Alfred L. Bush, Princeton, May 25, 1960.

> She'll rank our virtuous sage
> Amongst the first of men;
> And when she counts her sons
> Who earn'd immortal fame,
> She'll next to Washington's
> Record our Franklin's name.[5]

One would expect Peale and Rush—the sculptor and painter who, as the academy's committee, had arranged the purchase—to have had some valid reason for the attribution to Ceracchi, even if they could not remember the given name of the seller. [Jean] Simon Chaudron, the former owner, was a well-known person in the city and its French community, a clock-maker, jeweler, and silversmith, the artistic excellence of whose work Joseph Hopkinson had particularly praised in his annual address to the academy in 1810. Chaudron had been a charter member of the French Masonic lodge, *L'Amenité,* warranted at Philadelphia on May 20, 1797, and had continued to be very active in its affairs up until about 1810.[6] He was conspicuous as orator, poet, editor of *L'Abeille américaine* (1815–18), and one of the settlers of the French colony of Demopolis in Alabama in 1817. After 1810 he appears to have been on the wing in various enterprises, returning only occasionally to the city.

William Rush and Charles Willson Peale had both known Ceracchi and had been associated with him in the "Columbianum," Peale's short-lived art academy of 1795. Ceracchi was, like Chaudron, a Mason. These facts support the attribution to Ceracchi made by Peale, Rush, and Chaudron. Charles Henry Hart, on the other hand, has contended that their very familiarity with Ceracchi's name would have led them to confuse it with Caffiéri's.[7] He believed it probably one of the copies by John Dixey or Giuseppe

5. *Third Annual Exhibition of the Columbian Society of Artists at the Pennsylvania Academy* (Philadelphia, 1813), p. 5.
6. Information from Dr. William J. Paterson, Committee on Masonic Culture, R. W. Grand Lodge, F. & A.M., Philadelphia, Jan. 11, 1960. A portrait and biographical sketch appear in the *Poésies choisies de Jean-Simon Chaudron, suivies de l'oraison funèbre de Washington, par le même auteur,* Paris, 1841.
7. Hart and Biddle, *Houdon,* pp. 97–99.

Jardella, stone carvers employed by James Traquair of Philadelphia. One feature of the bust not in the original or in Ceracchi's known American work is the dead eye. This feature, suggesting a sculptor with a conservative respect for classic models, is present also in an early bust of the type definitely of native workmanship and marble, owned by the Independence Hall National Historical Park. Finally, Ulysse Desportes, leading authority on Ceracchi, sees no stylistic evidence in the bust that it is his, and doubts that Ceracchi, an original artist, would have given personal attention to the production of a copy.[8] Ceracchi returned to Europe in 1795, and the most likely conjecture appears to be that the bust was sent to Chaudron by his agency or from his studio, but was not his own work.

Joseph Nollekins described the Roman sculptor Ceracchi as "a short thin man, with a piercing black eye, and a very blue beard."[9] He had come to London in 1774, making portraits, effusive classical compositions, and exhibiting at the Royal Academy. On April 29, 1783, Dr. Jan Ingenhousz, physician to the Emperor of Austria, mentioned to Franklin that "Ceraqui" was in Vienna and eager to share in the erection of monuments to the heroes of American liberty.[10] Franklin discouraged the idea, which echoed Caffiéri's importunate ambition. Ceracchi, however, a restless, turbulent spirit, came to America in the year of Franklin's death, 1790, remaining until the summer of 1792, and was back again from 1794 to 1795. He was well received by leading citizens, yet soon learned the truth of Franklin's advice. His dream of a hundred-foot marble monument to Liberty found neither public nor private sponsors.[11] William Bingham gave him some assistance at the time of the arrival of the Lazzarini statue.[12] He was elected to the A.P.S. on Jan. 20, 1792. On Feb. 6, 1795, he presented to the society a bust

8. To the author, Aug. 18, 1961.
9. J. T. Smith, *Nollekins and his Times, 2,* 120. Information from Ulysse G. Desportes, 1957. Anderdon Collection (British Museum).
10. Franklin Papers (A.P.S.), *27,* no. 69.
11. Albert Ten Eyck Gardner, "Fragment of a Lost Monument," *Metropolitan Museum of Art Bulletin, 6* (1948), 190.
12. William Bingham to Nicholas Low, March 26, 1792, with copy of letter to Ceracchi (H.S.P.).

of David Rittenhouse, its president, who had aided him financially and with whom he had explored the Pennsylvania quarries in search of statuary marble.[13]

That Franklin may have been among Ceracchi's subjects is possible, and his most probable source, either in Philadelphia or Italy, would have been the Caffiéri. The gigantic bust of Minerva which once adorned the hall of the House of Representatives and is now owned by the Library Co. of Philadelphia is now securely attributed to him. He may also have made the bust of Franklin which Henry Wansey saw over the door of the same chamber in the summer of 1794.[1] That bust may have passed into private hands after the removal of the capital from Philadelphia, but there is no evidence by which to trace it to Simon Chaudron and the Pennsylvania Academy.

> 17 Undated. Bust, attributed to Giuseppe Ceracchi. Marble, ht. 21¼ in. The bust appears to be a faithful copy of the Caffiéri original. The pupils of the eyes are indicated. The scarf and the folds of the coat are close to the original. *Owner:* The Henry E. Huntington Library and Art Gallery, San Marino, Cal.

Constantia Abert offered the bust for sale to John Bigelow on Dec. 22, 1888, as "an original bust of Benj. Franklin by Ceracchi," and in an undated letter replying to Bigelow's inquiry of Jan. 4, 1889, stated that it had been purchased from the artist by Alexander James Dallas (1759–1817), that he had presented it to his "sister," Sophia Dallas Bache (wife of Richard Bache, Jr., son of Sarah Franklin Bache, and grandson of Benjamin Franklin). Sophia Dallas Bache "under straitened circumstances" had sold the bust to William P. Bryan, a Philadelphia merchant. Bryan bequeathed it to his wife, who had been Constantia Abert's great-aunt (oldest sister of her father's father, Col. J. J. Abert of the Corps of Topographical Engineers). Mrs. Bryan had bequeathed it to her brother, Col. Abert, who had given it to his son,

13. William Bartram, *Memoirs of the Life of David Rittenhouse* (Philadelphia, 1813), pp. 418–22.

1. Henry Wansey, *Journal of an Excursion to the United States* (Salisbury, 1796), p. 112.

Charles Abert, the husband of Constantia Bache. In this way the bust Constantia had known in her childhood had come into her own possession. The letter was accompanied by photographs, one of which had been made by the Post Office Department for the 1¢ stamp then in use.[2]

Sophia, actually the daughter of A. J. Dallas, had married Richard Bache in 1805, the year after Ceracchi had been executed in France on the charge of conspiring to assassinate Napoleon. In May 1871 Constantia Abert had offered the bust for sale to the M.H.S.[3] In 1906 it was on loan at the Corcoran Gallery, Washington. Its last private owner, Robert Walker Abert, stated on April 21, 1924, that it was a work of Ceracchi and that it "has been in my family except for a short interval since it was made."[4] It was sold soon after to its present owner. The bust is said to be identical with that described below, and to have come into family ownership at the same time.

18   Undated. Bust, attributed to Giuseppe Ceracchi. *Owner:* Boston Public Library.

The bust, said to be identical with that described above, and to have come into the Franklin family at the same time, was presented to the Boston Public Library in 1897 by Frank Wood, who gave the following account of it:

> The white marble bust of Benjamin Franklin, now in Bates Hall, that I presented to the Public Library, was made by Joseph Ceracchi an Italian sculptor and was studied from life. He made two, the other one is in the Corcoran Library at Washington, D.C. It is an exact duplicate of the one in the Library, although not in as good condition.[5]

This is presumably the bust of which Charles Hodge wrote to Jared

2. Union College, John Bigelow Papers, transcripts kindness of W. J. Bell, Jr. A similar statement by Charles Abert, 1897, is quoted in Clarence Winthrop Bowen, ed., *The History of the Centennial Celebration of the Inauguration of George Washington* (New York, 1892), p. 461; illust., p. 524.
3. *Proceedings of the M.H.S., 12* (1873), 81.
4. To George Simpson Eddy (Eddy Papers, Princeton University).
5. Frank Wood to Boston Public Library, Jan. 12, 1906.

Sparks on Oct. 19, 1835: "When Mrs. Bache (Mrs. H's. mother) went to Virginia several family pictures & a bust of Dr. Franklin were sent to the Academy of Arts. The bust is still there, but the pictures have been lost."[6] Mrs. Hodge's mother was Catharine Wistar Bache (1773–1814), and her husband, William Bache, an elder brother of Richard, the father of Sophia, to whom the similar bust described above had belonged. A portrait deposited by her at the Pennsylvania Academy of the Fine Arts in 1813 was released to William J. Duane on July 6, 1858.[7] The bust was "claimed by Mrs. Benj. Bache" on July 1, 1863.[8]

> 19　Undated. Bust, attributed to J. J. Caffiéri. Marble, ht. 26 in. (not including base). The pupils of the eyes are indicated. A unique feature is the addition of a fringe on the scarf. *Owner:* Detroit Institute of Arts.

This large and finely sculptured bust was in 1928 attributed to Caffiéri by Louis Réau, well-known authority on 18th–century French sculpture.[9] It had recently been discovered by Arthur S. Byne, in Madrid, where it had been preserved for some sixty years as the figure of a saint. It is, however, unsigned, and there is no record of Caffiéri's having ever repeated this work in marble. It may have been copied in Spain from the cast which, presumably, William Carmichael brought to Madrid. It is characterized, however, by that forward inclination of the head not present in the original and which (whether originating there or elsewhere) is first seen in early Philadelphia versions. Another conjecture might be that the work formed part of the collection of Josef de Jaudenes y Nebot, Spanish Chargé d'Affaires at Philadelphia, who had purchased from Ceracchi a "Washington" intended for the sculptor's monument to American Liberty, and who returned to Spain in 1796.[1] If so, costume and proportions indicate that it was not in-

6. Sparks Papers.

7. Minutes, Pennsylvania Academy of the Fine Arts. This was the portrait painted by Madame Lavoisier (see DUPLESSIS: "Gray Coat," No. 6). By her will, Catherine Wistar Bache left the painting to her daughter, Catherine Wistar Bache, and to her son, Benjamin Franklin Bache, "a marble bust and pedestal of his great grandfather, Benjamin Franklin."

8. Archives, Pennsylvania Academy.

9. Réau, "Le Buste en Marbre," pp. 167–72.

1. Gardner, "Fragment of a Lost Monument," p. 190.

tended as part of the monument. The bust came into its present ownership as the gift of Mr. and Mrs. Edgar B. Whitcomb in 1950.

> 20   Undated. Drawing, by unknown artist. Pencil on paper, oval, 8¾ x 7¼ in., mounted on paper, 12 x 10 in. Profile, to left, after a bust of the Caffiéri type. Inscribed on the reverse of the paper on which the drawing is mounted, "A Portrait of Benjamin Franklin / Benjn. West." *Owner:* A.P.S., Philadelphia.

The drawing has that forward inclination of the head which, though not present in Caffiéri's original, adds an air of thoughtfulness to many later versions. It is similar in this respect to early engravings from the Caffiéri, such as James Akin's, published by William Duane, Philadelphia, in 1809, or the London version by Thomas Holloway. These, however, are profiles to the right, of the right side of the face, and the drawing is not a reversal of that, but a view of the left side, in which the lobe of the ear is shown.

According to a label on the back of the frame, the drawing was in the West sale of 1898. It is illustrated in Sydney George Fisher's *True Benjamin Franklin* as "recently sold with other property of Benjamin West, and purchased by the Hon. S. W. Pennypacker, of Philadelphia, by whose permission it is reproduced. It is supposed to be a drawing by some unknown artist of the bust by Ceracchi."[2] It was reproduced simultaneously in the *P.M.H.B.* as an "original portrait" by West, owned by Samuel W. Pennypacker.[3] At the sale of the Pennypacker library in 1905, it was purchased by John Wanamaker. Dr. A. S. W. Rosenbach was its purchaser at the Wanamaker sale on May 25, 1938, at the price of $850.[4] It was sold by him in that year to its present owner.

The inscription on the back, though apparently in West's hand, is not specifically a statement of authorship, nor does the style of the work relate it to West. The most reasonable surmise would relate the drawing to those years when West was gathering from widespread sources, for use in projected history paintings, all the authentic material he could on Franklin's appearance.

2. Fisher, *The True Benjamin Franklin*, p. 350.
3. *P.M.H.B.*, 23 (1899), 46.
4. Eddy Papers.

See DUFOURNY (formerly attributed to Caffiéri); FRAGONARD, Nos. 1, 2; HOUDON, No. 8; SÈVRES, Nos. 8, 9; WEDGWOOD, No. 5.

CARMONTELLE, LOUIS CARROGIS DE (1717–1806)

> 1   Ca. 1780–81. Drawing. Ink, crayon and water color on paper, 11⅝ x 5⅝ in., cut to margin and mounted. Gray hair. Brown suit with maroon tint. White stockings and black shoes. Chair white touched with gold and upholstered in blue. Light gray hat on table partly covering printed paper, "LES LOIS / DE LA PENSILVANIA." Gray wall at left. At right, pale blue sky with ships. Inscribed on the back in ink, "Eripuit Coelo fulmen septum / que tirannis" and in pencil, "on l'a vu desarmer / les Tyrans et les Dieux." *Owner:* Herbert Clark Hoover, New York. Pl. 28.

Since the print from this drawing was published in April 1781, the portrait must have been made early in that year or late in 1780. The artist, Louis Carrogis, called Carmontelle, was a member of the household of the Duc d'Orléans in the varied role of professor of mathematics, librarian, dramatist, and stage designer. He left at his death a collection of some 300 such portraits, little whole-lengths in color in which accuracy and precision were combined with a charming spontaneity. He had the independence and naïveté of the accomplished amateur. Horace Walpole had in 1767 praised his work in general for its delicacy, assurance, and lack of artificiality.[5] Much of it was engraved, some by himself. A few years earlier than the "Franklin," his drawing of the Calas family, center of a cause célèbre in which Elie de Beaumont (see GREUZE, No. 1) had acted for the defense, had been engraved by Delafosse who made many prints from his work.[6]

A collection of Carmontelle's drawings is at the Musée Condé in Chantilly. There is no record, however, of the "Franklin" having been a part of it. On July 4, 1927, Abel Doysié sent word to George Simpson Eddy that the drawing would soon come up for sale.[7] In November 1928 it was purchased by Edward B. Robinette

---

5. Lewis and Smith, *Walpole's Correspondence, 2,* p. 27.
6. *Notes and Queries,* 2d ser. *1,* 179.
7. Eddy Papers.

from the Daniel Farr Co., Inc. Mr. Robinette presented it to Herbert Hoover, with whom he had been associated in Belgian Relief.

    2   1781. Line engraving by François Denis Née (1732–1817), after the drawing by Carmontelle. Engraved surface, 12¼ x 7½ in. "L. C. de Carmontelle, Del. Née Sculp. / On l'a vu désarmer les Tirans et les Dieux. / A Paris chez Née rue des Francs-Bourgeois, Porte St Michel, / A.P.D.R." The paper shown in the design was inscribed, "LES LOIX / DE PENSILVA- / NIE." Pl. 28.

Publication of the print was announced in the *Journal de Paris* of March 31, 1781. It was noted in the *Mercure de France,* April 7, 1781, under the heading, "Gravures":

> Portrait en pied de M. Franklin, gravé sur le dessin de M. de Carmontel. Prix 1 livre 4 sols. A Paris, chez M. Née, Graveur, rue des Francs-Bougeois, & à Versailles, chez M. Giraud, Negociant, au coin de la rue & place Dauphine. Au bas du Portrait on lit cette épigraphe: On l'a vu désarmer les Tyrans & les Dieux.[8]

It may be noted in the description of the original drawing by Carmontelle that Turgot's famous Latin epigram is written on the back of it in ink, and below that, in pencil, the French translation of it which appears on the face of this engraving. The translation is the work of Félix Nogaret, a poetaster and amateur of the arts, to whom the ideas of the Enlightenment came as a heady draught. Nogaret's initial friendly advance to Franklin was that least likely to elicit a warm response. He had written, on March 2, 1781, a long letter of the most fulsome personal praise, expanding this into a long discussion of the great need for a better translation into French of the Turgot epigram. An artist, he wrote, had recently presented himself, and had consulted Nogaret upon a portrait of Franklin which he was engraving.[9] Learning that the

8. "Full-length portrait of M. Franklin, engraved after the drawing by M. de Carmontel. . . . Below the Portrait this epigram appears: They have seen disarm the Tyrants and the Gods" (*4, 47*).
9. Franklin Papers (A.P.S.), *21,* no. 87.

print represented its subject "dans l'inaction," Nogaret advised the addition of a table on which an electrical machine, books, and other objects characterizing a great scientist should be placed. This idea, he affirmed, had been adopted, and he then launched into the matter which really interested him, the translation of the epigram to be placed upon the plate, coming up, after a long analysis, with "On l'a vu désarmer les tyrans et les dieux." The rest of the 11-page letter demonstrates its writer's poetic skill and fancy. It may be guessed that Née had come to Nogaret for a suitable inscription for his plate. Nogaret made his suggestion about a table and still life apparently without realizing that the design was Carmontelle's and already fixed. Later, he was to commission a portrait of Franklin for himself (see CASTRIQUE).

> 3   1781. Line engraving by François Denis Née, after Gaspard Duché de Vancy (d. 1788). Plate size, 12 5/8 x 17 15/16 in. Engraved surface, 10¼ x 16½ in. "Dessiné par Duché, d'après nature au Chateau de Ferney en 1781. Gravé par Née. / CHAMBRE DU COEUR DE VOLTAIRE / Pays de Gex No. I / N. B. Pour les Vues du Chateau de Ferney il faut avoir recours aux deux Estampes que nous en avons donné dans les Tableaux Pittoresques de la Suisse No. 155, et au No. 161, du même Ouvrage pour la Vue du Tombeau de Voltaire à Ferney." A view of a room with a memorial obelisk in a curtained niche, a curtained bed, a clock, and on the walls a view of the entry into Paris of Henry IV and forty portraits of Voltaire's friends and associates. Among them is "M. le Dr. Franklin," profile, to left, with spectacles, in an oval frame.

The little portrait has been accepted as a version of the Carmontelle profile, engraved also by Née and at the same time, to which he has added the spectacles. The plate appeared in the first of a sumptuous series of twelve folios issued at Paris between 1781 and 1796, *Description générale et particulière de la France, ou Voyage pittoresque de la France, avec la description de toutes ses provinces, ouvrage national, dedié au Roi, et orné d'un grand nombre de gravures, executées avec le plus soin, d'après les dessin des artistes par une société de gens de lettres.* Here the text makes clear that this engraving is to be taken as an actual view of Voltaire's private chamber, and implies that the portraits are represented as actually there:

> Ce seigneur [the Marquis de Villette, owner of the château] en a fait prendre le dessin qu'il a eu la bonté de nous confier, en nous permettant d'en insérer la gravure dans notre collection. Cette chambre est toujours restée depuis ce tems dans l'état où on la voit ici. Elle est ornée des portraits les plus ressemblans de la plupart des connoissances et amis de Voltaire, et des personnes qualifées avec qui il étoit en relation.[10]

Franklin's "Account of Family Expenses" notes as of April 1, 1781, "Nee, for the Description of France &c. 84."[1] Its inclusion in this large work at this time indicates that it must have been made before the Carmontelle print, but the Carmontelle drawing may still have been its source. Duché was in London in 1784, his portrait of Viscenzo Lunardi, the aeronaut, being engraved there at that time. He was in California with the La Pérouse expedition in 1786, and lost his life in the Pacific two years later.

CASTRIQUE

1782. Miniature. Unlocated.

In April 1782, just at the beginning of the negotiations with the peace commissioners from London, William Temple Franklin consulted Félix Nogaret as to the address of a painter, presumably to make a new portrait of his grandfather. On May 24 Nogaret wrote to Franklin begging him to pose for a miniature.[2] The painter would catch a likeness within the space of two hours only, would do the work at no cost to anyone, and the picture was to be a gift for Mme. Nogaret who had long been importuning it. In a letter

---

10. "This noble gentleman has had made of it the drawing which he has had the goodness to entrust to us, permitting us to add the engraving to our collection. This room has always remained as one sees it here. It is ornamented with the most lifelike portraits of most of the acquaintances and friends of Voltaire, and of notable people known to him." ("Pays de Gex. No. 1." Information from Abel Doysié, Paris, 1960.)

1. Franklin Papers (A.P.S.).

2. Franklin Papers (University of Pennsylvania), *6,* no. 28.

dated July 1782 he expressed his and Madame's gratitude for the work, just then received from the artist.[3]

The artist is identified in the letter of May 24 as one who had 15 days before painted a portrait of the new Archbishop of Paris, Leclerc de Juigné. The engraving of that portrait, surrounded by allegorical designs conceived by Nogaret, is inscribed, "Pinxit Castrique." Castrique is known only as a miniaturist of the late 18th century whose work is characterized by a fine stroke technique and by grayish tones.

In Chap. 8, above, the fragmentary evidence on this picture is given more fully, and the inferences which may be drawn from it discussed. The miniature may have been no more than another copy of the Duplessis pastel, the artist forced to that recourse by Franklin's unwillingness to pose, just as Joseph Wright had been at the same time. It may also have been the original of that dashing likeness apparently intended to express the sense of triumph accompanying the final achievement of victory which was engraved for Lavater's *Essai sur la physiognomie* (Pt. II, 1783), and which is repeated in miniatures attributed to Jean Baptiste Weyler, Jacques Thouron, and signed by "D.C." See WEYLER.

CATHELIN, JACQUES LOUIS (1739–1804)
1779. Line engraving. See FILLEUL, No. 2.

CERACCHI, GIUSEPPE (1751–1804)
Ca. 1790–95. Busts (attributed). See CAFFIÉRI, Nos. 16–18.

CHAMBERLIN, MASON (d. 1787)
1 1762. Painting. Oil on canvas, 50½ x 40¾ in. Eyes with yellow-brown iris, black pupils. Mole on left cheek. Indentation, perhaps a scar, below corner of mouth at right. Gray wig. Violet-brown suit. Background predominantly brown and yellow, with a dark green curtain, center, and steel bells and rods at left. Green upholstery on the chair back. Books at extreme left appear indistinctly. Signed at bottom, left, "M. Chamberlin pinxt. 1762." *Owner:* Wharton Sinkler, Philadelphia. Pl. 4.

3. Ibid., 7, no. 14.

218

The painting was commissioned by Franklin's friend, Col. Philip Ludwell, III, a wealthy Virginian who had settled with his family in Westminster a few years before. Franklin states that it was made "just before" his departure for Philadelphia, that is, in late July or early August 1762.[4] It was included in the exhibition of the Society of Artists opening May 14, 1763, as, "Portrait of a Gentleman: half length." A print published shortly after suggests that this may have been a part of the arrangement between the artist and Col. Ludwell. The artist, who had begun life as a merchant's clerk, owed his success both to the production of well-defined, accurate likenesses and to good business management. Franklin preferred this portrait to that by the contentious artist-electrician, Benjamin Wilson.

Philip Ludwell died on March 25, 1767, leaving three daughters, Hannah Philippa, Frances, and Lucy. The portrait was inherited by Lucy, who, on May 14, 1769, married John Paradise, a member of Johnson's Club and the owner, as was she, of properties in Virginia. He died in 1795. She returned to America in 1805. The painting remained in London, where it was purchased by Joshua Bates (1788–1864), a native of Weymouth, Mass., who had been sent to England as the business representative of W. R. Gray of Boston. There he entered into partnership with John Baring, and later became a member of the firm of Baring Bros. In 1856, after correspondence with Jared Sparks on the subject, he presented a copy of it by George Dunlop Leslie (1835–1921) to Harvard College.[5] The original portrait descended to his daughter, the wife of Sylvain van de Weyer, Belgian ambassador at London, and to his grandson, Col. Victor van de Weyer. It was still at this old residence, 21 Arlington St., when the entire property was put up for sale on Dec. 18, 1912. Sold for £2,940 at Christie's, it came to the Knoedler Galleries in New York. Owned for a time by George Palmer of New London, Conn., it was again offered for sale by the Rosenbach Galleries in 1926. See also above, pp. 57–60, and Pl. 4.

4. See above, Chap. 4, n. 19.
5. Sparks Papers. Another copy by Leslie, formerly owned by John Milnes, Lupset Hall, near Wakefield, Yorkshire, came into the possession of Percy Avery Rockefeller, whose son, Avery Rockefeller, presented it to Yale University in 1926. Both copies are in the 50 x 40 in. size. The books and other detail are shown in them more clearly than in the darker original canvas.

2   1764. Replica of the above. Destroyed.

On Nov. 15, 1763, William Franklin wrote from Burlington, N.J., to William Strahan who had agreed to look after his interests in London, "My father desires Mr. Chamberlyn would make a good copy of his Picture which was done for Col. Ludwell. Let it be put in a handsome Gilt Frame, and sent over, as soon as it can be well done, to him."[6] That the picture was to be Benjamin Franklin's gift to his son's new home appears in another letter from William to Strahan of Dec. 18, 1763. His wife, he writes, "would likewise be glad to have my father's picture from Mr. Chamberlyne's (which I wrote for in my last) and mine from Mr. Wilson's as our dining room remains unfinished for want of them."[7] His earlier letter is endorsed by Strahan, "June 22: 1764 gave Mr Chamberlin the Order."

The painting may be presumed to have been sent in due course to America, and eventually to have been destroyed with other of William Franklin's property. The loyalist Governor of New Jersey was arrested in June 1776, and held a prisoner in Connecticut until the end of October 1779. In the meanwhile, his wife had sought refuge in New York with all of his moveable property. There she died, and there, soon after, all of the property was destroyed in a fire. William's own statement of his loss cites:

> A Variety of elegant Household Furniture, suitable
> for a large Government House, Pictures, Prints, &c.
> and a large Library containing many scarce and valuable Books and curious Manuscripts respecting the
> first settlement of America, &c. &c. which were burnt
> in the King's Stores at New York, where they were
> lodged for safety by Mrs. Franklin, on the evacuation
> of New Jersey, who died previous to the fire, at which
> time I was a prisoner in Connecticut.[8]

3   1763. Mezzotint by Edward Fisher (1730–85), after Chamberlin. Plate size, 14⅞ x 10⅞ in. "M: Chamberlin pinxt. E:

6. Pierpont Morgan Library.
7. Charles Henry Hart, "Letters from William Franklin to William Strahan," *P.M.H.B., 35* (1911), 435.
8. Public Record Office, London. Loyalist Claims, A. O. 13.

Fisher fecit. B: Franklin of Philadelphia L. L. D. F. R. S. Sold by M Chamberlin in Stewart Street, Old Artillery Ground, Spittalfields. Price 5s." Pl. 4.

The print, published in competition with that by McArdell after Wilson's portrait, was preferred by Franklin, perhaps because of the character of the likeness and of the artist, perhaps also in friendship for those concerned with its sale. It was probably not begun when in November 1762, William Franklin wrote to Strahan of his offer to "take 100 of them."[9] With William it was in part, at least, a commercial venture.[1] An impression at the M.H.S. bearing Mather Byles' inscription that he had received it from Philadelphia on March 15, 1764, is the earliest record of Franklin's many gifts of these prints, and by this we can infer that his supply had been shipped to him from London late in the previous year. In sending one to Thomas François Dalibard, whom he had met in Paris, Franklin wrote, on Sept. 22, 1769, "As I cannot soon again enjoy the Happiness of being personally in your Company, permit my Shadow to pay my Respects to you. 'Tis from a Plate my Son caus'd to be engrav'd some years since."[2] This probably refers to William's offer to underwrite the project with a large order. The young governor seems not to have realized the time and labor the task required.

Samuel Okey on March 16, 1775, wrote to Henry Pelham from Newport, R.I., on the idea of a mezzotint of Dr. Winthrop "as a Companion to the Ingenious and Learned Dr. Franklin. I remember the size of the Plate as I may well do, as laying the Ground for it in London for that scraped by Fisher. I think it sold for five Shillings Ster'g."[3] See also above, pp. 57–60.

4 1773. Line engraving by François Nicolas Martinet (b. 1731), after the mezzotint by Fisher. Plate size, 8 3/16 x 5 5/16 in. "Dessiné et Gravé par F. N. Martinet / Il a ravi le feu des Cieux / Il fait fleurir les Arts en des Climats sauvages. /

9. Quoted above, p. 58.

1. Benjamin Franklin to William Franklin, April 20, 1771 (Franklin Papers, A.P.S., *45*, no. 37).

2. Ibid., *45*, no. 35 C.

3. "Letters and Papers of John Singleton Copley and Henry Pelham," *Collections,* *71* (M.H.S., 1914), 309.

L'Amérique le place à la tête des Sages / La Grèce l'auroit mis au nombre de ses Dieux." Frontispiece to *Oeuvres de M. Franklin . . . traduites de l'anglais sur la quatrième edition par M. Barbeu Doubourg, avec des additions nouvelles et des figures en taille douce,* Paris, 1773. Franklin's wide mouth has been narrowed and his features almost imperceptibly refined. The two moles on cheek and chin are clearly shown. Ornamental buttons have been added to the pocket of the waistcoat. Pl. 4.

The print amused its subject. He wrote to Deborah on Sept. 1, 1773, "There is a new Translation of my Book at Paris, & printed there, being the 3rd Edition in French. A Fifth Edition is now printing here. To the French Edition they have prefixed a Print of me, which tho' a Copy of that by Chamberlin, has got so French a Countenance, that you would take me for one of that lively Nation."[4] The Duc de Croÿ, however, meeting Franklin soon after his arrival in France on Jan. 23, 1777, reported, in spite of the spectacles on his nose and his no longer wearing a wig, "La ressemblance est parfaite dans la belle estampe à la tête de la traduction in–4° de ses oeuvres sur l'électricité."[5]

A sepia drawing, 6½ x 4½ in. in size, is listed in the sale catalogue of Godefroy Mayer as "probably the model for Martinet's engraving."[6]

5　1777. Line engraving by John Lodge (d. 1796), after the mezzotint by Fisher. Engraved surface, 7 x 4¼ in. "Ubi Libertas, ibi patria / BENJAMIN FRANKLIN, L.L.D. & F.R.S. / 'Those who would give up Essential Liberty to purchase / a little Temporary Safety, deserve neither Liberty nor / Safety.' Address of the Assembly of Pennsylvania, in 1755. / Engraved from an Original Picture by Jnº. Lodge. / Printed according to Act of Parliament, for J. Almon, in Piccadilly, London, 21st. April, 1777." Frontispiece to *The Remembrancer; or, Impar-*

---

4. Franklin Papers (L.C.).
5. "The resemblance is perfect in the beautiful print at the head of the translation in quarto of his works on electricity" (De Croÿ, *Journal inédit, 3,* 295).
6. *No. 30. Old Paintings, Drawings, Miniatures,* p. 8, no. 42.

tial *Repository of Public Events. For the Year 1777* (London, 1778). Pl. 5.

John Almon (1737–1805), bookseller and journalist, intimate friend of John Wilkes, friend also of Lord Temple, Burke, and Franklin, had been active for years in liberal causes and the politics of the opposition. *The Remembrancer* opens fire by reprinting the Pennsylvania constitution of 1776, follows with Paine's "American Crisis," and continues with volleys of American news, propaganda, and predictions of an American victory. It is an initial effort, of which there were to be others, to use Franklin's personal prestige almost to the point of placing him at the head of a movement to liberalize British policy and even to reform the structure of the government. It seems possible to assume some connection between the publishers of this book and the creators of the bronze medal described below, with its very similar purpose and inscription.

6   1777. Medal by unknown artist, after the mezzotint by Fisher, or the line engraving by Lodge. Bronze, diam. 1 25/32 in. (4½ cm.). Obverse: "B. FRANKLIN OF PHILADELPHIA L.L.D. O. F.R.S" with head of Franklin three-quarters to left, wearing a turbanlike cloth cap. Open shirt collar. Reverse: "NON IRRITA FULMINA CURAT" with tree threatened by storm clouds and lightning. In Exergue: "1777 +." Pl. 5.

The medal at once suggests the Dixon miniature of 1757, the only other portrait showing Franklin wearing the loose cap with which a gentleman, at home, replaced his wig. Nor is it derived from the Cochin engraving of 1777. In this Franklin wears spectacles, the fur cap rather than a cloth cap, and ordinary dress instead of an open collar. The Cochin, also, shows the right side of the face. Here the left side is shown, as in the Dixon miniature. The face, in pose and detail, is based upon the Chamberlin portrait, probably as reflected in the Lodge print. We must assume that the cap has been added by an artist who had heard of Franklin's arrival in France wearing an unusual substitute for a wig and who, having no clear idea of its character, added the type of informal headgear with which he was familiar and, as a natural concomitant of it, the open shirt-collar.

This assumes a date of early 1777, after Franklin's arrival in France but before the Cochin print or Nini medallion had reached England. The plus sign added to the "1777" creates a doubt as to whether it be date of issue or commemorates a period of activity. 18th-century origin is assured by the fact that the British Museum's example came to it by bequest of Clayton Mordaunt Cracherode (1730–99). Herbert A. Grueber's frequently reiterated statement based on the motto, "Non irrita fulmina curat" (he stands impervious to the futile thunderbolt), that the medal commemorates Franklin's appearance before the Privy Council in 1774, is unacceptable.[7] A passage in a letter of the spy Edward Bancroft, from London, Feb. 21, 1777, to Silas Deane in Paris, gives us a glimpse of British conjecture as to Franklin's new appearance and to that degree at least may be related to the history of this medal. "You will see by the enclosed card (drawn by a son of 177 [Dr. Joseph Priestley]) what ideas are here formed of the appearance of 64 [Franklin] in his Canadian Cap. Make my most respectful compliments to him."[8] Several passages in the letters of Josiah Wedgwood, written from Staffordshire to his partner, Thomas Bentley, then managing the London end of their business, give us in veiled terms what I believe to be the key to the mystery.

In April Wedgwood wrote, "We have some good Doctr. Franklins (will the courtiers believe it?) out of the kiln today."[9] These must have been among the first of the new blue and white portrait cameos, though the mold would have been that from which the earlier Franklin medallions in one color had been made. By July, however, he takes a very different attitude toward the making of a ceramic reproduction of a portrait whose subject he fears to name but which must have been this same bronze medal of Franklin. Franklin, it may well be inferred, had in that brief interval become a much more controversial figure. Also, there was a wide difference between the portrait cameos and a medal. The cameos

7. Herbert A. Grueber, "English Personal Medals," *Numismatic Chronicle, 11* (1891), 101.

8. *Collections* (N.Y.H.S., 1886). *Deane Papers, 1,* 496.

9. As quoted by Lady Farrer in her very freely edited edition of the *Letters of Josiah Wedgwood*, pp. 349–50, under the date April 19, 1777. William Billington, of the Wedgwood Museum, states that the letter is undated, but assumed to be of April 16. The Franklin cameo is listed in the Wedgwood catalogue of 1777.

were issued like engravings to satisfy the curious, and the subjects might be good or bad. A medal did formal honor to its subject and implied a strong allegiance on the part of the person who issued it. In July Bentley sent two pieces to Wedgwood to be reproduced, presumably for sale in London. One was a mold for a medal of the romantic and enlightened tyrant of Sweden, Gustavus III, the ally of France, who had granted his people freedom of the press and had been honored in an ode by Voltaire. The other was an actual medal which Wedgwood names only as "the Brazen head." He wrote back to his partner on July 17, 1777:

> I mention'd to you before my having receiv'd the K. of Sweden, & the Brazen head, & I was giving them out to be made in the common course of business, when a thought or two came across my mind which made me pause, & lay them by, 'till I could canvas the matter a little more at my leisure.
>
> My first hasty thought was, that the two characters we were going to celebrate were very different! One had just enslav'd a Kingdom. I need not say how the other is employ'd. It cannot be right to celebrate them both—Perhaps neither. I may think one of them worthily employ'd, but many circumstances may make it highly improper *for me*, & *at this season,* to strike medals to his honor.[1]

And two days later:

> My objections to striking medals from the Bronze you sent me rather increase. It would be doing no service to the cause of *Liberty in general,* at least so it appears to me, & might hurt us very much individually. Nay the personage is himself at this time more absolute than any Despot in Europe, how then can he be celebrated, in such circumstances as the Patron of Liberty? Besides, if France should declare herself openly an Ally &c &c I am from that moment an

1. Farrer, p. 372. Original at the Wedgwood Museum, Barlaston, Stoke-on-Trent, England.

enemy to both, & the case being very probable, I would not bring myself into so whimsical a situation as you may easily conceive, by throwing these circumstances together a little in your mind, I might add, that as the two Powers may be said to act really as Allies against us, though for political reasons without the form of a public declaration, the event of this conceal'd warfare may be more fatal to us than an open rupture, & I may, as a subject of the British Empire, declare my self an enemy to all its enemies & their Allies though I may curse most bitterly those who have brought us into the dilemma of calling those our enemies, who were, & might have continued to be, our best friends. But I have not fully settled these matters in my own mind. When I have I will acquaint you of it, & in the meantime your sentiments will have great weight with me in this, as they have *in all cases whatsoever*—But do not send them by the post.[2]

Josiah Wedgwood's inner conflict, his warm sympathy for America and his personal friendship for Franklin against his patriotic duty and the danger of continuing opposition to the government, ended in a decision against reproducing "the Brazen head," but in favor of the Swedish piece. A letter of Aug. 8 indicates that subversive matter was still coming from London and the head of the firm still hesitating over it. "The Rattle Snake is in hand," Josiah wrote. "I think it best to keep such unchristian articles for *Private Trade*."[3] See above, pp. 109–12.

> 7   Ca. 1805–50. Miniature by unknown artist, after the painting by Chamberlin. Opaque water color on ivory, rectangular, 4 5/16 x 3 5/8 in. Coloring essentially the same as the original. Crack in ivory at right, through the window. A printed catalogue entry on the back of the frame reads, "BENJAMIN FRANKLIN : MINIATURE ON IVORY / American School, late XVIII Century." *Owner:* A.P.S., Philadelphia.

2. Ibid.
3. Ibid., p. 375.

The miniature is significant only as a portrait of Franklin in an unusual form and as an early record of the Chamberlin painting. It may be the miniature of the same subject and size formerly owned by Francis Wellesley of Westfield Common, near Woking, England, whose collection was brought together over a relatively short period of time with the assistance of George C. Williamson, then the leading authority on the art of the miniature. The collection was exhibited at the Victoria and Albert Museum in 1914–15. The Franklin is not listed in the literature on the collection until its appearance as no. 59 in Sotheby's catalogue of the sale of the Francis Wellesley miniatures on June 28, 1920.[4] It is there described as holding the accession no. 720 in the Wellesley collection and with the note that it "appears to be the finished study for the well-known portrait." The size is given as 4½ x 3¼ in. It was purchased by "Bois" for £29. Sotheby's sale of the properties of Col. Abel Henry Smith and others on March 11, 1931, included paintings of various schools from the collection of H. G. Bois, but this portrait was not among them. The miniature was purchased by its present owner from Edmund Bury, dealer, on Aug. 1, 1953. See above, pp. 57–60.

CHEVILLET, JUSTE (1729–90)

1 1778. Engraving. See DUPLESSIS, "Fur Collar," No. 2.

2 Ca. 1778. Drawing. See DUPLESSIS, "Fur Collar," No. 24.

COCHIN, CHARLES NICOLAS, THE YOUNGER (1715–90)

1 1777. Original copperplate, engraved by Augustin de Saint Aubin (1737–1807), after a drawing by Cochin. Etched and engraved, 8 3/16 x 5 7/8 in. "35ᵉ / BENJAMIN FRANKLIN. / Né à Boston, dans la nouvelle Angleterre le 17. Janvier 1706. / C. N. Cochin filius delin. 1777. Aug. de St. Aubin Sculp. / Dessiné par C. N. Cochin Chevalier de l'Ordre du Roi, en

4. Weymer Mills, "Historic Miniatures. The Francis Wellesley Collection," *Century Magazine, 89* (1914), 202–07. *Catalogue of a Collection of Miniatures in Plumbago, etc., Lent by Francis Wellesley, Esq. 1914–15* (London, Victoria and Albert Museum, Dept. of Paintings, 1915). G. C. Williamson, ed., *A Handlist of the Miniatures and Portraits in Plumbago or Pencil Belonging to Francis and Minnie Wellesley* (Oxford, 1914).

1777, et Gravé par Aug. de St. Aubin Graveur de la Bibliotheque du Roi." The "35ᵉ" is very finely inscribed at the upper left corner of the plate (upper right of the print), outside the composition. The line in Latin is within the composition at the base, and obscured by the shading. With the plate, Yale University owns an unfinished proof of the print with the title, "BENJAMIN FRANKLIN," differently placed. Various other intermediate states of the print are recorded. *Owner:* Yale University, William Smith Mason Collection. Pl. 10.

The original drawing by Cochin from which the plate was engraved is not known to be extant. It is not mentioned in the sale of his estate of June 21, 1790, nor has it been found in the collection of his own work which he himself mounted and preserved.[5] In the sale of the estate of the engraver, on April 4–9, 1808, only a proof in quarto of the engraving itself appears.[6] The drawing was probably made in January or February, 1777. Publication of the print was first announced in the *Journal de Paris* of June 16, 1777. The *Mercure de France* carried the following in July:

> *Portrait de Benjamin Franklin,* né à Boston dans la Nouvelle-Angleterre, le 17 Janvier 1706, dessiné par Ch. N. Cochin, Chevalier de l'Ordre du Roi, en 1777, & gravé par Augustin de Saint-Aubin, Graveur de la Bibliotheque du Roi; prix 2 liv. 8 f. A Paris, chez M. Cochin, aux Galleries du Louvre, & M. de Saint-Aubin, rue des Mathurins, au petit Hôtel de Clugny.
>
> Ce Portrait d'un homme très celébre dans les sciences & dans la politique, est fort rassemblant, & la gravure en est agréable & pittoresque.[7]

The print is above all a news picture. Because of it, the sensational fact of Franklin's arrival in France and the sensational costume which so effectively dramatized his role as envoy from the New World to the Old reached every part of Europe, creating an image of tremendous value to Franklin's purpose. It is an accu-

5. At Philadelphia Museum of Art. Zigrosser, "Premier Dessinateur," pp. 40–47.
6. H. Mireur, *Dictionnaire des Ventes d'Art* (Paris, 1911–12), no. 81.
7. July, 1777, *1,* 173.

rate likeness and a perceptive characterization, but its importance and its contemporary impact is as news. It was not a formal portrait and was never repeated on canvas as such by any artist of established reputation. Repetitions there were without number and in every imaginable medium, but almost all of small size and a transient character: prints, ceramics, watch faces, and the like. The earliest dated engraving after it is by Johann Christian Gottfried Fritsch, Hamburg, 1778. In a curious allegorical print published anonymously in May 1779, "Le Tombeau de Voltaire," the motif of fur cap and spectacles is carried out in a full-length figure, semi-nude, bow in hand, and so made to represent the savage nobility of the American continent.[8] The end of its news interest is marked by the publication ca. 1780 of an altered copy of it engraved by Pierre Adrien Le Beau (b. 1744) after a drawing by Claude Louis Desrais (1746–1816), two minor artists of the time.[9] Desrais has revised the portrait to accord with the dignity due the representative of a recognized power at the Court of France. The portrait, reversed, is in a similar oval frame, with the same title. A ribbon tied in a bow ornaments the top of the oval. The spectacles have been removed, and a stylish cap lightly trimmed with fur substituted for the shapeless Canadian headgear. Franklin now wears a fur-lined satin dressing gown and a lace shirt-frill. The face is the same, but the other changes are so marked that the piece has occasionally been accepted as a new likeness. Some 15 years later the Desrais engraving was readapted to the taste of the revolutionary era in a popular color print by the Citoyenne F. Montalant.[1]

The copperplate of the original Cochin-Saint Aubin print, whose design was to be so widely re-echoed, was in the sale of the Edwin Babcock Holden Collection, American Art Gallery, New York, April 21, 1910. It is listed under no. 1230, "Four copies, and the original copper plate. As a lot." These, with other states of the

8. Described in Bachaumont, *Mémoires, 14,* 456, not without a word of ridicule for its discordant elements. The print, in which Ignorance is seen as interrupting the homage paid to Voltaire's memory by the four continents, was answered by another, "Le Tombeau de Voltaire foudroyé," in which the figure of Religion dominates the scene.

9. "BENJAMIN FRANKLIN / Né à Boston dans la Nouvelle Angleterre, / le 17 Janvier 1706. / Desrayes del. Le Beau scul. / A Paris chès Esnautes et Rapilly, rue St. Jacques à la Ville de Coutances. A.P.D.R."

1. Renouvier, *Histoire de l'art,* p. 246.

print, came thence into the collection of the late William Smith Mason. See above, pp. 96–9, 108–09.

> 2   Ca. 1777. Painting by an unidentified artist, after the Cochin-Saint Aubin engraving. Oil on canvas, 22½ x 18¾ in. Light brown eyes. Gray hair under the brown fur cap. Very dark magenta coat against a dark green background. At the lower left, painted in large script, "Franklin." *Owner:* A.P.S., Philadelphia.

The painting was purchased in Berlin in 1949 by Miss Edna K. Kassell of the Scientific Research Division, Military Security Board. The dealer from whom she acquired it stated that it had come from Frau Jacob, a descendant of the Wille family. This provenance was investigated and substantiated in part by a "good-sized photograph of the Wille salon in Bremen, taken at about the turn of the century; it shows the Franklin portrait hanging over the mantel."[2] There were, at the turn of the century, German painters of the name of Wille, but the significance of the picture lies in its probable ownership by one of the family active in Paris during Franklin's residence there, either Jean Georges Wille (1715–1808), engraver and designer, or his son, Pierre Alexandre Wille (1748–1821), painter and engraver. Even a copy from the print made by an artist to whom Franklin's appearance would be known would have some of the authority of a life portrait. The name of the subject placed upon the face of the canvas follows a practice common among engravers to avoid errors in identity. The subject faces to the left, rather than to the right, the pose perhaps being reversed to facilitate copying on the plate. The painting is one of the few copies in which the strong pleasantness of the original is retained. There has been some overpainting, however, by later owners, and only parts of the 18th-century paint surface are visible.

Miss Kassell had the painting cleaned by a Berlin restorer, Fernand Wohlenberg, who believed the painting to have the quality in mouth and eyes of a life portrait, and assigned it to the French School, ca. 1750–70. He saw some slight variation from the Cochin print and chose the flattering explanation of an earlier life portrait. The picture is certainly related to the Cochin print, though

2. Miss Kassell to the author, June 27, 1950.

it is hardly possible that its history and the full value of its likeness can ever be discovered. Neither the Wille father or son made an engraving of Franklin. Nor is there evidence by which to associate the painting with Johann Martin Will, of Augsburg, author of an enlarged Cochin-type mezzotint of Franklin and of other portraits of popular figures, all of an inferior quality. The painting was purchased from Miss Kassell by its present owner in 1950.

> 3 1778. Painting by John Trumbull (1756–1843), after the Cochin-Saint Aubin engraving. Oil on panel. 5⅜ x 4⅜ in. (sight). Gray fur cap. Brown eyebrows. Brown eyes. Lilac-brown suit. Gray background. *Owner:* Yale University Art Gallery.

Until its recent discovery and identification by Theodore Sizer, the painting was known only through the entry in Trumbull's list of work done before his first trip to Europe. It appears there as No. 39, "Head of Dr. Franklin—a fur cap—from a French print."[3]

Richard Bache had written his father-in-law on Jan. 31, 1778, acknowledging receipt of the "engraver's and potter's performances," referring undoubtedly to the Cochin print and the Nini medallion.[4] The two pieces were the first reflections of their envoy's appearance in France to reach the Americans. This little copy of the print was the first oil portrait of Franklin to be painted in America since Feke's of more than 30 years before. In Boston at the same time Trumbull copied the head of Peale's new portrait of Washington which had just been brought from Philadelphia by John Hancock.

> 4 1790. Medal by J. M. Lageman, adapted from the Cochin portrait. Silver, diam. 1 9/16 in. Obverse: "BENJAMIN FRANKLIN" with profile portrait to right, wearing fur cap; in exergue: "OB. XVII APRILIS MDCCXC." Reverse: "FULMINIS TYRANNIDISQUE DOMITOR" with globe surmounted by cap, electrical machine, writing materials, &c.; in exergue: "LAGEMAN FECIT."

3. Theodore Sizer, ed., *The Autobiography of Colonel John Trumbull* (New Haven, 1953), p. 55. Theodore Sizer, *The Works of Colonel John Trumbull* (New Haven, 1950), p. 25. Theodore Sizer, "Colonel Trumbull and a Newly-Found Portrait of Dr. Franklin," *Art Quarterly, 24* (1961), 327–31, with illustration.

4. Franklin Papers, University of Pennsylvania, *2,* no. 2.

The Amsterdam medalist appears to have been the first to adapt the Cochin likeness to full profile, memorializing Franklin in a way which shows how, though it was no longer acceptable in court circles, the simple figure in fur cap remained a popular image of the sage and humanitarian.[5] There is a similar profile in an unmarked plaque in bronze, oval, 2⅜ x 1⅞ in.

CURTIUS (KURTZ), PHILIPPE MATTHIAS GUILLAUME (1737–ca. 1800)
    Undated. Waxwork bust or figure.

In Paris, on September 14, 1779, young Elkanah Watson visited the Salon du Louvre, and was delighted to find Franklin represented there in painting and sculpture. In the evening, on his way to theatre, he took in a waxwork show:

> But first view'd a collection of wax-work in the vicinity; in Entering at the door a surly century [*sic*] rather obstructed our passage—in passing I was surprised to observe this supposed century to be artificial—the door keeper told me it was a Bostonian; tho' Intirely foreign—as it resembles an old swiss with whiskers. The variety of these works are too numerous to detail—the most striking, however, was that of the celebrated Voltaire, who is closely Ingaged with a table full of books, papers &c. before him; and his countenance Expressed Every sensation of a philosopher.[6]

A "Franklin" he did not see or did not mention, and just when Franklin's likeness joined those of Voltaire, Rousseau, Frederick the Great, Catherine the Great, Cagliostro, Hyder Aly, Blanchard the Aeronaut, and the others is not known. This popular and successful attraction of the boulevards is first identified as under the proprietorship of Curtius in Louis Sebastien Mercier's *Tableau de Paris* of 1783:

5. Illust. in *Verslagen om trent 's rijks versamelingen van geschidnis en kunst, 74* (1953), opp. p. 108.
6. Watson Papers, New York State Library.

Les figures en cire du sieur Curtius sont très-célèbres
sur les Boulevards, & très-visitées; il a modelé les
rois, les grands écrivains, les jolies femmes, & les
fameux voleurs; on y voit Jeannot, Desrues, le comte
d'Estaing & Linguet; on y voit la famille royale assis
à un banquet artificiel: l'empereur est à côté du roi.
Le crieur s'égosille à la porte: *Entrez, entrez mes-
sieurs, venez voir le grand couvert; entrez, c'est tout
comme à Versailles.* On donne deux sous par personne, & le sieur Curtius fait quelquefois jusqu'à
cent écus par jour, avec la montre de ces mannequins
enluminés.[7]

Leonard Cottrell, in 1951, was the first to make the presumptive
identification of Curtius of the waxwork with the sculptor Philippe
Mathias Wilhelm Curtius, who had been received into the Academy
of Saint Luc in 1778.[8] Perhaps in association with Christophe An-
dreas von Creutz, a German seal-cutter of the early 18th century,
he had formerly been cited as Christopher Curtius or Creutz, as
John Christopher Curtius, or simply as Curtius, the variant of
his German name by which he identified himself with Marcus
Curtius, the legendary hero of ancient Rome.

A hint as to the possible origin of the waxwork lies in a letter
of the sculptor Gardeur (q.v.) published in the *Journal de Paris*
of Sept. 20, 1778, the year of Curtius' admission to the Academy of

7. "The wax figures of Curtius are very popular on the boulevards, and much
visited; he had modelled kings, great writers, pretty women and notorious thieves; one
sees here Jeannot, Desrues, the Count d'Estaing & Linguet; one sees the royal family
seated at an artificial banquet: the emperor is beside the king. The barker bawls at the
door: 'Come in, come in, gentlemen, come see the great banquet; come in, it's every bit
the same as Versailles!' One pays two sous apiece, and Curtius sometimes takes in a
hundred crowns a day by the display of these colored manikins." (*3*, Amsterdam, 1783,
40–41.)

8. Cottrell, *Madame Tussaud* (London, 1951), pp. 18–25. Jules Guiffrey, *Histoire de l'Académie de Saint Luc* (Paris, 1915), p. 241, lists the name as Philippe
Mathias Wilhem Curtius. Further confirmation appears in an "Inventaire alphabeti-
que des documents relatifs aux artistes Parisiens conserves aux archives de la Seine,"
published in the *Bulletin de la Société de l'histoire de Paris et de l'Ile de France*
(1906), p. 82. Here Philippe Matthias Guillaume Curtius, painter and sculptor, is
listed as "demeurant 20, boulevard du Temple. Succession, an III. Domaine, cart. 521,
doss. 314."

Saint Luc. Here he accuses his former partner, Couasnon, of selling "his models to form the collection of busts in wax which one sees on the boulevards," and among them that of the Emperor, Gardeur's work alone.[9] Mercier's description, above, cites particularly the portrait of the Emperor Joseph II, brother of Marie Antoinette. Certainly, Curtius appears to have been more entrepreneur than artist. The ghost-written autobiography of his niece and successor, Mme. Tussaud, describes him as "John Christopher Curtius," a medical man from Berne who had progressed from anatomical models in wax to this more remunerative work.[10] Here also he is described as having excelled in enamel painting, and as having derived a large part of his income as a dealer in paintings.[1] His only appearance in a public exhibition occurred in 1791, after the liberalization of the Salon, with a colored wax bust of the Prince Royal. Both the merit of his work and his place as an original artist have been frequently denied.[2] An article on Curtius in the *Dictionnaire de la conversation* (Paris, 1858) describes his figures as life-sized, costumed, but with the qualification "more or less," as to resemblance.

It would seem certain that the character and success of Curtius' show at Paris must have been derived from the innovations of Patience Wright in London. Her contribution there had been a perfected realism and the use of subjects familiar to her public. On the other hand, she encouraged a better clientele by not including the notorious criminals with them in the exhibition. There is no evidence of any association with Curtius during Mrs. Wright's visit to Paris. The Curtius show moved steadily in this direction, the "comme à Versailles" shifting with the Revolution to the victims of the guillotine, a point of emphasis still much to the fore at Madame Tussaud's. Mme. Tussaud, succeeding her uncle as proprietor, took the show on tour through England and to a permanent place as one of the sights of London.

There seems always to have been a "Franklin" in the exhibition,

9. P. 1111.
10. Hervé, *Madame Tussaud's Memoirs and Reminiscences,* pp. 5–6.
1. Ibid., p. 17.
2. Maurice Dreyfous, *Les Arts et les artistes pendant la période révolutionnaire* (Paris, n.d.), p. 231. Renouvier, *Histoire de l'art,* p. 19. Maze-Sencier, *Le Livre des collectionneurs,* p. 677.

from Paris days to the present. Fire, war, and time, however, have wrought changes in the collection, and it is difficult to accept the present likeness as certainly an exact repetition of the original one.[3] Nor can one accept unquestioningly the legend of high gentility implicit in all the Tussaud literature, nor the claims of young Marie Grossholtz, afterward Tussaud, to have been an intimate of the intellectual group in Paris, to have known Franklin well, and herself to have modeled him in wax.

Both small wax profiles and small portraits in wax in high relief have been attributed to Curtius, including a high relief portrait of Franklin of which there are several variant examples. There appears to be no actual support for this attribution beyond the fact that a similar high relief "Death of Voltaire" has for many years been exhibited at Madame Tussaud's as a work of the founder.[4] See WEYLER, No. 9.

DARCIS, JEAN LOUIS (d. 1801)
    1795. Stipple engraving. See HOUDON, No. 11.

DEBROUX, LOUIS
    1777. Miniature. See GREUZE, No. 9.

DEJOUX, CLAUDE (1732–1816)
    1777. Bust. Hand-worked plaster, ht. 59 cm. Signed, "Cl. Dejoux Ft. 1777." *Owner:* Musée de la Coopération Franco-Américaine, Château de Blérancourt, Aisne, France. Pl. 15.
The artist, born at Vadans near the Swiss border, had studied at Marseilles, entered the studio of Guillaume Coustou at Paris, and in 1768 went to Rome with Pierre Julien, remaining there until 1774. He was admitted to the Académie Royale de Peinture et de Sculpture on March 28, 1778, and received as academician on July 31, 1779. His "morceau de reception" on this occasion was a "Saint Sebastian." Bachaumont rather frigidly avers that he might

3. Illust. in John Theodore Tussaud, *The Romance of Madame Tussaud's* (London, 1920), opp. p. 23.
4. Illust. ibid., opp. p. 26. Small profiles illust. opp. p. 21. A similar "Death of Voltaire" is described in *Some Works of Art Belonging to Edward Tuck in Paris* (London, 1910), p. 62, no. 79.

have chosen a better subject.[5] He exhibited regularly at the Salons, but his portrait busts, shown near those of Houdon and Caffiéri, seem not to have invited favorable comparison.

There can be no doubt, however, of the importance and merit of his portrait of Franklin. There is a warm immediacy in the likeness which carries with it the feeling of an artist charmed and excited by his subject. This may be the earliest bust of Franklin. It surely antedates that made by Caffiéri at the close of the year, though another, by Dufourny de Villiers, may have preceded it. There is no contemporary record of the work other than the artist's signature. He seems never to have exhibited it, and it survives in this one unique example. Louis Réau believed the bust by Berruer, with some small variations, to have been based upon it.[6] Points of similarity also suggest that Houdon's bust of Franklin, not made from life, may have been influenced by it.

DE MEAUX, FRANÇOIS
    1784. Drawing. See DUPLESSIS, "Fur Collar," No. 24.

DESRAIS (DESRAYES), CLAUDE LOUIS (1746–1816)
    Ca. 1780. Line engraving. See COCHIN, No. 1.

DIXON, C.
    1 1757. Miniature. Ivory, 2 x 1½ in. Mounted in a plain gold case to be worn as a pendant. Flesh tints faded. White turban cap. Reddish purple banyan, yellow waistcoat, and white shirt. Background stippled in dark gray. Signed, center right, "C.D." On the paper with which the ivory is backed, "Franklin" is written in pencil. On a piece of cardboard in the back of the case "Dr. Benjamin Franklin" is written in the same hand. *Owner:* Museum of Fine Arts, Boston. Pl. 2.

The miniature was painted in October 1757, and sent by Franklin to his wife on Jan. 21, 1758, with the request that she forward it to his sister, Jane Mecom. (See above, pp. 47–52.) Only "a white medallion of Dr. Franklin," presumably the Sèvres piece which he had given her, is mentioned in Mrs. Mecom's will of 1794, and

5. *13, 232.*
6. Réau, "Le Buste en Marbre," p. 167.

it may be assumed that she had already probably given the miniature to her daughter Sarah, Mrs. William Flagg, of Boston. In
1858 it was owned by Mrs. Flagg's unmarried daughter, Sarah, of
South Lancaster, Mass. Sarah Flagg's will of 1881 does not mention it, and we may again assume that she had already given it to
one of her heirs, her cousin, Franklin Greene, of Rhode Island.[7]
Franklin Greene, son of Franklin Greene and grandson of Elihu
Greene, was a great-grandson of Mrs. William Flagg. He had two
daughters, Agnes Love and Emily. Agnes married Joseph Williams
Balch, of Boston, and their son, Dr. Franklin Greene Balch, received the miniature as the gift of his aunt Emily. He placed it on
loan at the Museum of Fine Arts, Boston, in 1899, and made the
loan a gift in 1943.

> 2   Ca. 1790–95. "Franklin crowned by Minerva." Double
> miniature by unidentified artist. Altered copy after Dixon.
> Oval, ca. 2½ x 2 in. Set in gold to be worn as a pendant. The
> portrait of Franklin is three-quarters to right, the likeness an
> inexpert copy from Dixon, with natural hair substituted for
> the turban and the costume brought into the style of 1790. At
> upper left the figure of the goddess, armed with helmet and
> shield, holds a conjoined crown and cap over Franklin's head.
> Inscribed around the edge, "MINERVA presents her favorite
> SON doct. B. FRANKLIN the greatest Genius & Philanthropist
> that Boston or America ever produced with this cap of Knowl-
> edge & crown of Fame & Glory." On the opposite side is a
> miniature of Samuel Hubbart (b. 1766), three-quarters to
> left, a young man in the costume of ca. 1790–95, a conventional
> and very competently painted miniature of the period. Both
> portraits are illustrated in *Antiques, 36* (1939), 222. That of
> Franklin is illustrated in Bowen, *Centennial Celebration,* p.
> 444. *Owner* (1940): Col. Henry Mather Greene, Los An-
> geles.

The portrait has a history of continuous ownership in the Frank-

7. A note written by James M. Dodd, Boston, Oct. 23, 1858 (owned by the New
England Historic Genealogical Society), refers to Sarah Flagg of South Lancaster as
the owner of "a miniature of Dr. Franklin taken during his lifetime." Other information on the provenance of the miniature has been received from Dr. Franklin Greene
Balch and from the Museum of Fine Arts, Boston.

lin family. It is one of the group of portraits and other heirlooms described by Mrs. Russel Hastings in her article, "Some Franklin Memorabilia Emerge in Los Angeles," *Antiques, 36,* 222–26, and *37* (1940), 122–25. Preserved with the miniature in its leather case is a slip of paper reading, "Mrs. Franklyn to / Mr. Gooch." This evidence, apparently referring to Mrs. John Franklin who had died in 1768, and apparently in the hand of her executor, Tuthill Hubbart, is discounted by Mrs. Hastings as probably transferred to the miniature from some other one of the heirlooms. Her thorough and careful study of the provenance of the objects indicates that the miniature had belonged originally to Mrs. Samuel Partridge, the Betsy Partridge who on Oct. 24, 1778, had begged Franklin for a miniature of himself to "Ware on the Neck," and had been disappointed by the receipt of a Sèvres medallion instead. She draws an inference, almost certainly correct, that this is the miniature listed in 1814 among the jewelry in Mrs. Partridge's estate. The "one miniature setting" there entered was purchased at the sale of her effects by Thomas Waldron Sumner, whose wife was a niece and namesake of Mrs. Partridge.[8]

Mrs. Hastings discusses and dismisses various theories as to the identity of the young man on the opposite half of the piece, unaware of the answer given in the earliest documentation of it. This appears in *The Crayon, 5* (1858), 330: "There is in the possession of Miss Sumner a curious miniature of Franklin on ivory, taken at a much later period in his life. It represents Minerva also; she is placing upon the brow of the philosopher a laurel chaplet, and the cap of knowledge." Here the second miniature is described as that of Samuel Hubbart, a grandson of Mrs. Elizabeth Gooch Hubbart, who had married John Franklin as his second wife. It is here attributed "undoubtedly" to Malbone, from whose hand the portrait of Franklin "undoubtedly was not." Actually, it is probable that the portrait of Hubbart was originally the principal piece in the setting, and that of Franklin made as an ornamental backing piece in lieu of hairwork or some other form of allegorical design.

This must have been, therefore, Betsy Partridge's miniature of a favorite nephew. The Miss Sumner who owned it in 1858 must have

8. Hastings, "Franklin Memorabilia," p. 224. See genealogical chart opposite.

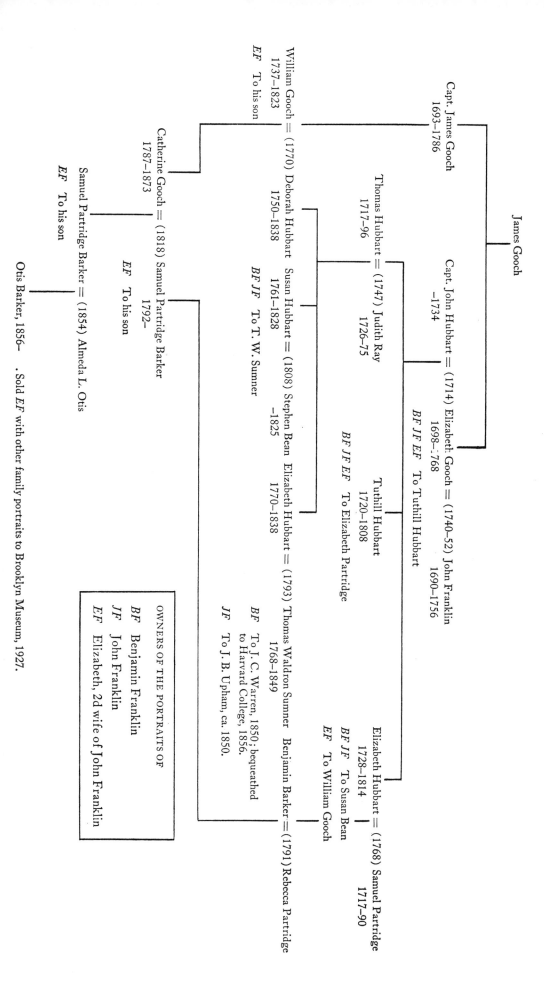

James Gooch

Capt. James Gooch
1693–1786

William Gooch = (1770) Deborah Hubbart
1737–1823   1750–1838
EF To his son   *BF JF* To T. W. Sumner

Thomas Hubbart = (1747) Judith Ray
1717–96   1726–75
BF JF EF To Elizabeth Partridge

Capt. John Hubbart = (1714) Elizabeth Gooch = (1740–52) John Franklin
-1734   1698–?768   1690–1756
                                         BF JF EF To Tuthill Hubbart

Catherine Gooch = (1818) Samuel Partridge Barker
1787–1873
EF To his son

Samuel Partridge Barker = (1854) Almeda L. Otis
1792–
EF To his son

Susan Hubbart = (1808) Stephen Bean   Elizabeth Hubbart = (1793) Thomas Waldron Sumner   Benjamin Barker = (1791) Rebecca Partridge
1761–1828   -1825   1770–1838   1768–1849
BF JF To T. W. Sumner   *BF* To J. C. Warren, 1850;
                                          JF To J. B. Upham, ca. 1850.

Tuthill Hubbart
1720–1808
BF JF EF To Elizabeth Partridge

Elizabeth Hubbart = (1768) Samuel Partridge
1728–1814   1717–90
BF JF To Susan Bean
EF To William Gooch

BF To J. C. Warren, 1850; bequeathed
to Harvard College, 1856.
EF To William Gooch

JF To J. B. Upham, ca. 1850.

OWNERS OF THE PORTRAITS OF

BF   Benjamin Franklin
JF   John Franklin
EF   Elizabeth, 2d wife of John Franklin

Otis Barker, 1856– . Sold *EF* with other family portraits to Brooklyn Museum, 1927.

been Eliza Partridge Sumner, the eldest child and at that time the only unmarried daughter of Thomas Waldron Sumner. From her it passed to a younger sister, Mrs. Elihu Greene, an ancestor of its recent owners.

DUCHÉ DE VANCY, GASPARD (d. 1788)
    1781. Line engraving. See CARMONTELLE, No. 3.

DUCREUX, JOSEPH (1737–1802)
    1782. Pastel. Unlocated.
Ducreux worked also in oil and miniature, but excelled in pastel, a skill he had acquired as the only student of Maurice Quentin de la Tour. He had the good fortune to be sent to Austria in 1769 to make the portrait of the Archduchess Marie Antoinette. He returned to Paris with the titles of Baron and "Premier Peintre de la Reine," and as a member of the Imperial Academy of Vienna. He was repeatedly presented without success, however, for membership in the Royal Academy of France, rejections laid to his reckless criticism of that body. He was a close friend of Greuze, who had placed himself in a similar position. He appeared frequently in the Salons after 1791, and in 1791 exhibited also in London. He was at this time attracting attention by a self-portrait and other studies in expression, laughing, grimacing, and yawning.[9] His portrait of Du Pont de Nemours, 1795, was engraved by Cathelin. His work is rarely signed and has often passed as that of other artists.[10] His sudden death was followed by a collapse of his reputation, and the high quality of his work was for many years ignored or forgotten.

At the Salon de la Correspondance of 1782 Ducreux exhibited one piece, a portrait of Franklin in pastel. The portrait was not in the large collection of his work owned in 1864 by his great-granddaughter.[1] It was not in the sale of his paintings at the Hotel Drouot, Paris, March 16–17, 1865. There is no other contemporary documentation of it, with the possible exception of a note from "Ducreux" in May, 1782, inviting William Temple Franklin to a

9. Prosper Dorbec, "Joseph Ducreux," *Gazette des Beaux Arts, 36* (1906), p. 199.
10. Ibid., p. 205.
1. Emile Bellier de la Chavignerie, "Pahin de la Blancherie," *Revue universelle des arts, 20* (1865), 119–24.

musical entertainment and supper.[2] That the portrait was never engraved suggests that it may have been a copy rather than an original likeness. The possibility that the splendid pastel now at the New York Public Library may be a copy by Ducreux rather than an original study by Duplessis is unsupported by evidence (see pp. 130–31). Another conjecture would relate Ducreux's pastel to the new likeness in miniature of 1782, which may have originated with Castrique, and which was repeated by the enamelists Weyler and Thouron.

An oil portrait attributed to Ducreux and identified as Franklin serves only to illustrate again that Franklin was not the only member of the Paris intelligentsia to wear his own hair and knot a scarf about his neck.[3]

DUFOURNY DE VILLIERS, LOUIS PIERRE

1777. Bust. Plaster, stained black to represent bronze. Ht. 30 in. including circular socle. *Owner* (1930) : D. A. Bernstein. Pl. 15.

Though shown at the Panama Pacific International Exhibition, San Francisco, 1914, the work is not known to have been illustrated or described until the publication of an article by Charles Messer Stow in the *Antiquarian,* November 1930:[4]

> The Caffieri bust illustrated on page 58, from the collection of Mr. D. A. Bernstein of Sound Beach, Connecticut, was in Chavagnac, the chateau of the Marquis de Lafayette, in 1792 and 1883, according to documents presented by the descendant of the French Revolutionary hero, who brought it to America. How Lafayette got the one illustrated herewith, which was in the Château de Chavagnac, is a matter for pure conjecture until definite evidence appears.

2. Franklin Papers (A.P.S.).

3. Described, but not illustrated, by Louis Guimbaud in "Benjamin Franklin et les artistes," *Art et curiosité, 3* (1925), 4–5.

4. "The Franklin of Caffiéri and his Contemporaries," *Antiquarian, 15* (1930), 58–60.

Yet one might say with safety that it was a gift from the subject.[5]

It is clear that the bust is not the work of Caffiéri, and it is regrettable that the documents of 1792 and 1883 were not fully quoted or described. In the purity of his conjecture the writer lights a candle before one famous name after another while failing to present evidence which might actually illumine the history of the piece. The document of 1792 may have been an inventory of the property of the Marquis, a common enough sort of document in that troubled period. That of 1883 was probably the photograph which accompanied the bust when it was offered for sale by Sotheby and Co. on March 5, 1937. A plaster cast of Houdon's "Washington" with the same provenance and ownership was also offered at that time. The catalogue notes that "Photographs showing the busts in the home of Lafayette and the original affidavit accompany the lot."[6] The "Franklin" was unsold at £65 and remained in the possession of Mr. Bernstein, the date of whose eventual disposal of it is not known.[7] Here is unsatisfactory and yet, withal, fairly acceptable evidence that the bust had actually been a possession of Lafayette. This provenance is a link in the very tenuous chain of evidence by which it can be identified as the lost work of Dufourny de Villiers and a cast from the first sculptured portrait of Franklin made after his arrival in France.

On March 8, 1777, Jean Baptiste Jacques Elie de Beaumont (1732–86), a jurist who figures largely in the intellectual life of Paris, wrote to Franklin in terms of "tendre vénération," asking that he sit to Dufourny de Villiers for a bust. He added a curious personal reinforcement of the request: from the sculpture, he proposed to have a painting made to hang in his library with the portraits of other friends of humanity:

5. Ibid., p. 60. The bust is not listed in John E. D. Trask and J. Nilson Laurvik, *Catalogue De Luxe of the Department of Fine Arts, Panama,* Pacific International Exhibition (San Francisco, ca. 1915), but this need not discredit the statement of its having been shown at the fair.

6. Sotheby and Co., Catalogue No. 94 B. The bust is also described, as to be sold, in *Apollo, 25* (1937), 174.

7. Information from Messrs. Sotheby and Co., Dec. 13, 1960.

241

Monsieur,

J'ai l'honneur de vous présenter Monsieur du fourny de villiers l'un de nos dignes membres de la société d'Emulation dont j'ai eu l'honneur de vous parler. Consacré aux arts par goût il ne croit pouvoir faire un plus noble et plus patriotique usage de ses talens que de consacrer à sa patrie le buste de l'illustre Franklin qu'un autre hemisphere menace de nous ravir et qui pourtant devroit se croire citoyen du monde entier si l'estime, la reconnaissance et le respect sont des titres d'incolat et de cité. Je joins mes priéres aux siennes, Monsieur, pour vous prier de lui accorder cette faveur dont il est digne par le prix qu'il y attache et en cela je vous sollicite pour moi-même, me proposant ensuite de m'assurer d'après ce buste votre portrait pour le placer dans ma bibliotheque au rang des amis de leur patrie et de l'humanité.

J'ai l'honneur d'être avec un tendre vénération ... [8]

Dufourny, to whatever degree he may have been "consecrated by taste to the arts," never attained an eminence in them. He contributed a long letter on the "Architecture des Salles de Spectacles" to the *Journal de Paris* of Sept. 30, 1780.[9] His watch mechanism and speaking tube were brought to Franklin's attention as important modern improvements.[1] As early as Jan. 24, 1778, he had expressed to Franklin his interest in becoming a citizen of Philadelphia, and he followed the American war with a warm partisanship, occasion-

8. "I have the honor to present to you M. Du Fourny de Villiers, worthy member of the Societé d'Emulation, of whom I have had the honor to speak to you. Dedicated to the arts by taste, he believes that he cannot make a nobler and more patriotic use of his talents than to bestow upon his country the bust of the illustrious Franklin, whom another hemisphere threatens to take from us and yet who should believe himself a citizen of the entire world, if esteem, recognition and respect are certificates of citizenship. I add my supplication to his, Monsieur, begging you to accord him this favor, of which he is made worthy by the value which he attaches to it, and in that I solicit you for myself also, intending to obtain your portrait after this bust, in order to place it in my library among the friends of homeland and humanity." (Franklin Papers, A.P.S., *5*, Pt. II, no. 99.)

9. *2*, 372–76.

1. Franklin Papers (A.P.S.), *26*, no. 28; *27*, no. 198.

ally communicating with Franklin upon one or another aspect of it.[2]

As late as 1822 Dufourny was remembered in Paris as having been a distinguished architect at the time of the outbreak of the Revolution.[3] He was elected president of the "Club des Droits-de-l'homme" in 1790 and president of the "Societé des Amis de la Constitution, séants aux Jacobins de Paris," the famous Jacobin club, in 1791.[4] In 1792, with Jacques Louis David and others, he was a member of the "Commission Conservatrice des Monuments," established for the preservation of expropriated works of art.[5] He was one of four architects appointed in 1793 to study the conservation of buildings while obliterating from them "ces signes qui blessent les yeux des Républicains."[6] He reported on maps found in the Tuilleries and elsewhere, on the furnishings at Chantilly, and was with Fragonard, Gérard, and others on artists' juries.[7] In 1793 he presided over the *Directoire* of the Department of Paris.[8] An irrepressible orator, he spoke to his ideal of liberty alone, making both friends and enemies in the rival parties. Arrested by order of Robespierre, he was saved from death in 1794 by Robespierre's fall. Returning to the fray, he was arrested again as a terrorist, again narrowly escaping the guillotine. The British Museum records 19 pamphlets from Dufourny's hand, including an "appeal for moderation" of 1795 incongruously entitled, *Allégeance! Justice! Vengeance! Vengeance!! Vengeance!!! Vengeance!!!! Vengeance!!!!!*

His death is said to have occurred soon after that last escape.[9] The Dufourny who was in 1800 one of the "Conservateurs au Musée Central des Arts" at the Louvre was perhaps the architect Léon Dufourny (1760–1818).[1]

2. Franklin Papers (A.P.S.).

3. Arnault, *Biographie Nouvelle, 6,* 135.

4. F. A. Aulard, *La Société des Jacobins, recueil des documents pour l'histoire de Club des Jacobins de Paris, 3* (Paris, 1885–97), 32.

5. Louis Tuetey, *Procès-verbaux de la Commission des Monuments, 1,* (Paris, 1902), vii n.

6. Ibid., p. xix.

7. Ibid., pp. 159, 164, 172, 185, 214–15, 312–14. Renouvier, *Histoire de l'art,* p. 17.

8. Tuetey, *1,* 130n.

9. Arnault, *6,* 135.

1. Marc Furcy-Raynaud, *Inventaires des sculptures exécutées au 18ᵉ siècle pour la direction des bâtiments du Roi* (Paris, 1927), p. 443.

Aulard's history of the Jacobins describes a meeting of the club on Sunday, Dec. 18, 1791, honoring friends of the Revolution overseas.[2] The flags of Great Britain, the United States, and France were paraded into a scene of the wildest enthusiasm and to cries of "Vive la liberté! Vive la nation! Vivent les trois peuples libres de l'univers!" After appropriate addresses it was moved that the busts of Dr. Price and Dr. Franklin should be placed beside that of Mirabeau, and that a voluntary subscription effect this purpose. Busts of Rousseau and Sidney were promptly called for by others, at which point M. Dufourny came forward with an offer:

> M. DUFOURNY.—Par vénération pour la mémoire du docteur Franklin, je demande à la Societé la permission de lui offrir un buste de ce grand homme que j'ai fait d'après lui. Ce sera pour moi une occasion de lui rendre hommage pour l'amitié dont il a bien voulu m'honnorer pendant sa vie.
>
> Cette proposition a été agrée avec applaudissements, et on arrête qu'il en sera fait mention honorable au procès-verbal. M. *le Président* veut, à cette occasion, faire un réponse à M. Dufourny, dans laquelle il le loue de ce qu'il a fait pour la Révolution. M. *Dufourny* rejette ces louanges, en disant qu'il n'a fait que ce que tout bon citoyen eût fait à sa place.—Les différentes motions sur les bustes mises aux voix, on arrête que ceux de Jean-Jacques, de l'abbé de Mably et de Sidney, seront joints à ceux de Price, de Franklin et de Mirabeau.[3]

2. Aulard, *3,* 290.

3. "M. DUFOURNY: In veneration for the memory of Dr. Franklin I ask the Society's acceptance of a bust which I have made of him. This will be an opportunity for me to do homage to the friendship with which he honored me during his lifetime. This proposal was accepted with applause, and it was voted to acknowledge it in the minutes. The President undertook on this occasion to reply to Mr. Dufourny with praise for what he had done for the Revolution. M. Dufourny rejected these encomiums, saying that he had only done as any good citizen would. Different motions on the busts were put to a vote, and it was decided that those of Jean-Jacques, the Abbe de Mably and of Sidney be added to those of Price, Franklin and Mirabeau." (Ibid., p. 291.) In making his gift, Dufourny not only emphasized his own personal acquaintance with Franklin but countered the possibility of the purchase of a bust from Houdon. Houdon had incurred the displeasure of the club by declining to enter a competition for a new bust of Mirabeau (ibid., *2,* 481).

A painting at the University of Michigan Museum of Art has come from almost exactly this time and place, and holds in its background what may well be a sketch of the Dufourny bust. It is a conversation piece by Jean Jacques Hauer (1751–1829), signed, "J. hauer 1791," and traditionally bearing the title, "Lafayette and Madame Roland Drawing a Plan for the Festival of the Federation." A seated lady holds on the desk before her the plan of a triumphal arch which she appears to be drawing under the direction of the officer in the uniform of the *Garde Nationale* standing beside her. Behind her are a harp and a harpsichord with the music of the *Ça Ira* upon it. On a chair where the officer has placed his hat is the *Moniteur Universel* for March 5, 1791.[4] High pedestals across the background hold the busts of Mirabeau, of Désilles, a young officer killed in the service of the Republic in 1790, of Franklin and of Rousseau. The "Rousseau," at upper right, casts the benediction of his glance down upon the scene, while the "Franklin" is so painted that he seems to smile across at the other. Franklin in this bust wears a neckcloth as in the Caffiéri, but it is not the Caffiéri. The sharp curve of its under surface down to the circular socle is the same as that from the Bernstein Collection. The smaller mouth and the line of cheek and chin at the left are the same. The button is missing and the scarf more tightly knotted, but these are details one would hardly expect the artist to follow in a freely-sketched representation.[5]

That the officer is actually Lafayette, then commander-in-chief of the National Guard of Paris, and the lady Mme. Roland, is not clearly established. Yet the painting is redolent with the burning ardor of the Revolution, and there is every reason to accept the unusual Franklin type shown in it as the work of the passionate Jacobin sculptor and architect, expert on theatrical settings.

The bust from the Bernstein collection is a softened, idealized Franklin, the age and solid characteristics of the face not in evidence. The mouth does not have the width and strength it should, though the mole at one side helps to identify it as Franklin's. I am

4. The *Moniteur* of this date reports a reorganization of the military service. Also a plea made by Victor Claude, Prince de Broglie (1757–94) in response to which his father, the Duc de Broglie, was permitted to retain his rank of marshal.

5. The painting is described and illustrated by Paul L. Grigaut, "Three French Works of American Interest," *Art Quarterly, 14* (1951), 350–51.

reluctant to believe that an artist as eminent as Jean Baptiste Greuze, he who made the portrait for the library of Elie de Beaumont, would actually have contented himself with copying a Dufourny bust. (See above, pp. 112–13.) Yet the fact remains that in both these portraits, sculpture and pastel, the same diminished mouth is shown.

The possibility that the original from which this cast was made may yet be extant appears in an entry in the Godefroy Mayer sale catalogue of 1910: "144. Life size terra cotta bust of Benjamin Franklin. He is represented full bust, head very slightly turned to left and a little bent, open collar and neck cloth, long hair falling on both shoulders. Admirable eighteenth century bust by an unknown artist, certainly executed from life. About 1780. Height of the bust 23½, with pedestal 30 inches. Fr. 7,500."[6]

DUMONT, FRANÇOIS (1751–1831)
     1779. Miniature. See DUPLESSIS, "Gray Coat," No. 2.

DUPLESSIS, JOSEPH SIFFRED (1725–1802)
There are three matrix portraits from which the innumerable repetitions of the Duplessis "Franklin" have descended:
1   The oil portrait signed and dated 1778, here listed as DUPLESSIS, "Fur Collar," No. 1.
2   The pastel, which may be either the original study for the above or a contemporary copy altered to suit Franklin's taste for simplicity in costume. It is described here as DUPLESSIS, "Gray Coat," No. 1.
3   The Joseph Wright portrait of 1782, based on the pastel, but in which the artist has slightly altered the face, changed the color of the costume, and added a chair back, and which, in deference to this claim to originality, is listed below as WRIGHT, JOSEPH, No. 1.
It should be noted that the "Fur Collar" was from the first regarded as a masterpiece of portraiture and copied by artists of outstanding as well as of lesser ability. That Duplessis showed a "Franklin" of this type at the Salon of 1801 is evidence that he was, in the

6. *No. 30. Old Paintings, Drawings, Miniatures*, p. 22.

twilight of his career, making replicas of the famous picture. However, neither Belleudy, his biographer, or other writers have attempted to distinguish the works of the master from what may be the finer copies. The artist, who used his signature sparingly, has signed only the original.[7] Apparently all repetitions of the "Gray Coat," on the other hand, are copies. All are French, while the Wright version, with red coat, went to Britain and was repeated only there.

A sort of genealogical chart of the paintings, engravings, sculpture, and other work derived from Duplessis, with an illustration by each, would reveal as nothing else could the fortunes of one portrait in the hands of copyists over a long period of time and in the eyes of the artists of different nations. The face would seem, as Franklin and his sister phrased it upon different occasions, not only to be as familiar as the moon, but as changeable. See above, pp. 125–31.

DUPLESSIS, "Fur Collar"
>   1   1778. Painting. Oil on canvas, oval, 28½ x 23 in. Hazel eyes with gray tint. Red coat with collar of light brown fur. Red waistcoat. Background greenish gray. Signed, at right, "J. S. Duplessis / pinx. parisis / 1778." In gilded oval frame ornamented at the top with a wreath of oak leaves and bay, below which a rattlesnake surmounts the frame, a branch of olive (for peace) lying with it at the left, and a branch of laurel (for victory) at the right. At the base of the frame a liberty cap, lion skin (for Britain), the club of Hercules, and a large scroll on which the single word, "VIR," is inscribed in black. *Owner:* Metropolitan Museum of Art, New York. Pl. 24.

Listed in the *Livret* of the Salon of 1779 as no. 128, "Le Portrait de M. Franklin. Tiré du Cabinet de M. de Chaumont," the ownership of the work by Le Ray de Chaumont is also attested upon the face of the engraving by Chevillet. It was a costly and splendid tribute. The *Journal de Paris,* in describing the opening of the Salon on Aug. 25, does not mention the portrait or Houdon's bust, but that such a compliment could be paid under royal auspices was not lost

7. Belleudy, *Duplessis,* p. 313.

upon others, the Americans in particular.[8] As early as May 4, 1780, Franklin was recommending that other artists copy this in preference to his posing for a new painting. (See JUDLIN.)

Unhappily, Le Ray's American investment, so liberally made and so inevitably hazardous, had brought him to the verge of ruin by the summer of 1780. Jonathan Williams reported to Franklin on Oct. 24 and again on Jan. 25, 1781, that his bankruptcy was imminent. It was a painful situation, with the continuing war and the financial prostration of the new republic largely to blame. Franklin could do little, though later, in 1789, he helped his friend's son collect the debts owed him by Congress, and by the time of his father's death in 1803 the young man had become an important figure in the development of the American frontier.

According to tradition, Le Ray de Chaumont retained the painting until 1791.[9] That would have been a propitious time for its sale, with the revival of Franklin's fame following his death the year before. Its purchaser appears to have been one of the brothers Périer, Jacques Constantin (1742–1818) or Auguste Charles, since it was from this family that it was purchased in 1919 by Col. Michael Friedsam, its last private owner.[10] They were engineers and mechanics concerned in the manufacture of paper, cotton spinning, sugar refinery, and a wide range of preludes to industrial revolution, but whose most famous accomplishment was the great "pompe à feu" of Chaillot, near Passy, which had begun operation late in 1778.[1] It was a steam-driven pump which raised water from the Seine to a reservoir, thence to provide the needs of the city.[2] Jacques Constantin Périer had been in England in 1777, negotiating with James Watt and facing the distrust of Watt's partner and Franklin's old friend, Matthew Boulton. Their two engines of English design and French construction, the "Constantine" and "Augustine," were visited by everyone. Franklin, whom Boulton

8. *Journal de Paris, 2,* Pt. I, 346–47.

9. Charles Sterling, *The Metropolitan Museum of Art. A Catalogue of French Paintings* (Cambridge, Mass., 1955), p. 172.

10. *New York Times,* Sept. 16, 1919, p. 1.

1. Bachaumont, *Mémoires, 12,* 137, 177.

2. A. L'Esprit, "Les Frères Perier, raffineurs de sucre," *Bulletin de la Société historique d'Auteuil et de Passy, 10* (1921), 16–23. "L'Ancienne Pompe à feu de Chaillot," Ibid., *3* (1898–1900), 90–94.

had been consulting on steam power back in 1766, met Périer and a representative of Watt at dinner on Dec. 30, 1780.[3] After the death of Jacques Constantin, Scipion Périer (1776–1821), chemist, manufacturer, and banker, took over the establishment at Chaillot. The Michael Friedsam collection, offered by bequest to the Metropolitan Museum, was accepted by its trustees on Dec. 21, 1931.[4]

> 2   1778. Line engraving by Juste Chevillet (1729–90), after the painting by Duplessis. Plate size, 11 15/16 x 8 1/16 in. Portrait to left, in oval border. "BENJAMIN FRANKLIN / Né à Boston, dans la nouvelle Angleterre, le 17 Janv. 1706. / Honneur du nouveau monde et de l'humanité, / Ce sage aimable et vrai les guide et les éclaire; / Comme un autre Mentor, il cache à l'oeil vulgaire, / Sous les traits d'un mortel, une divinité. Par M. Feutry. / Duplessis Pinxit Parisiis 1778. Chevillet Sculpsit. / Tiré du Cabinet de M. Le Ray de Chaumont & ca." Pl. 27.

The print publicized the American cause, emphasized Le Ray de Chaumont's adherence to it, and its publication was doubtless intended also to yield a profit or at least to meet the expenses involved. This it may well have done as it had a wide sale, competing well with the Filleul and other engravings, and sharing in public estimation the high place held by the portrait itself. The engraver, a competent, German-born craftsman, was a student and relative by marriage of Jean Georges Wille, the designer and engraver, in whose family a portrait of Franklin of the Cochin type has been discovered (see COCHIN No. 2). A small drawing of Franklin attributed to Chevillet is in the Princeton University Library, Carl Van Doren Papers. (See above, pp. 133–34.)

> 3   1801. Painting. Unlocated.

Jules Belleudy, his biographer, states that it was not until the Revolution, after the loss of his royal pension and his small fortune and with the handicap of fading eyesight, that Duplessis turned to painting replicas of earlier work.[5] The only supporting evidence for this, besides the existence of a small number of "Franklins" fine

3. Smyth, *Writings*, 10, 341.
4. *Metropolitan Museum of Art Bulletin*, 27 (1932), 4.
5. Belleudy, *Duplessis*, p. 253.

enough in quality to be his, is the presence of a replica in the Salon
of 1801, the year before his death. Belleudy was in error, however,
in identifying the painting of 1801 with an engraving by Pierre
Alexandre Tardieu, and in assuming that it was the original of the
"Gray Coat" type.[6] The engraving of the Salon of 1801 by Mon-
saldy and Devisme shows the portrait lightly sketched but unmistakably with the fur collar.[7] It shows also that the picture is in an
oblong frame, though matted or painted oval. This circumstance
associates it tentatively with the painting described below.

> 4   Ca. 1790–1801. Painting. Oil on canvas. Described in 1904
> as "Oval picture in a square frame. To the waist. Nearly full
> face, turning to the left. Red coat. The picture is said to have
> been painted in Paris, and on the back is written: 'Sent me
> from Paris, 1828: a memorial of Mr. Gallois. V. H.' . . . The
> picture is after Duplessis. With fur."[8] *Owner:* The Earl of
> Ilchester, London.

The picture is one of the very few with an unbroken history back to
a contemporary of the artist. Jean Antoine Cauvin Gallois (1761–
1828) figured in the political affairs of the Revolution, the Napo-
leonic era, and the Restoration. In his youth, as author of *Le Retour
de l'Age d'Or, ou le Regne de Louis XVI,* a poetic effusion of 1774,
he had been a friend of Cabanis and Mme. Helvétius, and a fervent
adherent to *les idées philosophiques.* In 1786 he translated from the
Italian Gaetano Filangieri's *La Science de la legislation.* With Du
Pont de Nemours and Condorcet he aided Fabre in his translation
of Robert A. Livingston's *Examen du gouvernment d'Angleterre,
comparé aux constitutions des Etats-Unis,* published in 1789. He had
a part in the Treaty of Amiens of 1802 and subsequent negotiations
with England.

Henry Richard Vassall Fox (1773–1840), third Lord Holland,
to whom Gallois bequeathed the portrait, had grown up and entered public life as a protégé of his uncle, Charles James Fox. In

6. Ibid., pp. 119, 216, 322.

7. Bibliothèque Nationale. Illust. in *Metropolitan Museum of Art Bulletin, 9*
(1951), 126.

8. *Catalogue of Pictures belonging to the Earl of Ilchester at Holland House*
(Privately printed, 1904), no. 220.

1791, the year in which Gallois entered public life, he visited France, meeting Lafayette and other political leaders there. He was in France again after the Treaty of Amiens. Like Gallois, he was a liberal and a writer of wide range, from statesmanship to poetry and plays. See above, No. 3.

>5 Undated. Painting. Oil on canvas, oval, 28½ x 22⅞ in. Gray hair. Hazel eyes. Background dark gray-green. An old label on the crossbar of the stretcher reads, "Portrait de Franklin / par Duplessis, tiré du Cabinet de M. de Chaumont / Voyez le . . . du Salon de 1779. No. 128." Illust. in *Proceedings of the A.P.S., 100* (1956), 377. *Owner:* Gilbert Bessot de Lamothe, Vaucluse, France.

>6 Undated. Painting. Oil on canvas, oval, 58½ x 72 cm. (28.34 x 23.03 in.). *Owner:* Comte Olivier de Lamothe-Mastin, Neuilly-sur-Seine, France.

The two canvases have been for many years in the same family. The first owner of one of them may have been either the Marquis or Marquise de Flamarens. Agésilas Joseph de Grossolles (1732–1818), Marquis de Flamarens, Baron de Montastruc et d'Orinque, Vicomte de Saint Martin, etc., married in 1767 Elizabeth Olympe Félicité Louise Armande du Vigier, daughter of the Procureur-Générale of the Parlement de Bordeaux and, through her mother, a member of the family of the powerful Comte de Maurepas. The couple receive passing, separate mention in Horace Walpole's Paris journals of 1767–71. The Franklin Papers contain an undated note from the Marquis, himself a military officer of high rank, asking Franklin to forward a letter to an officer serving in America.[1] It is also worthy of note that the twin brother of the Marquis, the Abbé de Flamarens, was the author of that earliest description of Franklin's appearance and popularity at the time of his arrival in France (see above, p. 98). The Marquis and Marquise had no children, but the lady became the mother of a daughter by the Comte de Provence, the future King Louis XVIII. The daughter, Mlle. Saulnier de la Marine, lived with her mother at the Château de Villiers-les-

1. Franklin Papers (A.P.S.), *70,* no. 90.

Maillets, Seine-et-Marne, where, according to family tradition, the portrait hung. She became the wife of Isaac Cox Barnet, American Consul at Paris, who is the first recorded owner of the portrait.

Isaac Cox Barnet was born at Elizabeth, N.J. on May 3, 1773, the son and grandson of physicians of that area. He first appears in France as Consul at Brest. When the consuls were withdrawn by President Adams in 1798, he was made Commercial Agent at Bordeaux. The new administration removed him from this post in 1801, though Benjamin Homans and Charles Pinkney strongly recommended him for another.[2] He remained in France and, with the restoration of the Bourbon regime in 1815, became Consul at Paris, continuing in that office until his death on March 8, 1833. He was acquainted with William Temple Franklin, at whose funeral in 1823 he was one of the few mourners. He figures as a successful, conscientious official. His portrait was drawn by Louis Boilly, artist of the painting of Houdon's studio, and published as a lithograph by Engelmann in 1831. It can probably never be determined whether he acquired the portrait from his wife or, as with so many American diplomats in Paris, purchased it there. The portrait was engraved several times, inscribed as his property or as that of his widow. A writer in the *Boston Daily Advertiser* of Oct. 1, 1858, states that he had seen the portrait "thirty years ago in the possession of Mr. Coxe Barnett, at that time consul from the United States in Paris, and had satisfactory evidence that it was the original by Duplessis." This suggests that Barnet's picture was No. 5, which bears the label identifying it as the original. Barnet had two sons, Charles and William Armand G., who traveled in the United States and may have settled there. The portrait became the property of his daughter, Caroline.

Caroline Barnet married Armand, Comte de Mastin. From her the picture descended again to a daughter, Alix Armande de Mastin, who lived at her ancestral home, the Château de Villiers, and died there, unmarried, in 1891. Her heir was a cousin, Etienne Bessot de Lamothe (1868–1939). At the château he found two almost identical portraits of Franklin. These he bequeathed to his sons, the present owners. That belonging to M. de Lamothe (No.

2. Information from National Archives and Reference Service. *Calendar of the Correspondence of James Madison* (Washington, 1894), pp. 361, 574.

5) was lent by him to the A.P.S. exhibition of Franklin portraits, from Jan. 17 to April 20, 1956, and is described and illustrated in the catalogue.[3]

> 7 Ca. 1790–1801. Painting. Oil on canvas, painted oval, 62 x 54 cm. (24.40 x 21.35 in.). Illust. frontispiece in Léon Honoré Labande, "Notes sur le Peintre Joseph Siffrein Duplessis et sur les Portraits de Franklin executés par lui," *Memoires de l'Académie de Vaucluse* (1898), pp. 393–402. Unlocated.

The original owner of the portrait was the Marquis de Vervins.[4] With the Revolution he became an *émigré,* and his mansion at Avignon was sold on Oct. 30, 1796, by the nieces of the Marchioness. It was purchased with all its furnishings by Jean Baptiste Antoine Bénazet Pamard, and became well known in after years as the Hôtel Pamard.[5] The "Franklin" is listed in a small catalogue of the paintings there, published ca. 1820.[6] In 1913 it was owned by his grandson, Dr. Alfred Pamard, who had been president of the Académie de Vaucluse since 1893.[7] It was sold in about 1914 to an unknown purchaser.

> 8 Ca. 1785. Painting, probably by Jean Valade (1709–87), after Duplessis. Oil on canvas, 28¾ x 23⅛ in. Brown fur collar. Reddish-brown coat and waistcoat. Olive-brown background. Gray spandrels with yellow edge. *Owner:* The Boston Athenaeum (on deposit at Museum of Fine Arts). Pl. 26.

In a letter dated Paris, Aug. 24, 1787, Jean Valade offered for sale to Thomas Jefferson a portrait of Louis XVI, recalling to the young American minister that it was from him he had purchased his portrait of Dr. Franklin.[8] Valade, a portrait painter, a member of the Royal Academy since 1754, had won praise in the Salons of earlier years but seems to have been in reduced circumstances at this time.

3. *Proceedings, 100* (1956), 377.
4. Probably Bonnevie de Vervins, but not clearly identified.
5. Information from Charles Le Gras, President of the Académie de Vaucluse, Sept. 19, 1953.
6. Léon Honoré Labande, "Notes sur le peintre Joseph-Siffrein Duplessis et sur les Portraits de Franklin exécutés par lui," *Mémoires de l'Académie de Vaucluse* (1898), p. 400. Belleudy, *Duplessis,* p. 86n.
7. Belleudy, pp. 85–86.
8. Original at Missouri Historical Society. Boyd, *Papers of Thomas Jefferson, 12,* 54.

He died on Dec. 12, 1787, at the age of seventy-eight.[9] Jefferson, in the catalogue of his collection, lists his "Franklin" as "2. Dr. Franklin, an original drawn for the Abbe Very by Greuse."[1] Coming to France in 1784 to succeed Franklin, he had emerged at once as a collector of art with a particular interest in securing fine portraits of distinguished contemporaries.[2] With this acquisition he set a precedent, becoming the first of the many members of our diplomatic corps who have purchased portraits, too often less-than-fine, of their great predecessor.

It must have been quite new when Jefferson bought it. The names of Greuze and Véri seem to have been carelessly applied to help the sale, for both Greuze and the Abbé were still living in Paris. The Abbé was the owner of a portrait of Franklin (see GREUZE, No. 3). His brother, the Marquis de Véri, had died and his collection gone on sale in Paris on Dec. 12, 1785. There were in it eleven works of Greuze, but no portraits of noted men.[3] Jefferson may have been there, for he had attended art sales at that time.[4]

The painting hung at Monticello until his death. It was inherited by Joseph Coolidge, Jr., from whom it was bought in September 1828 by the Boston Athenaeum for $200. It was then catalogued as having been painted for the Abbé de Véri by Greuze in 1782.[5] Edward Brooks' gift of a similar portrait (No. 11) to the Boston Public Library in 1858 led to a change in the attribution from Greuze to Duplessis. In 1876 it was deposited at the Museum of Fine Arts where it has since remained.

> 9   Undated. Painting by unidentified artist, after Duplessis. Oil on canvas, 21 x 15¾ in. Brown hair. Brown eyes. Brown coat. Background olive green brushed on lightly over yellow or buff. Very old canvas recently relined, adding an inch to its left edge. At lower left a piece of canvas 6 x 3 in. had been inserted. *Owner:* Independence Hall, Independence National Historical Park, Philadelphia. Pl. 26.

9. L. Vitet, *L'Académie royale de peinture et de sculpture* (Paris, 1861), p. 370.

1. Marie Kimball, "Jefferson, Patron of the Arts," *Antiques, 43* (1943), 166.

2. Ibid., pp. 164–65.

3. A. J. Paillet, *Catalogue de vente du cabinet de feu Monsieur le Marquis de Véri.*

4. Marie Kimball, *Jefferson. The Scene of Europe* (New York, 1950), pp. 114–15.

5. Mabel M. Swan, *The Athenaeum Gallery* (Boston, 1940), p. 116.

A modern label on the frame of this portrait states that it was painted by Joseph Siffred Duplessis "from life, and given by Franklin to Mme. Helvétius, Paris, 1770. Presented to President Truman by General Charles de Gaulle, at Washington, August 24, 1945." In June 1954 Mr. Truman presented the portrait to Independence Hall, Philadelphia.

This and the "Franklin" by Vanloo had been purchased ca. 1934 from the Marquise de Mun by the Cailleux Gallery, Paris. It was no. 28 in the gallery's exhibition, "Esquisses et Maquettes de l'Ecole Francaise du 18e Siècle," 1934, and in 1935 was in the exhibition at the Musée Galliera, "Auteuil et Passy d'Autrefois." At the time of their sale, the Marquise de Mun certified that both portraits had been continually in her husband's family, "Les deux portraits que possède M. Cailleux: 1. Portrait ovale aux lunettes, 2. Esquisse rectangulaire par Duplessis du portrait de Musée de Boston, ont fait partie de ma collection au château de Lumigny. Ils sont dans la famille de Mun depuis l'époque où Mme. Helvétius, arrière-grand-mère de mon mari, les reçut de Franklin dont elle était la grande amie."[6]

There can be no doubt of the long association of this painting with the De Mun family, which had been extremely close to Franklin during his residence in France and continued to hold his memory in reverence throughout the years. The origin of the painting, however, is open to speculation. Even Michel N. Benisovich's cautious acceptance that the portrait might have been painted by Duplessis "in one sitting—a not too long one" may be questioned.[7] The color of hair and eyes is incorrect, and the rough brushwork does not seem to have had the intention of marking out a likeness. The picture has some appearance of being an early copy, perhaps by an amateur using an older canvas, of an oval portrait, 80 x 60 cm., which came to the Musée Carnavalet in 1912 as the gift of Marc Furcy-Raynaud, art historian. This painting, with the smooth brushwork of 18th- or early 19th-century professional work, re-

6. "The two portraits owned by M. Cailleux: 1. Oval portrait with spectacles, 2. Rectangular sketch for the portrait at the Boston Museum, have been in my collection at the Château de Lumigny. They have been in the De Mun family since Mme. Helvétius, my husband's great-grandmother, received them from Franklin, her close friend." (Information from Jean Cailleux, Paris, July 28, 1953.)

7. "Duplessis in the United States," *Gazette des Beaux-Arts, 29* (1946), 285–86.

mains unfinished. Belleudy, generous in his attributions, describes it as an unfinished replica or copy.[8] In some fashion it is certainly related to the De Mun portrait.

10   Undated. Painting. Oil on canvas, oval, 71 x 57 cm. (27.95 x 22.44 in.).[9] *Owner:* Musée de Douai, France.

In 1852 the painting was presented to the Musée de Douai by Théophile Bra (1797–1863), a sculptor of Douai, where his father, Eustache Marie Joseph Bra (1772–1840), and his grandfather, François Joseph Bra (1749–1829), had lived before him. Aimé Ambroise Joseph Feutry, a poet and friend of Franklin who wrote the verses for the Chevillet engraving of the Duplessis portrait, died in Douai in 1789.

11   Undated. Painting. Oil on canvas, 27 x 21¾ in. Illust. in color in *The Pictorial Life of Benjamin Franklin,* Philadelphia, 1923. *Owner:* Boston Public Library.

The portrait is first recorded as the property of "Jarrey de Mancy" of Paris, who must have been Adrien Jarry de Mancy (1796–1862), a professor of history from 1820 to 1857, who had taught also at the *Ecole des Beaux Arts* and who had been one of the first to promote in France the English process of steel engraving. John Bigelow states that "it was offered to me by old De Mancy in 1852 for two thousand francs. There was a break in his history of it which led me to suspect that it might be a copy."[10] Samuel A. Green, librarian of the M.H.S., and Edward Brooks called to see it in the winter of 1854–55.[1] It was subsequently purchased by Mr. Brooks, who presented it to the city of Boston in 1858. The *Boston Advertiser* published a notice of it as then being "exhibited in the large library

8. Belleudy, *Duplessis,* p. 322.

9. As reported by the owner, ibid., p. 322. G. S. Eddy reports 73 x 60 cm. (Eddy Papers).

10. "Some Recollections of the Late Edouard Laboulaye," p. 32, quoted by Bowen, *Centennial Celebration,* p. 450. The owner's wife, Mme. Adèle Jarry de Mancy (1794–1854), was a daughter of the painter and designer, Jean François Lebreton (b. 1761) and herself a painter. She was the author also of works on drawing. Among her husband's works was *Iconographie instructive, ou Collection de portraits des personnages les plus célèbres de l'histoire moderne, accompagnés et entourés d'une notice biographique, chronologique et bibliographique,* Paris, 1827–28.

1. Bowen, p. 450.

hall," confusing its history with that of the portrait owned by Mrs. Barnet (No. 5), but for the first time pointing out the apparent error in the attribution of the Athenaeum's similar picture (No. 8) to Greuze.[2]

> 12 Undated. Painting.
> Oil on canvas, oval, 66 x 57 cm. (25.98 x 22.44 in.). Given to the Musée de Brest in 1881 by Félix Barret. *Owner:* Musée de Brest, France.

> 13 Undated. Painting. Oil on canvas, 30 x 25 in. Gray hair. Pale brown eyes. Light brown fur collar. Coat and waistcoat dull red. Blue shadow in stock and frill. Background olive-gray. Dark gray spandrels. *Owner:* The Brook, New York.

In 1883 Joseph T. Mason, U.S. Consul at Dresden, wrote to the M.H.S. and to other institutions of the discovery of this painting, then offered for sale at $1500.[3] It was owned by W. Krankling of Strehlen, Silesia, whose father, director of the Dresden Historical Museum, had purchased it in Courland.[4] In 1892 it was reported as the property of Mme. Helene Stauffre, an American, who had bought it at a little village in Saxony.[5] At this time it was purchased by Dr. Clifford F. Snyder, an American physician practicing in Berlin. It was exhibited at the Pennsylvania Academy of the Fine Arts in May 1893, remaining on loan there until 1907.[6]

> 14 Undated. Pastel. On paper, 30 x 25 in. Matted with opening 27 x 22¼ in. Background in tones of slate gray. *Owner:* Henry E. Huntington Library and Art Gallery, San Marino, Cal.

The portrait appears as no. 97 in the exhibition commemorating the centennial of Washington's inauguration in 1889, lent by Sam-

---

2. Reprinted in *The Crayon, 5* (1858), 330.

3. Reported to the society by Robert C. Winthrop, *Proceedings, 20* (1883), 263–64.

4. Bowen, p. 450.

5. Labande, "Notes sur le Peintre Joseph-Siffrein Duplessis," p. 400.

6. Pennsylvania Academy of the Fine Arts archives and minutes, Committee on Exhibitions, Jan. 24, 1894. During this period it was engraved by W. T. Bather, of New York.

uel Latham Mitchill Barlow of New York.[7] At his death, the Barlow collection was sold by the American Art Association on Feb. 10, 1890.[8] The work thereafter had frequent changes of ownership at private sale. Gen. Brayton Ives (1840–1914), financier and railroad executive of New York, a member of the Grolier Club and an active collector of books and works of art, sold it to Clarence S. Bement of Philadelphia, who was its owner in 1892.[9] It was exhibited at the Masonic Hall in Philadelphia and at the Grolier Club by Felix Isman of Philadelphia in 1906.[1] It was held by the Rosenbach Co. in 1926 at a price of $35,000, but remained unsold until purchased by its present owner in 1953.[2]

> 15   Undated. Painting. Oil on canvas, painted oval, 28¾ x 23½ in. Gray hair. Gray tint in eyes. Brown fur collar. Russet-brown coat and waistcoat. Background olive green. *Owner:* N.Y.H.S.

The painting was purchased by the N.Y.H.S., Louis Durr Fund, in 1892. A copy from Duplessis by Alexandre Roslin (1718–93) had been in the sale of Roslin's work on June 8, 1890, a fact which might support an attribution to the Swedish artist. Roslin had been received into the Académie Royale in 1753, and lived continually in Paris from 1775 to 1793, with a *logement* at the Louvre and a reputation as a leading competitor of Duplessis. He was represented by a portrait of Linnaeus in the Salon of 1779, and Du Pont de Nemours comments interestingly upon the two artists at this exhibition, considering Duplessis more successful in flesh tints, Roslin in fabrics.[3] The *Journal de Paris* on the same occasion echoes this comment, adding that Roslin was too liberal with carnations, that

7. Bowen, *Centennial Celebration,* p. 451.

8. *Catalogue of the Art Collection Formed by the Late Samuel Mitchill Barlow* (American Art Association, Feb. 10–12, 1890), p. 61, no. 1000.

9. Bowen, p. 451.

1. *Catalogue of an Exhibition Commemorating the Two Hundredth Anniversary of the Birth of Benjamin Franklin at the Grolier Club of New York* (New York, Grolier Club, Jan. 1906). *Centenary of the Birth of Right Worshipful Past Grand Master Brother Benjamin Franklin* (Philadelphia, Grand Lodge of Pennsylvania, 1906), p. 321, no. 6.

2. The Rosenbach Company, *1776. Americana. A Catalogue* (Philadelphia, 1926), p. 31, no. 62.

3. *Archives de l'art français,* n.s. 2 (1908), 105–06.

Duplessis' was too gray, but that Duplessis had a great advantage in the sculptural feeling with which he modeled his subject.[4] Mme. Roslin was also a painter of portraits.

16 Undated. Painting. Oil on canvas, oval, 27⅝ x 22¼ in. Inscribed on the back, "Peint par Duplessis pour obliger Monsieur le Vicmte de Buissy." *Owner:* Metropolitan Museum of Art, New York.

The painting was presented to the Metropolitan Museum in 1895 by George A. Lucas. Formerly attributed to Duplessis, it is now described by the Museum as "Workshop of Duplessis." No explanation of the inscription has been discovered.[5]

17 Undated. Painting by unknown artist, after Duplessis. Oil on canvas, oval, 25 x 21½ in. Illust. in *Benjamin Franklin Gazette* (1930), p. 109, and in sale catalogue cited below. Unlocated.

The portrait was offered for sale by the Ehrich Galleries, New York, in 1931. Its last private owner, Mrs. Mary T. Newman, stated that it had come from an ancestor living at Bordeaux during the Revolution who had married a French countess. Harold Louis Ehrich wrote to George Simpson Eddy on July 14, 1931, that Mrs. Newman could not "tell you now the name of the ancestor who married the French countess."[6] In the sale of paintings from the Ehrich Galleries on April 18, 1934, it is catalogued as having come from the collection of Nathan Haley (d. 1840), and as having been owned subsequently by Jeremiah Haley, by his widow, Maria, by T. Newman, and Mrs. Mary T. Newman.[7]

18 Undated. Painting. Oil on canvas, 30 x 25 in. *Owner:* Yale University Library, William Smith Mason Collection.

---

4. *Journal de Paris, 2,* Pt. I, 359–60.

5. On Jan. 14, 1777, the Baron de Bissy reminded Franklin of a dinner engagement with other friends and insurgents. Franklin Papers (A.P.S.), *72,* no. 69. He figured in the Salon de la Correspondance as an inventor, *Nouvelles de la République des Sciences et des Arts,* 1779, p. 50.

6. Eddy Papers.

7. *Important Paintings by Old Masters from the Ehrich Galleries* (New York, American Art Association, April 18–19, 1934), p. 108, no. 140. Illust.

The first known owner of this portrait was Robert Charles Winthrop (1809–94), U.S. Senator and for thirty years president of the M.H.S., who had taken a keen interest in the history of Franklin portraiture and in the acquisition of good examples for the city of Boston. The painting was ordered sold in 1924 in settlement of the estate of the widow of Robert C. Winthrop, Jr. It was purchased by William Smith Mason on Jan. 7, 1925.

19   Undated. Painting. Oil on canvas, oval, 28½ x 22½ in. Gray hair. Gray tint in eyes. Olive-green background. 18th-century gilt frame inscribed, "BENJAMIN FRANKLIN" and "DUPLESSIS." *Owner:* Harvard University, William Hayes Fogg Art Museum.

The painting comes from the collection of the Earl of Rosebery (1847–1929). Its descent in this family has not been traced. It was no. 41 in the Rosebery sale, Christie's, London, May 5, 1939. It was purchased from Scott and Fowles, New York, by Grenville L. Winthrop and bequeathed by him to the Fogg Museum.

20   Undated. Painting. Oil on canvas, 28 x 24 in. Gray hair. Hazel eyes. Henna coat with golden-brown fur collar and coat edged with same fur. Henna waistcoat, buttons, and loops. Background in brown tone with spandrels in upper corners. *Owner:* Mutual Assurance Co., Philadelphia.

The portrait is said to have been bought at the sale of pictures belonging to an artist named Vandenburgh by W. H. Robertson, U.S. Vice Consul at Paris, who made the purchase on the advice of Edward Everett.[8] Shortly after, in 1850, it became the property of Charles Augustus Stetson (1810–88) of the Astor House, New York. He gave up the management of the hotel in 1868, retiring to his home at Swampscott, near Boston. His son, Charles, continued the management until 1875. On Jan. 2, 1876, the painting was purchased by its present owner for $1000.

21   Ca. 1779–85. Miniature, possibly by A. N. B. Graincourt, after Duplessis. Water color on ivory, oval, 1 9/16 x 1 5/16 in. (sight). Iron-gray hair. Claret coat and waist-

8. Hart, *Pennsylvania Academy of the Fine Arts ... Loan Exhibition of Historical Portraits, December 1, 1887–January 15, 1888* (Philadelphia, 1887), no. 159.

coat. Brown fur collar. Olive-gray background. Set in gold case ornamented with gold ribbon at the top and floral wreath below. Originally made to be worn as a brooch. Altered to be worn as a pendant while owned by William J. Duane. "B. Franklin" in an oval engraved on the back. Reproduced in color as frontispiece in *The Record of the Celebration of the Two Hundredth Anniversary of the Birth of Benjamin Franklin, Under the Auspices of the A.P.S., 1,* Philadelphia, 1906. *Owner:* Philadelphia Museum of Art. Pl. 24.

The miniature was presented by Franklin to his daughter. In family tradition it is firmly associated with Jean Sicardi's miniature of Louis XVI which, set with diamonds, was presented to Franklin by the King on the occasion of his return to America in 1785. It was believed to have been painted "at the request of" or "by order of Louis XVI, King of France, about 1782–85," and Mrs. Bache has been cited as authority for the statement that the king intended his own portrait for the departing minister, this other to be "sent by him to Mrs. Franklin."[9] There is no mention of it in the register of royal gifts, nor has it the appearance of one. The tradition indicates that it was a gift, perhaps of the artist, and that both miniatures came to Philadelphia on Franklin's return.

The portrait descended from Sarah and Richard Bache to their daughter, Deborah, who married William J. Duane, and to their granddaughter, Elizabeth Duane, who married Archibald H. Gillespie. A great-granddaughter, Ellen, Mrs. Edward Parker Davis, was its last private owner. It was listed as no. 1 in Stan V. Henkels Catalogue No. 1356, *Relics of Benjamin Franklin, Estate of Ellen Duane Davis,* June 16, 1924. The miniature had by that time attained enormous fame. It had been copied in oils, engraved, reproduced in color and on a postage stamp. It was bought by Dr. A. S. W. Rosenbach for $7,000.[10] Two years later it was priced at $18,500.[1] It came to the Philadelphia Museum as the gift of Mrs. Edward S. Harkness in 1932.

J. J. Foster states that Duplessis is not to be regarded as a

9. Gillespie, *A Book of Remembrance,* p. 27. M. Atherton Leach Papers (Genealogical Society of Pennsylvania), *13,* 111.
10. Eddy Papers.
1. *1776. Americana,* p. 31, no. 63.

miniature painter, "but he is known to have painted a miniature of Dr. Franklin."[2] The possibility, however, is so exceptional that it cannot be accepted upon mere assumption. Duplessis lived in a time of considerable specialization in art, was a slow workman in his preferred medium, and more than fully occupied in it. It is doubtful that his eyesight was equal to such work. It is obvious, too, that his portrait was copied freely by others, with Franklin himself encouraging artists to do so, rather than submit to the rigor of posing. It is reasonable to suppose, therefore, that this ivory is one of those copies, and indeed the supposition adds interest to it, for there is a noticeable difference in the contour of the face, a fullness in the lower part, which suggests that the painter may have seen enough of his subject to venture a certain revision. Judlin's miniature was a copy, perhaps of this sort. Castrique's of 1782 may have been. The most likely guess, however, would identify it with the miniature exhibited by Antoine Noël Benoît Graincourt at the Salon de la Correspondance in 1779. That was recorded as almost identical in size and, as we know of no patron for whom it was made, a little more likely to have come back to Franklin as the gift of the artist.

22   Ca. 1778–85. Design for a miniature by Francis Lainé (1721–1810), after Duplessis. Pen-and-ink drawing, oval form indicated at base, indicated size of oval about 2 x 1⅜ in. Body to left. Head slightly inclined to left. "Franklin" written in reverse characters above the head. Reproduced with Plate 38 in *Francis Lainé, Peintre de la Cour de France sous Louis XVI, maître de l'Académie de Saint Luc, membre de la Société Royale de Londres. Son Cahier d'esquisses. Reproduction facsimile des 68 planches. Notice par Frédéric Rossel. Préface par Henri Clouzot,* Montbéliard, 1923. *Owner:* Claude Rossel, Montbéliard, France. Pl. 24.

The inscription in reverse emphasizes the fact that the drawing faces in the same direction as Chevillet's print, to the left, while Duplessis' painting is to the right. It would appear that in transferring his design to ivory it would be reversed, and that his model was

2. Joshua James Foster, *Dictionary of Painters of Miniatures* (London, 1926), p. 101.

therefore the painting rather than the print. The *Cahier d'esquisses* gives us a clear view of Lainé's place in the profession. Many portraits appear there, but with them a preponderance of frivolous and amorous designs, indicating that he specialized in *tabatières* and the like, and did a good business with the young man who enjoyed an erotic titillation with his pinch of snuff. He was a rover. Born in Berlin of French Protestant parents, he had traveled in India as a young man, returning to a life divided between Paris and London.[3] He had been received in the Académie de Saint Luc in 1773 and exhibited there in 1774.[4] He exhibited at the Society of Artists in London in 1776 and 1777, and at the Royal Academy in 1786, 1788, and 1789. Though cited as "Membre de la Société Royale de Londres," he was not a member of the Royal Society, the Royal Society of Arts, or the Royal Academy. He may have permitted some such distinction to be applied to him in France, as in England he allowed himself to be known as "Painter to the Court of France."[5] He is known to have been in Paris in 1777 and 1784.[6] He was there during the Revolution, and his last years were spent in Passy.[7] He was a clever and competent miniaturist, who worked both on ivory and in enamel. He gained a certain fame also as the inventor of pictorial hair work, the originator, therefore, of the innumerable mortuary designs in this sombre medium so popular during the 19th century.[8]

Lainé's sketchbook contains also a small drawing of the head and shoulders of a man wearing some sort of court or ecclesiastical robe.[9] A later hand has penciled "Franklin" on the margin. The portrait resembles Franklin, but is not a convincing likeness. A frame containing 15 miniatures is preserved with the sketchbook in the family collection, and one of these has been identified erroneously as Franklin.[1]

3. L. Fontaine, *Un Miniaturiste Français Inconnu en France. Francis Lainé* (Montbéliard, 1923), pp. 7 ff.

4. Guiffrey, *Académie de Saint Luc,* p. 339.

5. Fontaine, *Miniaturiste,* p. 60.

6. Ibid., pp. 62–63.

7. Ibid., p. 14.

8. Ibid., pp. 50–56. Examples are illustrated.

9. *Cahier d'Esquisses,* Pl. 46.

1. Fontaine, *Miniaturiste,* p. 98. Illustrated opp. p. 104, center of bottom row.

23　Ca. 1786. Miniature by Francis Lainé, after Duplessis. Unlocated.

Lainé exhibited a miniature of Franklin at the Royal Academy, London, 1786, and with it a "Triumph of Cupid and the Graces" and a "Marie Antoinette, the Present Queen of France." The "Franklin" may be supposed to have been based on the sketch described above, probably in the same size, and may have had the name similarly inscribed on it. An oval enamel of this type, but slightly larger (2⅛ x 1¾ in.) is preserved in the Musée Municipale, Carpentras (see Pl. 24).

24　Ca. 1784. Drawing by De Meaux, after the Chevillet engraving from Duplessis. Pencil on paper, 9 5/16 x 6 5/16 in. Figure to the left, in oval border. Inscribed below, "de Meaux delit. / LE DOCTEUR FRANKLIN né en 1706." *Owner:* Miss Frances M. Bradford, Philadelphia.

The drawing is an heirloom in the family of Polly Stevenson, the widow of Dr. William Hewson, who visited Franklin at Passy in the winter of 1784–85, bringing with her his godson, William, and her two other children. The drawing was Franklin's gift to her youngest, the ten-year-old Elizabeth.[2]

Painting, attributed to West. See WEST, No. 4.

DUPLESSIS, "Gray Coat"

1　1778. Pastel. On paper, 28 x 23 in. Gray hair. Hazel eyes indicated by gray within touches of brown. Pale blue-gray coat and waistcoat. A red line at the left indicates a chair back (not present in the "Fur Collar" type, but clearly developed in Joseph Wright's version). An inscription on the back of the picture reads:

Benjamin Franklin, à 77 ans; peint en 1783 par Duplessis; donné par Franklin lui-même à M. Louis le Veillard, gentilhomme ordinaire de la Reine, son ami et voisin à Passy. Joseph Sifrède Duplessis, Académicien, né à Charpentras, s'est distingué par une belle intelligence, les effets de la lumière, sur les chairs et

2. *Bi-Centenary of the Birth of Brother Benjamin Franklin,* p. 322.

accessoires un pinceau, bien senti et un coloris vrai. Les personnages de distinction dans ses portraits sont posés avec noblesse et dans des attitudes bien choisies. Il a peint le portrait de Louis XVI, ceux de M. et Mme. Necker, et des plusieurs grandes [dames] de la cour. (Les trois siècles de la peinture le [*sic*] France par Gault de St. Germain, 1808). Swiback l'élève le plus distingué de Duplessis, a surpassé son maître.[3]

An old label on the front of the frame, presumably derived from the above statement, reads, "Benjamin FRANKLIN à 77 ans / PEINT PAR JH. SD. DUPLESSIS 1783 / Donné par FRANKLIN lui même." *Owner:* New York Public Library. Pl. 25.

The pastel is probably the original study by Duplessis, made in this medium to save his subject the tedium of long sittings, and presented to him by the artist on the completion of the oil. This and alternative theories are listed above, pp. 129–31.

Charles Henry Hart argued that Joseph Wright's canvas of 1782 must be the original of the pastel, rather than an altered copy after it.[4] This theory falls before the fact that Franklin had had the miniature for Georgiana Shipley, described below, painted from the pastel in 1779.

The attribution of the pastel to Duplessis is supported by Franklin's statement that the Shipley miniature was a copy from Duplessis. William Temple Franklin owned a "Gray Coat" in oil

3. "Benjamin Franklin at 77; painted in 1783 by Duplessis; given by Franklin himself to M. Louis le Veillard, gentleman in waiting to the Queen, his friend and neighbor at Passy. Joseph Sifrède Duplessis, Academician, born at Carpentras, distinguished himself by his great intelligence, the effects of light on flesh and accessories, a sensitive brush and true color. He painted the portrait of Louis XVI, those of M. and Mme. Necker and of several great ladies of the court. (*Les Trois Siècles de la peinture en France* by Gault de Saint Germain, 1808.) Swiback, the most distinguished of Duplessis' students, surpassed his master." As indicated, the statement is a direct quotation from Pierre Marie Gault de Saint Germaine (1754–1842), *Les Trois Siècles de peinture en France* (Paris, 1808), p. 289. The writer, however, injects his own note of admiration for Jacques François Joseph Swebach (1769–1823), who had come as a boy from Metz to Duplessis' studio, and who had exhibited at the Salon de la Correspondance in 1782 at the age of 14. He was also known by the French translation of his name, Fontaine (see below, n. 8).

4. Charles Henry Hart, "An Original Portrait of Dr. Franklin, Painted by Joseph Wright," *P.M.H.B., 32,* 325.

which he believed to be by Duplessis.[5] William's statement carries more weight as regards the original than his own copy. The earliest engravings from the pastel were made by Pierre Alexandre Tardieu (1756–1844) in 1795 and 1797, both attributed to Duplessis on the plate.[6]

Happily, this great portrait has a known and unquestionable history of ownership. At his departure from France in 1785, Franklin gave the picture and the manuscript of his autobiography to his friend Louis Guillaume Le Veillard (1733–94), Mayor of Passy. Le Veillard died at the guillotine in the summer of 1794, the last days of the Terror, when Mme. Filleul suffered the same fate. Portrait and papers remained in the possession of his daughter until her death in 1834. M. de Sénarmont, a cousin, was the next heir.[7] He must have been the anonymous owner of the portrait and autobiography listed in the *Manuel de L'Amateur d'Autographes* (Paris, 1836), with a glowing description and the note that they might be purchased to adorn the library of some rich and enlightened gentleman.[8] The rich and enlightened gentleman did indeed appear, but not until thirty years later. John Bigelow (1817–1911), who had been in Paris as Consul General and as Minister from 1860 until September 1866, learned of the situation of the portrait and papers just on the eve of his return to America. From London, he authorized William H. Huntington to make the purchase from the owners, Paul and Georges de Sénarmont, grandnephews of Le Veillard, and this was accomplished on Jan. 26, 1867.[9] The portrait subsequently adorned both the Lenox Library and the private library of Mr. Bigelow. On May 13, 1908, it came as his

5. Engraved by Charles Pye, 1817, as after Duplessis.

6. Frontispiece to B. Franklin, *The Way to Wealth,* (Paris, 1795), and frontispiece to *Vie de Benjamin Franklin, ecrite par lui-même . . . tradui . . . par J. Castera* (Paris, An VI). Belleudy is in error in identifying these as from a second, later version by Duplessis, shown at the Salon of 1801 (*Duplessis,* p. 322).

7. John Bigelow, *Works of Benjamin Franklin, 1* (New York and London, 1904), 21.

8. Pp. 336–39. The *Manuel* is the work of P. Jul. Fontaine, identified as "Bibliographe, Membre de la Deuxième Classe de l'Institut Historique, Correspondant de l'Académie d'Evreux, etc." That the author may have been related to the artist so highly commended on the inscription on the back of the pastel, or its writer, is conjectural (see above n. 3).

9. Bigelow, *1*, 10–22. Max Farrand, ed., *Benjamin Franklin's Memoirs,* Parallel Text Ed. (Berkeley and Los Angeles, 1949), pp. xxx–xxxi.

gift to signal the opening of the new central building of the New York Public Library, where it hangs today.[1]

> 2 1779. Miniature attributed to François Dumont (1751–1831), after Duplessis. Water color on ivory, circular, diam. 2 in. (sight). Gray-brown hair. The flesh tints have faded, leaving the blue and green shadow tones predominant. Deep olive-brown background. Set in a circle of gold on the lid of a tortoise-shell snuffbox, 2⅜ inches in diameter, 1 inch in height. *Owners:* Elsie O. and Philip D. Sang, River Forest, Ill. Pl. 25.

The miniature was Franklin's gift to Georgiana Shipley, the daughter of one of his oldest friends of the English days, the Bishop of Saint Asaph. The young lady had studied art, shared in her father's classical scholarship, and was wholeheartedly united in the Whig liberalism of their circle. She wrote to Franklin from London on May 1, 1779, mentioning Johnson's lives of the poets with regret that the work should have been "in part tainted with his own odious political principles," and went on to a pleasanter subject:

> Numberless are the prints & medals we have seen of you, but none that I quite approve, should you have a good picture painted at Paris, a miniature copied from it would make me the happiest of beings, & next to that, a lock of your own dear gray hair would give me the greatest pleasure; my father has had a wax model taken of him, it is not yet finished, but if it should prove like, I will manage to send you one, in the meantime I enclose a shade, which I think you will be pleased with.[2]

Franklin had already sent her one of the little Sèvres medallions which he was giving to friends. She acknowledged it on the 12th: "This moment I have received from Mr. Digges your kind letter & valuable present. . . . A lock of your hair from a head I value so much, is all I have now to desire."[3] But fondly, carrying out her

1. *New York Public Library Bulletin, 12* (1908), 343–45.
2. A.P.S.
3. Ibid. See Sèvres, No. 1.

request to the letter, he had already written that the miniature would be sent. She replied on June 6, 1779: "You absolutely spoil me, my dear Doctor Franklin, by your indulgence, for I now expect, with the utmost impatience, the copy from Du Plessis's picture; altho before I received your last letter I was perfectly happy and content with the small head you had the goodness to send me by Mr. Digges."[4] The miniature was delivered to her by William Caslon, the London type founder. Her thanks followed on Feb. 3, 1780:

> How shall I sufficiently express my raptures on receiving your dear delightful letter & most valuable present. the pleasure I felt was encreased if possible by the sight of the beloved little lock of Hair. I kissed both that & the picture 1000 times: the miniature is admirably painted, the artist (whose name I wish to learn) appears inferior to none we have here in England: as for the resemblance, it is my very own dear Doctor Franklin himself, I can almost fancy you are present, nay I even think I see you smile at the excess of my happiness. while I am writing it lies on the table before me, it will ever be my constant companion, & not only make me happier but better as long as I live, "fingar et ad mores, te recolendo, tuos."[5]
>
> The whole family are as much delighted with the picture as myself, my father says, he perfectly recollects the serious yet cheerfull contenance & the superior mind, that used to convince and charm him.[6]

On May 26 she sent him her own self-portrait in water colors, and with it renewed thanks for the "beloved picture," which had, however, she confessed, "one *bad* effect, the temptation it gives me to take snuff, as an excuse for looking at it very very often."[7] A few years later, in 1784, William Temple Franklin borrowed it from

4. Ibid.
5. "I shall be shaped in thy character by the recollection of thee."
6. A.P.S.
7. Ibid.

her for the use of Benjamin West, and it is a principal source of West's head of Franklin in his picture of the signing of the treaty of peace. (See WEST, No. 1.)

Her sister wrote in 1785 to tell Franklin of Georgiana's "unfortunate marriage" to the impecunious Francis Hare-Naylor. He had already heard of it from Georgiana herself, asking his advice as to a "safe and honourable Retreat" in America. The couple, however, remained in Europe. Georgiana died in Lausanne in 1805. The miniature passed to her eldest son, Francis George Hare (1786–1864), and then to her grandson, the traveler and author, Augustus John Cuthbert Hare (1834–1903). While in his possession it was first described and illustrated in Paul Leicester Ford's *Many-Sided Franklin* of 1899.[8] In his will, dated Sept. 6, 1902, "Dr. Franklin's snuff box and the muffineer of Lady Jones" were bequeathed to Theodore Julius Hare (1839–1907).[9] It was inherited by his son, Marcus Leonard Theodore Hare, and by his grandson, Major Theodore Robert Marcus Mordaunt-Hare. On April 20, 1959, it was purchased at Sotheby's by John Fleming of New York.

The attribution of the miniature to François Dumont rests primarily upon an entry in Franklin's Cash Book, Passy, Sept. 4, 1779, "Paid M. Dumont for the Miniature for Miss Shipley in England 8 Louis."[1] Earlier entries record payments to Dumont, a steward or servant, but it is unlikely that this individual had served as agent in procuring the picture, since his wages were paid in full and the account with him closed on Aug. 8, 1778, and since the one is "Dumont" in every instance, and the other "M. Dumont." Moreover, stylistically, the portrait is attributable to this artist who, then at the beginning of his career, was in time to rank with Isabey as a miniaturist. Arriving in Paris from Lorraine in 1769, Anne Vallayer had allowed him to paint her portrait as a proof of his skill. He was received into the Académie Royale on April 26, 1788, with Joseph Siffred Duplessis as his sponsor.[2]

3   1779. Miniature by unidentified artist, after Duplessis.

8. P. 470.
9. Will, Somerset House, London.
1. Franklin Papers (A.P.S.).
2. Jean Georges Wille, *Mémoires et Journal, 2* (Paris, 1857), 175.

Opaque water color on ivory, oval, 1½ x 1⅛ in. Gray hair. Eyes with yellow pupil and black iris. Light-gray coat and waistcoat. Plain red-gold case. 1 7/16 x 1 3/16 in. Altered to a brooch by a yellow-gold oval to which the pin is attached. Hair work at the back in a small oval, with light brown and pale sandy locks intertwined. *Owner:* Miss Lydia Spencer Moncure Robinson, Paoli, Pa. Pl. 25.

According to a wholly credible family tradition, the miniature was Franklin's gift to Mariamne, daughter of William Alexander, upon the occasion of her marriage to his grandnephew, Jonathan Williams, Jr., on Sept. 12, 1779. This same tradition was probably Edward Everett Hale's source when he wrote in 1888 that, "When Miss Alexander, his young friend, was to marry Mr. Jonathan Williams, son of his nephew and correspondent, Franklin asked her what wedding present he should give her. She asked for his portrait."[3] Hale is in error, of course, in adding that he then sat to Martin for the large portrait on canvas which also descended in the family. That picture had been made a dozen years earlier and must have been still in Scotland. The miniature was the gift, and the brown and yellow hair are that of the bride and groom.

Young Jonathan Williams had been at Nantes as an American commercial agent when Franklin had arrived in the Loire in December 1776. William Alexander was also in France with his family, and wrote to Franklin on March 1, 1777, to warn him that he was surrounded by spies. Elkanah Watson, who walked from Paris to Passy and from there rode with the Franklins to the wedding at Saint Germain, remembered that William Alexander was himself suspected of being a spy.[4] Spies there were, but the Americans suspected everyone but the guilty few among themselves. Jonathan himself had long been torn between the calls of love and patriotism, and had written to Franklin two years before that his affair with "Miss A." was "totally at an end on acct of the War between her country & mine."[5] France and America had become allies that year, and this other international alliance, so long postponed, was an auspicious event for the entire American community.

3. Hale, *Franklin in France*, 2, 3.
4. E. Watson, *Men and Times of the Revolution*, pp. 108–09.
5. Feb. 19, 1777 (Franklin Papers, A.P.S., *37*, no. 56).

There is no early documentary record of the miniature. Jonathan Williams wrote to Franklin from Nantes on Dec. 1, 1782: "Inclosed is a Letter for Mrs. Williams which contains a miniature Picture belonging to her please give it to Billy to forward by some safe private hand."[6] This probably refers to a portrait of himself. Jonathan and Mariamne accompanied Franklin back to America in the summer of 1785. The miniature passed to their only daughter, Christine, who in 1806 married Thomas Biddle (1776–1857) of Philadelphia. Their son, Henry Jonathan Biddle (1817–62), married Mary Deborah Baird, and by the terms of her will the miniature was given to her son, Spencer Fullerton Baird Biddle, U.S.N. (married but childless), for his lifetime, passing then to her "eldest grandchild," its present owner.

> 4 Ca. 1779–83. Painting or pastel. The portrait is known only through a small engraving published with William Temple Franklin's edition of his grandfather's writings. The figure faces to the left, in an oval border, with the inscription, "FRANKLIN / ERIPUIT COELO FULMEN SEPTRUMQUE TYRANNIS. / Engraved by Chas. Pye, from an original Picture by Duplessis, / in the possession of Wm. Temple Franklin, Esqe. / Published by Henry Colburn, London, Octr. 1817." The light shade of the clothing indicates the gray color, a closer cross-hatching being required to represent the red of the Wright version. The engraver, since the likeness would be reversed, shows button holes rather than buttons on the clothing. Unlocated.

Literal acceptance of the inscription would indicate a replica by Duplessis in oil or pastel. A note from Arthur Lee, Paris, Sept. 19, 1779, may refer to this picture or to a print: "Mr. A. Lee presents his compts. to Mr. W. T. Franklin & has the honor of sending him an order for the delivery of the picture of his Grandfather, of which Mr. Lee begs his acceptance."[7] That the original pastel was given to Le Veillard in 1785 certainly suggests that Franklin's grandson had a portrait of his own at that time. Since in 1784 William had borrowed Georgiana Shipley's miniature for Benjamin

6. Franklin Mss. (H.S.P.).
7. Franklin Papers (A.P.S.), *108*, no. 99.

West's use, it is possible that this painting was made for him from that, in West's studio.

The young man, like his grandfather, seems to have made little distinction between copies and originals. On July 18, 1817, he promised Samuel Starbuck, a relative, that he would soon send "the first Impression of a Print of him I have just had engraved here for the Memoirs of his life. . . . This print I consider as the best likeness of Dr. Franklin in the latter part of his life that exists."[8]

William's will, dated Oct. 24, 1814, does not mention the portrait, but leaves most of his belongings to his mistress, Hannah or Anne Collier. This is confirmed by a codicil of May 6, 1823, after his marriage to her.[9] His widow continued to live in Paris.[10] The portrait if extant might therefore be in either England or France.

> 5   Ca. 1785. Painting. Oil on canvas, 73 x 60 cm. (28.74 x 23.63 in.). A chair back, at the left, is more clearly indicated than in any other early version. Reprod. by *Proceedings of the A.P.S., 100* (1956), 378. *Owner:* Mme. d'Herouville de Carpentier, Villers sur Mer, Calvados, France.

The first owner of the painting was Franklin's dear friend and neighbor, Mme. Brillon. Presumably, she had had it made at the time of his departure from France. It has remained in the possession of her descendants and has always been attributed by them to Duplessis.[1] The list of its owners follows:

Anne Louisa Boivin d'Hardancourt (1744–1824), who on Oct. 2, 1763, married M. Brillon de Jouy, an official of the *Parlement*.

Their daughter, Cunégonde Brillon de Jouy (1764–1831) who in 1783 married Marie Antoine Pâris d'Illins, General of Brigade, killed in action on Nov. 8, 1809.

Their son, Raoul Pâris d'Illins, who married Beatrice Michel de Boissy.

Their daughter, Alix Pâris d'Illins, who became the wife of Alfred Legrand des Cloizeaux, a member of the Académie des Sciences.

8. Franklin Papers (L.C.).
9. A.P.S.
10. Charles Hodge to Jared Sparks, Sept. 14, 1837 (Sparks Papers).
1. Bernard Faÿ to George Simpson Eddy (Eddy Papers).

Their daughter, Marie des Cloizeaux, wife of the Vicomte Charles d'Herouville, owner of the Château de Villers sur Mer, Calvados.[2] It has remained there, first in the possession of Rear Admiral d'Herouville de Carpentier, and then of his widow.

> 6 1788. Painting by Marie Anne Pierrette Paulze Lavoisier (1758–1836), after Duplessis. Oil on canvas, 28⅜ x 22⅞ in. Gray hair. Brown eyes. Dark gray coat. Yellow chair back upholstered in red. Very dark background. Stenciled on back, "Thomas Allen / Restorer / of / oil paintings / Philada. / 1837." *Owners:* Miss Anne Stockton and Mrs. L. Wardlaw Miles, Princeton, N.J.

The portrait was sent from Paris to Philadelphia as the gift of the artist. Franklin's acknowledgment of it was written on Oct. 23, 1788:

> I have a long time been disabled from Writing to my dear Friend, by a severe Fit of the Gout, or I should sooner have return'd my Thanks for her very kind Present of the Portrait, which she has herself done me the honour to make of me. It is allow'd by those who have seen it to have great Merit as a Picture in every Respect; but what particularly endears it to me, is the Hand that drew it. Our English Enemies when they were in Possession of this City and of my House, made a Prisoner of my Portrait, and carried it off with them, leaving that of its Companion, my Wife, by itself a kind of Widow: You have replac'd the Husband; and the Lady seems to smile, as well pleased.[3]

This and the similar painting she retained for herself are the only canvases attributed to the artist, but it is known that after her marriage to Antoine Laurent Lavoisier she studied painting and draw-

2. Ibid. Labande, "Notes sur le Peintre Joseph-Siffrein Duplessis. . . ." p. 401, states that it was then held by M. de Guestiers, of Paris, who had inherited it from his maternal grandfather, M. Pâris d'Illins.

3. Archives Nationales, Paris.

ing with David, and her drawings illustrating her husband's chemical experiments bear witness to her skill and precision.[4]

The picture passed from Franklin to his daughter, Mrs. Richard Bache, and to William Bache (1773–1814), who married Catherine Wistar. Their daughter, Sarah, married the Rev. Charles Hodge who, on Oct. 19, 1835, informed Jared Sparks that the portrait had been lost. "When Mrs. Bache (Mrs. H's. mother) went to Virginia several family pictures & a bust of Dr. Franklin were sent to the Academy of Arts. The bust is still there, but the pictures have been lost."[5] The lost paintings were recovered by the academy in 1858, and delivered to Catherine Wistar Bache, daughter of William Bache and elder sister of Mrs. Hodge.[6] From her the portrait of Franklin descended to a son of Charles Hodge, Archibald Alexander Hodge, then to Mary Hunter Stockton and her sister, Sarah Bache Stockton, and finally to its present owners.

> 7 1788. Painting by Mme. Lavoisier, replica of No. 6. Unlocated.

The picture has been reported as owned by the family of Chazelles, in France, descendants of Lavoisier.[7] Bernard Faÿ described it on Sept. 21, 1926, as "assez belle . . . mais non pas d'une facture magnifique."[8] In 1936 it was offered for sale, as by Duplessis.[9]

> 8 Ca. 1794–1803. Painting. Oil on canvas, 22 x 18¼ in. Gray-brown hair. Background mottled olive-brown. Damage to the left background has been repaired with some overpainting. The picture has been relined and may have been cut down in size. *Owner:* Mrs. Theodore Douglas Robinson, Mohawk, N.Y.

The first recorded owner of the portrait was James Monroe, who

---

4. Denis I. Duveen, "Madame Lavoisier," *Chymia, 4* (1953), 17–18. Denis I. Duveen and Herbert S. Klickstein, "Benjamin Franklin and Antoine Laurent Lavoisier," *Annals of Science, 11* (1955), 124; illust. pl. 6.

5. Sparks Papers.

6. Pennsylvania Academy of the Fine Arts, minutes, June 14, 1858, recording that the picture had been "Found in Mr. Gratz's attic." A receipt signed by Thomas Birch, Keeper, records the original deposit, including "Marble Bust of Dr. Franklin / China Bas relief of do. / One portrait of Do." (Academy archives.)

7. Eddy Papers.

8. Ibid.

9. Ibid.

obtained it either while Minister to France, 1794–96, or during his mission to France in 1803. It has remained in his family to the present time. A copy by Charles Bird King is in the Redwood Library, Newport, R.I.

> 9   Undated. Painting. Oil on twilled canvas, 28 x 22½ in. Gray hair. Light brown eyes. Coat and waistcoat very pale gray-blue. Brown chair back upholstered in red. Background dark to light gray. *Owner:* National Portrait Gallery, London.

Purchased by the National Portrait Gallery in June, 1871, the portrait was attributed by Sir George Scharf to F. Baricolo because of its close resemblance to one he had seen in 1865 "in which the colour of the coat was of a deep crimson," inscribed on the back, "Painted, at Paris, by F. Baricolo, 1783."[1] (See J. WRIGHT, No. 7.) The similarity of the chair backs suggests that the painting may have belonged to the family of Mme. Brillon (No. 5).

> Painting, "Treaty of Paris." See WEST, No. 1.

DUPRÉ, AUGUSTIN (1748–1833)

> 1   1783. Design for a medal. Pencil drawing on paper, 6 3/16 x 9 7/16 in. At right, portrait of Franklin, profile, to left, in a circular border inscribed, "BENJ. FRANKLIN MINIS. PLEN. DES ETATS UNIS DE LAMERIQ." and below, "MDCCLXXXIII." At left, circular design for reverse, with a winged "Genius of Liberty" taking flight, a staff and liberty cap in his right hand, a flame burning on his head, a broken scepter and fallen crown beneath his feet. His left hand is extended toward a circular temple surmounted by a lightning rod. Above him is inscribed, "JE VOLE A L'IMORTALITE." In lower left corner of the paper, a sketch of globe, caduceus, lamp, and other attributes, with stamped signature in blue ink in oval border, "A. Dupré fecit." At lower right, stamped initials "N.D." in circle (Narcisse Dupré, son of the artist). *Owner:* Boston Public Library. Pl. 20.

From Philadelphia, on Sept. 4, 1786, Franklin sent his sister two medals "struck as Compliments to your Brother, One by the Lodge

---

1. George Scharf, *Historical and Descriptive Catalogue of . . . the National Portrait Gallery* (London, 1888), p. 175.

of the Nine Sisters, of which he was President, the other by a private Friend."[2] These are undoubtedly the Masonic medal by Bernier and one of those by Dupré for which this drawing is a study. The "private Friend" was the artist himself, to whom Franklin had given some of the Congressional commissions, a fact borne out by the inscription on the actual medal, "SCULPSIT ET DICAVIT," "engraved and dedicated."[3] Charles Saunier emphasizes the fact that Dupré owned a little "maison de plaisance" at Auteuil, near Franklin's home, and ventures to state that he and Franklin often met and traveled to Paris together.[4] Among his American medals is the "Libertas Americana" of 1782, conceived and ordered by Franklin as his personal tribute to the American armed forces and their French allies. Later, Dupré designed medals for the private mint of Franklin's friend, Matthew Boulton, at Birmingham. He was a man of an inquiring, inventive turn of mind, had a particular interest in printing, his daughter having married one of the Didots, and he had been the first to suggest the stereotype process.[5]

The drawing was purchased in 1888 "from the Dupré family," together with a group of medals, proofs, and dies, by the Boston Public Library as an addition to its "Green Collection of Frankliniana." The purchase was arranged by William S. Appleton.[6] Earlier, alternative designs for the reverse of the medal are owned by the A.P.S.[7]

A small Sèvres medallion of the type which Franklin frequently gave to friends is also in the Boston Public Library collection. It would have been characteristic of Franklin to have given it to Dupré for use in this likeness. If Dupré's "Franklin" is based rather upon the profile of the Houdon bust, as seems almost certain, it has nonetheless been given a feeling of more placid strength,

2. Van Doren, *Benjamin Franklin & Jane Mecom*, p. 281.

3. Carl Zigrosser, "The Medallic Sketches of Augustin Dupré in American Collections," *Proceedings of the A.P.S., 101* (1957), 535–50.

4. "Les Médailles Françaises de l'Independance Américaine," *Les Arts, 172* (1918), 6.

5. Zigrosser, "Dupré," p. 535.

6. *Bookman, 22* (1905–06), 443–44. City of Boston, *Document 13, 1889. 37th Annual Report of the Trustees of the Public Library*. William S. Appleton, "Augustin Dupré and his Work for America," in *Proceedings of the M.H.S.*, ser. 2, 5 (1890), 348–52.

7. Zigrosser, "Dupré," pp. 541–43. Illust.

with a trace of humor only as lightly indicated as is possible within these small dimensions. Medalists realize more keenly perhaps than others the value of a standard likeness of a great figure, a fact which may have influenced Dupré and certainly had a part in the extensive imitation of his work by others coming after.

2 1784. Medal. Silver, bronze, or brass, diam. 1¾ in. Obverse: profile to left as in drawing. Inscribed around edge, "BENJ. FRANKLIN NATUS BOSTON XVII JAN. / MDCCVI." Signed on *tranche* of shoulder, "DUPRE F."; Reverse: "Genius of Liberty" as in the drawing, but the figure more erect, the temple placed at the left and the fallen crown and scepter at the right. Inscribed around the edge, "ERIPUIT COELO FULMEN SEPTRUM QUE TYRANNIS." In exergue: "SCULPSIT ET DICAVIT / AUG. DUPRÉ ANNO / MDCCLXXXIV." Pl. 20.

3 Ca. 1783. Medal. White metal proof, diam. 2 cm. (13/16 in.). Same profile and inscription as the obverse of the above. *Owner:* Boston Public Library.

Acquired from the Dupré family with the original design. "It is not known whether this is a preliminary study for the larger medal or a project for a coin or tiny medal."[8]

4 1786. Medal. Silver or bronze, diam. 1¾ in. Obverse: same as No. 2. Reverse: inscribed within a wreath of oak leaves, "ERIPUIT COELO / FULMEN / SEPTRUM QUE / TYRANNIS." Below: "SCULPSIT ET DICAVIT / AUG DUPRE ANNO / MDCCLXXXVI." A restrike with a slight variation in the design of the reverse is recorded.[9]

5 1790. Medal. Brass, diam. 1 11/16 in. Obverse: bust of Franklin, to right. Inscribed, "BENJ. FRANKLIN, MORT EN 1790." Signed on shoulder, "DUPRE F." Reverse: blank.

ELMER, STEPHEN (d. 1796)
1780. Painting. Oil on canvas, 30 x 25 in. Ruddy flesh tints. Green robe with sable collar over a light brown coat or waist-

8. Ibid., p. 544.
9. Melvin and George Fuld, "Medallic Memorials to Franklin," *Numismatist,* *69* (1956), 1403.

coat. Right hand holds the *London Evening Post*. Under the left hand is a copy of Richard Price's pamphlet, *Observations / on the Nature of / Civil Liberty, / the Principles of / Government, / and the / Justice and Policy / of the War with America,* London, T. Cadell, 1776.[1] Dark brown background. Signed, lower right, "S. Elmer. 1780." *Owner:* Edward Eberstadt & Sons, New York. Pl. 13.

Perhaps no Franklin portrait has been the subject of more doubt and speculation than this, a situation which the present study may not wholly resolve. It could not be from life, since all the portraits with natural hair are from French or American sources. Franklin wore spectacles, not pince-nez, though here one may plead an artist's unwillingness to obscure a part of the face by the supporting bar. That the picture represents Franklin at all has been seriously questioned. Elmer himself never publicly identified the subject of his piece. The identification as Franklin is documented by two of the engravings made from it after Elmer's death. These are based upon an engraving made and published by Thomas Ryder (1746–1810) of London, made when the picture was still new: "Painted by S. Elmer. Engraved by T. Ryder. / THE POLITICIAN. / Published as the Act directs May 1, 1782, by T. Ryder and Sold by A. Torre and J. Thane, No. 28 Hay Market." A new engraving, from this, appeared as frontispiece to *The Life and Works of Benjamin Franklin,* Bungay, Brightly and Childs, 1815. This first published identification of the subject received confirmation in a republication from Ryder's original plate, July 1, 1824, by Z. Sweet, London, with the altered title: "THE POLITICIAN. / [DR. BENJ: FRANKLIN]."

No denial of this acceptance of the likeness as Franklin's, within the lifetime of many who had known him, was ever made. The features could not be those of Richard Price, whose pamphlet figures so prominently. They resemble more closely those of the mad politician Labilliere, whose portrait Joseph Wright painted in 1780, with some of his favorite reading including the *Evening Post* of Jan. 1, that year. Ryder's engraving of "The Politician" dates the

1. Preface dated Feb. 8, 1776. On Feb. 13 Joseph Priestley sent a copy to Franklin. Carl B. Cone, *Torchbearer of Freedom. The Influence of Richard Price on Eighteenth Century Thought* (Lexington, University of Kentucky, 1952), p. 76.

Evening Post, "Jan. 1, 1776," the date which, though now illegible, must have been on Elmer's painting.

The few facts we have on the life of Stephen Elmer are, though only in a small degree, suggestive. "He resided chiefly at Farnham in Surrey, where he dealt as a maltster, and where he thought himself conveniently situated to pursue his favorite study, but which he intimated to be much more pleasant than profitable to him."[2] He also had a London address, and his "favorite study" had made him a member of the Society of Artists and an Associate of the Royal Academy. He was accounted by some the best painter of still life in England, and was known both as "little Elmer," and as "the celebrated painter of dead game."[3] His best patrons appear to have been the sporting gentlemen who brought these latter subjects to him, and if he had any political inclination, one would expect it to be close to theirs. Certainly there is no evidence of his being in any way sympathetic with Franklin or the pro-American group. A manuscript note in a Royal Academy catalogue of 1777 identifies him as "Old Elmer,"[4] and one glimpses him, all in all, as a crotchety oldster with a spirit of fun and far more impulse to deride than to extol the radical politicos of his day.

In that Academy show of 1777 little old Elmer exhibited "A Politician," along with "Fox and pheasant," "Partridges," "Basket of Strawberries," "Fowls" and a "View of Farnham Castle." This "Politician" of 1777 is otherwise unrecorded. It was probably a very similar picture to the "Politician" of 1780, with the same newspaper and pamphlet of 1776, but the figure may have been different. A plausible theory might be that the first picture satirized Franklin as an answer to the adulation he was then receiving in the anonymous medal (CHAMBERLIN, No. 6) and elsewhere, and that, this work having met with some approbation, the artist was moved to paint another, with a revised likeness, in answer to the renewed acclaim of Franklin in the publication of his *Political, Miscellaneous and Philosophical Pieces,* edited by Benjamin Vaughan and published by J. Johnson, London, 1779, with an en-

2. Edward Edwards, *Anecdotes of Painters who have been Born or Resided in England* (London, 1808), p. 233.
3. Whitley Papers.
4. Anderdon Collection.

graving based upon the new Sèvres medallion. This portrait engraving could be the source of Elmer's painting, with the head slightly turned from profile and with the addition of the glasses and different costume. The costume may have been that of his 1777 version. As to the pose, Martin's portrait of Franklin had not been engraved, but it was possible that it was known to Elmer and others, and that "The Politician" was in some measure a parody on it.

It is possible also that Elmer's source was not the engraving in the *Political, Miscellaneous and Philosophical Pieces,* but the very similar portrait published in the *Political Magazine and Parliamentary, Naval and Literary Journal* for October 1780.[5] This might be a shade closer to the painting and, like the painting, faces to the right. It accompanies a bitterly hostile "Life and Character of Dr. Franklin," who is there declared to be the "author and encourager of the American rebellion," to have early "manifested his inclination for mischief," and whose "dark machinations" after he "came to be noticed as a politician" are traced in detail.[6]

It may be surmised that Elmer had known Franklin by sight, though his work must have been based on available sources. That his intention was to satirize seems certain, and that a picture so conceived could be reissued posthumously in its subject's honor throws a new light on the invulnerability of Franklin's fame.

In 1799, after the artist's death, his nephew and heir, William Elmer, placed his work on sale as "Elmer's Sportsman's Exhibition" in a room in Haymarket.[7] One of the many sold was "The Politician—an old man reading news, kit-cat size, thirty guineas."[8] The remaining pictures were destroyed by a fire on Feb. 6, 1801.

In 1885 the painting was presented by W. H. Huntington to the Metropolitan Museum.[9] The Huntington Collection was retired to storage in 1906, and many pieces not essential to the Museum's purpose were sold afterward. This canvas, sold in 1956, was purchased by Prosper Guerry, and bought from George P. Guerry by

5. *1,* opp. 631.
6. Ibid., p. 631.
7. Edwards, *Anecdotes,* pp. 233–34.
8. Ibid., p. 234.
9. Bowen, *Centennial of the Inauguration of George Washington,* p. 458; illust., p. 464.

its present owners. A replica or early copy is in the U.S. Embassy, Paris.

FEKE, ROBERT (Ca. 1706/10–ca. 1750)

> Ca. 1738–46. Painting. Oil on canvas, 50 3/16 x 40 2/16 in. Brown wig with highlights on curls. Dark brown eyes. Greenish-black coat. Very dark green waistcoat. Black hat under left arm. Posed against a brown wall, at left. Background at right a green, barren landscape ending in green hills. Crudely painted gray-white clouds separate the hills from the gray-blue sky above. *Owner:* Harvard University. Pl. 1.

According to William Sawitzky, "Overcleaned and repainted to such an extent that it is now impossible to say with certainty who originally painted it."[1] The Fogg Museum corroborates this statement. The attribution to Feke is based primarily upon pose and composition, and is supported by Feke and Franklin associations in Boston, Newport, and Philadelphia. Consideration has also been given to John Greenwood, who with Joseph Badger was active in Boston at the time when it might have been painted there.

The painting descended in his family from John Franklin (1690–1756), elder brother of Benjamin, to Thomas Waldron Sumner, from whose estate it was purchased by Dr. John C. Warren. It was bequeathed by Dr. Warren to Harvard College in 1856. Two of the three family portraits owned by John Franklin, that of his wife (Pl. I) and this of his brother, are extant. The third, of himself, is unlocated. See above, pp. 24–45.

FILLEUL, ANNE ROSALIE (1752–94)

> 1 1778 or 1779. Painting. Oil on canvas, 910 x 725 cm. (35.82 x 28.54 in.). Half length behind a table on which are a map, "PHILADELPHIA," and spectacles. Body slightly to left and head to right. Bottle-green dressing gown trimmed with brown fur, over a white satin waistcoat. Shirt open at the collar. Right hand extended over the map. The lower part of the painting, at the map, has suffered some damage.[2] *Owner:* a descendant of the artist (name withheld), France. Pl. 23.

1. Quoted in *Antiques, 36* (1939), 222.
2. Abel Doysié to George Simpson Eddy, Aug. 9, 1923 (Eddy Papers). The painting is now in a modern frame.

The portrait was retained by the artist and is still owned by her descendants. They have the record of the purchase of a frame for it in 1779, and date the painting as in that year or in 1778. It is the work of a pretty and talented young woman, the daughter of Blaise Bocquet, a fan painter and the proprietor of a bric-a-brac shop in Paris. She married Louis Filleul in 1777, and at that time as a mark of favor, the queen had given her the post of concierge at the château of La Muette, bringing the couple a small income. She painted little thereafter, and the portrait of Franklin is one of her last works. Her home was not far from Franklin's and they had probably met socially. The painting, however, represents an investment by her father, who sponsored the publication of the engraving after it described below. The artist's connection with the court led to her death at the guillotine in 1794.[3] A property inventory made by the revolutionary government in 1793 mentions the portrait. "Mme. Filleul. Portrait de Franklin peint a mis-corps par la femme susdite, estime 120 livres."[4] There are no replicas, and as far as is known copies have been made only from the engraving.

> 2   1779. Line engraving by Louis Jacques Cathelin (1739–1804), after the painting by Mme. Filleul. Plate size, 14 3/16 x 11 in.; engraved surface, 13¼ x 9¼ in. "BENJAMIN FRANKLIN / Né à Boston le 17 Janvier 1706. / Eripuit coelo fulmen septrumque tyrannis. Peint par Madame Filleul. Gravé par Cathelin, Graveur du Roi. / A Paris chez M. Bocquet rue Comtesse d'Artois vis-à-vis celle Mauconseil."

Mme. Filleul's painting must have been made expressly for this engraving, published by her father. Cathelin had been admitted as academician of the Académie Royale in 1777, and exhibited his "Franklin" at the next Salon, that of 1779.[5] It was praised by a contemporary critic as a better resemblance than the bust by Houdon or the painting by Duplessis.[6]

3. Bouvier, "Un Concierge de Passy en l'An II," pp. 110–28.
4. Eddy Papers. From Archives Nationales, F.17.1267, Dossier.
5. *Livret,* p. 51, no. 263.
6. Belleudy, *Duplessis,* p. 87n, quoting Lesuire, "Le Mort vivant au Salon."

3   1780. Line engraving by unidentified artist. Plate size, 12⅞ x 8½ in.; engraved surface, 10½ x 8 in. "N.L.G.D.L.C.A.D.L. del et sculp. / BENJAMIN FRANKLIN / Ministaire plénipotentiaire à la Cour de France pour la République / des Provinces unies de l'Amérique Septentrionale. / Né à Boston le 17 Janvier 1706. / A Paris chez Bligny Lancier du Roi, Md. d'Estampes, Peintre, Doreur et Vitrier, Cour du Manège aux Tuilleries." Added at the right of this inscription is another, "Présenté à son Excellence / quelle à accepté le 14. / Juillet 1780. / Par son très Humble et très Obéissant / Serviteur BLIGNY." The portrait is shown in an oval frame held by a figure of Diogenes, lantern in hand and his tub in the background. The stone at his feet is inscribed, "STUPETE GENTES! REPERIT VIVUM DIOGENES." In the foreground, a shepherd's crook and a broken yoke. At lower right, a map inscribed, "AMERIQ. SEPTENT." covered by flame and lightning, from which a phoenix (looking very much like the American eagle) arises. At upper left, a liberty cap on a spear and the dove of peace, released, soaring into the sky.

The identity of artist and engraver remains hidden under that imposing array of initials. The letters might possibly indicate two persons with the same surname, N.L.G.D.L. and C.A.D.L., but thus far various theories have defied verification. The Philadelphia Museum owns the original pencil drawing from which the plate was engraved. It is on pale green-gray paper, 4 1/8 x 3 3/16 in., lightly ruled in squares for copying, cut to oval, and affixed to a counterproof of an earlier engraving of Cardinal Fleury in which the Diogenes figure was used. The discovery of this drawing enabled Carl Zigrosser to reconstruct in detail the origin of the Franklin print in the hands of H. T. Bligny, "a Parisian print publisher of no great standing," who made it his business to buy up and rework old engraved plates in this fashion.[7] Bligny's presentation of the work to Franklin on July 14, 1780, gained him some business through the following year, as there are entries in Franklin's *Account of Family Expenses* on Sept. 24, 1780, and July 12,

7. Carl Zigrosser, "Franklin Portraits in the Rockefeller Collection," *Philadelphia Museum of Art Bulletin, 44* (1948), 25, 27.

1781, for frames and prints bought of him.[8] Bligny advertised the print, with others, in the *Journal de Paris* of Jan. 21, 1781.

The print was echoed in an engraving by J. Pelicier in 1782, on a plate 9¾ x 6⅜ in., and with symbolism stressing the phoenix motif.

FISHER, EDWARD (1730–85)

 1763. Mezzotint. See CHAMBERLIN, No. 3.

FRAGONARD, JEAN HONORÉ (1732–1806)

 1 1778. Drawing, "Le Docteur Franklin Couronné par la Liberté." Sepia and pencil drawing, 47 x 35.5 cm. (18.49 x 13.06 in.). Bust of Franklin (after Caffiéri) on terrestrial globe, right foreground, is embraced by a winged youth. Liberty, at left, descends toward it, a wreath extended in each hand. Signed, lower left, "fragonard." Inscribed, below, in the same hand, "Frankelin." Reproduced in the catalogues of both sales noted below. *Owner* (1924–29): Marius Paulme. The origin of the drawing is documented by the engraving made from it and related correspondence (see below, No. 2). It was made for the Abbé de Saint Non, a distinguished amateur, enabling him to give Franklin, in a highly complimentary form, a demonstration of the new technique of aquatint engraving. The drawing itself is first recorded in the sale of the collection of Jean Ferrier of Aix-en-Provence, Hôtel Drouot, Paris, Dec. 24, 1924.[9] It was purchased by Marius Paulme, whose collection was sold at the Galeries Georges Petit, Paris, on May 13, 1929.[1]

 2 1778. Engraving by Jean Claude Richard de Saint Non (1727–91), after No. 1. Aquatint, plate size 9½ x 8 in. "Le Docteur Francklin couronné par la liberté."[2] The composition of the drawing is reversed. A liberty cap on a pole and rays of light have been added over the figure of Liberty. The inscription, "AMERIQUE" has been added on the globe and, to the scroll

 8. Franklin Papers (A.P.S.).
 9. Illust. opp. p. 9.
 1. Illust. p. 49.
 2. The *Catalogue des dessins anciens, gouaches & pastels . . . composant la collection de M. Marius Paulme* (Paris, Galerie George Petit, May 13, 1929), cites a print inscribed "Fragonard del.," "Le Docteur Couronné par la Liberté," and "L'Abbe de St. Non. Inve et sculpsit 1778" (p. 50).

under the bust, "Cons . . tutions / du Gouvernment / de Pensilvanie / Art. 1."[3] In foreground, a fasces with olive branches. Pl. 17.

On April 17, 1778, the Abbé de Saint Non wrote to Baron Gagnare de Joursanvault, a collector who sought examples of all his prints, commenting upon his alteration of the design and the circumstance under which the print had been made:

> Quant à la petite observation que vous m'avez faite sur l'estampe du docteur Franklin, si vous avez connaissance de l'Iconologie, vous devez rappeler qu'un bonnet en l'air, soutenu d'une picque ou un baton, est l'emblème de la liberté, comme une lampe l'est de l'étude, ou les balances de la justice; ainsi il était impossible de la caractériser autremont; la mal seulement, dans la gravure, c'est que ce fatal bonnet est trop mordu d'eau-forte et est devenue trop coloré, au lieu que, dans le dessin, il reste absolument dans la vapeur; mais je vous prie de considérer que cette plaisanterie a été faite dans une matinée et uniquement pour donner à cet homme célèbre qui désirait savoir comment on gravait dans ce genre là, une idée de ce procédé. Je n'ai pas, là-dessus, plus de prétention, et l'a-propos, l'intention en font tout le mérite. Vous faites beaucoup trop d'honneur à mes talents dont vous avez trop bonne idée.[4]

3. The inscription on the scroll reflects the recent appearance of the *Recueil des loix constitutives, des colonies angloises confederées sous la denomination d'Etats Unis de l'Amerique septentrionale*, published at the Hague in 1778 with a dedication to Franklin. It was reviewed in the *Journal de Paris*, June 19, 1778. This print, followed by that of Carmontelle, had its part in presenting Franklin not only as liberator but as legislator of the New World.

4. "As for your hint on the print of Dr. Franklin, if you are aware of the iconography, you will recall that a cap held aloft on pole or baton is the emblem of Liberty, as a lamp is of Knowledge, or the scales of Justice; thus it is impossible to characterize it otherwise; the only trouble with the print is that that fatal cap is too deeply bitten by the acid and is too dark, while in the drawing it floats in the air; but I beg you to consider that this little piece has been made in the space of one morning and solely to convey to this celebrated man a conception of engraving in this technique, an idea of the process. I claim no more for it, and after all, the merit is in the intention. You honor and reckon my talents too highly." (Louis Guimbaud, *Saint-Non et Fragonard, d'après des documents inédites*, Paris, Le Goupy, 1928, pp. 186–87.) Guimbaud interprets the letter as indicating that the design also was Saint Non's.

Saint Non, an amateur, had been one of the first followers of Jean Baptiste Le Prince, inventor of the aquatint process. His *oeuvre* includes 92 works, most of them made in 1766 and 1767. This plate was the only one made in 1778.[5] Portalis and Beraldi give us a pretty picture of Franklin coming to luncheon with Saint Non, to be taught the secret of etching in this new manner, the preparation of the plate, the printing, the pulling of the first impression—"Quelle agréable surprise pour le Brutus de l'Amérique!"[6] From two undated notes from Madame Brillon to Franklin, however, it appears that Saint Non sent the first example to Franklin through her hands, claiming that if so received it would have a greater merit in his eyes, and that through her also he transmitted to him twelve other impressions to be sent to his friends in America.[7]

Of these, one impression, of course, went to Sally, and was shown by her husband, Richard Bache, to various friends. This we know from a letter written by the fiery-tempered Timothy Matlack and published in the *Pennsylvania Gazette* of March 31, 1779. He excoriates Bache for having attacked the Pennsylvania constitution, particularly on the point of its unicameral legislature, reminding him that "your venerable father-in-law" had openly supported this feature, and goes on to use the print, with its allusion to the constitution of Pennsylvania, to drive home his point. "This print must have been intended for some friend of the Patriot and Philosopher, and have been handed to you by mistake." In September 1779 the firm of Bache and Shee was formed "for the purpose of doing commission business," and Franklin's aid in promoting it was solicited.[8] It would appear from the Franklin Papers that the firm's dealings left some unhappy memories in France, among those investors who suffered losses being M. Brillon and the Abbé de Saint Non.

3   1778. Etching by Marguerite Gérard (1761–1837), after a design by Fragonard. Etched surface, 19 x 14½ in. "ERIPUIT

5. Ibid., p. 201.

6. Roger Portalis and Henri Beraldi, *Graveurs du dixhuitième siècle, 3* (Paris, 1880–82), 491–92. Guimbaud also gives a charming report, pp. 166–67.

7. Franklin Papers (A.P.S.), *70,* no. 326; *43,* no. 60.

8. Richard Bache to Benjamin Franklin, Sept. 18, 1779 (A.P.S.).

COELO FULMEN, SEPTRUMQUE TIRANNIS / AU GENIE DE FRANK-
LIN." Pl. 33.

The print is an allegory illustrating the famous epigram of Turgot.
Franklin, in classic drapery, is seated in the clouds with America
at his side. At a backward gesture of his left arm, Minerva wards
off the lightning with her shield. The right arm, outstretched in
anger, signals Mars to leap upon the figures of Tyranny and Avarice, overthrowing them. Fragonard's original design for it was
probably made early in 1778 when the Franco-American alliance
was impending. In this drawing, the face of Franklin is not a likeness. Publication of the print was announced in the *Journal de
Paris* of Nov. 15, 1778:

> *Estampe nouvelle, dédiée au Génie de Franklin.*
> L'Auteur ingénieux de cette composition, M. *Frago-
> nard,* Peintre du Roi, a voulu rendre le vers latin
> appliqué à *Franklin: Eripuit coelo fulmen, scep-
> trumque tyrannis,* qu'on lit au bas de l'Estampe.
>
> Inspire par ce vers, qui remplit l'idée & les con-
> noissances profondes de *Franklin* & de sa sagesse dans
> la révolution du Nouveau Monde, le Peintre l'a
> représenté tout-à-la-fois opposant d'une main l'Egide
> de Minerve à la foudre, qu'il a sçu fixer par des Con-
> ducteurs, & de l'autre ordonnant à Mars de combattre
> l'avarice & la tyrannie; tandis que l'Amérique, noble-
> ment appuiée sur lui & tenant un faisceau, symbole
> des Provinces-unies, contemple avec tranquilité ses
> ennemis terrassés. Le jet simple & rapide de cette
> composition est aussi clair & aussi facile que le vers,
> que l'on a voulu peindre aux yeux. C'est avec cette
> dignité qu'il sied aux talens de célébrer le vrai mérite
> & les grandes actions.
>
> Cette Estampe, gravée par la Dlle. Marguerite
> *Gérard,* d'après les dessins & sous les yeux de M.
> Fragonard, son beau frère, a le mérite estimable aux
> yeux des Artistes, celui de rendre dans la gravure
> l'esprit de l'Auteur. On n'y a point cherché ce soin,
> ces beaux travaux & ces graces essentiel aux ouvrages

de burin; on n'a désire que d'exprimer par la pointe les touches hardies & spirituelles du dessin, avec la même rapidité, que le dessin lui-meme a été éxecute, & il nous semble que l'on y a réussi.

Cette Estampe paroit, & se trouve chez M. Fragonard, Peintre du Roi, aux vieux Louvre, du côté de la Colonade. Le prix est de 4 livres.[9]

Despite this indisputable contemporary attribution of the design to Fragonard and the print to Marguerite Gérard, questions have been raised as to authorship, and also as to whether the print be etching or aquatint. Louis Guimbaud describes it as "une tentative de Frago dans le domaine de l'aquatinte."[1] Fragonard's original design, first recorded as in the collection of François Hyppolyte Walferdin (1795–1880), is now the property of Wildenstein and Co., New York. In this drawing the face of Franklin is not a likeness. A proof of the print in the Walferdin collection was inscribed, "l'Apothéose de Franklin : gravé par Marguerite Gérard à l'âge de

9. *"New print, dedicated to the Genius of Franklin.* The ingenious author of this composition, M. Fragonard, Painter to the King, has sought to depict the Latin verse applied to *Franklin, Eripuit coelo fulmen, sceptrumque tyrannis,* which one reads at the base of the print.

"Inspired by this verse, which summarizes the spirit and profound understanding of Franklin and his wisdom in the New World revolution, the Painter has represented him at once turning aside the lightning with Minerva's shield, as his lightning rods have done, and with the other commanding Mars to attack Avarice and Tyranny; while America, nobly attendant on him and holding a fasces, symbol of the united provinces, calmly watches the overthrow of her enemies. The simple and rapid line of this composition is as clear and as facile as the verse, which the painter wanted to transform into a visual image. It is with this dignity that he has turned his talents to celebrate true worth and great deeds.

"This print, engraved by the Dlle. *Gérard,* after the drawing and under the direction of M. Fragonard, her brother-in-law, has the merit, dear to artists, of rendering in engraved line the spirit of the author. Here they have not aimed at that meticulousness, those beautiful works and those graces essential to the products of the burin; they have only sought to catch by the point the sure and sensitive touches of the design, with a rapidity equal to that with which the drawing was executed, and it seems to us that they have succeeded . . ." (Pp. 1278–79.)

An account of the print, largely a translation of this, but cited as having been found in "the Gazette of Amiens," was published in the *Pennsylvania Packet,* June 3, 1780, and reprinted in the *Connecticut Gazette* of June 30. See also Jeanne Doin, "Marguerite Gérard," *Gazette des Beaux-Arts, 8* (1913), 430.

1. Guimbaud, *Saint-Non,* p. 212.

seize ans, en 1772. Homage à mon maître et bon ami Frago."[2] The genuineness of the inscription has been doubted.[3] If spurious, however, the correctness of the attribution remains.

The composition is repeated in three or four additional drawings for which claims of their being the original design have been made. Michel Benisovich mentions "L'Homme qui a enlevé la fourche du Ciel et le sceptre aux tyrans," in the collection of Lady Mendl, Paris.[4] In Godefroy Mayer's sale catalogue of 1910 a drawing, "Au Génie de Franklin," 21 x 15½ in. in size, is attributed to Marguerite Gérard and described as "very probably the model drawing from which Fragonard etched and Miss Gerard finished the well-known engraving of Franklin."[5] A wash drawing, then the property of Clarence S. Bement of Philadelphia (d. 1895) is illustrated in Bowen, *Centennial Celebration,* p. 484. A drawing from the Hampton L. Carson collection appeared as no. 1264 in the Edward Babcock Holden sale of April, 1910, and is now in the William Smith Mason Collection at Yale. These last two may be the same work. The illustrations show a lack of force and original quality.

Undated drawing. See HOUDON, No. 9.

FRITSCH, JOHANN CHRISTIAN GOTTFRIED
See COCHIN, No. 1.

GAGE, G.
Messrs. Puttick and Simpson's *Catalogue of the Well Selected and Useful Stock of the Late Mr. John Tayleure, Printseller, of Adelaide Street, Strand* (London, Aug. 28, 1861), lists on p. 9: "110. *FRANKLIN* (DR. BENJ.) An appointment of Deputy-Postmaster, signed by him as Post-Master General of the Northern District of North America, 1761. Letters of persons named Franklin. Drawing of Benjamin Franklin, drawn at Boston by G. Gage; etc." Unlocated.

2. Roger Portalis, *Les Dessinateurs d'illustrations au dix-huitième siècle* (Paris, 1877), p. 244. Goncourt, *L'art du dix-huitième Siècle, 3,* 253.
3. Georges Grappe, *La Vie de Jean Honoré Fragonard* (Paris, 1942), p. 213n.
4. Benisovich, "Duplessis in the United States," p. 286.
5. *No. 30. Old Paintings, Drawings.*

GARDEUR, JEAN NICOLAS (ca. 1777–1808)
 1777, 1778, or 1779. Bust (?). Unlocated.

The work is unknown today, and its history rests entirely upon the following letter from Franklin's old friend, Barbeu Dubourg, dated "30ᵉ mars," and addressed to him at Passy:

> J'ai l'honneur de souhaiter le bonjour à Monsieur franklin et le prie de permettre que Mr. Gardeur qui a fait les portraits de la famille Royale &c, dans un genre tout nouveau, profite de l'occasion pour faire le sien sans le gener dans la meme séance qu'il a accordée pour ce matin meme à ce que j'ai oui dire à un autre Peintre. J'espére qu'il en rendura un petit buste agréable au public et surtout à son très humble serviteur
>
> Dubourg[6]

The date of the letter may be March 30, 1777, 1778, or 1779 (Dubourg died in Dec. 1779). In 1777 Gardeur and Jean Louis Couasnon (1747–1812), sculptors working in partnership, had made life portraits of Louis XVI and Marie Antoinette. From the terra cotta, these were reproduced by means of plaster molds *en carton,* that is, in papier-mâché, painted in lifelike colors and with the eyes represented in enamel.[7] The material was one for which new uses were being explored. Decorative forms of all sorts could be made from it, and it was even being used in the construction of carriage bodies by the summer of 1778.[8] By the autumn of that year the partners who had applied it to the fine arts had separated. Their mutual recriminations, recorded in an exchange of letters in the *Journal de Paris,* are a good source of information on the new technique.[9] It began with a friendly notice of Gardeur from the pen

6. "I have the honor to wish M. Franklin good day, and to beg him to grant Mr. Gardeur who has made the portraits of the royal family &c, in an entirely new medium, permission to paint his, without disturbing him, at the same sitting that I understand he has granted for this same morning to another painter. I am hopeful that he will produce a small bust acceptable to the public and above all to his very humble servant Dubourg." (Franklin Papers, A.P.S., *70,* no. 83b.)

7. Maze-Sencier, *Le Livre des collectionneurs,* p. 589. Stanislaus Lami, *Dictionnaire des sculpteurs, 1* (Paris, 1910), 363.

8. *Journal de Paris, 2,* 85–86. Bachaumont, *Mémoires, 12,* Sept. 29, 1778, 121.

9. *Journal de Paris, 2* (1778), 970–71, 1049–50, 1082–83, 1111.

of Pahin de La Blancherie, and continued with Couasnon's scornful attack and Gardeur's defense. La Blancherie, young and warm-hearted, was holding the first of those *assemblées* which were to become the Salon de la Correspondance, a project which had been inaugurated in the preceding May with the endorsement of Franklin and other prominent persons.

Gardeur had been a fan-maker, then merchant, then modeler-sculptor, and in the latter category was admitted to the Académie de Saint Luc in 1778.[1] That he had delivered Dubourg's letter to Franklin is obvious from its presence in the Franklin Papers. There is, however, no bust of Franklin which can be attributed to him, and since the painted papier-mâché pieces were to be made in quantity, it seems doubtful that Franklin's portrait was produced in that medium. Both Gardeur and Couasnon continued to appear in subsequent years at the Salon de la Correspondance, the first with decorative pieces, the second with portraits from life, but neither with a "Franklin."[2] Dubourg's letter, however, implies the publication *en carton* of "a little bust acceptable to the public." His reference to having heard that "another Painter" was making Franklin's portrait at the same time is of interest as possibly dating a different work. If the year of the letter is 1777, the "painter" was the sculptor Dufourny. If, as more likely, it is 1778, it was probably de L'Hospital.

GÉRARD, MARGUERITE (1761–1837)
   1778. Etching. See FRAGONARD, No. 3.

GIVONNE, MLLE. DE
   1, 2   1783, 1784. Pastel by Mlle. de Givonne, and copy after it by an unidentified artist. Unlocated.
Marie Anne Henriette Payan de l'Étang, Baronne de Bourdic (1746–1802) had formed a friendship with Franklin during a visit to Paris in 1783. Her pleasant intimacy with him provoked an

---

1. Guiffrey, *Académie de Saint Luc,* p. 300.
2. *Nouvelles de la république des sciences et des arts,* March 23, 1779, p. 60; April 20, 1779, p. 75; May 25, 1779, p. 125; July 11, 1781, p. 8; Nov. 28, 1781, p. 86. Chavignerie, "Les Artistes Français du XVIIIe Siècle," *Revue universelle des arts, 19* (1864), 363; *20* (1865), 260.

anonymous "Epître à Madame la Baronne de Bourdic, sur ses relations avec le Docteur Franklin," first published in the *Journal de Paris* of July 5, 1784.[3] She was a poetess, aglow with all the enthusiasms of the hour. We have another glimpse of her in that year as associated, along with several other noble ladies, in the "Société Patriotique Bretonne," in whose temple the revered title was the simple word "Citoyenne."[4] Her estate was in Uzès in the south of France, near Nîmes and not far from Avignon. After her return there in 1784, she wrote the Doctor in tender recollection of their friendship and to enlist his interest in behalf of a friend of her father's.[5] In a delicately flattering introduction to this request she tells him that she has brought home with her the little "portrait au crayon" which Mlle. de Givonne had made at his house the year before, and beneath which she had placed an inscription composed by herself:

> Cest le craÿon d'une jeune beauté
> qui rassembla ces traits, a laventure?
> Ce simple hommage a tant de verité
> que lart s'en etonne et murmure,
> Lapotre de la liberté,
> Sort *encore* une fois des mains de la nature.

She adds that from this small portrait and from a very recent recollection of Franklin, an artist has made "une ressemblance parfaite."

The poem implies that good fortune, rather than skill, had enabled the young beauty to recreate the features of the philosopher with such verity that Art, amazed, was moved to murmur in recognition, "L'Apôtre de la liberté." We have thus the record of a small pastel adorned with the poem which the lady modestly states to have been "bien plus l'ouvrage du coeur de Mde. de Bourdic que celui de son esprit," and a copy from it, presumably a larger piece, and certainly a more finished and accurate one. The artist of the original is unidentified. She may perhaps have been one of a group

3. Aldridge, *Franklin and His French Contemporaries*, p. 157.

4. Bachaumont, *Mémoires, 26,* June 20, 1784, 70–71.

5. "Does the crayon of a young beauty catch by chance these features? This simple homage has such truth that art stands self-perplexed, and murmurs, 'The apostle of Liberty emerges once again from the hands of nature'" (Franklin Papers, A.P.S., *41,* Pt. II, no. 139).

of ladies whom Mme. de Bourdic had introduced to Franklin at Passy.[6]

GOSSET, ISAAC (1713–99)

    1   1766. Wax profile attributed to Isaac Gosset; formerly attributed to Patience Wright. Head and shoulders, unmounted. Ht. 3 5/16 in. Width at bust, $2\frac{1}{8}$ in. Break across body repaired. Small piece broken from waistcoat, lower left, and bow of the queue ribbon missing. *Owner:* A.P.S., Philadelphia.

By the time of his death at his home in Kensington on Nov. 28, 1799, Isaac Gosset had become something of a celebrity. "The late Mr. G. invented a composition of wax, in which he modelled portraits in the most exquisite manner. . . . In the line of his art he may be said to have been *unique,* as the inventor of the inimitable materials with which he worked and of which the secret is now in the possession of his son, the learned and Rev. Isaac Gosset, D.D."[7] It is not known exactly in what way his wax composition was superior to that of other modelers. It was firm, durable, and of a very pale yellow color, thus imitating well, as the early wax modelers sought to do, the work of their predecessors, the carvers in ivory. At the same time, he had the advantages of the softer material, with which he could catch his final likeness directly from the subject, with speed and immediacy. He had learned the art from his uncle, Matthew Gosset (1683–1744). His brother, Gideon, is said to have been also a modeler, though no works by him are recorded. The Gossets are an ancient French family who had come to England as Huguenot refugees.[8]

"Isaac Gosset, Wax Modeller," appears in the catalogues of the Society of Artists from 1760 to 1776. No. 206 in the catalogue of 1767 is his "Portrait of a Gentleman; in wax, a model," which may have been his Franklin portrait.

The little profile described here is the only one with a continuous history of ownership. It has always been in the family of Mrs. Margaret Stevenson, with whom Franklin lodged in London. It must

6. Ibid., *43,* no. 127.
7. *Gentleman's Magazine, 69* (2), (1799), 1088–89.
8. Mary H. Gosset, "A Family of Modellers in Wax," *Proceedings of the Huguenot Society of London, 3* (1892), 540–68.

have been his gift to her or to her daughter, Polly, of whose impending marriage Deborah Franklin was inquiring in her letter of Dec. 13, 1766, quoted below. Polly Stevenson became the wife of Dr. William Hewson and in 1786 emigrated to Philadelphia. The last private owner of the portrait, Miss Frances M. Bradford, is their great-great-granddaughter. It was acquired by its present owner in 1960.

The attribution to Gosset rather than to Patience Wright is discussed below.

> 2, 3   1766. Wax profile attributed to Isaac Gosset, and ceramic reproduction attributed to Josiah Wedgwood. Unlocated.

It appears from Franklin's correspondence and other sources that a wax portrait was made by Gosset probably while he was posing for the painter David Martin, and that he sent one of the profiles to his wife in Philadelphia in 1766 and, early in 1767, sent her two small ceramic reproductions of it, one of which was set in a ring. (See above, pp. 72–4.)

It is largely on these conclusions that the attribution of the portrait type to Gosset rather than to Mrs. Patience Wright has been based. Gosset was active in 1766 in a pattern of associations which included the allied Scotch artists, Allan Ramsay and David Martin.[9] That Gosset made a wax of Jean Jacques Rousseau at the time when Ramsay was painting Rousseau and Martin Franklin is a reinforcement. Gosset is known to have supplied models to Wedgwood, and Franklin's letters of March and June, 1767, leave room for almost no other inference than that he had in his possession some of Wedgwood's early experimental pieces, forerunners of the famous cameo portraits. The surviving wax "Franklins" appear to be characteristic in every way of Gosset's work. Mrs. Wright did not come to England until 1772 and, with all the attention she attracted, there is no contemporary evidence of her ever having made small profiles in wax. Such a profile of Washington, ca. 1789, has an early attribution to her, but was more probably the work of her son, Joseph Wright, or her sister, Rachel Wells. All the primary sources mention only her lifesize and superbly lifelike heads and figures. See TASSIE, No. 1; WEDGWOOD, No. 1.

9. Whitley Papers, 612.

4 Ca. 1766. Wax profile attributed to Isaac Gosset. Ht. 3 in. Queue and queue ribbon lacking from the wig. The piece is otherwise exactly reproduced in the ceramic portraits of 1775 and later by Wedgewood and Tassie (q.v.) and in the bronze uniface medal (No. 7). Mounted on a dark background in an oval frame. *Owner:* Dr. Philip Bate, Victoria and Albert Museum, London. Pl. 9.

Until 1957 the piece carried the identification of an earlier owner, "Man in wig (Bishop Percy?)."

5 Wax profile. Duplicate of the above. Ht. 3 in. Crack across neckline. Mounted on glass with black background. Illust. in *N.Y.H.C. Quarterly Bulletin, 9* (1925), 7. *Owner* (1936): Richard T. Haines Halsey, New York.

6 Wax profile. Copy of No. 1. Ht. 3¾ in., width 2½ in. Creamy white wax on black cardboard. In frame, 6 x 7 in. Illust. in *Harvard Tercentenary Exhibition. Catalogue of Furniture, Silver, Pewter, Glass, Paintings, Prints* (Cambridge, Mass., July 25–Sept. 21, 1936), pl. 11. *Owner:* Metropolitan Museum of Art, New York.

From the collection of the Rev. Glenn Tilley Morse, who attributed it to Daniel Bowen (1766–1856). The collection was bequeathed to the Metropolitan Museum in 1950.

7 1766. Uniface medal by unidentified artist, after Isaac Gosset; formerly attributed to William Mossop. Bronze, diam. 1 9/16 in. "BEN^N. FRANKLIN L.L.D." Profile, to left, with bust shortened to fit the circular area and waistcoat omitted, making the figure appear less stout. Pl. 9.

An attribution of this medal to William Mossop (1751–1805), first made in 1891 by Herbert A. Grueber, has been repeated in almost all subsequent listings. "Though not signed, it appears to be an unfinished work of William Mossop, Sr."[1] Grueber adds the unreasonable assumption, also repeated, that the medal celebrates the conferring of the LL.D. degree upon Franklin by the University of Saint Andrews in 1757 (actually 1759). It has been assumed that it antedates 1762, since the Oxford D.C.L. of that year is not re-

1. Grueber, "English Personal Medals," p. 101.

corded upon it. Mossop's signed pieces are in a soft and distinctive style totally unlike this. His first medal was produced in 1782, and there is no "Franklin" in the list of his works.[2]

A clue to its actual origin appears in the similar uniface medal of 1766, by Frans Gabriel Leclerc, honoring Jean Jacques Rousseau (see above pp. 71–2). The "Franklin" may not be by Leclerc, but both are from works by Gosset, and the implication that they were issued at the same time, in response to a related public interest and for the same collectors, is clear.

GRAINCOURT, ANTOINE NOEL BENOÎT (1748–1823)

> 1779. Miniature. Exhibited at the Salon de la Correspondance on Aug. 11, 1779, as "*Le Portrait de M. le Docteur Franklin en mignature, oval d'un pouce six lignes de haute sur un pouce trois lignes de large, par M. Graincourt, Peintre de M. le Cardinal de Luynes, rue de la Jussienne. Le précieux fini fait reconnoître & applaudir M. Graincourt.*"[3] Unlocated.

The ligne being equal to .089 in., the miniature was an oval, 1.6 x 1.33 in. That "High finish brings recognition and always applause to M. Graincourt," testifies both to the technical high quality of the work and the importance of the artist to M. de La Blancherie, manager of the Salon. Graincourt was "peintre et pensionnaire de M. le Cardinal de Luynes," and the Cardinal a "protecteur du salon de la Correspondance."[4] Graincourt's lasting fame rests upon a biographical history of the French navy, written and illustrated also under the patronage of the Cardinal.[5] The work was illustrated by the author with portraits, all of them copies, and these too had appeared in the Salon de la Correspondance. The Walters Gallery owns a signed miniature by Graincourt, 1⅝ inches in diameter, which seems to bear out La Blancherie's accolade of praise, it being distinguished chiefly by the rendering of the costume in fine detail.

2. J. T. Gilbert, *A History of the City of Dublin, 2* (Dublin, 1861), xiii–xix.

3. *Nouvelles de la république des sciences et des arts* (Aug. 17, 1779), p. 214. Chavignerie, "Artistes Français," *Revue universelle des arts, 20* (1865), 321.

4. Ibid. Paul d'Albert de Luynes (1703–88).

5. *Les Hommes illustres de la Marine françoise, leurs actions mémorables et leurs portraits,* Paris, 1780. Late editions erroneously name the author as "Alfred" Graincourt.

The shape and size of the ivory of Graincourt's *Franklin* suggests that this might be the miniature which Franklin brought home from France and presented to his daughter (DUPLESSIS: "Fur Collar," No. 21, Pl. 24).

GREENWOOD, JOHN (1727–92)
    Ca. 1738–46. Painting. See FEKE.

GREUZE, JEAN BAPTISTE (1725/6–1805)
    1   1777. Pastel. Paper, oval, 31½ x 25⅛ in. Hair gray at top; at left, brown tinged with gray; at right, brown. Eyes with gray iris, dark brown pupils. Blue coat lined with brown fur. Blue tint in white satin waistcoat. Plain linen jabot. In contemporary gilt oval frame bearing label, "397 Greuze." (See above, pp. 112–14.) *Owner:* James Lawrence, Jr., Boston. Pl. 22.

Commissioned by Elie de Beaumont in March 1777, it was completed by June 30, when Bachaumont gives it a word of praise: "M. Greuze, ce Peintre excellent pour les têtes de caractère, s'est emparé de celle de M. Franklin, dont on voit l'esquisse. Il y a beaucoup de resemblance & d'expression."[6] Bachaumont also attests that a formal portrait, from this sketch, was ready for Elie de Beaumont by July 25 (see below). The sketch was retained by the artist until its acquisition by a friend of his later years, Nicolas Nikitich Demidov. Demidov—courtier, soldier, and philanthropist—had been born near St. Petersburg in 1773. He lived for a time in Paris in the same house as Greuze, and would seem to have acquired a number of his works at that time.[7] For reasons of health, he settled in Italy, bringing with him a vast collection of art and transforming an abbey at San Donato, near Florence, into a palace, where he died in 1828. Two sons, Paul and Anatole, succeeded him. The elder died in 1840. Anatole established a silk factory at the place, and purchased the title of Prince from the Grand Duke of Tuscany. His death in 1870 was followed by the dispersal of the

6. Bachaumont, *Mémoires, 10,* 164. This praise is enlarged upon on Sept. 6, ibid., p. 216.
    7. Louis Réau, "Greuze et Russie," *L'Art et les artistes,* n.s. *1* (1919–20), 282.

family collections.[1] The pastel is listed in the catalogue of the sale (Pt. IV, p. 185) as no. 397, and was bought by James Lawrence of Boston for 660 francs, a price considerably below those paid for other works of the same artist.[2] He bequeathed the portrait to his widow, who then married Thomas Liddall Winthrop. She bequeathed it to her son, James Lawrence, whose son of the same name is its present owner.

The advice given by Greuze to Joseph Ducreux, that he make a careful study before each painting, bears out his own procedure in this instance.[3] Greuze was an artist noted for the strength of his portraiture, which could be forthright and masculine as well as alluringly sentimental.[4] Here he was on a good footing with his subject, being, as was Elie de Beaumont also, a member of the Lodge of the Nine Sisters. Yet in his likeness the strength of the mouth is diminished, the lines of the face softened somewhat, and the costume perhaps unduly elegant. He chose to show the right side of the face, as Duplessis did, probably in order to leave the moles on cheek and lip in shadow, but Duplessis' is the stronger work. In spite of Bachaumont's praise and statement of July 25, quoted below, that the portrait would be engraved, no print was published from it, a circumstance which seems to indicate that contemporary criticism had somewhere touched the easily wounded sensitivity of the artist.

Greuze in his portrait in oil for Elie de Beaumont, changed the coat from blue to green and painted a lace jabot. Early copies with this feature are therefore derived from that work rather than from the pastel which he had kept in his possession. Contemporary evidence supports the existence of only one other replica by Greuze, that made for the Abbé de Véri (No. 3). The fact, however, that Greuze was the most widely known artist to make a Franklin portrait, commanding the highest prices on the market, has led to innumerable attributions to him of portraits of this and other types.

1. Frits Lugt, *Les Marques des collections de dessins & d'etampes* (Amsterdam, 1921), no. 2127.

2. Bowen, *Centennial Celebration,* p. 452. H. Mireur, *Dictionnaire des ventes d'art, 3* (Paris, 1911–12), 365.

3. Camille Mauclair, *Greuze et son temps* (Paris, 1926), p. 95.

4. Louis Hautecoeur, "Greuze, Portraitiste," *L'Art et les artistes,* n.s. 8 (1924), 169–73.

2 1777. Painting. Oil on canvas, 28½ x 22¾ in. Dull green coat trimmed with brown fur. White waistcoat. Lace jabot. Dark olive-gray background. See above, pp. 112–14. *Owner:* Mrs. Arthur Lehman, New York. Pl. 22.

On March 8, 1777, Jean Baptiste Jacques Elie de Beaumont (1732–86) asked Franklin to pose to the sculptor Dufourny de Villiers, stating that he would have a portrait painted from the bust to hang in his library with those of other friends of humanity. Instead, Greuze made a study in pastel from life, and from this an oil painting, the completion of which was noted by Bachaumont on July 25 in the following terms:

> On a dit que le Sr. Greuze faisoit le portrait de M. Franklin qui ne manquera pas d'être gravé. M. Elie de Beaumont Avocat célebre par son éloquence, par ses intrigues & par un génie romanesque, a disposé d'avance dans son cabinet une niche pour ce personage illustre, entre d'autres grands hommes anciens & modernes qu'il y a placés, & a fait d'avance cette inscription pour mettre au bas: *Alterius orbis Vindex, utriusque Lumen.*[5]

Of the many portraits attributed to Greuze, others have been linked also to the name of Elie de Beaumont. That described here has the best claim to this provenance. It is said to have been purchased in Paris by a Mr. Graham in 1828, as having come from the estate of Elie de Beaumont, who died there on Jan. 10, 1786. It was inherited by his son, J. C. W. P. Graham, of London, and by him bequeathed to Henry Anson Harton, of Burton-on-Trent. It was acquired by Thomas B. Clarke, and purchased from his collection by its present owner.

3 Ca. 1777. Painting. Oil on canvas, oval, 75 x 67 cm. (29.54 x 26.37 in.). Green coat trimmed with fur. White waistcoat. See

5. "It is said that Sr. Greuze has painted the portrait of M. Franklin and that it will not fail to be engraved. M. Elie de Beaumont, the attorney celebrated for his eloquence, his intrigues and romantic spirit, has a place ready on his wall for this illustrious personage, among other great men of ancient and modern times whom he has placed there, and has composed in advance an inscription for the frame: *Champion of the one world, and the light of both.*" (*Mémoires, 10,* 183.)

above, pp. 114–16. *Owner* (1936) : The Marquise de la Tourette, France.

It is established that two replicas of his original pastel of Franklin came from the studio of Greuze, that for Elie de Beaumont, cited above, and a second made for the Abbé Joseph Alphonse de Véri (1724–99). Véri's journal records his pride in having won Franklin as a friend and in having entertained the great American in his home. He asked Franklin's permission to hang a portrait there, in lasting evidence of their relationship. This was a common courtesy of the times, one which often becomes misinterpreted in tradition as the gift of a portrait from the subject:

> Si je vieillis autant que ce bienfaiteur de l'humanité, je me vanterai, auprès de mes petits-neveux, d'avoir connu ce grand homme, de l'avoir souvent reçu chez moi et d'avoir obtenu de lui qu'il se laissât peindre par Greuze pour que j'eusse son portrait de la main de ce grand maître. Ce portrait me suivra partout jusqu'au tombeau. Je le chéris d'autant plus, qu'étant ressemblant, Greuze y a peint toute la noblesse d'une âme libre, toute la sagesse d'une tête bien organisée et toute la sagacité d'un homme d'état.[6]

The portrait described above was owned ca. 1920 by the Baronne de Précourt, and was stated at that time to have come from the collection of the Abbé de Véri.[7] It passed to its later owner by inheritance.

4   1781. Pastel by Simon Petit, after Greuze. Exhibited at the Salon de la Correspondance on Aug. 23, 1781, as a pastel, after Greuze, "portant deux pieds de haut, un pied huit pouces de large" (25.52 x 21.32 in.).[8] Unlocated.

6. "If I should outlive this benefactor of humanity, I shall boast to my grand-nephews, of having known this great man, of having often received him in my home and of having obtained his consent to his being painted by Greuze in order that I might have his portrait by the hand of this great master. This portrait will be with me to the grave. I cherish the more in that, with the resemblance, Greuze has depicted there all the nobility of a free spirit, all the wisdom of an orderly mind and all of a statesman's sagacity." (De Witte, *Journal de l'Abbé de Véri, 1,* 21n.)

7. Eddy Papers. Camille Mauclair, *Jean Baptiste Greuze* (Paris, 1905), no. 1124.

8. *Nouvelles de la République des Sciences et des Arts,* 1781, p. 63.

The exhibition was accompanied by a note on the young artist and his patron, the Marquis de Véri, from which it may be inferred that the pastel was copied from the "Franklin" owned by the Abbé de Véri, brother of the marquis:

> Ces ouvrages, faits d'après M. Greuze, promettant un artiste dans leur jeune auteur. On en aura l'obligation à M. le Marquis de Véri, amateur aussi éclairé que bienfaisant, possesseur d'un superbe cabinet de l'École française, qu'il semble n'avoir formé que pour l'avancement des jeunes artistes. Sa munificence ne consiste pas seulement à les y reunir en tout temps; il pourvoit encore à leur besoin; il n'y a pas de dètails dans lesquels il n'entre avec eux, pour leur faciliter les moyens de travailler sans inquiétude et sans perte de temps.[9]

It was Simon Petit's first exhibition. His paintings were also shown at the Exposition de la Jeunesse of 1784, at the Salons of 1795 and 1796, and at the Exposition de l'Elysée in 1797.[10] A genre subject, "Le Bouquet de Violettes," engraved by him about 1805, bears the signature, "S. Petit p. et sc. An 13."[1] His brother, Claude François Henri Petit de Villeneuve, also exhibited at the Salon de la Correspondance in 1781, and had an active career as a painter until his death in 1820.[2]

5 Undated. Pastel by Jacques Samuel Louis Piot (1743–1812), after Greuze. Paper, oval, 55 x 46 cm. (21.65 x 18.11 in.). "Pepper and salt" hair. Gray eyes. Blue coat with brown fur. White waistcoat. Lace jabot. Dark gray background. *Owner:* Musée Cantonal des Beaux-Arts, Lausanne.

9. "These works, made after M. Greuze, give promise of an artist in their young author. That will be thanks to M. le Marquis de Véri, a connoisseur as enlightened as he is generous, owner of a superb collection of the French School, which he seems to have formed only for the advancement of young artists. His munificence consists not only in bringing them together there at all times; he watches their needs; he has gone into every detail with them, in order to enable them to work without worry and without loss of time." (Chavignerie, "Les Artistes français," *Revue universelle, 21,* 90.)
10. Ibid., p. 89. Benezit, *Dictionnaire.*
1. Witt Library, London.
2. Chavignerie, "Artistes," *Revue universelle, 21,* 90.

The artist was a native of Lausanne and died in that city, but had been active in Paris. In 1837 the portrait was presented to the Museum of Fine Arts in Lausanne by Professor Levade (1748–1839).[3]

6   Undated. Pastel by unidentified artist, after Greuze. Paper, oval, 20 x 17 in. Blonde hair touched with brown. Blue-gray eyes. Blue coat with fur collar. White waistcoat. Lace jabot. Gray background. Illust. in sale catalogue of H. Muller & Co., Amsterdam, June 11–14, 1912, no. 737. *Owner:* French and Co., New York.

In the listing cited above the portrait is described as by "Pastelliste Francais 1766," and as having come from a branch of the Martini family, its owners since the 18th century. Included in the sale was a copy of *La Science de Bonhomme Ricard, par Benjamin Franklin, l'histoire du sifflet et le testament de Fortuné Ricard,* Paris, n.d., bearing the signature of H. B. Martini–Van Geffen.

7   1846. Painting by George Peter Alexander Healy (1813–94), after Greuze. Oil on canvas, 33 x 27 cm. (12.99 x 10.62 in.). Light brown hair. Blue eyes. Brown coat. Plain linen jabot. *Owner:* Musée National de Versailles.

This copy, like others, is chiefly of interest as a record of its original. It was recorded in 1892 as having been painted from a second pastel by Greuze, also the property of Prince Demidov, which was lost at sea on its way to Russia.[4] However this may be, the plain linen shirt ruffle does set it apart from other copies and associate it with the original.

8   Undated. Painting by an unidentified artist, after Greuze. Oil on canvas, oval, 29 x 23¾ in. Light brown hair. Brown eyes. Green coat with brown fur. White waistcoat. Lace jabot. Dark background. *Owner:* DeEtte Holden Cummer Museum Foundation, Jacksonville, Fla.

By its traditional family history, the painting was Franklin's gift to a goddaughter, Mary Willing (1740–1814), afterward the wife of Colonel William Byrd, III. It was inherited by her daughter,

3. Information from the owner and from the Eddy Papers.
4. Bowen, *Centennial Celebration,* p. 452.

Evelyn Taylor Byrd, wife of Benjamin Harrison. Its subsequent owners in three generations all bore the name of George Evelyn Harrison. The last of these left it jointly to two daughters, Mrs. Frederick C. McCormack and Mrs. Louis Fagan, from whom it was purchased in 1959 by Ninah M. H. Cummer.

> 9   1777. Miniature by Louis de Broux, after Greuze. Ivory, oval, ca. 2⅛ x 1¾ in. Dull green coat. Lace jabot. Signed, lower right, "de broux / 1777 (?)." *Owner* (1958): Michel Bernstein, Issy-les-Moulineaux, France.

The miniature is apparently the earliest of many "Franklins" of the Greuze type. Greuze was not a miniaturist, but his work was always popular with the artists in this medium, and many unsigned pieces are attributed to him.

> 10   1785. Miniature by "D.C.," after Greuze. Enamel in gold frame, oval, height, 4½ in. Green coat with brown fur. White waistcoat. Lace jabot. Signed, right, "D.C. / 1785." Illustrated in the catalogue of the sale at Sotheby's on May 16, 1957, and in *Connoisseur, 140* (1957), 59. Unlocated.

The miniature was formerly in the J. P. Morgan collection. This and another enamel of Franklin similarly mounted were probably made by the artist to meet the demands of Franklin's friends at the time of his departure from France. See WEYLER.

HARDY, BERNHARDT KASPAR (1726–1819)
   Wax high relief attributed to Hardy. See WEYLER, No. 9.

HAUER, JEAN JACQUES (1751–1829)
   1791. Painting of bust. See DUFOURNY.

HEALY, GEORGE PETER ALEXANDER (1813–94)
   1846. Painting. See GREUZE, No. 7.

HESSELIUS, GUSTAVUS (1682–1755)
   Ca. 1736–37. Painting. See JOHNSON.

HOUDON, JEAN ANTOINE (1741–1828)

    1 1778. Bust. Terra cotta, ht. 41 cm. (13.14 in.). Signed at back, "houdon f. 1778." *Owner:* The Louvre, Paris. Pl. 18.

A letter in the Franklin Papers from Houdon to an unknown correspondent, dated Nov. 8, 1783, mentions "le lendemain du jour ou vous avez la bonté de me présenter à Mr. Le Docteur Franklin."[5] Here is conclusive evidence that, while they must have been together often at Masonic and other affairs, there had been no earlier formal presentation. Houdon's portrait, therefore, was made from casual observation, without the study and careful measurements which make Caffiéri's the more accurate likeness. Houdon's is the better characterization. These two great Franklin busts are generally distinguished by the fact that Caffiéri's wears a loosely tied scarf at the neck, and Houdon's a plain stock. There are subtler and more ponderable differences. In Caffiéri's the hair frames the face. Here, in Houdon's, it is brushed back over the ear, bringing at once a sense of alertness not present in the other. In Caffiéri's the eyeballs gaze forward as in contemplation and the mouth is still. Here the eyes glance to the observer's left and the lips are slightly parted as if with a word upon them. That rendering of the eyes was new to this conservative art, and the more striking then because of its novelty. Métra, in an entry of Nov. 14, 1778, which in addition gives us a more precise dating of the bust, remarks upon this feature. All Paris, he says, was crowding to Houdon's studio to see his "Rousseau" and his "Franklin": "On n'a point d'idée de la ressemblance frappante de ces portraits. M. Houdon a une manière qui lui est propre pour rendre les yeux. Jamais on n'a poussé plus loin la sculpture dans ce genre. Elle est, selon moi, au-dessus de le peinture."[6] There is a penalty to this freedom. Sculpture changes in aspect with different lights and points of view, and the "Franklin" is susceptible to this. It has a ray of humor at one time, a look of restriction and concern at another. The former, happily, is more usual, but the latter can be found and is recorded from an early date

    5. Franklin Papers (A.P.S.), *30,* no. 77.

    6. "One has no idea of the striking resemblance of these portraits. M. Houdon represents the eyes in a way of his own. He has not been surpassed in this form of sculpture. It is, as I see it, above painting" (Métra, *Correspondance secrète, 8,* 1787, p. 117).

in Chevillet's engraving after a drawing from the bust by Michel Honoré Bounieu (1740–1814).

At the Salon of 1779 Houdon exhibited the "Franklin," together with other terra cotta busts of Rousseau, Molière, the bust and statue of Voltaire intended for the Empress of Russia, and marble busts of Antoine Le Fère de Caumartin, Marquis de Saint Ange, and the Marshal Antoine Chrétien, Comte de Nicolai.[7] He was amply avenged, as Bachaumont observed while praising their vivid and convincing characterizations, upon those amateurs who had been commenting upon his apparent lack of employment.[8] He showed an enlarged revision of the work (No. 11) in the Salon of 1791.[9] This last was probably the "'Franklin." in his auction sale of Oct. 8, 1795, a period of financial difficulty.[1] Lami, however, cites this as perhaps the original terra cotta, which may subsequently have been repossessed by the artist.[2] A list of Houdon's work drawn up by himself about 1784 includes the bust of Franklin as no. 59 bis., and a later addition to it, perhaps made after his death, also lists a bust of Franklin as no. 116.[3]

In the posthumous sale of Houdon's work on Dec. 15, 1828, no. 27 was the terra cotta bust of Franklin.[4] Its purchaser was François Hippolyte Walferdin (1795–1880), a physician who was serving as chief of the Bureau à l'Administration des Douanes, a member of the Société Géologique de France, editor of Diderot, and a participant in other learned projects. He was known as a collector of terra cotta in later life, owning a number of Houdons and Nini medallions.[5] He also owned the original study for Fragonard's Franklin allegory before the addition of the portrait. The bust he bequeathed to the Louvre.[6]

7. *Livret* (1779), pp. 44–45.
8. Bachaumont, *Mémoires, 13,* 229–30. Lettre III, Sept. 22, 1779.
9. *Livret* (1791), p. 37.
1. Hart and Biddle, *Houdon,* p. 261.
2. Lami, *Dictionnaire des sculptures,* "Houdon."
3. *Archives de l'art français* (1907), pp. 203, 208.
4. Hart and Biddle, *Houdon,* p. 302, quoting from the only known copy of the sale catalogue, at the Bibliothèque Nationale.
5. Maze-Sencier, *Livre des collectionneurs,* p. 605.
6. Grimm, *Correspondance littéraire, 14,* 297n. Musée du Louvre, *Catalogue des sculptures* (Paris, 1922), p. 62.

Georges Giacometti states that his master, the sculptor Gustave Jean Baptiste Deloye (1838–99), had made a cast from the bust for M. Walferdin and from this had made a number of exact duplicates in terra cotta easily mistaken for originals, the only noticeable difference being a slight shrinkage of the clay in firing.[7] They were worked over with a tool before firing, even to a signature on the shoulder, "Houdon ft. 1778." In one of the two examples in the William Smith Mason Collection at Yale, the date is "1777."

In a subsequent revision the artist defined more clearly the easy pleasantness of his characterization, and made certain changes in the proportion and costume of the figure. See below, Nos. 11–14.

2, 3, 4, 5   Ca. 1778–79. Plaster casts by Houdon, from the original terra cotta bust. Unlocated.

Louis Réau remarks upon the prodigality with which Houdon published examples of his portraits, giving casts to institutions and individuals wherever his generosity was appreciated.[8] In his angry denial of Caffiéri's claim to being the official sculptor of the United States, William Temple Franklin reveals that as against Caffiéri's gift of a single cast, Houdon had given his subject four.[9] How Franklin disposed of the four busts is not recorded. Quite possibly, he gave one to Jonathan Williams (described below, No. 6). One might assume that the three extra busts had been disposed of by March 1779, when he ordered three casts from Caffiéri for shipment overseas, but this need not be the case. Franklin may have had a preference for the Caffiéri, or more probably, had an agreement with the artist as to future purchases. At all events, we find William Temple Franklin sending a bust by Houdon to the Salon de la Correspondance of February, 1783, as a contribution to its "Collection des hommes célèbres," together with a cast of the Caffiéri (Caffiéri, No. 10).[1]

Two invitations from the Abbé du Rouzeau, Secretary of the

7. Giacometti, *Le Statuaire Jean Antoine Houdon, 2,* 172.
8. Réau, "Le Buste en Marbre," p. 169.
9. April 3, 1785 (Franklin Papers, A.P.S., *104,* no. 156a). Hart and Biddle, *Houdon,* pp. 88–89.
1. Chavignerie, "Artistes français," *Revue universelle, 20,* 328. *Nouvelles de la République des Sciences et des Arts,* 1783, pp. 70, 78.

Lodge of the Nine Sisters, ca. 1784, summon the membership to the "not too solemn" inauguration of a bust of himself presented by Franklin.[2] The artist is not named. The Musée de Paris, an affiliate of the lodge, had already received a bust as Houdon's gift (described below, No. 7).

> 6   Ca. 1778–79. Cast. Plaster. Signature at back, "houdon f. 1778." Mounted on socle so that the figure leans forward.
> *Owner:* American Academy of Arts and Sciences, Boston.

The minutes of the A.P.S., Aug. 15, 1800, record the presentation of the bust by Franklin's grandnephew, Jonathan Williams: "Mr. Williams presented to the Society a bust of their late president Dr. Franklin (by Houdon) the thanks of the Society were returned to Mr. Williams for his donation." Since Jonathan Williams had been in France and in constant touch with Franklin during the war it is possible that this bust was one of the four casts described above.

In December 1802 Joseph Sansom, who had just returned from a tour of England and the Continent, presented to the society a plaster cast of a bust by Flaxman, after Houdon. Having two very similar portraits of its founder, it was proposed in the society to give the older one to the American Academy of Arts and Sciences in Boston, retaining this newer piece with which the famous name of Flaxman also was associated. Col. Williams' permission was solicited. His rather stiff reply of Feb. 16, 1803, agreed to the proposition and reaffirmed the authorship of the bust: "I did myself the honour of presenting to the American Philosophical Society a Cast of the Bust of Dr. Franklin from an Original by the celebrated Houdon."[3] By a resolution of Feb. 18, 1803, therefore, the bust, repaired and packed by Robert Welford, was sent to Boston as his gift.[4]

The American Academy occupied a room in the building of the Boston Athenaeum during most of the period of 1817–99. In 1828 the Athenaeum took into its collection four busts by Houdon which Joseph Coolidge, Jr., had inherited from his father-in-law, Thomas

2. Franklin Papers (A.P.S.), *40,* no. 66; *107,* no. 159.

3. Archives, A.P.S.

4. Minutes, A.P.S. Welford, bill to A.P.S., March 14, 1803, Yale University. Printed acknowledgment signed by J. Q. Adams for the American Academy of Arts and Sciences, Sept. 7, 1803, Indiana University, Jonathan Williams Collection.

Jefferson. One of these, the "Lafayette," was a purchase, while the others, the "John Paul Jones," "Washington," and "Franklin," remained on loan, a fact recorded in the minutes as late as 1865.[5] The "Washington" and "Lafayette" have remained with the Athenaeum, but by 1911 the "Jones" had disappeared and it was found that the institution had only one Franklin in its care. By a reasonable conjecture, the "Jones" had been lent to the old Boston Museum, sold with other properties at its dispersal, and is now at the Boston Museum of Fine Arts.[6] The Boston Museum catalogue of 1849 lists a "Franklin" by Houdon.[7] However, photographs show that the second work was at the Athenaeum late in that century or early in this.[8]

On Oct. 14, 1911, it was suggested that the Athenaeum, holding only one bust of Franklin and in doubt as to its ownership, either surrender it, or give a cast of it, to the American Academy, and the trustees responded by presenting the bust itself to the sister institution.[9] When some years later the academy left its Newbury St. building and moved to Brookline, the bust was again deposited with the Athenaeum.

From the provenance of the two works it is clear that the Athenaeum had returned to the academy that which was rightly the academy's property. The photographs show that the busts were of different types, this one a direct cast of Houdon's original of 1778, the other larger, differently costumed, and of a later date (see below, No. 13). This had been made when Jonathan Williams was at Paris, and may have been one of the four given to Franklin by the artist. The other dates from ca. 1789, the year when Thomas Jefferson left Paris for Monticello, with his collection of Houdon works.

> 7   1783. Cast. Unlocated.

Antoine Court de Gébelin (1725–84), littérateur, antiquary, and anthropologist, had been in touch with Franklin upon matters of

5. Mabel Munson Swan, *The Athenaeum Gallery, 1827–1873* (Boston, 1940), p. 165.

6. Ibid., pp. 166–67.

7. *Catalogue of the Paintings, Portraits, Marble and Plaster Statuary . . . in the Collection of the Boston Museum* (Boston, 1849), p. 24, no. 15.

8. Eddy Papers.

9. *Proceedings of the American Academy of Arts and Sciences, 47,* 830–32.

mutual interest since 1777. Much of this correspondence related to the *Loge des Neuf Soeurs* and to an affiliate of it, the "Musée de Paris," a creation of Court de Gébelin. It had been founded on Nov. 17, 1780, in the second year in which Franklin had been Venerable of the Lodge, as the "Société Apollienne," a cultural organization open to non-Masons. It became soon after the Musée de Paris and, with various ups and downs, lasted into the 19th century as the "*Lycée* and *Athenée.*"[1]

Franklin was present at its assembly of March 6, 1783, celebrating the successful conclusion of the American war for independence. He listened closely to the works in prose and verse which were read in honor of the birth of the new republic. He himself was, of course, the honored symbol of it all: "On fait l'inauguration de son buste, presenté par M. *Houdon,* aux acclamations de tous les spectateurs," after which followed the dinner and concert, and finally, as a climax to all, the head of the new nation's representative was itself crowned with laurel and myrtle.[2]

> 8   1778. Bust. Marble, ht. 17½ in.; with base, 22½ in. Signed at back, "houdon f / 1778." Some slight damage to marble at coat and waistcoat. The likeness, essentially identical with the original terra cotta (No. 1), appears to have been strengthened, particularly at cheek and chin. *Owner:* Metropolitan Museum of Art, New York. Pl. 18.

The bust is the first piece of sculpture acquired by the Metropolitan Museum, and is still prized as one of its most valuable possessions. It came to the museum in 1872 as the gift of John Bard (1819–99), brother-in-law of the museum's first president.[3] It was long supposed to have belonged originally to Franklin's close friend, Dr. John Bard (1716–99), but actually had been inherited by Mrs. William Bard, mother of the donor, from her father, Nicholas Cruger. Cruger, who had offered it for sale at $1000 in 1836, had purchased it from Eleuthère Irénée du Pont (1771–1834) whose father, Pierre Samuel du Pont de Nemours (1739–1817), had tried

1. Amiable, *Un Loge maçonnique,* pp. 187–204.
2. It is described in Bachaumont, *Mémoires, 22,* 154–55, under the date, March 11, 1783. There is a misprint in the account: "lundi" should read "jeudi."
3. In *Metropolitan Museum of Art Bulletin, 15* (1956), 16–17.

to sell it on the sculptor's behalf to the national or a state government.[4]

The bust, with other works, had been shipped to America by Houdon at the time of his visit in 1785. They came, however, by a different ship and did not arrive until after he had completed his portrait of Washington and returned to France at the end of the year. Thomas Jefferson, who had brought the sculptor over for this purpose, was informed of the matter by Francis Hopkinson, from Philadelphia, on May 1, 1786: "Some busts and casts of Mr. Hudon's Workmanship arrived here soon after he left us. They are in Mr. Pine's Care, but not yet unpack'd, Mr. Pine having been all Winter in Maryland, where he has had great success."[5]

In what is probably the outstanding work of his American career, Pine has left a record of his possession of this bust. David Martin's introduction of a bust of Newton into the background of his portrait of Franklin represents what had become something of a trade mark of his work, the introduction of a piece of sculpture appropriate to his subject. Similarly, Pine had often painted in a large marble bas-relief of some selected great figure. In his portrait of Samuel Vaughan, now owned by the A.P.S., he used this device, the profile here being of Franklin and painted from the Houdon marble. After Pine's sudden death in 1788, the responsibility for the sale of the bust was taken over by Houdon's friend and countryman, Du Pont.[6]

> 9 Undated. Drawing by Jean Honoré Fragonard (1732–1806), after the bust by Houdon, 1778. Sepia drawing, 10 15/16 x 9 3/8 in. Head, to left, nearly full-face. Inscribed, lower left, "B. Franklin." Illust. in *Allen Memorial Art Museum Bulletin,* Oberlin College, *8* (1951), no. 8. *Owner:* Art Institute of Chicago.

4. Du Pont de Nemours, April 20, 1800 (Longwood Library). Helen C. Frick, "Madame Jean Antoine Houdon," *Art Bulletin, 29* (1947), 209, quoting Du Pont to Mme. Houdon, Oct. 30, 1801. Du Pont to Thomas Jefferson, Jan. 20, 1802 (Jefferson Papers, L.C.) quoted in Hart and Biddle, *Houdon,* p. 106. Du Pont to Jefferson, Feb. 20, 1802, quoted in Gilbert Chinard, *The Correspondence of Jefferson and du Pont de Nemours* (Baltimore, 1931), p. 39. Jefferson to James Monroe, Feb. 28, 1802 (Jefferson Papers, M.H.S.). Du Pont to Jefferson, April 24 and April 30, 1802 (Longwood Library).

5. Boyd, *Papers of Thomas Jefferson, 9,* 440.

6. Frick, "Madame Jean Antoine Houdon," p. 209n.

The drawing, probably made soon after the exhibition of the terra cotta in 1779, is the first use of Houdon's work as the source of a portrait study by another artist, a use repeated often and with almost unfailing success from that time to the present.

The drawing was acquired by its present owner from the collection of Albert Meyer, Paris.

> 10   Ca. 1801. Cast of bust by John Flaxman (1755–1826), after the bust by Houdon, 1778. Plaster, ht. 26½ in. *Owner:* A.P.S., Philadelphia. Pl. 21.

The bust was presented to the A.P.S. by Joseph Sansom (1767–1826), who had just returned from a tour of England, France, and Italy. The gift is recorded at the society in its minutes of Dec. 3 and 17, 1802, Jan. 21, 1803, and in the donor's letter, in which he states: "It is a Cast, in Plaister of Paris, by Flaxman the Elder, of London, after the celebrated Original by Houdon, the first French sculptor of the age." The lower part of the bust is larger than the original (four buttons rather than three), and the whole likeness has been smoothed and softened, losing character in the process. It has been mounted so that the head leans forward, giving it a more venerable aspect. Soon after the receipt of this bust the Society arranged the presentation of its cast from Houdon's original to the American Academy of Arts and Sciences in Boston, and this bust, which has been remounted on its socle with a forward inclination, was probably so altered in imitation of the Flaxman at this time. Hiram Powers (1803–73) made several marble busts apparently based, with further slight modification, upon this work.

> 11   Ca. 1789. Bust, enlargement and revision of No. 1. Ht. 33.07 in. (see below, No. 13). The pleasant characterization of the head is strengthened. The figure is modeled almost at half-length, and is draped in the folds of a robe of ceremonial dignity, beneath which the stock and waistcoat of contemporary costume can be seen at the neck. Unlocated.

Houdon's original of this revised "Franklin" is unlocated. Its date and the circumstances under which it was made are open to speculation. While Houdon made other busts with the figure nearly half-length and the arms nearly to the elbow, this shows the right arm protruding as a stump, an unattractive feature which might be explained by the theory that the artist contemplated a statue and wished thus to suggest the larger rendering. In 1789 he was discussing with Jefferson the possibility of an equestrian "Washington," and the possibility of a large memorial to Franklin might well have been in mind. Jefferson apparently purchased a cast of this bust at that time (see below, No. 12). It is possible also that some word had reached Paris of William Bingham's intended gift of a statue of Franklin for the Library Co. of Philadelphia, the commission which was carried out by Francesco Lazzarini, 1790–91. If so, it must have been indirectly, for Bingham and Jefferson were in correspondence at the time, but upon other matters.

This must have been the "Franklin" shown by Houdon at the Salon of 1791. The fact that his original of 1778 had been exhibited there is evidence that this was a new or revised work, as it was exceptional to present the same work twice under these auspices. Two copies from it further document this new version. A stipple engraving, 10½ x 9 in., by Jean Louis Darcis (d. 1801) after a drawing by Guillaume Guillon Lethière (1760–1832) shows it in profile from the left side (the engraving, facing to right, has been reversed in printing). A proof of this at the Philadelphia Museum of Art is inscribed, "Le Thiere delt. 1795. Darcis Sculpt. 1795." The A.P.S. holds on deposit from the Metropolitan Museum a drawing, 20 x 15¾ in., made from the bust at almost full-face by Jean Jacques François Lebarbier (1738–1826). This also was published as a stipple engraving by Pierre Michel Alix (1762–1817), undated, but with the acknowledgment, "Dessiné par le Barbier l'Aîné d'après le Buste de Houdon."

12   Ca. 1789. Bust, cast from No. 11. Unlocated. Pl. 19.
This bust is the larger of the two Houdon "Franklins" which were present in the rooms of the Boston Athenaeum through most of the last century. One of these, a cast of the orginal terra cotta of 1778, is the property of the American Academy of Arts and Sciences (see above, No. 6). The other, in this markedly revised version, was deposited at the Athenaeum on March 11, 1828, by Joseph Coolidge, Jr. It had been inherited by him, together with the busts of John Paul Jones, Lafayette, and Washington, from his father-in-law, Thomas Jefferson. It has been assumed that Jefferson's pay-

ment of a thousand francs to Houdon on July 3, 1789, covered the purchase of these four casts, and that he brought them back with him to Monticello on his return from France in the autumn of that year.[7] There are no later transactions of the sort with Houdon recorded in his correspondence.

Photographs of the bust bear witness that it was extant late in the last or early in the present century.[8] In 1911, however, only one of the two Franklin busts, that belonging to the American Academy, was present in the Athenaeum's collection.

> 13 Undated. Bust, cast from No. 11. Plaster, ht. 84 cm. (33.07 in.); lgth. 60 cm. (23.62 in.). *Owner:* Musée des Beaux Arts, Angers, France. Pl. 19.

Georges Giacometti cites this only surviving example of the type as formerly in the possession of the sculptor Pierre Jean David d'Angers (1788–1856), "Par les lettres du grand sculpteur angevin à son ami Mercier (lettres inédites, datées de 1839, données par le peintre Lenepveu au musée), on sait le cas qu'il faisait des trois Houdon qu'il possédait (les plâtres de Mirabeau, de Franklin et la terre-cuite originale de Dumouriez)."[9]

> 14 Marble bust by Domenico Menconi, after Houdon. Ht. 26 in. The head is close to Houdon's revised work of ca. 1789 (No. 11), but is slightly inclined forward. Less of the body is represented. The neck is bare, and the hair falls on bare shoulders within folds of drapery. The eye pupils are not indicated. Signed on the back, "Do. Menconi / f . . . " *Owner:* A.P.S., Philadelphia. Pl. 21.
>
> 15 Marble bust. Ht. 23 in. Head and costume similar to the above. Signed at the back, "J. A. HOUDON 1780." *Owner:* William Rockhill Nelson Gallery of Art, Atkins Museum of Fine Arts, Kansas City. Pl. 21.

On Jan. 2, 1863, Dr. George Bacon Wood (1797–1879), having

7. Boyd, *Papers of Thomas Jefferson, 15,* 238.
8. Eddy Papers.
9. "From the letters of the great Angevin sculptor to his friend Mercier (unpublished letters, dated 1839, given to the museum by the painter Lenepveu), one learns of the value he placed upon the three Houdons he owned (the plasters of Mirabeau, Franklin and the original terra cotta of Dumouriez)" (Giacometti, *Le Statuaire Jean Antoine Houdon, 2,* 171). Jules Eugène Lenepveu (b. Angers, 1819; d. Paris, 1898).

recently returned to Philadelphia from Italy, presented to the A.P.S. a marble bust by an obscure Tuscan sculptor, Domenico Menconi. The minutes record:

> Dr. Wood, the president, presented to the Society a marble bust of Franklin, on a tall cylindrical pedestal of dark scagliogla. Dr. Wood gave the order to an artist of Florence M. Manconi [*sic*] to execute this life size reduction in marble of a gigantic plaster bust of Franklin in the private collection of Mr. Packinham [*sic*] (a banker in Rome) at his residence in Florence. Mr. Powers the American sculptor had himself executed a copy of this bust for his own studio. Dr. Wood had the same artist to copy, life size, a gigantic plaster bust of Washington in the same collection. Both the plaster busts are ascribed to Houdon.

Mr. Packenham, owner of the "gigantic plaster" original of this work, was an Englishman, senior member of the banking firm of Packenham and Smyth of Leghorn, where he lived.[1] The firm was represented at Florence by another Englishman, Mr. Maguay, and known as Maguay, Packenham and Smyth. It had also an office in Rome. Hiram Powers had business dealings with Mr. Packenham, was often his guest at Leghorn, but is not known to have made any sculpture for him. Powers did own a cast of the 1778 Houdon bust which had been obtained for him in Paris by G. P. A. Healy. He made some marble versions of his own from it, bringing a new Victorian suavity to both the face and the 18th-century costume.

The most striking feature of the Menconi bust is the departure from the 18-century costume used in both of the Houdon "Franklins" of which we have contemporary documentation. Instead, there is the bare neck and that arrangement of drapery over the shoulders in folds which give a classic dignity to the piece without the distinctive details of actual classic dress. Drapery of this sort

1. Information on Packenham and Powers from Mrs. Clara Louise Dentler, Sept. 5, 1961.

was a favorite device of Powers, who sometimes sculptured a toga, but preferred this more conventionalized classicism. When he showed a subject "à l'antique" it was, like Menconi's work, with the dead eye. Powers is not known to have made such a "Franklin," but he did sculpture a "Washington" after Houdon, with the variation of the drapery in this form and the dead eye.

Some still-undiscovered relationship appears to exist between Menconi's bust and a marble of markedly more subtle and sensitive workmanship now at the William Rockhill Nelson Gallery of Art, Atkins Museum of Fine Arts, Kansas City. This piece, slightly smaller, has the same bare neck and the same arrangement of drapery. The eye pupils are indicated. Its attribution to Houdon and the authenticity of the signature have been affirmed by experts. It was first recorded and reproduced in an article by the late Louis Réau, in *Connoisseur,* June 1948.[2] It is described there only as having come from "a private collection." In 1955 it was acquired by the Nelson Gallery as "indirectly from a descendant of Le Ray de Chaumont, to whom the bust had presumably been given by Franklin."[3] This provenance is open to question, as Franklin would hardly have made so expensive a present to a friend who was virtually bankrupt in 1780, nor would Le Ray have purchased it.

The Menconi is apparently a copy from this, or from a very similar work. Obscure as the connection is, the Menconi is the earliest documentation of the Nelson Gallery type, bringing it back, at least, to Florence, 1862. It is of incidental interest that another Florentine sculptor and contemporary of Menconi, Pasquale Romanelli, also made a similar Franklin head, with bare neck and the forward inclination but without the shoulders represented, a work now in the Mason Collection at Yale.

Boilly's painting of Houdon's studio, 1805 (see below, No. 16), shows a bust apparently in classic dress, but with the figure in the much smaller proportions of the work of 1778.

2. "A Great French Sculptor of the Eighteenth Century, Jean-Antoine Houdon," *Connoisseur, 121* (1948), 76–77.

3. Information from Ross E. Taggart, Senior Curator, to Leonard W. Labaree, Nov. 30, 1959.

16 1805. Painting of bust, by Louis Leopold Boilly (1761–1845). *Owner:* Musée des Arts Decoratifs, the Louvre, Paris. Pl. 20.

"Houdon dans son atelier modelant le buste de Laplace," signed and dated 1805, is a work composed with care and authority. The Witt Library, London, records six interiors of artists' studios by Boilly. Another of Houdon with similar background but showing him at work on a nude figure, among his students, is in the Musée de Cherbourg, and a drawing of it is also extant. This work has the clear intention of recording both the artist and his oeuvre. In the rank of busts at the upper right of the picture, a "Franklin" is shown in profile. Here the proportion of the body represented is about the same as in the terra cotta of 1778, but the costume is different. It is not the open drapery of the bust dated 1780 (No. 12), but might be accepted as showing in part the lines of the bust of ca. 1789 (Nos. 12–14).

See BERNIER; CAFFIÉRI, No. 14; DUPRÉ; SÈVRES, No. 7.

JOHNSON, SAMUEL (1684–1755)

Ca. 1736–37. Posthumous portrait of Francis Folger Franklin (1732–36), the likeness presumably based in part on that of Benjamin Franklin. Oil on canvas, 33 x 24¾ in. Dark eyes. Sandy hair with a reddish tinge. Red dress and blue cloak. The child's hand is extended toward a macaw, now represented only by a streak of red. Background at right, heavy foliage; at left, red-brown bank with olive-green lawn beyond, white mansion in distance, blue mountains rising in far distance. Much surface paint has been lost, probably during the first century of the painting's existence, since in the earliest reproduction, made by James Bryan Hall, Sr., for James Parton's *Life and Times of Benjamin Franklin* (1864), the engraver seems to have had to reconstruct as well as copy. The earliest photographic reproduction, in Gillespie, *A Book of Remembrance*, p. 18, shows the painting much as it is today. It was restored by Stephen S. Pichetto, New York, 1937. *Owner:* Mrs. James Manderson Castle, Jr., Wilmington, Del. Pl. 1.

316

The portrait has been continuously in family ownership. It passed by inheritance to Mrs. Edward P. Davis, a great-granddaughter of Benjamin Franklin, after whose death it was sold at auction on June 16, 1924.[4] Its purchase by Mrs. William Pepper (Henrietta D. Bache) continued it in the possession of another branch of the family. It was inherited by its present owner from her father, Franklin Bache (1869–1946).

The attribution to Samuel Johnson is conjectural. It is supported by evidence showing that Johnson was a painter of portraits and that at the time of the child's death he was a near neighbor and friend of Franklin. The composition of the portrait is based upon a popular mezzotint, "The Lord Euston," by John Smith, 1689, after Sir Godfrey Kneller, 1685 (Pl. 1), and Johnson was the type of painter likely to have been dependent upon mezzotint models in such work. Franklin was also on intimate terms with Gustavus Hesselius (1682–1755) whose style is more mature and academic, and with John Winter (d. 1782), a craftsman painter who does not appear on the Philadelphia scene until 1740. An attribution to Robert Feke has been suggested, but is unsupported by stylistic or other evidence. A suggestion that the painting may be the work of Simeon Soumain, New York and Philadelphia silversmith, appears to be based on a misreading of "Simeon" for "Limner" in Franklin's Ledger E, 1756. See above, Chap. 2.

JUDLIN, ALEXIS (ca. 1770–1810)
1780. Miniature, probably after Duplessis. Unlocated.
The miniature was painted at the order of Pierre Simon Fournier le Jeune (b. 1750; living 1789). He was a son of Pierre Simon Fournier (1712–68), author of *De l'Origine et des productions de l'imprimerie primitive en taille de bois,* 1759, and the *Manuel typographique* of 1764–66. Fournier le Jeune had supplied Franklin with types, had made a special font for him, and later supplied the typefoundry with which Benjamin Franklin Bache returned to Philadelphia. In the spring of 1780 he asked Franklin's permission to have a miniature painted of him. Franklin agreed, but as usual protested against the discomfort of posing and suggested

4. Stan V. Henkels, *Catalogue No. 1356. Relics of Benjamin Franklin. Estate of Ellen Duane Davis* (Philadelphia, June 16, 1924), no. 2.

a copy from the fine portrait in the large owned by de Chaumont. On May 4, fearing that he may have been misunderstood, Franklin apologized for his poor command of the French language, affirmed his willingness to go to the trouble of posing, but protested that he was not prepared to pay for the work if that had been the other's understanding.

> Quand j'ai fait mention de M. du Plessis, c'était pour dire, qu'ayant fait un bon Portrait de moi au grand pour M. de Chaumont, votre Artiste pouvoit le copier ce Portrait en Miniature pour vous. Mais comme vous aimiez mieux le faire tirer d'après nature, j'ai consenté, pour vous obliger, de donner des Séances à tel Artiste que vous voudriez employer, quoique ce soit une chose très ennuyante pour moi, & que je l'avais déjà refusé à plusieurs.[5]

Fournier replied with delightful tact and enthusiasm that if the miniature cost as much as twenty louis he would give them with pleasure, that two or three sittings would be the most beautiful gift he had ever received, doing honor to himself and to his posterity, and he gave his letter to be delivered at Passy by the painter himself. To the artist, however, Franklin would appear to have been persistently not at home. It was on June 25, just at that time, that Franklin met Thomas Digges' similar request with the frank statement that he was "perfectly sick" of sitting for his picture. Finally, on July 15 Judlin left a letter of Fournier's at Franklin's door, and with it one of his own:

> Monsieur
>
> Comme je n'ai pas eu l'honneur de vous trouvez chez vous, j'ai laissé un lettre de la part d'un Mr: de votre connaissance, au quel vous avés permis de vous faire peindre, comme cela vous serés trop incommode

5. "When I made mention of M. du Plessis, it was to say, that having made a good portrait of me in the large for M. de Chaumont, your artist could copy this portrait in miniature for you. But as you prefer one taken from life, I have consented, to oblige you, to give sittings to whatever artist you wish to employ, although this will be a very trying thing for me, and I have already refused it to others." (Franklin Papers, A.P.S., *70*, no. 6.)

de vous transporter chez moi et que je ne pourés point
non plus vous donner des séances chez vous, si vous
pouviés me confier pour quelque jour un portrait
de vous qui fut resemblant j'aurés le plaisir de con-
tenter celui qui désir votre portrait vous pouvés être
assuré Monsieur que j'aurés tout les soins possible
pour le portrait que vous me pretterés. J'ai l'honneur
d'être

    Monsieur

        Votre très humble Serviteur
        Judlin peintre de la Reine[6]

We do not know what portrait figured in this capitulation. Probably Franklin had then in his house the "Gray Coat" pastel, and
had recommended Chaumont's "Fur Collar" oil for copying because it was the more famous and more distinguished piece. We can
only surmise, but the chances seem to favor the miniature's being
a copy of the pastel (see DUPLESSIS, "Gray Coat," No. 1).

One thing is clear: Judlin succeeded in contenting his patron.
Fournier wrote to Franklin on Aug. 15, glowing with gratitude and
declaring that the picture gave him a million times the pleasure he
had anticipated, that he and his wife would treasure it all their lives.
When in 1781 Franklin ordered a special script type, Fournier
printed the sample sheet with Feutry's "vers mis au bas du Portrait de M. Franklin," the same that adorned the Chevillet engraving of the Fur Collar Duplessis.[7] Thirty years later, a bust
of Franklin presided over the activities of the Fournier foundry,
the workmen pointing it out to the American visitor with ex-
clamations of "Excellent Franklin!"[8]

6. "As I have not had the honor to find you at home, I have left a letter on behalf
of a gentleman of your acquaintance, for whom you consented to be painted. As it will
be too inconvenient for you to come to me, and as I can no longer give sittings at your
house, if you will entrust to me for a few days a portrait of yourself with a good resemblance, I shall have the pleasure of giving satisfaction to him who desires your
portrait. You may rest assured, Monsieur, that I shall take every possible care of the
portrait you lend me..." (Franklin Papers, A.P.S., *19,* no. 25.)

7. Luther S. Livingston, *Franklin and His Press at Passy* (New York, 1914), p.
196.

8. "William McCulloch's Additions to Thomas's History of Printing," *Proceedings of the American Antiquarian Society, 31* (1921), 185. See also UNKNOWN ART-
IST: SCULPTURE, No. 4.

Judlin had exhibited miniatures at the Royal Academy, London, from 1773 to 1776, and so may have had some slight previous acquaintance with Franklin. His miniature of the Chevalier d'Eon, London, 1776, at the Victoria and Albert Museum, is in the oval form popular in England, so that this French work may have been either oval or circular. His ivories are signed "Judlin" and sometimes dated, but it is unlikely that a copy would be signed. His work elicited some contemporary praise, and he is said to have succeeded well in giving an air of nobility to his portraits.[1] At the Salons of 1791 and 1793 he exhibited both portraits and allegorical compositions on revolutionary themes: "Equality," "The Republic," "The Rights of Man."

KING, CHARLES BIRD (1785–1862)
    Painting. See DUPLESSIS "Gray Coat," No. 8.

LAINÉ, FRANCIS (1721–1810)
    Ca. 1778–85. Drawing and miniature. See DUPLESSIS "Fur Collar," Nos. 22, 23.

LAVOISSIER, MME. (1758–1836)
    1788. Painting. See DUPLESSIS "Gray Coat," No. 6.

LAZZARINI, FRANCESCO
    1790–91. Statue. See CAFFIERI, No. 12.

LEBARBIER, JEAN JACQUES FRANÇOIS (1738–1826)
    Ca. 1795. Drawing. See HOUDON, No. 11.

LE BEAU, PIERRE ADRIEN (b. 1744)
    Ca. 1780. Line engraving. See COCHIN, No. 1.

LEMIRE, otherwise, CHARLES GABRIEL SAUVAGE (1741–1827)
    Ca. 1785. Statuette group, Louis XVI and Franklin. Bisque porcelain statuette. Ht. of figures and base, 12⅞ in. Base 8¾ in. long, 4 15/16 in. wide. The king, in armor, at left, extends

1. Maze-Sencier, *Livre des collectionneurs*, p. 531.

to Franklin a document on one page of which is inscribed in gold, "INDÉPENDENCE / DE L'AMÉRIQUE" and on the other, "LIBERTÉ / DES MERS." Maker's mark on back of base, "NIDERVILLE." The figures are uncolored. The example at the Metropolitan Museum is entirely so. In that at the H. F. du Pont Winterthur Museum the base is marbleized on all four sides in white and shades of red and gray. Pl. 29.

The Niderville factory in Lorraine was known chiefly for its statuettes in hard paste, modeled by, or under the supervision of, the director of its studios, Charles Sauvage, called Lemire. Founded in 1760, the factory was acquired in 1780 by Adam Philippe, Comte de Custine (1740–93), French general of the Seven Years War, who served also with the French forces in America. He entered active service again in support of the French Revolution, suffering there, however, misfortunes which led to his death on the guillotine. The factory was under the general management of François Lanfrey when this piece was issued. While the statuette has always been attributed to Lemire, there is no identifying mark or other confirmation. Lemire joined the Sèvres factory about 1808, exhibiting at the Paris Salons from that year until 1809.

While not from life, the head and figure of Franklin must be accepted as having authentic value. A piece in the collection of William J. Hoppin was recorded in 1878 as the only known example.[2] An inferior copy in bronze, the figures differently placed, is recorded in the photographic collection of the Bibliothèque Nationale. A rare woodcut also preserved in the Bibliothèque Nationale provides an early documentation of the statuette group, from which it is obviously derived.[3]

LESLIE, GEORGE DUNLOP (1835–1921)
    1856. Painting. See CHAMBERLIN, No. 1, and Pl. 4.

LETHIÈRE, GUILLAUME GUILLON (1760–1832)
    1795. Stipple engraving. See HOUDON, No. 11.

---

2. *L'Art, 15* (1878), 141–42.
3. Entitled, "Liberté des Etats-Unis reconnue par la France." Signed, lower left, "Lörtschen." Illust. in Bernard Faÿ, *Franklin, the Apostle of Modern Times* (Boston, 1929), p. 438.

LEVASSEUR, JEAN CHARLES (1734–1805)
   1778. Line engraving. See BOREL.

L'HOSPITAL, J. F. DE
   1   1778. Painting. Oil on canvas, oval, 25¾ x 19½ in. Gray
   hair. Gray eyes. Coat and waistcoat a dark claret. Background
   olive-gray. Signed, lower right, "J. f. DeLhospital / pinx^t. /
   1778." *Owner:* University of Pennsylvania, Philadelphia. Pl.
   22.

The following signed statement accompanies a photograph in the
Library of Congress Print Collection:

> Washington, D.C., November 18, 1913.
>   This portrait of Benjamin Franklin was painted in
> Paris in 1779 from life for his friend Count St.
> Morys.
>   It was given in 1837 [1831 or 1832. See below] by
> the grand-daughter of Count St. Morys to Lieutenant
> Ritchie while the latter was a guest at the family
> château of Houdainville, Dept. of Oise, France.
>   On Commodore Ritchie's death in 1870, it was
> given by his sister, Miss Ritchie, to Medical Director
> Joseph Beale, U.S. Navy.
>   On the death of Dr. Beale in 1887, it came into the
> possession of his son Joseph Beale, who is the present
> owner.
>
> > Joseph Beale,
> > 2301 Massachusetts Avenue,
> > Washington, D.C.

On June 16, 1914, Mr. Beale presented the portrait to the University of Pennsylvania on behalf of the Beale family and as a memorial to his father, Dr. Joseph Beale, an alumnus of the college, class of 1831.
   Etienne Bourgevain Vialart, Comte de Saint Morys, was born in Paris in 1772, the son of a "conseiller à la grandchambre de Parlement."[4] Father and son were emigrés in 1790, and the father

4. Michaud Frères, *Biographie universelle* (Paris, 1811–62).

killed at Quiberon in 1795, fighting for the restoration of the monarchy. The son traveled in Sweden and Russia. His *Voyage pittoresque de Scandinavie* (London, 1802) was followed by other works, historical and political. Returning from England after the Peace of Amiens in 1804, he was suspected of complicity in the royalist plot to destroy Napoleon by an infernal machine, was imprisoned, and then placed under surveillance at Houdainville, near Beauvais, Oise, where his father's once splendid château was falling into ruin. In 1814 he was active in promoting the restoration of the Bourbons, was ultimately rewarded with an army commission, but was never restored to his father's great estate. At the château he gathered about him a large library and what amounted in time to a museum both of natural history and the arts of the Middle Ages.[5] This work was cut short by his death in a duel on July 21, 1817, but was continued by his son-in-law, M. Schillings, an officer of the old army. He was survived also by his widow and a widowed daughter, Mme. de Gaudechart. Mme. de Gaudechart was probably the "grand-daughter" who gave the portrait of Franklin to Lieutenant Ritchie.

Robert Ritchie was born in 1798, the son of a Philadelphia merchant of the same name. He died in Philadelphia on July 6, 1870. In his long career in the Navy, from 1814 to 1867, there is only one occasion upon which he might have been traveling in France. He was a lieutenant on the *Java* at Port Mahon and cruising in the Mediterranean from 1829 to 1831. In May of that year he applied for a three-month leave of absence. "My health is a little impaired by hard service."[6] In 1833 he left for the West Indies in command of the schooner *Grampus,* serving thereafter in South American and Pacific waters.[7] It was probably, therefore, in the summer of 1831, but possibly in 1832, that the young man, traveling between Paris and Amiens, stopped at the Château of Houdainville which had become one of the tourist attractions of the region, met the lady, and departed with the painting.[8]

5. *Guide pittoresque du voyageur en France, contenant la statistique et la description complète des 86 Départements* (Paris, 1838), *2,* 28–29.
6. Ritchie to John Boyle, May 13, 1831 (H.S.P.).
7. Information from Naval Academy, National Archives, and *Navy Register.*
8. University of Pennsylvania records, from the family, give 1832 as the date of acquisition.

Dr. Joseph Beale was also a Philadelphian. He entered the Navy in 1837. Orders dated May 6, 1869, assigned him to special duty at Philadelphia, bringing him there at the time of Commodore Ritchie's death.[9]

If Jean Nicolas Gardeur's hope that he might share a sitting with another artist occurred in 1778, the other artist was probably L'Hospital, and the painting was in progress on March 30 of that year. The picture has the appearance of a life portrait, but the obscurity of the painter makes it likely that he was a provincial or amateur artist. It is needless to speculate upon whether he may have been related to Guillaume François Antoine de L'Hospital (1661–1704), whose mathematical treatise Franklin knew and had purchased for the Library Co. "Hospital, peintre, 1763–64" is included in the list of painters, decorators, and gilders employed at the Sèvres manufactory.[1] Schidlof mentions "de L'Hospital" as a French painter of the end of the 18th century, and cites a portrait of an artist in miniature with this signature in the possession of Warneck, a dealer in Paris.[2] A feminine softness in the characterization suggests that the artist may have been a woman.

Where the portrait may have been during its owner's services at sea, from 1833 to 1867, is not known. That it may have been with his family in Philadelphia is suggested by the use of this portrait type on the one dollar bank notes of the Merchants and Planters Bank, Savannah, Ga., of June 1, 1859, engraved by "Danforth, Wright & Co., Philada. & New York." It was on the Danforth, Wright & Co. letterhead, Philadelphia, New York, and Cincinnati, in 1856, and on a stock certificate of the Spring Garden Institute, Philadelphia, engraved by the American Bank Note Co. of that city and dated Nov. 22, 1865.[3]

2   Ca. 1778. Painting. Oil on canvas, oval, 27⅞ x 22¼ in. Gray hair. Gray eyes. Brown coat and waistcoat. Brown back-

9. *Navy Register,* 1868, 1870.

1. Georges Lechevallier-Chevignard, *La Manufacture de porcelaine de Sèvres. Histoire de la manufacture, 1738–1876, 2* (Paris, 1908), 133.

2. Leo Schidlof, *Die Bildnisminiatur in Frankreich* (Vienna and Leipzig, 1911), p. 319.

3. Bella C. Landauer, *Some Ephemeral Portraits of Lincoln and Franklin from the Collections of Bella C. Landauer* (New York, 1935), unpaged.

ground. The signature, "De Lhoopin / pinxit," appears to be an early restorer's effort to recreate the original after over-painting the background. *Owner:* Mrs. A. Wright Post, New York.

A signed statement by William Warner Hoppin (1807–90), grand-father of the present owner of the painting, reads:

> This portrait of Dr. Benjamin Franklin was painted for and under the immediate inspection of Queen Marie Antoinette in her apartment at the Petit Tria-non near Versailles. At the time of the pillage of the Royal Palaces during the revolution in 1792–3, it was consigned to the care of one of the Queen's at-tendants of whom it was afterward purchased by Dr. Swediaur in Paris, who had been the intimate friend of Franklin. At his death in 1825, it became the prop-erty of the Rev. Edward Forster he being the residu-ary legatee of the said Dr. Swediaur. The artist's name is De L'hoopin. In the winter of 1847 being in Paris and hearing through the Banking House of Greene & Co., of the existence of this Portrait, and the earnest wish of Mrs. Forster then an aged lady of about 80, that it might become the property of an American Citizen, I purchased the same of Mrs. Forster. Original papers showing the authenticity of the Portrait are now in my possession. In the winter of 1889 this painting was taken from its original can-vas and transferred to its present canvas and restored by J. A. Hooper of Providence, R.I.
>
> Wm. W. Hoppin[4]

The first part of this statement is so rich in romantic implications as to savor more of legend than of fact. Some confirmation of its association with the queen and her private apartments would be a

4. Statement preserved with the painting. A similar statement by the writer's son, William Warner Hoppin, dated New York, Nov. 15, 1892, accompanies a photograph of the portrait in the British Museum, Department of Prints and Drawings.

most interesting addition to the Franklin iconography. Ownership by Dr. Franz Xaver Schwediauer (1748–1824), Austrian physician and friend of Franklin, is wholly credible. That this is not the portrait of Franklin engraved in London in 1783 as "From a Painting in the Possession of F. Schwediauer, M.D., in Newman Street" (see WRIGHT, No. 9) seems to bear out the story that he had acquired it during the Revolution.

The Rev. Edward Forster (1769–1828) studied medicine and law at Oxford, and in 1796, after the death of his first wife, entered the Church. In 1799 he married Lavinia, only daughter of Thomas Banks, R.A., sculptor. In 1801 he was elected a Fellow of the Royal Society. He published various books, including his *British Gallery of Engravings,* for which his wife drew title pages and vignettes, but these ventures involved him in financial losses and led to his removal, with his wife and daughters, to Paris in 1815. In 1818 he was appointed Chaplain to the British Embassy, a post which had been created at his own suggestion. He died in Paris on Feb. 18, 1828, leaving his entire estate to his wife.[5] The portrait was exhibited at the Luxembourg Museum in 1830 as the property of Mme. Forster and as having been painted from life by De L'Hospital.[6] It is clear that the signature must have been legible at that time, though the artist's initials do not appear.

Its purchaser in 1847 may have associated the altered name with his own. William Warner Hoppin had been traveling in Europe from 1839 until that year. He was Governor of Rhode Island from 1854 to 1856. The portrait has descended through his son to his granddaughter.

3　Undated. Painting. *Owner* (1936) : Clinton N. Hunt.
The catalogue of Guido Bruno's American Autograph Shop, Merion Station, Pa., November 1941, lists a full-page folio letter of James Strong, New York, 1840, with "Interesting description of a painting of Dr. Franklin, in his possession, painted from life in Paris, about 1777 or 78, by J. F. De l'Hospital. Places its worth at

5. *Dictionary of National Biography.* Will, Somerset House, London, dated April 23, 1816.

6. Emile Bellier de la Chavignerie and Louis Auvray, *Dictionnaire Générale des artistes de l'école français, 1* (Paris, 1882), 1046.

$500.00. . . . He states that he is a bachelor, has no home and the painting 'that would not shame Titian' should be in better hands than his."[7]

This may be the painting which in 1842 was listed as no. 82 in the October exhibition of the Apollo Association in New York, as by J. F. De L'Hospital and as the property of D. Elliot.[8] Other entries show Daniel Elliot to have been a member of the Committee of Management of the American Art Union from 1840 to 1843, and to have exhibited other paintings, landscape and genre.[9] The New York directories show him to have been in the paper business in partnership with Gaius C. Burnap and Nathan Babcock. He does not appear in the directories after 1846.

Again, these two citations may also apply to a portrait described and illustrated in the *Benjamin Franklin Gazette,* May 1936, whose original owner according to this account had been Walter Hunt (1796–1859), in whose family it had descended.[1] The illustration shows it to be very similar to the Ritchie and Hoppin portraits. Walter Hunt appears in the New York directories from 1834 to 1854 as a designer and engineer. He has been cited as the inventor, in about 1853, of a cartridge for firearms.[2]

> 4   Undated. Painting, enlarged copy after De L'Hospital. Oil on canvas, 41 x 33 in. Half length, to right, seated in a black chair upholstered in a mottled red. Gray coat and waistcoat. Holds silver spectacles and dark red handkerchief in lap. Background greenish gray, with column at right. *Owner:* W. H. Lowdermilk and Co., Washington, D.C.

Possibly an early American copy of one of the smaller portraits, this canvas is described in the *Benjamin Franklin Gazette* of March 1932 as having been "for generations" in the family of Charles Lee Frank, who had purchased it originally from a Washington family by the name of Saunders.[3] It has been attributed to Benjamin West

7. *American Clipper. Catalogue of American Autograph Shop,* (Nov. 1941), p. 294, no. 94.

8. Bartlett Cowdrey, *American Academy of Fine Arts and American Art-Union, 1816–1852, 1* (New York, 1953), 298.

9. Ibid., pp. 106, 298, 346, 394.

1. Cover illust. Text on p. 8.

2. *National Cyclopedia of American Biography, 10,* 476.

3. Cover illust. Text on p. 4.

by Dr. Holmes of the National Gallery.[4] In 1929 P. J. Moore certified to its having a provenance identical with that of the Hoppin portrait, and Gaston Neumans, Knight of the Order of the Crown of Belgium, former pupil of the Royal Academies of Antwerp and Brussels and former expert of the Hôtel Drouot, made a formally certified attribution to Duplessis.[5]

LODGE, JOHN (d. 1796)
    1777. Line engraving. See CHAMBERLIN, No. 5.

LOO. See VANLOO

McARDELL, JAMES (1728–65)
    1761. Mezzotint. See WILSON, No. 5.

MANÉ
    1778. Ivory medallion. See SEVRES, No. 2.

MARTIN, DAVID (1737–98)
    1   1766. Painting. Oil on canvas, 49 x 40 in. High complexion. Moles on left cheek and below under lip are clearly shown. Blue coat with gilt buttons and gold braided buttonholes. Red cloth cover on table. Leather bound books with colored labels and gilt tooling. No legible writing on books or papers. Bust of Isaac Newton in new bronze. Chair upholstered in red, with gilded ornamental carving at the top, surmounted by an eagle. Red curtain at upper left behind bust. Brown background. *Owner:* The White House, Washington. Pl. 8.
The eagle surmounting the chair back, a symbol difficult to associate with Franklin or with 18th-century London, must be presumed a later addition. It does not appear in any replica or copy. It is not in the copy of this work by James Reid Lambdin (1807–89), and so cannot be attributed to Thomas Birch, who prepared the painting for the annual exhibition of the Society of Artists and

4. Frick Art Reference Library.
5. Yale University, Mason Collection.

Pennsylvania Academy, opening in May 1814.[6] If an addition, however, it is certainly of early date, a fact borne out both by examination of the canvas and by the emblem itself, which resembles the eagle of the Society of the Cincinnati more than the emblem in its later forms. The "Scotch Pebble sleeve buttons" shown in the picture are mentioned in the will of Louis Bache, Sept. 5, 1819.[7]

The following, preserved with the picture by its successive owners, is the most authoritative documentation of its origin:

> The portraite of Benjamin Franklin, LL.D., was painted by Martin, in London, when the Doctor was about sixty years of age. It was ordered and paid for by Robert Alexander, then of the House of William Alexander and Sons, of Edenburgh, and was designed to perpetuate the circumstance of his advice, given in consequence of the perusal of certain important papers. . . . After the death of Robert it descended to his Brother, William Alexander. Jonathan Williams, a grandson of Dr. Franklin's sister, having married the daughter of William Alexander, the portraite has been given to them, to decend to the eldest male heir perpetually as the joint representative of both Parties. . . .
>
> This disposition is hereby confirmed.
> January 1, 1806.
>
> Jona. Williams
Mariamne Williams
>
> Note.—Doctor Franklin was so well satisfied with Mr. Martin's performance & the likeness was deemed so perfect, that he was induced to have a copy made by the same Artist at his own expense, & it was sent to his Family in Philadelphia. It was after his death, left by his will, to the Supreme Executive Council of Pennsylvania, of which he had been the chief, & was

6. On June 18, 1814, Colonel Jonathan Williams, its owner, paid Birch $15.00 "for repairing the portrait of Dr. Franklin" (Jonathan Williams Papers, Indiana University).

7. H.S.P., Bucks County Wills, Bk. 9, p. 365.

accordingly suspended in their chamber. By the new Constitution, the Council of State was abolished & this poor portraite, became an abandoned orphan, without having any place in which it had a right to hang itself.

The celebrated Peale, a declaired enemy of everything unnatural—took pity on the wretched outcast and has humanely hung it up among his natural curiosities in the Philadelphia Museum.

The foregoing memorandum is copied from the original, in the Handwriting of my Father, Jonathan Williams, and the signatures are those of himself and my Mother. . . . By virtue of the direction contained in it, the above mentioned portraite passed to me, and has continued in my posession since his death. . . .

I hereby in accordance with the disposition made by them bequeath it to my eldest male heir.
November 1, 1828.

Henry J. Williams.[8]

Henry J. Williams, whose quizzical statement on the fate of the replica owned by Franklin (see below, No. 2) is appended to the earlier certification, was quoted by Dr. Thomas Hewson Bache as having enlarged upon his father's account of how the original picture came into being; he was reported as saying that Robert Alexander had been involved in a property dispute into which Franklin had been drawn as an arbitrator, and that Mr. Alexander, in order to celebrate the final decision rendered in favor of himself, had had Franklin painted in the act of studying one of the deeds.[9] There is no record of such a transaction, nor indeed of any dispute other than a friendly one between Franklin and Robert Alexander as rival poets in 1759.[1] See above, pp. 74–9.

8. As printed in *The Record of the Celebration of the Two Hundredth Anniversary of the Birth of Benjamin Franklin, 1* (Philadelphia, 1906), xvii–xviii. Slightly variant versions of the statement were given the author by Dr. Williams B. Cadwalader, owner of the portrait in 1956, and are quoted by Albert P. Brubaker, "The Martin Portraits of Franklin," *P.M.H.B., 56,* 252–53.

9. Bowen, *Centennial Celebration,* pp. 453–54.

1. Forbes, *Curiosities of a Scots Charta Chest,* pp. 180–81.

The portrait remained in the possession of descendants of Jonathan and Mariamne Williams until its acquisition by the Knoedler Galleries of New York and its purchase by Mr. and Mrs. Walter H. Annenberg of Philadelphia. Their gift of it to the White House collection was announced on January 27, 1962.

> 2 1767. Painting, altered replica of No. 1. Oil on canvas, 49½ x 39½ in. Chairback upholstered in red damask, with no ornamental carving. *Owner:* Pennsylvania Academy of the Fine Arts, Philadelphia.

The date of the painting is recorded in the last codicil to Franklin's will, June 23, 1789: "My picture, drawn by Martin, in 1767, I give to the Supreme Executive Council of Pennsylvania, if they shall be pleased to do me the honor of accepting it, and placing it in their chamber." His "Journal" accounts of Nov. 27, 1767, note the payment of £12.12.0 to "D. Martin Limner."[2] Liking the portrait himself and finding it much admired by others, Franklin ordered this replica, though he already had Wilson's portrait, and his son a replica of Chamberlin's. That he did not underwrite the publication of a mezzotint, as Martin may well have hoped, would be due to the fact that he still had his supply of Fisher's after Chamberlin, and was still sending them to friends in the years following.

The evidence is not entirely clear, but he seems to have kept the picture in London until 1771, and then to have sent it to Philadelphia. On April 20, 1771, he wrote to his son that he was sending William's portrait, which had been left with Jeremiah Meyer to be copied in miniature, and "other pictures . . . for my own house."[3] On Aug. 14 he wrote to Deborah replying to her acknowledgment of their arrival:

> I am glad to hear of all your Welfares, and that the Pictures &c. were safe arrived. You do not tell me who mounted the great one, nor where you have hung it up. Let me know whether Dr. Bond likes the new one better than the old one; if so the old one can be return'd hither to Mr. Wilson the Painter.

2. Franklin Papers (A.P.S.).
3. Ibid., *45,* no. 37.

You may keep the Frame, as it may be wanted for
some other picture there.[4]

Here the "new one" and the "old one" are portraits of himself by
Benjamin Wilson (Nos. 1 and 3). The "great one" may have been
the three-quarter length by Wilson (No. 4), though there is no
reason to believe that this was ever owned by Franklin, and the surmise that it was sent to America seems to have no foundation. It
could not have been the Chamberlin three-quarter length, since
that was William's and intended for his home. It must, therefore,
have been the Martin three-quarter length. Franklin's use of the
word "great," as with the first Wedgwood profiles, refers simply
to comparative size. The question as to "who mounted the great
one" probably indicates that it had been shipped rolled. Franklin
made further suggestions about it in a letter to Deborah of March
19, 1772, but some of the words have been torn away and the
reader can only guess their import. "I wonder that the Picture coud
not [hang on the] stairs. I think it would have hung [in the] Passage. It might have been mou[nted] . . ."[5]

It had probably been mounted by Charles Willson Peale. Peale
made a long sojourn in Philadelphia in the latter part of 1771, and
again in the summer of 1772. In a letter of July 29, 1772, he wrote
that his brother, James Peale, "is now making a copy of a fine piece
of Mr. Franklin."[6] The high quality of the copy suggests its attribution to both brothers rather than solely to the younger, then in-
experienced James (see below, No. 5). The Peales may have retained the original for some time, perhaps even during the war.
Had it been then in the Franklin house it would probably have
been carried away by the retreating British, who took with them his
portrait by Wilson (No. 1).

Years later it came back to the Peales as, in Henry J. Williams'
phrase, "a wretched outcast." On May 14, 1790, the Supreme Executive Council of Pennsylvania had gratefully accepted Franklin's
bequest of it to adorn their Council Chamber.[7] The Council had
been abolished by the adoption of the new state constitution of 1790,

4. Ibid., *46*, Pt. II, no. 76.
5. Ibid., no. 79.
6. Peale-Sellers Papers.
7. *Pennsylvania Archives*, 4th ser. *4*, 101.

but the painting did not become actually an "outcast" or "orphan" until the removal of the state government to Lancaster in April 1799 had left the old State House unoccupied. When Peale moved his museum into it in the autumn of 1802, the state's paintings of Franklin, Washington, and Thomas Wharton were still there, and he hung them in his museum gallery. He scrupulously acknowledged their ownership and published it in his gallery catalogue of 1813. Arrangements made soon after to send the pictures to Lancaster were never carried out, and they were included in the final sale of the gallery at auction in 1854. The "Franklin" and "Washington" were at that time purchased by Edward Ingersoll for his brother-in-law, Henry Pratt McKean. They passed to his son, Thomas McKean, whose children in 1912 deposited them in the Pennsylvania Academy of the Fine Arts. On July 19, 1942, the "Franklin" was given to the Academy by the two surviving daughters of Thomas McKean, Maria McKean Allen and Phebe Warren McKean Downs. See above, pp. 77–8.

> 3   1772. Painting, replica of No. 2.[8] Oil on canvas, 50 x 40 in. Signed, lower right, "D. Martin, pinxt / 1772." *Owner:* Dr. Alexander J. Alexander, Lexington, Ky. Pl. 8.

The actual date of the painting is probably earlier than 1772, since the evidence indicates that Franklin's replica (No. 2), from which it was made, had been sent to Philadelphia in 1771. Probably it was painted at the same time as the other, in 1767, and the signature added by the artist at the time of sale. Its purchaser was Franklin's old friend, John Sargent (ca. 1715–91), merchant and banker, a director of the Bank of England, a Member of Parliament from 1754 to 1761, and from 1765 to 1768. Their friendship and business relationship, begun in 1759, was close and cordial. At the time of Franklin's return to Philadelphia in 1762, Sargent, Aufrere and Co. had contributed two gold medals to be given as prizes in oratory at "your college," the subject to be "Reciprocal Advantages arising from a perpetual union between Great Britain and her Colonies."[9] Mr. Aufrere, also a friend, acquired a portrait, noted below (No.

8. Erroneously described as a replica of No. 1, Martin's original, in Sellers, *Portraits and Miniatures by Charles Willson Peale,* p. 80.

9. Thomas H. Montgomery, *A History of the University of Pennsylvania* (Philadelphia, 1900), p. 365.

6). In 1772 Franklin's account was with Sargent, Chambers and Co.

The two friends scrupulously refrained from communication during the war, but renewed the correspondence in 1783, and young William Temple Franklin was staying at the Sargent house in London in 1784. Franklin wrote to him there on Oct. 18, 1784, sending his love to Mr. and Mrs. Sargent. On Nov. 14 Mr. Sargent returned their thanks "after the hearty old English manner," for a print of himself which Franklin has sent from Paris.[1] From this charming couple the portrait descended to a Mrs. Larpent and to her son, George Larpent, of Cockerell, Larpent and Co., London. George Larpent sold it in 1850 to Alexander John Alexander, bringing it back into the family for whom the original had been painted.[2] Robert Alexander (1767–1841), a brother of Mariamne, had also emigrated to America, settling first in Virginia and then on a plantation, "Woodburn," in Woodford County, Kentucky. His eldest son, Alexander John, as heir to the Scottish family estates of Airdrie and Cowdenhill, became a British subject, was educated at Oxford, and in 1842 succeeded to the lands of his uncle, Sir William Alexander. His younger sister, Mary Belle, had also come to England, where in 1859 she married Henry Charles Deedes of the Indian Office. The portrait hung at Airdrie House. Robert C. Winthrop saw it there in 1875, but in reporting on its history confused it with the original in Philadelphia (No. 1).[3] In 1892 it was at Henry Deedes' home, Binderton House, Chichester, Sussex.[4] Sometime after the death of Mrs. Deedes the portrait was sent to the American heir, Alexander John Aitchison Alexander, whose son is presently its owner.

> 4 Ca. 1775–85. Painting, altered replica of No. 1. Oil on panel, 11½ x 8½ in. Lilac-gray suit. Green table-cover. Calf-bound books with red labels, yellow tooling, and green tops. Book lying flat on table has red pages. The bust of Newton is gray. Red curtain, upper left, appears to have been over-

1. A.P.S.
2. Bowen, *Centennial Celebration,* p. 454, quoting a letter from Henry Deedes to B. F. Stevens.
3. *Proceedings of the M.H.S., 14* (1876), 10–11.
4. Bowen, p. 454.

painted in lower part. Chair carving as in the original. Green protective paint on back. *Owner:* John G. Shelley, Roxburghshire, Scotland.

Long supposed to be a work of Alexander Nasmyth (1758–1840), whose style is similar to that of David Martin, the portrait was recently attributed to Martin by Mr. R. E. Hutchison, Director of the Scottish National Portrait Gallery, on the basis of Martin's other portraits of Franklin and the existence of other small sketches in oil by Martin. These sketches appear to have been hastily made memoranda of his compositions, not intended for sale. The likeness is softened and without the strength of the original, though the smiling face is acceptable as another aspect of the sitter. The coloring is not the same, nor carefully chosen. The picture is the only replica in which the ornamental chair back appears, and was therefore probably made in Edinburgh from the original, no doubt between 1775, when Martin settled there permanently, and 1785, when Mariamne and Jonathan Williams, owners of the original, removed to America.

5   1772. Painting, copy of No. 2 by Charles Willson Peale (1741–1827) and James Peale (1749–1831). Oil on canvas, 49 x 38½ in. *Owner:* A.P.S., Philadelphia.

From Franklin's letters it appears that he sent his own replica of Martin's portrait from London to his Philadelphia home in the summer of 1771 (see above No. 2). It would appear also that it arrived unmounted, that Charles Willson Peale was employed to stretch it, and that this copy was made while he then had it in his possession. On June 29, 1772, he wrote to John Beale Bordley that his younger brother, James, "is now making a copy of a fine piece of Mr. Franklin."[5] The copy remained in the possession of Charles Willson Peale and has always been accepted as his work. The excellence of the painting, at a time when James Peale was still at the beginning of his career, indicates the work of both brothers, or that James Peale's copy was a different picture, now lost.

On Aug. 20, 1776, John Adams visited Peale's painting room, and wrote home mentioning Franklin's as among the portraits he had

5. Peale-Sellers Papers (A.P.S.).

seen there.[6] When Peale founded his gallery of heroes of the Revolution in 1782 the copy of Franklin was in it. Soon after Franklin's return from France on Sept. 14, 1785, Peale replaced this picture with a new life portrait. On Dec. 16 he presented the copy to the A.P.S., with a polite note to its secretary:

> As I have always considered the *American Philosophical Society* in the most respectable point of view; and as it is natural for every one to express his Sensibility in that manner which accords best with his own Habits & Line of business, I do myself the Honour to present to the said Society, through your hands, a Portrait of their Venerable President, his Excellency Dr. Franklin, coppied from a much admired Painting of Mr. Martin.[7]

The gift may have been inspired in part by the fact that the Society then had in prospect the erection of a building of its own. The members in returning their thanks requested him to retain the picture until "the Society shall have a convenient Place for its reception."[8] Peale, then embarking on his career in the sciences, was elected to membership in the following year, and in 1794 moved his new museum of natural history into the recently completed Philosophical Hall. The old copy from Martin, therefore, remained in his care until his retirement to Germantown in 1810.

6   Ca. 1784–90. Painting, altered copy of No. 3 by Benjamin West (1738–1820). Oil on canvas, 50 x 40 in. Blue coat, from which the gold braid is omitted. Red cloth on table and red drapery in background. *Owner:* Estate of John D. Rockefeller, Jr.

The painting follows the replica owned by John Sargent. The omission of all gold braid from the coat reflects changing fashions in dress rather than the taste of artist or patron. The patron was almost certainly Mr. Sargent's business partner, George Rene Aufrere (1715–1801). He was the son of a French Huguenot

6. C. F. Adams, *Letters of John Adams and his Wife Abigail Adams,* p. 216.
7. Archives of the A.P.S.
8. Minutes of the A.P.S., Dec. 16, 1785.

clergyman, the Rev. Israel Antoine Aufrère (1667–1758).[9] His marriage in 1746 to Arabella Bate had brought him a substantial fortune.[10] Like Mr. Sargent, he served in Parliament, being Member for Stamford from 1765 to 1774.[11] He was a connoisseur and collector of art, and with both Sargent and Franklin, a friend of Benjamin West. It may be inferred that in 1784, when West was eagerly looking for portraits of Franklin to use in projected historical works, he borrowed Sargent's Martin among the others. It was a likeness not suited to his purpose, but it was the Franklin whom his old friends remembered and was particularly suited to them. This and the copies described below came from his studio as a result. Whether they are by his hand or an assistant's cannot be determined.

The earliest documentation of West's version of the Martin portrait is the mezzotint from it published by Edward Savage in 1793.[12] The identification with West's work appears in the lack of gold braid and by Savage's own statement in a letter to George Washington, sent on Oct. 6, 1793, with gifts of his "Washington" and "Franklin" mezzotints:

> The portrait of Doctor Franklin, which is published as the companion, is done from a picture in the possession of Mr. West, President of the Royal Academy. The picture has been done some years and was thought very like when done. I have the pleasure to inform you that both of those prints are approved of by the artists. Particularly Mr. West, whose Friendship and servility [*sic*] I have the honor to receive.[1]

George Rene Aufrere had one child, Sophia, who in 1770 married Charles Anderson, 1st Baron Yarborough (1748/9–1823). Their son, Charles Anderson-Pelham, 1st Earl of Yarborough

9. Winifred Turner, "The Aufrere Papers. Calendar and Selections," *Publications of the Huguenot Society of London, 40* (1940), xvi, 112, 162n.

10. Joseph Farington, *The Farington Diary, 3* (London, 1922–28), 77–78.

11. Gerrit P. Judd, IV, *Members of Parliament, 1734–1832* (New Haven, 1955), p. 109.

12. "D. Martin Pinxt. E. Savage Sculpt. / BENJAMIN FRANKLIN, L.L.D. F.R.S. / London, Published Septr. 17, 1793 by E. Savage, No. 50 Hatton Garden."

1. Charles Henry Hart, "Edward Savage," *Proceedings of the M.H.S., 19* (1905), 7.

(1781–1846), was made Earl of Yarborough and Baron Worsley in 1837. In 1806 he married Anna Maria Charlotte Simpson, heiress of her uncle, Sir Richard Worsley of Appuldercombe (1751–1805), a well-known antiquary, Member of Parliament, and Fellow of the Royal Society, known also as a patron of Benjamin West. Sir Richard was formerly thought to have been the original owner of this painting. The present Earl of Yarborough has very kindly searched the list of paintings owned by Mr. Aufrere (ca. 1790), the catalogue of the Worsley collection at Appuldercombe (1837), as well as catalogues of the paintings at the family seat at Brocklesby Park, 1814 and 1841. No "Franklin" appears. He agrees that the provenance of the painting would probably be from George Aufrere, and has suggested that its omission from the lists may be explained by the relegation of the portrait of Whig and rebel to a limbo in the attic.[2] In 1846 a "Franklin" attributed to West and owned by the Earl of Yarborough was exhibited by the "British Institute for promoting the fine arts in the United Kingdom."[3] In 1856 the family list at last acknowledges the presence of Poor Richard.

With the turn of the century, however, two portraits of the Martin type were present in the collection, the other a small "cabinet size" piece, also without the gold braid, but with the coat vermilion instead of blue (see below No. 8). The large painting was sold in the Carlisle sale, Sotheby's, on May 6, 1926.[4] It was purchased by Messrs. Duveen for £3,300.[5]

7   Ca. 1784–90. Painting, altered copy of No. 3 by Benjamin West. *Owner:* Earl Stanhope, Chevening, Sevenoaks, Kent. Franklin, in his London years, was close to those learned and practical men, Philip, 2d Earl Stanhope, and his son, Lord Mahon. They had the same taste for simplicity in dress and manner, the Earl at one time being pushed aside by the doorkeeper of the House of Lords with the friendly warning, "Honest man, you have

2. Earl of Yarborough to the author, Dec. 20, 1959.
3. Catalogue (London, 1846), no. 52.
4. No. 10, p. 9. Illust.
5. Information from Sotheby and Co. (Eddy Papers).

no business in this place." His reply had been merely to regret the opinion.[6] This unpretentiousness is reflected in the small portrait of Franklin, apparently acquired from West after the war. John Sargent, when reopening his correspondence with Franklin on Jan. 3, 1783, added a word on the continuing friendship of "my neighbor Lord Stanhope."[7] Lord Stanhope died in 1786. It may have been either the old Earl or the new who commissioned the little portrait. The younger man had married Lady Hester, daughter of William Pitt, Earl of Chatham, in 1774, at the time when Chatham, Stanhope, and Franklin were so deeply concerned in American affairs, and that strange creature, the sculptress Patience Wright, was hovering on the shadowy fringe of their deliberations. The 3rd Earl, however, quarreled with all the members of his family, bequeathing everything that he could to others. The portrait, according to its present owner, he left "to the father of Mr. Deane Franklin Walker who, in 1860, kindly gave it back to my grandfather, the 5th Earl Stanhope. The picture still hangs here at Chevening."[8] The painting is recorded at the National Portrait Gallery, London, with a sketch and color notes made by Sir George Scharf in 1892. There is a woodcut illustration in Ford's *Many-sided Franklin,* p. 266. A copy has been presented to the Franklin memorial in his Craven St. home.

> 8 Undated. Painting, copy by unknown artist. Oil on canvas, 19 x 16 in. Vermilion coat, without gold braid. Green chair and table cover. Blue curtain. *Owner:* The Earl of Yarborough, Brocklesby Park, Lincolnshire. Pl. 8.

The difference in coloring suggests that the painting is a copy of Edward Savage's mezzotint after the altered copy by Benjamin West (No. 6). That larger portrait owned by the Earl of Yarborough was sold at Sotheby's on May 6, 1926. This painting is listed in Sotheby's catalogue of June 30, 1926, but was not sold.[9]

6. William Stanhope Taylor and John Henry Pringle, eds., *The Correspondence of William Pitt, Earl of Chatham, 4* (London, 1840), 55n.

7. A.P.S.

8. To the author, Aug. 20, 1953.

9. *Catalogue of Pictures by Old Masters* (London, Sotheby and Co.), p. 26, no. 114.

9   Undated. Painting, copy by unknown artist. Oil on canvas, 21 x 15½ in. Vermilion coat without gold braid. Green table cover and chair. *Owner* (ca. 1930) : Mrs. George A. Plimpton, New York.

Apparently a replica of the above, the portrait is said to have come from the collection of Lady Larking, lady in waiting to Queen Victoria, of Bournemouth, England.[1] It is described and illustrated in the catalogue of the sale of the collection of John Anderson, Jr., American Art Association, New York, April 6, 1916.

MARTINET, FRANÇOIS NICOLAS (b. 1731)
    1773. Line engraving. See CHAMBERLIN, No. 4.

MENCONI, DOMENICO
    Ca. 1860. Bust. See HOUDON, No. 14.

MERCER, WILLIAM (1773–1850)
    1786. Miniature. See C. W. PEALE, No. 6.

MONIÉ
    1778. Medallion (?), probably after Nini or Sèvres. Bronze, chased and gilded. Unlocated.

Samuel Jackson Pratt (1749–1814), clergyman, actor, author, and adventurer, was a tall, well-spoken fellow with an energetic step and manner. Known only by his literary pseudonym, "Courtney Melmoth," and accompanied by "Mrs. Melmoth," he was introduced to Franklin by Barbeu Dubourg, as an English writer in sympathy with the American cause. With Dubourg's friendly letter, dated Nov. 14, 1777, Melmoth presented him with an ode of his own composition. Franklin appears to have been charmed by him, to have welcomed his services as a pamphleteer, and to have been willing to pay for them. On Jan. 1, 1778, Ralph Izard of South Carolina wrote Franklin asking for an interview. On the next day Courtney Melmoth who happened to be staying at the same hotel, made the same request. The two, with their wives, met

1. Courtauld Institute, Witt Library, London. Frick Art Reference Library, New York.

at Franklin's house. What we know of the meeting comes from an undated letter from Franklin to the Englishman:

> I should have been flattered exceedingly by Mrs. Melmoth's showing the least Inclination for one of those Portraits, when Mrs. Izard accepted the other, and should have presented it to her with the greatest Pleasure. She did not appear to desire it, and I did not presume it of Value enough to be offered. Her Quarrel with me on that account is pleasing. The Reconciliation, when I can obtain it, will be more so. At present another Lady has put it out of my Power to comply with the Terms. M. de Chaumont, at whose Pottery in the Country they were made, receiving a request from Petersburgh for one of them, to gratify the Curiosity of the Empress, & having none in town, he got from me the only one I had left, and has sent it away. But I am promis'd another soon, & shall seize the first Moment of making my Peace with it. In the meantime, I hope you will intercede for me, in that heart where I am sure you have an Interest. Accept my Thanks for the Books, from the Reading of which I promise myself a good deal of Pleasure. Please to accept also the Trifle enclos'd, and believe me with most sincere esteem . . . [2]

The letter replies to one containing an "Impromptu" poem which Mr. Melmoth states that Mrs. Melmoth had written. Franklin's unwonted courtliness of tone makes one suspect that he had succumbed to the Melmoth manner, the pretty actress, and the flattering to-do over his portrait. It would rather appear, however, that his friends pursued their advantage too far. On March 15 the artist Monié came to Franklin's door bearing a new portrait of him, the exact character of which is unknown but which, by the most reasonable conjecture, was a bronze ormolu casting from the Nini terra cotta which Franklin, in his letter, had promised to give

2. Franklin Papers (L.C.).

to Mrs. Melmoth. Mrs. Melmoth was to have accompanied him, but did not. Instead, he bore two letters of introduction:

Sir,

Some few Days ago the Bearer, Monsieur Monié, was recommended to me by a friend who sent, with him, the inclos'd card. He proves himself a man of singular ingenuity by those Portraits he will have the pleasure to shew you, and I hope your judgment of them will tally with that which your grandson was pleas'd to pass on them yesterday. If that is the case I shall have reason to congratulate myself upon being the Instrument of introducing a patriotic Artist to the attention of so amiable a Protector as Dr. Franklin. Agreeable to the tenor of the Inclos'd Billet, Mrs. Melmoth would have accompanied Mr. Monié, but she is unluckily prevented this pleasure by Indisposition.

I am Sir

your most obed: servt:

Courtney Melmoth.[3]

The "Inclos'd Billet" is in French, and signed only with a seal showing the De Mailly arms surmounted by a coronet.[4] It is a polite introduction of M. Monié, an excellent artist who just completed "le portrait de M. franklin en bronze ciselé et dorée en or moulu," to Mme. Melmoth, a friend of the writer. Monié had been prompted to make the portrait solely by enthusiasm and the pleasure of the task, but unhappily he was not rich. An appeal was made therefore to the "inspirations de Madame Melmoth pour engager Mr. Franklin à recompenser généreusement l'artiste." There is no evidence that Franklin was moved to do so. His accounts, however, show payments of 932 livres to "Courtney Melmoth a Political Writer" on Feb. 6, 1778, and 288 more on May 15.[5]

3. Franklin Papers (A.P.S.), *8*, no. 171.
4. Ibid., *48*, no. 73. The writer might be any lady or gentleman of the name, among the possibilities, Barnabé Augustin de Mailly (1732–ca. 1793), goldsmith and enamel painter, and Charles Jacques de Mailly (1740–1817), whose medallions on a gold snuff box are at the Walters Gallery, Baltimore.
5. Franklin Manuscripts (H.S.P.), *7, 13*.

In June the Melmoths made a hurried and secret departure from Paris, leaving a pattern of debts behind them. It is possible that the Monié portrait was a wholly independent venture, as the De Mailly letter indicates, yet it is more probable that Courtney Melmoth had undertaken to cap the incident of the Nini medallion by returning it to his patron transmuted into gold, and then had been himself unable to pay the bill. He was in London in the following year, his wife on the stage as Queen Elizabeth, and he writing what is perhaps his most lasting work, the epitaph for David Garrick's monument in Westminster Abbey.

Forrer records a medalist who signed a portrait medal of Charles Dommey, "Monié F." and who made counters for the six corporations of the merchants of Paris, 1780.[6] A Nini medallion in gilded bronze is privately owned in Philadelphia.

NÉE, FRANÇOIS DENIS (1732–1817)

1781. Line engravings. See CARMONTELLE, Nos. 2, 3.

NINI, JEAN BAPTISTE (1717–86)

To Storelli's authoritative description of the famous Nini medallions this work adds only the new discovery that the Franklin portraits were not original with Nini, but were adapted by him from drawings by two other artists.[7] The nine types recorded by Storelli are therefore listed here under two headings: NINI: WALPOLE and NINI: VALLAYER-COSTER.

That he worked from others' studies and probably never even saw his subject, does not impugn the artistry of Nini's charming portraits. His interpretation of his sources is skillful and sensitive. Great pains went into their making. Each piece was modeled in wax preparatory to the casting of the terra cotta mold. Each letter, the tiny ornaments and electrical symbols, the imaginary coat of arms devised for Franklin, and the signatures were added from separate molds, and each emerging medallion was finished by hand. The originals have a sharpness and clarity not found in imitations or modern reproductions.

There are stories of bulk shipments of the original medallions

6. L. Forrer, *Biographical Dictionary of Medallists, 4* (London, 1904–30), 126.
7. A. Storelli, *Jean Baptiste Nini. Sa Vie. Son Oeuvre. 1717–1786,* Tours, 1896.

being discovered years after they had left the factory but had failed to reach the outlet to which they had been consigned. A letter from Boulogne-sur-Mer, dated Dec. 26, 1879, apropos of the fur cap type (NINI: WALPOLE, Nos. 1, 2), mentions a consignment intended for America but held for years in the customs house at Nantes, and at that time owned by M. Anatole Montaiglon.[8] This is perhaps the same lot which Forrer describes as six cases of medallions wrapped two by two in strong paper and consigned to America in 1779. The ship was wrecked off Noirmoutier, but part of the cargo saved and brought back to the customs warehouses. In about 1830 the boxes were sold to agents of the Navy. A collector, M. Myrvoix, bought four of them and in 1876 sold two to an official at Angoulême, from whom some specimens found their way to England in 1899.[9] Storelli mentions six cases found at the Château de Chaumont where the factory had been located, and Bowen refers to a find of a hundred there in 1849.[1] Hale cites the discovery of a number in a Bordeaux warehouse in 1885, "as fresh as on the day when they were first baked."[2]

NINI: WALPOLE

    1   1777. Medallion by Jean Baptiste Nini, after a drawing by Thomas Walpole (1755–1840). Terra cotta, diam. 4⅝ in. (slight variations reported). Bas-relief profile to left, wearing fur cap. Inscribed within circular self-frame border, " . B. FRANKLIN . . AMERICAIN ." Name and title are each preceded and followed by a minute cluster of four dots. In relief on the *tranche* of the shoulder a shield emblazoned with lightning rod and thunderbolt and surmounted by a crown. Impressed on tranche of the shoulder, "NINI / F 1777." Below this, by border, in relief, "1777." On reverse, impressed number of the potter, "169." Pl. 10.

By March 1, 1777, Franklin was settled at Passy in that small house on the grounds of the Hôtel Valentinois which had been offered for his use by Donatien Le Ray de Chaumont. This gentleman was

8. Vaillant to an unnamed correspondent (Sartain Papers, H.S.P.).
9. Forrer, *4*, 271–72.
1. Storelli, p. 23. Bowen, *Centennial Celebration*, p. 460.
2. Hale, *Franklin in France*, *1*, xvi.

also owner of the faïence factory at the historic Château de Chaumont near Onzain, 122 miles to the south. Nini, the squat and jovial Italian artist, an engraver turned sculptor, had been his manager of the factory since 1772. The earliest dated reference to the Franklin medallion is in a letter of Jonathan Williams to William Temple Franklin, from Nantes, June 17, 1777, "Pray ask M. de Chaumont to let me have 3 or 4 of the Doctor's profiles which he has made at his manufacture de Fayency."[3] From this we may infer that they had first appeared in Paris a week or two earlier.

"The clay medallion of me you say you gave to Mr. Hopkinson," Franklin wrote to his daughter in Philadelphia, "was the first of the kind made in France."[4] Only the Chaumont medallions are described as "clay." Franklin refers to those made soon after at Sèvres as "china." It must have been this medallion and a Cochin engraving, sent from Passy on July 19, 1777, which Richard Bache acknowledged on Jan. 31, 1778: "I am obliged . . . for the Engraver's and potter's performances, the latter is reckoned the best likeness of you."[5]

There is one extant example of the type with recorded contemporary ownership. It is inscribed in the handwriting of the recipient, "Presented to C. W. Peale. By Mons. Gerard French Minister to the United States." Joseph Matthias Gérard de Rayneval arrived at Philadelphia on July 12, 1778, and sailed again for France on Oct. 21, 1779. His portrait was painted by Peale shortly before his departure. The medallion was sold with other Peale properties on March 27, 1919, and is now owned by the A.P.S.[6]

On Dec. 11, 1777, Franklin wrote to Thomas Walpole, an English banker who had been living in Paris but was then in London, "From a Sketch Dr. B[ancroft] had which was drawn by your ingenious & valuable Son, they have made her Medallions in *terre cuit*. A Dozen have been presented to me, and I think he has a Right to one of them. Please to deliver it to him with my Compliments."[7] It is another curious association of Edward Bancroft with portraits of the man whom he was betraying. Bancroft, from London, on

3. Franklin Papers (A.P.S.), *101,* no. 23.
4. June 3, 1779 (Smyth, *Writings, 8,* p. 347).
5. Franklin Papers (U.P.), *2,* no. 2.
6. Henkels, *Catalogue No. 1232,* no. 1. Illust.
7. From the original, courtesy of the owner, Mr. D. Holland, London.

Feb. 21, 1777, sent to Deane, in Paris, a drawing by Joseph Priestley's son, a conception of what Franklin may have looked like in his fur cap.

Walpole's drawing, which must have been made very soon after Franklin's first arrival in Paris, may have shown the fur cap. It must certainly have included the spectacles. Both would have been difficult to translate into a bas-relief profile without obscuring the likeness. Nini's final solution was to omit the glasses and add the fur cap of Jean Jacques Rousseau. The variant types, listed below, with spectacles or with liberty cap, are apparently experimental efforts to solve these problems to the satisfaction of Le Ray de Chaumont. See MONIÉ; WEDGWOOD, No. 2.

2   1777. Small model of the above. Diam. ca. 3½ in. Storelli states that in general this type has a point in relief in the last line of the frame, above the head of Franklin, and a fleur-de-lis impressed on the reverse.

3   1777. Alternative design, with spectacles. Diam. 3½ in. The bar of the spectacles is made to pass below the eye in order not to obscure it. No self-frame or inscription. Coat of arms on tranche of shoulder. Pl. 10.

4   1777. Finished model of the above. Inscribed within circular self-frame, "*FRANKLIN* *AMERICAIN*." Coat of arms on tranche of shoulder, with impressed signature, "NINI F." Below signature, "1777." Illust. in Storelli, p. 115.

5   1777. Alternative design, with liberty cap. Inscribed within self-frame, "*B * FRANKLIN * AMERICAIN*." Signed and dated as above. Illust. in Storelli, p. 117.
A copy, with a liberty cap in different form and without arms or signature, is in the Metropolitan Museum, New York.

6   1778. Altered and enlarged version of No. 1. Diam. ca. 6¼ in. Inscribed within self-frame, "B. FRANKLIN DIRIGE LA FOUDRE ET BRAVE LES TIRANS." To separate the words of the inscription Nini uses parts of his coat of arms device, a hand holding a rod, and a bolt of electricity. The coat of arms is in relief on the tranche of the shoulder and beside it the impressed

signature, "I. B. / NINI. / F." In relief, below, "I B NINI F MDCCLXXVIII."

The original Nini medallion with fur cap (No. 1) had performed with astonishing success its function of popularizing Franklin's mission to Paris, and outranks in circulation and historic importance all subsequent versions. With the consummation of the Franco-American alliance, however, in the spring of 1778, Franklin had become the official representative of a foreign power at the court of France and the publication of a likeness consistent with this ministerial status was thought appropriate. Nini therefore enlarged the likeness and omitted both cap and costume in order to give a classic dignity to the piece. His estimate of Franklin's baldness must have been based upon descriptions. Versions of the type are dated both 1778 and 1779. Its rarity, and the dating of the type which succeeded it, indicate that it was made late in the one year and discontinued early in the other.

> 7 1779. Redated repetition of the above. The signature in relief at the base reads, "I B NINI 1779." Pl. 11.

NINI: VALLAYER-COSTER

> 1 1778–79. Medallion by Jean Baptiste Nini, after a drawing by Anna Vallayer-Coster (1744–1818). Terra cotta, diam. 6¼ in. Same self-frame and inscription as NINI: WALPOLE, No. 6. Same coat of arms on tranche of shoulder. Impressed signature on base of bust, "I B NINI F / 1778." In relief below coat of arms, "I B NINI F 1779." For attribution of the type to Vallayer-Coster, see above, pp. 104–07.

The most marked difference in the new likeness is in the hair, which here falls to the shoulder. The bald area on the crown is larger, but there is a tuft of hair at the forehead. How to represent in sculpture an area of very thin hair posed a problem for the sculptors which Nini solved in this unique way.

> 2 1778–79. Recast of the above, with new inscription. Inscribed, ERIPUIT CŒLO FULMEN SCEPTRUMQUE TIRANNIS." The Latin inscription, shorter than the French, has enabled Nini with his little symbolic device of both rod and lightning.

"CŒLO" only, is flanked on one side by the rod, on the other by the electricity. The signature in relief at the base reads, "NINI F 1779."

3   1779. Recast of the above, with new date. The signature in relief at the base reads, "I B NINI F MDCCLXXIX." Pl. 11.

NOTTÉ, CLAUDE JACQUES (ca. 1754–1837)
   1779. Drawing. Unlocated.
At the Salon de la Correspondance, Feb. 11, 1779, there was exhibited "*Le portrait de M. le docteur Franklin,* dessiné au crayon, avec des allégories, par *M. Notté,* peintre, rue du Four S. Germain, chez M. Delaporte, maître charron."[8] The artist lodging at the master wheelwright's was one of many unknowns whom M. de La Blancherie delighted in introducing to the public at his Salon. He showed other works, indicating a preference for full-length figures and groups. There is no clue as to the character of his "Franklin," save that it was in crayon and had an allegorical accompaniment of some sort. It may have been from life, since the notice does not specify a copy, and Notté, as a member of Franklin's Lodge of the Nine Sisters, would have had opportunities there, and perhaps elsewhere, to observe his subject. Three years later, La Blancherie had praise for the coloring in his "Tableau représentant un jeune homme dans l'attitude de l'enthousiasme de la composition."[9]

According to Bouchot, Notté was twenty-nine years of age when he exhibited his "Jeune homme," and is seen again in the turmoil of the French Revolution, an inspired and active painter and at the same time a captain of the National Guard whose duty it was to furnish guards to the guillotine and the prisons.[10] Thieme-Becker records him as a miniaturist, a native of Nanteuil-sur-Marne, who had studied at the academy at Rouen. He exhibited at the Salons du Louvre, 1793 and 1795.

Notté is the author of a spirited representation of John Paul Jones in the midst of "le combat du 22 7bre 1779 contre le Captain Pearson," standing by his shattered bulwark, a cutlass in his right

8. *Nouvelles de la république des sciences et des arts* (Feb. 16, 1779), p. 20. Chavignerie, "Les Artistes Français," *Revue Universelle, 21* (1866), 43.
   9. *Nouvelles,* June 26, 1782, p. 188.
   10. Henri François Xavier Marie Bouchot, *La Miniature Française. 1750–1825, 1* (Paris, 1907), 130.

hand while with his left he pulls one of the five pistols from his belt, smoke rolling, guns blazing, spars falling around him. This was engraved in mezzotint by Johann Martin Will (1727–1806) at Augsburg. Will, with fine impartiality, had published in the same size portraits of George III as an admiral receiving the salutes of his fleet, and of Benjamin Franklin, after the Cochin print, with a fur-lined coat added to set off the fur cap.

PALLIÈRE, ETIENNE

> Ca. 1778. Allegorical drawing of a quayside, with figures. Pen, crayon, and sepia on paper, 12 x 16¾ in. (sight). *Owner:* Yale University, William Smith Mason Collection. Pl. 30.

Franklin and Louis XVI are brought together in this lively scene, the one in fur cap and glasses to assure recognition, the other in royal armor. The piece is a reflection of Franklin's immediate fame in the contemporary scene, with no authenticity as portraiture whatever. Pallière was a designer of Bordeaux, and the work is highly appropriate to that locale. It was published as an engraving (engraved surface 12⅝ x 17¼ in.). A water color is listed in the sale catalogue of Godefroy Mayer.[11] Yale's drawing and an engraving from it were in the Edwin Babcock Holden collection from which they were acquired by William Smith Mason.[1]

PEALE, CHARLES WILLSON (1741–1827)

> 1 Ca. 1767. Pencil sketch of Franklin (?) with a young woman. In diary. Page size, 3¾ x 6 in. See above pp. 80–1. *Owner:* A.P.S., Philadelphia. Pl. 28.

> 2 1785. Painting. Oil on canvas, 23 x 18¾ in. Brownish gray hair. Hazel eyes, with gray tone and highlights predominating over the yellow. Silver spectacles. Violet-brown coat and waistcoat. Background greenish gray. *Owner:* Pennsylvania Academy of the Fine Arts, Philadelphia. Pl. 37.

11. *No. 30. Old Paintings, Drawings, Miniatures.* This drawing is listed as no. 52, p. 10, "Franklin obteint de Louis XVI l'envoi d'une armée pour secourir les Etats-Unis d'Amérique." A second drawing is listed as no. 51, p. 10, "L'Independance de l'Amérique reconnue," with idealized portraits of Franklin, Washington, and Rochambeau. No. 52 is now owned by Mrs. John W. Baber, Arlington, Va.

1. Robert Fridenberg, *The Edwin Babcock Holden Collection. Unrestricted Public Sale* (New York, American Art Galleries, 1910), no. 1278. "The original drawing, which is included, is attributed to Desrais and the engraving is believed to be by Pallière."

Franklin returned to Philadelphia from France on Sept. 14, 1785. The portrait was painted soon after for the artist's gallery of heroes of the Revolution, and remained with "Peale's Museum" until the sale of the paintings in 1854. It was purchased at that time by Joseph Harrison, and from the sale of the collection of his son, Joseph Harrison, Jr., on Feb. 26, 1912, was purchased by its present owner.

3   1787. Mezzotint. Plate size and engraved surface, 6⅜ x 5⅝ in. Oval within rectangular shaded area. Inscribed on oval border, "HIS EXCELLENCY B. FRANKLIN L.L.D. R.R.S. PRESIDENT OF PENNSYLVANIA, & LATE MINISTER OF THE UNITED STATES OF AMERICA AT THE COURT OF FRANCE." Within border, under bust, "C.W.Peale pinxt. et Fecit 1787." The figure is to the right, reversing the pose of the painting. Pl. 37.

The print is one of a series published in the Constitutional Convention year. Peale wrote to Dr. David Ramsay on Feb. 2, 1787:

> But of late I have begun another great work, the making of mezzotinto prints from my collection of portraits of illustrious personages. This undertaking will cost me much labor, as I am obliged to take the plates from the rough and doing the whole business myself, even the impressing. I have just finished one of Dr. Franklin, which I am giving out as a specimen of the size and manner I intend this series of prints.[2]

4   1789. Painting, enlarged replica of No. 2. Oil on canvas, 36 x 27 in. Thin gray hair. Gray eyes behind silver spectacles. Dressing gown of blue flowered brocade lined with pink silk. Pinkish lavender waistcoat. Silver inkstand, lightning rod and manuscript on table. Lightning rod in hand. Background, red curtain at right and at left a cloud from which lightning strikes a building below. *Owner:* H.S.P., Philadelphia.

The manuscript on the table is covered with minute writing:

> In every stroke of lightning, I am of opinion that the stream of electric fluid, moving to restore the equilibrium between the cloud and the earth, does always previously find its passage, and mark out, as I may

2. Peale-Sellers Papers.

> say, its own course, taking in its way all the conductors
> it can find, such as metals, damp walls, moist wood,
> &c., and will go considerably out of a direct course,
> for the sake of the assistance of good conductors; and
> that, in this course, it is actually moving, tho' silently
> and imperceptibly, before the explosion, in and
> among the conductors; which explosion happens only
> when the conductors cannot discharge it as fast as they
> receive it, by reason of their being incompleat, dis-
> united, too small, or not of the best materials for con-
> ducting. Metalline rods, therefore,

The above quotation may well be the longest painted inscription in any portrait. It reveals the artist's intention and the earnestness with which he pursued it. The portrait memorializes Franklin's career as a scientist, concentrating for the purpose upon his greatest and most famous discovery, the lightning rod.

At its meeting of June 17, 1789, the A.P.S. commissioned Peale to paint a new portrait of its president, absent from the meeting because of illness. The members had been discussing his malady and its expected fatal termination, and did not realize that Peale had already presented them with a portrait (MARTIN, No. 5). Peale, who had also been absent from the meeting, assumed that a new life portrait was wanted. He went to Franklin's house and began the portrait, but found his subject too ill to pose without pain. He therefore based his work upon his likeness of 1785, showing the invalid in dressing gown rather than business suit, and bringing in the attributes designed to give the canvas its monumental character.

On Dec. 2, 1791, the society commissioned Peale to paint the portrait of its second president, David Rittenhouse. Apparently by verbal agreement, the older portrait of Franklin, Peale's copy after Martin, was hung in the newly-erected Philosophical Hall, and the new one retained by the artist. Peale may have sold it to John Barclay (1767–1816), Mayor of Philadelphia, whose son, James Joseph Barclay, presented it to the H.S.P. in 1852.

5 Undated. Painting. Unlocated.

In 1834 the painter James Reid Lambdin (1807–89) listed portraits by and after Peale in the catalogue of his museum at Louisville, Ky. Among them was a "Portrait of Franklin, an original."

> 6   1786. Miniature, copy of No. 2, by William Mercer (1773–1850). Unlocated.

Billy, the young deaf mute, whose father, General Hugh Mercer, had been killed at the Battle of Princeton, was with Charles Willson Peale as a student from 1783 to 1786. Peale wrote to his guardian, Genl. George Weedon, on April 3, 1786, that the boy had copied in miniature "my late portrait of Dr. Franklin."[3] The miniature, he wrote, had been lent to Mr. Fitzhugh of Virginia.

> 7   Ca. 1851. Miniature after No. 2, by Rembrandt Peale (1778–1860). Copper (?), rectangular, ca. 4 x 3¼ in. To left, without spectacles. Dark coat. Light waistcoat. Curtain in upper left background. Inscribed on back, "Mrs. Peale reciprocates / your kind remembrance. / Respectfully / Rembrandt Peale." Unlocated.

A letter dated Philadelphia, April 8, 1851, is the only documentation of Rembrandt Peale's work as a miniaturist:

> Mrs. DeBonneville
>   Dr Madam
>   I do not hesitate to say that it would be unpleasant to me in relation to Mr. Huntington for me to make a copy of Mercy's Dream. I am very gratified at your appreciating the Miniature on Ivory of Thomas Jefferson. This I consider the best Portrait of Mr. Jefferson I have executed. I very much appreciate your Commission to paint on Copper the leading figures in the Colonial Government Twelve in all, at the price of $150—each.
>   Mrs. Peale sends her kindest
>   remembrance.
>   I remain
>   Respectfully
>   yours
>   Rembrandt Peale.[4]

3. Ibid.
4. From the estate of John N. Laurvik. Present location unknown.

This miniature, presumably one of the twelve alluded to, was discovered in Boston in 1933, and offered for sale in Philadelphia by Edmund Bury in that year.

> 8 Ca. 1851. Drawing, related to the above. Ink and crayon on paper, 12⅝ x 10¼ in. To left, as above, without spectacles. Blue eyes. Pink in face. Lilac shadows in coat and jabot. Green tint behind each shoulder. Signed, lower right, "Rembrandt Peale." Inscribed on the back, "Please accept Mrs. Peale's / best remembrances / She reciprocates / your kind remembrance to her / R. P." Illust. in *P.M.H.B., 80* (1956), 10. *Owner*: R. Norris Williams, II, Philadelphia.

The drawing is first recorded in the catalogue of Guido Bruno's American Autograph Shop, Merion Station, Pa., April 1941. It was purchased by its present owner in 1955 from a dealer who had acquired it in New York. See MARTIN, No. 5; PINE.

PEALE, JAMES (1749–1831)
1772. Painting. See MARTIN, No. 5.

PEALE, REMBRANDT (1778–1860)
Ca. 1851. Miniature and drawing. See C. W. PEALE, Nos. 7, 8.

PELICIER, J.
1782. Line engraving. See FILLEUL, No. 3.

PERIER
Undated. Drawing. See UNKNOWN ARTIST: DRAWINGS, No. 1.

PETIT, SIMON
1781. Pastel. See GREUZE, No. 4.

PINE, ROBERT EDGE (1730–88)
Ca. 1787. Painting. Oil on canvas, 26½ x 21½ in. Three-quarters to right. Gray hair. Brown eyes. Silver spectacles. Dark gray-green chair. Olive-green background. Illust. in *Exhibition of American Portraits, Collection of John Fred-*

erick Lewis (Philadelphia, 1934), p. 108, no. 214. *Owner:* Franklin Institute, Philadelphia. Pl. 37.

William Sawitzky, reviewing this collection, believed the attribution to Pine probably correct. The work has the blurred quality which characterizes Pine's later canvases, due, apparently, to failing eyesight. According to its owner in 1924, "It was bought by me about ten years ago from the estate of Gilbert L. Parker, deceased, of Philadelphia, and is probably the last portrait of Franklin ever painted."[5] Its marked similarity to Charles Willson Peale's mezzotint of 1787 suggests that it was based upon that, with free revision from the artist's personal recollection of Franklin's appearance. It may be that the portrait was intended in part for use in Pine's projected historical painting, "The Congress Voting Independence," which was still unfinished at his death in November 1788 (see SAVAGE). Daniel Bowen purchased this work and most of the other show pieces in Pine's estate, exhibiting them first at his museum in New York, and then at his Columbian Museum in Boston where they were, by all accounts, destroyed in the fire of Jan. 15, 1803.[6] There is no evidence that Pine's half-length portrait of Franklin shared any of this history. It is not in the list of works which Pine's widow hoped to sell by lottery in 1790, nor in the list of Bowen's museum. It was probably sold, therefore, shortly before or soon after Pine's death. It came to its present owner as the gift of Mrs. John Frederick Lewis in 1933. See HOUDON, No. 8; SAVAGE.

PIOT, JACQUES SAMUEL LOUIS (1743–1812)
    Undated. Pastel. See GREUZE, No. 5.

POWERS, HIRAM (1805–73)
    Undated. Bust. See HOUDON, Nos. 10, 11.

PRATT, MATTHEW (1743–1805)
    1   Ca. 1790–95. Tavern sign. Unlocated.
Late in his career, Matthew Pratt painted signs. These, as the work

5. Eddy Papers.
6. James M. Mulcahy, "Congress Voting Independence," *P.M.H.B., 80* (1956), 80–85.

of a skilled portraitist who had studied in London with West, stood out as the best in the city and lingered long in public recollection. He shared honors here with George Rutter, whose "Franklin" after Martin, painted at about the same time, attracted much notice.[7] Pratt's, a group scene, is mentioned in Watson's *Annals* in the section on "Taverns":

> The sign of a cock picking up a wheat ear drew the public attention to Pratt, who painted also "the Federal Convention"—a scene within "Independence Hall"—George Washington, President; William Jackson, Secretary; the members in full debate, with likenesses of many of those political "giants in those days"—such as Franklin, Mifflin, Madison, "Bob" Morris, Judge Wilson, Hamilton, &c. This invaluable sign, which should have been copied by some eminent artist, and engraved for posterity, was bandied about, like the *casa santa* of Loretto, from "post to pillar," till it located in South street near the Old Theatre. The figures are now completely obliterated by a heavy coat of brown paint, on which is lettered Fed. Con. 1787.[8]

Dunlap's information on the piece was derived from Mordicai N. Noah, the critic and playwright:

> He says a prologue he wrote when a boy "was probably suggested by the sign of the Federal Convention at the tavern opposite the theatre (the old theatre in South-street). You no doubt remember the picture and the motto: an excellent piece of painting of the kind, representing a group of venerable personages engaged in public discussions. The sign must have been painted soon after the adoption of the federal constitution; and I remember to have stood 'many a time and oft' gazing, when a boy, at the assembled

7. John Binns, *Recollections of the Life of John Binns* (Philadelphia, 1854), pp. 182–83.
8. Watson, *Annals of Philadelphia, 1,* 468.

355

patriots, particularly the venerable head and spectacles of Dr. Franklin, always in conspicuous relief."[9]

There is at least some reason to suppose that this "venerable
head and spectacles" may have been based upon the silhouette of
Franklin painted by Joseph Sansom in 1789 or 1790. John Archibald Woodside, one of the most skillful and gifted of the "ornamental painters" of the early 19th century, appears to have been
an apprentice or journeyman of Pratt.[10] He opened his own studio
in 1805, the year of Pratt's death. The collection of Joseph Sansom's silhouettes came to its present owner through Woodside's
heirs, and may have been acquired by Woodside either directly
from Sansom or from Pratt. Edward Savage used the Sansom profile in his "Congress Voting Independence," but it was, of course, a
much more accurate representation of the Franklin of the Convention than the Franklin of 1776. See SANSOM, No. 1.

2   Undated. Painting. See WILSON, No. 6.

PRIESTLEY, JOSEPH, JR. (1768–1833)
    1777. Drawing. Unlocated.
Edward Bancroft wrote to Silas Deane, from London on Feb. 21,
1777, "You will see by the enclosed card (drawn by a son of 177
[Dr. Priestley]) what ideas are here formed of the appearance of 64
[Franklin] in his Canadian Cap." See CHAMBERLIN, No. 6.

RAMAGE, JOHN (ca. 1748–1802)
    Ca. 1787. Miniature. Ivory, oval, 1 7/8 x 1 7/16 in. Gray hair.
    Hazel eyes with gray tone predominating. Black spectacles.
    Blue coat and waistcoat. Background mottled light brown and
    olive. Very plain gold case to be worn as pendant. *Owner:*
    British Society for International Understanding, London. Pl.
    37.
The attribution to Ramage is supported by the pointed oval shape
of the ivory and its scalloped border in the case. Both are characteristic of his work, though Ramage did occasionally mount

9. Dunlap, *Arts of Design, 1,* 102.
10. Joseph Jackson, "John A. Woodside, Philadelphia's Glorified Sign-painter,"
P.H.M.B., 57 (1933), 59–60.

miniatures for other artists. During the whole of the period between Franklin's return to America and his death, Ramage was a resident of New York. Since Franklin remained in his home city, it must be assumed that Ramage visited Philadelphia, perhaps attracted by the gathering of the Constitutional Convention, although there is no supporting evidence of his having done so. The nearly full-face pose is similar to his "Washington" of 1789 and may have been selected as of greater dignity and force than the usual three-quarter view.

The miniature is believed to have an unbroken history of ownership in the Franklin family. In 1898 it was inherited from her father, Albert D. Bache, by Miss Caroline D. Bache and was presented by her to its present owners, occupants of Franklin's former home in Craven St., London.

REICH, JOHN MATTHIAS (1768–1833)
   1806, 1807. Medals. See SANSOM, Nos. 5, 6.

RENAUD, JEAN MARTIN (1748–1821)
   Ca. 1790. Medallion. See SÈVRES, No. 6; UNKNOWN ARTIST: DRAWINGS, No. 2.

ROSLIN, ALEXANDRE (1718–93)
   Undated. Painting. See DUPLESSIS, "Fur Collar," No. 15.

RUSH, WILLIAM (1756–1833)
   1   1787. Bust. Wood, ht. 21 in. *Owner:* Yale University Art Gallery, New Haven. Pl. 38.
The origin of the bust is recorded in the diary of Noah Webster, Philadelphia, Feb. 9, 1787: "Wait on Mr. Rush, Carver, for a Bust of Dr. Franklin, for Mr. Isaac Beers, N. Haven."[11] And on April 14: "Send to New York Dr. Franklin's Bust, Some Grammars, &c."[1] And "Paid . . . For M Isaac Beers, for a Bust of Dr. Franklin £2.6.10 Penns. currency dollars at 7/6."[2]

11. Emily Ellsworth Ford Skeel, ed., *Notes on the Life of Noah Webster, Compiled by Emily Ellsworth Fowler Ford, 1* (New York, 1912), 210.
   1. Ibid., p. 213.
   2. Ibid., p. 213n.

During this and the preceding year Noah Webster had been on terms of cordial intimacy with Franklin who had endeavored, without success, to persuade the young man to take up his project for alphabet reform.[3] Isaac Beers (1742–1813) had apparently ordered the portrait as an ornament or sign for his bookstore and publishing house in New Haven. His partner, Hezekiah Howe, published the first edition of Webster's *American Dictionary of the English Language.* The bust is made not to rest on a pedestal, but to hang from a wall, a feature which has caused it to be mistaken for a ship's figurehead.[4] It is said to have been in the possession of Yale College since 1804.[5] The earliest documentation of it is in a small notebook bearing on its cover the misleading title, "Watch / Quarter / and / station / bill. / U.S. Brig Perry / Lt. Comdr. A. H. Foote." Here Mrs. Augustus Russell Street, mother-in-law of Andrew Hull Foote, wife of the founder of the Yale School of the Fine Arts and granddaughter of Isaac Beers, has listed paintings and other objects belonging to the college, and including: "Bust of Dr. Franklin carved by Rush. This work of art, taken from life, was presented by Dr. Franklin to his friend Isaac Beers Esqr of N. H."[6] The lines of old age, so clearly apparent in the sculptured mouth, establish the correctness of Mrs. Street's statement that the work was made from life.

2   Undated. Full-length ship's figurehead. Unlocated.
Nearly thirty years after his death, Abraham Ritter recalled of William Rush:

> The figureheads of most all of our merchant ships were the work of his hand, and generally admitted to be good likenesses of their originals. His "William Penn," "General Washington," "Franklin," "Voltaire," "Rousseau," and "General Wade Hampton," with many others, were amongst the prominent specimens of his art.

3. Ibid. *2,* 471.
4. "A Franklin Figurehead by William Rush," *Antiques, 39* (1941), 83–84. Pauline A. Pinckney, *American Figureheads and their Carvers* (New York, 1940), p. 172.
5. *New Haven Register,* Nov. 22, 1953, p. 2.
6. Yale University.

They were full-length, life-like, full-dressed figures, the generals in regimentals, and the others in
plain garb.[7]

Scharf and Westcott also cite this figure of Franklin as full-length.[8]
It was probably, as Ritter suggests, a carving for a merchant ship.

3 1815. Bust-size ship's figurehead. Unlocated.
The 74-gun U.S. Ship *Franklin,* built in Philadelphia in 1815, bore
on her prow a bust of the Caffiéri type mounted in scroll work.[9]
It is documented in Navy records as by Rush.[10] The ship was considered a masterpiece of naval architecture and had a distinguished
career.[11] Her figurehead has been erroneously identified with
the bust by Rush at Yale, described above.[12] This *Franklin,* third
American warship of the name, was broken up at Portsmouth, New
Hampshire, in 1853, and replaced by a steam frigate authorized
in 1854, whose figurehead, by Woodbury Gerrish of Portsmouth, is
now at the U.S. Naval Academy.[1]

SAINT AUBIN, AUGUSTIN (1737–1807)
1777. Line engraving. See COCHIN, No. 1.

SAINT NON, JEAN CLAUDE RICHARD, ABBÉ DE (1727–91)
1778. Aquatint. See FRAGONARD, No. 2.

SANSOM, JOSEPH (1767–1826)
1 Ca. 1789. Painted silhouette. Paper, 4 13/16 x 3 11/16 in.
Profile, to right, ht. 2½ in. Inscribed below, "Dr. Benjamin Franklin, F. R. S. / Sometime Governor of Pennsyl-

7. Abraham Ritter, *Philadelphia and her Merchants* (Philadelphia, 1860), p. 104.
8. J. Thomas Scharf and Thompson Westcott, *History of Philadelphia, 2* (Philadelphia, 1884), 1066.
9. Drawing by Thomas Birch reproduced in *P.M.H.B.,* 75 (1951), 189, and in
Howard I. Chapelle, *History of the American Sailing Navy* (New York, 1949), p.
280.
10. Pinckney, *American Figureheads,* p. 85; illust. of figurehead, opp. p. 80.
11. "The Franklin 74 that carried Mr. Rush to England is confessedly (even by
the ministerial papers in England) the finest vessel in every respect in the world"
(Robert Ralston to William Bedlow Crosby, Jan. 21, 1818, Dickinson College Library).
12. "A Franklin Figurehead by William Rush," *Antiques, 39* (1941), 83–84.
1. Chapelle, p. 540. Pinckney, *American Figureheads,* p. 60.

vania / Aged 84." At upper right, in pencil, "51." Though its exact date is not determined, the profile must stand as the last life portrait of Franklin. See above, pp. 181–84. *Owner:* T. Morris Perot, III, Philadelphia. Pl. 39.

This silhouette has been removed from an album containing profiles of other Philadelphians of the time. The volume was inscribed by the father of its present owner:

> Silhouettes
> Purchased in 1899 from the Misses Woodside (1853 North Twenty-first St., Philadelphia, Pa.) being balance of a collection left them by their grandfather, an artist, who had received it from Joseph Sansom. As the collection contained no likeness of a member of the family of the Misses Woodside, they sold part of the collection to others, and the balance to me.

The ladies living at 1853 North Twenty-first were, by the city directory of 1898, Josephine and Margaret Woodside. In the next year's volume they are at a different address, with Josephine listed as "dressmaker," and it was presumably in connection with this change that the sale of the silhouettes occurred. They are believed to have been the daughters of the painter Abraham Woodside (1819–53) and the granddaughters of John Archibald Woodside, Sr. (1781–1852), the "ornamental painter" whose signs, banners, and easel paintings gained him a considerable reputation in Philadelphia.[2] Woodside would seem to have begun his career as a journeyman for Matthew Pratt, and it is possible that the profile of Franklin was used in a famous tavern sign of Pratt's representing the Constitutional Convention. See PRATT.

2   Ca. 1796–1801. Painting by Edward Savage (1761–1817), after the silhouette by Joseph Sansom, "The Congress Voting Independence." Oil on canvas, 19¾ x 26½ in. Interior of Independence Hall, Philadelphia, with a group of figures. Benjamin Franklin, full-length, seated, to left, knees crossed and hand on chin. White hair. Spectacles. Brown suit. Black shoes with silver buckles. *Owner:* H.S.P., Philadelphia. Pl. 39.

2. Jackson, "John A. Woodside," pp. 58–65.

The painting was acquired ca. 1892–93 by Charles Henry Hart from the collection of "the old Boston Museum, on Tremont Street," and was identified by him as the unfinished work of Robert Edge Pine (see PINE), afterward completed by Edward Savage.[3] The painting was purchased from him by the H.S.P. in 1904. In 1956 James M. Mulcahy reviewed the history of the picture, showing that Hart's association of it with Pine's work was not wholly substantiated, and presenting the conclusion that it is entirely a work of Edward Savage, begun in Philadelphia about 1796, with continuing additions interrupted by his death in 1817.[4] The figure of Franklin must have been added before his removal from Philadelphia in 1801. The other figures are from various sources, including Pine. Savage was not given to acknowledging his many debts to other artists, and made no acknowledgment to Pine. However, had he been able to add some luster to the work by announcing the original composition as Pine's, he would have done so. The *Catalogue of the Paintings, Portraits, Marble and Plaster Statuary . . . in the Collection of the Boston Museum* lists this work as "Signers of the Declaration of Independence and view of the Hall where it was adopted. An original picture by E. Savage."[5]

It is open to question whether Savage's profile of Franklin, the most prominent foreground figure in the painting, is taken directly from Sansom's silhouette or from some other source, such as Matthew Pratt's "Constitutional Convention" (see PRATT). It is certainly more true to Franklin as Philadelphians remembered him in his latter years than anything derived from an earlier source could have been.

> 3 Ca. 1800–17. Original copperplate engraved by Edward Savage after No. 2, unfinished. Copperplate, engraved surface, 18 9/16 x 25 11/16 in. No inscription. *Owner:* M.H.S., Boston.

Harold E. Dickson attributes the engraving to Savage himself, largely on its inexpert character.[6] In 1818 the artist's son offered

3. Charles Henry Hart, "The Congress Voting Independence," *P.H.M.B., 29* (1905), 1–14; "Edward Savage," pp. 1–19.

4. Mulcahy, "Congress Voting Independence," pp. 74–91.

5. Boston (1847), 11, no. 127.

6. Harold E. Dickson, *John Wesley Jarvis, American Painter, 1780–1840. With a Checklist of his Works* (New York, 1949), pp. 46–47, 56.

the plate for sale to John Trumbull, who rejected the offer.[7] It was presented to the M.H.S. in 1859. A number of proof impressions have been taken from it.

4   Undated. Silhouette by Augustin Amant Constant Fidèle Edouart (1789–1861), probably after No. 2.

The profile is illustrated in a group of "Portraits cut from sculpture or paintings by Edouart when visiting America," pl. 54 in E. Nevill Jackson's *Silhouette Notes and Dictionary* (London, 1938).

5, 6   1806, 1807. Medals by John Matthias Reich (1768–1833), after designs by Joseph Sansom.

Joseph Sansom's "History of the American Revolution in a series of medals" commemorates three events: "The Declaration of Independence," "The Recognition of Sovereignty," and "The Retirement of Washington." These complete the series. No others were made, though he had intended the series as "a commencement of a Medallic History of the United States."[8] His designs were carried out at the U.S. Mint by a medalist of German birth who, as Jean Mathieu Reich, had been employed in the French capital while Franklin was there, and who had settled in Philadelphia in 1800. There he was employed as engraver and diesinker at the Mint. He also engraved banknotes.[9] In later years he was a typefounder. In 1811–14 he exhibited his medals, including one of Franklin, at the Pennsylvania Academy of the Fine Arts. Joseph Sansom, while he presented examples of the medals to various institutions in the city, scrupulously withheld his name from all public announcements of them. They were for sale at the watchmaker's and jeweler's shop of Simon Chaudron, 12 South Third St.[1] Chaudron was owner of the marble bust attributed to Ceracchi (see CAFFIÉRI, No. 15). Sansom's first Franklin medal follows the Caffiéri type (see below, C). His second is after Houdon (see below, D), and he probably

7. Mulcahy, "Congress Voting Independence," p. 88.
8. Curator's Record, A.P.S., Aug. 19, 1825, statement accompanying the presentation of three silver medals.
9. James Maxwell and William Fry to Reich, Sept. 9, 1816 (Library Co. of Philadelphia).
1. *Poulson's American Daily Advertiser,* Nov. 26, 1807, p. 3, col. 4.

used the Flaxman version which he himself had brought back from London and presented to the A.P.S. (see HOUDON, No. 10).

The Sansom medals are listed below, Franklin's profile appearing in C and D. They were struck in gold, silver, bronze, and white metal, diam. 1⅝ in.

> A 1805. "Retirement of Washington, 1797." Obverse: profile of Washington. Inscribed, "G. WASHINGTON PRES. UNIT. STA." Reverse: Shield on pedestal. Inscribed, "COMMISS. RESIGNED: PRESIDENCY RELINQ." In exergue, "1797."

On Dec. 28, 1805, the *United States Gazette* reported that "A medal worthy of the illustrious Washington has been executed in Philadelphia by a German artist (J. Reich) upon the designs of a person of taste, under the inspection of the Director of the Mint, the librarian of the Philosophical Society, and other gentlemen of professional ability or acknowledged judgment."[2] In 1885 the dies were reported as still owned by Sansom's descendants.[3]

> B 1806. "Recognition of Sovereignty, 1783." Obverse: profile of Washington. Inscribed, "G. WASHINGTON C.C.A.U.S." Reverse: an eagle with an olive branch in its beak and lightning issuing from its talons hovers over a portion of the globe inscribed, "UNITED STATES." Above, "1783."

"Medal of Washington, struck for the donor," was given to Peale's Museum on Sept. 8, 1806.[4]

> C 1807. "Recognition of Sovereignty, 1783." Obverse: profiles of Franklin and Washington, to left. No legend. Franklin's portrait is after the Caffiéri bust. Reverse: same as B.

The accolated profiles recall the similar treatment of Louis XVI and his queen in Reich's memorial medal of 1793.[5]

> D 1807. "Declaration of Independence, 1776." Obverse: profile of Franklin, to right, after Caffiéri. Inscribed, "LIGHTNING

2. William Spohn Baker, *Medallic Portraits of Washington* (Philadelphia, 1885), p. 36. The Peale's Museum Accession Book (H.S.P.) corroborates under the date, Jan. 1, 1806, that the medal was struck in Dec. 1805.
3. Baker, p. 37.
4. Peale's Museum Accession Book.
5. Michel Henin, *Histoire numismatique de la Révolution française, 1* (Paris, 1826), pl. 53, nos. 545–46.

AVERTED TYRANNY REPELL'D." Reverse: a beaver gnawing at the base of an oak tree. In exergue: "1776."

"2 medals of B. Franklin, struck for the donor" were given to Charles Willson Peale's Philadelphia Museum on Nov. 10, 1807.[6] These were probably those recorded here as C and D. The Philadelphia news in *Poulson's American Daily Advertiser,* Dec. 1, 1807, reported:

> History and the Fine Arts.
> Yesterday were presented to GEORGE CLYMER, Esquire and DR. BENJAMIN RUSH, as the only surviving Representatives for Pennsylvania, in the Congress, that declared *The Independence of the United States,* fine impressions of the Medal, lately struck in Philadelphia, in commemoration of that splendid event.

OBVERSE
A head of BENJAMIN FRANKLIN,
Taken from Houdon's Bust,
INSCRIPTION
LIGHTNING AVERTED: TYRANNY REPELL'D.
REVERSE
THE AMERICAN BEAVER,
Nibbling at THE OVERSHADOWING OAK OF BRITISH
POWER, on the Western Continent.
Date
1776.[7]

The profile, of the Caffiéri type, is erroneously attributed to Houdon, a familiar error, Caffiéri being apparently unknown in America at this time.

SAUVAGE, CHARLES GABRIEL (1741–1827)
    Ca. 1785. Porcelain statuette group. See LEMIRE.

SAVAGE, EDWARD (1761–1817)
    See MARTIN, No. 6; SANSOM, Nos. 2, 3.

6. Peale's Museum Accession Book.
7. P. 3, col. 4.

SÈVRES

A prolonged search, generously aided by Marcelle Brunet, scholarly archivist of the Manufacture Nationale de Sèvres, has failed to produce any explicit record of the origin of the Sèvres portraits of Franklin. They were all small pieces of an inexpensive, popular type, intended for ready sale to enthusiasts and not at all in a class with the formal and magnificent wares upon which the reputation of the manufacture rests. There are three portrait types:

1. A circular profile medallion (No. 1), possibly after a drawing from life. The hair resembles that in the Caffiéri bust, but a more conventional costume is shown. It is here dated 1778.

2. A small bust (No. 7) reproducing Houdon's of 1778, here dated ca. 1779.

3. Two small busts (Nos. 8, 9) which appear by the features, arrangement of hair, and costume to have been copied from the Caffiéri bust, and a circular profile medallion (No. 10) apparently from the same source. These are undated.

All are in the unglazed porcelain prized by the manufacture for its resemblance to marble. The busts were made to be mounted upon socles of the famous Sèvres blue, decorated with gold and glazed.

> 1   1778. Profile medallion. Unglazed porcelain. Diam. 1⅝ in., with variations. The diam. of the model at Sèvres is 12 cm. Profile, to right. The hair covers the ear in a manner very similar to the same view of the Caffiéri bust. Stock and shirt ruff. Four buttons on the coat. Sèvres mark on the back. Some examples with self-frame ruled in gold. Pl. 12.

This is the most popular and successful of the Sèvres "Franklins," its authenticity well endorsed by contemporaries.[8] The artist is unknown. It has been wrongly attributed to Jean Martin Renaud (see below, No. 6), and to A. Stöttrup, an obscure German engraver.[9] It appears to have been issued in the late summer or autumn of 1778. On Dec. 18 of that year, one of Franklin's English friends, Christopher Baldwin, wrote to him, "I was lately

8. By Franklin's sister (Van Doren, *Benjamin Franklin and Jane Mecom*, p. 267) ; by Benjamin West, as "strong," in 1782 (Hale, *Franklin in France, 2,* 20).

9. Apparently on the basis of Stöttrup's print after the piece, in Anderson Galleries sale catalogue, New York, Dec. 18, 1928, p. 30.

shewn an excellent little profile, but it did not please me so well as that with your wig—tho I knew it instantly, and its so excellently well done, that I wished much to be possessed of it—but your friend withstood all my importunitys."[1] Writing again from London on March 5, 1779, Baldwin identified the piece. "The profile I alluded to, is I am told, about 2½ inches long, of the Royal Manufactory of Sauve—Miss Watkins promises to kiss it the moment it comes to hand—so that your experiment will certainly be tried."[2] Franklin repeated the experiment, the exact nature of which must be guessed, by sending an example also to Georgiana Shipley, who acknowledged its receipt on May 12, 1779. This piece is identified by the engraving made from it in London soon after (see below, No. 4). It may be assumed that this also is the medallion which Mané had copied in Oct. 1778 (see below, No. 2). It is certainly also that which Pierre Eugène du Simitière was carefully mounting in his collection in Philadelphia in September 1779, on a ground of black velvet in a round black frame with the inner molding gilded, and which he entered in his record as "a small profile bust in basso relievo representing Dr. Franklin made of the French porcelain of Seves [sic] near Paris (Mr. Joseph Wharton)."[3] Joseph Wharton, Jr., had visited Franklin at Passy in the spring of that year. On Dec. 11, 1779, Michael Hillegas was writing from Philadelphia to obtain examples of both the Nini and Sèvres medallions: "two or 3 of the several Busts of Doctor Franklin which are done in a kind of brownish or Redish Earth & put in Round Frames, like pictures, about 3 inches in diameter, Also of those done in a kind of China of ye same size."[4]

Franklin kept a supply of the medallions at hand, and gave them as souvenirs to friends and callers. This practice appears to have begun in the spring of 1779 and to have continued through his residence in France. He sent his "little Head in China" to Betsy Partridge on Oct. 11, 1779. This must have been the "white medallion of Dr. Franklin" mentioned in Jane Mecom's will.[5] The iron cast-

1. Franklin Papers (A.P.S.), *12*, no. 205.
2. Ibid., *13*, no. 168.
3. *P.H.M.B.*, *13* (1889), 364.
4. Ibid., *29*, 237.
5. Van Doren, *Benjamin Franklin and Jane Mecom*, p. 352.

ing over the fireplace of Catherine Ray Greene in Warwick, R.I., had probably been made from Mrs. Mecom's piece.[6] Only one of the gift medallions has continued in family ownership. This was given to Capt. Timothy Folger (1732–1814) when he visited his relative at Passy, and is now owned by Mrs. Harry Armstrong, his descendant.[7] See TASSIE, No. 2; WEDGWOOD, No. 3.

2 1778. Copy of No. 1 by Mané. Unlocated.
On Oct. 18, 1778, M. Mané wrote to Franklin that he had presented to the Académie Royale des Sciences "plusieurs Medaillons éxécutés au Tour" or turned on the lathe, that Franklin's portrait was one of the number, and that, with this letter, he was enclosing an identical example of it.[8] The likeness, he wrote, had been taken from "un modèle en Porcelaine de la Manufacture Royale." The letter is docketed, "M. Mané with an Ivory Medallion."

Beginning in the following year Mané appears frequently as an exhibitor in Pahin de La Blancherie's Salon de la Correspondance, showing both models of heavy mechanical equipment and fine jeweler's work such as watch cases and cane heads.[9] He is listed variously as goldsmith, jeweler, and mechanician, and his address given as the rue des Arcis. The Salon had been established in May 1778, with the endorsement of a committee of the Académie des Sciences, headed by Franklin. Although the work does not mention Mané, it is possible that the medallion he had presented to the Académie is the original from which an engraving of a turned medallion copied from the Sèvres piece was made for the *Manuel du tourneur, ouvrage dans lequel on enseigne aux amateurs, la manière d'exécuter sur le tour à pointes, à lunette, en l'air, excentrique, à guillocher, quarré, à portraits & autres, tout ce que l'art a produit de plus ingénieux & de plus agréable,* Paris, 1796.[10]

6. Illust. in *A.P.S. Library Bulletin* (1946), opp. pp. 30, 31.

7. Illust. in Will Gardner, *The Clock that Talks and What It Tells* (Nantucket Island, Mass., 1954), p. 100. Here erroneously dated 1769. Timothy Folger's oath of allegiance to the United States (Franklin Papers, A.P.S., *74,* no. 15) is dated Passy, July 8, 1781.

8. Franklin Papers (A.P.S.), *12,* no. 54.

9. *Nouvelles de la république des arts et des lettres,* Feb. 9, 1779, p. 12; Feb. 23, 1779, p. 29; June 15, 1779, p. 149; June 22, 1779, p. 158; July 10, 1782, p. 205.

10. *2,* Pl. 35.

3   Ca. 1779. Copy of No. 1, painted in grisaille, oval, with gold border, on Sèvres coffee cup. Inscribed, "BENJAMIN FRANKLIN." Pl. 12.

Two examples are known, one at the Victoria and Albert Museum, and one owned by Mrs. Herbert A. May, Washington. The latter is accompanied by its saucer, similarly decorated at the center with emblems of the Franco-American alliance. Pierre Verlet suggests that these may have been from the set purchased in 1779 by the Comte de Saint-Simon.[1]

4   1779. Line engraving after No. 1, by unidentified artist. Profile, to left, without border or background. Plate size, 5½ x 3¾ in. Height of engraved portrait, 3 3/16 in. "B. FRANKLIN, L.L.D. F.R.S. / Born in Boston in New England, Jan 17th. 1706 / NON SORDIDUS AUCTOR NATURAE VERIQUE."

The print appeared as frontispiece to Franklin's *Political, Miscellaneous and Philosophical Pieces,* London, 1779. Benjamin Vaughan, editor of the work, wrote to Franklin on June 17, 1779, that it had been taken from a large medallion with the same likeness as that on the smaller piece which Franklin had sent to Georgiana Shipley.[2] Years later he declared that he had selected this likeness for his frontispiece as the best then available. "After seeing a variety, I chose the face and figure most like him."[3] Franklin gave a copy of the book to his sister, who also praised the portrait. "Your Profile," Jane wrote, "Done more to your Likenes than any I have heartofore seen."[4]

It is probable that many of the subsequent engravings of the type were made from this print rather than from the ceramic piece. The profile appeared, to the right, with the addition of a background and allegorical scene in an engraving by Robert Pollard (1755–1838) to illustrate a hostile account of Franklin in the *Political Magazine, 1* (1780), 631 (Pl. 13). In Italy it was copied by the Florentine engraver, Carlo Lasinio, in a print published in

1. Pierre Verlet, *Sèvres. Le XVIII Siècle* (Paris, 1953), p. 42.
2. Franklin Papers (A.P.S.), *14,* no. 190.
3. To Jared Sparks, June 17, 1835 (Sparks Papers).
4. Van Doren, *Benjamin Franklin and Jane Mecom,* p. 267. Illust. in Carl Van Doren, *Jane Mecom,* New York, 1950.

1783.[5] In Germany it was engraved by C. G. Nestler, 1780, and by Daniel Berger (1744–1824) in 1783.[6] In America an engraving, to left, in an oval border, was made by John Norman (ca. 1748–1817) in 1782. The motto, which was repeated in many engravings, had been suggested to Benjamin Vaughan by the Bishop of Saint Asaph.

> 5   Ca. 1779. Profile medallion after No. 1, by Richard Champion (1743–91). Porcelain, oval, 8¾ x 7⅛ in. (British Museum). The profile, to right, is surrounded by a gilded wreath and this by a frame of sculptured flowers. Also published without ornamentation, oval, 3 x 2½ in., white figure on blue ground (Fogg Museum).

Hugh Owen states that the attribution of the plaque to Champion is established by the existence of a small piece from the same mold, without the border but with the Bristol mark on the back.[7] The floral decoration was characteristic of the Bristol pottery founded by Richard Champion, Whig politician and active friend of the American cause, who had founded the business in 1773 in competition with Wedgwood and the Staffordshire potters. Five years later, due largely to the effect of the war on business, his fortunes were at a low ebb. In November 1780 he was offering his patents for sale to Wedgwood.[8] In 1781 he sold out to another Staffordshire firm, and a few years after emigrated to South Carolina where he became something of a public figure.[9] He presented two examples each of his Franklin and Washington medallions to George Washington.[10] An example which is still preserved in the Franklin family acquired a legendary origin. The will of Catherine, widow of Dr. William Bache, Jan. 31, 1821, bequeathed it "To my daughter

5. Pace, *Benjamin Franklin and Italy,* p. 291 ; illust. p. 99.

6. *The Edwin Babcock Holden Collection,* compiled by Robert Fridenberg (New York, American Art Galleries, April, 1910), no. 1429.

7. Hugh Owen, *Two Centuries of Ceramic Art in Bristol* (Gloucester, 1873) p. 93.

8. Farrer, *Letters of Josiah Wedgwood,* p. 604.

9. G. H. Guttridge, ed., *The American Correspondence of a Bristol Merchant, 1766–1776. Letters of Richard Champion* (Berkeley, Cal., 1934), pp. 4–7.

10. Ibid., p. 5. Anna Wells Rutledge reports that one of these was in the Lewis sale, purchased by A. G. Murphy (Henkels catalogue, p. 15, no. 657, illust.), and another mentioned in the will of Eleanor Custis Lewis, 1850, "Profile in flowers of B. Franklin for C. & L. Conrad."

Sarah Bache I give a Seve [*sic*] china medallion of Doctor Franklin, which was presented by Louis the Sixteenth of France to the daughter of Doctor Franklin."[1]

> 6   Undated. Profile medallion, altered copy of No. 1, by Jean Martin Renaud (1748–1821). Terra cotta, diam. 3 in. (without frame). Bust three-quarters to right, head in profile to right. Drapery over shoulders and chest bare. Under the bust a liberty of fur, dividing the inscription, "VI RS." Ornamental circular border. Signed, faintly, on tranche of shoulder, "J. M. Renaud." The whole set in a circular wooden frame.
> *Owner:* Metropolitan Museum of Art, New York.

The discovery of this unique portrait in a Paris bric-a-brac shop by George A. Lucas was announced by Paul Leicester Ford in May 1894.[2] Charles Henry Hart illustrates and describes it in his article on the Franklin portraits in *McClure's Magazine, 8* (1897), 267, giving the over-all diameter as 5 inches. Hart assigns the date 1785 to the piece, as George Whately of London acknowledged the receipt of a medallion from Franklin on July 22, and as that year is close to the first dated record of Renaud's work in Paris. This is insecure evidence, as there is nothing to show that Franklin's gift was not one of the Sèvres pieces of which he kept a supply at hand. It is more reasonable to assign the work to Renaud's active period during the French Revolution and the Empire. The inscription, "VIRS," must have been borrowed from that on the frame of the original Duplessis portrait and repeated in engravings, "VIR." The obvious error of the fourth letter may account for the rarity of the medallion.

Renaud's little bas-reliefs, shown at the Salon de la Correspondance in 1787, were praised for tasteful design and precise execution, declared to be "très-spirituelle," and much sought after by connoisseurs.[3] He exhibited frequently at the Louvre from 1798 to

1. Copy of will (A.P.S.). Sarah's husband, Dr. Hodge, repeats the statement in a letter to Jared Sparks, Oct. 19, 1835 (Sparks Papers). The plaque is reproduced in the catalogue, *Benjamin Franklin and his Circle* (New York, Metropolitan Museum of Art, 1936), no. 68.
2. "A New Portrait of Franklin," *Scribner's Magazine, 15* (1894), 617–18. Illust.
3. *Nouvelles de la république des sciences et des arts* (March 8, 1787), p. 132.

1817. He is said to have been employed as a modeler at Sèvres.[4] Impressed by the similarity of his new discovery to the Sèvres medallions, George A. Lucas attributed these also to Renaud. To establish the attribution he had both Sèvres types (Nos. 1, 10) cast in metal with "J. M. RENAUD" inscribed under the shoulder in the manner of a signature.

> 7 Ca. 1779. Bust, after Jean Antoine Houdon's bust of 1778. Unglazed porcelain. Published in three heights, 40, 26, and 18 cm. On socle of Sèvres blue, decorated with gold.

The model preserved at Sèvres is a cast of Houdon's "Franklin" of 1778, with the signature, "houdon 1778." The earliest documentation of a Sèvres bust of Franklin may refer to this piece. It is a letter of April 10, 1779, from Richard Bennett Lloyd in London to William Temple Franklin, asking, "if you will get me His Bust (One of those made of the Seve [sic] China) have it set on a blue stone with a gold border."[5]

> 8 Undated. Bust, by unidentified artist. Unglazed porcelain, ht. 8⅞ in. Head very slightly turned to right. Hair covers the ears almost entirely. A scarf, tight about the neck, extends from throat into the waistcoat. Two buttons on the coat and one on the waistcoat. Mounted on blue socle, ht. 2⅛ in., marked in gold, "Franklin" (Yale University, Mason Collection). The model at Sèvres is 39 cm. high; three buttons on the coat. Pl. 14.

This and the two pieces described below appear to be copies from the Caffiéri bust, with slight variations from the original and from each other. On April 28, 1777, just after the completion of Caffiéri's work, Franklin dined at Sèvres in company with Jean Jacques Bachelier, head of the decorative studios there, M. Parent, Director of the Manufacture Royale, and Le Ray de Chaumont.[6] Bachelier, a philanthropist and connoisseur of wealth and taste, was founder of the Ecole Royale de Dessin, a charitable drawing school

---

4. Forrer, *Biographical Dictionary of Medallists*. Marcelle Brunet, archivist of the Manufacture Nationale, reports no record of his presence there.

5. Franklin Papers (A.P.S.), *47*, no. 145.

6. Bachelier to Franklin, April 27 (Ibid., *5*, no. 168). Their host was Melchior (?) Parent; the Sèvres archives have no contemporary record of his full name.

for the working class, and his liberal educational projects were the subject of later correspondence with Franklin. One of them was to be the establishment of a technical school in America. It is possible that these three pieces, less attractive in characterization than the Sèvres medallion of 1778 (No. 1) or the Sèvres bust after Houdon (No. 7), were first attempts, later rejected, as some of the Nini medallions had been. It is hardly credible, however, that the Manufacture Royale would have issued a Franklin portrait before the official recognition of the new republic. The government, as with Borel's print, was careful to avoid any premature suggestion of alliance. Again, there is a complete lack of documentation or of early copies of these pieces. Finally, the large size of the buttons on the coat suggests a date in the 1790s. The three works are almost certainly posthumous echoes of Franklin's popularity.

The portrait has been attributed to Josse François Joseph Leriche (1738–1812), apparently on the basis only of his long association with Sèvres. There is no supporting evidence in the Sèvres archives or museum. Although Caffiéri's bust, shown at the Salon of 1777, was purchased by the state, there is also no evidence that he was required, as was generally stipulated, to provide Sèvres with a small model for reproduction in biscuit. Other models of his are preserved there, marked with his characteristic signature, "Fait par J. J. Caffiéri," and the date.[7]

> 9   Undated. Bust, by unidentified artist. Unglazed porcelain, ht. 7⅜ in. Likeness the same as the above, with minor variations. Same arrangement of scarf. Three large buttons on right side of coat, half only of the lowest. Two buttons on the waistcoat. Finished below on a small square base on which is impressed "FRANKLIN" within an oblong border. On blue socle 2⅝ in. high (Yale University, Mason Collection). See above, No. 8.

> 10   Undated. Profile medallion, by unidentified artist. Unglazed porcelain, diam. of model at Sèvres, 15 cm. Profile, to right. The likeness follows that of the busts above (Nos. 1, 2), with minor variations. Scarf around the neck similarly ar-

7. Guiffrey, *Les Caffiéri,* p. 299.

ranged. Three buttons on the coat. Pl. 14. See above, No. 8. See ELMER.

STAFFORDSHIRE

Ca. 1762–72. Statuette, attributed to Ralph Wood (1716–72). Cream-colored porcelain, ht. 13½ in. The stout figure stands on a square pedestal. The right hand is extended as if holding the kite string, and the head looks upward as toward the kite. The left hands holds a book against the hip. A fur-lined mantle extends from the left shoulder to the feet. A medal is suspended by a ribbon about the neck. Pl. 44.

The figure honors Franklin's fame more clearly than Franklin himself. The costume is that of a Continental gentleman of the early years of the 18th century, linking the piece inescapably to the German factories where the art of pottery sculpture had been revived, with German imports and imitations nourishing the growth of the industry in England. The English potter has here apparently taken the elements of a German figure and rearranged them to honor the famous American. The medal might pass for the Royal Society's Copley award. The robe might represent Franklin's academic degrees. The Metropolitan Museum owns an example in which the robe is trimmed with royal ermine. The same figure with a different pose of the head is recorded. The pedestal is similar to that of the "Gamekeeper" and other figures attributed to Ralph Wood of the well-known family of craftsmen in this medium. While the likeness has no authenticity or importance as a portrait, it has gained acceptance. Frank Falkner, in his *Wood Family of Burslem,* praises "the lifelike expression of the American philosophe."[8] See SUZANNE.

SUZANNE, FRANÇOIS MARIE (ca. 1750–ca. 1802)

1793. Statuette. Terra cotta, ht. 14¾ in. The figure stands on a flat base by a broken column. His right hand holds a scroll. His hat is under his left arm. Pl. 29.

The figure first appeared in the Salon of 1793, listed in the *Livret*

8. London (1912), p. 16.

as no. 62 and as "Francklin en pied. Terre cuite, de 14 pouces de proportion. Par Suzanne."

The artist, son of a sculptor active in mid-18th century Paris, had studied in Rome and had been a friend of Jacques Louis David, whom he again accompanied to Italy in 1779. His figure of Franklin followed others of Rousseau, Voltaire, and Mirabeau which he had offered in homage to the legislative assembly of July 11, 1792. Though a posthumous likeness, the portrait was acceptable to those who had known Franklin well by sight, as Suzanne himself may have done, and is important as one of the few representations of the complete figure.

Examples of the terra cotta are at the Metropolitan Museum and the Walters Gallery. It proved enormously and immediately popular, and has been repeated in bronze and other metals, in marble, plaster, china (including the Staffordshire "Old English Gentleman" and "General Washington"), and in every size from miniature to life. Numerous variations of costume and pose occur. Perhaps the earliest engraving from it is a thoroughly Anglicized version, "BENJAMIN FRANKLIN L. L. D.," published by H. D. Symonds, Aug. 27, 1796.

TARDIEU, PIERRE ALEXANDRE
    See DUPLESSIS, "Fur Collar," No. 3; "Gray Coat," No. 1.

TASSIE, JAMES (1735–99)
Rudolf Erich Raspe in his *Descriptive Catalogue* of the work of Tassie, London, 1791, states that "Mr. Tassie has long modelled Portraits in Wax, in imitation of those executed by the ingenious Mr. Gosset. But as these are liable to be defaced, and wishing to render them perpetual, he was led to mould and cast them in his beautiful, hard, white, Enamel Paste."[9] Tassie had worked for Wedgwood from 1769 to 1774, and the two "Franklins" attributed to him are from models used also by Wedgwood.

    1   Undated. Profile medallion after Isaac Gosset. An exact copy of GOSSET, No. 1. Pl. 9.

    2   Undated. Intaglio seal, after SÈVRES, No. 1. Paste, oval,

9. *1,* 35–36.

1 1/16 x 13/16 in. Inscribed below, "PLUS ULTRA." An example is in the Scottish National Portrait Gallery.

THOURON, JACQUES (1749–89)
See WEYLER.

TRUMBULL, JOHN (1756–1843)

1   Ca. 1786–96. "The Declaration of Independence." Oil on canvas, 20⅞ x 30⅞ inches. Group portrait of thirty men, with the standing figure of Franklin in left center. Gray-white hair. Blue eyes. Dark gray dress. *Owner:* Yale University Art Gallery, New Haven. Pl. 27.

Sweeping aside an impressive fabric of spurious "Franklins" attributed to Trumbull, Theodore Sizer accepts as genuine only Trumbull's early copy of the famous fur cap print (see COCHIN, No. 3) and the figure in the "Declaration." That figure was not painted from life, and whatever preparatory studies may have been made are lost. Having abandoned his military career and formed his determination to become an artist, Trumbull embarked for London. He landed at Nantes in mid-May 1780, proceeded to Paris, and crossed to England in July. He carried a letter of introduction from his father to Benjamin Franklin, and Franklin at his departure gave him a letter of introduction to West. His portrait was based upon the personal recollection formed in this brief period, reinforced by the work of others, particularly the miniature after Duplessis which Franklin had sent to Georgiana Shipley.

In November, Trumbull was arrested in London in retaliation for the execution of John André, and held prisoner until the following summer. During his confinement he continued to paint and was visited by friends.[10] His arrest caused consternation among the Americans in the city, and was particularly alarming to Thomas Digges who had been aiding escaped American prisoners as Franklin's agent and whose name Trumbull had inadvertently mentioned in his examination by the police. Coming from France that spring, Digges had delivered the miniature which Franklin had sent as his gift to Miss Shipley. He had importuned Franklin for a portrait for himself, receiving in reply Franklin's well-known protest against

10. Sizer, *Autobiography of Colonel John Trumbull,* pp. 72n., 73n.

the tedium of posing for artists. On Aug. 18 he had sent to Franklin "porcelain representations of Washington & yourself," which may have been the Richard Champion pieces.[1] Digges, reporting to Franklin on Nov. 21, described Trumbull as an American gentleman "whom I never heard of before."[2] On Dec. 29 he wrote again under one of his numerous aliases, revealing a larger acquaintance with Trumbull's affairs.

> The porcelain is meant for you; & is the proof of the skill of a young artist here who may soon visit the person whose likeness it is.
>
> Mr. T——ll, before his misfortune, finished an exceeding good picture of W——n—full length & very much admired as a good painting. It is now engraving by a masterly hand & the print will be out in a few days. I am to have a companion to that picture, full length also, of the hoary headed F——n; which will also be engraved. I am sure it will be an equal good one to that already done of W——n. I know neither of these illustrious personages, but I am sure I shall be happy in holding in view good likenesses of the two first men of America. I think the young artist will be much helpt in the likeness of the lat[t]er by the little medallions, the miniature lately sent to a young lady in a snuff box, by former pictures in possession of Friends, & by the artist's recollection of the hoary head.[3]

Thus it appears that Trumbull had at this time a portrait of Franklin under consideration. His release from prison, however, was conditioned upon his leaving the country, and he chose to return to America. Not until January 1784 did he arrive again in

1. H.S.P.
2. William Bell Clark, "In Defense of Thomas Digges," *P.H.M.B.*, 77, 422.
3. H.S.P. Trumbull's "Washington," painted for L. de Neufville, a young Dutch merchant in sympathy with the American cause, is now at the Metropolitan Museum of Art (Sizer, *The Works of Colonel John Trumbull*, p. 62). The engraving, a mezzotint by Valentine Green, is dated Jan. 15, 1781. The companion print of Franklin did not appear.

West's studio. There he found Franklin's portrait again a matter of immediate interest in connection with West's proposed historical series on the American Revolution, the series which soon after devolved from West upon his student and became so large an object in Trumbull's later life.

He had no other meeting, however, with Franklin. He was again in Paris in 1785, but a month after Franklin's departure. In 1790 he reached Philadelphia just too late again. Franklin had received his letter enclosing that in which West commended the project and the young artist's "fource of genius & industry," but Franklin died a month before his arrival in the city.[4]

The Franklin of the "Declaration," in contemplative mood, glasses in hand, and dressed in simple black, is a characterization of strength and originality. The Duplessis is clearly its principal source but not obtrusively so. Only the detail of the eye color is clearly at fault.

> 2   1818. Replica of the above in life size. *Owner:* The United States, Rotunda of the Capitol.

TUSSAUD, MME. FRANÇOIS (MARIE GROSSHOLTZ) (1761–1850)
    See CURTIUS.

UNKNOWN ARTIST
    1   Amelia Barry, original owner. Unlocated.
One of his English friends, Amelia Barry, wrote to Franklin on July 3, 1777, in terms of tender regard. "Your Portrait, which receives additional value from being your gift, is the capital piece of my closet."[5] The picture may have been one of the mezzotints by Fisher after Chamberlin, of which Franklin had given many to friends.

> 2   A club in Marseilles, original owner. Unlocated.
On Dec. 14, 1778, three members of the Société du Parnasse in Marseilles wrote to inform Franklin of the convivial honors which

4. West to Franklin, Oct. 8, 1789; Trumbull to Franklin, Nov. 25, 1789 (Franklin Papers, A.P.S.), *36,* nos. 180, 186.
5. Ibid., *6,* no. 92.

had been offered him by the membership, glass in hand, on the previous day:

> Vous étiez au milieu de nous. Oui, Monsieur, votre
> portrait entouré de laurier étoit apposé dans l'endroit
> le plus apparent; à coté étoit le pavillon insurgent.
> Ce grave, ce vénérable franklin souriot à notre fête,
> il se joignoit à nos plaisirs, il prenoit part à notre
> joye. De ses yeux il partoit un feu électrique qui pas-
> soit jusqu'a nos âmes.[6]

To this Franklin returned a cordial reply. *L'Espion anglois* published a notice of the group under the earlier date, Marseilles, May 19, 1778.

> L'insurrection des Americains, Milord, a causé une
> si vive émotion dans Marseilles, qu'on y a institué
> une fête pour en conserver & célébrer la mémoire à
> perpetuité: c'est un *Club* à la manière angloise; il est
> composé de treize personnes, emblême de treize colo-
> nies unies. . . . J'ai été frappé en entrant dans la salle
> à la vue d'une foule de portraits représentant tous
> d'illustres insurgens, mais celui de M. Franklin a
> surtout attiré mes regards à cause de la devise: *Eri-
> puit coelo fulmen, sceptrum que Tyrannis:* elle y
> étoit inscrite depuis peu, & chacun en admira la
> vérité sublime.[7]

6. "You were in our midst. Yes, Monsieur, your portrait, wreathed in laurel, held the place of honor; beside it was the insurgent banner. This grave, this venerable Franklin smiled upon our festival, he joined in our pleasures, he partook of our joy. From his eyes he cast an electric fire which flowed into our souls." (Ibid., *12*, no. 196½a.)

7. "The insurrection of the Americans, Milord, has stirred such lively emotions at Marseilles, that they have instituted a fete to preserve and honor its memory into perpetuity: it is a *Club* of the English sort; it is composed of thirteen persons, representing the thirteen united colonies . . . I was struck on entering the hall by the sight of a crowd of portraits of all the famous insurgents, but that of M. Franklin caught my eye particularly because of the inscription: *Eripuit coelo fulmen, sceptrumque Tyrannis:* this was written not long ago, and everyone admired its sublime verity." *L'Espion anglois, 9* (1782–84), 79–81. Alfred Owen Aldridge has identified this as the earliest dated printing of the Turgot epigram.

3 Benjamin Smith Barton (1766–1815), original owner. Unlocated.

The minutes of the Pennsylvania Academy of the Fine Arts, March 13, 1816, record that "Mr. Pennington stated, that agreeably to the request of the late Dr. Barton he presented to the Academy two pictures, one of the Mr. Locke and the other Dr. Franklin, which belonged to the Doctor in his lifetime." Edward Pennington, an administrator of the estate, was also a director of the academy. In the inventory of the estate, which included a number of pictures, the only identified portrait is the "Picture of Dr. Franklin" hanging in the front room on the second story, a bedroom, and valued by the appraiser at $3.00.[8]

The academy long owned and exhibited its portrait of John Locke, variously attributed to Vandyck, Lely, and Kneller, but there is no record of its ownership of this portrait of Franklin.

UNKNOWN ARTIST : CARICATURE

Only the Philadelphia caricatures, made while Franklin was in the city, have a genuine value as portraiture. They present for recognition a face and figure known to all. The innumerable others use the prints or plaques as sources and give us only an idea as to which of these were most current at the place of publication. An exception is the French "Magnétisme Dévoilé" of 1784, an original likeness, though it depends on Franklin's spectacles as the point of recognition.

1 1764. Etching. Plate size, 7⅛ x 9⅞ in. Three couplets inscribed across the base:

> [Left]
> The German bleeds & bears ye Furs
> Of Quaker Lords & savage Curs

> [Center]
> Th'Hibernian frets with new Disaster
> And kicks to fling his broad brim'd Master

8. Register of Wills, Philadelphia.

[Right]
But help at hand Resolves to hold down
Th'Hibernian's Head or tumble all down

Israel Pemberton, representing the Quakers and holding a belt of wampum in his hand, rides the Scotch-Irish "Hibernian" and leads by the nose the blindfolded German on whose back an Indian is mounted. The Indian on *his* back carries a pack of goods marked with the initials of Israel Pemberton. Franklin stands at the left holding a paper which reads, "Resolved / ye Prop:ʳ / a knave / & tyrant / N C D / gov:ʳ Do." Pl. 6.

"Such a necklace of Resolves!" Franklin had written from Pennsylvania to a friend in London on March 30, 1764, "and all *nemine contradicente,* I believe you have never seen."[9] "N C D" abbreviates the then familiar Latin phrase for unanimous passage, which Franklin applies to the Assembly's condemnation of proprietor and governor. Franklin is himself the "help at hand" dubiously referred to in the last couplet. Between his legs is Joseph Fox, represented much as Henry Fox had been in a British caricature of 1762.[10] The frontier settlements deeply resented the independent "Friendly Association" headed by Israel Pemberton and Joseph Fox, which had supplied the Indians with goods in a privately supported effort to maintain the traditional Quaker policy of amity with them. Fox was accused of complicity in the Indian atrocities, and was said to have sent the friendly Indians who came as fugitives to Philadelphia to the barracks in order to augment his own fees as Barrack Master. See above, pp. 61–3.

2   1764. Etching. Engraved surface, 7¾ x 10 in. At the left, Israel Pemberton and an Indian squaw. In the center the "Paxton Boys" advance upon the defenders of the fugitive Indians, Joseph Fox in the foreground, the Friends meeting house in the background. At the right Franklin observes the scene from his library, wearing darkened glasses to suggest faulty vision. An appropriate verse of three couplets is inscribed under each part of the scene. Pl. 6.

Here, as in No. 1, Israel Pemberton's friendly interest in the In-

9. Smyth, *Writings, 5,* 225.
10. Long, *Mr. Pitt and America's Birthright,* opp. pp. 137, 409.

dians is given a broad and unfriendly interpretation. His title, "King Wampum," reflects resentment of the fact that in presenting the gifts of the Quaker "Friendly Association," he had received belts of wampum in return and, it was believed, had been mistaken by the Indians for a figure more powerful than the provincial officials. Pemberton was said to have made advances to a squaw at one of the Indian conferences, and she to have used the opportunity to steal his watch.

Some of the soldiers called out to defend the Indian refugees had, during a shower of rain, taken refuge in the Friends meeting house on High St. It was thereupon dubbed in derision "the new Barrack," in contradistinction to the barracks of 1758 in which the Indians were being held under a guard of regular troops. See above, pp. 61–3.

> 3   1764. Line engraving. Plate size, 7 1/2 x 12 15/16 in. No title. The plate derides and attacks the Quakers. At the left Israel Pemberton gives tomahawks to the Indian warriors. At the right Pemberton reenacts his affair with the squaw, featured also in No. 2. Joseph Fox approaches the group at the table with a threat to turn Presbyterian again. One of the seated Quakers expresses a doubt that Franklin's pamphlet, *Cool Thoughts,* will have warmth enough to affect the Paxton spirit. Franklin, in right center, watches the discordant scene with pleasure, exclaiming, "Fight Dog Fight Bear I am Content / If I but get the Gover." His wealth and preoccupation with science are represented by a purse in his right hand marked "Pensilvanᵃ Money" and a scroll in his left addressed "To Doctr. Pringle." See above, pp. 61–3. Pl. 7.

> 4   1764. Line engraving. Plate size, 9 x 14¾ in., with printed title, "The COUNTER-MEDLY, being a proper ANSWER to all the DUNCES of the MEDLY and their ABETTORS," and a long poem, the whole occupying a broadside of 22 x 17 in. Franklin is depicted in right center, observing, "See how these Palatine Boors / herd together." The devil, behind him, holds his *Narrative* and *Cool Thoughts,* while promising, "Thee shall be Agent BEN / For all my Realms." Pl. 7.

The long poetic effusion beneath the picture also plays upon the unfriendly reference Franklin had made to the German population as "Palatine Boors" in his *Observations Concerning the Increase of Mankind,* published in 1755:

> BLUSTRADO next presents himself to View,
> To his own int'rest and the Devil's true,
>   "They're Rogues and Rascals, Scoundrels, *German Boors,*
> Egregious Villains, perjur'd Sons of Whores,
> Who would turn honest Franklin out of doors."

The broadside belongs to the political campaign leading to the election of Oct. 1, 1764. It answers one of similar style and dimensions which had supported the party with which Franklin was allied, *The Election, a Medley, Humbly Inscribed to Squire Lilliput, Professor of Scurrility.* Squire Lilliput, otherwise the schoolmaster David James Dove, had probably had a large part in the contrivance of this rebuttal. Both apparently had the services of the same engraver.[1] See above, pp. 61–3.

> 5   Ca. 1784–85. Line engraving, "Le Magnétisme dévoilé." Plate size, 11⅝ x 13 in. Engraved surface, 10 1/16 x 11 7/8. Franklin, entering from the left with his colleagues, holds up the "RAPPORT / DES / COMMISS / AIRES," the rays from which shatter the tub and scatter the devotees and evil spirits of animal magnetism. Pl. 30.

Franklin's signature headed those of the nine eminent scientists whose *Rapport des commissaires chargés par le Roi, de l'examen du magnétisme animal,* first issued on Aug. 11, 1784, exposed the fraudulence and ended the activities of Friedrich Anton Mesmer and his partner, Charles Deslon. The mesmerists had been active and successful in Paris for six years. A central feature of their practice was a large wooden tub, from which metal rods extended to the patients, while soft music played.

The figure of Franklin belongs to no previous type, and yet depends for recognition upon the spectacles and the fur-lined coat. The coat may have been copied from the Lemire statuette. This likeness appears to have been the inspiration of the artist of a small drawing of Franklin presenting his grandson to Voltaire, appar-

1. The broadside is at the H.S.P. and the Library Company of Philadelphia. William Dunlap mentions this piece as one seen in his childhood, *Arts of Design, 1,* 148.

ently the sketch-design for an illustration. The original is in the Bibliothèque Nationale, and a reproduction in Willis Steell's *Benjamin Franklin of Paris* (New York, 1928), opp. p. 126.

6   1787. Etching, "Zion Besieg'd & Attack'd." Plate size, 14 x 18 in. See above, pp. 180–81. Pls. 38, 39.

UNKNOWN ARTIST: DRAWINGS

1   1783. Pencil drawing. Paper, diam. 3⅜ in. In circular frame. Profile, to right, with hat. Inscribed, lower right, "M. perier / ce 4 janvier / 1783." *Owner:* Walters Art Gallery, Baltimore. Pl. 13.

The profile may have been taken from the Sèvres medallion (see SÈVRES, No. 1). The hair and the addition of the hat make, however, a marked alteration. The inscription, placed where one would expect identification of subject rather than signature, has not been explained. An inscription behind the figure may have been erased and shaded over. The drawing appears to be the original of that described below.

2   Undated. Pastel. Paper, 6 x 4½ in. Profile, to right, with hat and spectacles. Circular border around the portrait, with title below, "Benjamin Franklin / né a Boston en 1706," crudely and incorrectly lettered. A printed statement framed with the drawing reads:

> from an Album formed by a Mr. Lacombe (died 1814), a man of letters and friend of Voltaire. This drawing is attributed to Jean Martin Renaud, a sculptor, who made a small medallion of Franklin in Terra Cotta; he was a relative of the engraver, Gilles Demarteau (b. 1729, d. 1776). From a descendant of his, Mr. Geo. A. Lucas, of Paris, procured the drawing and presented it to the W. H. Huntington Collection, Metropolitan Museum of Art, N.Y., 1898.

Owner: Metropolitan Museum of Art, New York.

The original owner of the album may have been Jacques Lacombe (1724–1811), author, compiler, and publisher. Mr. Lucas' attribution of the work to Renaud is based upon its similarity to the Renaud medallion he had discovered (see SÈVRES, No. 6). In the same fashion he had attributed all the Sèvres medallions to Renaud, issuing metal reproductions with Renaud's name added in the manner of a signature. Renaud, whose active career belongs to the early 19th century, can only be linked to this work by the most tenuous supposition. The familiar inscription giving the year of Franklin's birth, without a death date, might indicate that it was placed there in his lifetime.

The pastel appears to be a copy of that described above (No. 1), with the addition of spectacles.

UNKNOWN ARTIST RECORDED IN ENGRAVINGS

1   1783. Line engraving. Plate size, 4¾ x 4 in. Engraved surface, 4 5/16 x 3 3/4. Profile, to left. Pl. 13.

The portrait appears in Jean Gaspard Lavater, *Essai sur la Physiognomie, 2,* 286. Whereas Lavater's other portrait of Franklin (see WEYLER, No. 2), on p. 280 of the same section of the work ("De l'Homogénéite"), is cited as an example of faulty portraiture through which the physiognomist can only with difficulty discern the true features, here the features are accepted as consistent and right. The subject is not identified. The author states the profile to be that of a thinker, "plein de sagacité & de pénétration," a marvelous characterization of a man who could rise from small beginnings without effort, and could puruse his objectives with deliberate firmness but without obstinacy. Particular attention is called to the lines of the forehead and to the rounded end of the nose. The hair is described as soft and fine. In the first English edition of the work the likeness was identified as Franklin's.

2   1801. Stipple engraving by James Hopwood (ca. 1752–1819). Engraved surface 5¾ x 3⅝ in. "Engraved by J. Hopwood / from an original Picture in the Possession of the late General Washington. / Dr. Benjamin Franklin. / Pub: Nov. 1, 1801, by M. Jones, Paternoster Row."

Hopwood worked for British magazines of the early 19th century both as designer and engraver. This plate is probably derived from one of the prints after Chamberlin, with alterations in the hair and costume, and with a spurious provenance intended to give it distinction and authority.

> 3   1804. Stipple engraving by William Evans. Engraved surface 3 x 2⅜ in. "DOCTOR BENJAMIN FRANKLIN. / Engraved by Wm. Evans, from an original picture, / (the last painted) in the possession of Dr. Jas. Hamilton. / Published for Lackington, Allen & Co., Jany. 1, 1804."

The "original picture" has not been discovered, nor its presumed owner identified. No such painting is recorded in the wills of Dr. James Hamilton, of Finsbury Square, London, dated Dec. 15, 1826, nor of the Scottish physician (1749–1835), who was a famous and convivial character of Edinburgh. Whitfield J. Bell, Jr., has suggested as the most plausible identification the Irish James Hamilton for whom Joseph Priestley wrote a letter of introduction to Franklin on March 11, 1779, describing him as a friend of liberty and lover of science.[2] Benjamin Vaughan also wrote in his behalf to Franklin on April 23, 1780:

> This letter may perhaps be delivered to you by a Dr. Hamilton, a strict acquaintance and friend of Dr. Crawford and of whom Dr. Crawford speaks very honorably. He is an Irish gentleman, & having some little independency is upon a scheme of travelling for two years. I do not know that he will present this in person, but if he holds his intention of keeping company with *another* Irish physician to Paris (who is related to an American major,) you will probably hear of or see him; and it is well you should know that he is trust-worthy.[3]

The engraving may be an adaptation of the Charles Willson Peale mezzotint of 1787, and it is possible that, as with the preceding (No. 2), no source painting existed.

2. Franklin Papers (A.P.S.), *13,* no. 186. Named as "Mr. Hamilton" only.

3. L.C. Dr. Adair Crawford (1748–95), physician and chemist, a friend of Joseph Priestley as well as of Vaughan.

UNKNOWN ARTIST : MINIATURES

   1   Undated. "Licentious allegorical miniature." Oval, 3 x 2½ in. Unlocated.

The miniature is described in the sale catalogue of Godefroy Mayer: "Licentious allegorical miniature painting referring to Franklin's efforts to obtain assistance from the French Court in gaining the liberty of the American colonies. Extremely free representations of Louis XVI, Franklin and a female figure (England)."[4] It is further described as of the "finest possible" workmanship, and priced at 1,500 francs. The nature of the subject and the high quality of the technique suggest that this may have been the work of Francis Lainé (q.v.). Lainé's sketch book of his designs has been preserved by his descendants, but some drawings of a particularly libertine character have been destroyed by them.

   2   Miniature requested by Elkanah Watson. Unlocated.

After financial reverses suffered by himself and his partner in France in 1783, Elkanah Watson went to London where he joined a convivial circle of friends. On July 11 he wrote to William Temple Franklin asking that a miniature of Benjamin Franklin be made for "one of the most accomplish'd Ladys in the City of my particular acquaintance," who wished to have it set in a bracelet.[5] It was to be circular, 1½ inches in diameter. There is no evidence of any compliance with this request. His accompanying sketch shows a three-quarter length figure within the circle.

   3   Undated. Miniature owned by Thomas Jefferson. Unlocated.

Jefferson's catalogue of his works of art, now at the University of Virginia, includes a "Franklin," artist unidentified, as one of the "miniatures" in the "Tea Room" at Monticello.[6] Its character is obscured by the fact that Jefferson used the word "miniature" freely, applying it also to small prints.[7]

   4. Item no. 91 in his catalogue, *No. 30. Old Paintings, Drawings, Miniatures.*

   5. Franklin Papers (A.P.S.), *105,* no. 86.

   6. Marie Kimball, "Jefferson's Works of Art at Monticello," *Antiques, 59* (1951), 299.

   7. Information from James A. Bear, Jr., Thomas Jefferson Memorial Foundation, Sept. 27, 1961.

UNKNOWN ARTIST: PAINTING

Ca. 1782–83. Probably oil on canvas, ca. 29¼ x 23½ in. Unlocated.

On Feb. 10, 1786, Comte Antoine Jean Marie Thévenard (1733–1815) solicited the aid of Thomas Jefferson in obtaining a portrait of Washington of the same dimensions as the "Franklin" which he then owned: 27½ pouces high and 22 pouces wide, "le tout mesure de Paris, pied de Roi."[8] Head and bust were shown in life size, and were "a perfect resemblance."[9] Writing to Franklin on May 25, 1788, Thévenard mentions his pleasure in the portrait which, he says, had at that time adorned his home for five years.[10]

In his letter of Feb. 10, 1786, Thévenard had declared himself unable to choose between Wright and Peale, not knowing their work. It is unlikely, therefore, that his "Franklin" was a replica of Joseph Wright's portrait of 1782.

Thévenard, French admiral, was commandant at L'Orient, and in this position had been of considerable assistance to the American cause.[11] He became a correspondent of the Académie des Sciences in 1778 and was admitted to membership in 1786.

UNKNOWN ARTIST: SCULPTURE

1   Ca. 1778. Engraved gem. Unlocated.

In 1879 J. J. Guiffrey reported on "Pierre Gravés Représentant Voltaire et Franklin," from information found in the Archives Nationales. The gems were to be seen, ca. 1778, in the hands of the Sieur Bérard, and were described as 5 lignes in height and 3 in width (approx. ½ x ¼ in.). Bérard had specimens of the gems mounted in rings in a revolving setting, so that the head of Brutus, which graced the reverse of the "Franklin," could also be used as a seal. The "Voltaire" had the likeness of Sophocles on its reverse. The gems were priced at 12 louis.[12]

2   Ca. 1783–85. Snuffbox, with portraits of Franklin and

8. Boyd, *Jefferson Papers, 9,* 276.
9. Ibid., pp. 276, 545.
10. Franklin Papers (A.P.S.), *36,* no. 54.
11. Lincoln Laurenz, *John Paul Jones* (Annapolis, 1943), pp. 418–23.
12. *Nouvelles Archives de l'art français* (1879), pp. 434–36.

Washington. Circular box of composition with ivory and gold borders and lined with tortoiseshell, diam. 3 in. Molded wax or plaster figures under glass on lid and under base. On lid, Mercury and figures representing the United States in an allegorical composition inscribed, "AMERICANA PROSPERITAS." On base, a winged figure of Fame or Victory, in flight, holding in her left hand a wreath and in her right medallion portraits of Franklin and Washington ½ in. high and inscribed, "FRANKLIN" and "WASSINGTON" (*sic*). Illustrated in *Benjamin Franklin and His Circle. A Catalogue of an Exhibition* (New York, Metropolitan Museum, 1936), p. 31, and in *The Pictorial Life of Benjamin Franklin* (Philadelphia, Dill & Collins, 1923), n.p. *Owner:* William S. Coleman, Princeton, N.J.

In the will of Franklin's son-in-law, Richard Bache, dated Jan. 2, 1810, the box was bequeathed to his son, William, as "a french snuff box, on the top of which, is represented *American Prosperity,* and what it contains (which I know he will highly appreciate)." The contents were locks of hair of Benjamin Franklin and his daughter, Sarah Franklin Bache. The box has continued in family ownership to the present time. It is now on deposit in the Princeton University Library.

In style, the allegories and portraits suggest the suave and finished designs of Augustin Dupré (q.v.). See reference to snuffbox by Beyer, VANLOO, No. 3.

3   Undated. Wax conversation piece, Franklin, Rousseau, and Voltaire. Pl. 31 B. The three figures are seated, with two small boys, one black, one white, in an Elysian setting of foliage and water, the whole in a glass case with a painted background. The piece is recorded at the Caisse Nationale des Monuments Historiques as from the "Collection Rolland."[13] Unlocated. Pl. 31.

4   Ca. 1780–90. Model, "Franklin Experimenting." Composition, wood, &c. On wooden base with ornamental edge and

13. This might be the collection of pictures and "objets de haute curiosité" formed by M. Rolland, art dealer, and sold in Paris after his retirement from business on March 22 and days following, 1830.

checkered design. In glass case, ht. 10¼ in., base, 10¼ x 7⅞ in. (Example at Musée Municipale, Saint-Germain-en-Laye.) Pl. 31.

These small models, in which a cheerful and reasonably well depicted Franklin is shown seated at a table with electrical equipment, appear to have been manufactured in some quantity. Franklin wears a hat, which can be removed, and has natural hair. His face is turned upward as if to observe a descending bolt of electricity. A similar figure of Voltaire, writing, was also published. Two designs of round and square tables were used interchangeably with these figures.

John Bigelow obtained photographs of one of these "Franklins," with a letter from its owner, Mme. Guerin de Vaux, dated Paris, March 10, 1904, in which she traces its ownership in her family back to Franklin's friend, Fournier le Jeune:

> My father Mr. Fournier des Orves was indeed the great grandson of Fournier le Jeune, who was a great printer and possessed much knowledge, born in 1712, died in 1768.[14] My father was the last to bear his name; my sister Mme. de Thore and I are his direct descendants.
>
> Fournier le Jeune was very intimate with Franklin. At the time of my birth there still existed letters which they had exchanged and particularly the one which had accompanied the sending of the statue.[1] Unhappily they have been lost since, and I am sorry to be unable to send you any written proof of their relations.
>
> The name of the author is unknown.
>
> Other reproductions of the statue possibly exist as I know for certain that some statues of the same kind have been sometimes made—several in number.

14. These are the dates of Pierre Simon Fournier, le Jeune, whose son, Simon Pierre Fournier, le Jeune, was the one of Franklin's acquaintance.

1. The letter may have referred actually to the miniature of Franklin by Judlin painted for Fournier. The reference to the hair of the model later in the letter suggests that the miniature may have been mounted with a lock of Franklin's hair at the back of the case.

389

I know indeed two statuettes of Voltaire of the same type, and which are alike each other. (Mr. d'Allemagne's collection and Musée Carnavalet in Paris.) These statues are made of a white paste, gesso or other composition; they have been moulded and painted. The hair of the one we possess is certainly the real hair of the great Franklin, which has been stuck; the letter I named before mentioned it. The connaissor Mr. d'Allemagne declares them of German workmanship.[2]

The New York Public Library owns photographs of this piece and of one owned by Godefroy Mayer, Paris, 1906. A pair of the models of Franklin and Voltaire in the Lazienki Palace, Warsaw, the last residence of the King of Poland, is described and illustrated in *Gazette des Beaux Arts, 11* (1934), 245–46. The model at the Musée Municipale de Saint-Germain-en-Laye was acquired from the Ducastel collection in 1872.

5   Ships' figureheads. Unlocated.
On March 20, 1779, Messrs. Woestyn Brothers, of Dunkirk, informed Franklin that a 24-gun frigate privateer was being built at Havre under their orders, and begged that His Excellency would "nous accorder la faveur de le baptiser sous son nom Le franklin."[3] They added an earnest wish that he would interest himself and his friends in the impending voyages of this "corsaire." The ensuing correspondence reveals Franklin's hesitation to accept the honor while not in a position to make an investment in the enterprise. On May 11 the firm apologized for its importunity in the matter, but declared that the sculptor at Havre now needed only his acquiescence to complete the ornamentation of the ship.[4] A week later Franklin responded with his written consent and his hopes for the success of the adventure.[5]

A few years later, probably in 1781, Le Ray de Chaumont's young son filled an interval of boredom with a letter to his friend

2. *New York Public Library Bulletin, 10* (1906), 9.
3. Franklin Papers (A.P.S.), *13*, no. 210.
4. Ibid., *14*, no. 97.
5. Franklin Papers (L.C.). On April 25 the firm had declared its intention to name the ship in his honor even if he had no material interest in it.

William Temple Franklin. He was at an unnamed port engaged in the business of a ship about to sail, so engrossed in marine affairs that he felt sure his letter would smell of tar:

> Ce vaisseau ci est en bon ordre à present et tout prêt
> à partir ainsi que ceux qui doivent l'accompagner, on
> y a mis le médaillon de votre grand papa où son buste
> est representé de grandeur naturel et très ressemblant,
> je souhaite que les Anglais ne le prenne pas car ces
> gens la le bruleront tout vif avec leurs diable et notre
> pape.[6]

The word "medallion" might be misleading, and one must assume the young man to be as unused to artistic terms as he professed to be to the nautical.

A *Franklin* from Philadelphia was indeed captured at sea at about this time, and there are references in the Franklin Papers to a French letter-of-marque and to other vessels with the name. In later years it continued in the Navies of France and the United States. (See RUSH, Nos. 2, 3.) No other documentation of actual figureheads made in Franklin's lifetime, however, has been found.[7]

UNKNOWN ARTIST: SCULPTURE
Wax high relief after Weyler. See WEYLER No. 9.

VALLAYER-COSTER, ANNE (1744–1818)
See NINI: VALLAYER-COSTER

VANLOO, CHARLES PHILIPPE AMEDÉE (1719–95)
1   Ca. 1777–85. Painting. Oil on canvas, oval, 28½ x 22⅞ in. Gray hair. Gray eyes. Silver spectacles. Light brown fur collar on green coat. Dark green background. *Owner:* A.P.S., Philadelphia. Pl. 23.

6. Franklin Papers (A.P.S.), *107,* no. 166. "This ship here is in good order and ready to sail as soon as manned. They have put on her the medallion of your grand papa where his bust is shown life-size and very lifelike. I hope the English don't take her for they'd burn her alive with their devil and our pope."
7. For other later Franklin figureheads, see Pinckney, *American Figureheads,* pp. 119–20, 144, 172; L. Vernon Briggs, *History of Shipbuilding on North River, Plymouth County, Mass.* (Boston, 1889), pp. 195, 394.

Though the date of this most important painting cannot be precisely fixed, and though the name of the artist is fixed only by a plausible speculation, the fact that it was painted for, and in the taste of, Mme. Helvétius cannot be questioned. It was sold from the family of her descendants and the Château de Lumigny, Seine et Marne, where it had hung for almost 150 years, by the Marquise de Mun. Its purchaser was the Cailleux Gallery of Paris, by whom, through the agency of Gilbert Chinard, it was sold to the A.P.S. on Nov. 19, 1948.[8]

In 1933 it had been stated that the picture had been "made in England" and presented by Franklin to the Marquis de Mun as a "souvenir de tendre amitié."[9] It was exhibited in Paris in 1935 as a work of the French school and as the property of M. Cailleux.[10] The certification by the Marquis de Mun in 1944 states that the painting was Franklin's gift to a daughter of Mme. Helvétius: "La fille ainée de Madame Helvétius, Charlotte, épousa le Marquis de Mun et Franklin apporta ce portrait à la fille de son amie, lors d'une de ses visites à Lumigny."[11] The far more reasonable supposition that the portrait was commissioned by Charlotte's mother, to satisfy her own feeling of "tendre amitié," is established by a note written by Jean Baptiste Le Roy and published as an appendix to the "Eulogy" on Franklin delivered by the Abbé Fauchet in 1790: "Sa meilleure amie, celle chez qui il se livroit le plus volontiers à une conversation libre et amusante et où il aimoit à passer le tems que lui laissoient les affaires, la Ve d'Helvétius le faisoit peindre chez elle. 'Amusez moi, disoit-il à ses amis, ou vous aurez de moi le plus triste des portraits.' "[12]

8. Information from Jean Cailleux to the author, July 28, 1953, and from the A.P.S. A formal certification signed by the Marquis de Mun, Nov. 5, 1944, accompanies the picture.

9. Eddy Papers.

10. *Exposition. Auteuil et Passy d'autrefois au Musée Galleria . . . 18 mars–24 avril, 1935,* no. 225.

11. "The elder daughter of Madame Helvétius, Charlotte, married the Marquis de Mun, and Franklin brought this portrait to the daughter of his friend on one of his visits to Lumigny" (Gilbert Chinard, "Abbé Lefebvre de la Roche's Recollections of Benjamin Franklin," *Proceedings of the A.P.S., 94* (1950), 214).

12. "His best friend, she in whose home he relaxed most readily in free and amusing conversation and with whom he loved to pass what time he could spare from business, the widow Helvétius, had him painted there. 'Amuse me,' he told her friends, 'or you will have the most sorrowful portrait of me.' " (Ibid., p. 219.)

The portrait must be dated, therefore, within the ripening of this charming intimacy. Franklin had met Mme. Helvétius and her daughters in the spring of 1777. Beyond question a life portrait, the painting must be dated between that meeting and their separation in 1785. It would be natural to place it close to Franklin's famous "vengeons-nous" letter to the lady, written on Dec. 7, 1778.

The attribution to Amédée Vanloo is based upon the print by Pierre Michel Alix described below (No. 2), which appears to be founded upon this likeness, though the costume is simplified to meet the republican taste of ca. 1790, and which is inscribed "Vanloo Pinxt." The Vanloos were a large and a talented family of painters. One has been named as a neighbor of Franklin and Mme. Helvétius at Passy.[13] Louis Michel Vanloo (1707–71) had painted a portrait of Helvétius (engraved by both Augustin de Saint Aubin and by Alix) and a portrait of Mme. Helvétius. His portrait of Helvétius has some of the same smiling intimacy, as if his widow had asked this other painter for a similar portrayal of her new friend. A posthumous bust of Claude Adrien Helvétius had been made by Caffiéri, suggesting also that the lady may have been one of those who had urged Franklin to sit for the sculptor in 1777. Amédée Vanloo was the only one of the family at hand to have painted this work. He was a mature and competent artist.[14] Of some significance, too, is his predisposition for scientific subjects, a taste he shared with Wright of Derby. There is his "La Lanterne Magique" of 1764, now at the National Gallery in Washington. Of more significance is his "L'Electricité" shown at the Salon of 1777, and signed and dated in that year.[1] The crank of an electrical machine with a glass globe (such as that in Benjamin Wilson's print of Franklin) is turned by a man, while a girl stands on a stool, insulated by a cushion, and directs the current which is passing through her body down into a bottle of liquid held for her by a Negro page.

Vanloo's portrait of Franklin, obviously because of its intimate

13. C. Leroux-Cesbron, "Un Ami de Franklin: Le Veillard," *Bulletin de la Société historique d'Auteuil et de Passy, 10* (1921), 32.

14. Charles Oulmont, "Amédée Vanloo, Peintre du Roi de Prusse," *Gazette des Beaux-Arts* (1912), *2, 139*–50, 223–34.

1. Courtauld Institute, Witt Library, London. The painting is now in the Yousoupoff Collection, Petrograd.

and private character, was never exhibited while in family ownership, and its later history is documented by only a few copies.

2   Ca. 1790. Color aquatint after Vanloo, by Pierre Michel
Alix (1762–1817). Oval, engraved surface 9½ x 8 in. "Vanloo
Pinxt. P. M. Alix Sculpt. / Francklin. / A Paris chez Marie
François Drouhin, Editeur & Imprimeur-Libraire, Rue Chris-
tine, No. 2, Imprimé chez lui par Becket." Pl. 23.

The print is one of a series of portraits begun in July 1790 and
finished in Sept. 1797. The "Claude Adrien Helvétius," after Louis
Michel Vanloo, is dated 1793. At the Salon of 1795 Alix exhibited
the "Franklin," "Lavoisier," "Montesquieu," and "Helvétius." It
is said that during the Terror Alix burned many of his portraits
and that it was not until after the 9th Thermidor that he dared to
add "Bailly" and "Lavoisier" to the series.[2]

The substitution of a simple gray coat for the fur-trimmed costume of the original was undoubtedly in deference to revolutionary
feeling. Partly because of this change, the portrait has been listed
as after the likeness by Charles Willson Peale, 1785, engraved
in mezzotint in 1787. There are remarkable but probably wholly
coincidental similarities between the Peale and Vanloo portraits
in the treatment of the glasses, the hair where it crosses the ear,
and other features.

3   Ca. 1852–53. Pastel by Louis Mathieu Didier Guillaume
(1816–92), after an early copy from Vanloo. Paper, oval, 28¼
x 22⅞ in. *Owner:* Virginia Historical Society, Richmond.

There is no record of any replica or contemporary copy of Vanloo's
painting. This copy in pastel, however, was made from a portrait
which had been owned by a contemporary whom Franklin had
known well. It came to the Virginia Historical Society in 1853 as
the gift of William Campbell Rives (1793–1868), who had been
Minister to France from 1829 to 1830 and from 1849 to 1853. According to a letter from Rives, Nov. 14, 1853, he had "sought dili-
gently for some representation of an American subject by an eminent European painter" for the Society:

> I flatter myself, therefore, that in the Portrait of
> Franklin which I left in your possession a few days

2. Renouvier, *Histoire de l'Art,* p. 253.

ago, I am offering to the Historical Society of Virginia a memorial which they will be pleased to accept. It is from an undoubted original by Greuze, the most eminent French artist of the reigns of Louis XV and Louis XVI. The original could not be purchased for any price; and the painting now offered to the Historical Society, executed by a very superior Parisian artist, is the only copy ever permitted to be taken from it, which was accorded as a special mark of consideration for the institution to which it was destined, as well as a kindness to myself.

A brief history of the original painting may not be without interest to the Society.

It was obtained by the present possessor from a descendant of Beyer. Beyer, from a zealous practical application to the physical sciences, came to be employed by the French government to superintend the construction and arrangement of Paratonneres, or Lightning Rods, on the public edifices and monuments of Paris. This employment brought him into communication with the inventor of the Lightning rod, who was then the American minister at Paris.[3]

He goes on to recount the familiar legend of a gift from the great man to his friend: Beyer had invented "tablettes mecaniques" by which Franklin could write accurately without being seen, and Franklin had reciprocated with the portrait.

Beyer had indeed been in charge of placing the lightning rods on the public buildings of Paris, and was the author of a work on the subject.[4] He had been a correspondent of Franklin's from 1781 to 1785. He was the inventor of a musical instrument to which Franklin, at his request, had given the name "glass-chord."[5] On April 6,

3. *Virginia Magazine of History and Biography, 40* (1932), 77–78. Rives' description appeared also in the *Virginia Historical Reporter, 1* (Richmond, 1854), 12. The minutes of the society do not record the gift. *The Virginia Magazine of History and Biography, 34* (1926), 215; *35* (1927), 61, erroneously reports the donor as John Young Mason, Minister to France, 1853–59.

4. *Aux Amateurs de physique, sur l'utilité des paratonneres,* Paris, 1809.

5. "Note sur le glass-chord; par Beyer," *Journal de Physique, 48* (1799), 408.

1785, in the customary return for a kindness, he made Franklin a gift of a snuff box "que je me suis appliqué à vous faire, comme un faible marque de la reconnaissance."[6]

Apparently another individual also shared the favor of the owner of the original "Greuze." A very similar pastel in the same size was brought from France by Henry Shelton Sanford, who had been Secretary of the U.S. legation at Paris from 1849 to 1853. Rives' artist, Guillaume, a French portrait and landscape painter, settled in Richmond, Va., in 1857, having come to America a few years earlier.

VILLIERS
See DUFOURNY DE VILLIERS.

WALPOLE, THOMAS (1755–1840)
See NINI: WALPOLE.

WEDGWOOD
The Wedgwood "Franklins" are of secondary importance as portraiture, but were a primary historical factor in maintaining Franklin's reputation in England during the critical years of the war and in echoing his fame more lately and more broadly. They are listed here by type and by date of origin as nearly as that can be determined, without full definition of the various materials and sizes in which they have been published.

1   1766. Profile medallion, after Isaac Gosset.
Probably first issued in white creamware, after 1768 in black basalt, and after 1774 in the familiar cameos of white against blue, green, or gray jasper. See GOSSET, No. 1.

2   1777. Profile medallion, after Jean Baptiste Nini, with fur cap.
A few exact reproductions of the circular Nini, 4½ inches in diameter, were made. In the numerous and familiar oval cameo medallions of this type the Nini armorial mark on the shoulder is still often in evidence. See NINI: WALPOLE, No. 1.

6. Franklin Papers (A.P.S.), *33,* no. 74.

3   1778. Profile medallion, after Sèvres.
An exact duplicate of the Sèvres is at the Metropolitan Museum.
As an oval cameo, and in intaglio, the piece became one of the most
popular of the Wedgwood "Franklins." See SÈVRES, No. 1.

4   1778. Profile medallion with short hair and antique costume, attributed to William Hackwood (d. 1836). Pl. 11.
Wedgwood's "Classic Franklin," in sizes from the smallest to the
large 11 x 8 in. plaques, was issued through the years probably in
greater numbers than any other. The classic garb gave it, no doubt
intentionally, a certain timelessness, and at a juncture when the
Gosset type with its large bagwig was out of date, and the long-
haired French likenesses carried a certain hostile political implication. It is, furthermore, the only one of the group which can be
claimed as a Wedgwood creation. Whatever its sources, they have
been freely and strongly revised. It might reasonably be related to
the Nini plaques of 1778 and 1779. But the lines of the face in some
respects hold to the Gosset profile, and the presumptive dating
opens a possibility that it may have preceded the Nini of 1778. On
Aug. 24 of that year Josiah Wedgwood wrote from the Etruria
works to his partner, Thomas Bentley, in London mentioning an
error which he had corrected in the last issue of *Illustrious Moderns:* "The Dr. before Franklin was an error which I corrected as
soon as I saw it."[7] The pieces are for the most part stamped "FRANK-
LIN." One of this type, however, at the Fogg Museum, bears the
obtrusive "DR." before the name.

The Wedgwood Museum attributes the portrait to William
Hackwood, after Nini.[8] Due to the founder's subordination of the
individual artist to the firm name, the attribution is not documented.

The likeness is repeated in a small line engraving, ca. 1790–1800,
"H. Lips del. & sc. / BENJAMIN FRANKLIN," in which it appears as
a bust being crowned by Liberty, with at the base of its pedestal,
a cherub with a map of the hemispheres and the musical glasses.

5   1779. Bust, from a cast or copy after Jean Jacques Caffiéri.
A pattern model of the bust, ht. 28 in., is preserved in the Wedg-

7. Archives, Josiah Wedgwood and Sons, Barlaston, Stoke-on-Trent.
8. Harry M. Buten, *Wedgwood and Artists* (Merion, Pa., 1960) pp. 20, 56.

wood Museum, Barlaston, and was formerly attributed to Patience Wright.[9] Its making obviously depended upon the importation of a cast of the original from France. The clue to the date is a letter from Wedgwood to his partner, May 30, 1779:

> This letter, let me tell you whilst I remember, serves, chiefly, to advise you of a box we send by the coach to day containing amongst other things a head of *Newton* & another of Franklin, to make a trio with the *Priestley* already sent. If these give satisfaction to the Doctor, *as far as they go,* I shall be very happy, & we will jogg on with a few more, though probably not with the rapidity the Dr. whirls every thing into that lies within the reach of his vortex. Pray look at these heads with a view to their price. I think they should be cheap to sell quantities of them, but whether they should be @ 21ˢ–27ˢ, or 31/6 I must leave for you to determine upon comparing them with other things.[10]

No attribution of the Wedgwood version of the bust can be made, and it was probably produced without alteration directly from the Caffiéri. It is interesting to note, however, that Giuseppi Ceracchi was with the firm at this time and that the model of the Priestley bust referred to bears his signature.[1] See CAFFIÉRI, No. 1.

WEST, BENJAMIN (1738–1820)

1   1784–85. "The Treaty of Paris." Figure of Franklin in a group portrait of the peace commissioners. Oil on canvas, 28½ x 36½ in. Franklin has dark gray-brown hair. His costume is very dark. John Jay is dressed in light olive-tan, John Adams in light tan, Henry Laurens in red. William Temple Franklin's figure belongs to the unfinished part of the painting, sketched over an undercoat of pale gray. Above, blue sky with

9. Frederick Rathbone, *Catalogue of the Wedgwood Museum, Etruria* (Etruria, 1909), p. 106.

10. Wedgwood Archives. William Billington, Curator, to the author, March 26, 1960, states his belief that the impatient "Doctor" to whom reference is made must have been Priestley, correspondence with Dr. Price having ceased at this time, and because of a reference on May 9, 1779, to "3 more heads in the box for Dr. Priestley."

1. Rathbone, p. 73.

clouds. *Owner:* Henry Francis du Pont Winterthur Museum, Winterthur, Del. Pl. 27.

Early in April 1782 Caleb Whitefoord, master of wit and persiflage, Franklin's old friend and neighbor of Craven St. days, called upon him at Passy to introduce Richard Oswald and to initiate the formal discussions of a treaty of peace. He was back in London at the end of the month and delivered a letter from Franklin to Benjamin West. On April 28 West replied with expressions of continuing regard and with news of his wife and sons, one of whom was Franklin's godchild: "It allways gave me and Mrs. West the greatest satisfaction to hear of your health—a confirmation of which I have not only received by our friend, but have now before [me] in a Bust, which he procured two or three days past, the likeness is strong and time seems to have made but little impression on the Original . . . "[2]

It is natural to suppose that at this juncture the English friends of Franklin, both for his sake and for that of a satisfactory political reconciliation, would come forward as they did with renewals of friendship. Portraiture was involved in this effort, and the bust brought to West may have been intended for use in a painting. The possibility of historical works in which Franklin would be cast with prominence must have occurred at this time. West, old friend that he was, had never painted Franklin from life. The source materials which he assembled beginning at this time were: the bust brought by Whitefoord and perhaps retained by West;[3] the Sèvres medallion; David Martin's portrait, 1772, owned by John Sargent (see MARTIN, No. 3); Joseph Wright's portrait, 1782, owned by Whitefoord (see J. WRIGHT, No. 5); and the miniature after Duplessis owned by Georgiana Shipley (see DUPLESSIS, "Gray Coat," No. 3). He made separate use of a copy or engraving after Weyler (see No. 2, below).

William Temple Franklin's letter to his grandfather, dated London, Nov. 9, 1784, holds the earliest documentation of "The Treaty of Paris": "I have, tho' with some Difficulty, procur'd for Mr.

---

2. Franklin Papers (A.P.S.), *25,* no. 49.

3. The plaster cast of a bust of Franklin is listed in *Catalogue of the Last Part of a Superb Collection . . . formed by the late Benjamin West* (London, Christie, 1820), p. 36.

West the Miniature you sent Georgiana and he is now doing your Head from it in the picture of the signing of the Treaty."[4] John Quincy Adams, who was present when his father's likeness was added, ca. 1785–88, enlarges the record:

> 1817, June 6th. Mr. West—Spent the evening with us. He told me that he had in the year 1783 made a sketch for a picture of the peace which terminated the war of the American Revolution, which he would send me to look at the next morning, as he accordingly did. I then recollected having seen it before, at the time when my father was sitting to him for his likeness in it. The most striking likeness in the picture is that of Mr. Jay. Those of Dr. Franklin, and his grandson W. T. who was Secretary to the American Commission, are also excellent. Mr. Laurens and my father, though less perfect resemblances, are yet very good.[5]

Franklin's dark costume gives him a dramatic prominence in the composition, though beyond this it is primarily a group portrait, with little suggestion of the enactment of a great event in history. In January 1784 John Trumbull returned to West's studio and eventually assumed, as a personal and professional mission, the series of historical paintings on the American Revolution, which West had begun in this unfinished piece. A small sketch by Trumbull at the H.S.P. indicates that he had considered carrying out the theme in a composition of his own, in which Franklin was to be dramatized by a central position between opposing groups at a long table.

At the sale of West's paintings in 1820 this was purchased by Joseph Strutt (1765–1844), of the family prominent in cotton manufacture. It passed to his nephew, Edward Strutt, who became Baron Belper of Belper in 1856, and who died in 1880. It was purchased from the 2d Lord Belper by John Pierpont Morgan (1837–

4. Franklin Papers (A.P.S.), *32,* no. 168. Also, Georgiana Shipley to Benjamin Franklin, Nov. 6, 1784 (Bache Papers); Mr. and Mrs. Sloper to W. T. Franklin (Franklin Papers, A.P.S., *108,* no. 7).

5. J. Q. Adams, *Memoirs, 3* (1874), 559, quoted in the exhibition catalogue, *Benjamin West* (Philadelphia, 1938), pp. 38–39.

1913). It was first exhibited in the United States at the Brooklyn Museum in 1917.[6]

Two other paintings after this work and of approximately the same size are recorded, but without contemporary documentation.

> 2   Ca. 1805–15. "Franklin drawing Electricity from the Sky." Oil on paper, 13¼ x 10 in. White hair. Dark eyes. Figure dressed in black and wearing a red cloak blown upward by the storm, seated on a blue-gray rock, his right hand extended upward to the key and electric fire, his left holding a paper. The kite string is held by cherubs at right, the nearest draped in yellow and that behind him in red with an Indian head ornament, and above them a second kite is tossed aloft. Two others, with electrical equipment, at left. Storm clouds and lightning overhead. *Owner:* Wharton Sinkler, Philadelphia. Pl. 35.

Using the Weyler likeness as his source, West has brought into this picture all that his "Treaty" had lacked in drama, and based his portrait more on recollection and imagination than on his sources. The earliest documentation is in a letter from Charles Robert Leslie to William Dunlap, ca. 1833:

> It ought to be known, if it is not, that at the time Mr. West made his noble present to the Pennsylvania Hospital, his pecuniary affairs were by no means in a prosperous condition. He was blamed by those who did not know this, for selling the first picture he painted for them; but he redeemed his pledge to them, and I can bear witness of his great satisfaction, when he heard that the exhibition of it had so much benefited the institution. He had begun his own portrait to present to the hospital. It was a whole length on a mahogany pannel; he employed me to dead color it for him. He had also made a small sketch of a picture of Dr. Franklin, to present with it. The doctor was seated on the clouds, surrounded by naked boys, and the experiment of proving lightning and electricity to be the same was alluded to.[7]

6. *Brooklyn Museum Quarterly,* 4 (1917), 81; illust. p. 78.
7. Dunlap, *Arts of Design, 1,* 86.

Leslie went from Philadelphia to London in 1811, returning only briefly to America in 1833. It was in 1811 that West had felt under the necessity of selling his "Christ Healing the Sick," promised to the Pennsylvania Hospital. The replica painted for the hospital is signed and dated 1815. Before sending the gift, originally promised in 1801, he had insisted that a suitable exhibition hall be built. In March 1816 he wrote to the Board of Managers:

> When the Room is so much advanced as to ascertain the Time of it's Completion, and in a dry state to receive the Picture, I will have it ship'd for Philadelphia with it's Frame in a safe and proper Manner—I wish it to be placed opposite the Entrance into the intended Room, midway of which on each side, there should be a low Fire place for warming the Room in Winter, and over which Fireplaces I will compliment each with a Picture.[8]

While he may well have thought to have this little work published as an engraving, he may also have considered it, in larger size, for a situation over one of the fireplaces—his own portrait above one, and this of the founder of the institution above the other. The painting, however, remained in the possession of West's descendants until the sale of a part of his estate in 1898.[9] It appears next in the sale catalogue of Godefroy Mayer's collection.[1] It was brought to the United States by Kennedy and Co., and sold to its present owner.

> 3. Undated. Copy by unknown artist, after West (?). Unlocated.

On Feb. 28, 1783, Governor Thomas Pownall (1722–1805), who had retired to England from the colonial service in 1760, wrote to Franklin from Richmond, Surrey: "P.S. I am this day made happy by having received & hung up an excellent Portrait of you, my old friend—copied from that which West did for you."[2] This statement

---

8. *Pennsylvania Hospital Bulletin, 8* (1950–51), 9.

9. *Catalogue of the Collection of Pictures, Drawings and Sketches Which Have Remained in the Possession of the Family Ever Since His Death* (London, Christie, Manson and Woods, March 18–19, 1898), p. 16, no. 140.

1. *No. 30. Old Paintings, Drawings,* p. 15, no. 83.

2. Franklin Papers (A.P.S.), *27,* no. 151.

implies that West had painted a life portrait for, and of, Franklin. This could only have occurred before 1775. It is possible that the writer's memory was at fault and that the picture was after one by Wilson or some other artist. In 1875 the portrait was owned by the Rev. C. C. Beaty-Pownall. A letter from Franklin, which had been kept in the back of the frame had been lost, apparently destroyed by a servant. The picture was at this time "Thought to be by Copley, and is understood to have been given to Governor Pownall by Franklin himself."[3]

4   Undated. Painting, attributed to Benjamin West. Unlocated.

On July 2, 1864, William John Duane (1780–1865), who had married Franklin's granddaughter, Deborah Bache, wrote to James Parton whose biography of Franklin had just appeared, complaining that the descendants of members of the old Proprietary party still hated the memory of Franklin. He expressed anger that a portrait of Franklin, bequeathed to the Pennsylvania Hospital, had disappeared and that no serious inquiry had been made as to its whereabouts.[4] The 1906 exhibition of Frankliniana at the Masonic Temple, Philadelphia, included a "Copy by Welsh, A.D. 1855, of Benjamin West's portrait of Franklin, at the Pennsylvania Hospital. Loaned by the Select and Common Councils of Philadelphia."[5] After its purchase of a large segment of the old Peale's Museum portrait gallery in 1854, the city had made an effort to fill certain conspicuous gaps. The copy (Pl. 26), by Thomas B. Welch (1814–74), must be the Franklin listed as no. 43 in the catalogue of the Independence Hall collection published in 1855.[6] This work shows a somewhat altered version of the "Fur Collar" Duplessis, enlivened by a bolt of lightning across the left background. No record of the original has been found in the minutes of the hospital, nor has the bequest to the hospital been identified. No apparent

3. Robert C. Winthrop, "Remarks," *Proceedings of the M.H.S., 14* (1875), 161.
4. Milton E. Flower, *James Parton, the Founder of Modern Biography* (Durham, N.C., 1951), p. 75.
5. *Bi-Centenary of the Birth of Right Worshipful Past Grand Master Brother Benjamin Franklin* (Philadelphia, 1906), p. 321.
6. *Catalogue of the National Portraits in Independence Hall* (Philadelphia, 1855), p. 14.

original of the Welch copy has been found. A portrait of the same type but with marked differences in detail is owned by the American Scenic and Historic Preservation Society, and hangs at Philipse Manor Hall, Yonkers, N.Y. (Pl. 26). It was formerly the property of Henry Theodore Tuckerman (1813–71), poet and art critic, and was purchased by the society from Fleming Tuckerman on March 19, 1909.[7]

> Drawing by unknown artist, attributed to Benjamin West. See CAFFIÉRI, No. 20.

> Paintings. Altered copies by Benjamin West. See MARTIN, Nos. 6, 7.

WEYLER, JEAN BAPTISTE (1747–91)

The "Franklins" of the type variously attributed to Weyler and to Jacques Thouron (1737–89) began presumably with a miniature on ivory or paper, which was translated at once into the permanent medium, enamel. Almost all the known versions are in small size, and the piece was undoubtedly intended at its inception to shine by its vigor and intensity from a jewel-like setting. The identity of the artist of the original is obscured in part by the fact that the enamelists of the 18th century frequently copied the compositions of others, and with a virtuosity to which connoisseurs sometimes granted the respect due to original art.

The possible origin, and possible attributions of this type are discussed in Chap. 8, bringing into view two other artists, the miniaturist Castrique and the miniaturist who signed his enamels "D.C."

> 1 Ca. 1782. Miniature, by Jean Baptiste Weyler. Enamel, oval, 25/32 x 19/32 of an in. White hair tinged with gray. Black costume. Brown background. Reverse, dark green. Setting 2 1/2 x 2 1/16 in., of gold ornamented with pearls and enamel. To be worn as a pendant. *Owner:* Charles Clore, London. Frontispiece.

This is probably the miniature listed in the Lenoir sale, Paris, 1874:

---

7. *Scenic and Historic America, 4* (1935), 21–22. A Benjamin Wilson portrait owned in Philadelphia (see WILSON, No. 3) was at one time also attributed to West.

"498. Medaillon ovale peint sur émail et attribué à Weyler. Portrait de Franklin. Cadre en or gravé à chainette."[8] It is fully described and illustrated in the catalogue of the David-Weill collection, Paris, 1957.[9]

> 2 1782–83. Line engraving, by an unidentified artist. Plate size, 4 x 3 5/16 in. Published in Lavater, *Essai sur la physiognomie, 2,* 280, the dedication of which is dated Zurich, May 31, 1783. No title or inscription. The textual matter is headed "Quatorzième Fragment. De l'Homogénéité. Addition G." Pl. 36.

This is the earliest dated example of the portrait type and was probably drawn and possibly engraved in the year preceding the publication of the book. It was presumably also derived from Weyler's miniature (No. 1) or a painting very similar to that or the others described here. If so, the artist sharpened and conventionalized the whole to accord with a medium from which clear definition is expected. He also added the ornamental loops and tassels to Franklin's coat. (See below, No. 9.)

Lavater does not mention Franklin's name in characterizing the subject of the portrait. He states that he cannot find a single exact truth in the picture, concedes that the brow is in accord with hair and chin, but sees the mouth as too tightly closed and too undulating in shape. Through these imperfections of the artist he can nonetheless discern the character of a man not easily trifled with and whose presence alone would overawe base and corrupted minds. The subject is identified as Franklin in the index to the volume. The engraving was probably Benjamin West's source for his "Franklin Drawing Electricity from the Sky" (WEST, No. 2, Pl. 35).

> 3 1783. Copy in oil by an unidentified painter (Italian and Mason), after a miniature in enamel by Weyler. Unlocated.
> The letter of June 24, 1783, in which a member of the Masonic

8. "Oval medallion painted on enamel and attributed to Weyler. . . . Gold frame with chain-work engraving" (*Catalogue des diaments, bijoux . . . miniatures . . . dépendant de la succession de Mme. V*[e]*. Lenoir,* Paris, Hôtel Drouot, May 18–23, 26–30, 1874, p. 74).

9. Gillet, *Miniatures and Enamels from the D. David-Weill Collection,* p. 526, no. 381.

lodge at Carcassonne informed Franklin of his reception into that branch of the brotherhood and of the presence at the ceremony of a portrait by "un peintre excellente Italien et Maçon," copied from a miniature by "Veilles," is quoted above, p. 171. The lodge subsequently passed out of existence, and no such portrait is now owned by the fraternity, either at Carcassonne or at Paris.

It is open to speculation whether or not this may be the oil portrait of the type which came on the market in the Franklin bicentennial year. On March 30, 1906, Augustus Biesel sent a photograph of the painting, "by Greuze," from Paris to the A.P.S., where it is still preserved. On May 22 he wrote to Joseph George Rosengarten of the society, that the "Greuze" was to be sold in London, at Christie's.[1] Christie's catalogue entry completes the description: "GREUZE: Portrait of Benjamin Franklin, in dark dress. Oval— 28½ in. by 23 in."[2] It was purchased at the sale by "Pollock."

> 4   Ca. 1782–89. Miniature, by Jacques Thouron. Ivory, oval, 3 3/16 x 2 3/8 in. White hair. Brown eyes. Dark gray coat with light brown facing. Louvre inscription on the back, "24864 de l'inventaire de 1832. Thouron. Pt. de Franklin." *Owner:* The Louvre, Paris. Pl. 34.

This and its replica in enamel (No. 5) are held by the Louvre without other record of provenance than the inventory of 1832, "which seems to prove that they came from the royal collections."[3]

> 5   Ca. 1782–89. Miniature, by Jacques Thouron. Replica of No. 4. Enamel, oval, 3 3/8 x 2 9/16 in. Same coloring as the ivory (No. 4), but slightly darker in tone. Louvre inscription on the back, "Touron Peintre en émaux de Genève. + vers 1789. Beauvais, 24863 de l'inventaire de 1832." *Owner:* The Louvre, Paris. Pl. 34.

> 6   Ca. 1782–89. Miniature, by Jacques Thouron. Unlocated.

A Milanese connoisseur, the Marquis Girolamo d'Adda, purchased the miniature in Geneva in 1849. He seems to have known the Thouron family at Geneva, and he published an account of Thou-

1. Archives, A.P.S.
2. Sale from various sources, Christie, Manson and Woods, London, May 31, 1906, p. 6. Marked catalogue at Frick Art Reference Library.
3. Information from Abel Doysié, Paris, Dec. 2, 1960.

ron's life, in which he states that several members of the royal family had commissioned portraits of Franklin, among them the two pieces at the Louvre.[4] An excellent engraving of his miniature was made for him in 1850 by Carlo Raimondi, Director of the School of Engraving in Parma.[5]

George Simpson Eddy reported a Thouron miniature at the Filangieri Museum, Naples, April 3, 1927.[6] This, however, is no longer there.[7]

> 7 1785. Miniature, by "D.C." Enamel, diam. 2¼ in. Inscribed on the back, "Le Dr. Franklin / Avril 1785." Also, "+ + + / D C P" *i.e.* 3 firings, D. C. pinxit. Also, "2 couche de fondan / use / poli au feu." See p. 175. *Owner:* Georges Wildenstein, New York. Pl. 34.

> 8 1785. Miniature, by "D.C." Enamel, oval, ht. 4¼ in. Gray hair. White cravat. Red coat. Inscribed on the back, "Le Docteur Franklin." Unlocated.

The work is recorded in the catalogue of the sale at Sotheby's, London, May 16, 1957. Two enamels were offered in the same lot, no. 37, this and another "Franklin" after the portrait by Greuze. The copy from Greuze is signed, right center, "D. C. / 1785." Both are identical in size and in identical gold frames with berried olive branches surmounted by chased gold ribbon ties and bearing the maker's marks of Gabriel Sebastien Beau. They were formerly in the J. P. Morgan collection, and were purchased by a collector in Buenos Aires.[8]

> 9 Ca. 1785–95. Polychromed wax high-relief portraits published for popular sale with variations in detail. Attributed to Bernhardt Kaspar Hardy (1726–1819) and to others. Pl. 34.

The pose of the head, the free treatment of the hair, and the orna-

4. M. Mignet, *Vita di Franklin,* trans. G. d'Adda (Milan, 1870), pp. xxxviii–xl. Cited, with additional material, by Pace, *Benjamin Franklin and Italy,* p. 295.

5. Plate size, 7 3/16 x 5 3/8 in. "B. FRANKLIN / Dal dipinto sopra smalto di Giacomo Touron / presso il Marchese Girolamo d'Adda in Milano / Raimondi incise." Pace, pp. 294–95; illust. p. 310.

6. Eddy Papers.

7. Director of the museum to the author, Sept. 10, 1957.

8. Information from Messrs. Sotheby and Co. The pieces are recorded also in *Connoisseur, 140* (1957), 59.

mentation on the coat in certain versions indicate that the work was derived originally from the Lavater engraving (No. 2). The pieces are most often and most reasonably attributed to Hardy, of Cologne, and are certainly of German manufacture. The figures are set in a shadow-box frame with varying backgrounds in which one frequently finds a tablet bearing the famous "ERIPUIT COELO FULMEN SEPTRUMQUE TYRANNIS" and surmounted by a trumpet. The simpler example at the Musée Carnavalet (Pl. 34) has gray hair, brown dress, and is set against a background of red cloth only, in a frame 7 in. high, 8⅝ in. wide, and 2¾ in. in depth. Some versions wear a fur-trimmed coat, borrowed perhaps from the Lemire statuette or a German engraving after it. Examples are illustrated in J. Bennett Nolan, "A Long-Lost Franklin," *Antiques, 19* (1931), 184, 186, 187, "Lightning on Franklin Waxes," *Antiques, 19,* 436, the Bibliothèque Nationale photograph collection, and the sale catalogue of the Kohler collection, Vienna, 1917.[9] This last illustrates also a use of the same head, with different attributes, to depict "Die Genügsame," an old man clutching his bread and water in a representation of "Frugality."[1]

The waxes of this type have no value as portraiture, but are of interest as a farther echo of Franklin's fame. They reveal also the popularity of Lavater's monumental work and the effort of these more distant artists to correct the likeness in the light of his criticism by emphasizing old age in the eyes and by endeavoring to make the mouth more expressive of Franklin's character as Lavater interpreted it.

WHITEFOORD, CALEB (1734–1810)
1762. Caricature. Unlocated.
In his letter to Whitefoord, dated Dec. 7, 1762, Franklin's allusion to the "Piece from your own Pencil" as "a strong and striking likeness, but . . . otherwise such a picture of your Friend, as Dr. Smith would have drawn, black, and all black," follows a reference to a humorous print and is followed by a comment on American paint-

9. P. 238. *Kunstauktion von C. J. Wawra . . . versleigerung der Sammlungen Dr. Kohler* (Vienna, Jan. 30, 1917), no. 357.
1. Ibid., no. 365.

ing. Whitefoord, wit and connoisseur, whose literary bent was for concise verbal statement, had undoubtedly enclosed in his letter not only a "humourous and sensible Print" but an imaginative pictorial conception of his correspondent. (See above, pp. 60–1.)

WILSON, BENJAMIN (1721–88)

    1   1759. Painting. Oil on canvas, 30 x 25 in. Gray-white wig. Eyes with yellow iris, dark brown pupils. High complexion. The mole on Franklin's left cheek, only, is shown. Lumpy texture around the left side of the head suggests overpainting to alter the line of the wig. Brown coat with cloth-covered buttons. Background very dark brown. In middle to lower left background, lightning from a cloud strikes a small church spire. Signed and dated, lower right, "B. Wilson / 1759." *Owner:* The United States, White House. Pls. 2, 3.

As an experimenter and writer on electricity, whose work Franklin had read and recommended to a friend in 1752, Benjamin Wilson would have been one of the first to come into his circle of acquaintance after his arrival in London in 1757. Wilson was continuing his experiments, but was also at the height of his reputation as a portrait painter. Franklin commissioned him to paint his own portrait and a replica for his friend, Dr. Thomas Bond, a portrait of his son, William, who had accompanied him to London, and a portrait of his wife from a small canvas painted in Philadelphia.[2] Portraits of Sally and Franky had also been sent from Philadelphia, and he applied to Wilson to paint the whole family in a conversation piece. This the artist declined to do. (See above, pp. 52–3.)

Commissioned in 1758 and completed in 1759, the painting of her husband was probably sent at once to Mrs. Franklin in Philadelphia. There is an indirect reference to it in her letter to him of June 13, 1770. On July 14, 1778, at the end of the British occupation of Philadelphia, Richard Bache reported to Franklin:

> I found your house and furniture upon my return to Town, in much better order than I had any reason to expect from such a rapacious crew . . . Some books and musical instruments were missing. A Captain

2. The portrait, on a canvas 29¾ x 24⅞ in., was purchased by the A.P.S. in 1953.

Andre also took with him the picture of you, which hung in the dining room. The rest of the pictures are safe, and met with no damage, except the frame of Alfred, which is broken to pieces.[3]

John André, who with other officers had been quartered in Franklin's house, was then an aide on the staff of Maj. Genl. Sir Charles Grey, to whom he gave the portrait. Until 1906, it hung in Howick House, the Northumbrian home of the Greys. On March 31, 1906, Albert Henry George Grey, 4th Earl Grey and Governor General of Canada, announced his intention of returning it to the United States as part of the bicentennial celebration of Franklin's birth.[4] It arrived on April 14, directed to the President of the United States, and has since remained, often in storage, at the White House. It was lent to the Franklin exhibition at the A.P.S., from Jan. 17 to April 20, 1956, and was briefly seen in that period, once more beside the portrait of Deborah from which it had been separated for 178 years.[5]

2   1759. Painting, replica of No. 1. Unlocated.
The portrait was Franklin's gift to Dr. Thomas Bond of Philadelphia. After his return to America in 1762, Franklin noticed a crackle in the paint, and upon his return to London brought this to Wilson's attention. The artist blamed a new type of varnish, but agreed to paint a new picture on the condition that the old one be sent back to him. See below, No. 3.

3   Commissioned ca. 1765; received, 1771. Painting, replica of No. 1. Oil on canvas, 30¼ x 25¼ in. Hair in wig not clearly defined; parted in center. Eyes with yellow iris, dark brown pupil. Mole on left cheek. Light brown coat. Background very dark with reddish brown streaks at lower left and lower right, perhaps representing a stormy sky. *Owner:* Mrs. James Manderson Castle, Jr., Wilmington, Del.

3. H.S.P.
4. Charles Henry Hart, "The Wilson Portrait of Franklin; Earl Grey's Gift to the Nation," *P.M.H.B., 30,* 409–16. *Record of the Celebration of the Two Hundredth Anniversary of the Birth of Benjamin Franklin,* pp. xv–xvii. Minutes, A.P.S., April 20, 1906, p. 74.
5. Described and illust. in *Proceedings of the A.P.S., 100* (1956), 371.

The painting replaced Franklin's earlier gift to Thomas Bond (No. 2). Dr. Bond wrote in acknowledgment on July 6, 1771: "Good Mrs. Franklin has presented Me with a new Picture of you, which has been much visited, and much admired, it is generally agreed there is in it a remarkable sensible meaning, added to a most striking Likeness. I must sincerely thank you for this additional Instance of your Friendship."[6] Franklin wrote to Deborah from London on Aug. 14, 1771: "Let me know whether Dr. Bond likes the old one better than the new one; if so the old one is to be return'd hither to Mr. Wilson the Painter. You may keep the Frame, as it may be wanted for some other Picture there."[7] Deborah having failed to make the matter clear, Franklin wrote more explicitly to Dr. Bond on Feb. 5, 1772:

> When I was at your House I observed that the Paint of the Picture you had was all cracked. I complain'd of it to the Painter. He acknowledged that in that Picture, and three others, he had made a Trial of a new Varnish which had been attended with this mischievous Effect; and offer'd to make Amends, if I would sit to him again, by drawing a new Picture gratis, only on this condition, that the old one should be return'd to him. I wrote this to Mrs. Franklin, who should have acquainted you with it, but I suppose forgot it. He was 5 or 6 years in finishing it, having much other Business. If therefore you like the new one best, please to put the old one in a Box, and send it by the next Ship hither, as the Painter expects to have one or the other returned.[8]

It may be supposed that Franklin did pose again, in compliance with the artist's stipulation. The painting, however, appears to be, with very slight alterations, a replica of that of 1759. It is clear from the lack of any crackle in the painting that Dr. Bond did return the old canvas and retain the new.

Dr. Bond died on March 4, 1784, leaving a family of seven chil-

6. Franklin Papers (A.P.S.), *3*, no. 67.
7. Ibid., *46*, Pt. II, no. 76.
8. A.P.S.

411

dren. The painting is not mentioned in his will. The assumption, unsupported by evidence, is that the painting came into the possession of Edward Duffield, later one of Franklin's executors. It passed to his grandson, Edward Duffield Ingraham (1793–1854), lawyer and author, son of Francis and Elizabeth (Duffield) Ingraham. It was then described as "a present from Franklin, supposed to have been done by West."[9] At the sale of Mr. Ingraham's library in 1855 it was bought by Franklin's great-grandson, Dr. Thomas Hewson Bache, and in 1912 or 1913 was purchased from the estate of Dr. Bache by his nephew, Franklin Bache. It was inherited by his son, Charles Bache, whose sister is its present owner.

> 4   Ca. 1760. Painting, enlarged replica of No. 1. Oil on canvas, 50 x 40 in. Brown coat. Green curtain in right background. Table with roll of papers in right foreground. *Owner:* Knoedler Galleries, New York. Pl. 2.

The painting was undoubtedly made for the publication of the mezzotint from it (No. 5). The artist may then have sold it, or, if one of his patrons had invested in the print, it would have passed into his hands. Probably from the time of its painting until its sale in 1946, it hung at Quiddenham Hall, Norfolk, the seat of the Earls of Albemarle. There also hung the full-length portrait of Washington, captured at sea by Capt. George Keppel on Sept. 3, 1780. Capt. Keppel's prize had been the American packet *Mercury*, bound for Holland with the late President of Congress, Henry Laurens. He had with him the draft of a treaty with the Dutch, and Peale's new painting of Washington was intended as a gift to the Stadtholder. In tradition, the "Franklin" was said also to have been in Laurens' baggage.[10] This, however, cannot be credited. There is no record of the painting's ever having gone to America. Nor can it be believed that Laurens would have carried with him for such a purpose the long-outdated portrait of another diplomat already in Europe. It is far more probable that some member of the family, which included a governor of Virginia, had acquired the painting when new, because of his interest in Franklin and

9. Jared Sparks' notes, ca. 1839 (Sparks Papers). Watson, *Annals of Philadelphia, 1,* 533; illust. opp. p. 523.

10. Prince Frederick Duleep Singh, *Portraits in Norfolk Houses* (Norwich, ca. 1928), p. 147.

American affairs. One who might have done so is the admiral, Augustus Keppel, second son of the 2d Earl of Albemarle, a strong Whig who from 1761, when the mezzotint from the painting was published, until 1780, was in Parliament, a friend of Burke and foe of the "King's Friends."

The painting was purchased by the Knoedler Galleries at Sotheby's on Feb. 13, 1946.

> 5   1761. Mezzotint by James McArdell (1728–65), after No. 4. Plate size, 13⅞ x 9⅞ in. "B. Wilson pinxt. Js. McArdell fecit. / B. Franklin of Philadelphia. 1761 / L.L.D. F.R.S." Pl. 2. The mole on Franklin's left cheek is strongly indicated. That on the chin is not shown. The book, without title in the painting, is marked, "Electric[1] / Exp[ts]." The static electricity machine with glass globe has been added to the still life on the table, right foreground. In the left background, lightning strikes a town as in the painting, but above this, light is shown breaking through the clouds in a symbolism not used by Wilson.

For later impressions the date 1761 was erased from the plate. In 1794 a new print, either a copy or an extensive revision of the plate, was published by the London printsellers, Laurie and Whittle. The head had been altered as to likeness, with the addition of glasses, and bears no resemblance to Franklin.

> 6   Ca. 1762–72. Painting by Matthew Pratt (1734–1805), altered copy after Wilson. Oil on canvas, 29 x 24 in. Eyes with yellow iris, dark brown pupils. Complexion rather swarthy. Mole on left cheek, but not under left lip. Olive-green coat and waistcoat with crudely painted highlights. Background very dark with tones of green and brown. Pale red lines at right, over the shoulder, may indicate a curtain. Lower left background shows indistinctly a village struck by lightning, while a light area at the upper right follows the cloud depiction in the mezzotint (No. 5). *Owner:* American Scenic and Historic Preservation Society, Philipse Manor Hall, Yonkers, N.Y. Pl. 3.

The eyes are similar to Wilson's painting, but various other details, including the highlights, suggest dependence on the mezzotint. If not a life portrait, as has long been supposed, the painting still has authority as the work of an artist who knew Franklin well by sight. It may have been painted in Philadelphia or in England.

The painting was acquired by Charles Henry Hart from Mrs. Charles P. Jackson (Rosalie Vallance Tiers), a great-granddaughter of the artist. It was purchased from Hart by Alexander Smith Cochran on March 12, 1908, and in 1929 bequeathed with his entire collection to the American Scenic and Historic Preservation Society.[1]

WINTER, JOHN (d. 1782)
See JOHNSON.

WOOD, RALPH (1716–72)
See STAFFORDSHIRE.

WRIGHT, JOSEPH (1756–93)
1   1782. Painting, altered copy of DUPLESSIS, "Gray Coat," No. 1. Destroyed.

It was Joseph Wright's great good fortune to be chosen to paint a portrait of Franklin for Richard Oswald at the beginning of the peace negotiations in the spring of 1782, a painting from which he might have expected to do a prosperous business in replicas for the rest of his life. (See above, pp. 151–54.) It was his great misfortune to lose the original from which this harvest might have been reaped, by shipwreck on his voyage to America.

The painting was a copy from the famous Duplessis pastel, with the color of the dress changed to red, a chair back indicated, and the lines of Franklin's face slightly altered from life. There can be little doubt that the young artist was chosen not only as an American but for his complaisance in the matter of his subject's unwillingness to undergo the tedium of posing. His letter of August 1782, just before embarking for America, asking for "leave to make another Copy," and apologizing, "as I may be in some measure troublesome and he must be tired of seeing me so constantly," implies

1. *Scenic and Historic America, 4* (1935), 20, 27.

Franklin's presence in the operation. His statement, "The last I did Mr. Whitford has been pleased to take from me," implies also that he had sold his first original and had now to make a new matrix for his American replicas. That version must have been with him when he embarked from Nantes in October and been lost with the ship. The portrait type was unknown in America until a version (No. 3) was brought from England to Boston in 1860.

> 2 1782. Painting. Oil on canvas, 31¾ x 25½ in. Gray hair. Hazel eyes. Dull red coat and waistcoat. Yellow chair back upholstered in dark green. Olive-brown background. Mounted on a panel. Inscribed on the back, "Benjamin Franklin by J. S. Duplessis presented by Benjamin Franklin to Richard Oswald who negotiated on behalf of the government with Franklin in Paris 1782 and was chief negotiator of the treaty with the United States." An old label on the back reads, "The property of the late R. A. Oswald Esq. J. P. of Auchincruive, Ayrshire, N. B." A modern label, "B. Franklin by Duplessis. Above was written on back of canvas before it was mounted on panel by M. O'Brien & Son." Also printed label of the "House of O'Brien, Chicago." The frame is similarly labeled. Richard Alexander Oswald, then owner of the painting, wrote on April 14, 1892, "With a magnifier I can trace on the back of the picture in red the remains of 'Mons. Oswald.' I have little doubt from the 's' the picture is by a French artist."[2] *Owner:* Yale University, New Haven.

The painting made for Richard Oswald during the peace negotiations of 1782 is presumably the original both of replicas by Wright and of copies by British artists. Richard Oswald died on Nov. 6, 1784, at Auchincruive, Ayrshire, the estate which he had purchased in 1759. The estate and with it the portrait was inherited first by his nephew, George Oswald, and then by George Oswald's son, Richard Alexander Oswald, the Laird of Auchincruive who triumphed over Lord Panmure of Brechin and Navar ("The Generous Sportsman") in the "grand main of cocks" at Hallion's in

2. R. A. Oswald to Clarence Winthrop Bowen (Boston Public Library). Also *Magazine of American History,* 27 (1892), 472.

Edinburgh.[3] In 1841 portrait and estate passed to a cousin, James Oswald, merchant in Glasgow. He had already inherited from his father a second portrait (No. 3) which he gave to a friend, Joseph Parkes, leaving the "Ambassador's Portrait," as it was called, hanging where it always had at Auchincruive. (See Chart, p. 418.) It was at Auchincruive on March 18, 1898, when its owner, a later Richard Alexander Oswald, wrote of it as follows to the Librarian of the Boston Public Library:

> The Ambassador's Portrait still hangs where it has ever hung and that is in this house. . . . The picture you have is one which belonged to my Great Grandfather, hung in his House of Shieldhall and was removed by my Great Uncle—his son—to his House in Glasgow where people now alive saw it.
>
> He—my Great Uncle James Oswald M. P. for Glasgow, succeeded to this House and Property the year I was born, 1841, but he never lived here and handed over House and Property to my Uncle Alexander Oswald my Father's Elder Brother, and I well remember as a Boy of 13 or perhaps before, having the picture now hanging here of Franklin pointed out to me as the picture given by Franklin to Mr. Oswald in 1780 or so. This will bring us to 1854; Since when I am certain the picture has never left this House.
>
> James Oswald died in 1853 and you will see that Mr. Charles Sumner says, dates (57) and (59) in speaking of Mr. Parkes "he called it a Greuze."
>
> There is no reason it should not be a Greuze, for both the Shieldhall and the Auchincruive picture might be a replica of the other.[4]

Richard Alexander Oswald's attribution of the painting to Duplessis was based upon its similarity to the engraving of that owned by William Temple Franklin and by what appeared to be French script in the "Mons. Oswald" on the back. He pursued the

3. John Kay, *Series of Original Portraits,* 1 (Edinburgh, 1838), p. 426n.
4. Boston Public Library.

legend that Franklin and his ancestor had exchanged portraits, but was led to the conviction that this could not have been. "Mr. Oswald had a personal objection to being painted and I doubt if he was ever placed on canvass. Zoffany attempted to paint him in the background of his portrait of Mrs. Oswald, but Mr. Oswald made him paint it out, and I believe he exists behind a cloud in that picture —the only one he ever was under."[5]

The painting was purchased from the estate of Richard Alexander Oswald by Gabriel Wells and sold to William Smith Mason in 1922. It was first attributed to Wright by George Simpson Eddy.[6] It came to Yale University with the Mason collection in 1936.

3   Ca. 1782. Painting, replica or copy of No. 2. Oil on canvas, 30⅝ x 24 in. *Owner:* Boston Public Library.

The portrait may be presumed to have been commissioned by Richard Oswald, owner of No. 2, and to have been given by him either to his brother, Dr. James Oswald, or to his nephew, Alexander Oswald of Shieldhall. Alexander Oswald bequeathed it to his son, James, who in 1841 became by inheritance the owner of both portraits. (See Chart, p. 418.) James Oswald, a Member of Parliament for Glasgow, presented it to Joseph Parkes. Charles Sumner saw it at his house in 1857 and 1859, recalled that it was then attributed to Greuze, and recalled its owner as "a very remarkable person, extensively known in London, full of information, fond of pictures, and much interested in our country, with an excellent American library & with an American wife born in Pennsylvania & grand-daughter of Priestley."[7] (See above, No. 2.)

Sumner wrote to Gardner Brewer of Boston about the picture, from Washington, Dec. 10, 1859:

> Mr. Parkes is an eminent literary character & lawyer & he authorized me to say that the Franklin portrait might be had for £250. Its authenticity, of course is beyond question. As a portrait by Greuze (the two in Boston are by Duplessis) painted for the British

5. Ibid.
6. George Simpson Eddy to William Smith Mason, May 19, 1924 (Eddy Papers).
7. Boston Public Library. The first published reference to the painting, then owned by Parkes, appeared in the *Edinburgh Review* (1854), p. 33.

negotiator, & coming from his family, it has an historic interest of the highest character, even if its artistic merit were not great.[8]

Both Mr. Palfrey and President Sparks, he added, had seen the picture and knew it well. On Jan. 12, 1860, Parkes accepted an offer of 200 guineas for the painting. He added that it needed no "Barbaric 'cleaning.' Not 6 years ago I had the old varnish off & new varnish (without oil) put on [by] a Mr. Bates—an eminent 'Restorer,' since deceased. Mr. Bates then told me, that the lineaments of the Portrait were so fine that any future cleaning, in the common scouring mode, would seriously injure the Painting.'"[9]

On March 7, 1872, Gardner Brewer presented the portrait to the trustees of the Public Library of the City of Boston as an addition to its new collection of Frankliniana.[1] It was still attributed to Greuze in 1883.[2] Charles Henry Hart considered the painting a copy, but by a better hand than Wright's.[3]

> 4   1782. Painting. Oil on canvas, 30 x 25 in. Inscribed on the back, "This picture of Dr. Franklin was painted at Paris in 1782, & was presented by him to Mr. Wm. Hodgson, of Colman Street, as a token of his Regard and Friendship."
> *Owner:* Corcoran Gallery of Art, Washington, D.C. Pl. 25.

The original owner of the portrait was Franklin's friend, William Hodgson (1745–1851), who during the war had handled financial affairs for him in London. From London Hodgson wrote to Franklin on Oct. 14, 1782, congratulating him on his improved health and looking forward to his completing "that great and famous work" which would prove that the liberties of mankind are not to be trifled with. Apropos of certain business matters, he added: "If the above Bill on Lorient is honored will you please to apply the whole or what part you please to Mr. Wright for the picture, which when proper opportunity offers, I am expecting."[4]

The picture presumably came on the market after Hodgson's

8. Boston Public Library.
9. Parkes to J. S. Morgan (ibid.).
1. Ibid.
2. *Proceedings of the M.H.S., 20* (1883), 359.
3. Frick Art Reference Library.
4. Franklin Papers (A.P.S.), *26,* no. 39.

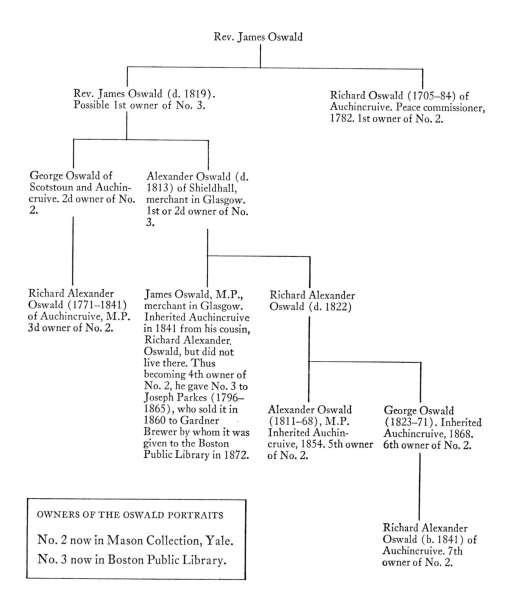

Rev. James Oswald

Rev. James Oswald (d. 1819). Possible 1st owner of No. 3.

Richard Oswald (1705–84) of Auchincruive. Peace commissioner, 1782. 1st owner of No. 2.

George Oswald of Scotstoun and Auchincruive. 2d owner of No. 2.

Alexander Oswald (d. 1813) of Shieldhall, merchant in Glasgow. 1st or 2d owner of No. 3.

Richard Alexander Oswald (1771–1841) of Auchincruive, M.P. 3d owner of No. 2.

James Oswald, M.P., merchant in Glasgow. Inherited Auchincruive in 1841 from his cousin, Richard Alexander Oswald, but did not live there. Thus becoming 4th owner of No. 2, he gave No. 3 to Joseph Parkes (1796–1865), who sold it in 1860 to Gardner Brewer by whom it was given to the Boston Public Library in 1872.

Richard Alexander Oswald (d. 1822)

Alexander Oswald (1811–68), M.P. Inherited Auchincruive, 1854. 5th owner of No. 2.

George Oswald (1823–71). Inherited Auchincruive, 1868. 6th owner of No. 2.

Richard Alexander Oswald (b. 1841) of Auchincruive. 7th owner of No. 2.

OWNERS OF THE OSWALD PORTRAITS

No. 2 now in Mason Collection, Yale.

No. 3 now in Boston Public Library.

death at the great age of 106. It next appears as owned by Graves, the print seller and successor to John Boydell. Henry Stevens (1819–86) who, with his brother, Benjamin Franklin Stevens (1833–1902), was an American and dealer in Americana living in London, wrote of it as follows to J. S. Morgan on Nov. 28, 1882:

> My Dear Mr. Morgan,
>
> I have seen the Portrait of Franklin by Duplesis at Graves's. It is no doubt a genuine portrait & is in good order. When Mr. Graves (who is an old friend of mine) saw that I knew something of Franklins portraits (Painted & engraved) he told me that he had written to you & hoped you would take it at 150 Guineas, & that you had looked in last evening & thought a 100 right to fetch it. I then told him that I had seen you yesterday & you had spoken of it & that was the reason of my curiosity to see it. After some conversation he said that he felt pretty sure of selling it at the 150 Guineas even if you did not have it & that he thought Mr. Scharff would take it for the National Portrait Gallery. Now only at the beginning of this month I met Scharff at Murrays dinner & he said "Well you havn't found us a Franklin yet." This has been a greeting of his these ten years. I therefore feel pretty sure that Scharff will take it if you do not.[5]
>
> Mr. Graves at last said "Well, I thought to have 150 Guineas, but if you think that too much I will make it less to Mr. Morgan. I replied that it was no business of mine, but I hoped that he would secure it, but perhaps you had better drop a little. He said Will 150 pounds do? & I said a "little more." He finally said make it £140, and I will clean it up, put it in a nice carved frame with plate glass, all in clean & first rate order, the extras to cost me £10. So that is equivalent to £130. for the portrait as it is. I told him I would report to you & he said he would hold it subject to your decision until next Saturday.

5. The National Portrait Gallery had bought its "Franklin" (see DUPLESSIS: "Gray Coat," No. 9) in 1882, eleven years earlier.

It seems to me that this portrait is well worth the
£140. done up. Duplesis painted several replicas
with variations. This presented by Franklin himself
to his friend Hodgson . . . [*illegible*] unquestionably
one of the finest.

I hope I have not put my foot in it by calling to see
it. I did not mention your name until Mr. Graves
told me that he had offered it to you.

The writing on the back is old and probably of the
time, but it is not in Dr. Franklin's hand. I hope you
will secure the portrait.[6]

It was Stevens who arranged the sale of the portrait in 1885 to
William Wilson Corcoran (1798–1888), whose gallery in Washington had been begun in 1859 and incorporated by Congress in
1870.[7]

5 1782. Painting. Oil on canvas, 30 x 25 in. Steely gray hair.
Hazel eyes. Darkish brick red coat and waistcoat. Background,
at right gray with a green cast graduating into darker green
with a gray cast at the back of the head, left. Lately an inscription has been painted across the top of the canvas, "BENJ.
FRANKLIN. LL.D." *Owner:* The Royal Society, London.

The portrait was purchased from the artist in 1782 by Caleb
Whitefoord, who had come to Passy with Richard Oswald to
negotiate a treaty of peace. Two years later, he lent the portrait to
West for his group portrait of the peace commissioners (see WEST,
No. 1). To William Temple Franklin, who was to be included in
this painting, he wrote on June 30, 1784:

Some time ago, our old friend Mr. West, having
the opportunity of seeing three of the American
Plenipo's here, & wishing to transmit their Portraits to Posterity in some Historical picture, made
a sketch of the signing of the Preliminary Treaty, to
which I contributed a material part by lending him

6. Stevens letter press copy book, *2, 587*, property of Henry Stevens, Son and Stiles,
London. Information from Whitfield J. Bell, Jr.
7. Charles Henry Hart, "An Original Portrait of Franklin, Painted by Joseph
Wright, belonging to the Royal Society, London," *P.M.H.B., 32, 325.*

the Portrait of your Grandfather by Mr. Wright which I brought with me from Paris. There is only wanting (To make it compleat) a head of the Secretary of the American Commission, which Mr. West requests you will send us. A miniature will do; but it should be *in Colours*; & the attitude of the Head, *looking over the right shoulder*. I have promised the Portrait of your Grand Father, when Mr. West can spare it, to Mrs. Hewson; who from her long acquaintance and great veneration for him, I thought highly deserving of such a present. I reserve a copy of it for myself, & have given one to Mr. Strahan.

You had once thoughts of visiting this capital; pray is there any prospect of our having the pleasure of seeing you here?[8]

William did come in November, and West added his portrait to the group at that time. He also visited Georgiana Shipley and arranged for the loan of her snuff box miniature to West. It is quite possible that in each instance West reciprocated by having the young men in his studio make copies of the pictures lent or even doing them himself. This might account for William's own portrait of his grandfather (see DUPLESSIS, "Gray Coat," No. 4), and would explain Whitefoord's plan to "reserve a copy of it for myself," and his gift of "one to Mr. Strahan." It seems clear, however, that he did not give Mrs. Polly Hewson his original, retaining a copy. She emigrated to Philadelphia in 1786, and there is no record in her will or elsewhere to the effect that she owned such a painting. It would have been known and copied in America, and it would have been preserved among the carefully treasured heirlooms of her descendants. Moreover, Whitefoord's statement in the letter quoted below, "painted by Mr. Wright," has, coming from a connoisseur of art, all the authority of a clear attribution.

On Feb. 25, 1791, acknowledging his election to membership in the A.P.S., Whitefoord added in a postscript:

It is a curious coincidence of circumstances, that on the day and hour when your letter arrived, acquaint-

8. Franklin Papers (A.P.S.), *106,* no. 45a. Hart, "Original Portrait," pp. 322–23.

ing me of my Election into the American Philosophical Society, I received a letter of Thanks from
the Royal Society here, for a Portrait which I had
presented to them, of my honoured friend, your late
worthy President. It is an excellent Resemblance
of that truly Great man and useful Philosopher; and
was painted by Mr. Wright, an American Artist,
whom I employed at Paris in the year 1782. It is now
added to the Heads of illustrious Persons, in the
Royal Society's Great Room; and Doctor Franklin is
grouped with his immortal Brethren in Philosophy,
Newton, Boyle, and Locke.[9]

6   Undated. Painting. Oil on canvas, 31 x 26 in. Gray hair.
Hazel eyes. Claret coat, waistcoat, and buttons. Chair back
yellow with dark green upholstering. Background dark olive-
brown. *Owner:* Pennsylvania Academy of the Fine Arts, Philadelphia.

The portrait was listed in the catalogue of the collection of Joseph
Harrison, Jr. (1810–74), mechanical engineer, of Philadelphia,
as "No. 56. UNKNOWN. 'Portrait of B. Franklin.' . . . Purchased
from the late Wm. Vaughan, Esq., London, a contemporary of
Franklin, and always considered by him an original portrait."[1]
William Vaughan (1752–1850) was the younger brother of Benjamin Vaughan who had daringly published an edition of Franklin's writings in London during the war, with an engraving after
the Sèvres medallion as frontispiece. He was a London merchant
and insurance executive whose scientific interests had made him a
Fellow of the Royal Society and a member of the Linnaean Society
and Royal Astronomical Society. The portrait was purchased for its
present owner at the sale of a part of the Joseph Harrison collection.

7   1783. Painting, copy by Francesco Baricolo, after Joseph
Wright. Oil on canvas, 24⅜ x 21 in. (sight), and 32¾ x 28 in.
(including frame). "Dark blue-gray hair. Dark hazel eyes.

9. Hewins, *The Whitefoord Papers,* pp. 211–12.
1. *Catalogue of Pictures in the Gallery of Joseph Harrison, Jr., Rittenhouse
Square, Philadelphia* (ca. 1870), p. 6.

Eyebrows broad dark sepia. Cheeks, lips and nostrils deep pink. Face shaded crudely with bluegray & sepia brown. A very harsh and poorly painted picture." Signed on back of canvas, "F. Baricolo Pinsi / Parigi 1783."[2] Unlocated.

The portrait was painted for Dr. Edward Bancroft, Secretary to the American commission in Paris and the English spy who so pathetically clung to his personal admiration for the man he was betraying. It was offered to the National Portrait Gallery in 1865 by the Rev. T. Davis Lamb, of the Rectory, West Hocking, with the following letter:

> I have lately come into possession of a Portrait, in oils, of Dr. Franklin, the American Minister. . . .
>
> Dr. Franklin sat for it in 1783 & presented it to my grand father Dr. Bancroft, his private secretary. It has never been out of our family.
>
> In addition to its value as a work of art, it possesses great interest from the following incident, when Dr. Franklin was in England some years previously, he had been treated with great want of respect (as he thought) by the Privy Council before whom he appeared. On his return home he declared his intention never to wear the same clothes again, till he put them on to sign the treaty of American independence.
>
> This he did sign in 1783—and wore the same suit of clothes. He wore them once more when he sat for this portrait, at my grandfather's special request.

The purchase, offered at 200 guineas, was declined by the trustees of the gallery at their meeting in July 1865, the director, however, preserving both a sketch and descriptive notes on the picture. Its similarity to the portrait purchased in 1871 (DUPLESSIS, "Gray Coat," No. 9) led to the attribution of that canvas, for a time, to Baricolo.

Francesco, or François, Baricolo, painter and engraver, was an obscure figure, living in Paris. This, the only painting identified as his, has brought him a disproportionate measure of fame. As an

2. Notes of Sir George Scharf, July 22, 1865, archives of the National Portrait Gallery, London.

engraver he was somewhat less obscure, a portrait of Necker and a few works in color being recorded.

8 Ca. 1783–84. Painting, copy after Joseph Wright. Unlocated.

Caleb Whitefoord, in his letter of June 30, 1784 (see above, No. 5), states that he has given a copy of his portrait by Wright "to Mr. Strahan." Franklin's old friend, William Strahan, printer, Member of Parliament, died on July 9, 1785. His will, recorded at Somerset House, leaves his personal effects to his son, Andrew. Andrew, who also knew Franklin and who carried on the printing business, would have been the logical one to have succeeded to the portrait. There was also an elder son, George, and a daughter, Margaret Penelope, the wife of John Spottiswoode, a son-in-law, Andrew Johnston, and grandchildren and nephews.

Early examples of the Wright type which might possibly be associated with this or with the two other unlocated pictures noted below are in the collection of T. E. Hanley (28 x 24 in.) and the Mason Collection, Yale University (30 x 25 in.).

9 1783. Line engraving by William Angus (1742–1821), after a painting or copy of a painting by Joseph Wright. Plate size, 6 7/8 x 4 5/16 in. "EUROPEAN MAGAZINE / BENJ. FRANKLIN, L. L. D. / W. Angus Sculp. / From a painting in the Possession of F. Schwediauer, M. D. in Newman Street. / Publish'd April 1st, 1783, by J. Fielding, Paternoster Row, J. Sewell, Cornhill, & J. Debrett, Piccadilly." The engraving first appeared in the *European Magazine* of March 1783. The heavy shading of the coat indicates that the original was the dark red of the Joseph Wright type.

There is every reason to suppose that Dr. Franz Xaver Schwediauer, Austrian physician, associate of Ingenhousz, Pringle, and other friends of Franklin, might have been the owner of a portrait of Franklin. Arriving in Paris from London on Sept. 17, 1782, he had written Franklin asking for an interview that he might communicate his plan for a reformed penal code. Newman St., his London address, was also that of Benjamin West. At the outbreak of the French Revolution he was drawn again to Paris, remained, and died there on Aug. 27, 1824. At his death he is said to have owned a quite different portrait of Franklin (see L'HOSPITAL, No. 2). In 1855 "T.H.B." of Philadelphia inquired in *Notes and Queries* as to the whereabouts of Schwediauer's painting in the engraving, but received no reply.[3]

10   Ca. 1825. Lithograph by Thomas Kelly, after a painting or copy of a painting by Joseph Wright. The New York Public Library owns a lithograph of Franklin, Joseph Wright type, 8 13/16 x 7 5/16 in., inscribed, "Thomas Kelly. From an Original Portrait, given to Arch'd Hamilton Rowen Esq. / by Dr. Franklin in 1776 at Paris / Drawn on stone by T. Kelly and Printed by A. H. R. Leinster St."

Kelly was an amateur lithographer of New York City. This work is tentatively dated 1825. Archibald Hamilton Rowen is not identified. If made from an actual painting, it must have been the first of the Wright type to come to America.

11, 12   Undated. Paintings, copies after Joseph Wright.
An early copy from the collection of Lord Northbrook was sold at Sotheby's in 1931 and is recorded in the photograph collection of the National Portrait Gallery, London. Its owner was a descendant of Sir Francis Baring (1740–1810), founder of Baring Bros. and Co., one of whose sons figured in American history as Lord Ashburton, while another married a daughter of William Bingham, of Philadelphia.

Another strong early copy was painted for Sampson Vryling Stoddard Wilder (1780–1865), who spent many years as a banker in Paris, and also traveled extensively in England. This work is attributed in family tradition to John Vanderlyn, who had enjoyed the friendship and patronage of Wilder. Vanderlyn was in England in 1805. It is now owned by Mrs. Robert M. Tappan, of Needham, Mass.

13, 14   Undated. Paintings.
To his letter to William Temple Franklin, dated August 1782 (see p. 153), Joseph Wright added a postcript saying that he had thought of making the portrait he would take with him to America

3. 2d ser. *1*, 12.

"the size of my mother's, or the other little one you saw." At least two such small "Franklins" of the type are extant, but without any record of their origin.

One, 12½ x 9½ in., was purchased from the collection at the Château de Réau, Saintes, by George F. Baker of New York.[4]

The other, 14 x 12 in., was in the collection of Herbert Lee Pratt.[5] This may be the same as that formerly owned by H. N. Stevens, London.[6]

WRIGHT, PATIENCE (1725–86)

> 1   1772. Wax sculpture. Life-size bust, in natural color and with natural hair. Probably exhibited as a clothed figure, with hands. Unlocated. (See Pls. 40, 41.)

On Feb. 1, 1772, when she wrote her will on board the *Nancy,* about to sail from New York harbor, Patience Wright was famous up and down the colonial seaboard and was setting out to conquer London with such a show of marvelously lifelike figures as that capital had not seen before. In this effort the middle-aged widow with the loud voice and the piercing eye was to be entirely successful. She must have just arrived when Franklin wrote on March 30, 1772, in reply to the letter she had brought him from his sister Jane in Boston. He promised Jane that he would recommend the lady to his friends. Patience had brought him one of those surprises which were the key to her success, an amazingly lifelike bust of his old friend Cadwallader Colden. A week later, on April 6, Henry Marchant, after visiting Mrs. Salmon's waxworks in Fleet St., a long-established London spectacle, noted in his diary that there was "a much superior Piece to any I saw here at Dr. Franklin's. The Bust of Lieut. Govr. Colden of New York done by one Mrs. Wright late of New York just arrived here to set up her Business."[7]

Mrs. Wright found quarters at 30 Great Suffolk St., the Strand, and proceeded to fill them—this being the secret of her popularity —with well-known individuals and character types faultlessly re-

4. Frick Art Reference Library.
5. Ibid.
6. Bowen, *Centennial Celebration,* p. 451.
7. Manuscript diary owned by Miss Alice Clarke and Miss May Harris. From copy at A.P.S., p. 13.

produced. Franklin was there in effigy, and in the others known to have been present one can see the pattern of his introductions: Mrs. Catherine Macaulay, the historian whose new liberal viewpoint had won her many admirers, David Garrick, the Earl of Chatham, Lord Lyttelton, and John Wilkes.[8] Franklin wrote to his wife on April 6, 1773, that he had somehow incurred the displeasure of Mrs. Wright. It is probable that Patience, who had entered into a friendly relationship with the Penn family, had been induced by them to pay less attention to Franklin. She may have taken his portrait out of her collection, since later descriptions make no mention of it. See above, pp. 84–95.

2 1772. Wax sculpture, replica of No. 1. Complete figure, with sculptured head and hands. Unlocated.

As echoes of her success in London, Mrs. Wright at once began to send duplicates back to New York to enhance the exhibition maintained by her sister, Rachel Wells. Mrs. Wells moved the show to Philadelphia, where Mrs. Wright's only son, Joseph, had been in school in the care of another of his aunts. This probably occurred when Congress assembled in the city. Charles Willson Peale paid a shilling each admission for his sisters on Oct. 5, 1776.[9] John Adams was there on May 10, 1777, and describes two rooms, one with the parable of the Prodigal Son in a waxwork tableau, the other with "the figures of Chatham, Franklin, Sawbridge, Mrs. Macauley, and several others."[1] He mentions also "another historical piece" of Elisha restoring to life the Shunammite's son. This had been a subject of Benjamin West's, and to copy the painting in water color had been Peale's first exercise as a student in West's studio. It is reasonable to infer that Peale had collaborated in the making of the wax group and, if so, it was probably in return for lessons, since he was making waxwork figures of his own at a later period.

After the war, Mrs. Wells was living with others of her family at her childhood home in Bordentown, N.J. She had the figures there, though no visitor has left a description of their exhibition. She received in 1785 "a Present of a Lott in Bordentown to build

8. *New York Gazette and the Weekly Mercury,* Nov. 9, 1772.
9. Diary (Peale-Sellers Papers).
1. C. F. Adams, *Familiar Letters of John Adams and His Wife,* p. 271.

her a Museum on." This information appears in a curious letter of Dec. 16, 1785, written assuredly by Mrs. Wells, but purporting to be the anonymous communication of an aged and infirm statesman "that was first in Congress," begging Franklin to arrange a similar gift for Mrs. Wright. Mrs. Wright could thus be persuaded to return from London to "Lay her bons" on native soil, and be rewarded for her services as a secret agent: "Mr. Hancock & others of our oldest members allways alowed that her inteligence was the best we receivd them by the hand of her sister Wells who found them in ye wax heads she then sent to her &c &c by her Last Latters she Cant be content to have her bons Laid in London."[2] Patience did, however, lay her bones in London, and Rachel hers in faraway New Jersey. Rachel's will, dated Sept. 17, 1795, and proved March 23, 1796, left the wax figures to her brother, John Lovell. According to the inventory, now missing, there were then 33 figures in the collection.[3]

3   Undated. Replica or copy of No. 1. Destroyed.
Much of Patience Wright's correspondence with Franklin during the Revolution concerns the plight of Ebenezer Smith Platt, a young American held in London on a charge of treason. He came of a Long Island family, as did she, and she had known him well in New York, where, in 1774, he was in the watch and clock business.[4] The war, in which his brother, Richard, figured as an aide to Genl. Montgomery at the storming of Quebec, and one of their uncles as a member of Congress, saw Ebenezer embarked on an adventurous mercantile career, ending with his arrival in London as a prisoner.[5] With the waxwork artist pleading his cause and Franklin perhaps an agent in the matter, he was in time released and promptly married her daughter, Elizabeth. The couple returned to America with a waxwork show and settled in New York. Ebenezer, who had been ailing as a prisoner, died. Elizabeth spent her last years with her aunt in Bordentown, where she wrote her will on Sept.

2. Franklin Papers (A.P.S.), *44*, p. 76.
3. Elmer T. Hutchinson, ed., *New Jersey Archives. Volume 38. Calendar of New Jersey Wills, 9* (Newark, 1944), 404.
4. *Arts and Crafts in New York, 1726–1776*, p. 159.
5. G. Lewis Platt, *The Platt Lineage* (New York, 1891), p. 48. Elizabeth Wright to Benjamin Franklin, Feb. 13, 1777 (Franklin Papers, A.P.S., *5*, no. 56).

4, 1792, and it was proved twelve days later. Her estate was very small and included no waxwork.[6]

From the slender evidence of his advertisements in the New York papers, it appears probable that Daniel Bowen, who was buying up museum exhibits of all sorts, had purchased the Platt collection after Ebenezer's death. His "Lord North," advertised on June 11, 1788, must have come from Mrs. Wright's in London. So also his "King, Queen, and Prince of Wales of Great-Britain, habited in cloaths which were presented by the King," advertised on Oct. 3, 1789.[7] On Oct. 10, 1793, Bowen called attention to other figures of particular interest, among them "Dr. Benjamin Franklin sitting at a table with an Electrical apparatus," and "Mrs. Platt, the late Celebrated American Artist in Wax Work."[8] When Bowen established his Columbian Museum in Boston, the first item listed in the "Large Collection of Wax-Work (large as Life)" was a figure of "The late Dr. Benjamin Franklin."[9] The museum was destroyed by fire in 1803 and again in 1807.

4   1781. Wax sculpture. Destroyed.

The portrait, a head only, was made for Elkanah Watson. It was not from life, but made at the Hôtel d'York, Faubourg Saint Germain, in Paris, where he and Mrs. Wright were staying, and was then taken out to Passy in order to pass comparison with the original. After Mrs. Wright's return to England, Watson played numerous pranks with the head and with a suit of clothes given him by Franklin for the purpose. It was broken, many years later, after his return to America. See above, pp. 145–51, and Pl. 41.

6. *Archives of the State of New Jersey. 1st series. Volume 37. Calendar of New Jersey Wills, 8* (Jersey City, 1942), 286.
7. Rita Susswein Gottesman, *The Arts and Crafts in New York, 1777–1799.* (New York, 1954), p. 386.
8. Ibid., p. 388.
9. Photo. of broadside, author's collection.

INDEX

Francis Folger Franklin, ca. 1736–37, by Samuel Johnson (?). Courtesy of Mrs. J. Manderson Castle, Jr.; photo courtesy of Frick Art Reference Library

The Lord Euston, mezzotint by John Smith, 1689, after Sir Godfrey Kneller, 1685. Courtesy of the New York Public Library

Benjamin Franklin, ca. 1738–46, by Robert Feke. Courtesy of Harvard University

Mrs. John Franklin, by John Greenwood. Courtesy of the Brooklyn Museum

Benjamin Franklin, 1757, by C. Dixon. Courtesy of the Museum of Fine Arts, Boston

Self-portrait. Signed "C. D. / Se ipse / p / 1748" by C. Dixon. Courtesy of the Victoria and Albert Museum

Benjamin Franklin, by Benjamin Wilson (WILSON, no. 4). Courtesy of Knoedler Galleries, New York

Benjamin Franklin, 1759, by Benjamin Wilson (WILSON, no. 1). Courtesy of the White House, Washington; photo by Victor Amato

Benjamin Franklin, mezzotint by James McArdell, 1761 (WILSON, no. 5). Courtesy of the New York Public Library

Benjamin Franklin, 1759, by Benjamin Wilson (WILSON, no. 1. Infra-red photograph, revealing detail). Courtesy of the White House, Washington; photo by Victor Amato

Benjamin Franklin, by Matthew Pratt (WILSON, no. 6). Courtesy of the American Scenic and Historic Preservation Society; photo by Lawrence D. Thornton

Self-portrait, by Benjamin Wilson. Courtesy of the Earl Spencer; photo courtesy of National Portrait Gallery

Mrs. Deborah Franklin, by Benjamin Wilson, after an unidentified artist. Courtesy of the American Philosophical Society

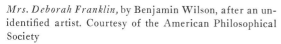

Benjamin Franklin, 1762, by Mason Chamberlin (CHAMBERLIN, no. 1). Courtesy of Wharton Sinkler

Benjamin Franklin, by George Dunlop Leslie, after Chamberlin. Courtesy of Yale University

Benjamin Franklin, mezzotint by Edward Fisher, 1763 (CHAMBERLIN, no. 3). Courtesy of the Philadelphia Museum of Art, Mrs. John D. Rockefeller Collection

Benjamin Franklin, engraving by François Nicolas Martinet, 1773 (CHAMBERLIN, no. 4). Courtesy of Yale University

Benjamin Franklin, engraving by John Lodge, 1777 (CHAMBERLIN, no. 5). Courtesy of the Philadelphia Museum of Art, Mrs. John D. Rockefeller Collection

Benjamin Franklin, anonymous medal, 1777 (CHAMBERLIN, no. 6). Courtesy of the American Numismatic Society

Early and late 19th century versions engraved by S. Topham, John Romney, and W. J. Alais. Courtesy of Yale University

Political Unrest in Pennsylvania, 1764, by an unknown artist (UNKNOWN ARTIST: CARICATURE no. 1). Courtesy of the Historical Society of Pennsylvania

The March of the Paxton Men, by an unknown artist (UNKNOWN ARTIST: CARICATURE no. 2). Courtesy of the Library Company of Philadelphia

Franklin and the Quakers, 1764, by an unknown artist (UNKNOWN ARTIST: CARICATURE no. 3). Courtesy of the Historical Society of Pennsylvania

Rebuttal to the Pro-Franklin "Medley," by an unknown artist (UNKNOWN ARTIST: CARICATURE no. 4). Courtesy of the Historical Society of Pennsylvania

The COUNTER-MEDLY, being a proper ANSWER to all the DUNCES of the MEDLY and their ABETTORS.

Benjamin Franklin, 1766, by David Martin (MAR-TIN, no. 1). Courtesy of Knoedler Galleries, New York

Benjamin Franklin, by David Martin, 1772 (MAR-TIN, no. 3). Courtesy of Dr. Alexander J. Alexander

Self-portrait, by David Martin. Courtesy of the National Gallery of Scotland

Benjamin Franklin, by an unidentified artist (MARTIN, no. 8). Courtesy of the Earl of Yarborough

Benjamin Franklin, 1766, by Isaac Gosset (GOSSET, no. 4). Courtesy of Dr. Philip Bate, Victoria and Albert Museum

Benjamin Franklin, ceramic medallion by James Tassie, after Gosset. Courtesy of the National Gallery of Scotland

Benjamin Franklin, medal by unidentified artist (GOSSET, no. 7). Courtesy of Yale University

Jean Jacques Rousseau, black basalt plaque by Wedgwood and Bentley, after a wax bas-relief by Isaac Gosset. Courtesy of Mr. and Mrs. Louis Henkels; photo by Sylvia R. Cuden, Buten Museum of Wedgwood

Jean Jacques Rousseau, mezzotint by David Martin, 1766, after the painting by Allan Ramsay. Courtesy of the British Museum

Benjamin Franklin, 1777, engraving by Augustin de Saint Aubin, after a drawing by Charles Nicolas Cochin (COCHIN, no. 1). Courtesy of the Philadelphia Museum of Art, Mrs. John D. Rockefeller Collection

Benjamin Franklin, engraving by Pierre Adrien Le Beau (1748–ca. 1800), after a drawing by Claude Louis Desrais (1746–1816); the Cochin altered to accord with the subject's new ambassadorial dignity. Courtesy of the Bibliothèque Nationale

Benjamin Franklin, 1777, medallion by Jean Baptiste Nini, after a drawing by Thomas Walpole (NINI: WALPOLE, no. 1). Courtesy of the National Portrait Gallery, London

Benjamin Franklin, a trial, with the famous spectacles (NINI: WALPOLE, no. 3). Courtesy of Max Slater; photo courtesy of the Massachusetts Historical Society

Benjamin Franklin, 1778, the fur cap removed (NINI: WALPOLE, no. 7). Courtesy of the Bibliothèque Nationale

Benjamin Franklin, 1779, the final version, after a drawing by Anne Vallayer-Coster (NINI: VALLAYER-COSTER, no. 3). Courtesy of the Fogg Museum of Art

Self-portrait, Anne Vallayer-Coster. Courtesy of the Musée National de Versailles; photo courtesy of Archives Photographiques, Paris

Benjamin Franklin, the "Classic" medallion by Wedgwood (WEDGWOOD, no. 4). Courtesy of the Fogg Museum of Art

Benjamin Franklin, 1778, the original model (SÈVRES, no. 1). Courtesy of the Manufacture Nationale de Sèvres

Benjamin Franklin, 1778, unglazed porcelain medallion (SÈVRES, no. 1). Courtesy of the Henry E. Huntington Library and Art Gallery

Benjamin Franklin, the medallion painted on china, at Sèvres, ca. 1779 (SÈVRES, no. 3). Courtesy of Mrs. Herbert A. May

Benjamin Franklin, "M. perier ce 4 janvier 1783" (Unknown Artist: Drawings, no. 1). Courtesy of the Walters
Art Gallery, Baltimore

Benjamin Franklin, in Lavater's *Essai sur la Physiognomie,* 1783 (Unknown Artist Recorded in Engravings, no. 1). Courtesy of Yale University

Benjamin Franklin, engraving by Robert Pollard, 1780 (see Elmer; Sèvres, no. 3). Photo by
James F. Steinmetz

Benjamin Franklin, by Stephen Elmer, 1780. Courtesy of Edward
Eberstandt and Sons, New York

Benjamin Franklin, original plaster model (SÈVRES, no. 10). Courtesy of the Manufacture Nationale de Sèvres

Benjamin Franklin, original model (SÈVRES, no. 8). Courtesy of the Manufacture Nationale de Sèvres

Benjamin Franklin, porcelain bust (SÈVRES, no. 8). Courtesy of the Fogg Museum of Art

Benjamin Franklin, 1777, bust by Claude Dejoux. Courtesy of the Musée de la Coopération Franco-Américaine, Château de Blérancourt

Benjamin Franklin, 1777, bust attributed to Louis Pierre Dufourny de Villiers. Courtesy of Sotheby and Company, London

Lafayette and Madame Roland (detail), by Jean Jacques Hauer (see DUFOURNY). Courtesy of the University of Michigan Museum of Art

Benjamin Franklin, 1777, the original terra cotta (CAFFIÉRI, no. 1). Courtesy of the Bibliothèque Mazarine, Paris; photo at left by Alvin Eisenman

Benjamin Franklin, 1777, the original terra cotta (CAFFIÉRI, no. 1). Courtesy of the Bibliothèque Mazarine

Benjamin Franklin, the cast from the Salon de la Correspondance (CAFFIÉRI, no. 10). Courtesy of the Royal Society of Arts

Benjamin Franklin, copy by an unidentified Italian sculptor, ca. 1790–1800 (CAFFIÉRI, no. 13). Courtesy of the American Philosophical Society

Le Docteur Franklin Couronné par la Liberté, aquatint by the Abbé de Saint Non, 1778 (FRAGONARD, no. 2). Courtesy of the Philadelphia Museum of Art, Mrs. John D. Rockefeller Collection

Benjamin Franklin, copy attributed to Giuseppe Ceracchi (CAFFIÉRI, no. 16). Courtesy of the Pennsylvania Academy of the Fine Arts

Benjamin Franklin, 1778, the original terra cotta (HOUDON, no. 1). Courtesy of the Louvre, Paris; photo at left courtesy of Archives Photographiques, Paris

Benjamin Franklin, marble bust brought to the United States by the artist (HOUDON, no. 8). Courtesy of the Metropolitan Museum of Art, Gift of John Bard, 1872

Benjamin Franklin, the cast owned by Thomas Jefferson (HOUDON, no. 12). Photo courtesy of Yale University

Benjamin Franklin, the only extant example of the type (HOUDON, no. 13). Courtesy of the Musée des Beaux-Arts, Angers, France

Benjamin Franklin, the cast owned by Thomas Jefferson (HOUDON, no. 12). Photo courtesy of Yale University

Benjamin Franklin, "Le Barbier L'ainé daprès Le Buste de houdon" (see HOUDON, no. 11). Courtesy of the American Philosophical Society (on deposit from the Metropolitan Museum of Art)

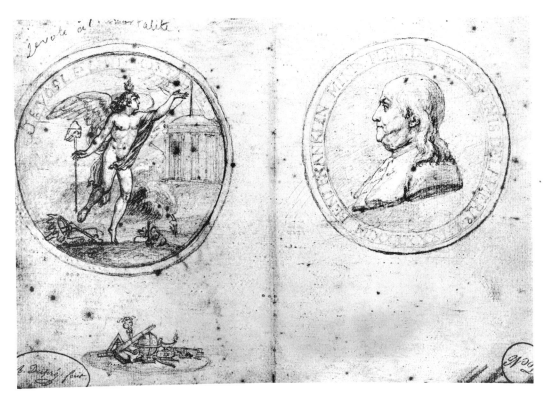

Benjamin Franklin, original design for the medal, 1783, by Augustin Dupré (DUPRÉ, no. 1). Courtesy of the Boston Public Library

Atelier de Houdon (detail), by L. L. Boilly; the bust of Franklin appears directly over that on which the artist is working. Courtesy of the Musée des Arts Decoratifs, Louvre, Paris; photo courtesy of Archives Photographiques, Paris

The Genius of Franklin, reverse of the medal by Dupré, 1784 (DUPRÉ, no. 2). Courtesy of Yale University

Benjamin Franklin, medal by Jean François Bernier, 1783. Courtesy of the American Philosophical Society

Benjamin Franklin, copy by John Flaxman (HOUDON, no. 10). Courtesy of the American Philosophical Society

Benjamin Franklin, copy by Hiram Powers. Courtesy of Yale University

Benjamin Franklin, marble bust by Domenico Menconi (HOUDON, no. 14). Courtesy of the American Philosophical Society

Benjamin Franklin, marble bust signed "J. A. Houdon 1780" (HOUDON, no. 15). Courtesy of the William Rockhill Nelson Gallery of Art, Atkins Museum of Fine Arts, Kansas City

Benjamin Franklin, 1777, pastel by Jean Baptiste Greuze (GREUZE, no. 1). Courtesy of James Lawrence, Jr.

Benjamin Franklin, painting by Jean Baptiste Greuze, 1777 (GREUZE, no. 2). Courtesy of Mrs. Arthur Lehman

Self-portrait, painting by Jean Baptiste Greuze. Courtesy of the Louvre, Paris

Benjamin Franklin, 1778, painting by J. F. de L'Hospital (L'HOSPITAL, no. 1). Courtesy of the University of Pennsylvania

Benjamin Franklin, ca. 1777–85, painting by Charles Philippe Amédée Vanloo (VANLOO, no. 1). Courtesy of the American Philosophical Society

Benjamin Franklin, aquatint by Pierre Michel Alix, ca. 1790 (VANLOO, no. 2). Courtesy of the Philadelphia Museum of Art, Mrs. John D. Rockefeller Collection

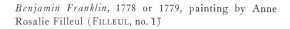

Benjamin Franklin, 1778 or 1779, painting by Anne Rosalie Filleul (FILLEUL, no. 1)

Self-portrait, painting by Anne Rosalie Filleul

Benjamin Franklin, 1778, painting by Joseph Siffred Duplessis (DUPLESSIS: "Fur Collar," no. 1). Courtesy of the Metropolitan Museum of Art, New York

Self-portrait, painting by Joseph Siffred Duplessis. Courtesy of the Musée Municipale de Carpentras, France

Benjamin Franklin, drawing by Francis Lainé (DUPLESSIS: "Fur Collar," no. 22). Courtesy of Claude Rossel

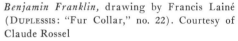

Benjamin Franklin, miniature given by Franklin to his daughter (DUPLESSIS: "Fur Collar," no. 21). Courtesy of the Philadelphia Museum of Art

Benjamin Franklin, miniature in enamel (see DUPLESSIS: "Fur Collar," no. 23). Courtesy of the Musée Municipale de Carpentras, France; photo by F. Meyer

Benjamin Franklin, pastel by Joseph Siffred Duplessis (Duplessis: "Gray Coat," no. 1). Courtesy of the New York Public Library

Benjamin Franklin, 1782, painting by Joseph Wright (Wright, no. 4). Courtesy of the Corcoran Gallery of Art

Benjamin Franklin, the snuffbox miniature for Georgiana (Duplessis: "Gray Coat," no. 2). Courtesy of Elsie O. and Philip D. Sang

Benjamin Franklin, the miniature for Mariamne (Duplessis: "Gray Coat," no. 3). Courtesy of Miss Lydia Spencer Moncure Robinson

Benjamin Franklin, painting from the family of Madame Helvétius (DUPLESSIS: "Fur Collar," no. 9). Courtesy of Independence National Historical Park, Philadelphia

Benjamin Franklin, the painting owned by Thomas Jefferson (DUPLESSIS: "Fur Collar," no. 8). Courtesy of the Museum of Fine Arts, Boston

Benjamin Franklin, painting attributed to Benjamin West (WEST, no. 4). Courtesy of the American Scenic and Historic Preservation Society; photo by Lawrence D. Thornton

Benjamin Franklin, painting by Thomas B. Welch (see WEST, no. 4). Courtesy of Independence National Historical Park, Philadelphia

The Declaration of Independence (detail of Benjamin Franklin), by John Trumbull. Courtesy of the Yale University Art Gallery

Benjamin Franklin, engraving by Juste Chevillet, 1778 (DUPLESSIS: "Fur Collar," no. 2)

The Treaty of Paris, by Benjamin West, 1784–85. Courtesy of the H. F. du Pont Winterthur Museum

Presumed sketch of Franklin and a friend, by Charles Willson Peale, 1767 (PEALE, no. 1). Courtesy of the American Philosophical Society

Benjamin Franklin, ca. 1780–81, drawing by Louis Carrogis de Carmontelle (CARMONTELLE, no. 1). Courtesy of Herbert Clark Hoover

Benjamin Franklin, engraving by François Denis Neé (CARMONTELLE, no. 2). Courtesy of the Philadelphia Museum of Art, Mrs. John D. Rockefeller Collection

Benjamin Franklin, terra-cotta statuette by François Marie Suzanne, 1793. Courtesy of the Metropolitan Museum of Art, Bequest of Annie C. Kane, 1926

Benjamin Franklin, terra-cotta statuette by François Marie Suzanne, 1793. Courtesy of the Walters Art Gallery, Baltimore

Louis XVI and Benjamin Franklin, porcelain group by Lemire. Courtesy of the H. F. du Pont Winterthur Museum

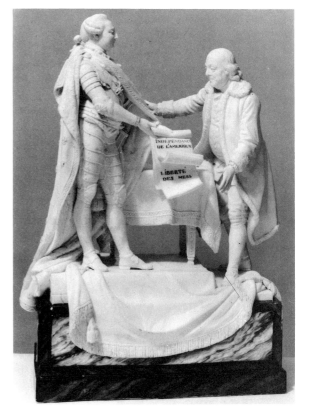

Le magnétisme dévoilé, engraving, ca. 1784–85 (UNKNOWN ARTIST: CARICATURE no. 5). Courtesy of the Bibliothèque Nationale, Paris

Allegory of the Franco-American Alliance, by Etienne Pallière, ca. 1778. Courtesy of Yale University

Benjamin Franklin Experimenting, a well-preserved figure of the type, though lacking hair and spectacles (UN-KNOWN ARTIST: SCULPTURE no. 4). Courtesy of the Musée Municipale de Saint-Germain-en-Laye

Franklin, Rousseau, and Voltaire, from the Rolland Collection (UNKNOWN ARTIST: SCULPTURE no. 3). Photo courtesy of Archives Photographiques, Paris

L'Amérique Indépendante, 1778, engraving by Jean Charles Le Vasseur, after a drawing by Antoine Borel (BOREL). Courtesy of the Philadelphia Museum of Art, Mrs. John D. Rockefeller Collection

Eripuit Coelo Fulmen Sceptrumque Tiranis, 1778, etching by Marguerite Gérard, after a design by Jean Honoré Fragonard
(FRAGONARD, no. 3). Courtesy of the Philadelphia Museum of Art, Mrs. John D. Rockefeller Collection

Benjamin Franklin, miniature on ivory by Jacques Thouron (WEYLER, no. 4). Courtesy of the Louvre, Paris

Benjamin Franklin, miniature in enamel by Jacques Thouron (WEYLER, no. 5). Courtesy of the Louvre, Paris

Benjamin Franklin, miniature in enamel by "D. C.," 1785 (WEYLER, no. 7). Courtesy of Georges Wildenstein

Benjamin Franklin, polychromed wax high-relief (WEYLER, no. 9). Courtesy of the Musée Carnavalet, Paris

Franklin Drawing Electricity from the Sky, painting by Benjamin West (WEST, no. 2). Courtesy of Wharton Sinkler

280   QUATORZIEME FRAGMENT. DE L'HOMOGÉNÉITÉ

ADDITION G. ·

Un bon Physionomiste devroit savoir distinguer dans chaque portrait inconnu, les traits qui sont vrais, de ceux que le Peintre a manqués ou altérés; ceux qui sont dans la nature, de ceux qui en sortent. *Un seul trait* parfaitement vrai devroit lui suffire pour déterminer & pour rétablir tous les traits qui ne sont vrais qu'à demi, ou qui ne le sont pas du tout. Quant à moi, je ne me vanterai point d'être parvenu à ce degré de sagacité, à cette infaillibilité de tact; cependant il m'est arrivé quelquefois d'en approcher plus ou moins, & de faire dans ce genre des expériences assez heureuses. Quoiqu'il en soit, il seroit difficile d'y réussir pour le portrait ci-joint, où je n'apperçois pas une seule partie qui soit *dans l'exacte vérité*. Tout ce que j'en puis dire, c'est que le front s'accorde avec la chevelure, & parti- culièrement avec le menton. D'après ces traits je suppose que dans l'Original les paupières sont plus ridées, celle de dessus beaucoup plus précise & plus avancée; & les parties du visage proprement dites, mieux prononcées en général. Je suis également sûr que la copie ne rend pas entièrement l'expression de la bouche, déjà si belle : elle doit être moins fermée & moins ondoyante. Malgré les imperfections de ce portrait, j'y démêle encore le caractère d'un homme auquel on ne sera pas tenté de se jouer aisément, & dont la seule présence doit imposer aux ames lâches & corrompues.

Essai sur la Physiognomie, engraving by an unknown artist (see WEYLER, no. 2)

Benjamin Franklin, mezzotint by Charles Willson Peale, 1787 (C. W. PEALE, no. 3). Courtesy of the American Philosophical Society

Benjamin Franklin, 1785, painting by Charles Willson Peale (C. W. PEALE, no. 2). Courtesy of the Pennsylvania Academy of the Fine Arts

Benjamin Franklin, painting by Robert Edge Pine, ca. 1787. Courtesy of the Franklin Institute, Philadelphia

Benjamin Franklin, ca. 1787, miniature attributed to John Ramage. Courtesy of the British Society for International Understanding, London

Benjamin Franklin, 1787, bust in wood by William Rush (RUSH, no. 1). Courtesy of the Yale University Art Gallery

Zion Besieg'd & Attack'd, 1787, by an unknown artist (UNKNOWN ARTIST: CARICATURE no. 6). Courtesy of the Library Company of Philadelphia

Zion Besieg'd (detail), by an unknown artist (UN-
KNOWN ARTIST: CARICATURE no. 6). Courtesy of the
Library Company of Philadelphia

Benjamin Franklin, ca. 1789, painted silhouette
by Joseph Sansom (SANSOM, no. 1). Courtesy of
T. Morris Perot, III

Congress Voting Independence (detail), painting by Edward Savage, ca. 1796–1801. Courtesy of the Historical Society of Pennsylvania

Patience Wright, engraving from the *London Magazine,* 1775

William Pitt, Earl of Chatham, wax figure by Patience Wright. Courtesy of L. E. Tanner, C. V. O. F. S. A., Keeper of the Muniments and Library Westminster Abbey; photo courtesy of the Victoria and Albert Museum

William Pitt, Earl of Chatham, head of the figure by Patience Wright. Courtesy of L. E. Tanner, C. V. O., F. S. A., Keeper of the Muniments and Library, Westminster Abbey; photo courtesy of the Victoria and Albert Museum; photo by R. P. Howgrave-Graham, Westminster Abbey Library

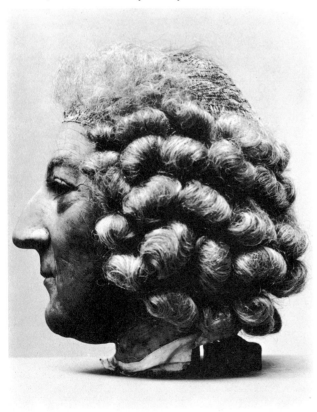

Benjamin Franklin's coat, in which the wax figure of Franklin was dressed (WRIGHT, PATIENCE, no. 4). Courtesy of the Massachusetts Historical Society

Patience Wright, drawing by John Downman (from G. C. Williamson, *John Downman,* London, 1907), original unlocated; reproduced with the kind permission of the publisher, Studio Books

"Eliza," Mrs. John Hoppner, daughter of Patience Wright, engraving by J. Kingsbury, after a drawing by John Hoppner. Photo by John R. Freeman and Company

Major Peter Labilliere, Christian Patriot and Citizen of the World, mezzotint by H. Kingsbury, after a painting by Joseph Wright. Courtesy of the British Museum; photo by John R. Freeman and Company

Benjamin Franklin, "by Greuze"; Mr. Mason added the picture to his collection, though doubting the identification; a similar portrait is recorded at the Bibliothèque Nationale. Courtesy of the William Smith Mason Collection, Yale University

Self-portrait, painting by Johann Kupetzky (1667–1740); this and another version have passed as "Benjamin Franklin, by Snyder." Courtesy of the Massachusetts Historical Society

David Middleton, by Thomas Gainsborough; formerly in the collection of the Marquis of Lansdowne, and for many years identified as Franklin, probably because of its similarity to an 18th century French print by P. Maren. Courtesy of Murray Seasongood

Benjamin Franklin, "by James Peale"; actually Gunning Bedford by Charles Willson Peale. Courtesy of Samuel Herbert McVitty

BENJ. FRANKLIN.

Benj. Franklin, engraving by Peter Maverick, after a painting by George Catlin; actually Tapping Reeve (1744–1823), Connecticut jurist

The Versailles Portrait, engraving by Gustave Levy; probably an idealized portrait of Jean Jacques Rousseau; no such painting is now in the gallery at Versailles

Franklin and his Wife, double miniature by Jean Baptiste Weyler; now unlocated; illustration from the catalogue of the Mannheim Collection sale, Paris, March 14, 1913

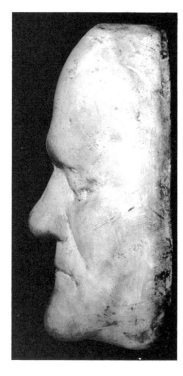

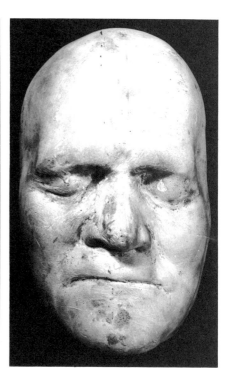

Death mask of Franklin, discovered by Lawrence Hutton in a collection of phrenological masks; in the center, the official *Franklin of the phrenologists,* a cast from a Caffiéri bust. Courtesy of the Princeton University Library and the Anatomical Museum, University of Edinburgh

Benjamin Franklin, terra-cotta bust by an unidentified artist; unlocated. Photo courtesy of Archives Photographiques, Paris

Benjamin Franklin, Staffordshire figure, ca. 1762–72, attributed to Ralph Wood (STAFFORDSHIRE). Courtesy of the American Philosophical Society